I0854253

HARLAXTON COLLEGE
R27994Y0544

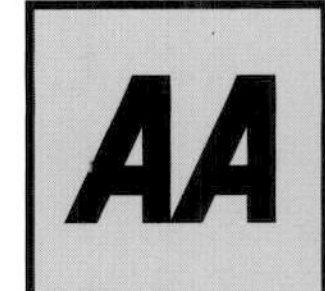

WALKS THROUGH BRITAIN'S HISTORY

Produced by AA Publishing

First published 2001
Reprinted 2001 and 2003
New edition with new walks 2011

Published by AA Publishing (a trading name of AA Media Limited, whose registered office is Fanum House, Basing View, Basingstoke, Hampshire RG21 4EA; registered number 06112600).

ISBNs: 978-0-7495-6862-7
and 978-0-7495-6863-4 (SS)

A CIP catalogue record for this book is available from the British Library.

The contents of this book are believed correct at the time of printing. Nevertheless, the publishers cannot be held responsible for any errors or omissions or for changes in the details given in this book or for the consequences of any reliance on the information it provides. This does not affect your statutory rights. We have tried to ensure accuracy in this book, but things do change and we would be grateful if readers would advise us of any inaccuracies they may encounter.

We have taken all reasonable steps to ensure that these walks are safe and achievable by walkers with a realistic level of fitness. However, all outdoor activities involve a degree of risk and the publishers accept no responsibility for any injuries caused to readers whilst following these walks. For more advice on using this book and walking safely see pages 12–13.

Some of these routes may appear in other AA walks books.

Visit AA Publishing at theAA.com/shop

Walks written and compiled by:
Martin Andrew, Chris Bagshaw, Kate Barrett, Bill Birkett, Sheila Bowker, Michael Buttler, Nick Channer, Liz Cruwys, Paddy Dillon, Rebecca Ford, David Foster, John Gillham, Paul Grogan, David Hancock, Des Hannigan, Tom Hutton, Tony Kelly, Dennis Kelsall, Deborah King, Christopher Knowles, John Manning, Terry Marsh, Andrew McCloy, Moira McCrossan, John Morrison, Andrew Noyce, Nicholas Reynolds, Beau Riffenburgh, Julie Royle, Jon Sparks, Ann F Stonehouse, Hugh Taylor, Anthony Toole, Ronald Turnbull, Sue Viccars, David Winpenny.

Editor: Charles Phillips
Design: Keith Miller
Picture Research: Liz Allen
Proofreader: Ann Stonehouse
Index: Marie Lorimer

For AA Publishing:
Managing Editor: David Popey
Image manipulation and internal repro:
Neil Smith and Natalie Sternberg
Production: Stephanie Allen
Editorial Assistant: Rebecca Needes
Cartography provided by the Mapping Services Department of AA Publishing

Printed and bound by Leo Paper Products, China

A04147

Right: *Medusa head mosaic from a Roman villa at Bignor, West Sussex*

AA

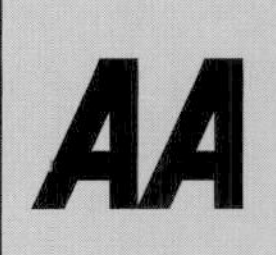

WALKS THROUGH BRITAIN'S HISTORY

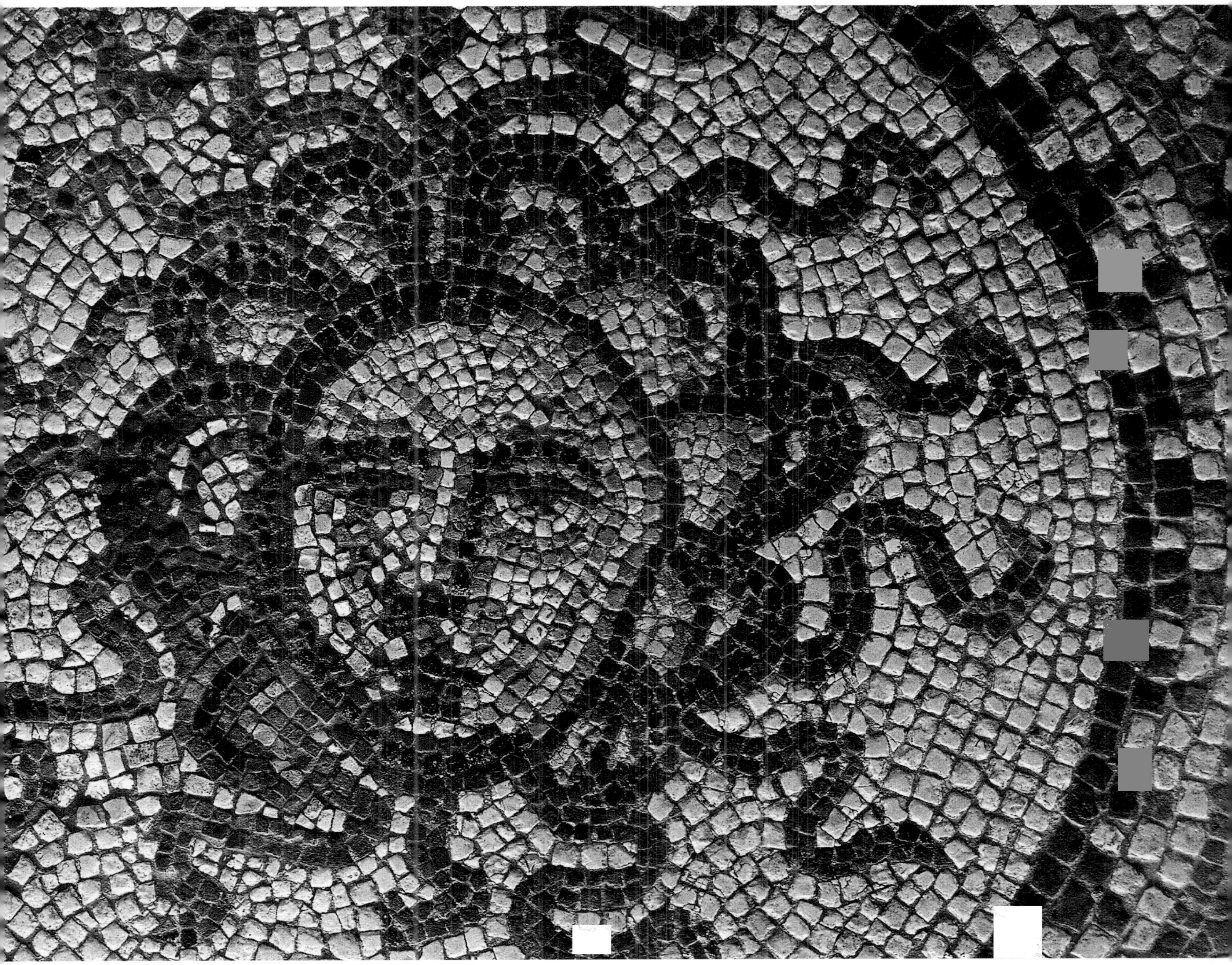

Contents

THE VICTORIAN AGE 1837–1901

THE EDWARDIAN AGE 1901–1918

DEPRESSION AND WAR 1918–1945

MODERN BRITAIN 1945–PRESENT

Pages 6–7: *A stretch of Hadrian's Wall at Cuddy's Crag – a Roman structure built to keep out the Picts of the North*

Walking Through History

Walks Through Britain's History brings you the opportunity to combine two wonderful aspects of living on this lovely island. You can follow carefully planned routes through beautiful and varied settings that change in character from mellow farmland to sweeping panoramas, from wild moorland to dramatic seascapes, from small villages to historic cities – often within just a few miles of each other, and each aspect itself changing with the seasons. But these are not simply scenic walks through town and country – they tread some of the lesser-known paths of Britain's long, rich and fascinating history. You will soon discover that wherever you go in Britain, something exciting and memorable happened, sometimes only a hundred years ago, sometimes more than a thousand.

Some elements of history remain hidden – occasionally to be unearthed briefly by archaeologists, pored over with awe and wonder, and then covered up again to preserve them. Others are visible as small fragments or as reconstructions – a portion of a Roman fort, for example. Yet there are still so many historically fascinating remains in Britain, often things that we take for granted as part of the landscape – hill-forts and henges; castles, abbeys, churches and chapels, both intact and ruined; railways and canals; country houses and gardens; and fortifications guarding the vulnerable coastlines. All these things are evidence of Britain's social and economic progress – of 'civilisation'.

Creating a Landscape

The British landscape is not completely natural, as we might expect it to be, but is more often than not man-made. Forests were once cleared to make room for agriculture, then new forests were planted as hunting grounds; vast open areas were enclosed by hedges (and then opened up again, bringing about a shift in the balance of wildlife); whole tracts of land, such as the fenland in East Anglia, were drained and 'reclaimed' for farming; mineral-rich areas were intensively mined, leaving the landscape ravaged and spent; even the remote, rugged Highlands of Scotland were made accessible by the building of roads and bridges.

Bringing the Landscape to Life

Walking in Britain is made exciting not only by the physical signs of the country's history, but also by a wealth of associated legends and of colourful characters – some very real and others, if not totally imaginary, at least moulded and romanticised into something more than they really were. The solid but nonetheless often flamboyant and intriguing figures of kings and queens, churchmen and aristocrats, inventors, philanthropists and rogues, as well as the common man going about his everyday life, sit alongside romanticised figures such as the Welsh

Above: *A Byzantine plate discovered in the Anglo-Saxon burial site at Sutton Hoo*

Right: *The Bayeux Tapestry depicted in contemporary cartoon strip the Conquest of 1066 – this is part of a replica held in Reading Museum*

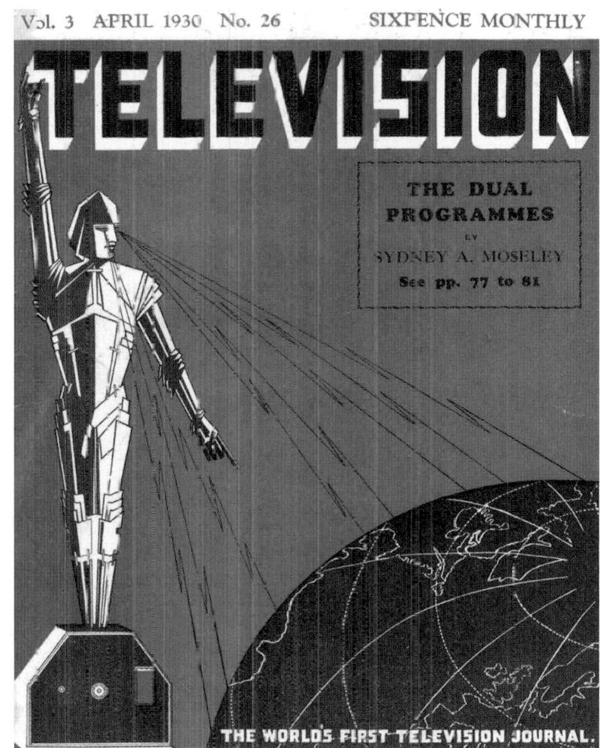

bard Taliesin or the iconic Scots William Wallace and Rob Roy. It is little wonder that, over many centuries, countless writers, poets, artists and even musicians have been moved to celebrate – and record for posterity – the history, landscape and legends of the land. As you take a walk through Britain's history yourself, you will begin to appreciate what inspired them.

Prehistory Gives Way to History

Our survey of British history begins towards the end of a period that lasted for many hundreds of centuries and is known loosely as 'prehistoric' – the time before written history. This era has been divided by archaeologists into 'ages', and the years covered here (4500 BC to AD 43) are subdivided according to the material being used by Britons at that time for making tools – hence the Stone Age, the Bronze Age and the Iron Age. During this era, the Celts arrived from Europe and settled in southern Britain and in Ireland.

Then came the Romans, who created an imperial outpost and for almost four hundred years inhabited much of the island, imposing their culture upon the earlier settlers, and driving the Celts westwards into Wales and Cornwall. Their departure in AD 410 left the country open to further invasion, which came in the form of tribes from northern Europe – Angles (from whom the name 'England' is derived), Saxons and Jutes. In the 9th century came the Vikings, raiders and settlers from the Scandinavian countries of Denmark and Norway. During this time, also, Celts from Ireland – 'Scots' – settled in northern Britain, absorbing the native Pictish tribes into their culture and giving birth to Scotland.

Normans Usher in the Middle Ages

Early in the second millennium after the birth of Christ came the last of the invasions, that of the Normans in 1066, led by one of the most famous figures in British history – William the Conqueror. The Conquest marks the opening of the medieval period. From this point to the present day, plenty of blood has been shed in wars fought against other countries, and sometimes within Britain, usually over rights to the throne. There have been many threats of invasion, from the Spanish, from the Dutch, from the French, from the Germans; but invaders have repeatedly and often heroically been held at bay.

The medieval age ended in 1485 with the conclusion of one of the most bitter and complex civil confrontations, the Wars of the Roses, and the accession of Henry Tudor as King Henry VII. Periods of history now began to be measured according to the name of the royal house in power – Tudor (1485–1603) and Stuart (1603–1714) – or by the names of the kings or queens – Georgian (1714–1836), Victorian (1837–1901) and Edwardian (1901–1910).

The Modern Age

The 20th century was largely marked by the two World Wars and their aftermath, by the end of Britain's empire and by profoundly challenging changes to the country's industry. Moving into the 21st century Britain is coming to terms with the development of a multinational, multiracial country, and rapid technological advance.

The walks included in the book represent a cross-section of historical events. The places around which the walks are based have been placed into the era in which they have a special historical significance, even though the cities (in particular) may have connections with several eras. Canterbury, for example, was originally a Roman city, but is best known as a centre of pilgrimage following the martyrdom of St Thomas Becket in 1170 and in *The Canterbury Tales* of Geoffrey Chaucer (1343–1400), so it is placed in the 'Medieval' section. Similarly, Dartington Hall in Devon is a splendid medieval mansion with a long history but is best known for the Dartington Hall educational trust established there by Leonard and Dorothy Elmhirst in 1935, and so it is placed in our chapter covering this period between the First and Second World Wars, 'Depression and War'.

Top: *Since the early 20th century advances in technology and communications have transformed Britain*

Left: *Scottish architect and designer Charles Rennie Mackintosh was a leading light of the Arts and Crafts Movement at the beginning of the 20th century*

History's Impact on the Land

During the period beginning with the New Stone Age (from about 4500 BC), much of the British landscape was recovering from the ravages of the last Ice Age, and the hunter–gatherer lifestyle was slowly giving way to a more settled existence. Evidence of this new way of life is found in the prehistoric monuments dating from this period – stone circles, hill-forts, burial mounds and figures cut into chalk hills.

The Romans, whose arrival heralded a completely different civilisation, made use of some of the Iron Age hill-forts, as well as establishing many settlements of their own. They brought with them new methods of building, engineering, administration and farming, new foods and wine, a new language and a new religion – Christianity. Although much of their building has long since disappeared below ground, Britain is rich in evidence of the Roman occupation – their characteristic long, straight roads; fragments of walls in cities; orderly military defences; excavated remains of sumptuous villas with their wonderful mosaic floors and sophisticated central heating systems; and the complex baths.

The Romans' departure saw the disintegration of much of what they had established – cities fell into ruin, villas and temples were abandoned, and the country was overrun with pagan invaders. Yet gradually order was restored, and a new civilisation began. Christianity was re-established. Churches and monasteries were built, and the first illuminated manuscripts were created. Anglo-Saxon 'kingdoms' were formed and laws were established. The landscape was dotted with Saxon villages. Forest was cleared and the land ploughed into long, narrow strips for cultivation. Remains excavated from Saxon burial sites, such as the burial ship of Raedwald of East Anglia at Sutton Hoo, Suffolk, indicates the great wealth of the chiefs.

Above: *Axe heads, elegantly shaped, can be dated to the Bronze Age*

Right: *The 'Virgin Queen', Elizabeth I, presided over a golden age in British history*

Vikings – and Normans

Violent Viking invasions interrupted the Saxons' ordered lives, but eventually the Vikings, too, settled into an ordered existence, and the cultural similarities they shared with the Saxons enabled them to live relatively peacefully, side by side. The Saxons by now lived under a united kingdom; it was a crack in the strength of the crown that allowed renewed Viking attacks towards the end of the 10th century, resulting in the reign of the Danish king, Canute. The line of succession became more complicated, and the death of King Edward 'the Confessor' in 1066 opened England up to invasion from a new quarter – Normandy, in northern France.

With the Norman Conquest, led by a triumphant William of Normandy, came a period of rapid change. William made his presence felt by erecting castles. Often built on the sites of Roman defences, the first castles were usually of the wooden 'motte and bailey' type, later replaced by much sturdier stone castles, the remains of which can be seen throughout the country. The other architectural legacy of the Norman period lies in the religious buildings – from small country churches to the great monastic foundations with their magnificent cathedrals. Although many of these were rebuilt through the medieval period, becoming ever more elaborate, the rounded arches and heavy decoration that typify Norman, or Romanesque, architecture are still visible in most cathedrals.

The French language was introduced, but the sound Anglo-Saxon system of law and administration was retained and developed. Medieval new towns were laid out to a geometric plan, and vast areas of forest were planted as hunting grounds. The age of chivalry was born. Centres of learning were founded, including the universities of Oxford and Cambridge and some of the famous public schools. This was also a time of constant wars, and of terrible plagues that claimed the lives of rich and poor alike.

The Tudor Age, then Civil War

The accession of Henry VII ended the Wars of the Roses and restored peace to England. The reign of his son, the notorious Henry VIII, saw the birth of the navy and building of defences around the southern coastline, as well as the founding of new colleges and schools. The King's desperate bid to provide a male heir to the throne resulted in a break with the Church in Rome and the introduction of the English Protestant Church. The consequences were far reaching. They included many years of religious conflict, while the Dissolution of the Monasteries also meant the destruction of countless medieval treasures. In spite of all Henry's efforts, it was a female heir who was to become the other great Tudor – Queen Elizabeth I. During the age of 'the Virgin Queen', exploration to far lands began in

earnest; literature, painting and music flourished as never before; and the distinctive black-and-white timbered buildings now known as Tudor style appeared. But there was no heir to carry on the Tudor name, and it was the Stuart king of Scotland – son of Mary, Queen of Scots, executed by Elizabeth – who succeeded her.

In the mid-17th century internal conflict erupted: Crown and Parliament fought for political power, involving much of the population of Britain. For a short while, Parliament triumphed; but the death of Parliamentarian leader Oliver Cromwell led to the restoration of the monarchy. This century also saw yet another destructive plague, while the Great Fire of London enabled architect Sir Christopher Wren to make his elegant mark in the rebuilding of the city.

Industrial Revolution, Modern Life

Everyday life had for many centuries revolved around farming the land, both for providing crops and for breeding sheep – the wool trade brought great prosperity, and many of the rich medieval towns were built by wealthy wool merchants. But a great change was waiting in the wings that would transform large parts of Britain – the Industrial Revolution. Great leaps in technological advancement during the Georgian and Victorian eras lured people into the towns, where factories provided employment. Towns developed rapidly with new homes to accommodate this labour, while some philanthropic factory owners built whole villages for the purpose. The whole of Britain was opened up, with new roads, bridges spanning rivers and shipping canals for transporting the produce of underground mines. Even the impenetrable Highlands of Scotland could now be reached by road. The introduction of train travel completed the new-found freedom. Working people who had always stayed close to home began to take trips to the seaside or into the country. Towards the end of the 19th century, the wealthy could enjoy another revolutionary form of transport – the motor car.

The early years of the 20th century – the Edwardian era – are portrayed as a golden age. Modern civilisation was in place, but life still proceeded at a relatively gentle pace. Then came the First World War, followed by a mixture of shock and grief and an almost unnatural jollity in the 'Roaring Twenties'; then years of depression, and before the world could properly draw breath, came the Second World War. Air raids over England left gaping holes and smouldering rubble where once buildings had stood; families were separated as children were sent away to the country for safety, and in some cases were never reunited; women worked the land and assembled munitions in the factories while their menfolk were scattered around the world.

After the Wars and Into a New Century

In the decades after the Second World War Britain had to come to terms with the loss of its empire and with economic difficulties that saw a transformation of the industrial landscape – the closures of coalmines, steel plants and docks. In the wake of these came regeneration projects that revitalised former industrial areas through the opening of parks and heritage centres. There also were causes for celebration that brought their own challenges, including the rise of computing and service industries, immigration leading to a multiethnic and increasingly pluralistic society and a greater understanding of ecological priorities. In the first decade of the 21st century the threat of international terrorism and renewed economic difficulties brought new problems, but Britain and its people remained vibrant, determined and optimistic, with an enduring interest in treading the paths of history across the beautiful British landscape.

Top: *Medieval jousting was a chivalrous affair, as portrayed in Geoffrey Chaucer's* The Knight's Tale

Left: *Our local museums are a treasure trove of historical artefacts – this statue of an unknown king is in the Bowes Museum, at Barnard Castle*

Following the Walks

Each of the 12 sections in the book contains nine mapped, circular walks, ranging from one-and-a-half to ten miles in length. The directions for the walks are clearly numbered and annotated. They not only guide you through the walk, but also include useful tips such as where a track might become muddy, or what to look out for if the footpath has temporarily disappeared because, for example, a field has been ploughed. Each map is accompanied by an review of the walk's historical background, as well as one or more information boxes giving background on other points of interest, either at the site itself or a short distance away, in the local area.

***Right:** The Battersea Shield is a remarkable bronze relic of the Iron Age, discovered in the mud of the River Thames at Battersea Bridge, London*

Feature Walks

One walk in each section is chosen to encapsulate key qualities of the period's history and character and is presented as a feature walk. These walks give you the opportunity to experience history up close and at first hand – for instance, to tread on the battlefield where William the Conqueror triumphed in 1066, to walk through Stratford-upon-Avon in the footsteps of William Shakespeare, or to gaze up at the iconic London Eye, the giant riverside wheel built to usher in the new millennium but now a fixture and a key attraction in the capital city. Many of these feature walks will appeal to readers with children, as there is plenty to enjoy here even for reluctant young walkers.

Route Information

A panel accompanies each walk to give details of the total distance, terrain, conditions underfoot, parking, public toilets and any special conditions that apply, such as restricted access or level of dog friendliness. The minimum time suggested for the walk is for reasonably fit walkers and doesn't

***Below:** The 1930s Hoover Building in Perivale, London, is one of Britain's most celebrated Art Deco structures*

allow for stops. An indication of the gradients you will encounter is shown by the rating ▲▲▲ (no steep slopes) to ▲▲▲ (several very steep slopes). Walks are also rated for their difficulty – those rated ●●● are usually shorter and easier with little total ascent. The hardest walks are marked ●●●.

Parking and Getting Started

Many of the car parks suggested are public, but occasionally you may find you have to park on the roadside or in a lay-by. Please be considerate when you leave your car, ensuring that access roads or gates are not blocked and that other vehicles can pass safely. The start of each walk is given as a six-figure grid reference prefixed by two letters indicating the 100-km square of the National Grid to which it refers. Each walk has a suggested Ordnance Survey Explorer map where you'll find more information on using grid references.

Dog Friendliness

Keep your dog under control at all times, especially around livestock, and obey local byelaws and other dog control notices. Remember, it is against the law to let your dog foul in many public areas, especially in villages and towns.

The route information often contains specific advice regarding the dog friendliness of the walk. Not all routes are appropriate for dog walkers, so please read the advice provided before setting out.

Walking in Safety

All these walks are suitable for any reasonably fit person, but less experienced walkers should try the easier walks first. Although each walk here has been researched with a view to minimising the risks to the walkers who follow its route, no walk in the countryside can be considered to be completely free from risk. Walking will always require a degree of common sense and judgement to ensure that it is as safe as possible.

Route Map Legend

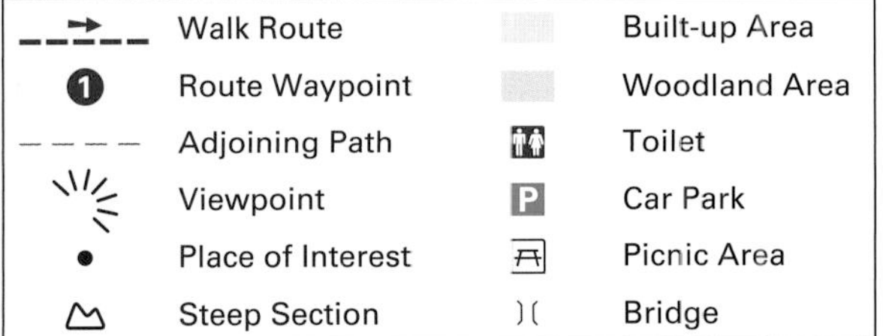

	Walk Route		Built-up Area
1	Route Waypoint		Woodland Area
	Adjoining Path		Toilet
	Viewpoint	P	Car Park
•	Place of Interest		Picnic Area
	Steep Section	)(	Bridge

- ❑ Be particularly careful on cliff paths and in upland terrain, where the consequences of a slip can be very serious.
- ❑ Remember always to check tidal conditions before walking along the seashore.
- ❑ Some sections of route are by, or cross, busy roads. Take care and remember traffic is a danger even on minor country lanes.
- ❑ Be careful around farmyard machinery and livestock, especially if you have children with you.
- ❑ Be aware of the consequences of changes in the weather and check the forecast before you set out. Carry spare clothing and a torch if you are walking in the winter months. Remember that the weather can change very quickly at any time of the year, and in moorland and heathland areas, mist and fog can make route finding much harder. Don't set out in these conditions unless you are confident of your navigation skills in poor visibility. In summer, remember to take account of the heat and sun; wear a hat and sunscreen, and carry spare water.
- ❑ On walks away from centres of population, you should carry a whistle and survival bag. If you do have an accident requiring the emergency services, make a note of your position as accurately as possible and dial 999.

Top: *Chimneys first became common in the Tudor period – these, decorated in the Tudor style, are typically tall*

Left: *Heraldry is celebrated in a coat of arms at the Victorian Gothic Castell Coch, near Cardiff*

AGE OF MYSTERY

For hundreds of thousands of years before recorded history began, people were living in Britain and shaping its landscape. Their world remains, on the whole, a mystery – although several of its monuments survive, scattered across third-millennium Britain. These include evocative circles of standing stones, burial chambers and hill-forts.

Life for Britain's inhabitants hardly changed over hundreds of centuries: the most dramatic upheavals were caused by the weather. During several ice ages, glaciers provided a land bridge with Europe; in between, when the ice melted, Britain was an island again. Meanwhile, people wandered back and forth, adapting to the world around them.

Ancestors of modern humans made and used stone tools in Britain up to 1.2 million years ago: fragments of stone tools found in Happisburgh, Norfolk, in 2010 suggest that early humans called *homo antecessor* ('Pioneer Man') may have lived there in that period. Also in East Anglia, butchered animal remains from 700,000 BC indicate that by this date early humans were using stone tools to cut animals up. Early Britons lived as nomadic hunters and gatherers, making tools of flint and shelters of animal-hide and wood.

In about 25,000 BC another ice age hit, and settlement was interrupted. When it resumed, about 10,000 years later, the settlers were 'modern' humans, *homo sapiens*. They lived in caves, wore furs and bone jewellery, hunted with spears and knives and used sophisticated language.

By the 3rd millennium BC, Britain's neolithic communities were felling the trees that covered most of the country, creating clearings for crops and grazing. They shifted materials across land on sledges, or along the coasts and rivers by boat – on hide-covered coracles that are still used in Wales and Ireland today. During this era plain pottery was produced; tomb chambers and monuments built for the dead; and by 3000 BC work had begun on Stonehenge.

THE METAL AGE

An old way of life seemed to be changing from about 2750 BC – as well as customs for dealing with the dead. Collective burial in chamber tombs gave way to cremation in henges or individual burial in round barrows. Here, skeletons were surrounded by decorated pottery beakers, tools and ornaments made of gold and the new alloy – bronze. The Bronze Age revolved around farming, but other industries flourished, too. Any reasonably sized settlement had its weaver, potter, carpenter, leatherworker and, of course, metalworker. By 1000 BC these settlements were being fortified with circular walls and palisades and earth ramparts, as migrating groups from the north competed for resources.

After 600 BC a new group of tribes from Central Europe began settling in Ireland and Britain. The Celts had enjoyed trading links with the British for many years, but now they took centre stage. Using bronze and iron, the Celts produced weaponry and ornaments embellished with swirling designs. They also made ploughs, enabling the most difficult soils to be worked. In the hierarchical Celtic society, slaves were at the bottom; freemen paid rent and produce to the tribal leaders, and the upper echelons of society included warriors and druids. Religion permeated every part of life: gods and spirits inhabited trees, rocks and pools; sorcery and magic, woven into songs and stories, were passed down verbally and recited at court or round the central hearths of their circular houses.

KEY SITES

Isle of Arran, Ayrshire: Standing stones, cairns and huts dating back to 3000 BC.

Avebury, Wiltshire: Remains of stone circle and ceremonial centre from c.3000–2100 BC.

Swinside, Cumbria: Late Stone Age or Early Bronze Age stone circle, c.2000 BC.

Chains Barrow, Exmoor, Devon: Bronze Age burials from c.2000 BC.

Brown Clee, Shropshire: Iron Age hill-fort.

Uley, Gloucestershire: Iron Age hill-fort on the edge of the Cotswold escarpment, 6th century BC.

Uffington, Oxfordshire: Figure of galloping horse cut in chalk hillside, perhaps in 1st century AD.

Left: The Avebury Stone Circle (c.2600 BC) contains local sarsen stones up to 19ft (6m) tall.

500,000 BC Ancestors of modern humans (*homo heidelbergensis*) leave the earliest human remains so far discovered in Britain at Boxgrove, West Sussex.

225,000–200,000 BC Neanderthal man (*homo neanderthalensis*) uses caves as seasonal shelters. Neanderthal teeth of this date were found in Pontnewydd Cave, Clwyd.

27,000 BC The earliest burials in Britain are believed to have occurred during this time. A ceremonial burial of a young man in a shallow grave took place in Pavilan Cave, Gower Peninsula, Wales.

25,000 BC Ice covers the world as the last Ice Age begins, interrupting settlement but allowing people to move between continents.

16,000 BC Ice still covers most of Britain and Europe, as the Ice Age reaches its height.

10,000 BC Last glaciers disappear from Britain; the Upper Palaeolithic ('Early Stone') Age begins.

10,000 BC Early inhabitants use harpoons for fishing, and simple bone and stone tools and implements.

Back to the Stone Age on Arran Moorland

A bracing walk leads past the fascinating remains of stone circles, cairns and huts inhabited by Scotland's earliest settlers

Arran is famous for its archaeological remains, which date as far back as the Mesolithic Period or 'Middle Stone Age' (8000 BC–4000 BC). The greatest concentration can be found on the wild, windswept Machrie Moor. It was here that people settled from the earliest of times and have left the remains of their hut circles, chambered cairns and standing stones.

The earliest inhabitants settled here around 8,000 years ago; across millennia settlements were created and the first simple monuments erected. Within this small area of moorland there are more than 40 stone circles, standing stones, chambered tombs and hut circles, making it the finest Neolithic and Bronze Age site in Scotland. (The dates assigned to these periods vary according to the region; in Scotland, Neolithic or 'New Stone Age' means 4000 BC–2000 BC, while the Bronze Age lasted 2000 BC–750 BC.)

Most visitors to Machrie Moor head straight for the three large, red sandstone pillars, the tallest of which stands slightly over 18ft (5.5m). These stones were once part of a much larger circle; the other stones have fallen or been removed. No one is certain what function these Bronze Age circles performed, but it is likely that they had a religious significance. Many stone circles are precisely aligned to particular celestial events such as the rising of the midsummer sun; they possibly also fulfilled seasonal functions, indicating when to carry out certain rituals or plant and harvest crops.

Where Fingal Ate

Other early Arran inhabitants had another explanation for the circles. According to legend, the giant Fingal – a Scottish form of the Irish warrior Finn MacCumhail – put his dog, Bran, in the outer circle and tied it to a stone with a hole in it to stop it wandering while Fingal had his meal in the inner circle. The double circle still has the name of 'Fingal's Cauldron Seat'.

The dwellers on the moor lived in round huts, the remains of which are still visible. There is no explanation as to why or when they departed, but one theory is that climate change forced them to move to a more sheltered part of the island. Since they left, the area has become covered by a blanket of peat bog. There is undoubtedly more to discover beneath this protective layer.

Below: *Auchagallon Stone Circle, c.2000 BC, was built around a burial mound*

Right: *Standing stones known as 'Fingal's Cauldron Seat' are the remains of another stone circle on Machrie Moor*

Walk 1 Standing stones on the Isle of Arran

Explore Scotland's finest Stone and Bronze Age remains on Machrie Moor

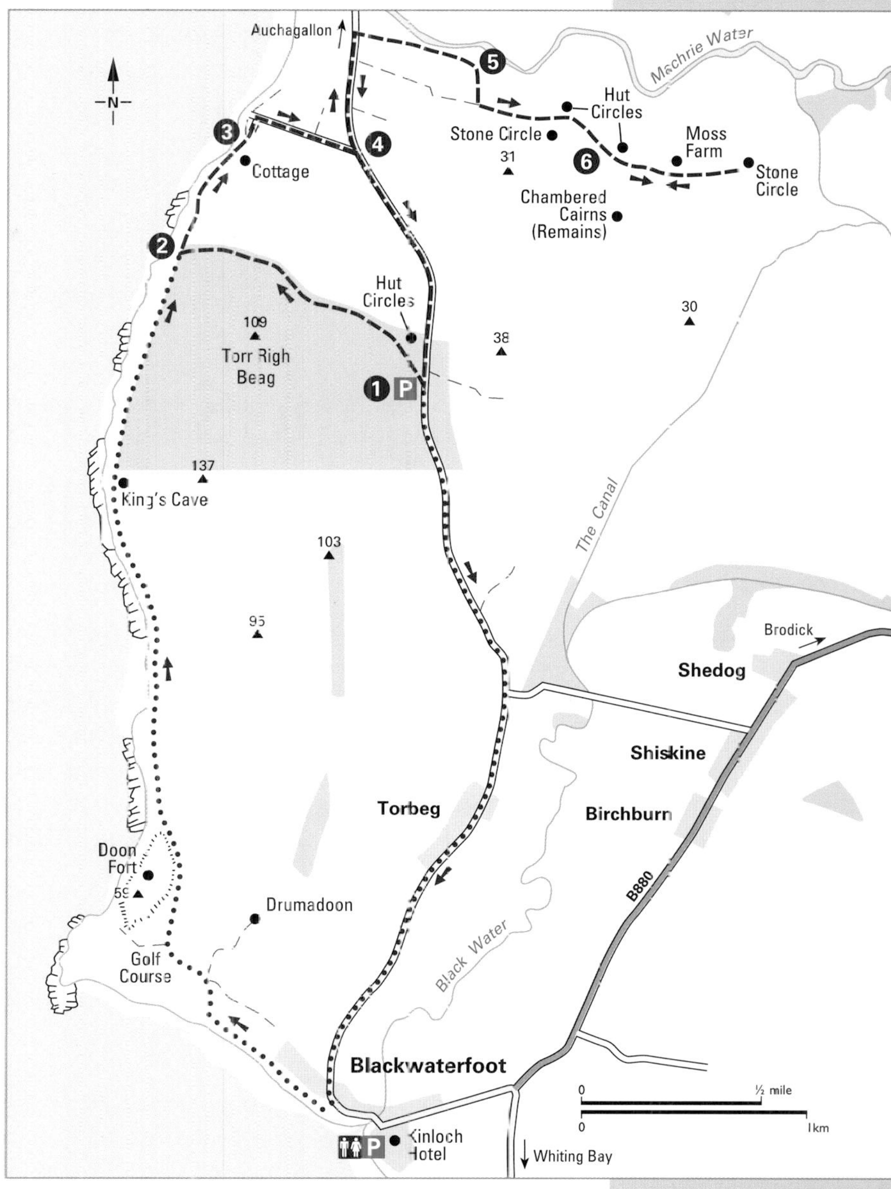

1 From the car park take the footpath signed for 'King's Cave' going through woodland, past the site of some hut circles and by the edge of the woods until it heads downhill towards the sea. Look out for a waymarker on the right, pointing back in the direction you have just walked.

2 Turn right onto a faint path, in summer overgrown with bracken. In a short distance, climb through a wire fence. Cross this field and go through a gate, then head downhill, aiming for a white cottage.

3 At the left end of the cottage go through a gate at the corner of the garden wall and along a farm road between two fences. Keep on this road, passing a cottage on the right, and then keep right at the fork.

4 When the road ends at a T-junction with the A841, turn left. Continue to the signpost for 'Machrie Moor standing stones'. At the sign turn right, climb over a stile and then follow the access road. This rough track passes through two fields.

5 In the second field, when you are nearing the far left-hand corner, you will come upon a megalithic site. Nothing is to be seen above ground, actually, and the site was only identified by archaeologists after flints were found that proved to be around 7,000 to 9,000 years old. After identifying the site, continue on the road to the much later Moss Farm road stone circle, which dates to around 2000 BC.

6 From here the track continues, passing the deserted Moss Farm then crossing a stile to the main stone circles of Machrie Moor. After inspecting these, return to the stile and take the Moss Farm road back to the A841. Turn left onto this and walk for approximately 1.5 miles (2km) to return to the car park.

Extending the Walk – the Bruce's Spider
Whether King's Cave is actually where Robert the Bruce met his fabled spider is not known, but he certainly spent some time hiding there during the Wars of Independence in the 14th century. To visit the cave, walk down the road into Blackwaterfoot then follow the coastal path north, behind Doon Fort. Once past the cave, you can either continue on the main walk from Point 2 onwards, or turn right to return to the start.

Distance 5.5 miles (8.8km)

Minimum time 3hrs

Ascent/gradient 114ft (35m) ▲▲▲

Level of difficulty ●●●

Paths Footpaths, rough tracks, road, 3 stiles

Landscape Seashore, moor

Suggested map OS Explorer 361 Isle of Arran

Start/finish Grid reference: NS 898314

Dog friendliness On lead near livestock; see signs

Parking King's Cave car park

Public toilets Car park at Blackwaterfoot

WHILE YOU'RE THERE

North of Machrie Moor, in a remote position overlooking Machrie Bay, stands the Auchagallon Stone Circle. Thought to be a Bronze Age kerbed cairn, this once had a continuous kerb of sandstone blocks around its edge, and is 3,000–4,000 years old. Many of the blocks are now missing, but what remains is a stone circle enclosing a burial cairn, the finest burial site on the island. There are 15 sandstone uprights arranged in a circle of 47ft (14.3m) diameter. The stones arrayed downhill of the cairn (to its west) are taller than those arranged to the east, on the uphill side. The site was excavated in the 1800s and a stone box of the kind usually used for burials was found in the central cairn, but little more is known of the results of this investigation; the stone circle and cairn have not been excavated in the modern era. The stone circle commands breathtaking views. This evocative site in a lovely setting is well worth a visit.

10,000 BC Inhabitants begin to describe their world using drawings in caves. Drawings of a horse and a man discovered in the caves of Creswell Crags, Derbyshire, are believed to date from this period.

8000 BC The Mesolithic ('Middle Stone') Age begins in Britain; hunters and fishers spread across the country.

6000 BC Settlers arrive in Crete, in the Greek Islands.

6000 BC Neolithic farming communities develop in southeast Europe.

4500–4000 BC Neolithic farmers and craftsmen arrive in Britain from Western Asia. They clear forest, colonise the land and build stone and timber houses.

4300 BC In Brittany and Ireland the first megaliths (large stone monuments) are built.

3500 BC The plough, developed in Asia and spread from there, is introduced to Britain and Europe.

3300 BC In Egypt town settlements begin to appear along the Nile Valley, and hieroglyphics come into use.

Romancing the Stones in the Preseli Hills

A walk along a prehistoric highway leads past the site from which bluestones were transported to Stonehenge

The Pembrokeshire Coast National Park is best known for its stunning coastline. Britain's smallest National Park is in no place further than 10 miles (16.1km) from the sea, and this furthest point was an extension of the boundaries to incorporate one of the most important historic sites in the United Kingdom, the Preseli Hills.

A circular walk around the most interesting sites of the Preseli Hills is almost impossible: the uplands form an isolated east–west ridge that would at best form one side of a circuit linked with a lengthy road section. Instead of taking this less than ideal option, this walk forms a narrow figure-of-eight to scale the most spectacular hill on the ridge and trace the line of the famous dolerite outcrops, or carns. It then makes an out-and-back sortie to an impressive stone circle. The route is packed with interest.

Carn Menyn's Bluestones

It was from Carn Menyn, one of the rocky tors that crown the marshy and often windswept hills, that the bluestones forming the inner circle of Stonehenge were taken in *c.*2600 BC. These bluestones, or spotted dolerite stones to give them their proper name, would have each weighed somewhere in the region of 4 tonnes and must have been transported more than 200 miles (320km) in total. To this day we cannot explain how or why.

The Stonehenge story, significant as it may be, is only part of the historic and at times mystical feel of this narrow upland. The track that follows the ridge is an ancient road, dating back more than 5,000 years. It's probable that it was a safe passage between the coast and settlements inland at a time when wild predators such as bears and wolves roamed the valleys below. Gravestones line the track, perhaps of travellers or traders who were buried where they died, while a number of standing stones dot the hills.

King Arthur's Resting Place?

West of Carn Menyn, beneath another outcrop named Carn Bica, is a stone circle known as Beddarthur. Small by comparison to Stonehenge or Avebury, its oval arrangement of 2ft–3ft (0.6m–1m) high stones is claimed to be the burial place of King Arthur; *bedd* means 'grave' in Welsh. There are certainly links between the legendary historical hero and the area; it is suggested that the King and his brave knights chased Twrch Trywyth, a magical giant boar, across these hills before heading east.

Bottom: *Dolorite boulders on a snowy Carn Menyn*

Below: *Legends of King Arthur claim that he was buried at the Beddarthur stone circle*

Walk 2 Welsh mountain mysteries

Follow a 5,000-year-old road to a possible burial site for King Arthur

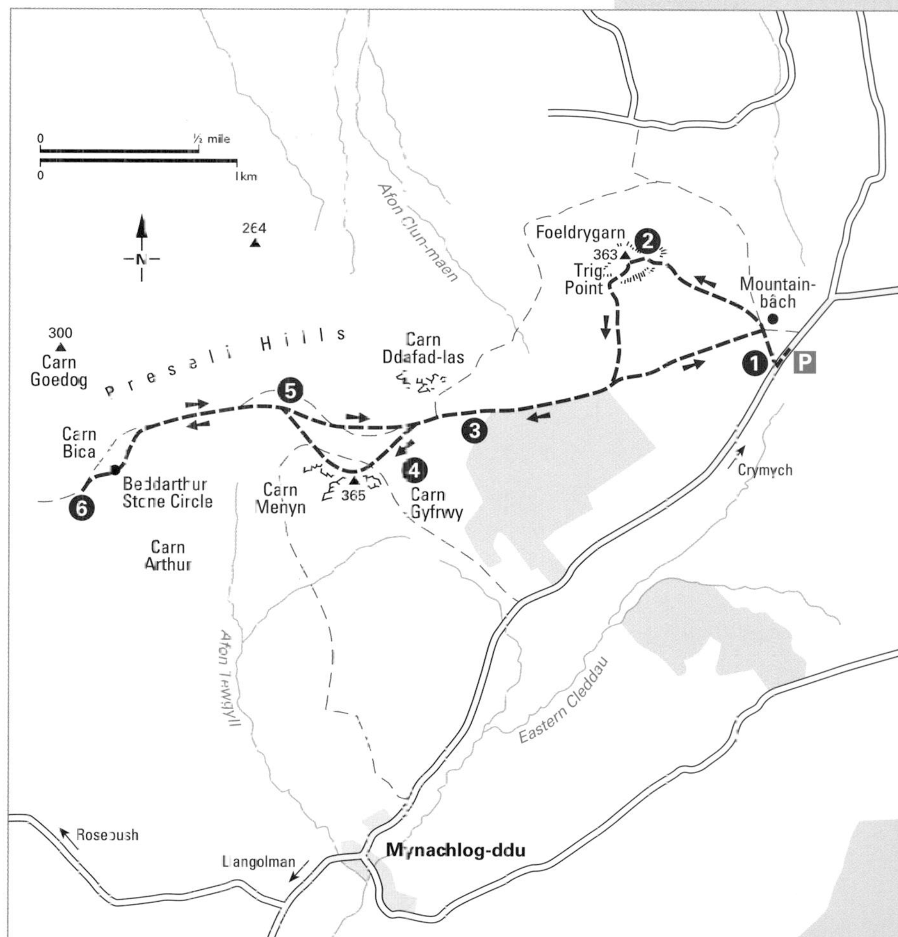

1 Walk to the left out of the lay-by on the lane from Crymych, then turn right up a stony track. When you reach the gate, keep going straight ahead for another 100yds (91m) or so, and then fork left onto a grassy track, which soon becomes clearer as it winds its way up the hillside. Follow this all the way to the rocky cairns and trig point on Foeldrygarn.

2 Bear left at the summit and locate a grassy track that drops steeply to the south. Cross the heather-clad plateau beneath, aiming for the left-hand corner of a wood. When you meet the main track, turn right to walk with the edge of the wood on your left.

3 Leaving the wood, the path climbs slightly to some rocky tors. The second of these, the one that's closest to the track, has a sheepfold at its base. Shortly after this, the path forks and you follow the left-hand track down to the nearest of the group of outcrops to your left.

4 This is Carn Gyfrwy. Continue on faint paths to the larger outcrops ahead, then curve right away from the stones and drop slightly to Carn Menyn, the lowest of the bunch, perched precariously on the edge of the escarpment. The path becomes clearer here and drops slightly into a marshy saddle that can be seen ahead.

5 In the saddle you'll meet the main track. Turn left and follow it steadily up towards Carn Bica, which is visible on the hillside ahead of you. Just before this, you'll cross the circle made by the stones of Beddarthur.

6 Turn around and retrace your steps back to the saddle. Climb slightly to pass the tor with the sheepfold and stay on this main path to walk beside the plantation once more, now on your right. At the end of this, drop on a grassy track down to the gate. Turn right onto the lane and continue back to the car park.

HOW WERE THE BLUESTONES MOVED TO STONEHENGE?

Were the bluestones hauled northwest overland then by sea on rafts around St David's Head, Land's End and up the Hampshire Avon? Or were they hauled southwest to Milford Haven, then taken by sea to the Bristol Avon, then overland again and along the River Wyle and the Hampshire Avon? Some geologists argue that the stones were carried by ice sheets in c.46,000 BC. However tests in 1994 suggested that the stones had been exposed to air for no more than 14,000 years – well after any possible ice transport. Moreover, neither they nor any other stones on Salisbury Plain have glaciation marks on them.

Distance 5.5 miles (8.8km)

Minimum time 2hrs 30min

Ascent/gradient 560ft (170m) ▲▲▲

Level of difficulty ●●●

Paths Mainly clear paths across open moorland, no stiles

Landscape Rolling hills topped with rocky outcrops

Suggested map OS Explorer OL35 North Pembrokeshire

Start/finish Grid reference: SO 165331

Dog friendliness Care needed near livestock

Parking Small lay-by on lane beneath Foeldrygarn

Public toilets None on route but plenty of sheltered nooks and crannies

Note Navigation very difficult in poor visibility

A Wonder of the Prehistoric World

An enthralling Ridgeway walk reveals the scale and complexity of some of Britain's finest ceremonial monuments

Avebury's great stone circle is one of the most important megalithic monuments in Europe: the circle, which dates to 2600 – 2100 BC and is constructed from local sarsen stones, was enclosed in a massive earthen rampart nearly 1 mile (1.6km) in circumference. The main circle comprised 98 standing stones, each 9–19ft (3–6m) tall and weighing up to 20 tonnes; other smaller circles stood within. Today only 27 stones remain of an original total of 200. The area of the circle was 28.5 acres (11.5 ha) and it was divided into four sections by roadways. One can only wonder at the skill, vision and beliefs, not to mention the sheer dogged hard work, that enabled the peoples of that time to move huge stones and dig thousands of tons of earth to create such landscapes.

On Windmill Hill

Archaeological evidence from Windmill Hill, near Avebury, indicates that there was a flourishing community in the area by 3700 BC. Early farmers had started to clear the forest for agriculture, and – in addition to hunting wild animals – they reared cattle, sheep and pigs for meat. They made tools from flints, animal bones and antlers; and clothes, tents and thongs from animal skins. They made – and in time decorated – pots, and ground flour on quern stones. They also held seasonal gatherings on the top of Windmill Hill – evidence has been found in ditches there of ritual feasting and human burials.

In the Sanctuary

At around the same time the first chambered tombs were constructed for burials. Roughly contemporary with Windmill Hill is West Kennett Long Barrow, which was in use for 1,500 years. Huge and well preserved, it consists of passages and chambers constructed from local sarsen stones. As the skeletons found here were incomplete, it is thought that the dead may first have been laid to rest – and rot – in the Sanctuary, a temple on nearby Overton Hill.

The purpose of the Sanctuary is one of Avebury's many enigmas. There is nothing to see today besides a mass of small posts representing a series of buildings dating to *c.*3000 BC. The Sanctuary was linked to the Avebury stone circle by an avenue of standing stones, suggesting that it had a ceremonial function. Even more of a mystery is the reason for the construction of Silbury Hill, the manmade conical mound that stands beside the A4 and is passed on the walk. The construction of this, the largest manmade mound in Europe, must have required 80 million manhours of labour; the people who built it used only antlers for picks and animal shoulder blades for shovels. In 1776 archaeologists sank a shaft 100ft (31m) down from the top of the mound, looking for evidence

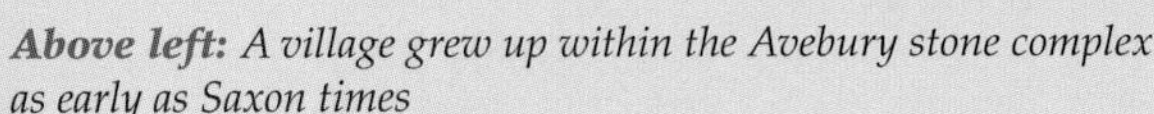

Above left: *A village grew up within the Avebury stone complex as early as Saxon times*

Left: *Sunrise at Avebury catches the mysterious megaliths*

Walk 3 Avebury – pagan pastures

Roam freely to explore the remains of a 3,000-year-old ceremonial complex

1 From the car park, walk to the main road and turn right. In 50yds (46m), cross and go through a gate with a blue bridleway sign. Pass through another gate and follow the path alongside the river. Go through two more gates and cross two stiles, passing Silbury Hill.

2 Beyond a gate, walk down the right-hand field-edge to a gate and the A4. Cross over and turn left, then almost immediately right through a gate. Walk down the gravel track and cross a bridge over a stream. The track soon narrows to a footpath. Go through a kissing gate and turn sharp left.

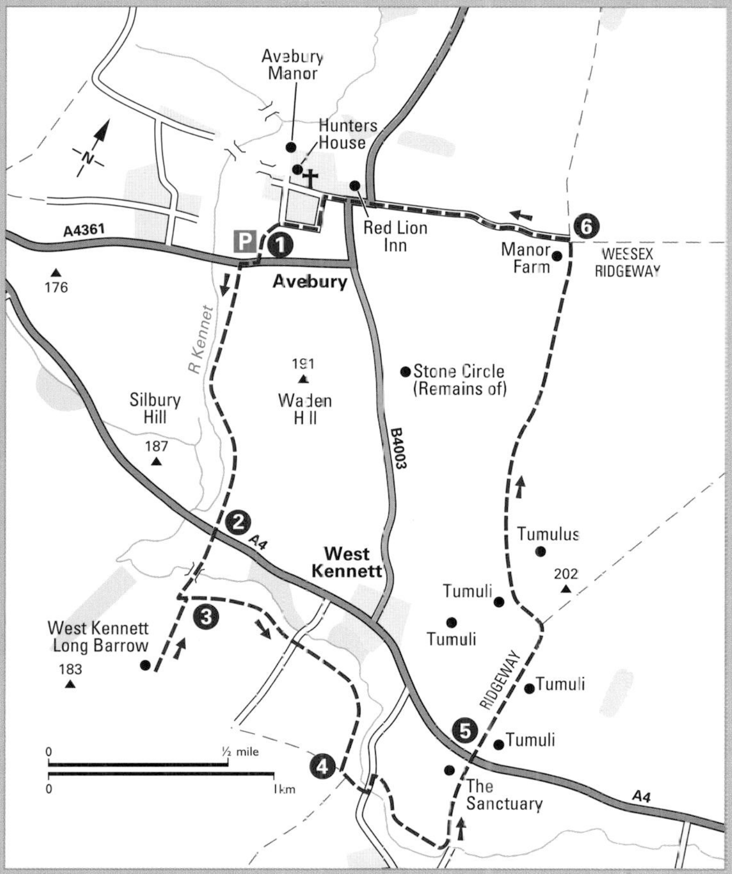

3 To visit West Kennett Long Barrow, shortly turn right. Otherwise go straight on around the left-hand field-edge to a stile and continue along a track. At a staggered junction, keep ahead across a stile and walk along the right-hand field boundary. Keep to the right in the corner by a redundant stile, and cross the stile on your right in the next corner and proceed up a narrow footpath.

4 At a T-junction, go left and descend to the road. Turn left, then just beyond the bridge, take the bridle path sharp right. Follow the right-hand field-edge to a gap in the corner and turn sharp left following a track uphill. At the top you'll see tumuli on the right and the Sanctuary on the left. Continue to the A4.

5 Cross the A4 and head up the Ridgeway. After 500yds (457m), turn left off the Ridgeway onto a byway. Bear half-right by the clump of trees on a tumuli and keep to the established track, eventually reaching a T-junction by a series of farm buildings, Manor Farm.

6 Turn left, signed 'Avebury', and follow the metalled track through the earthwork and straight over the staggered crossroads by the Red Lion Inn. Turn left opposite the National Trust signpost and walk back to the car park.

Distance 5 miles (8km)
Minimum time 2hrs 30min
Ascent/gradient 262ft (80m) ▲▲▲
Level of difficulty ●●●
Paths Tracks, field paths, some road walking, 4 stiles
Landscape Downland pasture, water-meadows, woodland and village
Suggested map OS Explorer 157 Marlborough & Savernake Forest
Start/finish Grid reference: SU 099696
Dog friendliness Keep dogs under control across pasture and National Trust property
Parking Large National Trust car park in Avebury
Public toilets Avebury

of burials; when none was found they plugged only the top of the shaft, leaving a void that collapsed in heavy rains in December 2000. You are not allowed to climb the hill.

Ceremonial Route

The walk leads along part of the Ridgeway, an ancient track with a magnificent view of Avebury's setting. You pass Silbury Hill, the West Kennett Long Barrow, the Sanctuary and the remains of the stone circle. The Stone Avenue is the 1.5-mile (2.4km) ceremonial route lined with standing stones that ran from the southern entrance to the Sanctuary. Some of the original stones in the first section have been excavated and restored; some were reused as building materials in the village; and some, like many of Avebury's stones, remain underground, where they were buried in the medieval period.

AVEBURY AND ALEXANDER KEILLER

Avebury today owes as much to archaeologist Alexander Keiller as to the vision of our ancient ancestors. Heir to a marmalade fortune, he was able to indulge his passion for archaeology. In the early 1930s he came to Avebury, which had a thriving community within and around the stone circle, and determined to restore it to its original glory. He purchased land, excavated stones and – a matter of controversy today – re-erected fallen stones, setting up markers to replace those he believed to be missing. Trees were cleared and buildings within the circle demolished. Some villagers left the area while others moved to new houses in nearby Avebury Truslow. After the Second World War, Keiller sold the site to the National Trust.

3200 BC Sumerians develop a writing system on clay tablets. In Britain, stone circle building begins – for example, at Castlerigg in Cumbria.

3000 BC The first monument is constructed at Stonehenge, in Wiltshire. It is a bank and ditch enclosure around 330ft (100m) in diameter, perhaps with a ring of 56 wooden posts.

3000 BC Neolithic communities fell trees to create clearings for crops and grazing for cattle. Production of pottery begins. Desertification in the Sahara begins as a result of clearing of forests by early farmers.

3000 BC The first urban civilisation in Crete develops.

2920 BC In Egypt, the reign of the pharaohs begins.

2900 BC In India, the Indus Valley civilisation arises.

2750 BC In Turkey, the city of Troy is founded.

Count the Stones at Swinside

A quiet ramble leads past Swinside Stone Circle, hidden in a hollow above the Duddon river estuary

***Top right:** A gold pommel mount for a dagger, part of burial relics dating to 2000* BC

***Above:** 'Sunkenkirk' – the Swinside stone circle*

Swinside Stone Circle has kept watch over this corner of the Lake District for 4,000 years or more. The circle is a late Neolithic or early Bronze Age structure, probably dating from *c.*2000 BC. About 95ft (29m) in diameter, the circle appears to be aligned on the midwinter solstice – the place on the horizon where the sun rises on 21 December. The tallest stone, at the northernmost part of the circle, is a pillar 7ft 6in (2.23m) high. At the southeast of the circle there is an obvious entrance consisting of a gap 7ft (2.1m) wide flanked by two portal stones situated just outside the main circle. From the centre of the circle the midwinter solstice sunrise is visible through these stones.

'Sunkenkirk'

Locally the stone circle is called 'Sunkenkirk', the name drawn from a legend relating how once, when a church was being built on the site, the labourers could make no progress because the Devil kept pulling the stones down into the ground during the night. It is also said that – as with many such stone circles around the country – a person counting the stones more than once will find that he or she arrives at a different number each time. With that in mind, it is perhaps best to say that there are more than 50 but fewer than 60 stones in the circle. (There are, in fact, 55 stones.)

A Quiet Corner

Most of the people you meet around the Duddon Valley have travelled no great distance; local folk have a high regard for the area's delights. The walk stretches almost all the way from a tidal estuary to the flanks of the high fells, taking in old coppice woodlands and pastures. Blast furnaces and charcoal burners once belched smoke into the air, and ships laden with pig iron sailed from the estuary, but that was a couple of centuries ago. There is a series of standing stones near Ash House towards the end of the walk, but there is no public access to them.

Walk 4 A Lake District gem at 'Sunkenkirk'

Taste the atmosphere of an ancient ceremonial or religious site at one of Cumbria's finest stone circles, in a lovely corner of the county

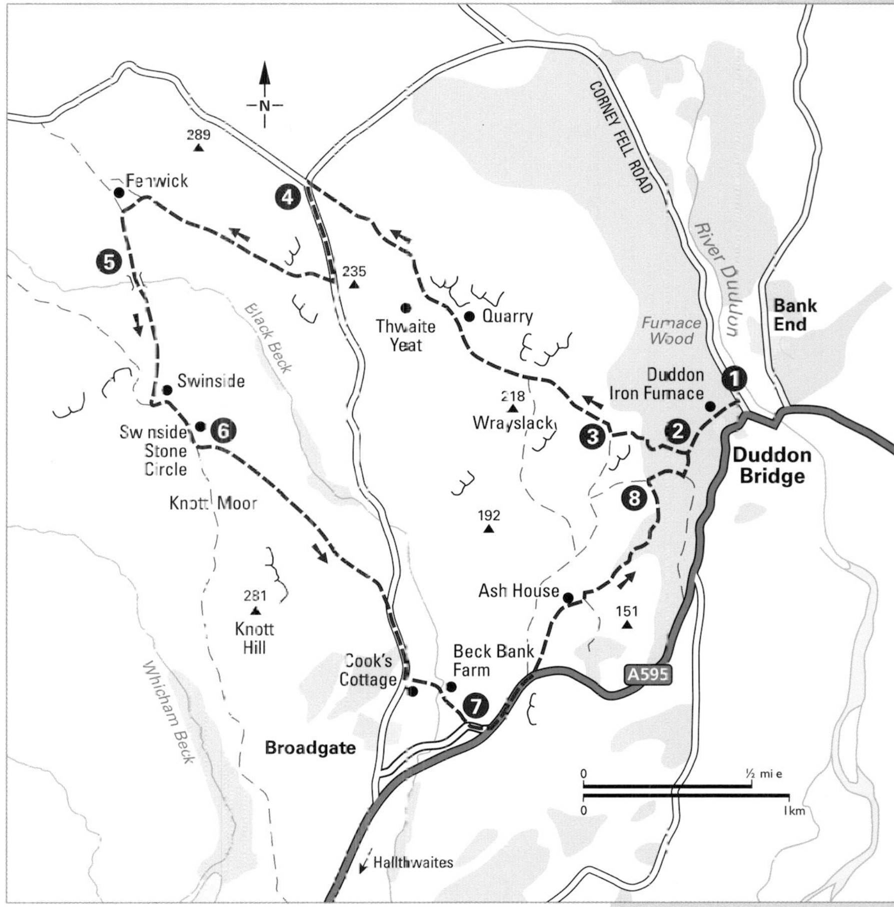

1 The Duddon Iron Furnace is on the left of the Corney Fell road, soon after the turning from Duddon Bridge. A public bridleway sign points up a track beside the ruins. At the last building, turn left up a woodland path marked by a bridleway sign hidden among brambles.

2 Cross a narrow access road and continue uphill. Turn right at a junction and keep on climbing. You will join a track leading further up the wooded slope, but watch for a gate in a wall on the left. Go through the gate and then follow a deep, narrow path flanked by bracken, crossing a low gap in the hills.

3 Turn right to reach a gate. Go through and follow a walled track. When another gate is reached, go through and turn left. A path running roughly parallel to a tall wall passes an old quarry near a farm called Thwaite Yeat. The path is vague on a moorland slope, but look ahead to spot a signpost at a road junction.

4 Turn left down a narrow road signposted 'Millom', and then turn right along a farm track. It crosses a dip and leads to a gate marked 'Fenwick'. Go through and follow the track almost to the farm, but turn left as indicated by a public footpath sign. Cross three stiles as the path leads down through fields to Black Beck.

5 Cross a footbridge and climb uphill, looking ahead to spot Swinside farm. Keep to the right of the buildings, but turn left to join and follow the access road away from the buildings. Swinside Stone Circle is in a field on the left.

6 Walk down the farm access road and continue along a tarmac road to Cook's Cottage. Just before the building is a stile and public footpath signpost. A field path and stile lead to Black Beck, and stepping stones lead to Beck Bank Farm. Two tracks lead from the farm to a nearby road. Use the one on the left. If the stones are uncrossable, retrace your steps to Cook's Cottage and turn left down the road, through Broadgate to a T-junction.Turn left, along the road past old mill buildings to rejoin the route at Point 7.

7 Turn left along the road and left again along a busy main road. Walk round a bend to find two farm roads signposted as public bridleways. Take the second one to Ash House. Leave the garden through a gate and turn left, over a stile. Turn right, by the fence along a narrow path. Another stile leads into woods. Walk uphill, then down to reach a marker post at a junction.

8 Turn right and walk downhill, then turn left at a junction. Keep right at another junction, following a path that was used earlier. Cross a narrow access road and proceed down to the Duddon Iron Furnace and the start of the walk.

WHILE YOU'RE THERE

The ruined Duddon Iron Furnace is visible from the start of the walk. Dating from 1736, this was one of eight rural blast furnaces in the area. Apart from the addition of an extra charcoal store, the structure has hardly changed from the day it was built. Information boards show the layout of the site, which included charcoal and iron ore stores, a wheelhouse, furnace, blowing house, casting house, office and slag heap. Ore and charcoal were fed into the furnace from the top of the site and pig iron left at the bottom. Ships sailing out of the Duddon Estuary transported the iron to Bristol and Chepstow for use in the shipbuilding industry. Small rural furnaces simply went out of business when bigger blast furnaces were constructed. Today the ruins are managed by English Heritage and are always open for inspection.

Distance 6 miles (9.7km)

Minimum time 2hrs 30min

Ascent/gradient 820ft (250m) ▲▲▲

Level of difficulty ●●●

Paths Good paths, some can be muddy, farm roads, 6 stiles

Landscape Wooded slopes, mostly rough pasture

Suggested map OS Explorer OL6 The English Lakes (SW)

Start/finish Grid reference: SD 197882

Dog friendliness On lead where sheep graze and on roads

Parking Parking space at Duddon Iron Furnace

Public toilets Nearest at Broughton-in-Furness

Note If Black Back is in spate, stepping stones are uncrossable and the detour adds 0.75 mile (1.2km)

2700 BC In Egypt Pharaoh Zoser builds the first pyramid at Saqqara.

2600 BC In Pakistan the Indus Valley cities of Mohenjo-daro and Harappa are built.

2600 BC Blue rhyolite stones are transported to Stonehenge from the Preseli Hills in Wales.

2575 BC In Egypt Pharaoh Khufu builds the Great Pyramid at Giza (near modern Cairo).

2500 BC At the foot of the Great Pyramid, Pharaoh Khafre builds the Great Sphinx.

2400 BC Near Avebury in Wiltshire, the first phase of building on Silbury Hill begins.

2000 BC Decorated pottery is produced in Britain, and stone chamber tombs are built. Complex village settlements, such as Chysauster in Cornwall, emerge.

Pinkery Pond to Moles Chamber

This upland tramp gives a taste of quintessential Exmoor among the barrows and tumuli of Bronze Age farmers

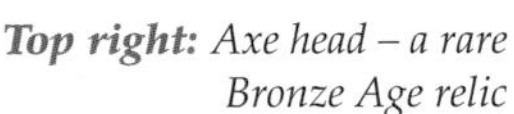

Top right: Axe head – a rare Bronze Age relic

Above: Decorated ornaments from a Bronze Age burial site

Below: Challacombe Longstone, with Longstone Barrow visible on the horizon

In about 2000 BC the hunter-gatherer lifestyle of the Stone Age came to an end on Exmoor. In the Bronze Age that followed we find traces of agriculture: the first farmers grew crops such as barley and kept livestock – mostly cattle and sheep. We also find round barrows – for example, Chains Barrow and Longstone Barrow – scattered across the moorland summits. Elsewhere in Somerset the standing stones are of the Bronze Age – charred wood accidentally buried under the stones can be carbon-dated.

It used to be thought that the change from the Stone Age to the Bronze Age came about by conquest: better swords and axes allowed the new people to kill or enslave the old. Today, tree pollen preserved in peat bogs can be dated very accurately, and shows that the clearance of the moors for farming was a gradual process. The scratch-plough was perhaps more important than the sword: the idea of settling and starting a farm conquered rather than a tribe. The climate was warmer and drier in those days, and the moorland was grass rather than peat. Large areas will have been hedged and banked for pasture: on Dartmoor, 25,000 acres (10,000ha) of Bronze Age enclosures have been mapped out.

High Society

The shepherds belonged to a wider social unit than the family or farmstead. At least some people were of sufficient importance to build up a collection of 50 or 60 axe-heads, implying that the Bronze Age farmers were not entirely peaceful people. We do not know why Bronze Age people chose to build their barrows on the bleakest of hilltops. Perhaps they were scared of the spirits of the dead and wanted to keep them out of the way, or perhaps a conspicuous barrow would intimidate the people on the next hill.

Walk 5 Bronze Age burial grounds high on the moor

Travel back 4,000 years to the time of Somerset's hardy first farmers

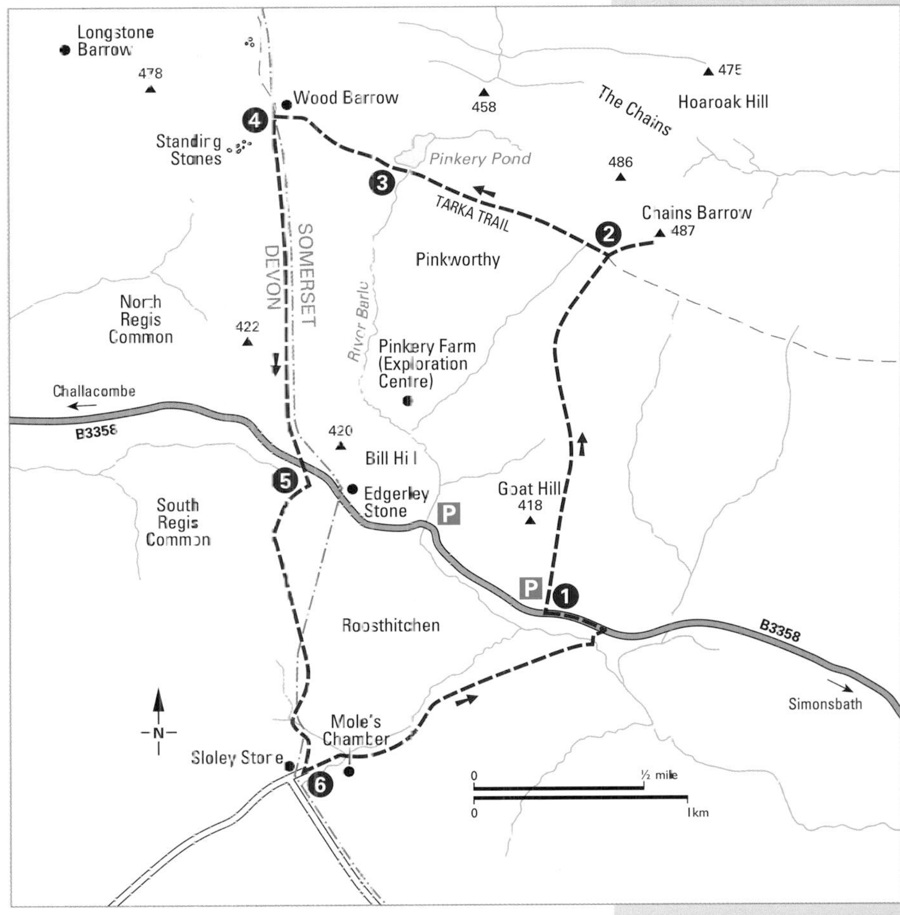

1 At the Simonsbath end of the pull-off is a gate with a bridleway sign for Chains Barrow. Go up the right-hand edges of two fields, then head 35yds (32m) left, to a gate. The way across the following rough moorland is marked by occasional blue-topped posts. Walk gently uphill, keeping parallel with a hedge away on the left. The marked way bends slightly right, up the crest of a wide moorland spur. At the top you will come to a bank which has a gateway.

2 A signpost indicates a sketchy path out over the moor to Chains Barrow. Return to the gateway and follow the path ahead, signed 'Pinkery Pond', running along and above the fenced bank. It leads across the moor top to Pinkery Pond; this is crossed on its dam.

3 Follow the fence as it continues uphill to a gate with a blue spot. Maintain your direction across moorland for 350yds (320m) to join a high bank and fence from the right, and follow this to Wood Barrow.

4 The gate ahead leads into Devon. Beyond, Wood Barrow is one of many put to more conventional use, originally by the Saxons, as markers of the Devon boundary. In front of Woodbarrow Gate turn left on a signed bridleway track, with a high bank on its right. This leads off the moor. Bear left around a sheep-pen made of metal crash barriers. A gate leads onto the B3358.

5 Cross the B3358 into a track signposted 'Mole's Chamber'. This climbs for 0.25 mile (400m) to a signpost. Here you must bear left, keeping to the left of a fence, for 550yds (503m). A junction of high banks soon comes into sight: take the gate ahead and go downhill to the left of the high bank beyond. Go straight downhill to the right-hand of two narrow gates, with a stream and the start of a track beyond. Follow this track up and to the right, until you reach a point just before the corner of a tarmac road. An inscribed boundary marker, the Sloley Stone, is just above the track.

6 Turn down sharp left, heading away from the road. Follow a faint old track that runs down across a stream to a narrow gate with a blue paint-spot. An improving path runs down to the right of the stream, gradually slanting up to a gate. Here join a larger track, and immediately after the gate keep ahead, slanting slightly downhill. A faint green track runs parallel with the river down on the left, to a signposted gate. Turn left on a concrete track, to join the B3358. Turn left to the parking pull-off.

CHALLACOMBE LONGSTONE

Standing above the village of Challacombe, the Challacombe Longstone is a slate slab 9ft (2.7m) tall, 4ft (1.25m) wide and just 10 inches (25cm) thick at its base. It was erected near the source of the River Bray, just below the ridge, and surrounded by bog – although in Bronze Age times the land was drier. Close by, and visible on the skyline, is the Longstone Barrow and the Quincunx, a collection of five stones with four aligned north, south, east and west and the fifth occupying the centre.

WHILE YOU'RE THERE

The Lynton & Barnstaple Railway, above Parracombe, runs just 1 mile (1.6km) across the very top of Exmoor, but gives passengers wide views westwards across Devon. There are plans to extend its narrow gauge steam service to the original terminus at Barnstaple.

The West Somerset Railway runs for 20 miles (32km) from Bishop's Lydeard to Minehead, through the Quantock Hills and along the coastline. A branch of the Old Great Western Railway, it is Britain's longest standard gauge steam railway.

Distance 5.75 miles (9.2km)

Minimum time 3hrs

Ascent/gradient 700ft (213m) ▲▲▲

Level of difficulty ●●●

Paths Narrow moorland paths following fences and some tracks, 1 stile

Landscape Bleak, grassy moorland

Suggested map OS Explorer OL9 Exmoor

Start/finish Grid reference: SS 729401

Dog friendliness Be aware of possible livestock, ponies and deer on open moorland

Parking Unmarked roadside pull-off on B3358 on Goat Hill

Public toilets None on route; nearest in Simonsbath car park

2000 BC In early Bronze Age Britain metal axes, daggers and spearheads are widely made.

2000 BC Elite individuals are buried in round barrows with goods including pottery and bronze daggers. An individual is buried at Lockington, Leicestershire, with two gold armlets, a copper dagger from Brittany and two pottery vessels.

1850 BC In Egypt engineers working for Pharaoh Senusret III cut a great channel 260ft (79m) in length and 34ft (10m) wide through cliffs at the Nile's First Cataract. The tunnel is navigable by warships.

1800 BC The first deep copper mines in the British Isles are dug. Mines are excavated at Great Orme in Wales and Mount Gabriel, County Cork, Ireland.

1792–1750 BC Hammurabi the Great establishes the Babylonian Empire. He collects Hammurabi's Code, one of the world's first law codes.

The 'Twelve Apostles' of Ilkley Moor

An excursion across Yorkshire moorland leads to an intriguing Bronze Age stone circle

The 'Twelve Apostles' is a ring of Bronze Age standing stones sited close to the meeting of two ancient routes across Ilkley Moor, a long ridge of millstone grit immediately to the south of Ilkley. The twelve slabs of millstone grit (there were more stones originally, probably twenty, with one at the centre) are arranged in a circle approximately 50ft (15m) in diameter.

The tallest of the stones is little more than 3ft (1m). The circle may well have been used for celestial observations. Some believe it was sited to align with the midsummer sunrise or used for observing the Moon; in folklore the site has associations with the Druids, priests of Iron Age and Bronze Age Britain.

'Cup and Ring' Carvings

The circle is the most visible evidence of 7,000 years of occupation of these moors. There are other, smaller circles too, and Ilkley Moor is celebrated for its Bronze Age rock carvings, many showing 'cup and ring' designs. The most famous of these rocks features a sinuous swastika, traditionally a symbol of good luck until the Nazis corrupted it.

In addition to Pancake and Haystack rocks, seen on this walk, there are dozens of other natural gritstone rock formations. The biggest and best known are the 'Cow and Calf', close to the start of this walk, where climbers practise their holds and rope work.

Above right: *Prehistoric 'cup and ring' rock carvings high on Rombalds Moor*

Below: *A sweeping view over the town of Ilkey, from the moor*

Walk 6 Ancient stones in a spectacular setting

Explore an historic landscape – and look out for Bronze Age 'cup and ring' carvings

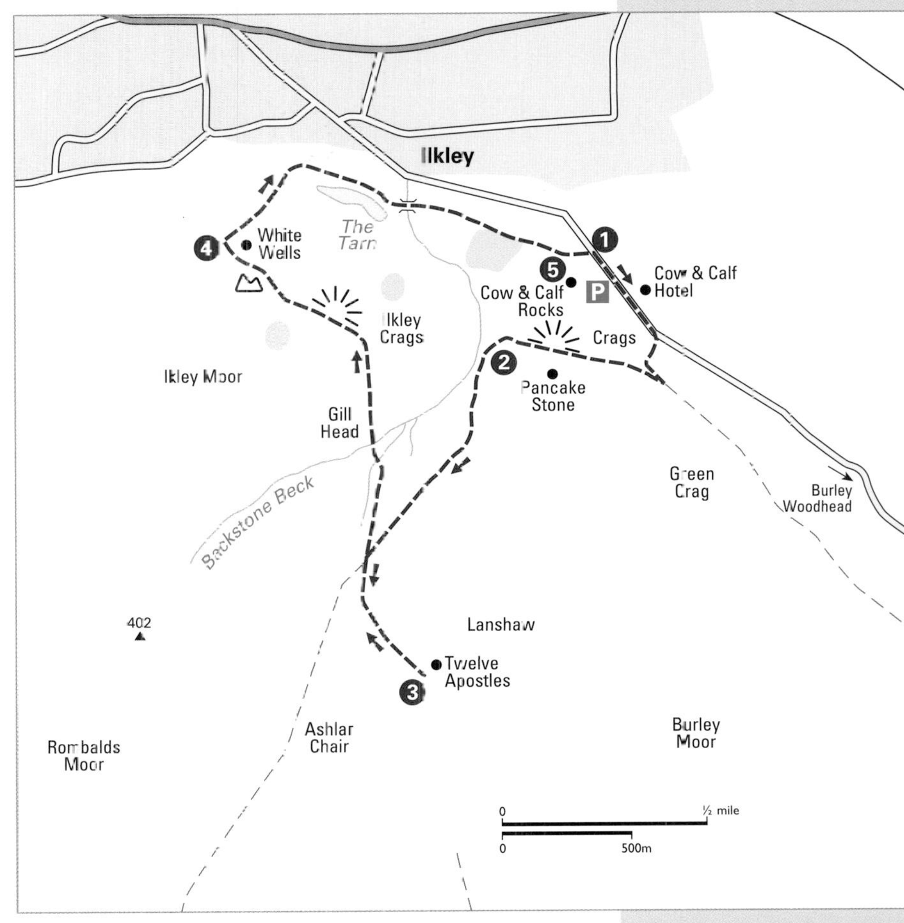

1 Walk up the road; 150yds (137m) beyond the Cow and Calf Hotel, where the road bears left, fork right up a grassy path. Scramble onto the ridge and follow it west past the Pancake Stone, enjoying extensive views over Ilkley and Wharfedale. Dip across a path rising along a shallow gully and continue beyond Haystack Rock, joining another path from the left. Keep left at successive forks, swinging parallel to the broad fold containing Backstone Beck, over to the right.

2 After gently rising for 0.75 mile (1.2km) across open moor, the path eventually meets the Bradford–Ilkley Dales Way link. Go left here, along a section of duckboarding. Pass a boundary stone at the top of the rise, and continue to the ring of stones known as the Twelve Apostles, just beyond the crest.

3 Retrace your steps from the Twelve Apostles, but now continue ahead along the Dales Way link. Bear right at a fork and cross the head of Backstone Beck. Shortly, beyond a crossing path, the way curves left in a steep, slanting descent off the moor below the ridge, levelling lower down as it bends to White Wells.

4 Turn right in front of the bathhouse, and follow a path across the slope of the hill past a small pond and falling below a clump of rocks to meet a metalled path. Go right, taking either branch around the Tarn to find a path leaving up steps at the end. After crossing Blackstone Beck, ignore a rising grass track and continue up the final pull to the crags by the Cow and Calf rocks.

5 It's worth taking a few minutes at the Cow and Calf to investigate the rocks and watch climbers practising their belays and traverses. From the rocks a paved path leads back to the car park.

HATLESS ON ILKLEY MOOR

The Yorkshire-dialect song 'On Ilkla Moor Baht'at' ('On Ilkley Moor Without a Hat') is reckoned to be Yorkshire's unofficial anthem; according to tradition, it was composed by members of a church choir from Halifax when they were on an outing to the moor. The song acts as a warning to a lover wandering on Ilkley Moor without a hat to court his beloved; because the winds are bitter and he has no headgear he might catch his death of cold and be eaten by worms, which will be eaten by ducks, and the ducks will be eaten by members of the choir.

Distance 4.5 miles (7.2km)

Minimum time 2hrs 30min

Ascent/gradient 803ft (245m) ▲▲▲

Level of difficulty ●●●

Paths Good moorland paths, some steep paths towards end of walk, no stiles

Landscape Mostly open heather moorland, and gritstone crags

Suggested map OS Explorer 297 Lower Wharfedale

Start/finish Grid reference: SE 132467

Dog friendliness Under control where sheep graze freely on moorland

Parking Car park below Cow and Calf rocks

Public toilets At White Wells visitor centre

WHAT TO LOOK OUT FOR

Many rocks on Ilkley Moor are decorated with 'cup and ring' patterns – including the Pancake Rock, near the start of this walk. Cup and ring patterns comprise a small hole or depression carved in the rock and surrounded by concentric rings. They are found in northern England, Scotland, Ireland and many other parts of Europe. Many more rock carvings can be found on the moor. The swastika pattern mentioned in the main text is on the Woodhouse Crag on the moor's northern edge.

The route passes White Wells, built in 1700 around a local mineral spring. Today it is a visitor centre but it was once an early health farm. As such it was a precursor of Ilkley's transformation from a village into a prosperous spa town. Dr William Mcleod arrived here in 1847, recognised the town's potential and spent 25 years creating a place where the well-heeled could 'take the waters' in upmarket surroundings. Dr Mcleod promoted the 'Ilkley Cure', a strict regime of exercise and cold baths.

1700 BC Copper and gold mining begin to develop in Britain. The settlers use these new materials to make sophisticated tools, weapons and jewellery. At Rillaton, Cornwall, an individual is buried with an exquisite gold cup fashioned to resemble a pottery beaker.

1600 BC In the Minoan Empire people worship a snake fertility goddess and make figurines of a woman holding a snake in each hand. There is evidence of animal and human sacrifice.

1100 BC In Britain the earliest hilltop settlements start to appear in places such as Cissbury and Herefordshire Beacon; they remain in use for the next 300 years, often built upon and greatly extended by successive generations.

Uffington's White Horse

A spectacular walk leads to the place where, according to legend, St George killed the dragon

High above the Oxfordshire countryside stands the chalk figure of a galloping horse. This noted landmark, 365ft (111m) long and 130ft (40m) tall, is cut into the turf of White Horse Hill at a height of 856ft (261m). The best time to see the horse is early on a summer's day or during the week in the middle of winter, when the crowds and the cars are scarce. It is then that the Uffington White Horse exudes its own peculiar air of mystery.

Regarded as far and away the most beautiful of all the British chalk hill figures, the horse is formed from a chalk-filled trench and, contrary to popular belief, not etched into the natural chalk. Its design is stylised, with an elegant, slender body and a distinctive beaked jaw similar to those displayed on early Iron Age coins. There have been countless theories over the years as to its age and exact purpose.

A medieval document records it as one of the wonders of Britain, along with Stonehenge, while some sources suggest it was cut some time during the 1st century AD. Others claim it was established to celebrate King Alfred's victory over the Danes at the Battle of Ashdown in AD 871. In more recent times, the age of the horse has been scientifically pinpointed by a series of archaeological digs and analysis of soil samples, indicating that it dates back almost 3,000 years, to the late Bronze Age or early Iron Age.

Unanswered Questions

The horse is not clearly appreciated other than from the air or from some distance away – which gives credence to the theory that the White Horse may have acted as a tribal banner or badge for the inhabitants of the Vale of White Horse below. What does it symbolise and why was this particular site chosen? There are no conclusive answers. Certainly the White Horse is closely associated with mythology. One legend claims that the figure is St George's steed and that the flat-topped chalk outcrop below, known as Dragon Hill, is where St George slew the beast. A bare patch on the summit is supposed to mark where the dragon's blood was spilt.

Above right: *The Rillaton gold cup (1700 BC) was discovered in a burial site in Cornwall, and is now held in the British Museum, London*

Below left: *The stone tomb at Wayland's Smithy (3700 BC–3400 BC) contained the remains of eight individuals, including a child*

Below right: *The highly stylised design of the White Horse also appeared on coins during the Iron Age*

Walk 7 Galloping figure on an Oxfordshire hillside

Take a downland ramble to discover the magic of one of Britain's greatest antiquities

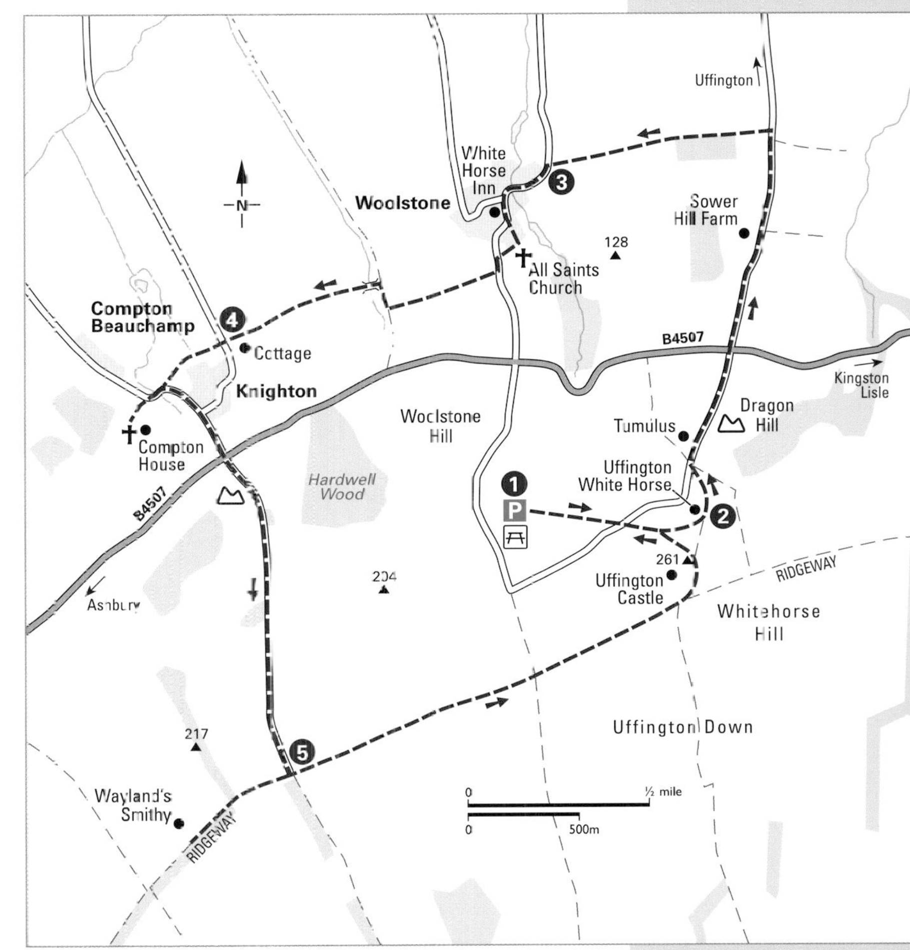

1 From the car park go through any gate to follow the outline of the grassy path along the lower slopes towards the hill. Make for a gate and cross the lane to join a bridleway. Make sure to keep left at the fork, by a bridleway waymark, and walk along to the head of Uffington's galloping White Horse.

2 Descend steeply on the path to the tarmac access road, keeping the chalk figure on your left. If you prefer to avoid the dramatic descent, retrace your steps to the lane, turn right and continue down to the junction with the B4507. Cross over and take the road towards Uffington, turning left at the path signposted to Woolstone. Go through a gate and keep the hedge on your right. Make for a stile in the field corner. Continue across the next field to a gap and cut through trees to the next gap. Keep ahead with the hedgerow on your left.

3 Through a kissing gate, turn left at the road and walk through the village of Woolstone. Turn left by the White Horse Inn and follow the road to All Saints' Church. At its metal kissing gate, veer right across the churchyard to a stile and gate. Cross a paddock to a further gate and stile. Turn left up the road for less than 100yds (91m) and turn right at the footpath sign. Walk for 0.25 mile (400m) with a hedge on your left side, across three fields, to a stile. Turn right and walk through the trees for about 150yds (137m), looking for a concealed footbridge on your left. Cross the footbridge to a field, head diagonally left to a stile and turn right. Follow the field-edge to a stile and aim ahead, across further fields and stiles, to a thatched cottage. As you pass the cottage to your left you will reach a road.

4 Cross the road and follow the D'Arcy Dalton Way on the opposite side. Take a stile into a paddock, then veer left to join a rough track to the road by the village sign for Compton Beauchamp. Cross over and take the drive to the church, next to the manor. Retrace your steps to the sign and walk up to the junction with the B4507. Cross over and climb quite steeply to the Ridgeway.

5 Turn right for 550yds (503m) if you wish to visit Wayland's Smithy. Otherwise, turn left and walk for 1 mile (1.6km). At the highest point on the track, about 50yds (46m) beyond a track junction, turn left. Go to the trig pillar, then left (visiting the fort first) and descend to rejoin the outward track, back to the car park.

WHILE YOU'RE THERE

Visit Wayland's Smithy, just off the route. This impressive 5,000-year-old long barrow occupies a remote and atmospheric location. It is so called because at one time it was said to be the workplace of the Saxon smith god Wayland. According to a local legend, any traveller who needed a new horseshoe had only to leave his animal overnight, together with a silver coin; when he returned in the morning he would find the coin missing and the animal fitted with a new shoe. Excavations in 1962–63 showed that there were two stages of construction: an oval barrow containing a wooden burial house was built in c.3700 BC and contained the remains of 15 individuals. A long barrow containing two stone chambers was built in c.3400 BC and contained seven adults and one child. Crowning Whitehorse Hill is Uffington Castle, an Iron Age hill-fort situated high on the Ridgeway. The hill-fort covers about 8 acres (3ha).

Distance 7 miles (11.3km)

Minimum time 3hrs 45min

Ascent/gradient 720ft (219m) ▲▲▲

Level of difficulty ●●●

Paths Ancient tracks and field paths, road (can be busy), 9 stiles

Landscape Vale of White Horse and exposed downland country on Oxfordshire/Berkshire border

Suggested map OS Explorer 170 Abingdon, Wantage

Start/finish Grid reference: SU 293865

Dog friendliness Under control or on lead in vicinity of the Uffington White Horse and along Ridgeway

Parking Large car park near Uffington White Horse

Public toilets None on route

1050 BC Phoenicians develop the first alphabet.

1003 BC King David unites Israel and Judah and founds the city of Jerusalem.

800 BC In Ancient Greece the poet Homer completes the *Iliad* and the *Odyssey*. (The *Iliad* is acknowledged to be the oldest work in Western literature.)

776 BC The first Olympic Games are held on the plains of Olympia, Greece, in honour of the Greek gods.

753 BC The Roman Empire is founded.

700 BC Britain enters the Iron Age. Iron revolutionises weapon- and tool-making and enables intensive farming and building of hill-forts.

Iron Age Hill-forts on Shopshire's Highest Hill

An exhilarating excursion visits former Iron Age sites on Brown Clee's upland commons

***Top right:** The view from Titterstone Clee to Brown Clee, Shropshire's highest peak*

***Above:** In many places on the Clees, Iron Age remains are overlaid by evidence of later mining*

Choose a clear day for this walk, because the astounding view from Abdon Burf, the higher of Brown Clee's twin summits, extends from the Cotswolds to Cadair Idris in Snowdonia. At 1,770ft (540m) tall, Brown Clee is Shropshire's highest hill, overtopping its sibling, Titterstone Clee, by 23ft (7m), and the Stiperstones by just 13ft (4m).

Brown Clee may be high, but it is not wild, although it appears to be so in places. In this area you have a perfect illustration of just how intensive rural land use can be. There is scarcely anything this hill has not been used for at one time or another in its long history.

Nobody knows when people started making use of the Clee Hills, but forts were built on Brown Clee in the Iron Age. Those on Abdon Burf and Clee Burf have been destroyed by quarrying. A third, Nordy Bank, still stands on Clee Liberty. Iron Age people hunted on the hills, and the tradition continued for centuries, with the Clees part of a royal forest for a time.

Brown Clee Hill must have been used for stock grazing after the hill-forts were built, or even before that. More recently, in the Middle Ages, all of the hillside above the encircling roads was common land, divided between parishes, while an outer ring of parishes also had grazing rights. Stock from the outer parishes was driven to and from Brown Clee on tracks known as outracks or strakerways, most of which are now footpaths or bridleways. Many are deeply sunken through long use, and commoners' sheep and ponies still graze Clee Liberty.

Medieval Mining

Mineral extraction also has a long history in the Clee Hills. Brown Clee is riddled with shafts and is said to be the highest ex-coalfield in Britain. Ironstone was dug from the coal measures from the Middle Ages onwards and fed a number of forges around the hill. More recently, a type of volcanic rock called dolerite (also locally known as dhustone) was exploited, mostly for road building, and the ruins of a stone-crushing plant still disfigure Abdon Burf. Wagons then transported the stone down a steep incline to the railway at Ditton Priors. Quarrying ceased in 1936 and the incline is now a footpath (though not a right of way), used in this walk to gain access to the hill. You can still see parts of the actual tramway in places.

Walk 8 Historic fortifications and a stunning vista

Wander free on Brown Clee to enjoy views of Nordy Bank fort – and far beyond

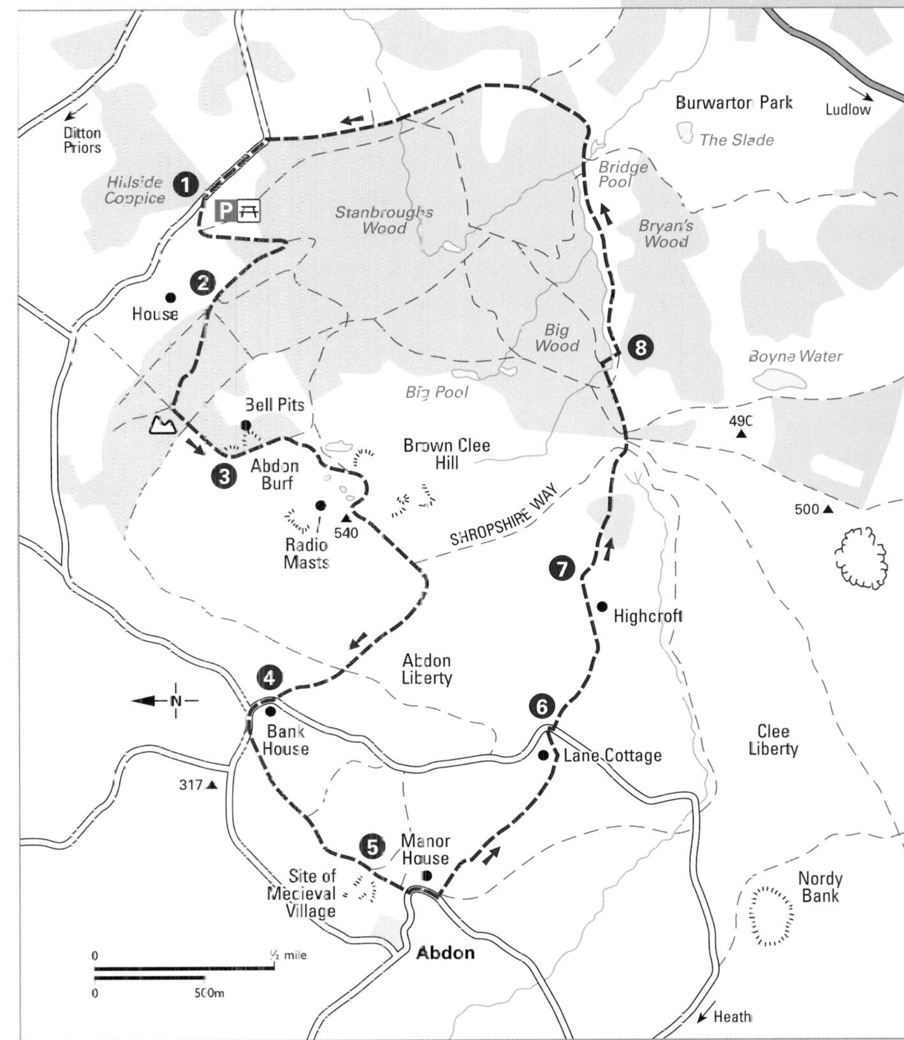

1 By the north end of the picnic field, a footpath climbs to the right then swings back left. Follow it into woodland, with conifers on the left. Soon go right on a level forest track which runs along the woodland edge, with a field on the right.

2 There are two houses just below the field. As you draw level with the second one, you will come to a turning circle on the left, where a path rises diagonally through a plantation. Follow this path to a steep straight track (the former tramway). Turn left, soon crossing a cattle grid into pastureland.

3 Continue less steeply, past conspicuous mounds of quarry spoil. The track turns sharp left. It's easy walking now to Abdon Burf, with its ugly masts and awesome views. From the summit, a rough path descends southwest (use the view indicator to confirm the direction). Follow it down to a line of posts. Go through these and keep descending by a fence. The path swings right, becoming a hollow way.

4 When you meet a lane, turn right, then go left at a junction and soon left again at a gate. The waymark points diagonally right, but instead go straight ahead along the left-hand edges of several meadows, and maintain the same direction as the path merges with the remains of an old green lane.

5 As you approach Abdon, a stile gives access to a garden. Go straight through, with signs directing you past the house and down a hollow way to a lane. Turn left, go past farm buildings and continue to a collection of barns. There's a stony track opposite – walk a few paces along it to a bridleway on the left. Follow it uphill. Where it appears to come to a dead end, enter the field on the right and continue until a stile gives access to a boardwalk in the garden of Lane Cottage.

6 Meet a lane and cross to a stile almost opposite. Climb steeply towards a fence/hedge on the skyline. Cross at a stile, continue to the far corner of the next field, then turn left on a track. At Highcroft, the track becomes a hollow way.

7 Go through a gate into pasture and follow the right-hand fence to the top corner. Pass through another gate and continue to a line of beeches on the summit ridge. Go forward through the beeches, then proceed straight on down a track, passing through woodland, plantation and finally bracken to a junction. Turn right.

8 The track crosses a stream. Fork left on a green path descending near the stream. When you meet a concrete track, make a turn to the left. After 600yds (549m) you'll come to a junction. Branch right here if you want the pub or bus stop at Burwarton. If not, keep left to return to the picnic site.

WHILE YOU'RE THERE

Visit the hamlet of Heath, situated to the west of Brown Clee. The renowned Heath Chapel stands alone in a field and is acknowledged to be the purest example of Norman church architecture in Shropshire. The nave and chancel have remained virtually unchanged for 800 years. Look out for fine examples of the Norman arch – see the chancel arch and the arch over the door – and the box pews.

Distance 7 miles (11.3km)

Minimum time 3hrs 30min

Ascent/gradient 1,460ft (445m) ▲▲▲

Level of difficulty ●●●

Paths Generally good, but boggy in places, 5 stiles

Landscape Hill, moorland, pasture and plantation

Suggested map OS Explorer 217 The Long Mynd & Wenlock Edge

Start/finish Grid reference: SO 607873

Dog friendliness Under strict control near sheep

Parking Verges by Brown Clee Picnic Area, on road west of Cleobury North

Public toilets None on route

605 BC King Nebuchadnezzar comes to power in Babylon, and his conquests include the enslavement of the Jewish people. He initiates the building of the Hanging Gardens of Babylon.

600 BC Tribes of warlike people, known as the Celts, reach Britain and Ireland. They settle in hill-forts, sow barley and have complex religious beliefs.

530 BC In northern India Prince Gautama embarks on life as an ascetic prior to founding Buddhism.

509 BC The Roman Republic is founded.

500 BC The inhabitants of a clifftop hill-fort at Hengistbury Head, Dorset, trade with tribes on the European mainland. Iron, silver and bronze goods are exchanged for pottery, tools and wine from the mainland. They use coins – this is one of a few pre-Roman sites where coins have been found.

330–320 BC Greek sailor Pytheas of Massilia (Marseilles) sails around the British Isles. He describes trade in Cornish tin – from sites at Land's End and St Michael's Mount – with the Mediterranean.

Uley and its Fort on the Hill

The ancient fort of Uley Bury is the centrepiece for a walk along the Cotswold escarpment

The Uley Bury hill-fort, near the village of Uley, dates to the 6th century BC and is one of the finest hill-forts in the Cotswolds. There are many hundreds of Iron Age forts throughout England and Wales. They are concentrated in Cornwall, Southwest Wales and the Welsh Marches, with secondary concentrations throughout the Cotswolds, North Wales and Wessex. The term 'hill-fort' is generally used in connection with these settlements, but this can be misleading: there are many on level ground and many, also, that were not used purely for military purposes – often they were simply settlements located on easily defended sites.

Below: *The narrow entrance to Hetty Pegler's Tump, a Neolithic tomb (c.3200 BC)*

Bottom: *Uley Bury makes the most of its natural defences high on the escarpment ridge*

Types of Hill-fort

There are five types of hill-fort, classified according to the nature of the site on which they were built. Contour forts were built along the perimeter edge of a hilltop; promontory forts were built on a spur, surrounded by natural defences on two or more sides; valley and plateau forts (two types) depended heavily on artificial defences and were located in valleys or on flat land respectively; and multiple-enclosure forts were usually built in a poor strategic position on the slope of a hill and were perhaps used as stockades. Uley Bury, which covers about 38 acres (15.4ha), is classified as an inland promontory fort. The fort falls away on three sides; the fourth side, which faces away from the escarpment, is protected by specially constructed ramparts that would have been surmounted by a wooden palisade. The natural defences – the Cotswold escarpment, facing west – were also strengthened by the construction of a wide and deep ditch, as well as two additional ramparts, an inner one and an outer one, between which the footpath largely threads its course. The three main entrances were at the northern, eastern and southern corners. These vulnerable parts of the fort would have been fortified with log barriers.

Although some tribespeople lived permanently in huts within the fort, most lived outside, either on other parts of the hill or in the valleys below. In an emergency, therefore, there was space for those who lived outside the fort to take shelter within. Eventually the fort was taken over by the Dobunni tribe – Celtic interlopers from mainland Europe who arrived about 100 BC. Uley Bury appears to have been occupied by the Dobunni throughout the Roman era.

Walk 9 Around the ramparts of an Iron Age settlement

Explore where settlers made the most of natural defences on a Cotswold hillside

1 From the main street locate the Uley Stores (on your left as you walk up the street). Walk along the narrow lane (to the right, as you look at the stores). Pass between houses as the lane dwindles to a track. Immediately before a stile turn right along a public footpath heading towards Uley church.

2 When the churchyard can be seen on the right, turn left to go up a narrow path beside a cottage. This path rises fairly sharply and brings you to a kissing gate. Pass through into a meadow. Climb steeply up the grassland towards woodland.

3 At the treeline veer to the left of the woods. In a corner on the far left of the woods go through a gate and follow a winding woodland path uphill. When you come to a fence, stay on the path as it bears left. Go through a gate to emerge from the woods. Stay on the path as it rises across grassland.

4 Follow the perimeter of the ancient Uley Bury in an anti-clockwise direction, with steep drops falling away to your right. When you meet a junction of paths go left along the edge of the hill, with wide and impressive views to the west. After about 600yds (549m), at a curve, you will see a stile that invites you to descend.

5 Ignore this stile; instead continue ahead. At the next corner go over a stile and continue to skirt the bury. When you have gone a further 250yds (228m), to the bury's southeastern point, bear right on a bridleway that descends between hillocks. Continue, dropping quite steeply through bushes to a gate (not the gate and stile visible 50yds/46m to your right). Descend to a stile.

6 Walk along the tarmac path, all the way to a cottage and then a kissing gate. Go through this and pass beside the cottage to arrive at a lane. Turn left here and follow the lane, soon passing the Uley Brewery, to reach the main road. Turn left, passing South Street, to return to the start.

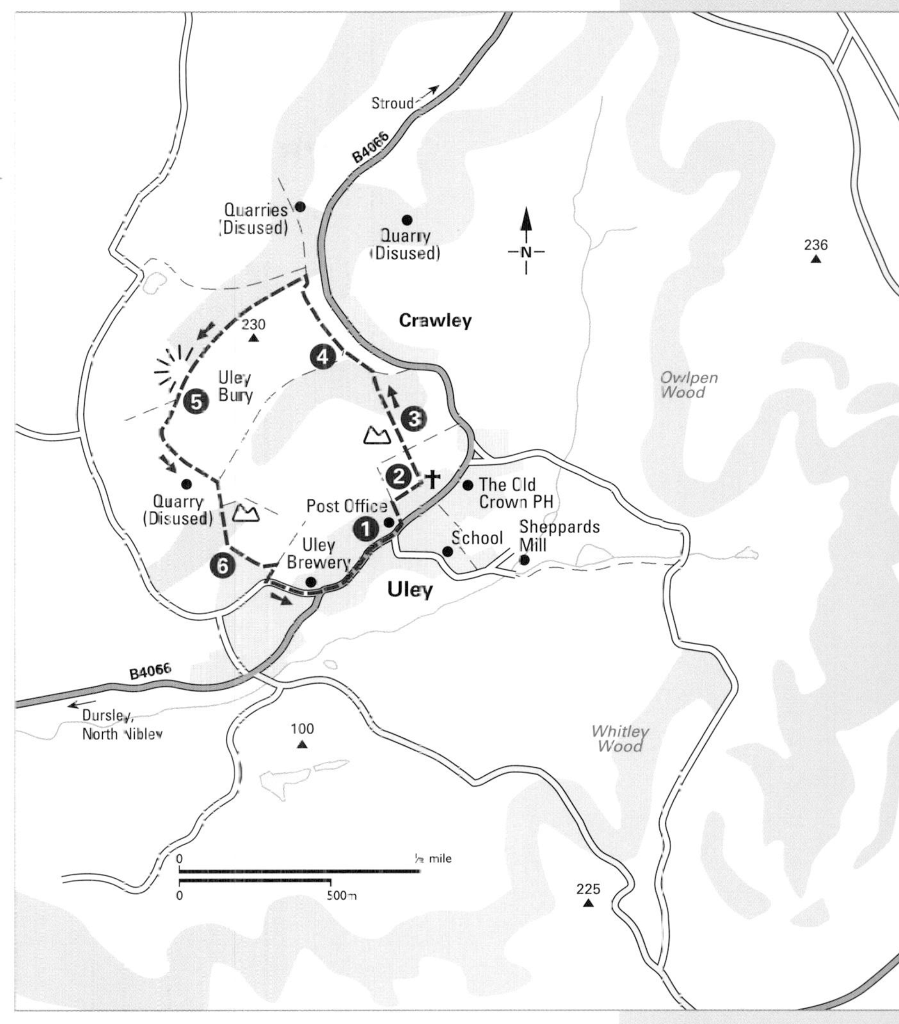

WHILE YOU'RE THERE

Just to the north of Uley Bury is Uley Long Barrow, better known as 'Hetty Pegler's Tump'. This is a Neolithic chambered tomb 120ft (37m) in length, 80ft (25m) wide and 10ft (3m) tall, dating to 3300–3200 BC. It is oriented east–west. A forecourt to the east of the mound gives onto a narrow stone doorway that leads into a passage 23ft (7m) long. Off the passage are three semicircular chambers: these would have contained cremated remains. The long barrow takes its name from that of Hester ('Hetty') Pegler, wife of the 17th-century owner of the field, Henry Pegler, while the word 'tump' was a slang name for a barrow or small rounded hill.

Distance 3 miles (4.8km)

Minimum time 1hr 30min

Ascent/gradient 345ft (105m) ▲▲▲

Level of difficulty ●●●

Paths Tracks and fields

Landscape Valley, meadows, woodland and open hilltop, 2 stiles

Suggested map OS Explorer 168 Stroud, Tetbury & Malmesbury

Start/finish Grid reference: ST 789984

Dog friendliness Suitable in parts but livestock on Uley Bury

Parking Main street of Uley

Public toilets None on route

CRICKLEY HILL AND OTHER IRON AGE FORTS IN THE COTSWOLDS

There are many notable Iron Age remains in the Costwolds. Remains of hill-forts are found at Little Sodbury, Painswick Beacon and Crickley Hill, among others. At Crickley Hill the oldest remains, of an enclosure and causeway, date all the way back to 3200 BC; in the 7th–6th centuries BC a triangular hill-fort of around 9 acres (3.6ha) was constructed behind a ditch and ramparts 16–22ft (5–7m) thick. Up to 100 people lived there. In the 6th century BC the fort was attacked, burned and abandoned. Around 400 arrowheads were found. At Painswick Beacon the triangular hill-fort was probably built in 500–100 BC.

ROMAN BRITAIN

AD 43–410

IMPERIAL OUTPOST

When the Roman emperor Claudius despatched troops to invade Britain in AD 43, he was tackling unfinished business. Ninety years earlier, Julius Caesar had led his warships on two raids against the 'barbarians' who lived on the northern edge of the Roman Empire.

Julius Caesar's campaigns in Britain in 55–54 BC yielded little more than a haul of prisoners and some good publicity back in Rome, but they left us with the invaders' accounts of life among the Celtic tribes – and one particularly vivid glimpse of the Druids of Anglesey, who faced their enemy across the Menai Strait, gesturing and praying, while wild-haired women waved flaming torches. A century later, the Emperor Claudius also found that the British Celts were a walkover.

Despite intertribal warfare and treachery, the Britons resisted the Romans for many years, notably under the leadership of Caratacus (Caradog), who, after his capture, was rewarded for his valour with 'honourable exile' in Rome. Others kept up the struggle, even after they were deemed 'client kingdoms'. One such group was that of the East Anglian Iceni people: in AD 60 their king's widow, Boudicca, took vengeance on the Romans for the rape of her daughters. The Romans, in turn, killed all suspected of rebellion.

In the following years the Romans overran Wales, northern England and southern Scotland. Eventually troops were withdrawn to go and face other conflicts – so northern Britain remained free of Roman rule, a division later marked by Hadrian's Wall, built from AD 122 onwards.

ROMAN LIFE

Britain was part of the Roman Empire for four centuries and, after the bloodletting of the 1st century AD, lived largely in peace with its masters. Even Hadrian's Wall was as much a customs barrier as a military border. In the period of diplomacy that followed, self-governing tribal authorities were established, called *civitates*: each elected its own magistrate, and was centred on a large town. Towns of varying size and importance flourished, with aqueducts, amphitheatres and temples.

Straight roads were built to speed communications, armies and goods across country. Many still function today. Roman religion mingled with British beliefs – in Aquae Sulis (Bath), the sacred springs of the Celtic water goddess, Sulis, were simply rebranded, and Sulis merged with the Roman goddess Minerva. Roman fashions and tastes were adopted by wealthy Britons, who Romanised their names, spoke Latin and built increasingly elaborate villas. The luxurious palace of Fishbourne, in Sussex, provided a perfect model – with its mosaics, underfloor heating and enclosed garden. The demand grew for imports such as olive oil, wine and glass, mainly for an elite; the daily drudge of most Britons carried on much as it always had.

DECLINE AND FALL

It all began to crumble in the 4th and 5th centuries AD. In AD 408–09 Saxons began raiding the British coasts, and two years later Emperor Honorius, struggling to contain troubles elsewhere, told the province to defend itself, without the aid of imperial muscle. Rome managed to maintain a hold on the northern isles for a few years afterwards – but its grasp was weakening. As the 5th century AD progressed, Britain entered another new phase of its history.

KEY SITES

Venta Icenorum, Norfolk : At Caistor St Edmund, the headquarters of the Queen of the Iceni, Boudicca, famous rebel against Rome in AD 61.

Brewood, Staffordshire: Where the Romans built a key section of Watling Street in *c* AD 100.

Hadrian's Wall: the 73-mile (117km) border at the northern edge of the Roman province in Britain was begun in AD 122.

Corstopitum, Northumberland: The Roman army built a fort and town at Corbridge in the 1st–2nd century AD.

Glannoventa, Cumbria: The Roman settlement at Ravenglass, built in the 2nd–3rd century AD, boasts a splendid bathhouse.

Left: At Housesteads fort on Hadrian's Wall around 800 soldiers guarded the Empire against Picts

AD **43** Emperor Claudius, determined to capture Britain, dispatches 50,000 Roman troops under the leadership of General Aulus Plautius. The army lands in Richborough, Kent, and heads for Colchester, the British tribal capital.

AD **47** The Fosse Way is established, running from Exeter to join the Ermine Street Way at Lincoln.

AD **48** Roman troops reach South Wales and, despite strong native resistance en route, overrun native hill-forts. Building of barracks commences at St Albans, Cirencester, Colchester and other strategic points.

AD **48** Claudius visits Colchester, to see the city taken and accept the surrender of the Celts. A Temple of Claudius is built as a centre of the imperial cult.

A Revolting Queen at Caistor St Edmund

A walk around a Roman fortress leads you in the footsteps of Queen Boudicca of the Iceni

When the Romans invaded Britain, they built arrow-straight roads, established well run, prosperous towns and developed industries such as tile-making, salt production and potteries. However, not all the local tribes were pleased to be part of the Roman Empire.

One rebel was Boudicca, who had been married to King Prasutagus of the Iceni. The trouble started when Prasutagus died in AD 60: he was barely cold in his grave before the Roman procurator's men arrived to grab property and money, and troops appeared to impose military law. One Roman insulted Boudicca, who responded with anger, and in retaliation the Queen was flogged and her daughters raped. News of this outrage spread like wildfire throughout East Anglia and the revolt was born.

__Above right:__ Boudicca, Queen of the Iceni, led a rebellion against the occupying Romans

__Below:__ The walk leads past St Edmund's Church, in the corner of the old Roman town

Boudicca's headquarters are said to have been at or near Venta Icenorum at Caistor. Contemporary accounts tell us that she was tall, with fierce eyes and a strident voice. She had a mane of tawny hair that tumbled to her waist and she wore a striking multicoloured tunic, a gold neck torc and a cloak held by a brooch. Female rulers were not unknown to the Iceni and they quickly rallied to her fiery speeches of rebellion and revenge. Other tribes joined the throng as Boudicca's army moved against the Romans, carrying huge shields and wearing their best battle gear.

The Rage of the Britons

From Venta Icenorum to Colchester they marched, probably using the recently completed Roman road. The army grew until it was 100,000 strong, all angry – and all determined to exact revenge on their hated oppressors. Meanwhile, Colchester was wholly unprepared for the attack, because the civilians had been assured there was nothing to worry about – they had well trained Roman soldiers to defend them. But as soon as the members of the garrison spotted the enormous, vengeful throng, they abandoned their posts and fled for safety inside the Temple of Claudius. The civilians were left to fend for themselves. A massacre followed.

No one was spared and as many as 20,000 were killed. The wooden town was burned to the ground and the stone temple fell two days later. Boudicca then moved on to London and St Albans, where the bloodshed continued.

The Triumph of the Romans

Roman general Suetonius marched to engage her army. The two forces met near St Albans. Suetonius' well trained army was outnumbered, but reports say that the Romans destroyed 80,000 of the larger force – an appalling number of dead for any battle; Boudicca probably poisoned herself after the defeat. Her legend lives on. This walk takes you through the lands she once ruled, some of it along the footpath, 38 miles (61km) long, named in her honour.

Walk 10 Base of a fearless British ruler who dared to defy the mighty Romans

Inspect the remains of the tribal settlement in which Boudicca inspired a bloody uprising

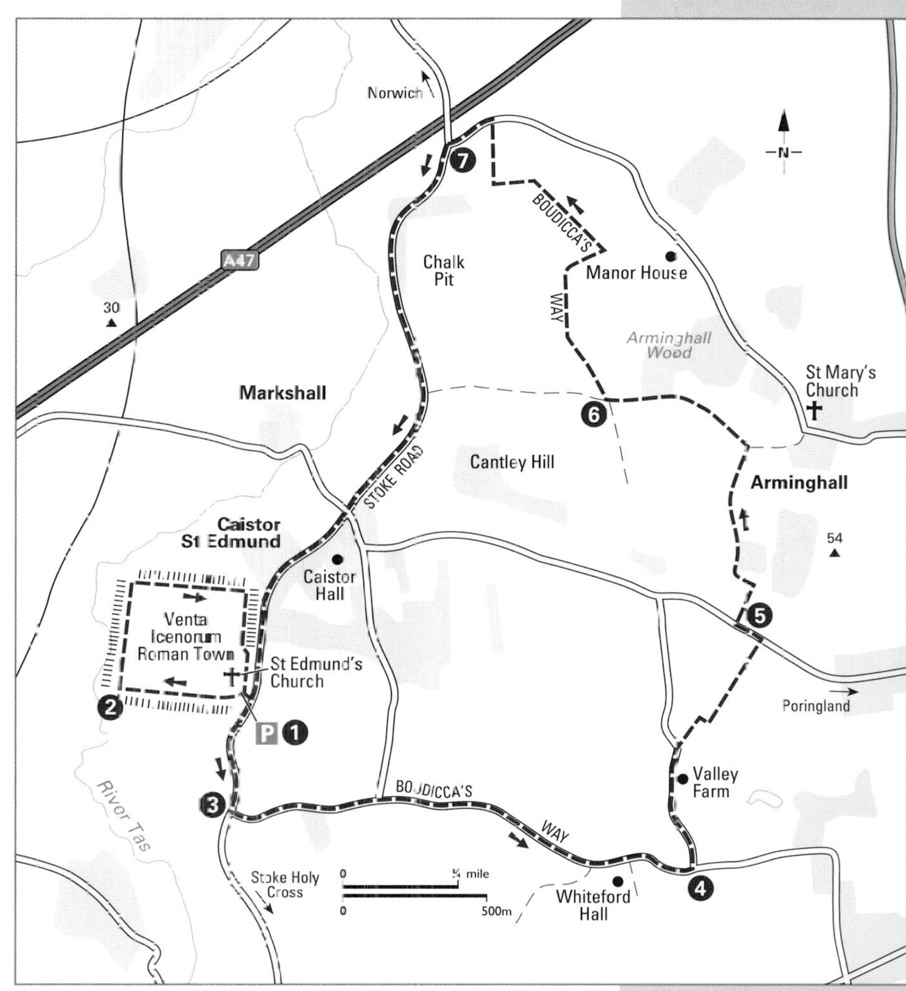

1 The first part of the walk follows the marked circular trail around Venta Icenorum, so go through the gate next to the notice board at the car park. The trail is marked by red and white circles. Climb a flight of steps, then go down six to reach the huge bank that protected the town, with a deep ditch to your left. Now head west, towards the River Tas.

2 Turn right by the bench, walk past fragments of old walls, then go right again when you reach a longer section of wall, still following the trail markers. Go through a gate, then walk along the side of the bank keeping a further stretch of wall to your right. Go up the steps, then descend again to the ditch on the eastern edge of the town. Carry on past St Edmund's Church and when you reach the car park, walk through it. Afterwards cross the road, then go through the gate opposite then turn right. You are now on Boudicca's Way.

3 Just after the brick cottages take the tiny unmarked lane to your left, still following Boudicca's Way. Go up a hill, keep straight at the next junction and keep walking until you see Whiteford Hall.

4 Turn left up Valley Farm Lane, following the yellow Boudicca's Way markers. After the farm, look for the footpath sign to your right. Take this and keep to your right, along the side of a hedge. Jig right, then immediately left and keep walking until you reach a paved lane. Turn left and then look for another footpath sign, which you'll find to your right.

5 Take the footpath, and follow the markers down a hill and up the other side. It's important to keep to the footpaths here, because there are plenty of signs indicating private property. At the top of the field, take the left-hand path through the woods, continuing to follow the yellow markers for Boudicca's Way.

6 At a four-way junction, go right across a field, still on Boudicca's Way. Continue around a chalk quarry until you see a gate to the right. Follow the path straight across the field. Turn left onto Arminghall Lane.

7 At the T-junction, go left using the gravel path and the verges. Descend a hill into the village of Caistor St Edmund, and follow signs for the Roman town, passing 17th-century Caistor Hall to your left. Keep walking until you reach the signs for Venta Icenorum, then turn right into the car park.

WHILE YOU'RE THERE

Take a few minutes to visit St Edmund's Church. The church was built in *c.*1050 and probably stands on the site of an earlier church or Anglo-Saxon manor house. King Edward the Confessor gave the church to the Abbey of Bury St Edmunds. The original nave survives and incorporates in its southwest part materials taken from the Roman town walls. The church porch and tower date to the 14th century. Inside, look for the 15th-century font, which is eight-sided and set on two steps – a design typical of East Anglia. It is decorated with images of an angel, a lion, an ox and an eagle (the emblems of the Four Evangelists Matthew, Mark, Luke and John), as well as the arms of St Edward the Confessor.

Local wild flowers are also worth seeking out. If you're taking the walk between June and September look for common knapweed, which has hairy pink flowers and was once used to treat sore throats. Common mallows are also pink, have a thick, round stem, and large reddish-mauve flowers. Also look for viper's bugloss, a member of the borage family, which has purplish-violet flowers.

Distance 6.25 miles (10.1km)

Minimum time 3hrs

Ascent/gradient 279ft (85m) ▲▲▲

Level of difficulty ●●●

Paths Paved road and public footpaths, several sets of steps

Landscape Rolling farmland and an archaeological site

Suggested map OS Explorer 237 Norwich

Start/finish Grid reference: TG 232032

Dog friendliness Dogs must be on lead in Roman town

Parking South Norfolk Council and Norfolk Archaeological Trust car park at Roman fort (free)

Public toilets None on route

AD 43–410

AD 50–51 Roman soldiers defeat the Ordovices of North Wales on the River Severn, and rebel chief Caratacus (Caradog) surrenders.

AD 52 Governor Didius Gallus builds a base for the XIV Legion at Wroxeter.

AD 61 Governor Suetonius Paulinus takes Anglesey.

AD 61 Boudicca, Queen of the Iceni, leads a revolt against the Romans but is defeated.

AD 64 Persecution of Christians begins in Rome under Emperor Nero after a fire destroys Rome and the Christians are blamed.

AD 65 Legion II Augusta garrison Gloucester.

What the Romans Did for Brewood

An easy country ramble explores a landscape across which the Romans built a major road

During the first years of the Roman occupation of Britain, in *c.*AD 100, the area to the north of Brewood was established as a main transport route. Here the Romans built Watling Street, which stretched from Londinium (London) all the way to present-day Wroxeter, just to the west of Shrewsbury, and was later extended to Chester. Watling Street was just one of the dozens of major roads built by the Romans across Britain; others were the Fosse Way (from Exeter to Lincoln) and Ermine Street (from London to York), and Watling Street.

Construction Methods

Roman roads in Britain were an extension of a systematic network that connected Rome to the four corners of its vast empire, a network built principally as a means of moving its great armies quickly and efficiently across occupied countries. In order to do this, the roads had to be exceptionally well constructed.

They were usually built on a raised embankment (to allow adequate drainage), made out of rubble obtained from drainage ditches built on either side. Next came the layer of sand, or gravel and sand, sometimes mixed with clay; and finally the whole thing was metalled with flint, finer gravel or even the slag from the smelting of iron. The finished road was often several feet thick, cambered to allow water to run off it and with kerb stones on each side to channel any excess water.

Enduring Legacy

Given the complexity of the roads, the huge distances covered and the fact that every single inch was laboriously built by hand, the continued existence today of so many Roman roads – or at least of their foundations – provides mute testimony to the mind-boggling efforts of their builders. In addition to being well designed and well maintained, Roman roads also invariably followed straight lines.

Today's A5 follows the route of Watling Street for much of its length, and you only have to glance at an atlas to see how much straighter it is than any modern road. This was achieved by lining up marker posts. The result meant both faster journey times and a much more efficient communications network. It is worth noting that the Shropshire Union Canal, along which the first part of the walks runs, was built along similar principles, raised on great embankments and built in a series of straight lines, ultimately to improve travel times. The canal bisects Watling Street just to the north of Brewood.

Above: *A Roman coin of the first century AD depicts a pipe-organ*

Below: *The A5 at Stretton follows the typically straight route of Roman Watling Street*

Walk 11 Roman road in Watling Street country

See where the Romans built a celebrated long-distance road with military precision

1 From the Bridge Inn car park, go straight across the main road and down some steps to the canal. Go right at the bottom of the steps and follow the canal tow path as far as the A5 and then through Stretton Spoil Banks to Bridge No 17 near Lapley Wood Farm.

2 Cross over the bridge and, at the concrete track, turn left for 100yds (91m). Just as this track bears right, go through the gate in the hedge to your right. Follow the hedge along the edge of the field and then along a dirt trail through a thin strip of woodland.

3 At the end of the trees, go through the gate directly ahead, and then head diagonally left across a field to its left-hand corner. Go through another gate and continue in the same direction, passing along the left-hand edge of the field. At the end of this long field go through another gate, and carry on across another small field to the edge of Whitegate Farm.

4 Skirt round the left-hand edge of the courtyard to reach the gate onto the A5. Take care crossing this busy main road and then head left for 50yds (46m) before turning right along the metalled farm road. Follow this as far as the Hawkshutts and, opposite the farmhouse, go left through a gate and head straight across the field, past the right-hand corner of the wood ahead, and across the next field to a gate ahead.

5 After going through the gate, bear right along a path through bushes and trees as far as the gate into another field. Bear slightly left here, aiming for the middle of the trees ahead, until you get to a gate and a gravel-surfaced farm track. Go right along this track, and then bear left along the road after Birk's Barn, following it as far as Leafields Barns.

6 Go over a stile on the right, then after a second beyond a driveway go diagonally left across a field in the direction of the church steeples until you get to a stile. Cross the stile and head right, around the edge of the field, to a line of trees down the middle. Head left here, following the line of trees as far as a gravel track. Go ahead up the track to the canal and then turn right, back towards St Mary's Church and the start.

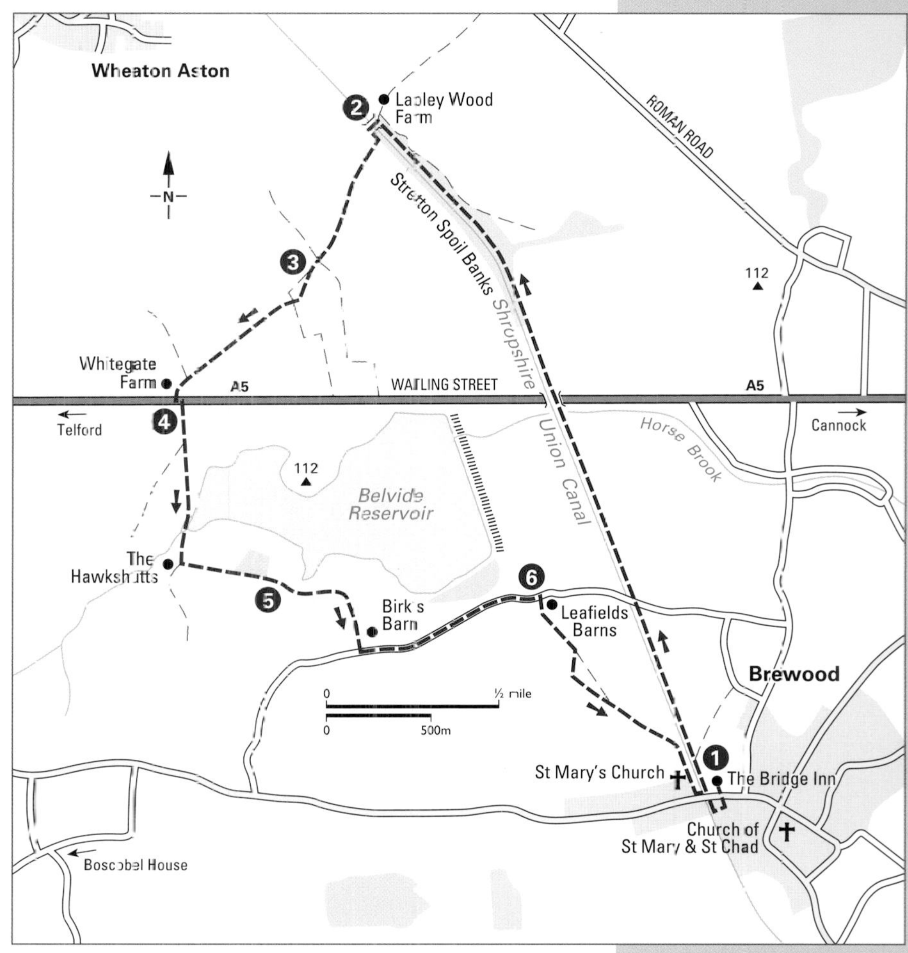

WHILE YOU'RE THERE

Boscobel House, 3 miles (4.8km) to the west of Brewood, is famous for the part it played in the English Civil War: Prince Charles (later King Charles II) – determined to reclaim the English throne when his father was executed on the orders of Parliament in 1649 – fought Parliamentary forces at Worcester in 1651, but his army was routed. Charles fled and hid at the hunting lodge of the Royalist Giffard family, where he concealed himself in an oak tree. Today, another oak grows on the site of the original tree and the house is a museum.

A visit to Brewood Church is also recommended. Colonel Carless, a Brewood soldier who fought alongside Charles at Worcester in 1651 and hid with him in the oak tree, is buried in the cemetery there. The church itself, dedicated to St Mary and St Chad, owes its surprising size to the fact that successive bishops of Lichfield owned a medieval manor nearby.

Distance 5.75 miles (9.2km)

Minimum time 2hrs

Ascent/gradient 75ft (23m) ▲▲▲

Level of difficulty ●●●

Paths Tow paths, grass trails and roads, 3 stiles

Landscape Canal, farmland and reservoir

Suggested map OS Explorer 242 Telford, Ironbridge & The Wrekin

Start/finish Grid reference: SJ 881088

Dog friendliness Must be kept on lead near livestock

Parking Ample side-street parking in Brewood

Public toilets None on route

AD 43–410

AD **65** Aquae Sulis (Bath) becomes an important Roman settlement. Today, Bath is one of the best preserved Roman towns in Britain.

AD **70–100** The Christian gospels are written.

AD **71–80** Fishbourne Palace in Sussex is built. The great Roman palace was probably built for Cogidubnus, King of the Regni tribe, recognised as a sub-ruler and created an honorary citizen of Rome.

AD **75** Governor's palace and basilica built in London.

AD **75–77** Roman forces, under the leadership of Agricola, establish a new frontier in Cambria (South Wales) and build a fort at Caerleon.

AD **77** Agricola is made Governor of Wales and stamps out further resistance from the Welsh.

Stones and Settlements on Tal y Fan

A bracing walks visits remains left by ancient settlers and their Roman conquerors

Tal y Fan is an outlier of the Carneddau range, and the most northerly 2,000ft (610m) hill in Wales. You can take the difficult option and climb it from sea level or you can use a peak-baggers' route that begins from Bwlch y Ddeufaen, 1400ft (427m) up in the hills above the Conwy Valley. If you do this, you will have wonderful views of Snowdonia and the North Wales coastline, and you will be following a centuries-old route used by Bronze Age and Iron Age tribesmen. These people would have used the route regularly, for they had large settlements all over the northern Carneddau. Great monoliths either side of the road give the pass its name – Bwlch y Ddeufaen ('Pass of the Two Stones').

The Bronze Age Hill Settlers and the Romans

When you climb to the top of Tal y Fan you can see the Bronze Age settlements in plan, for here on a great high plateau the Ordovices tribesmen could farm while watching out for their enemies from over the seas. The Roman invasion under Gnaeus Julius Agricola must have come as a shock to these primitive farmers. In AD 75–77 the invaders set up forts at Segontium (Caernarfon) and Canovium (Caerhun in the Conwy Valley).

When the Roman cohorts marched into the hills they made the Bwlch y Ddeufaen road their own, surfacing it and adding mileposts. The Ordovices were defeated: their great forts – such as Caer Bach, on the southern slopes of Tal y Fan – were abandoned. Today, Caer Bach lies beneath the turf and gorse, but its earth ramparts and a circle of stones are still visible. Looking down into the Conwy Valley, you can drift back in time and imagine those heartbreaking battles with the superior power of Rome.

Decline and Fall

As the Roman Empire declined, however, the native tribes returned to Tal y Fan, tending sheep on the high northern plateau and growing crops on the steeper southern flanks. Looking down to the castle at Conwy you are reminded that although King Edward I of England would come to conquer the region in the 13th century, it would take the land clearance and enclosure acts of the early 19th century to force the Welsh hill people away from their settlements.

Above: *Roman remains of the camp at Segontium, founded in Caernarvon in AD 78*

Below: *Spring flowers and a standing stone at Bwlch y Ddeufaen*

Walk 12 Through the Pass of the Two Stones

Look down from Tal y Fan on lands farmed by Bronze Age settlers and conquered by Romans

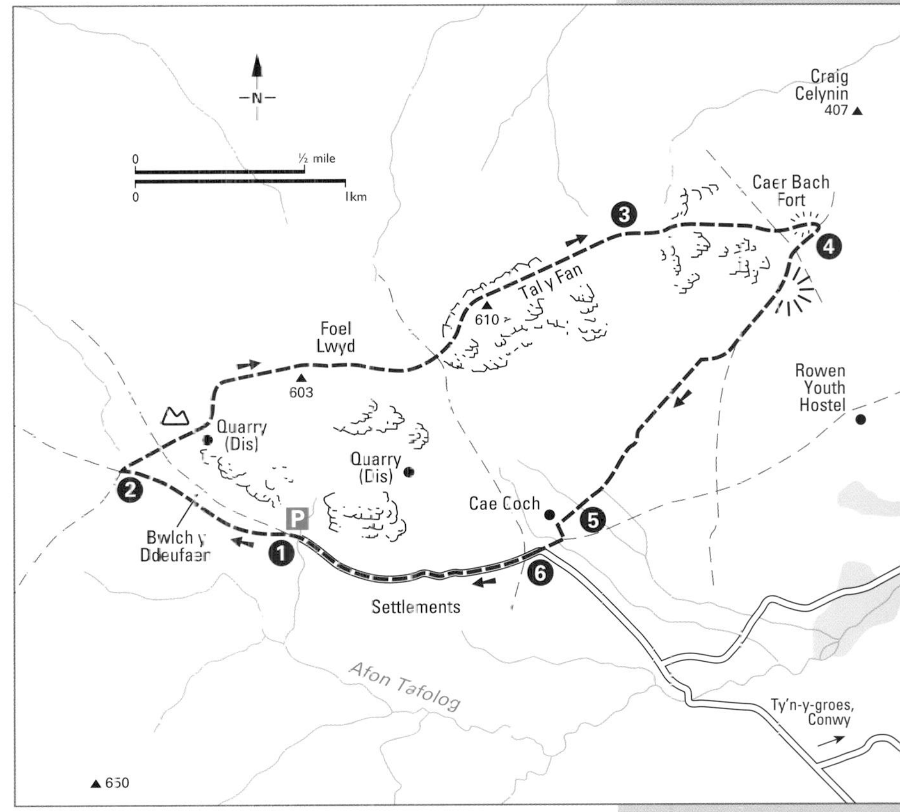

1 From the car park at the top of the metalled section of the road to Bwlch y Ddeufaen, continue along the road, which is now unsurfaced, and follow it past the ancient standing stones to the high pass itself, where you go through a gate in a crossing wall.

2 Turn right and follow the course of the wall, across the pass under three lines of electricity pylons, and then up the steep rocky slopes of Foel Lwyd. A narrow footpath continues, first descending to a little saddle, or col, then climbing to the even rockier summit of Tal y Fan.

3 The descending footpath still follows the line of the drystone wall, but stays with more even ground on the left. When the wall turns right, continue straight ahead, towards the prominent hill of Craig Celynin. Thread between outcrops to reach a little green valley running down to the right, where you look for the gorse-covered mound of Caer Bach Fort.

4 When you reach the remains of the fort turn right to follow a tumbled down wall heading southwest across high pastureland overlooking the Conwy Valley. Except for a short stretch this wall now acts as your guide, as do the frequent ladder stiles and locked gates sited in all the intervening cross-walls on the route.

5 The footpath becomes a cart track, which follows a route that passes beneath the whitewashed cottage of Cae Coch, before turning left to join the stony vehicle track that has come from Rowen Youth Hostel.

6 Turn right along the track, which soon joins the Bwlch y Ddeufaen road at a sharp corner. Go straight ahead along the road and follow it back to the car park.

Distance 5 miles (8km)

Minimum time 3hrs

Ascent/gradient 984ft (300m) ▲▲▲

Level of difficulty ●●●

Paths Cart tracks and narrow mountain paths, 7 stiles

Landscape Moor and mountain

Suggested map OS Explorer OL17 Snowdon

Start/finish Grid reference: SH 720715

Dog friendliness Can be off lead on high ridges, but should be kept under tight control in farmland

Parking Car park at end of Bwlch y Ddeufaen road, off B5106 Conwy–Llanwrst road

Public toilets None on route

THE SIGHTS OF CONWY

Conwy's imposing castle and adjacent walled town were built in 1283–88 by King Edward I of England. Along with the castles of Caernarvon, Harlech and Beaumaris (on Anglesey), Conwy was part of a ring of fortifications intended to enforce English rule on unwilling locals. These castles were all designed by Edward's supremely gifted architect Master James of St George. The one at Conwy stands on a narrow promontory overlooking the tidal estuary. It boasts eight forbidding drum towers connected by a curtain wall that is 15ft (4.5m) thick in some places. The walls of Conwy town contain no fewer than 21 towers and three gates; they average a thickness of 24ft (7.5m) and run for more than 1,300 yards (0.5km).

In addition, don't miss Plas Mawr in Conwy's High Street. This claims to be the finest surviving Elizabethan gentry town house in Britain and it's certainly an impressive building. It was built for Robert Gwydir, a merchant in the town, between 1576 and 1585. The lime-washed walls and opulent furnishings must have been breathtaking at the time. The house is open from late March to late October.

AD **79** The Romans establish a major camp in Deva (Chester) to protect the surrounding land from Welsh tribesmen and establish the Roman northern front.

AD **79** Mount Vesuvius erupts in Italy, burying Pompeii.

AD **81** The Romans build Trimontium (Newsteads fort) near Melrose in the Scottish borders.

AD **82** Agricola pushes the Roman frontier into Galloway and Ayrshire and defeats the Novantae tribe.

AD **85** People in the northern Pennines and the Scottish lowlands are finally subdued.

AD **87** Inchtuthill's fortress, still incomplete, is abandoned as Agricola returns to Rome and his conquests begin to diminish. Because of strong resistance by the Picts, Rome failed to conquer Scotland during their time in Britain.

The Romans of Corbridge

History lies around every corner in Corbridge, where the Romans built a series of forts and then a town

The Romans, under Agricola, first arrived in the region of Corbridge, Northumberland, in AD 79. They built a series of forts and finally established a town. The first small fort and bath-house was on a site 1 mile (1.6km) to the west of the later Roman town; in AD 84 they abandoned this structure and established a second fort on the site of their eventual town. The second fort burned down in *c.*AD 105 and was rebuilt. It was improved again in AD 120 when Hadrian's Wall was being erected as the northern frontier of the Empire, and again in *c.*AD 140 when, under Emperor Antoninus Pius, a second wall (the Antonine Wall) was built further north, between the River Clyde and the Firth of Forth.

The Antonine Wall was abandoned in AD 163, and after this date Corbridge was no longer a garrisoned fort. Nevertheless it developed into a town known as Corstopitum, strategically placed at the junction of Roman roads Dere Street (running from York to northern Britain) and Stanegate (running from Corbridge to Carlisle). The Romans had a fine bridge across the Tyne, and you can still see the remains of foundations when the water levels are low. The excavated remains of this town are just half a mile (800m) to the west of modern Corbridge, on the north bank of the Tyne. The early section of this walk passes near to them.

Defence Against the Scots

In Corbridge, Low Hall on Main Street has a fortified pele tower. These fortifications were added to defend against the Scots – both the Border reivers, who came to rob and pillage, and the Scots armies, who came to destroy. William Wallace, Robert the Bruce and King David II of the Scots all invaded, and all laid the town waste on their journeys south.

The centrepiece of modern Corbridge is undoubtedly St Andrew's Church, built in the Saxon era and with a Roman archway borrowed from the older settlement. The church was extensively modified in the 13th century, with the addition of aisles, transepts and chancel, and was restored during Victorian times. Around the back of the church you will come across another fortified house, this time the 13th-century Vicar's Pele – even the clergy were not immune from the wrath of the Scots. Before going down to the River Tyne, the route passes Town Barns, where novelist Catherine Cookson lived in the 1970s.

Above right: *A Roman ceremonial helmet, made of bronze in the 1st–2nd century AD*

Below: *Corbridge was a garrison town, the most northerly town in the Roman Empire*

Walk 13 At the Empire's northern frontier

Explore where Roman troops and settlers faced the anger of border raiders

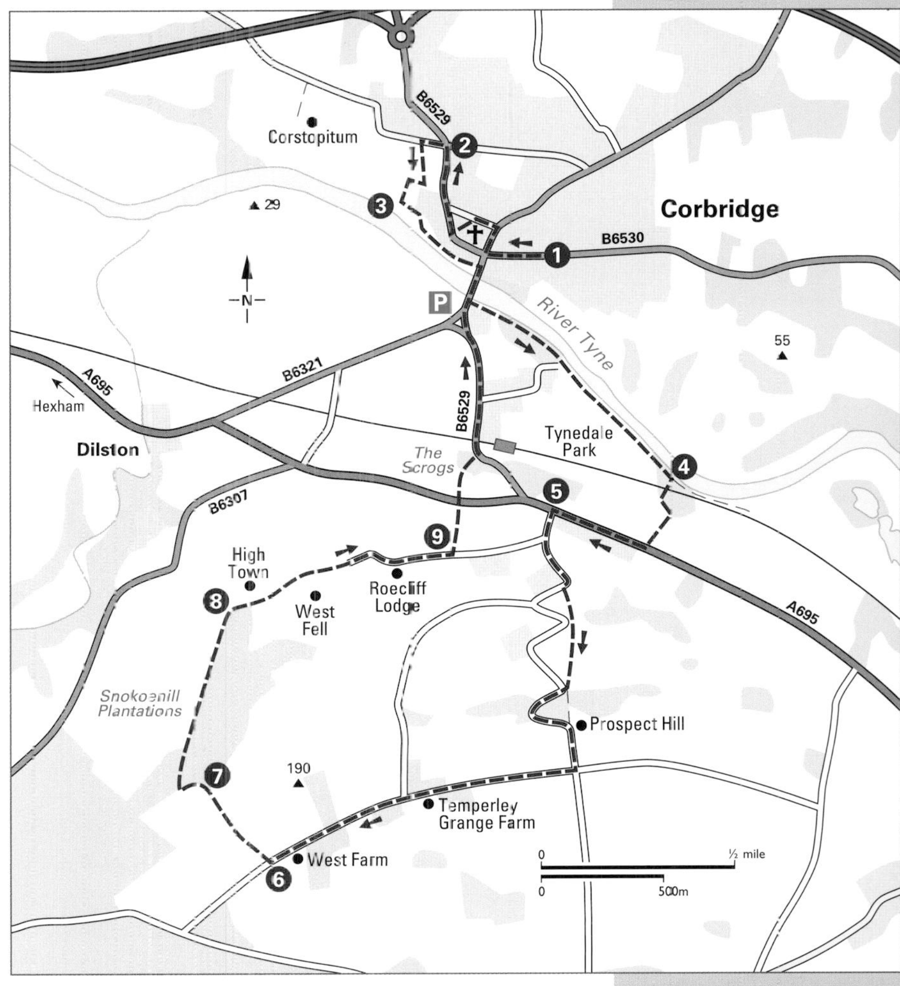

1 The walk begins at Low Hall Pele on the eastern end of Main Street. Head west down Main Street before turning right up Princes Street. At the town hall turn left to go along Hill Street, then, just before the church, turn left up the narrow street to pass the Vicar's Pele. Turn right at the Market Place and head north up Watling Street, then Stagshaw Road, which is staggered to the left beyond the Wheatsheaf Inn.

2 Go left along Trinity Terrace, then left again to walk along a footpath, which is signed 'West Green'. This path leads past Town Barns, the former house of celebrated novelist Catherine Cookson, to the Georgian house of Orchard Vale, where you turn right, then left along a lane to the river.

3 Turn left along Carelgate, then follow the riverside path towards the town bridge. Go over the bridge, then follow the south banks of the River Tyne on an unsurfaced track that passes the cricket ground at Tynedale Park before mounting a grassy embankment running parallel to the river.

4 Turn right up some steps, carry on over a ladder stile, then cross the railway tracks (taking care as you go). Another stile and some more steps lead the path through a wood and then you make your way across a field to meet the A695 road, where you turn right – follow the footpath that runs along the nearside.

5 Just beyond some cottages, turn left up a country lane, which zig-zags up Prospect Hill. Just after the first bend leave the lane for a southbound path that climbs fields. Just short of some woods the path meets a track where you turn right for a few paces to rejoin the lane. Follow this up to reach a crossroads at the top of the hill, where you turn right.

6 After passing Temperley Grange and West farms, leave the road in order to take a path on the right that follows first the right-hand side, then the left-hand side of a dry-stone wall across high fields and down to the Snokoehill Plantations.

7 Go through a gate to enter the wood, then turn left along a track running along the top edge. The track doubles back to the right, soon to follow the bottom edge of the woods.

8 Turn right when you have walked beyond a gate above High Town farm and then follow the track, which becomes tarred beyond West Fell.

9 Beyond Roecliff Lodge a path on the left crosses a field to reach the A695 road. Cross the road, and then follow the path as it continues and enters a copse known as the Scrogs, before joining the B6529 by Corbridge Railway Station. Walk along the road over the bridge and back into Corbridge itself.

WHILE YOU'RE THERE

Visit Corstopitum, where the two large granaries and the Fountain House are particularly impressive. The main street that runs through is the Stanegate. There are also remains of an aqueduct, a forum or marketplace, temples, barracks, military compounds, houses and an underground strongroom. Finds from the archaeological digs are kept in the museum. They include Roman armour, coins and personal artefacts, believed to date to AD 122–38 and to have been used when the site was a fort. Also on display is the celebrated Corbridge Lion, a sandstone sculpture of a lion crouching above an animal (perhaps a deer) that was initially used as decoration on a tomb but then reused as a fountainhead. Dated to the 2nd–3rd century AD, the lion was excavated at Corstopitum in 1907 by celebrated architect Sir Leonard Woolley.

Distance 6 miles (9.7km)

Minimum time 3hrs 30min

Ascent/gradient 525ft (160m) ▲▲▲

Level of difficulty ●●●

Paths Village streets, riverside and farm paths and lanes, 8 stiles

Landscape Small town and low hills

Suggested map OS Explorer OL43 Hadrian's Wall

Start/finish Grid reference: NY 992642

Dog friendliness Dogs should be on leads

Parking On town centre streets, or in free long stay car park over bridge

Public toilets On Princess Street between Hill Street and Main Street

AD **100** The Roman Empire is at its height. Paper-making is developed in China.

AD **100–200** Cirencester is established as the administrative centre for the West Country.

AD **122** Emperor Hadrian visits Britain. The building of Hadrian's Wall, of stone and turf, is begun to mark the frontier from present-day Bowness in the west to Newcastle in the east. Fifteen garrison forts are built along it to control the movement of local peoples.

AD **142** Antonine's Wall is built of turf, extending from the Clyde to the Firth of Forth, and marking Roman incursions into the Lowlands. Twenty years later the boundary reverts to Hadrian's Wall.

Raveglass: the Roman Port

This walk unveils a surprising Roman legacy in the Lake District National Park's only seaport

Ravenglass does not feel like a thriving port. The last tall-masted cargo ship sailed into the bay in 1914, and most visitors who come here, perhaps on 'La'al Ratty' from Eskdale, seem surprised to see the sea at all. The Lake District isn't really about the coast, after all.

But wind the clock back 2,000 years or so, and things were very different. In AD 78 or 79 General Julius Agricola was here contemplating the next steps in his imperial conquest of the islands. Over the Irish Sea were unknown tribes, hostile to Rome's expansion. Across the Solway, too, the legionaries' progress looked threatened.

Here on the tidal river bank, sheltered by the ever-shifting dunes on the seaward side, he built a hasty fort of earth and timber, leaving its day-to-day control to a garrison of Germans. Glannoventa ('the town on the river bank') grew in stature. As Hadrian asserted his control on Rome's northern frontier 50 years later, the fort was expanded to 3.6 acres (1.5ha) and formed the last outward face of a vast new barrier, which stretched all the way to the east coast at Tynemouth. Inland, the Roman road named the 10th *iter* ran up Eskdale to the garrison fort at Hardknott, then over the fells to Ambleside, Kendal and the roads to the south.

By AD 300 there was an extensive *vicus* or town in the lee of the fort and, at its eastern corner, a fine bathhouse. Of the fort itself there is little to see: more than 90ft (27m) has been lost to the ever-changing course of the estuary and the sea. The engineers of the Whitehaven and Furness Junction Railway were no more respectful: the railway line cuts the remaining fort in half, and the passage of time has concealed the rest.

Above right: *Every Roman fort had its bathhouse – these are the remains at Glannoventa*

Below: *A road links Glannoventa to the Roman fort at Hardknott Pass*

Walk 14 Remarkable survival of a distant era

Find hard evidence of the legionaries' taste for cleanliness in a Roman bathhouse

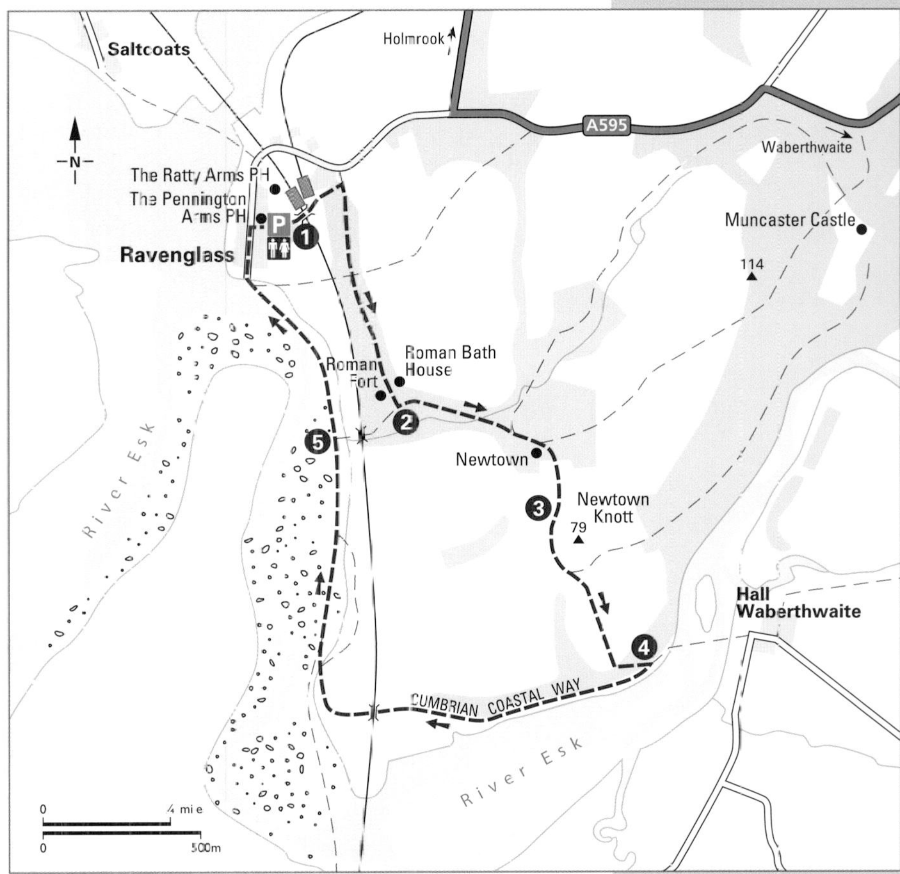

1 Leave the car park by the top-right corner, signposted 'Roman Bath House'. Cross the railway bridge and pass the station complex and children's play area on the left, following the snicketway beyond to a gate. Through this turn immediately right along a lane. Soon pick up a path on the left running parallel with the road, waymarked 'Muncaster'.

2 Shortly arrive at the Roman Bath House. Very little is visible of the Roman fort. Continue beyond the Bath House, keeping left at a junction with the signs for Muncaster. Stay on the main track as it winds round towards the farm buildings at Newtown. Ignore signs off to the left, but continue round the back of the farm buildings and on through a gate to a gateway in the boundary wall of the castle park.

3 Bear right through this along a muddy track, keeping the wall on your right as you skirt round the foot of Newtown Knott. (Newtown Knott is open access land, so you can scramble to its summit if you have the time). On the far side of the Knott, keep right, descending to a large gate in the wall. Walk down the field heading for a kissing gate at the bottom beyond a clump of gorse. Through this continue into the woods to a junction. Turn left and in a few paces turn right, by a Cumbria Coastal Way sign, which should have a current tide timetable.

4 Observe the warning notices about high tides here, and if it is safe to proceed, walk out through the gateway onto the marshy foreshore of the Esk Estuary. Turn right and follow the marshside path as it winds in and out of rushes and over little streams, finally straightening to pass under a railway bridge. On the other side continue round the corner, with the estuary now deepening and the spit of land supporting the Eskmeals dunes narrowing your horizon. Stay at the head of the beach, passing another railway bridge and ignoring the track that goes through it.

5 Just beyond, climb a flight of steps up the bank to a level, grassy area, where some benches boast fine views across the estuary and dunes to the open sea beyond. The grassy path descends back to shore level. Now follow the track in front of the houses to reach the floodgate at the bottom of Ravenglass's main street. Turn right here and walk up the street, turning right at the Pennington Arms to return to the car park.

MUNCASTER CASTLE

In 1208 land at Muncaster was granted to the Pennington family, and is still in the family's ownership today. The sandstone castle is a major addition to a 14th-century pele tower. Visitors get a guided tour (on audio tape, at least) by the present owner. Muncaster Castle is also the headquarters of the World Owl Trust, dedicated to owl conservation.

WHILE YOU'RE THERE

The bathhouse at Glannoventa was a state-of-the-art construction in the 4th century AD, and came complete with hypocaust underfloor heating. The four principal rooms of a Roman bath – the *laconium* steam room, the *tepidarium* for essential oils, the scalding hot *caldarium* and the icy plunge of the *frigidarium* – were all here. What is really remarkable about Glannoventa's bathhouse however, is that it survives in such good condition 1,700 years later: shown on modern maps as Walls Castle, the remarkable remnants stand up to 12ft (3.7m) high and even bear traces of their original plaster. In a niche on one wall a statue of the emperor or the goddess Fortuna would have watched over bathers.

Distance 3 miles (4.8km)

Minimum time 2hrs

Gradient 50ft (15m) ▲▲▲

Level of difficulty ●●●

Paths Road, grassy paths and tracks, some very boggy

Landscape Tidal marsh, foreshore woods and fields

Suggested map OS Explorer OL6 The English Lakes (SW)

Start/finish Grid reference: SD 085964

Dog friendliness One field grazed by sheep, rest suitable

Parking Ravenglass village car park

Public toilets At car park

Note The foreshore section of this walk may be impassable for up to 2 hours either side of high tides more than 23ft 7in (7.2m) at Barrow. Check tide times on BBC Cumbria website

AD 146 Rome invades Greece.

AD 154–55 With the help of reinforcements from Germany, Governor Julius Verus puts down a revolt by the Brigantes in the Pennines.

AD 160 In Rome, thousands die of the plague, causing a trading crisis that affects the economy.

AD 163 Governor Calpurnius Agricola retreats to Hadrian's Wall, unable to withstand Pictish assaults.

AD 170–80 Emperor Marcus Aurelius writes his philosophical *Meditations* while on camapaign.

AD 175 Some 5,500 Sarmatian cavalry, conscripts from north of the River Danube, are sent to Britain.

AD 200 The road system is completed in Rome.

AD 209 Emperor Severus travels with reinforcements to Britain to help counter attacks on Hadrian's Wall.

AD 250 Savage attacks by Saxons from northern Germany prompt the building of a series of forts on the south coast of England.

With the Romans and Celts at Farley

This secluded outing leads back 2,000 years through history on the Greensand ridge

Right: *Masonry indicates the temple's groundplan*

Below: *Ride Lane was once a Roman road*

High on windswept Farley Heath are the remains of a Romano-Celtic temple, one of the few Roman sites to have been found in Surrey. In Roman times, you would have reached this place along the branch road that led north-west from Stane Street – the busy London to Chichester highway – at present day Rowhook, on the outskirts of Horsham. On this walk you will twice cross the line of the Roman road – first near Winterfold Cottage and again on Ride Lane, just after the junction with Madgehole Lane.

Many Gods in Roman Britain

Roman and native gods were worshipped together in Britain, and distinctive Romano-Celtic temples evolved to accommodate the various rites. Designs generally consisted of a square or rectangular tower surrounded by a lean-to verandah. You can see the outline of the Roman temple's foundations just a few paces north of the car park at the start of your walk. The two concentric masonry squares are a modern reconstruction, built to show the ground plan that was discovered by poet and amateur archaeologist Martin Tupper in 1848 and confirmed by subsequent excavations in 1939 and 1995. The temple was built before the end of the 1st century AD. It was enclosed within a precinct wall, or *temenos*, which was also located during the excavations but has since been re-buried. Tupper's finds, which included several decorated bronze strips from a priest's sceptre, are now in the British Museum.

The temple was isolated, although there was a Roman villa just south of Pitch Hill, 3 miles (5km) back towards Stane Street. No other permanent buildings have been found inside the temple precincts. The temple remained in use until the end of the Roman occupation early in the 5th century, and it seems that the building burnt down some time before the year 450.

Walk 15 Where native and Roman deities met

Tread in the footsteps of pagan worshippers on picturesque Farley Heath

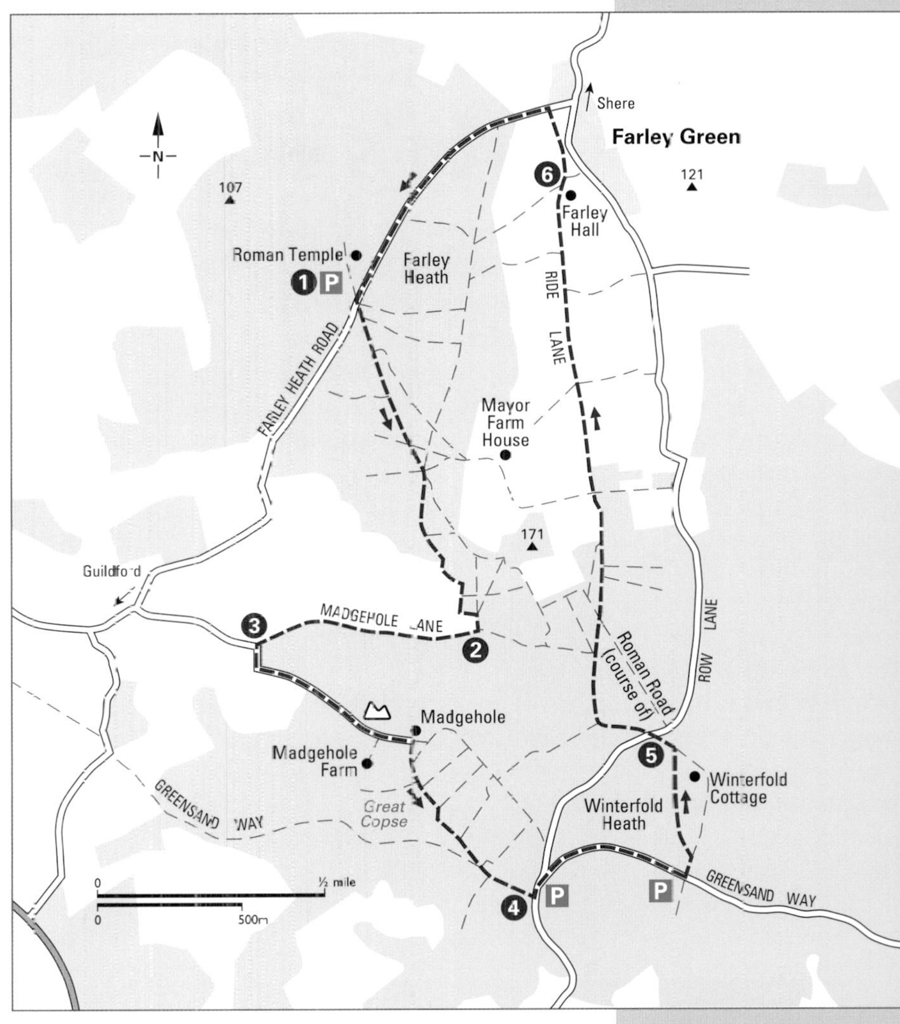

1 Stand in the car park facing the road and walk to the entrance on your right-hand side. Cross the road, and follow the signposted public bridleway across Farley Heath. Keep to the right at the first fork, and continue straight across when you get to the the sandy bridleway crossroads. Keep straight on again at the five-way junction, and take the fork to the right a few paces further on. Then, as the main track swings round hard to the left, continue down the woodland bridleway straight ahead. You'll wind gently down to a waymark post; turn right here, and follow the public bridleway for a further 70yds (64m) to a T-junction with Madgehole Lane.

2 Turn right and follow this deeply rutted, sunken lane until it meets a narrow tarmac road at a pretty, tile-hung cottage.

3 Turn left, signposted towards Winterfold, and climb through this delightful, sequestered valley past the rambling, half-timbered Madgehole Farm to Madgehole. Here you leave the tarmac and swing hard right, climbing steadily past a Christmas tree plantation on your left. Follow the waymarked bridleway as it winds right, then left, through Great Copse, and join the Greensand Way as it swings in from the right.

4 Turn left on to Row Lane and, after 150yds (137m), fork right towards Ewhurst and Shere. Follow the road over the brow of the hill, until you come to Car Park 5 on your right. Turn left here, onto an unsignposted footpath into the woods, and keep right at the fork 90yds (82m) further on. Almost at once, bear left off the main track, up a narrow footpath by the side of a wire fence. This leads you down beside the huge garden of Winterfold Cottage, to another waymarker post. Fork left here, and follow the public bridleway along the rough cottage drive until you reach Row Lane.

5 Cross over and continue along the bridleway. After around 200yds (182m) this bears hard right downhill onto Ride Lane, which will carry you all the way to Farley Green. Keep right when you come to the junction with Madgehole Lane, and then trudge steadily through this rutted, prehistoric landscape until gradually the banks roll back as you make your approach to Farley Hall.

6 Pass the lovely old half-timbered farmhouse on your right, and keep bearing left until you come to the top of the green. Bear left again, and follow Farley Heath Road back to your car.

Distance 5 miles (8km)

Minimum time 2hrs 30min

Ascent/gradient 574ft (175m) ▲▲▲

Level of difficulty ●●●

Paths Forest tracks and rutted lanes, running in water after rain

Landscape Remote wooded hillsides, occasional farms and cottages

Suggested map OS Explorer 145 Guildford & Farnham

Start/finish Grid reference: TQ 051448

Dog friendliness Can mainly run free, on lead on roadside section

Parking Forest car park (number 8) on Farley Heath

Public toilets None on route

WHILE YOU'RE THERE

After seeing the Farley Heath temple, you can see a Roman priest's headdress in Guildford Museum. Right next to the Castle Arch in Quarry Street, the museum houses Surrey's largest collection of archaeology and local history – from Palaeolithic hand axes to a collection of 17th-century pottery and glass. Needlework displays include samplers, patchwork and baby clothes. Pictures and artefacts illustrate aspects of local life. There is also a collection given by garden designer/planter Gertrude Jekyll – a notable figure in the Arts and Crafts Movement – that include a 16th-century napkin bearing an embroidered portrait of Queen Elizabeth I. The museum is open from Monday to Saturday; admission is free.

Along the Emperor's Wall

An energetic walk tours part of Hadrian's imposing fortification

After a visit in AD 122, Roman emperor Hadrian decided that his Governor of Britain, Nepos, would supervise the building of a great wall to repel the violent Picts and Britons of the north. They originally planned it to span the countryside between the River Irthing at Thirlwall and Newcastle, but added a turf wall that would extend to the west coast at Bowness on Solway.

The engineers were put to work, aided by Roman soldiers brought in from York, Caerleon and Chester. The first-built sections of the castellated wall were 15ft (4.5m) high and 10ft (3m) wide, although later sections were reduced in size in order to speed up the construction. On the northern side the Romans excavated an impressive V-shaped ditch, the *Berm*, 27ft (8.2m) wide and 9ft (2.7m) deep, except where defending crags made this measure unnecessary.

Milecastles and Turrets

Fortified gateways (milecastles) were sited along the length of the wall at intervals of one Roman mile (1.5km). These would allow passage for through traffic, and also act as a barracks for a garrison of eight soldiers. Between the milecastles, at intervals of one-third of a Roman mile (498m), were turrets which served as observation posts. Later, large forts such as Great Chesters, Carvoran and Housesteads were built close to the wall, and a second ditch, the *Vallum*, was dug on the south side to enclose the military area. This was a flat-bottomed trench 20ft (6m) wide and 10ft (3m) deep.

Wall under Threat

Following the Roman withdrawal from Britain the wall fell into decay and its crumbling masonry was used to build churches, farmhouses and field walls. After Prince Charles Edward Stuart ('Bonnie Prince Charlie')'s failed Jacobite rebellion in 1745 against the rule of King George II, Parliament demanded that a military road be built in the region. Unfortunately, this road used Hadrian's Wall as its foundations for many miles. It seemed that the wall would disintegrate into oblivion.

The fact that modern-day visitors can still view this spectacle is largely due to the efforts of entrepreneur and keen archaeologist John Clayton. In the mid-19th century he bought much of the land that contained the wall, and presided over

Above: *The Romans built thier wall straight up Crag Lough – one of Northumberland's highest cliffs*

Right: *The wall threads its way near Highshield Crags*

the early digs that unearthed its treasures. The foundations of the wall and its forts have since been lovingly restored. The museum at Chesters remains a testament to this great man.

As you stride out beside Hadrian's Wall and above the precipitous cliffs, it is not difficult to imagine the desolate times of the Roman cohorts patrolling along the high parapets.

WHILE YOU'RE THERE

Housesteads, which is in the care of the National Trust, is perhaps the most spectacularly sited of the wall forts, its position giving it commanding views across the Tyne Valley and Northumberland hills. The site contains foundations of granaries, barracks and a hospital.

Walk 16 A rampart to repel the northern Picts and Britons

See life from the perspective of both Roman soldier and Pictish warrior

1 From the car park descend to a grassy depression beneath Peel Crags. The path arcs left and climbs back to the ridge in a series of steps before following the cliff tops past Turret 39A and Milecastle 39.

2 There's another dip, then a climb to Highshield Crags, which overlook Crag Lough. Beyond the lake the footpath climbs past Hotbank farm.

3 At the next dip, Rapishaw Gap, turn left over the ladder stile and follow the faint but waymarked Pennine Way route across undulating moorland. The first stile lies in the far right corner of a large rushy enclosure. A clear cart track develops beyond a dyke and climbs to a ridge on Ridley Common where you turn half left to descend a grassy ramp.

4 The path slowly arcs right to meet and cross a fenced cart track at Cragend. Here a clear grass track zig-zags down to a moorland depression, with Greenlee Lough in full view to your left. At the bottom the ground can be marshy and the path becomes indistinct in places. A waymark points a sharp right turn but the path loses itself on the bank above it. Head north here, keeping the farmhouse of East Stonefolds at ten to the hour. The next stile lies in a kink in the cross wall.

5 Beyond this, turn half-left to traverse a field before going over a ladder stile and turning left along the farm track, which passes through East Stonefolds. The track ends at West Stonefolds. Walk through the farmyard, heeding the plea from the residents not to intrude too much on their privacy.

6 Past the house continue, with a wall to the left, along a grassy ride, and go over a step stile to reach a signposted junction of routes. Go straight ahead on the permissive path signposted to the Greenlee Lough Birdhide. The path follows a fence down to the lake. Ignore the stile unless you want to go to the hide itself, but instead continue alongside the fence.

7 Go over the next stile and cross wetlands north of the lake on a duckboard path, which soon swings right to a gate. Beyond this continue on the path, climbing northwest, guided by waymarker posts to the farm track by the clearfelled stumps of the Greenlee Plantation.

8 Turn left along the track and follow it past Gibbs Hill farm. Past the farmhouse a tarmac lane leads back towards the wall. Turn left at the T-junction to return to the car park.

Distance 8 miles (12.9km)
Minimum time 4hrs
Ascent/gradient 885ft (270m) ▲▲▲
Level of difficulty ●●●
Paths Mainly well walked National Trails, 16 stiles
Landscape Ridge and wild moorland
Suggested map OS Explorer OL43 Hadrian's Wall
Start/finish Grid reference: NY 750677
Dog friendliness Farming country, keep dogs on lead
Parking Steel Rigg (pay) car park
Public toilets Nearest at Housesteads information centre
Note Please don't damage the wall by walking on it

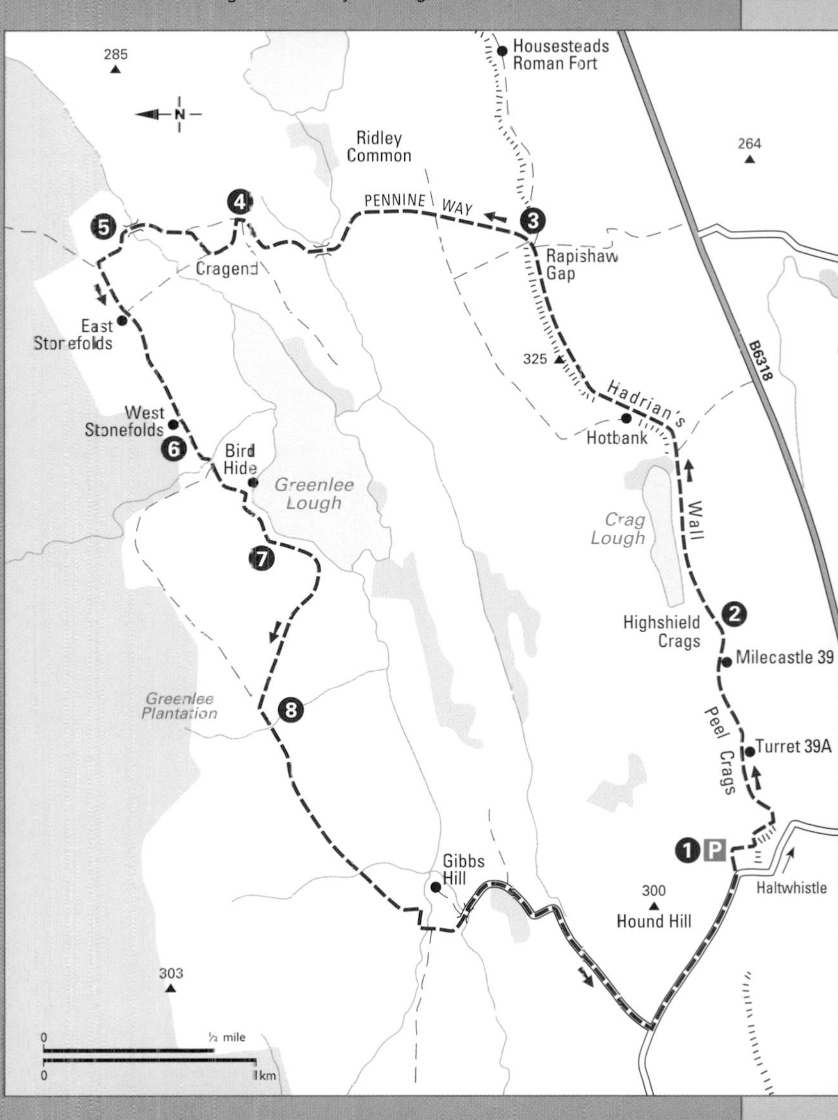

AD **254** St Alban, the first British Christian martyr, is executed, in Verulamium.

AD **270** A magnetic compass is used for the first time, in China.

AD **270** The Roman palace at Fishbourne, West Sussex, is abandoned after a major fire.

AD **277** A fort at Richborough, Kent, is one of several built on the southeast coast to repel Saxon raiders.

AD **286–293** Carausius rebels against Rome, declaring himself Emperor of Britain.

AD **300** The Roman fort at York is substantially rebuilt as a military headquarters.

AD **300** Emperor Diocletian decrees that Christians should be persecuted within the Empire.

AD **313** Under the Edict of Milan Christianity is officially tolerated within the Roman Empire.

AD **314** Three British bishops (including one from York) attend a church council at Arles in France.

Roman Remains on Epsom and Ashtead Commons

An engaging ramble leads through an historic corner of Surrey, where a Roman villa and bathhouse once stood on what is now a common

The two commons at Epsom and Ashtead are very ancient and date back to the 'Wildwood' that once covered much of England. As settlements grew up, the villagers had commoners' rights for grazing, collecting firewood and extracting gravel and clay. The woods were often pollarded, to produce straight, thin pieces of wood, and also to allow grass to grow underneath them so that cattle could graze.

In Roman times there was considerable activity in the area. Stane Street, which ran from London Bridge to Chichester, passes only one mile (1.6km) away. A Roman villa and bathhouse has been found in the northern part of Ashtead Common and it is thought it was located near a large tile factory and several clay pits. The villa had its own bathhouse area, and there was also a separate bathhouse, probably used by the men who worked in the tile factory. The complex was built in AD 67–79 but mainly occupied in AD 117–138, and after being rebuilt in AD 150 was completely abandoned by AD 200. The site was excavated in 1924–29; among the objects found were some gold jewellery, pottery and other objects used for religious or ritual purposes.

***Background:** Several Roman villas in Britain had beautiful floor mosaics like this one from Fishbourne (1st century AD)*

***Right:** A venerable hornbeam (*Carpinus betulus*), one of the key species conserved at Ashtead Common*

From Industrial Centre to Genteel Spa

Epsom's fortunes really picked up in the 17th century. Towards the end of the Elizabethan era it was discovered that the water in some of the ponds on the common was good for constipation, and Epsom Well was developed – it is now a wishing well in the centre of a housing development. Aristocrats came down from London to take the waters and Epsom became one of the most celebrated spas of the 17th century. Epsom Salts were prepared by boiling down the waters.

Later in the century, the existence of this spa led to the need to provide additional forms of entertainment. Horse racing was introduced and survives today as the Epsom Derby.

Valuable Trees

Ashtead Common is a National Nature Reserve, and both commons have been designated a Site of Special Scientific Interest. The ancient woodland has some very old trees, including more than 2,300 veteran oak pollards, some of which are upwards of 400 years old.

Walk 17 Where clay was dug and tiles made

Watch for birds, bees and butterflies among signs of the Roman past

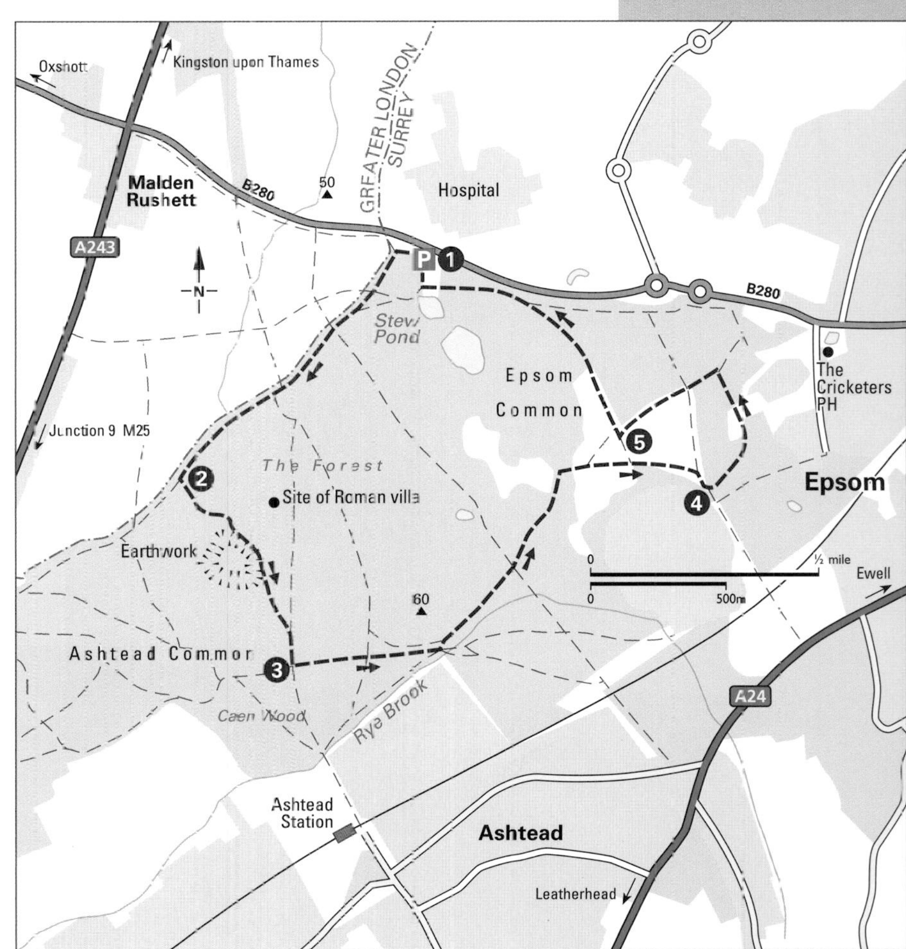

1 From the car park head away from the road past two wooden posts and past a notice board. Stick to the main path through woodland and cross a public footpath at a waymark post. At a fingerpost turn right following public bridleway 29, signed to Ashtead Common. Pass the noticeboard about Ashtead Common National Nature Reserve, and walk on with a field to the right. At the next fingerpost at a crossing with a public bridleway carry straight on, following the sign to Kingston Road. There are open fields and good views to the right. At the next cross-tracks there is a fingerpost and a noticeboard named Chessington View, and our way goes straight on, turning left and right, and keeping to the public bridleway for Kingston Road.

2 At the next fingerpost turn left following public footpath 32 over a wooden boardwalk. Soon there is a grassy area on the right, and you should take the path on the left and follow it round to the right. To the right at this point is a large earthwork. Walking past, there is a track from the left but ignore this and keep straight on. At the next fingerpost turn right following public footpath 32, then meet a broad track and turn right. Pass a fingerpost signing Concessionary Ride 2 on the left, and continue straight on along public bridleway 33.

3 At the next fingerpost on the right, turn left along public footpath 25 and go straight on past the crossing with public footpath 34. At the next cross-tracks, by a fingerpost, leave public footpath 25 and turn left. Within 15yds (14m) turn right and continue, ignoring any tracks on the right. Bear left and see the river restoration project on the right. Meet a T-junction with a public bridleway and turn left, than after 10yds (9m) turn right. Pass a noticeboard on the left and enter Epsom Common. At the next fingerpost, by the marker for West Heath, a track comes from the left but continue straight ahead anyway. After an open space on the left pass the Summer Horseride, also on the left, and the signpost for the Thames Down Link. Follow the path right and, by a fingerpost, continue along the main path, bearing right. Pass another fingerpost and a bench and continue straight ahead. Reach a fork, with houses and a noticeboard to the right.

4 Take the left fork and, in 25yds (23m), turn left at a fingerpost along a public bridleway signed 'Christchurch Road ½ mile' (805m). (To find The Cricketers pub, continue straight ahead at this point along the main path which leads to Stamford Green.) Our route is along the Summer Horseride. Meet a cross-tracks and turn left at a waymark post inscribed with 'Public Footpath 55'.

5 At the next cross-tracks, where there is a small sign on the left indicating the Thames Down Link, turn right. At the next cross-tracks turn left, and ignore the next tracks from left and right. Meet a gate on the right where the Thames Down Link and the Chessington Countryside Walk go right, but go straight on along public bridleway 29. Continue straight ahead past a noticeboard by open ground and reach an attractive stew pond on the left. Just past the stew pond take the path on the right to return to the car park.

WHILE YOU'RE THERE

Between Points 2 and 3 of the walk the route passes an ancient earthwork that is a large triangular site, possibly even older than the Roman villa. Some prehistoric finds and tracks have been discovered in the area of the earthwork. In the area near Cobham, Painshill Park is a superb 18th-century parkland, with follies, a grotto, beautiful vistas and even a working vineyard. There is a fine collection of North American trees and shrubs to be admired.

Distance 3.75 miles (6km)

Minimum Time 1hr 30min

Ascent/gradient Negligible ▲▲▲

Level of difficulty ●●●

Paths Generally broad paths, well marked

Landscape Commons and light woodland with views of farmland

Suggested map OS Explorer 146 Dorking, Box Hill & Reigate

Start/finish Grid reference: TQ 183612

Dog friendliness Good

Parking Epsom and Ashtead Commons Car Park, Christ Church Road

Public toilets None on route

AD 324 Emperor Constantine founds Constantinople (formerly Byzantium, and now modern Istanbul) as the new imperial city of Rome.

AD 337 On his deathbed Constantine formally converts to Christianity, but he is usually thought to have been a Christian at least since he defeated his rival Maxentius at the Battle of Milvian Bridge, in 312.

AD 367 Scots from Ireland, Picts from Scotland and Saxons and Franks from northern Europe attack Roman Britain, and the Emperor Valentinian dispatches Roman troops to restore order.

AD 410 Rome, under attack by Alaric the Goth, can no longer afford to support its troops abroad, and they are withdrawn from Britain. The Empire falls in AD 476.

Around the Roman Town of Alcester

This easy excursion leads through an old Roman town and picturesque woodland

Above: *Rome's first Christian emperor, Constantine the Great, is commemorated on a milestone found at Alcester*

Left: *The bridge over the River Arrow at Oversley Green dates back to the 16th century*

The Romano-British town at Alcester flourished in the 2nd–4th century AD. Named Alencestre, it covered 44 acres (18ha) and was built where the River Arrow makes a loop, west of its meeting with the River Alne. Unfortunately, Alencestre is now completely covered by the modern town, although from time to time new relics come to light, such as the Roman milestone commemorating Emperor Constantine (AD 306–337), which was excavated in the town in 1966.

Remains of defensive structures – including clay ramparts and a wall 9ft (2.75m) wide – have been found on the eastern edge of the Roman town. Archaeologists also found remnants of stone buildings that indicate two had floors of mosaic. They believe that Primrose Hill, which is crossed on the walk, was probably the site of a Roman fort. This would have commanded views of the rivers Arrow and Alne and the road south from Salinae (Droitwich Spa), called the 'Salt Way' after the region's main produce in the Roman era. Several bronze Roman pieces, including a harness ring used by cavalry, have been found on the hill.

Through the Forest of Arden

The walk takes you through the old part of Alcester and down Malt Mill Lane into Oversley Green. Beautiful Oversley Wood is a remnant of the Forest of Arden, and if you walk here in spring you will see a carpet of bluebells and may even spot a shy muntjac deer. The route goes close to the villages of Exhall and Wixford, with their black-and-white buildings, then returns over Primrose Hill, which rises 350ft (107m) above the Arrow Valley, offering a fine view of Ragley Hall to the left. Once over the busy A46 road you will pass several beautiful thatched cottages as you walk down Primrose Lane on the way back into Oversley Green.

Walk 18 Back to the days when Warwickshire was ruled by Constantine

Tour ancient woodland and take in wide views once enjoyed by Roman settlers and soldiers

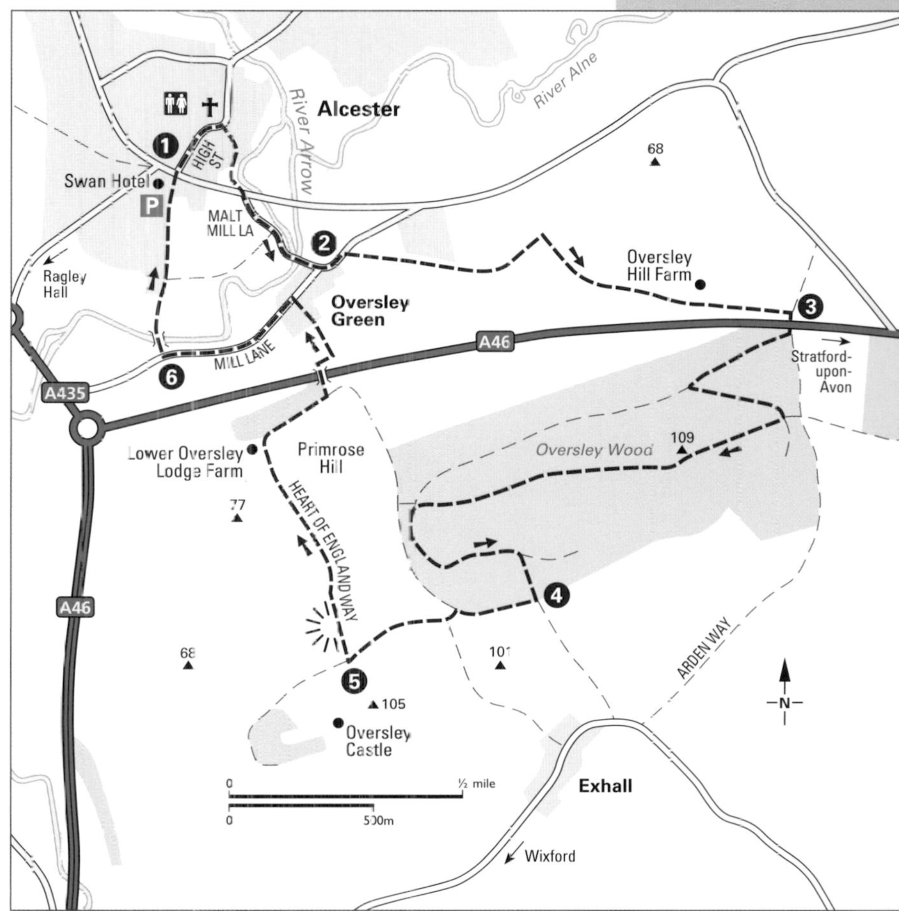

1 From the car park enter Bleachfield Street and go left to the old Stratford Road. Cross the road and then wander up High Street. Bear right past the impressive St Nicholas Church and at the corner of the road turn right down Malt Mill Lane. When you reach the bottom of the lane, go left through the public gardens and follow the tarmac footpath by the side of the River Arrow to reach the old Stratford Road again. Cross the road and go down the lane opposite into Oversley Green village, crossing the bridge over the River Arrow.

2 At the road junction bear left on Stratford Road, and in 80yds (73m) go right along a hedged footpath behind a row of houses. Cross a field via two kissing gates and walk past a golf driving range, crossing a stile to reach a kissing gate at a junction of paths. Do not go through it but go right here along the field edge, then through a field gate and across pastureland to join a track that passes through a kissing gate below Oversley Hill Farm before coming to a Severn Trent sub station.

3 Continue ahead across a stile and through a gate to go right, under the A46 road bridge, and bear right through the gateway into Oversley Wood. Take the metalled track into the wood for about 400yds (366m), then go left. In a further 400yds (366m) the metalled track arcs right. At a path crossroads, go right on a grass path steeply uphill and continue westwards over the crest of the hill, descending past a viewpoint bench back to the main metalled track. Now go left for 650yds (594m), then right at a bench onto a wide path to leave the wood over a stile.

4 Go right and walk along the edge of Oversley Wood to its corner. Continue ahead along the hedged track until you reach a farm lane, with Oversley Castle on the hillock to the left.

5 Go right along the lane and join the Heart of England Way. Walk up the lane towards some large grain silos by the side of Lower Oversley Lodge Farm. From the farm complex go right along the concrete lane and left through a handgate down to the footbridge over the busy A46. Cross and walk down Primrose Lane, passing a beautiful thatched house. At the T-junction go left along Mill Lane for about 650yds (594m).

6 After passing a fourth mobile home, go right, down a path and cross a footbridge over the River Arrow. Continuing ahead, the path becomes a lane by houses, with allotments to the right. Walk up Bleachfield Street back to the car park.

WHILE YOU'RE THERE

Take the opportunity to visit Ragley Hall, along the Evesham Road, set in 400 acres (165ha) of parkland. The home of the Marquess and Marchioness of Hertford, this was designed by Robert Hooke in 1680, and is one of the earliest and most handsome of England's great Palladian houses. The magnificent Great Hall contains some outstanding baroque plasterwork done by James Gibbs in 1750, and there is a large mural up the stairway. The decorations and furnishings in the Red Saloon have been superbly maintained and the room still looks as it did when designed by James Wyatt in 1780. The stables house a carriage collection, and 'Capability' Brown designed the gardens. There is also an adventure playground for children, and the Jerwood Collection sculpture trail. It is open Thursday to Sunday, 11am–6pm, daily during school holidays.

Distance 5.5 miles (8.8km)

Minimum time 2hrs 15min

Ascent/gradient 269ft (82m) ▲▲▲

Level of difficulty ●●●

Paths Pavements, field paths, woodland tracks and farm lanes, 3 stiles

Landscape Gentle rolling farmland, woodland and rural town

Suggested map OS Explorer 205 Stratford-upon-Avon & Evesham

Start/finish Grid reference: SP 088572

Dog friendliness Keep dog under control at all times

Parking Bleachfield Street car park, Alcester

Public toilets Bulls Head Yard car park, Alcester

INVASIONS AND SAINTS

The post-Roman era has been called the Dark Ages, although it was no intellectual desert. If there was a dark time, it was in the years of invasion, turbulence and change. The invaders themselves left no written records, but monks such as Gildas, Bede and Nennius chronicled the events of the period.

New masters replaced the Romans from 449, when German mercenaries – Saxons, Angles and Jutes – arrived at the invitation of a British leader, Vortigern. Their job was to help fend off foreign incursions, but instead they took the opportunity to establish their own rule in the south. Within 150 years much of the ex-Roman province was known as the Angles' Land – England. Meanwhile, the Britons continued to resist, mounting a campaign against this wave of invaders and settlers – commanded, according to legend, by King Arthur, who faced the Saxons in battle around the turn of the 6th century, culminating in a final battle on 'Mount Badon'. The site of this engagement is uncertain – some historians suggest the hill-fort at Little Solsbury Hill, Somerset, others a site in Cumbria.

Religion was also about to undergo a profound change. In 565 a Celtic missionary monk, Columba, travelled to the Pictish lands in the north, and converted first their king, Bride, and then his people to Christianity. Pope Gregory, 30 years later, sent a missionary party to do the same for the English, and, under the protection of King Ethelbert, his man Augustine became the first Archbishop of Canterbury. In the 7th century churches sprang up across the country; landowners eager to secure their place in the afterlife provided land and funds for monasteries that soon accumulated huge wealth and influence. This was 'the age of saints'. By now Britain was a patchwork of kingdoms, one of which, Mercia, set about swallowing up its neighbours by force and politics – particularly under its 8th-century king, Offa. His campaigns against the Welsh left an enduring legacy in Offa's Dyke, which still more or less marks the English-Welsh boundary.

Then, in 789, a lightning raid on the Dorset coast signalled the arrival of a new threat – the Vikings, or Norsemen. For years these adventurers made sorties from Scandinavia to plunder Britain's coasts and churches. Gradually the Norsemen established settlements – first in the north of Scotland, on Shetland and Orkney. But it did not go all their way. Britain's inhabitants fought back, sometimes successfully – Viking leader Ragnor Lodbrook was captured and thrown into a snake-pit. His son, Ivar the Boneless, took his revenge by slaughtering the Northumbrians at York, and establishing Danish ascendancy in northern England.

Alfred, King of Wessex (the West Saxons), rallied his people several times against the Danes. In 886 his truce with the Danes divided England between Wessex, Mercia and the Danelaw – but sporadic war continued between the Scandinavians and the Wessex kings. Danish attacks on the Picts wiped out their kingdom of Fortriu. In its place emerged Alba, kingdom of the Scots: the Scottish king, Constantine II, held the Danes at bay for 50 years.

Life in Britain was unpredictable and sometimes violent. But that was not the whole picture. Scholarship, art and poetry flourished. New towns developed, law and administration regulated life, while the Saxons marked out a system of shires and courts. Trade flourished and Britain became affluent enough to attract the ambitious William of Normandy.

KEY SITES

St Non's Bay, Pembrokeshire: The reputed birthplace of David, patron saint of Wales, in *c.*500.

Iona, Hebrides: Island where Irish monk St Colomba founded a 6th-century community.

Sutton Hoo, Suffolk: Anglo-Saxon cemetery containing ship burial of Raedwald (died *c.*625).

Bardney Abbey, Lincolnshire: Founded in *c.*675 by the Anglo-Saxon king of Mercia, Ethelred.

Offa's Dyke, Welsh borders: Border fortification built by Offa, King of Mercia in 757–96

Deerhurst Church, Gloucestershire: England's finest surviving Saxon church.

Left: *A footpath along Offa's Dyke on the English–Welsh border near Knighton, Shropshire*

449 Angles, Saxons and Jutes, led by Hengist and Horsa, land in Kent.

495 Cerdic lands in Hampshire to found the West Saxon Kingdom (Wessex).

500 Christianity wins converts throughout Ireland, Scotland and Wales as missionaries preach the Gospel.

500 The British or Welsh warlord later celebrated as King Arthur wins a great victory against the Saxons at Mount Badon.

500 St David is born in Pembrokeshire.

527 The East Saxon Kingdom (Essex) is founded. The first king is named Aescwine.

The Wells of the Rees

This strenuous walk along the Southern Upland Way treads in the footsteps of 4th-century pilgrims

Sitting 'on the hillside at the back of the sheiling called Kilgallioch', wrote Scottish cyclist and journalist Davie Bell in the mid-20th century, 'are three dome-shaped structures of great antiquity.' These were the Wells o' the Rees, the 'rees' in question being sheep pens surrounding the wells.

Popularly known as 'the Highwayman', Bell rode his bicycle all over the roughest parts of southwest Scotland in the 1930s and '40s and chronicled his exploits in a weekly column in the *Ayrshire Post*. He was intrigued by the 'Wells o' the Rees' and mounted several expeditions through thick bracken in search of them.

Today, the waymarked Southern Upland Way takes walkers to within 100yds (91m) of the wells and a signpost points them out. But when Davie Bell was roaming these moors, there were no long-distance footpaths or signposts. He eventually found the wells after getting directions from the farmer's wife at Kilgallioch. He described them as 'three piles of stones… skilfully constructed, with each well having a canopy and the shape of the whole like that of a beehive'. Made of flat stones and oval in shape they were 'streamlined into the hillside, with a recess over the well for a utensil'.

Above right: *The Hunterston Brooch, now in the National Museum of Scotland, is a masterpiece of Celtic craftsmanship*

Below right: *A distinctive stone 'beehive' marks one of the wells*

Below: *Christian carvings on the Laggangairn standing stones, on the Southern Upland Way*

Resthouse for Christian Pilgrims?

Locals told Bell that the wells were built by the Romans, but it seems more likely that they were made for early Christians on their way to Whithorn Priory. Established by St Ninian in 397, this was a centre for Ninian's mission to the Picts. The whitewashed church was called *Candida Casa* ('the White House'), and the name Whithorn derives from the Pictish translation of 'White House', Hwit Aerne.

According to the Revd C H Dick in his *Highways and Byways of Galloway and Carrick*, the wells may have been part of the ancient church and graveyard of Kilgallioch, which was near by, although when Dick walked across the moors from New Luce in 1916 he saw nothing in the way of ruins. The pilgrims' route to Whithorn was also the path followed by lepers on their way from Glenluce Abbey to the leper colony 1.5 miles (2.4km) north of Loch Derry at Libberland.

Walk 19 Refuge on the way to St Ninian's priory

Seek out the 'wells' where Scotland's earliest Christians rested

1 Cross a cattle grid and head west along the Southern Upland Way (SUW) on a well-surfaced forest road. Pass Loch Derry, on your right in just under a mile (1.6km) and then continue on the forest road, passing a signpost on the left to Linn's Tomb.

2 Follow the road as it curves to the right, then, following the SUW markerpost, turn left, leave the road and head uphill. It's a steep climb from here, on a well-trodden path with waymarkers.

3 Cross over a forest road and then continue on the uphill path heading towards the summit of Craig Airie Fell. Reach the summit at a trig point.

4 From the OS triangulation pillar, continue on a well-marked path towards a waymarker on the horizon. Turn left at the waymarker and head downhill on a footpath that twists and turns to another waymarker near the bottom. Turn right here and keep going until you reach the edge of the forest.

5 The SUW now follows a forest ride. Shortly you'll come to a clearing with a cairn on your left. Keep straight ahead following the waymarkers to the next clearing where a sign points left to the Wells of the Rees. Turn left and head downhill, across a dry-stone wall and then a gap in another wall. In winter you will find the wells easily but in summer, when the bracken is thick, you'll have to poke about a bit. The first two wells are on your right as you come through the gap and the other is off to the left.

6 Retrace your steps from here to the signpost and turn left. Continue along the Southern Upland Way to reach a junction with a forest road. Turn left and follow it to the end, then continue along a faint path, cross a wall and continue east towards Craigmoddie Fell.

7 Climb to the highest point then look to your left to Loch Derry then, to the right of it, Derry farm. Head in a straight line for Derry farm then drop down off the fell and pick up a path heading towards Loch Derry.

8 Follow this to go through a gate and on to the forest road. Turn right and return to Derry farm and the start.

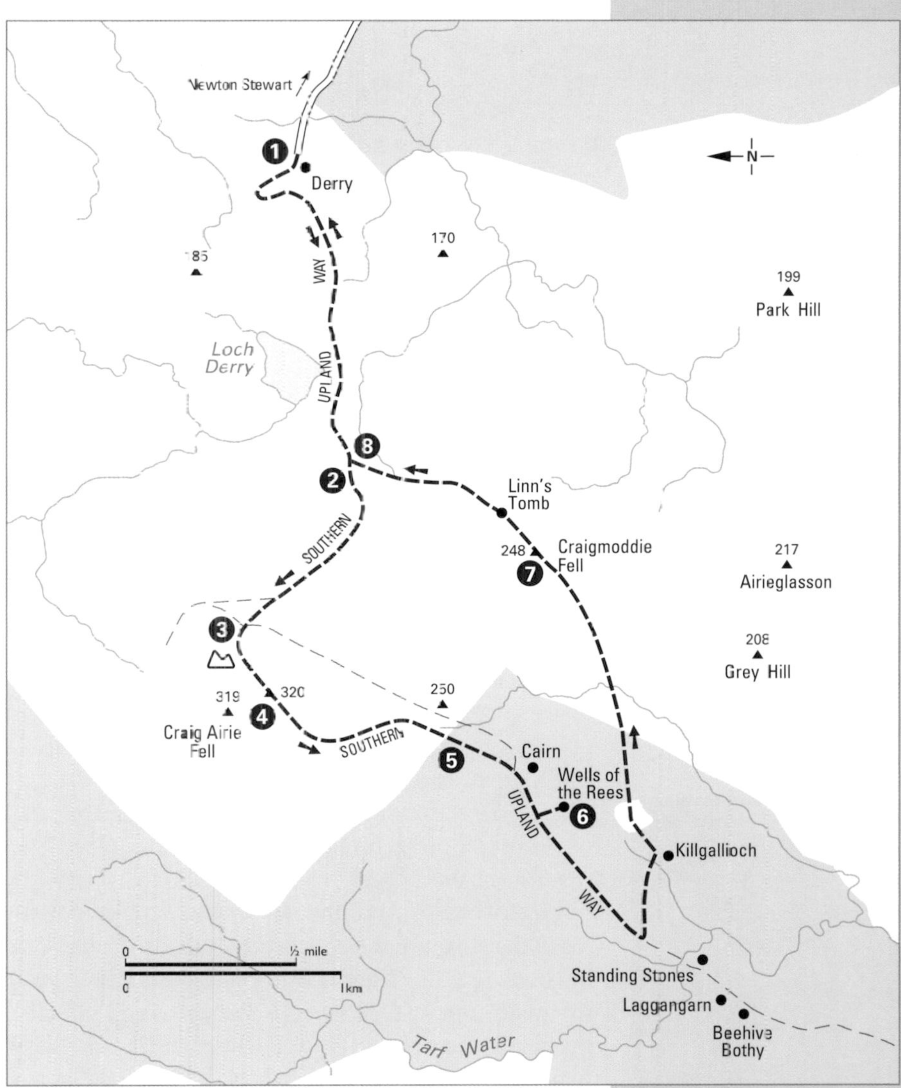

WHILE YOU'RE THERE

Visit the ruins of the Cistercian abbey at Glenluce. In a secluded position in the valley of the Water of Luce, this is a tranquil place to spend a few hours. The abbey was founded in *c.*1192 by the Earl of Galloway and was an important stopping point for pilgrims on their way to Whithorn. Look out for the remains of the 13th-century south transept and the late medieval chapter house (*c.*1500). This still has its vaulted roof; there is also a museum of monastic life. Much of the rest of the abbey is a ruin, which has been used as a source for building materials.

Distance 6.25 miles (10.1km)

Minimum time 3hrs 30min

Ascent/gradient 558ft (170m) ▲▲▲

Level of difficulty ●●●

Paths Forest roads, forest track, very rough ground

Landscape Hills, forest and loch

Suggested map OS Explorer 310 Glenluce & Kirkcowan

Start/finish Grid reference: NX 260735

Dog friendliness Keep on lead near livestock

Parking Near Derry farm

Public toilets None on route

531 In Persia (modern Iran) Khosrau I, the greatest king of the Sasanid dynasty, comes to the throne.

542 Irish monk St Brendan founds a monastery on the Isle of the Saints, in the southern Hebrides.

547 King Ida of the Angles founds the Kingdom of Bernicia with a capital at Bamburgh, Northumberland.

550 British priest Gildas writes his history, *The Ruin and Conquest of Britain.*

550 St David founds a monastery at St David's, Wales, on the site of the later cathedral.

563 St Columba lands on Iona; from here monks are sent out to establish missions on the mainland.

570 The Prophet Mohammed is born in Mecca.

571 The Kingdom of East Anglia is established.

585 The Kingdom of Mercia is established.

597 St Augustine arrives from Rome, and founds a monastery on the site of Canterbury Cathedral.

A Pilgrimage Around St Non's Bay

An attractive outing offers easy walking along the wonderful coastline that gave birth to Wales's patron saint

Below: *A stained-glass portait of St David at Castell Coch*

Bottom: *The rugged coastline near St David's*

This walk leads to a spot that can claim to be the very heart of spiritual Wales – the birthplace of St David, patron saint of Wales. David had immense influence on Welsh culture, but little is known about him. His mother is said to have been St Non, derived from Nun or Nonita, and to have been married to a local chieftain called Sant.

Legend suggests that David was born around AD 500: although a fierce storm raged throughout his birth, a calm light reputedly lit the scene; by the morning, a fresh spring had erupted near by, becoming the Holy Well of St Non. St David went on to be baptised by St Elvis at Porthclais, in water from another miraculous spring.

Windswept Headland

Shortly after the stiff climb out of Porth Clais, at point 4 on the walk, you round Trwyn Cynddeiriog, the headland that divides Porth y Ffynnon from St Non's Bay. This is where St Non and Sant, St David's parents, were said to have lived. A short distance further along the coast path, at the head of the bay, you see a footpath on the left that leads to a ruined chapel. This is thought to have been built in the 13th century on the spot where St David was born.

A path then leads to a gate, behind which you see St Non's Well and a grotto. Further up the hill is the newer chapel, dedicated to Our Lady and St Non. This was built in the 1930s using stone from other principle local evangelical sites, including the original chapel.

Man With a Mission

Judging from his parentage, David would have been well educated. According to tradition, he undertook a number of religious odysseys including one to Jerusalem, before he finally returned to his birthplace around AD 550. He then founded a church and monastery at Glyn Rhosyn, on the banks of the River Alun, on the site of the present cathedral of St David's. He set about spreading the Christian word to mainly pagan locals. St David's Day is celebrated on 1 March every year and St Non, who saw out her life in Brittany, is remembered on the day after.

St David's is little more than a pretty village, although it boasts the title 'city' on account of its magnificent cathedral. This is a wonderful place and does not seem any the worse for the large amount of tourism that it attracts. Known as Tyddewi – 'David's House' – in Welsh, the city grew to significance partly as a result of its coastal position at the western extreme of the British mainland: it would have been linked easily by sea with Ireland and Cornwall. As well as the cathedral and the ruins of the Bishop's Palace, it houses a plethora of gift shops; the National Park information centre, close to the car park, is one of the finest in the country.

Walk 20 Ruined chapel on a Welsh headland

Pay your respects at St David's reputed birthplace as you round Trwyn Cynddeiriog

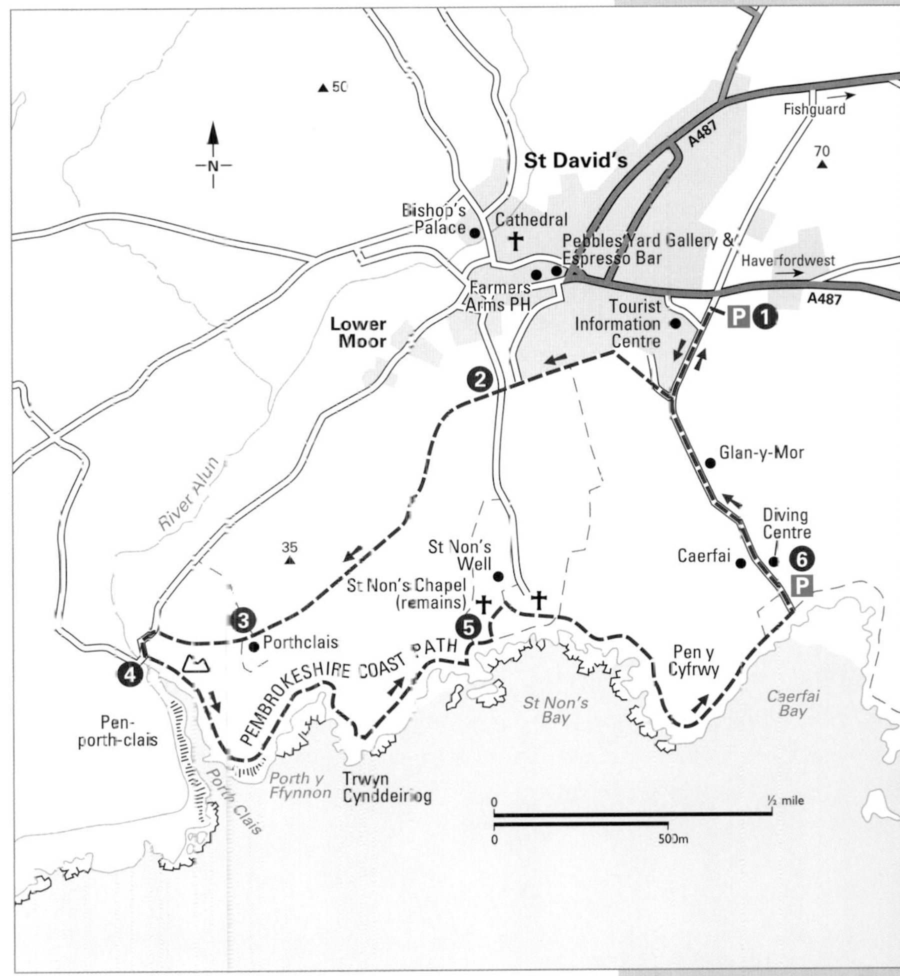

1 Turn left out of the car park in St David's and walk down the road, as if you were heading for Caerfai Bay. As the houses thin out, you'll see a turning on the right that leads to more dwellings. Take this turning, and turn left onto a waymarked bridleway. Follow this between hedges, past the end of a road and on to reach a junction with another road.

2 Walk straight across and take the waymarked path to a fork, where you keep right to continue to a stile. Cross and keep to the left of the field to another stile, where you keep straight ahead again. This leads to a farmyard, which is also a caravan park.

3 Go through the gate and turn left towards the farmyard and then right. As the drive swings left, keep straight ahead with the hedge to your right. Continue across this field and drop down between gorse bushes, keeping straight ahead at a crossroads of paths, to the road at Porth Clais. Turn left to the bottom of the valley and then, before crossing the bridge, turn left onto the coast path.

4 Climb up steeply onto the cliff tops and bear around to the left towards Porth y Ffynnon. The next small headland is Trwyn Cynddeiriog, where there's a grassy platform above the cliffs if you fancy taking a short rest. Continue into St Non's Bay and look for a footpath on the left that leads to the ruined chapel.

5 From the chapel, head up to a gate that leads to St Non's Well, and from there follow the path beneath the new chapel and back out onto the coast path. Turn left to climb easily onto Pen y Cyfrwy, continue around this and drop down towards Caerfai Bay.

6 You will eventually come out beneath the Caerfai Bay car park, where you turn left onto the road. Follow this road, past the Diving Centre and carry on until you reach St David's and the start of the walk.

Distance 3.5 miles (5.7km)

Minimum time 1hr 30min

Ascent/gradient 262ft (80m) ▲▲▲

Level of difficulty ●●●

Paths Coast path and clear footpaths over farmland, 2 stiles

Landscape Leafy countryside and dramatic cliffs

Suggested map OS Explorer OL35 North Pembrokeshire

Start/finish Grid reference: SM 757252

Dog friendliness On lead around St Non's Chapel and Well

Parking Pay-and-display car park in St David's

Public toilets Next to Tourist Information Centre

ST DAVID'S CATHEDRAL

St David's Cathedral is both architecturally stunning and spiritually moving. It stands on the site of the monastery David founded in the 6th century, which was a pilgrimage centre for centuries. In 1120 Pope Calixtus II decreed that two pilgrimages to St David's were the equivalent of one to Rome – an honour indeed; William the Conqueror visited to offer prayers in 1081, while King Henry II visited in 1171. The present cathedral was begun in 1181, but its 'new tower' fell down in 1220 and an earthquake in 1247–48 caused further damage. Under Bishop Gower in 1328–47 the cathedral's magnificent rood screen and the Bishop's Palace were built. The nave roof and its ceiling were constructed in 1530–40, and at the conclusion of this work the tomb of Edmund Tudor, 1st Earl of Richmond and father of King Henry VII, was installed in front of the high altar. Architect John Nash rebuilt the West Front in the years after 1793, and then the entire building was restored in 1862–70 by George Gilbert Scott, a proponent of the Victorian Gothic style in architecture. The cloisters were rebuilt and adapted to modern use in 2003–07. The cathedral and Bishop's Palace host a series of classical concerts every summer.

664 The Synod of Whitby opts to follow the doctrine of the Roman rather than the Celtic Church.

669 Theodore is named Archbishop of Canterbury by Pope Vitalian.

673 Theodore calls the Synod of Hertford, which gives Canterbury authority over the English Church.

731 The Venerable Bede, a monk at Jarrow Monastery, writes *An Ecclesiastical History of the English People.*

732 Frankish leader Charles Martel wins a famous victory over Islamic Saracens in the Battle of Tours.

779 Offa defeats the West Saxons and is recognised as the most powerful leader in England.

The Holy Island of St Columba

This circuit of parts of the island held sacred to the memory of a Celtic saint leads past his landing place in Coracle Bay

Top right: *The White Strand of the Monks, Iona*

Above: *Iona's Benedictine Abbey stands on the site of St Colomba's church*

In the early summer of AD 563, a middle-aged cleric crossed from Ireland to the remote and windswept island of Iona with 12 companions and the intention of setting up a monastic community. Columba (in Gaelic, Colum Cille, 'the Dove of the Church') did not intend to bring Christianity to a new country, indeed he had left his native Ireland under a cloud.

The problems had started with a dispute over copyright: Columba had secretly copied a psalter owned by St Finnian of Clonard, and Finnian had claimed ownership of the copy. The dispute became more complicated when a young prince accidentally killed an opponent during a game of Irish hockey and claimed sanctuary with Columba. A battle followed, for which Columba felt responsible. In penance for these events he accepted 'white martyrdom' – perpetual exile.

At the centre of Columba's settlement on Iona was a church of oak logs and thatch and, around it, huts for the individual monks. Columba himself slept on the bedrock, with a stone for a pillow. Larger huts of wattle were used as the dining hall, guest house, library and writing room. The monks' lives consisted of prayer, simple farming and study, and here Columba composed poetry in Latin and Irish.

Celtic versus Roman Christianity

Columba's Celtic Christianity spread from Iona across Scotland and led to the Northumbrian foundation of Lindisfarne, with its rich tradition of illustrated religious books such as the Lindisfarne Gospel. Here the faith came into contact with the Roman-style Christianity of continental Europe, brought to England by Augustine in AD 597. While the outward dispute was about the correct hairstyle for monks and the way to calculate the date of Easter, it seems that the Celtic Christianity was more personal and mystical, the Roman more authoritarian. The Roman version eventually dominated, but the Celtic was not fully suppressed. Columba, never officially canonised as a saint, is venerated in Scotland and Ireland to this day.

Iona Today

The spirit of Columba still dominates the island. From the low hill called Dun I, he blessed the island and community on the day of his death. The monks grew kale and oats on the machars (coastal lowlands) of Bay at the Back of the Ocean, over what is today the golf course. At the southern tip of the island is Coracle Bay, traditionally named as the saint's landing place.

Walk 21 Missionary base on magnificent Iona

See the ruins that so moved English writer and critic Samuel Johnson – and the hill from which St Colomba gave his last sermon

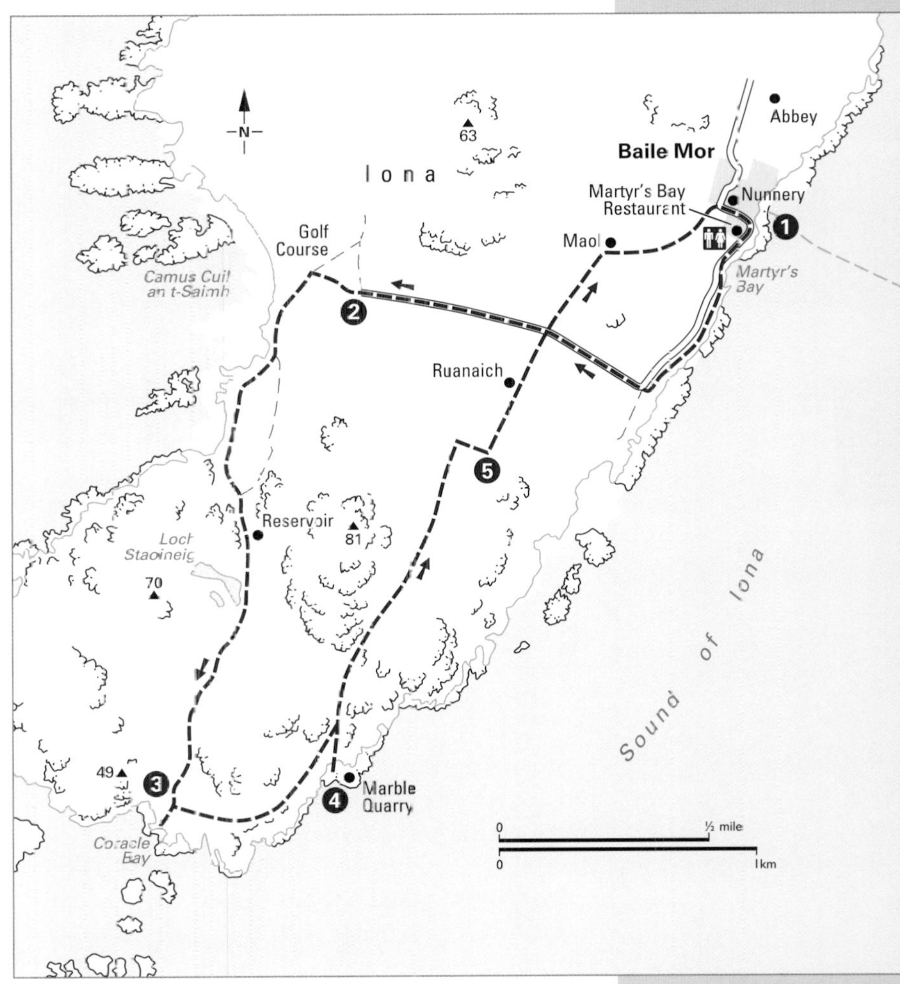

1 Ferries cross to Iona about every hour. Once on the island, take the tarmac road on the left, passing Martyr's Bay. After a second larger bay, rejoin the road as it bends right. Follow the road across the island to a gate on to the Iona golf course (dogs on leads).

2 Take the sandy track ahead, then bear left past a small cairn to the shore. Turn left along the shore to a large beach. At its end, bear left up a narrow valley. After 100yds (91m), pass a small concrete hut to join a stony track. It passes a fenced reservoir and drops to the corner of Loch Staoineig. Walk along to the left of the lochan on a path, improved in places, that runs gently down to Coracle Bay. Cross to the left of an area that shows the furrows of lazybed cultivation – fields drained to improve crop yields – and reach the shore just to the left of a rocky knoll.

3 Take the route ahead, following an indistinct path. If your ferry to the mainland leaves in less than 2 hours' time, you will need to return by the outward route and had better leave exploring the marble quarries for another visit. Otherwise, return inland for approximately 200yds (183m) and bear right into a little grassy valley. After 100yds (91m), go through a broken wall and then bear slightly left, past another inlet on the right. Cross heather to the eastern shoreline of the island. Bear left, above the small sea cliff, for 0.25 mile (400m). Turn sharp right into a little valley descending into the remnants of the marble quarry.

4 Turn inland, back up the valley to its head. Pass the low walls of two ruined cottages and continue in the same direction for about 200yds (183m) to a fence corner. Keep the fence on your left, picking a way through heather. Dun I with its cairn appears ahead – aim directly for it to reach the edge of fields, where a fence runs across ahead. Turn right along it to a small iron gate.

5 This leads to a track that passes Ruanaich farm to the tarmac road of the outward walk. Cross onto a farm track, which bends to the right at Maol. It reaches Baile Mor (Iona village) at the ruined nunnery. Just ahead is the abbey with its squat square tower, or turn right directly to return to the ferry pier.

A SIMPLE PLACE OF PRAYER

'That man is little to be envied, whose patriotism would not gain force upon the plain of Marathon, or whose piety would not grow warmer among the ruins of Iona,' wrote the renowned English writer and critic Samuel Johnson, who visited the island in 1773 in the company of his friend and later biographer James Boswell. Today's Iona Foundation is ecumenical – tied to no single denomination of Christianity – and it has restored the buildings within a tradition of simple craftsmanship and prayer. The grave of John Smith, Labour leader in the 1990s, lies in the northeast extension of the burial ground.

Distance 5.25 miles (8.4km)

Minimum time 3hrs 30min

Ascent/gradient 650ft (198m) ▲▲▲

Level of difficulty ●●●

Paths Tracks, sandy paths, some rugged rock and heather

Landscape Bare gneiss rock and Atlantic Ocean

Suggested map OS Explorer 373 Iona, Staffa & Ross of Mull

Start/finish Grid reference: NM 286240

Dog friendliness Keep on lead near sheep and on golf course

Parking Ferry terminal at Fionnphort on Mull

Public toilets Beside Martyr's Bay Bar

780 The construction of Offa's Dyke begins to create a defensive border between Wales and England.

789 Two centuries of savage Viking raids along the English coast begin with a raid in Dorset.

788–91 Charlemagne, King of the Franks, leads a triumphant campaign against Slavs and Avars.

800 The Christian community at Kells Monastery complete the superbly illustrated *Book of Kells*, now in Trinity College, Dublin.

825 Ecgberht, King of Wessex, wins the allegiance of his neighbour kingdoms and defeats Mercia at the Battle of Ellandun. By 827 Ecgberht was considered the most powerful leader in England.

Taliesin and the Twin Lakes

A gentle mountain walk visits two lakes, one fit to impress poets of the present and one that inspired many great bards of the past

Surrounded by woodland, lush pasture and craggy hills, Llyn Crafnant is serenely beautiful. The name Crafnant derives from old Welsh for 'valley of garlic' – and today, as in centuries past, the valley smells of wild garlic when the plant is flowering. The first part of this fine walk follows an undulating forestry track that gives a slightly elevated view of the lake. Little whitewashed cottages are arranged neatly in the lower pastures, while the slopes at the head of the valley are tinged with the russet of heather and the golden grey of the much-faulted crags which rise to the knobbly ridge crest. Here the summit of Crimpiau rules supreme.

After rounding the lake the route climbs out of the valley through the trees and zig-zags down into the upland hollow of Llyn Geirionydd. This is a wilder place altogether, one with barren hillsides and conifer plantations – although sometimes there are waterskiers on the lake to lessen the sense of wilderness. Another lakeside path follows, sometimes almost dipping into the lapping waters. Scaling a bluff you come to the spoil heaps of a huge old lead mine, one of many in the area. Unfortunately, the lake was poisoned by these lead mines and as a result, you will see no fish here.

Above right: *A monument commemorates Taliesin, the great Welsh bard*

Below: *Llyn Crafnant is a renowned Snowdonian beauty spot; it was dammed in 1874*

Although the lake waters cannot support life, two quite rare plants thrive on rocks from the spoil heaps. The forked spleenwort looks like a cross between grass and a moss, but it is actually a fern. It does not appear to mind the high toxicity, and neither does the alpine pennycress, a short hairless perennial with untoothed leaves growing stalkless from the stem and with clusters of small white or pale mauve flowers that appear between April and July.

Bard to Many Kings

On a grassy mound at the end of Llyn Geirionydd stands an obelisk topped with a cross. This imposing monument commemorates the 6th-century bard Taliesin (*c.*534–*c.*599), the earliest Welsh poet whose works have survived to the present day.

Taliesin was a compelling figure with a colourful history. He had connections to many royal courts of the time, including that of King Arthur (see box, opposite).

Eisteddfods at Llyn Geirionydd

Bardic traditions at Llyn Geirionydd did not die with Taliesin, for Welsh poet John Roberts (1828–1904) organised an Eisteddfod named 'Festival of the Geirionydd's Banks' in 1863 after a disagreement with the organisers of the national event. Roberts took the name Gwilim Cowlyd for these eisteddfods (festivals of poetry, performance and music).

The competition was held here until 1912, four years after Roberts's death, and each year attracted distinguished entries. Another poet, David Francis (1865-1929), performed under the name 'the Blind Harpist of Meirion'.

Walk 22 Lakeside haunt of renowned Welsh poets

Walk shores once paced by the great bard Taliesin – and his successors

1 Turn right out of the car park and follow the lane to the north end of Llyn Crafnant. Turn right again here, and follow the forestry track along the northwest shores of the lake, before taking the lower left fork.

2 Ignore a stile on the left, and instead climb with the forestry track. Keep watching for a later waymarked footpath on which you should descend left to cross a stream by a cottage, Hendre Bach. Turn left down a track, passing a couple of modern chalets.

3 Turn left along the road which heads back towards the lake. Leave this at a telephone box for a path, signposted 'Llyn Geirionydd' and waymarked with blue-capped posts. This climbs through the conifer forests and over the shoulder of Mynydd Deulyn.

4 Descend with the main winding forestry track, still following the obvious blue-capped posts. Ignore the track forking to the right – it leads to Llyn Bychan.

5 On reaching the valley floor, leave the track to go over a step stile on the left. The path then crosses a couple of meadows beneath Ty-newydd cottage before tracing Llyn Geirionydd's shoreline. Take your time to enjoy the views. At the northern end of the lake the path keeps to the right of a wall and meets a farm track.

6 Turn left and immediately right to reach the Taliesin Monument on a grassy mound. Descend to a green path heading north towards the Crafnant Valley.

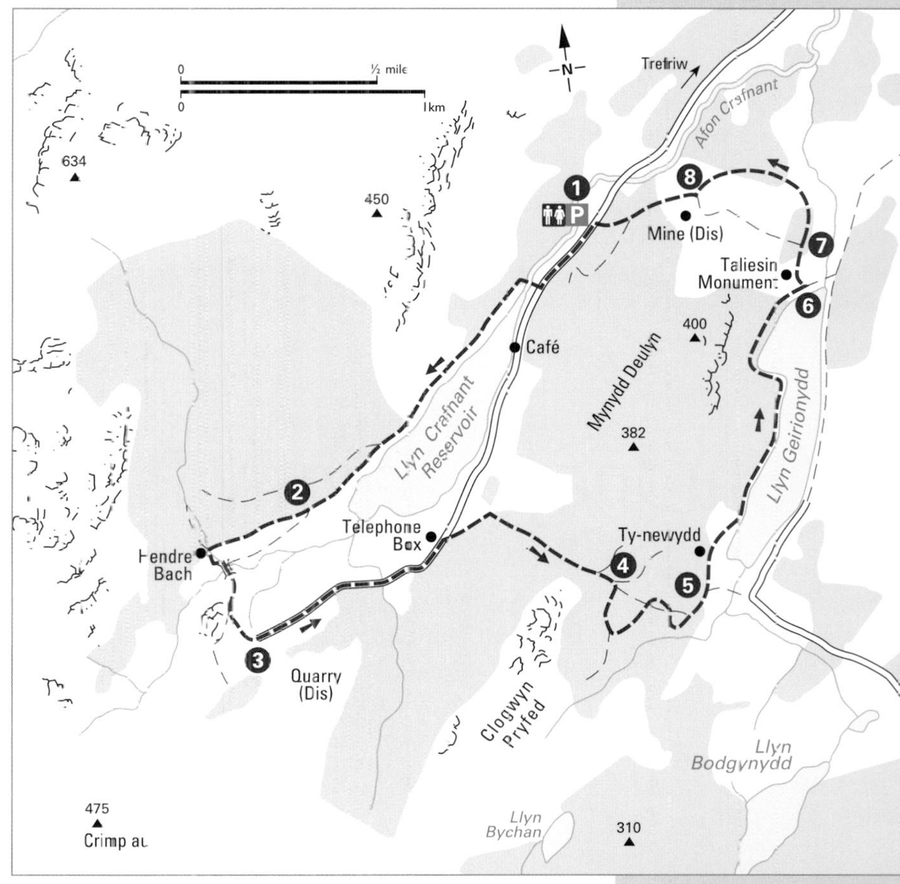

7 Veer left to cross a ladder stile and follow the undulating path ahead over wooded rock and heather knolls.

8 The path eventually swings left to reach an old mine. Here, take the lower track on the right which descends back to the valley road and the forest car park.

Distance 5 miles (8km)

Minimum time 3hrs

Ascent/gradient 984ft (300m) ▲▲▲

Level of difficulty ●●●

Paths Clear paths and forestry tracks, 5 stiles

Landscape Lake, afforested hillsides and woods

Suggested map OS Explorer OL17 Snowdon

Start/finish Grid reference: SH 756618

Dog friendliness Dogs could run free in forest areas

Parking Forestry pay car park, north of Llyn Crafnant

Public toilets At car park

THE BARD TALIESIN

Taliesin's name means 'Shining Brow' in medieval Welsh. Poems attributed to him survive in *The Book of Taliesin* (*c.*1275–1325); if they are indeed his work, they must have been transmitted orally for 600 years or more before being written down. Most scholars believe Taliesin to have been of Irish descent; he has been linked to legends as colourful as some of his poems, but we know that he lived for some time at the northern end of Geirionydd. In those days bards were resident at the courts of warlord kings, and Taliesin is said to have attended on at least three Celtic monarchs, including King Maelgwyn Gwynedd – who, according to a local monk, was one of the most sinful rulers in history. After a fiery row, the departing Taliesin predicted that a yellow creature would rise from Morfa Rhianedd (Llandudno) and kill the King – and it is known that when the King died in 547 there was an outbreak of yellow fever. Many of Taliesin's poems recount tales of magic and mystery, and some relate to the heroics of King Arthur. A great part of Taliesin's work praises Urien of Rheged, a northern leader whose kingdom occupied much of modern Cumbria and southwest Scotland and whose deeds are linked by some to those of Arthur. In some legendary traditions Taliesin himself is celebrated as a companion of King Arthur.

839 Aethelwulf accedes the throne of Wessex on the death of Ecgberht.

846 In India Vijayalaya funds the Chola Empire.

865 The Danish army lands in East Anglia and sweeps northwards, capturing York, before turning south and crushing every English kingdom except Wessex.

871–99 As King of Wessex, Alfred embarks on a determined campaign to push back the invaders, ordering massive warships, building fortresses and eventually driving the Danes from his territories.

875 The monks of Lindisfarne, fleeing from the Danes, take with them the illuminated Lindisfarne Gospels (now kept in the British Museum).

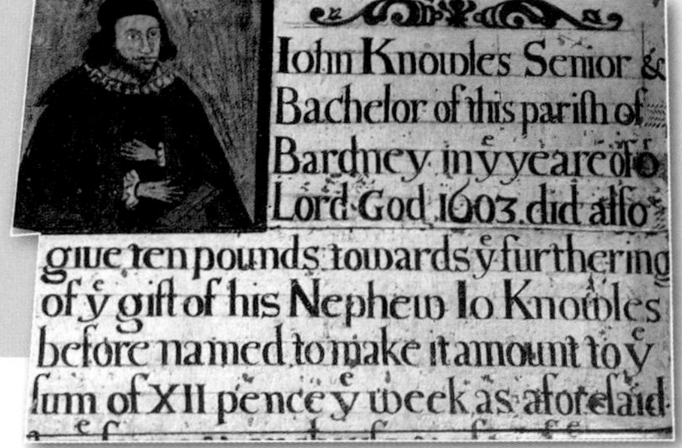

Bardney's Saintly Paths

An atmospheric outing leads to ruined abbeys east of Lincoln

Above right: *A charity board notes a donation in 1603 to fund rebuilding of St Lawrence Church in Bardney*

Below: *Gothic arches at Tupholme Abbey*

Bottom: *A barn owl on sentry duty beside the remains of Tupholme Abbey*

The valley of the River Witham, east of Lincoln, once housed nine monasteries or religious houses, attracted by the accessibility that the river afforded as well as the ecclesiastical standing of nearby Lincoln. The first to be built was Bardney, endowed by Ethelred, King of Mercia, and its fame and popularity were sealed when it became the shrine to St Oswald.

King Oswald was killed in battle in 642 and his body was brought to Bardney in 675 – although his head went separately to Lindisfarne Abbey and his arms to Bamburgh, both in Northumberland. According to the story, Oswald's remains arrived at night, and the monks at Bardney initially refused to allow the cart to enter. Suddenly a 'pillar of light' shone skywards from the coffin, convincing them that this was indeed a saintly person, and after that they never shut their gates. The local Lincolnshire saying for when someone leaves a door open is: 'Do you come from Bardney?'

Whereas the Benedictine monks of Bardney wore black habits, the Premonstratensian monks (from Prémontré, in France) at Tupholme Abbey, which is also visited on this walk, wore a white habit and cap and were known as the 'White Canons'. From Matins at 2am through to Compline at dusk, they spent their days in prayer and recitation, although they also found time to rear sheep, sell wool and import building stone via a canal-link to the River Witham. Beyond the solitary remaining wall of Tupholme Abbey is a field where canons dug fish ponds.

Viking Terror

Bardney Abbey was destroyed by Viking raiders in *c.*870 and the relics of St Oswald were moved to Gloucester. Just over two centuries later, in 1087, the site was re-established as a priory by Bardney's new Norman owner, Gilbert de Gant, and in 1116 Gilbert's son, Walter, made it an abbey. However, the fate of the monks was sealed by King Henry VIII, who seized all assets in 1536. A short-lived local rebellion in October 1536 only led to the execution of six Bardney monks. The monastery closed two years later.

Thereafter ruin was swift. Before long the site was raided for building material and had farm cottages built against it. In 1909-14 local vicar Charles Laing excavated the area: he traced the layout of the cloister, chapter house and so on, and published his detailed findings, but as the weather caused the newly revealed stonework to deteriorate it was eventually decided to cover up the ruins carefully. In 1998, the Lincolnshire Heritage Trust stepped in to save what was left.

Walk 23 Haunting outlines of a 7th-century abbey

Take an intriguing excursion to the former resting place of St Oswald

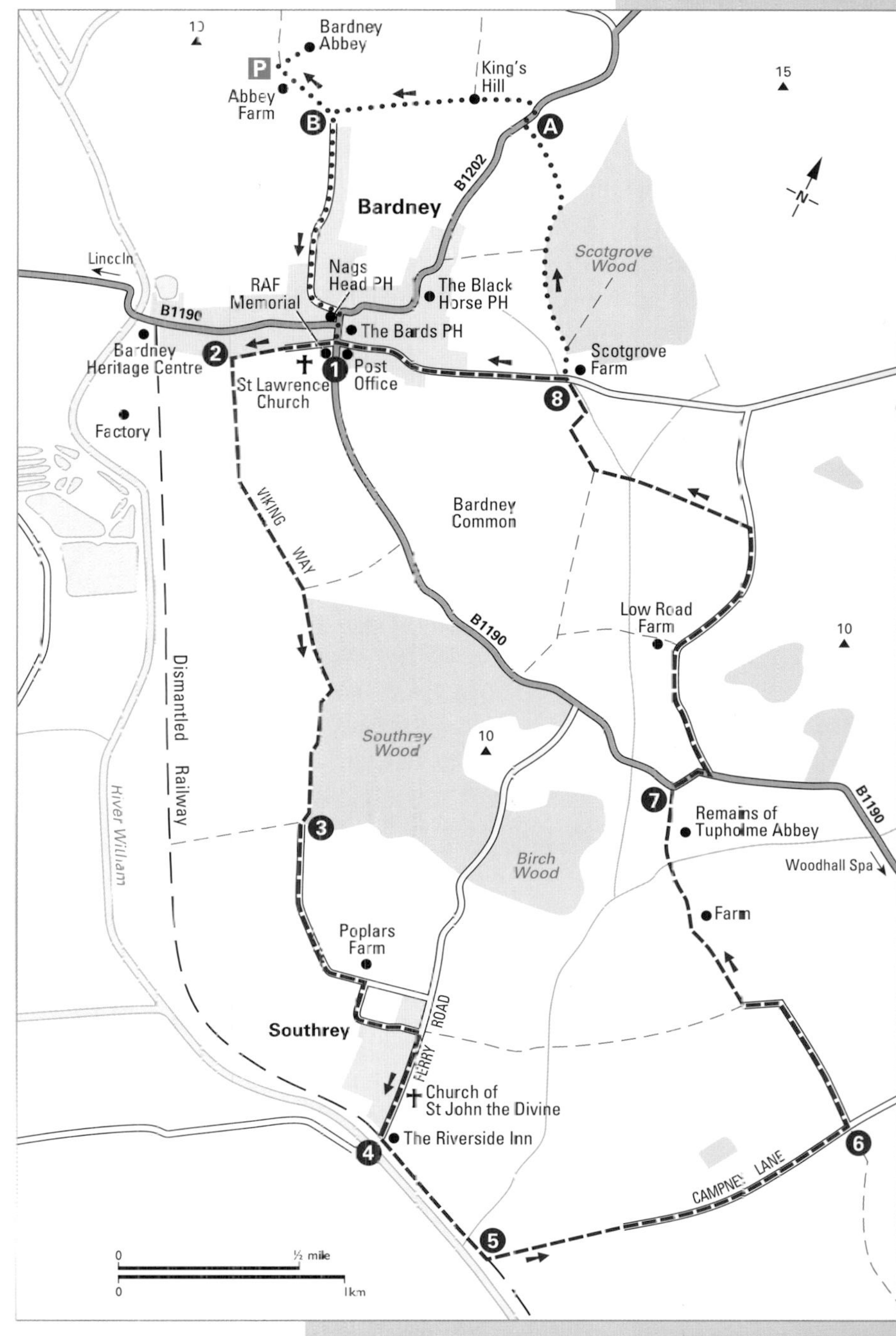

1 From the RAF memorial opposite Bardney's post office, walk along the adjacent Church Lane. Just beyond St Lawrence Church take the public footpath on the left.

2 At the end of the path turn left onto a wide track through the fields. Ignore the inviting permissive bridleways into Southrey Wood (left).

3 When the wood finishes continue along the main track. When it reaches the buildings of Southrey it swings left past Poplars Farm. Take the first road on the right. At the end of the road go right again to reach the Riverside Inn at the far end of Ferry Road.

4 Turn left onto the raised bank of the River Witham, now part of the Water Rail Way, and follow the old trackbed beside the river for 650yds (594m).

5 Go left at a public footpath sign and across a footbridge over a drainage dyke for a track across a field. Continue straight on as it turns into Campney Lane.

6 At the road junction turn left and, after a sharp left bend, turn right on to a signposted public bridleway. Follow this wide ride between hedges. Go through a gate and then past a farm to reach the remains of Tupholme Abbey.

7 Beyond the abbey turn right on the road, then left on a lane. About 750yds (686m) after Low Road Farm take the footpath between two fields on the left. When the dividing dyke appears, keep both it and the fence on your left. Cross a bridge and go through another field to turn right onto a cross track all the way to the road.

8 Turn left for the verge, then follow the pavement back into Bardney.

Extension

Leave the route where it turns left into the road opposite Scotgrove Farm (Point 8). Cross the road, go past the farm, and before the wooden barrier turn left on a wide ride. Keep Scotgrove Wood on your right. When the wood finishes go straight on to reach the road at the end (Point A). Turn right, cross over for a wide track across fields. Go straight at a junction of tracks until you reach the surfaced drive to Abbey Farm (Point B). Turn right through the farm buildings to reach the parking area for Bardney Abbey. The outlines of the buildings and layout are visible in the field to the right; look for the information board. To return to Bardney simply turn left at Point B and follow Abbey Road back through the houses, turning right opposite the Bards to reach the centre.

Distance 7.75 miles (12.5km) [*Extension* 9 miles (14.5km)]

Minimum time 4hrs [*Extension* 4hrs 30min]

Ascent/gradient Negligible ▲▲▲ [*Extension* ▲▲▲]

Level of difficulty ●●● [*Extension* ●●●]

Paths Flat and open arable land, punctuated by woodland

Landscape Easy field paths and bridleways

Suggested map OS Explorer 273 Lincolnshire Wolds South

Start/finish Grid reference: TF 120694

Dog friendliness Mostly good, watch for livestock

Parking Horncastle Road, centre of Bardney

Public toilets None on route (nearest at Woodhall Spa)

Royal Grave at Sutton Hoo

This atmospheric walk leads to the famous site of an Anglo Saxon burial ground

The discovery of an Anglo-Saxon ship burial at Sutton Hoo in 1939 shed new light on the Dark Ages and opened up a whole new chapter of English history. It all came about when Edith May Pretty, a widow with a keen interest in spiritualism, reported seeing visions of ghostly warriors dancing on the burial mounds near her home. She called in a local archaeologist, Basil Brown, to investigate and before long he had made his extraordinary discovery.

Many of the graves had been desecrated by robbers, but in one of the mounds he found the remains of a 90ft (27m) wooden ship with a burial chamber inside. The timber had rotted, leaving nothing but rusty iron rivets and a dark stain, but the treasures that survived included Byzantine silver, gold buckles and a bejewelled helmet, sword and shield. The only thing missing was a body, presumably decomposed.

Sutton Hoo Treasure

An inquest awarded the treasure to Mrs Pretty and she donated it to the British Museum, the single most generous gift that institution has ever received from a living donor. Archaeologists have been puzzling ever since over the identity of the missing man. Although weapon burials were not uncommon, the riches found at Sutton Hoo have led most experts to conclude that this was the burial ground of the early East Anglian kings, and that the burial chamber in the ship was that of King Raedwald, leader of the Wuffinga dynasty, who died around 625. He defeated Aethelfrith of Northumbria and was the first southern king to hold sway over the northern kingdom; he was an early convert to Christianity but

Above: *A reconstruction of the famous helmet found in the burial ship*

Below: *Drinking horns and harp (both reconstructed) from a Sutton Hoo grave*

Bottom: *At Sutton Hoo there are 17 burial mounds dating to the 6th–7th century on a site overlooking the River Debden*

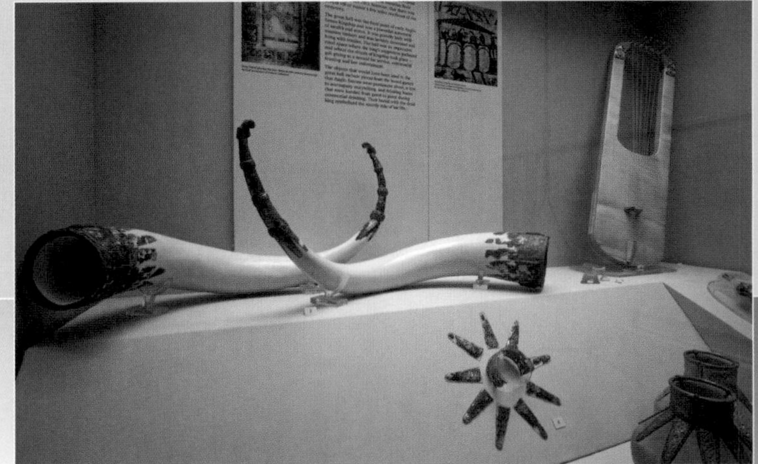

WHILE YOU'RE THERE

Visit the National Trust exhibition and treasury, which contains some of the original finds from Sutton Hoo. It is open daily in summer and on winter weekends, though times may vary throughout the year. From here, a signed pathway leads around the burial grounds. At weekends and in the summer holidays, members of the Sutton Hoo Society give guided tours of the site, with the opportunity to climb on the burial mounds.

allowed both Christian and pagan religion in East Anglia. In 2002 the National Trust opened an exhibition on the site with replicas of many of the items and some of the original treasures on display. There is a sword in its wooden scabbard, the sword-belt fittings exquisitely patterned in gold and red garnet from India. There is an ornamental shield, covered in golden dragons and eagles, and a warrior's helmet with designs of horsemen in wrought copper and bronze. The artists making the replicas were full of admiration for the skills of their Anglo-Saxon ancestors. 'They were highly sophisticated people with an appreciation of art and culture. Some of these objects are extremely difficult to make even today,' says the National Trust.

Most people agree that the new exhibition has made Sutton Hoo easier to understand. If, however, you prefer your lumps in the ground without explanation, come here at dawn or on a misty morning when the place still has an air of mystery about it: you just might see ghostly figures dancing on graves.

Walk 24 Burial of King Raedwald

Savour a taste of mystery in evocative surroundings

1 From the National Trust car park, take the signposted blue trail from behind the Visitor Centre, descending towards the River Deben on a gravel track. Turn left opposite the entrance to Little Haugh and turn right by a map of the Sutton Hoo Estate. The path narrows and turns left alongside a fence on its way to the river. Keep left around a meadow and climb the steps to the river bank, with Woodbridge visible on the opposite bank.

2 Turn left and walk along the river bank. The path is overgrown in places and the plank bridges can be slippery in wet weather but the views are superb. After 400yds (366m), climb the steps to your left to leave the river behind and turn left around a turf field. Keep to the edge of the field as it swings right and climbs between woodland to the left and a reservoir to the right.

3 Turn right at the top of a rise to follow a bridleway along the field-edge, with Deben Wood to your left. At the end of the wood the path swings half left across a field, then passes through a hedge onto a lane. You could turn left here for a short cut, picking up the walk again in 300yds (274m) at Point 6.

4 Keep straight ahead for 0.75 mile (1.2km), crossing the drive to Haddon Hall. At Methersgate Hall bear right around farm buildings, then left on a footpath beside a brick wall. Pass a pair of cannons on the lawn of the hall and continue ahead with the River Deben opening out in front of you. Go through a gate and turn left across a field, then go through another gate and turn right along a lane. Stay on this lane for 1 mile (1.6km) and as it bends left past Cliff Farm.

5 At the second three-finger signpost turn left along a field-edge track, passing an embankment on the right. Keep to the public bridleway as it swings left around an area of woodland. At the end of the woodland, keep straight ahead between fields and as the path becomes a broad grass track through trees, passing some cottages to reach a minor lane.

6 Turn right and stay on this lane for about 1 mile (1.6km) to the main road (B1083). Turn left and walk carefully along the verge for 400yds (366m), soon to take the footpath left opposite the road junction. When you see the burial mounds to your left-hand side, turn right to return to the Visitor Centre on a National Trust permissive path.

Distance 7.25 miles (11.7km)
Minimum time 3hrs
Ascent/gradient 262ft (80m) ▲▲▲
Level of difficulty ●●●
Paths Field-edge and riverside paths, farm lanes, short section of busy road
Landscape Farmland, woodland and River Deben
Suggested map OS Explorer 197 Ipswich, Felixstowe & Harwich
Start/finish Grid reference: TM 290493
Dog friendliness On lead on farmland and National Trust land (not allowed near burial mounds)
Parking National Trust car park – included in entry price for exhibition, or pay-and-display when exhibition closed (free to NT members)
Public toilets At National Trust Visitor Centre – walkers' toilets behind building are open when centre is closed

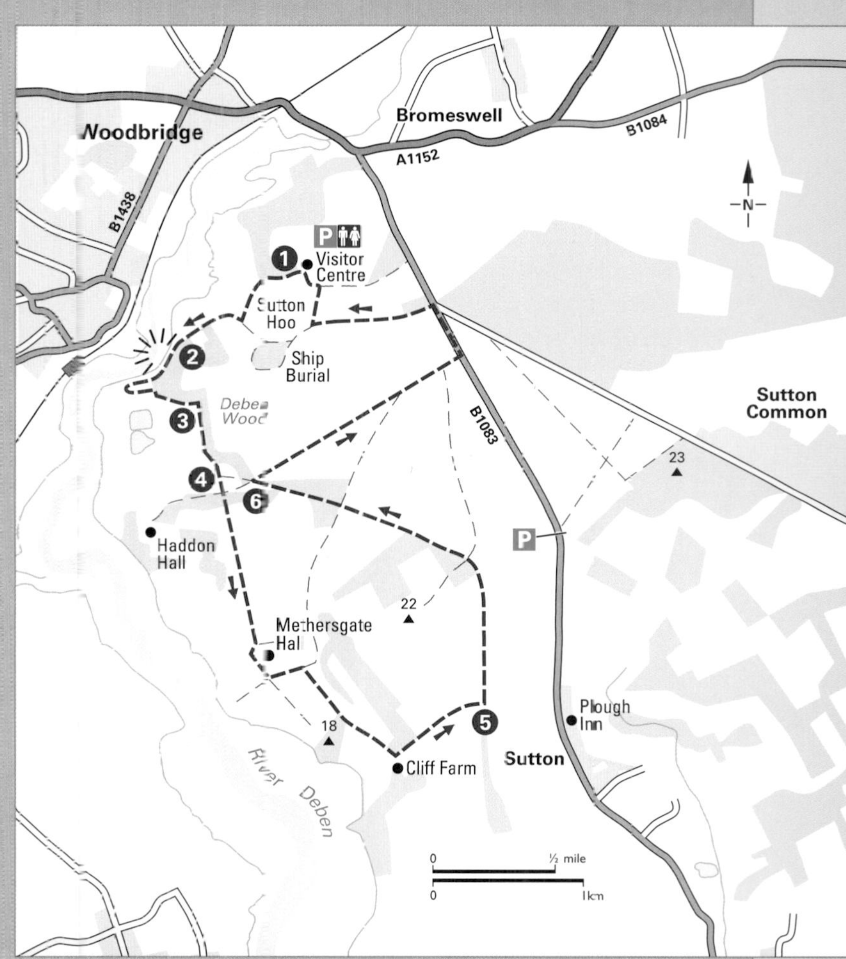

878 Alfred defeats the Vikings. He is recognised as ruler of the south and overlord of the north.

886 Alfred captures London and starts uniting the Anglo Saxons under the Wessex dynasty.

891–95 Monks complete the Anglo-Saxon chronicles and translate Bede's texts into Anglo-Saxon.

899–925 Alfred's son, Edmund, wins other English lands, defeating the Danes and advancing into East Anglia, Essex and central England.

925 The death of Edmund brings Aethelstan to power. He heads north and successfully beats back the intrusions of the fierce Viking leader Eric Bloodaxe, finally defeating him in 954.

Alfred's Greatness Remembered at Wantage

A fascinating walk passes the statue of a revered British king before heading for spectacular expanses of downland

King Alfred is one of those heroic figures we remember from the pages of school history books. His victories in battle and his reputation for scholarship and justice rightly earned him the title Alfred the Great. He is suitably commemorated in the Market Place of Wantage, the town of his birth. The striking marble statue of him at its centre was sculpted by Count Gleichen, Prince of Hohenlohne-Langenburg, and unveiled in 1877. As you pass by it, in the initial stages of the walk, note the battleaxe in one hand and manuscript in the other.

Soldier and Scholar

Alfred, the youngest son of King Aethelwulf, succeeded his brother Aethelred as King in 871, at a time when Viking invaders had overwhelmed most of England to the north of the Thames and Wessex was under constant attack. Seven years later Alfred defeated the Danish army at Edington in Wiltshire. He repelled another invasion in 885 and captured London the following year. He is also remembered for building a fleet, which earned him a reputation as 'father of the English navy', and creating a ring of fortified strongholds around his kingdom.

In addition to this, he was an educated man and as a child he travelled to Rome and to the Frankish court of Charles I, the Bald. He revived learning and translated many documents from Latin into Anglo-Saxon. He was instrumental in codifying the laws of his kingdom. He made a treaty that recognised the peaceful partition of England with one part – called the Danelaw – under Viking rule and law. The Danelaw was principally the kingdoms of Northumbria, East Anglia and parts of what is now the east Midlands.

A Mighty Battle

Yet most local people probably associate Alfred with the Battle of Ashdown, fought not far from Wantage in 871. The Danes held Reading, but it was Alfred's intention to entice them away from the river, which they commanded, and confront them on the downs. Alfred and his brother Aethelred encouraged the enemy to pursue them up the Kennet Valley; the two men then fell back towards the downs, with the Danes in hot pursuit. At Ashdown, they stood their ground. What happened next is not clear: the area surrounding the Ridgeway was guarded by forts and perhaps Alfred looked to them for help in his quest for victory. In the end Alfred won the day, sending the Danes packing – and proving that once they were away from their boats they were an easy target.

After a number of victories over the Danes Alfred was forced to retreat to the relative safety of the Somerset marshes. However, he had taken a positive first step in his efforts to resist the Vikings during the following years.

__Top:__ Interlaced decoration on a Viking silver brooch dated to c.900

__Left:__ A statue of Alfred in Wantage Market Place marks his birthplace in AD849

Walk 25 Where Alfred overcame the mighty Danes

Visit an area of country that holds a very special place in English hearts

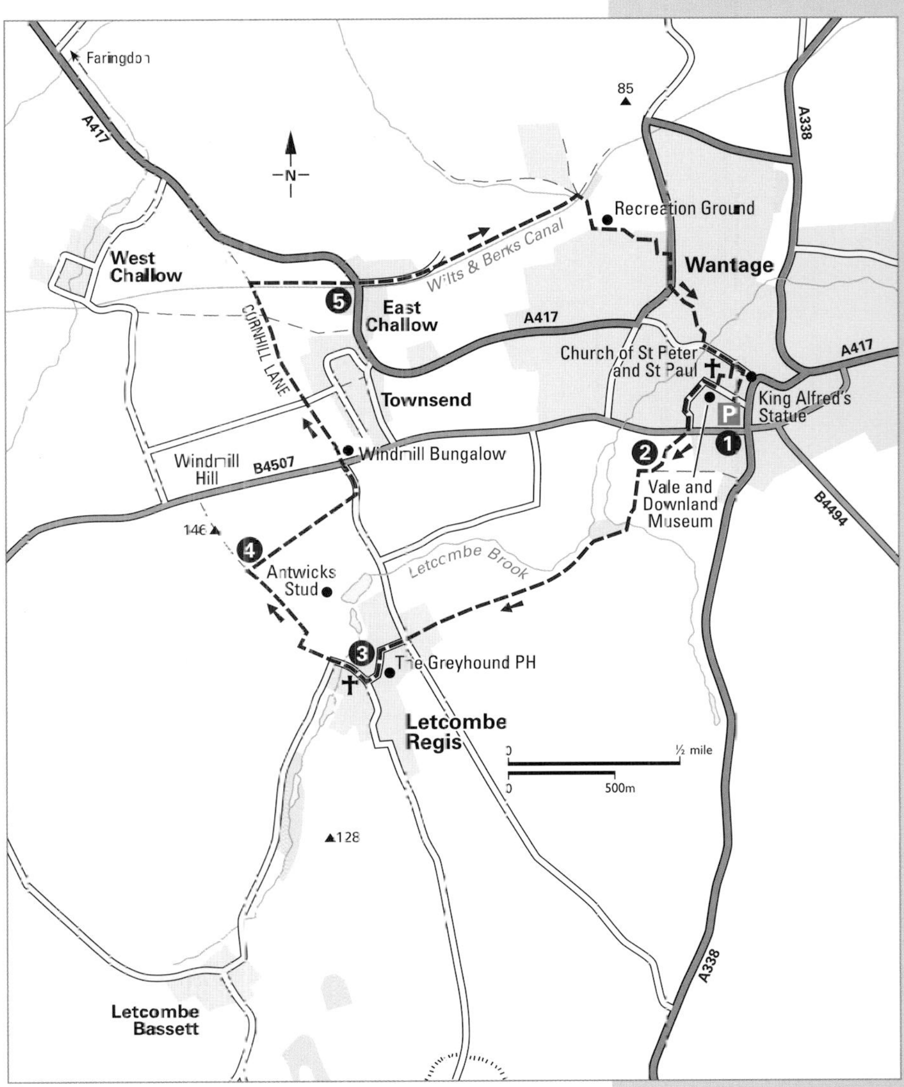

1 Pass the public toilets, then cross Church Street to take a covered walkway to the Market Place. To the right is the statue of King Alfred, but your route is left, following the signs for the museum. Approach the parish church of St Peter and St Paul and follow the road round to the left. Opposite you at the next junction is the Vale and Downland Museum (this is Church Street again). Turn right here, following Priory Road to its end. Cross this busy road (Portway) to a footpath to the left of the Croft.

2 Follow the clear tarmac path as it runs between fences and playing fields. At length you reach a housing estate; continue ahead into Letcombe Regis and make for the junction with Courthill Road. Keep it on your left and go straight ahead, past the Greyhound pub and a thatched cottage dated 1698, to a junction.

3 Turn right by the church, signposted 'Letcombe Bassett and Lambourn' and, when the road bends sharp left, go straight ahead. After a few paces the drive bends right. Keep ahead along a path between banks of vegetation, following it as it curves right, then swings left. Pass Antwicks Stud over to the right and climb gently between trees and bushes.

4 Turn right at the next intersection and follow the tree-lined track to the road. Turn left and make for the junction. Cross over, pass alongside Windmill Bungalow and follow Cornhill Lane. Begin a gentle descent, cross a lane by a school and continue down the slope. Keep ahead to a footbridge crossing the old Wilts & Berks Canal. Turn right and follow the tow path.

5 Take care in crossing the A417 road, then follow a works access road for 200yds (183m). Move right to walk alongside a section of restored canal. On reaching a tarmac drive, turn right to a row of houses. Turn left, pass a play area and follow a track to the right. Turn left, to some lock-up garages, then right but soon left to a mini-roundabout. Turn right, seeking Belmont (a street) on the left. Turn here, then fork right into a fenced path. Follow this, passing new housing, to Mill Street. Turn left, up to King Alfred's monument and the start.

Distance 5.25 miles (8.4km)

Minimum time 2hrs 30min

Ascent/gradient 150ft (46m) ▲▲▲

Level of difficulty ●●●

Paths Pavements, tow path, field paths and tracks, 1 stile

Landscape Town outskirts, farmland and downland

Suggested map OS Explorer 170 Abingdon, Wantage

Start/finish Grid reference: SU 397877

Dog friendliness On lead on town outskirts, in villages and if horses about

Parking Portway car park (enter from Church Street)

Public toilets At start

WANTAGE – A HISTORIC AND CULTURED TOWN

The final section of the walk runs alongside a restored section of the Wilts & Berks Canal. Opened in 1810 to connect the Kennet & Avon Canal with the River Thames, this was closed in 1914, but much of the route survives and restoration is ongoing. While in Wantage visit the Vale and Downland Museum, which describes itself as the starting point for exploring the Vale of White Horse. The Church of St Peter and St Paul dates in part to the 13th century; look out for the 15th-century misericords. If you like poetry visit the Betjeman Memorial Park, also in Wantage. Betjeman, who was Poet Laureate from 1972 to 1984, lived in Wantage for many years and celebrated the town in his poems.

955–59 Alfred's great grandson, Eadred, is king.

959 Edgar becomes king. He is crowned in 973 by St Dunstan, Archbishop of Canterbury, undergoing the first 'coronation' style ceremony.

975–78 The brief reign of Edward the Martyr ends in his murder on the orders of Aethelred, who succeeds him. In the same year, the Vikings begin another series of violent raids on English shores.

979–1016 Aethelred II, the Unready, unable to defend England against the Vikings, attempts to bribe the invaders before ordering the massacre of all Danes in England. He flees to Normandy and is restored only briefly to the throne before his death in 1016.

1016 Aethelred's son, Edmund Ironside, fights the Danish king Canute for the throne but is killed. Canute succeeds the throne as King of England.

1016–35 King Canute modernises English laws. In 1017 he divides England into four earldoms and marries Aethelred II's widow, Emma. England remains under Danish rule until 1066.

On Offa at Knighton

This walk covers a fine stretch of the earthwork built by Offa of Mercia in the 8th century

Knighton straddles the English–Welsh border, nine toes in Wales and one in Shropshire. Its Welsh name is Tref-y-clawdd, which translates as 'town on the dyke', a reference to its position on the great earthwork known as Offa's Dyke. Offa was ruler of the English kingdom of Mercia in 757–96, and the eponymous dyke is the longest archaeological monument in Britain, an impressive structure consisting mainly of a bank, with a ditch on the Welsh side.

Nobody is certain why Offa ordered its construction. At one time historians believed it was an agreed frontier, a way of defining the border or of regulating trade. Now many experts argue that after a period of instability with constant cross-border raiding, Offa decided to secure his frontier with a defensive boundary. Opinion has also changed on the extent of the dyke: historians formerly believed that it ran all the way from Treuddyn (north of Wrexham) to Chepstow, but now many think that the barrier may have been shorter than that: for example, recent work in Gloucestershire has suggested that the earthwork in the lower Wye Valley, previously accepted as part of Offa's Dyke, actually dates from a different period.

The Shropshire earthwork is certainly part of Offa's Dyke, however. Most of the best-preserved sections are in Shropshire, particularly on remote Llanfair Hill, a little to the north of this walk, which is also the dyke's highest point (1,410ft/430m).

The Dyke's Enduring Mysteries

To date, nearly 200 archaeological digs have been carried out on the dyke system. As far as its purpose is concerned, the only thing that has been concluded with any reasonable certainty is that it was built in such a way as to defend Mercia from the raiding Welsh. It was probably not simply an agreed frontier or a boundary marker. But, then again, if it was defensive, why have no traces of fortifications or palisading been discovered? Clearly, there is still much to learn.

Below: *Breathtaking views are a reward for energetic exertion on the Offa's Dyke Path*

Walk 26 An earthwork defence against the Welsh?

Skirt the Welsh–English border as you take a step back in time on Offa's Dyke

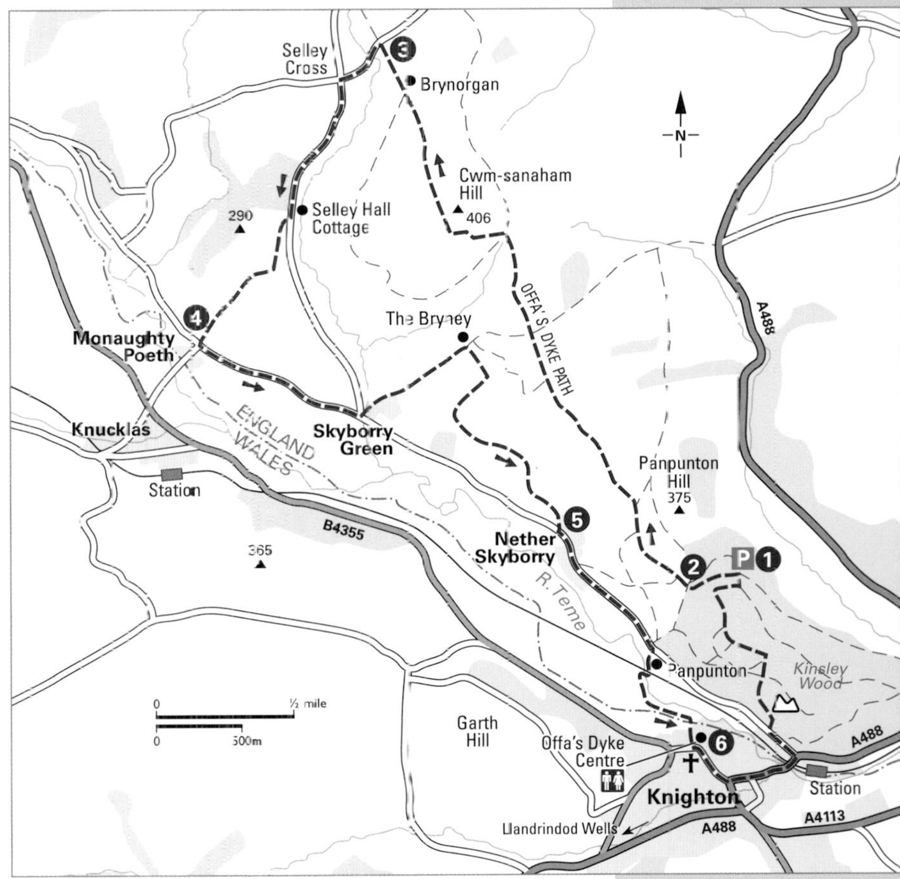

1 Adjacent to the car park, at the northern end of Kinsley Wood, is a meadow containing a barn. Walk along the left-hand edge of the meadow; at the crest veer away from the field-edge and descend through trees to Offa's Dyke Path (ODP).

2 Turn right and follow the ODP for about 2.5 miles (4km). The path runs above steep slopes falling to the west, following the dyke all the way. After rounding a combe, it climbs to the top of Cwm-sanaham Hill (1,323ft/406m), then continues northwards, soon descending very steeply to a white house, Brynorgan.

3 Meeting a road, leave the ODP, turning left, then left again at Selley Cross. After 0.5 mile (800m) or so, just beyond the Workhouse, go through the first gate on the right. Follow a vague path to the far side of a field, then turn right, heading to the top right corner. Cross a stile, then follow waymarks across several fields, to meet a lane at Monaughty Poeth.

4 Turn left for 0.75 mile (1.2km) to a junction at Skyborry Green. Turn left again, then right, joining a bridleway that climbs to the Bryney. Turn right behind the house. Don't join the obvious track just above but follow a narrow footpath along the hedge. It's waymarked at intervals as it works around the hill. Join a track at Balls Cottage and descend to the road at Nether Skyborry.

5 Turn left for 0.5 mile (800m), then right onto the ODP just before Panpunton farm. The path crosses the railway and the River Teme, then follows the Teme towards Knighton, crossing the border and turning right to the Offa's Dyke Centre.

6 Leaving the Centre, turn left through Knighton, then left again on Station Road. After passing the station, turn left on Kinsley Road. Join the first path on the right into Kinsley Wood, opposite Kinsley Villa and Gillow. Fork left after a few paces, then embark on a grindingly steep climb. The gradient eases before the path emerges from trees into scrub and across a forest road. Keep straight to the top of the ridge, then turn left to walk along it. The path descends to a track. Turn right to return to the start.

Distance 8 miles (12.9km)

Minimum time 3hrs

Ascent/gradient 1,542ft (470m) ▲▲▲

Level of difficulty ●●●

Paths Excellent on ridge, undefined across fields, 14 stiles

Landscape Steep hills overlooking the Teme Valley

Suggested map OS Explorer 201 Knighton & Presteigne

Start/finish Grid reference: SO 287734

Dog friendliness Can run free in Kinsley Wood, but sheep present elsewhere

Parking Informal car parking in Kinsley Wood, accessed by forest road from A488 (or park in Knighton, next to bus station or at end of Crabtree Walk, near Offa's Dyke Centre)

Public toilets In Knighton, off Broad Street, and Offa's Dyke Centre

OFFA'S DYKE NATIONAL TRAIL

Offa's Dyke National Trail, opened in 1971, is a splendid walk that runs for 177 miles (285km) from Prestatyn to Chepstow, following the earthwork for 30 miles (48km). The dyke has survived for 1,300 years, but has never been under such pressure as it is today. It has been damaged by agriculture, undermined by rabbits, threatened by development and now eroded by walkers. It is best to walk alongside the dyke, where the route has been realigned, rather than on top. Encouragingly, a conservation scheme has recently been initiated involving a partnership between the Offa's Dyke Path Management Service (based in Knighton), local farmers and interested bodies.

1031 Malcolm II of Scotland swears allegiance to King Canute.

1040 Harthacanute accedes the English throne and declares himself King of Denmark and England.

1042 Edward 'the Confessor' reigns in England. He causes unrest by appointing lands and titles to Norman barons over their English counterparts. In 1052 Edward orders the construction of Westminster Abbey.

1066 The death of Edward the Confessor leaves no heir and two ambitious men leap to claim the throne: William, Duke of Normandy, who cites a long-standing promise of inheritance, and Harold Godwineson, who insists the dying king bequeathed the throne to him.

A Rare Saxon Chapel at Deerhurst

An easy river walk takes in one of very few wholly Saxon buildings in England

Deerhurst, a pretty village on the banks of the River Severn, is endowed with a chapel and a church of particular, if not unique, significance. Both buildings hark back to that poignant period of English history immediately before the Norman Conquest. At the time of their arrival in England in the 5th–6th century AD, the Saxons were pagans. However, they were gradually converted through the influence of St Augustine and the preaching of the British or Celtic Church. Deerhurst was in the Saxon kingdom of Hwicce, an area that was converted to Celtic Christianity by Welsh missionaries.

Deerhurst Church

In 800 Aethelric, ruler of Hwicce, was inspired by a visit to Rome – and on his return set aside a large acreage of land at Deerhurst for a monastery. This became the most important monastery in Hwicce and indeed one of its monks, Alphege, was to become Archbishop of Canterbury in the early 11th century. The monastery, however, was partially destroyed by the Danes in the 9th century. Although a small monastic community stayed on, it was finally levelled at the time of the Dissolution of the Monasteries in the 16th century. Nonetheless, the monastery church at Deerhurst, once as important as Gloucester and Tewkesbury, has survived as the finest Saxon church in England. It contains some 30 Anglo-Saxon doors and windows as well as a 9th-century font.

Odda's Chapel

A short distance from the church is Odda's Chapel, one of only a handful of wholly Saxon buildings left in England. It takes its name from Earl Odda, a kinsman of Edward the Confessor. When his brother, Aelfric, died at Deerhurst in 1053, Odda had this chapel built, to be used as an oratory and to be served by the monastery monks. It owes its survival entirely to chance. The monastery and the chapel eventually became the property of Westminster Abbey. The chapel was later deconsecrated and subsumed into the adjoining abbot's house. After the monastery's dissolution in 1540 the abbot's house became a farmhouse and the existence of the disused chapel was quite forgotten. It was only in 1885, during restoration work on the house, that the chapel was rediscovered and its significance understood. The building you see today is one of great simplicity – a stone room with high walls and only two windows – but its antiquity, location, and its almost pristine state seem somehow awe-inspiring.

Near by, and also visited on this walk, is the village of Apperley. Here you'll see some very fine timbered houses, one of which is the post office. The Coalhouse Inn, on the river bank, was built in the 18th century to cater for the bargees who were transporting coal from the Forest of Dean upriver to Gloucester and Tewkesbury.

Above right: *An Anglo-Saxon copper gilt chalice belonging to Hexham Abbey*

Background: *An inscription from within Odda's Chapel*

Below: *St Mary's at Deerhurst is the finest Saxon church to survive in England*

Below right: *The interior of Odda's Chapel*

Walk 27 Monastic church and oratory chapel

Walk the Severn Way alongside an ancient religious settlement

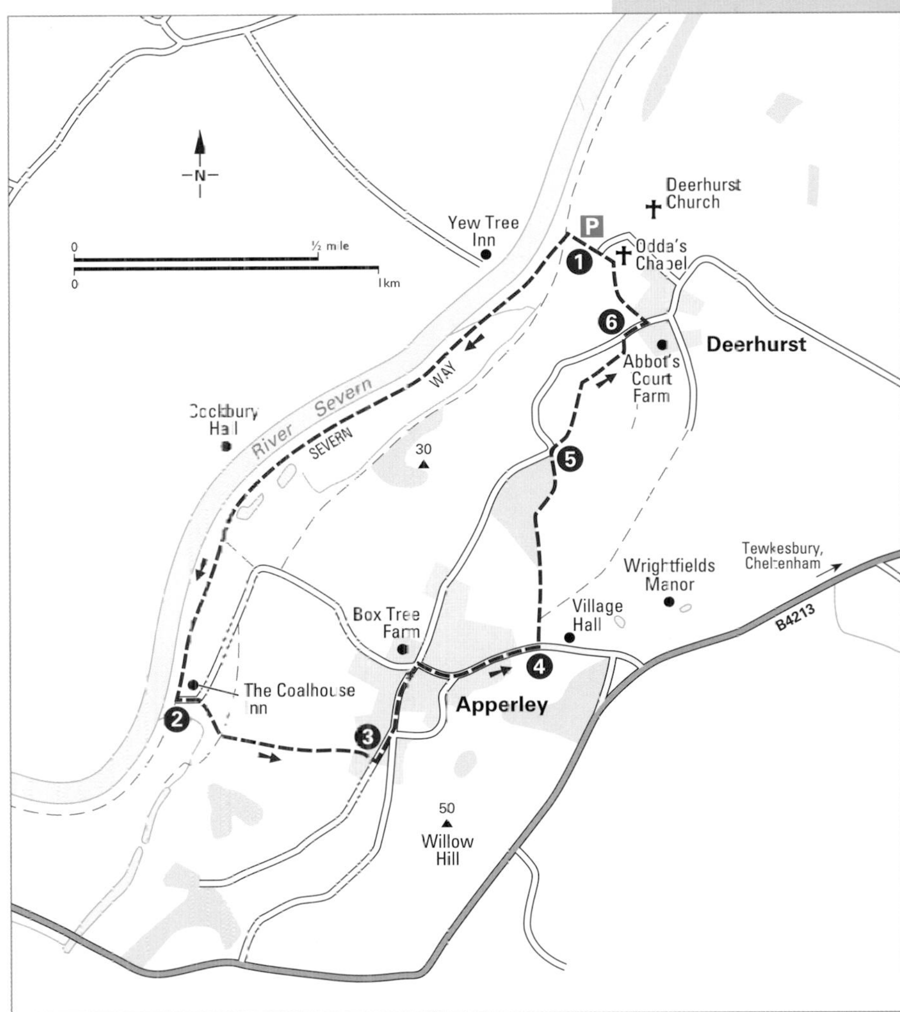

1 With Odda's Chapel behind you, turn left and then right through a gate to walk along a track as far as the river bank. Turn left to follow the Severn Way. Continue through a number of gates and over stiles, following an obvious path (which may sometimes be a little overgrown), with the river always keeping close by on the right. Eventually you will reach the Coalhouse Inn, set back a little to the left.

2 Turn left after the pub to follow a road. Once behind the pub turn right on a track for just a few paces. When the track veers left go straight ahead to a stile and cross into a field. Continue to another stile. In the following field go uphill to find another stile at the top, beside a gate. Go over the stile and follow the right-hand margin of the field to another gate. Go through, and continue to the road in Apperley.

3 Turn left to walk through the village. At a four-way signpost turn right, away from Box Tree Farm, heading along Sawpit Lane, towards Tewkesbury.

4 Just before the village hall turn left and walk across the playing fields to a stile. Cross and stay on the same line to arrive at another stile. Now follow the right-hand margin of a field and, later, a plantation, as it eventually curves right and brings you to a stile at a lane.

5 Go over to the lane and turn sharp right to reach a gate. Once in the field turn left to come swiftly to another stile. Cross this to enter another field and then walk down, crossing another stile to the right of a house. Carry on ahead until, after passing new barns on your right, you find a stile and finger post in the hedge to your left. (Look out for Odda's Chapel, which is visible beyond.) Go over to a road and turn right.

6 Continue to a flood gate. Turn left to walk atop flood defences alongside a private garden. Cross a stile into a meadow and continue diagonally right, to a stile and gate beside Odda's Chapel and the timbered building next to it. This brings you to a gate by your starting point.

WHAT TO LOOK OUT FOR

The first church on the site of St Mary's was built in the 7th century. It was rectangular, with a west porch. Then in the 9th century the apse was reconstructed and chapels added down the church's length. The foundations of the 9th-century apse can be seen outside the east end. In the west front the 10th-century Saxon tower is dominant in the centre; inside the tower look out for a Saxon sculpture of a Madonna and Child. Also inside the church look out for Saxon wolf-head decorations to either side of the main door and at the sides of the altar. In the Norman period the walls of the nave were knocked through to create side aisles. In the north aisle is a 9th-century font – one of the oldest in England.

TEWKESBURY ABBEY

Tewkesbury Abbey, for Benedictine monks, was established in 1087; the present building was begun in 1102 and consecrated in 1121. Stone used in the construction was imported from Caen in Normandy and transported up the River Severn; the tower and nave were completed in 1150. The imposing tower measures 148ft (45m) from the base to the top of the pinnacles, is 46ft (14m) square, and was hailed by architectural historian Nikolaus Pevsner as 'probably the largest and finest Romanesque tower in England'. In 1471, during the Wars of the Roses, a contingent from the Lancastrian army defeated at the Battle of Tewkesbury sought sanctuary here but were pursued and put to the sword by the Yorkists.

Distance 3.25 miles (5.3km)

Minimum time 1hr 30min

Ascent/gradient 115ft (35m) ▲▲▲

Level of difficulty ●●●

Paths Fields, pavement and riverbank, 12 stiles

Landscape Hills, villages and river

Suggested map OS Explorer 179 Gloucester, Cheltenham & Stroud

Start/finish Grid reference: SO 868298

Dog friendliness Off lead except near occasional livestock

Parking Car park (small fee) outside Odda's Chapel

Public toilets None on route

HIC WILLELM: DUX

ERA OF CONQUEST

Some time in the 1070s, Bishop Odo of Bayeux commissioned a tapestry to celebrate his half-brother Duke William of Normandy's victory at the Battle of Hastings in 1066. The resulting medieval action adventure, with spies, chases and violence, is our most vivid account of the Norman Conquest.

In the Bayeux Tapestry, the dying Edward the Confessor bequeaths his kingdom to William of Normandy; when Harold Godwineson takes the crown instead, William invades and kills his rival at the Battle of Hastings in 1066. Over subsequent years, William stamped out a succession of revolts, confiscating English lands and awarding them to his own men. The Normans proved that they had arrived and fully intended to stay; they brought with them new styles – the tapestry contrasts droopy-moustachioed Saxons with their shaven-headed enemies – and a new tongue, making Norman French the language of court and nobility. Among the most immediate effects of the invasion were the hundreds of stone castles that sprang up across the country, and the massive cathedrals that were built in Durham, Chichester, Ely, Norwich and elsewhere, often on the sites of Anglo-Saxon cathedrals. The Scottish king, Malcolm III, submitted to William at Abernethy in 1072, but continued to raid the Northumbrian territories; the English-Welsh border provided another flashpoint, where Norman lords were installed to make inroads into Powys and Gwynedd. But by 1086 England was secure and William could commission a survey of his possessions in the Domesday Book.

CRUSADES AND CONFLICT

The Norman dynasty held fast until another squabble over the crown turned into civil war between William's grandson, Stephen, and Stephen's cousin Matilda, wife of Geoffrey Plantagenet, Count of Anjou. In 1154 Matilda's son won the day for the Angevin cause, taking the crown as Henry II. Henry's marriage to Eleanor of Aquitaine created a vast empire that stretched from the Pyrenees to Scotland. Richard the Lionheart, Henry's heir, spent most of his time fighting Turks in the Holy Land. Along with pilgrimages, crusades were the main mass events of the time: crowds flocked to answer the rallying calls of churchmen such as Giraldus Cambrensis, whose chronicles provide a colourful glimpse of 12th-century life. Richard was succeeded by his brother John, whose bad press stems from the loss of his French lands and excessive cruelty to opponents. To keep the peace with his increasingly rebellious barons, John signed the Magna Carta in 1215, agreeing limitations on royal power and the rights of subjects.

By the 13th century Britain was an uneasy balancing act of feudal kingdoms and principalities, with the English king as overlord. This status was challenged in Wales by Llywelyn ap Gruffydd, who refused to pay tribute to Edward I. Edward's response was rapid and devastating: his troops forged through Wales, leaving a ring of mighty fortresses. The principality was divided into English-style counties and the King's heir, Edward, was made their nominal prince. In Scotland, Edward set about championing John Balliol, his candidate for the throne, in the face of opposition from Robert the Bruce. Although Edward's was successful in taking the Scottish 'Stone of Destiny' from Scone, the Scots were not beaten, and Britain entered the 14th century simmering with rebellions and resentments.

KEY SITES

Hastings, East Sussex: Battlefield on which William of Normandy defeated King Harold in 1066.

Llanthony Priory, Monmouthshire: Founded for Augustinian canons in c.1118.

Fountains Abbey, North Yorkshire: Founded by Benedictine monks from York in 1132.

Walpole St Andrew, Norfolk: Where King John may have lost his riches in the Wash in 1216.

Castell y Bere, Gwynedd: Castle built by Welsh prince Llywelyn the Great in c.1221

Stirling, Scotland: Scene of Scots patriot William Wallace's famous defeat of an English army in 1297.

Left: In this section of the tapestry, William delivers a rousing talk to prepare his men for battle at Hastings

Britain's Most Famous Battlefield

A trek back into history visits the field on which Duke William and King Harold fought for the English crown

Above: Under a hail of arrows, Normans triumph on the battlefield at Hastings

Below: Battle Abbey was built in 1070–94 with its high altar on the site at which King Harold was killed in the fighting

If one date from England's glorious past stands out more than any other, it is surely 1066. One of the most important and significant events of the last millennium, the Battle of Hastings represents a defining moment in British history.

Bloody Battle

Visit the battlefield and you can still sense something of that momentous day when William, Duke of Normandy, defeated Harold and his Saxon army and became William the Conqueror of England. See the spot where Harold is believed to have fallen and, by exercising a little imagination, you can picture the bloody events that led to his defeat.

William began by occupying a position on a hill about 400yds (365m) to the south of the English army, massed on a higher hilltop. Harold and his men fortified their formidable position and following abortive uphill charges on the English shield-wall, the Normans withdrew, unable to breach the defences. It looked for a time as if victory was within Harold's grasp, until William rallied his men and executed two successful strategies. One was to instruct his bowmen to shoot their arrows indiscriminately into the air, though William had no idea that one of them would hit Harold in the eye, fatally wounding him. The other was to create the impression that his armies were fleeing the battlefield. Sensing victory, the English gave chase but this was their downfall. The Normans rounded on them and decisively won the battle. William marched victoriously to London where, on Christmas Day, in Westminster Abbey, he was duly crowned King of England.

Walk 28 In 1066 country, where Normans won a famous victory

Seek out the spot at which King Harold was felled by invaders

1 Turn left out of the car park and follow the track to a gate. Keep left along the bridleway beside woodland, the path swinging left to a fingerpost and junction of paths. Bear off left with the 1066 Bexhill Walk marker and walk down the field-edge and through two gates. Join a track and keep ahead, soon to cross a drive via stiles, and follow the fenced path along the field-edge high above the road to a stile.

2 Cross the B2095 (take care – dangerous bend), walk along Telham Lane and take the private road right towards Peppering Eye Farm. Keep to the metalled drive for 0.5 mile (0.8km), passing Stumblet's Barn and crossing a stream to ascend to a junction of paths by Powdermill Cottage. Turn left along a track through the trees, drop downhill and bear off left with the waymarker across the centre of a field to cross a footbridge and enter Fore Wood (RSPB Nature Reserve).

3 Bear right and follow the yellow-arrowed route through the edge of the wood, turning right where the path curves left at a bench. Go left at the fingerpost, cross a footbridge and follow the path right through scrub, parallel with the stream. On reaching an open field, keep left around the field-edge, pass a pond and gently climb along a defined path along the top edge of a field. The path becomes a track through trees, passing another larger pond, then soon emerges into a field, keeping ahead along the field-edge to a junction of tracks.

4 Bear left, then right at a fork, curving left around a pond to reach a waymarker that stands close to some pheasant pens. Turn sharp right up the bank, enter woodland and continue to a stile and footbridge. Turn left to another stile, then right along the field-edge. Head across the field, and go through a gate.

5 Bear diagonally right downhill across the field to a gate and track. Just before some barns, climb the stile on the right to follow the arrowed path around Millers Farm to reach a gate. Rejoin the track and follow it out to a road.

6 Cross the road, pass beside a gate and follow the path through Powdermill Wood. Cross the top end of Farthing Pond, then bear sharp right and fork off left, uphill along a narrow path through woodland to a stile. Cross the field aiming to the right of a cottage to reach a stile. Turn right along a track, go through a gate and follow the 1066 Walk uphill through a field and soon afterwards retrace your outward route back to the car park.

WHAT TO LOOK OUT FOR

Before the Battle of Hastings, William vowed that if God gave him victory that day, he would build an abbey on the site of the battle at Senlac Field. Little of the church remains today. The abbey was enlarged and improved, but after the Dissolution of the Monasteries much of it was converted into a private house by Sir Anthony Browne, Henry VIII's Master of Horse.

Distance 5 miles (8km)
Minimum time 2hrs 30min
Ascent/gradient 448ft (140m) ▲▲▲
Level of difficulty ●●●
Paths Field and woodland paths, some road walking, 10 stiles
Landscape Gently undulating farmland and woodland
Suggested map OS Explorer 124 Hastings & Bexhill
Start/finish Grid reference: TQ 747156
Dog friendliness Enclosed woodland paths and stretches of 1066 Country Walk suitable for dogs off lead
Parking Pay car park at Battle Abbey
Public toilets Mount Street car park in Battle, Brede Lane in Sedlescombe and Battle Abbey

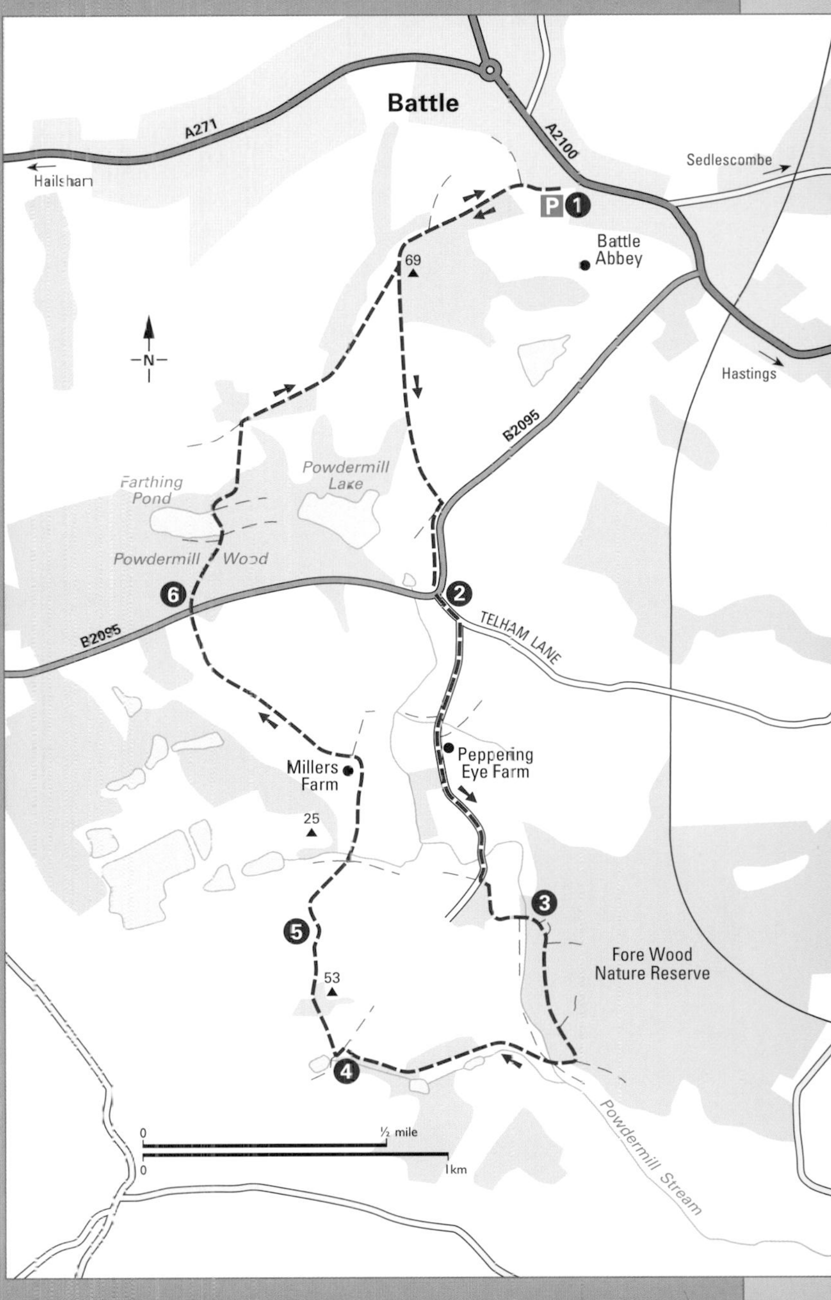

1066 After victory at the Battle of Hastings in October, Duke William of Normandy is crowned King William I in Westminster Abbey in December.

1067 Crushing a revolt, William I builds Exeter Castle.

1070 Building of Canterbury Cathedral begins after the original church is destroyed by fire.

1072 William I invades Scotland as far as the River Tay and demands that Malcolm III pay homage to him.

1078 The White Tower, the first part of the Tower of London, is begun. Construction takes 20 years.

1079 Winchester Cathedral foundations are laid, and the New Forest is created as a royal hunting area.

Barnard Castle

An instructive ramble leads round and about the Norman stronghold of 'old Barney'

The imposing fortress of Barnard Castle tops an 80ft (24m) crag that towers above the River Tees. The castle was built in 1112–32 for Bernard de Balliol, whose father Guy had fought side by side with William the Conqueror at the Battle of Hastings. William's son and successor, William Rufus, granted Guy lands that included the area in which this town arose. The stone castle replaced an earlier wooden fortification.

The Balliols would become a powerful force in the north, and John Balliol, with a little help from Edward I, would become King of Scotland in 1292. In the same century the little town that had grown around the castle was granted a charter for a market. The medieval layout of streets, yards and back alleys still exists today and many of the older buildings have survived.

Above right: *The picturesque ruins of Egglestone Abbey*

Below: *County Bridge, with the walls and ruined round tower of Barnard Castle behind*

The castle itself had a colourful history: it was captured by one of the prince bishops of Durham and in 1569, during the Rising of the North against Queen Elizabeth I, it was subjected to an 11-day siege. The damage inflicted made rebuilding necessary, though the round keep, added in the 14th century, survived.

Egglestone Abbey

At Point 3 on the walk the ruins of Egglestone Abbey are visible across the River Tees through pretty riverside woods, and then after crossing the river the abbey can be inspected more closely at Point 4. Founded around 1196 by landowner Ralph de Multon for the Premonstratensian order, the abbey was sold after the Dissolution of the Monasteries to Robert Streeley, who converted the cloisters into a house, which has long since been in ruins. The best-preserved part of the abbey is the church, which stands on a grassy knoll above the river. Look out for elegant double-lancet windows and its unusual mullioned east window. The abbey ruins attracted the eye of English artist J.M.W. Turner.

Later Visitors

In the latter part of the walk, back in the town of Barnard Castle – affectionately known as 'Old Barney' – the route leads along Galgate, a wide street once called Gallowgate (the place where the gallows stood). This was also the course of a Roman road that linked forts at Bowes and Binchester. In Market Place on the right look out for the former King's Head Inn, now called the Charles Dickens, where Dickens stayed while researching his novel *Nicholas Nickleby* (1839). Then on a street named the Bank don't miss the four-storey, 16th-century Blagraves House, now established as a restaurant, where Oliver Cromwell is supposed to have stayed during his visit to the town in 1648.

Walk 29 Fortress Balliol

Walk from Norman beginnings through centuries of history

1 From the car park go through the passageway signposted to the river. Go across Newgate Street and continue through another little ginnel, which leads through the churchyard of St Mary's, then out onto the riverside parkland of Demesnes.

2 Here turn left along a stony path, which angles down to the river. It passes Demesnes Mill, then follows the north bank of the Tees, with the river on your right.

3 You pass the sewage works (quickly if the wind is in the wrong direction). Ignore the upper-left fork of two paths and stay by the river to enter pretty woodland, which allows glimpses of the remains of Egglestone Abbey on the far bank. Go through the gate on to the road and turn right across Abbey Bridge.

4 Turn right at the junction on the far side of the bridge, then go left up the access track to view the abbey. Return to the road and follow it left, to pass Bow Bridge. A squeeze stile in the hedge on the right marks the start of the path along the south bank of the Tees. On the approach to a caravan park the path crosses fields and veers slightly away from the river.

5 Turn right along a surfaced track, down to the caravan park, and take the second drive on the left, which leads to a continuation of the riverside path.

6 Turn right over the footbridge back into Barnard Castle and go straight ahead into Thorngate. Turn left along Bridgegate. Where the road crosses the County Bridge, go straight on to follow a path that rounds the castle walls to the entrance. After visiting the castle, continue past the Methodist church to Galgate.

7 Turn right along Horse Market and continue to the Market Cross. Carry on down the Bank then, at the top of Thorngate, go left to Demesnes. Retrace your earlier steps back to the car park.

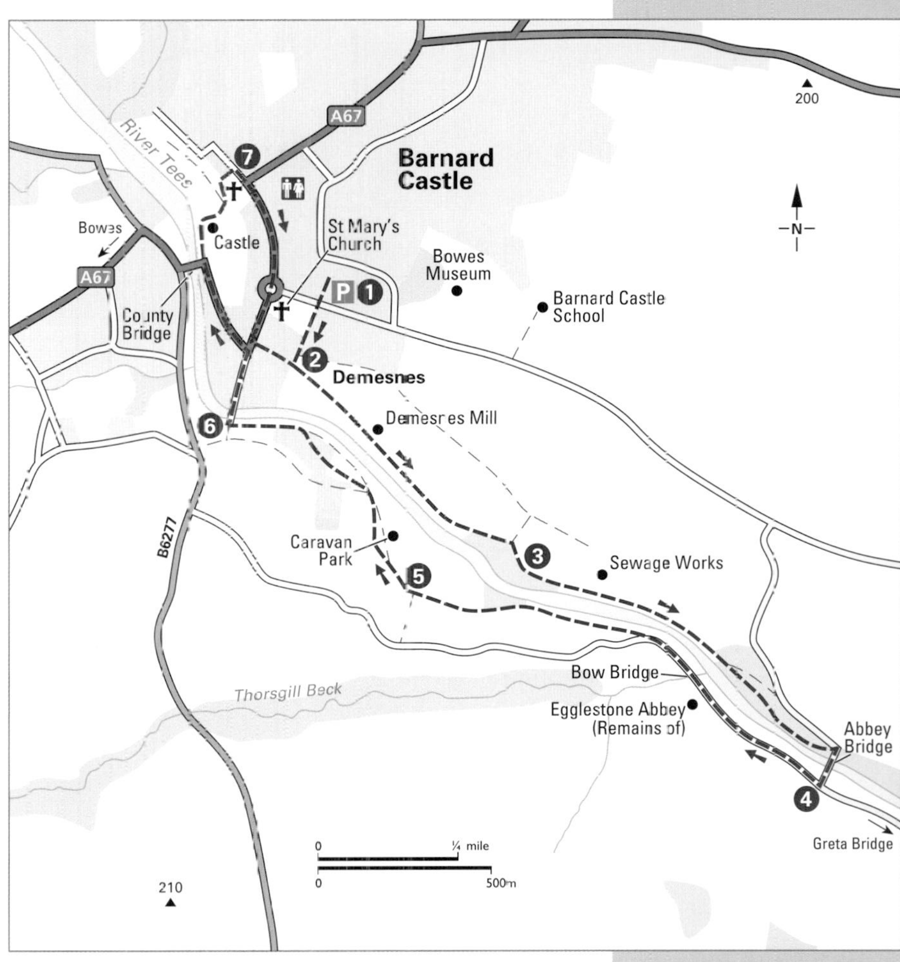

BOWES MUSEUM

When wealthy local businessman John Bowes married French actress Joséphine Coffin-Chevalier in 1852, they hired architect Jules Pellechet to build a château in Barnard Castle. The building was intended to house the couple's collection of art and treasures. Building took many years, and after Josephine's death in 1874 John more or less lost interest, then died himself in 1885; nevertheless, the building was completed under the guidance of trustees and opened to the public in 1892. Today at the Bowes Museum you can view furniture and ceramics, as well as paintings by Canaletto and J.M.W. Turner. The grounds are also magnificent. The museum is open 10am–5pm every day except Christmas Day, Boxing Day and New Year's Day.

Distance 4.25 miles (6.8km)

Minimum time 2hrs 30min

Ascent/gradient 165ft (50m) ▲▲▲

Level of difficulty ●●●

Paths Town streets and good paths, 6 stiles

Landscape Riverside and market town

Suggested map OS Explorer OL31 North Pennines

Start/finish Grid reference: NZ 051163

Dog friendliness Dogs should be on leads

Parking Pay-and-display car park at end of Queen Street between Galgate and Newgate

Public toilets By Morrisons supermarket off Galgate

1081 William I invades Wales as far as St David's.

1086 William I sets out to profit from his hard work and commissions the Domesday Book to survey all taxable lands and their owners.

1087 William I falls from his horse in France, and dies from his injuries. He is buried in Caen.

1087–1100 William II, a reputed tyrant and younger son of William I, takes the throne. He is killed while hunting in the New Forest: there is speculation about whether his death was an accident or murder. The place where he fell is marked by the Rufus Stone.

1093 The building of Durham Cathedral begins. It is a masterpiece of Romanesque architecture.

Llanthony and its Hills

A ramble along the southern end of the Vale of Ewyas leads past the evocative ruins of a 12th-century abbey endowed by a great Norman family

The ruins of Llanthony Priory occupy a remote and beautiful situation in the Vale of Ewyas. The priory, one of the first in Britain for Augustinian canons, was established in the Norman era and received several endowments of land from the Norman de Lacy family. According to tradition, the Norman knight William de Lacey was hunting in the valley of the river Honddu and took refuge in a 6th-century chapel reputedly founded as a hermitage by St David himself. William founded a church, and settled as a hermit; he was joined by Ernisius, former chaplain to King Henry I's wife, Queen Matilda, and a house of Augustinian canons was established on the site by *c.*1118.

Vulnerable Position

Llanthony became a notable religious centre, which at its largest held 40 canons, but its isolated position made it vulnerable to attacks during wars with the Welsh, and in 1134 the canons were forced to take refuge in Hereford, before, in 1136, establishing a second house, Llanthony Secunda, in a safer setting at Gloucester. Llanthony Secunda in time became the more important of the two houses, and the original, Llanthony Prima, became a retreat house and was reduced in status from abbey to priory. However, Llanthony Prima's fortunes revived towards the end of the 12th century after Hugh II de Lacy and his son Walter II de Lacy endowed it with land in Wales and income from churches in Ireland that were part of de Lacy landholdings there.

Gerald of Wales, the Archdeacon of Brecon, passed through Llanthony in 1188 while on a preaching tour of Wales to drum up support for the Third Crusade. Gerald – who is also known as Giraldus Cambrensis – made much of the abbey's remote setting, and said it was 'fixed amongst a barbarous people'. Yet Llanthony continued to benefit from de Lacy patronage and a new and large church was built there in 1200–30. In the 14th century, however, the priory declined once more, and by the time of the Dissolution of the Monasteries in 1538 there were just four canons at Llanthony. The priory was sold into private ownership and fell into the ruins seen today.

Among the later owners was the 19th-century poet Walter Savage Landor. He had landscaping work carried out in the valley, but had difficult relations with many of his neighbours.

Top: *An English silver coin bearing the image of King William II*

Above: *High arches mark the nave of the priory*

Walk 30 Remains of a once-grand Norman abbey

Visit a beautiful corner of Wales in which canons once braved 'a barbarous people'

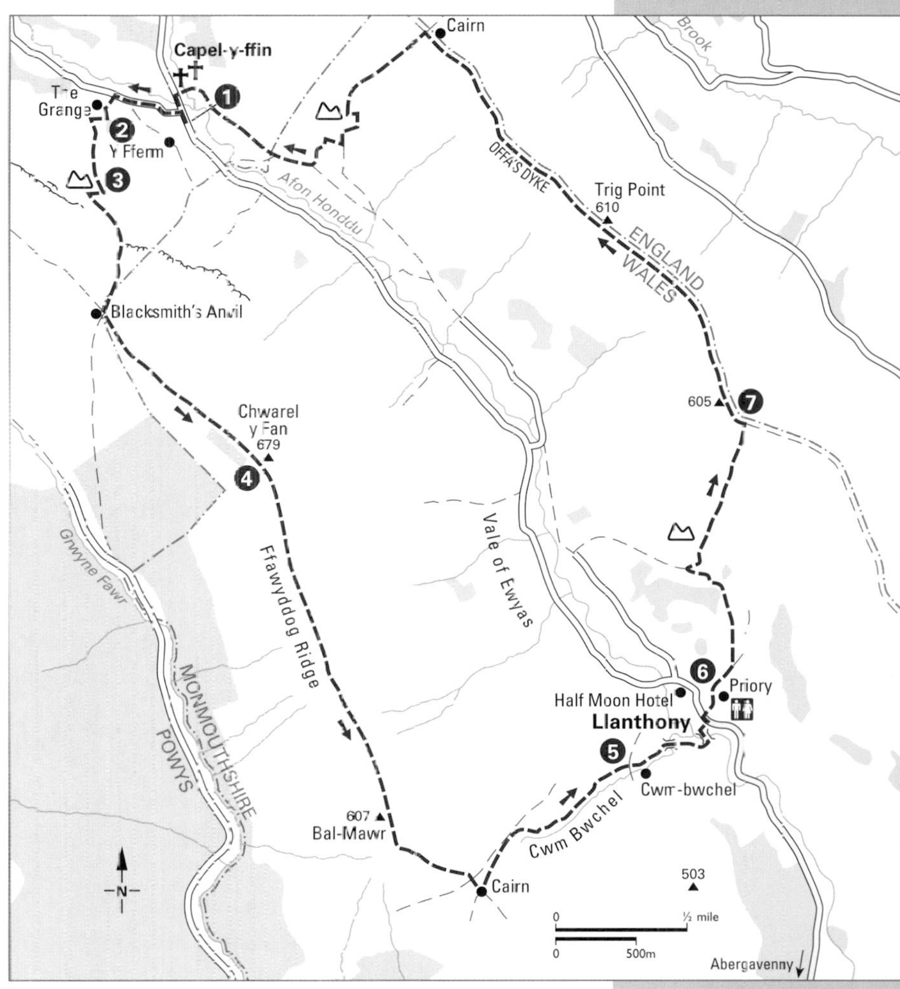

1 Walk towards the bridge, but before you cross it, bear left up a narrow lane, signposted to the Grange Pony Trekking Centre. Follow this along the side of the stream and past a footpath on the left, marked by a stone archway. Continue to a drive on the left, again leading to the trekking centre, and follow this up to a cluster of barns.

2 Keep right here and continue uphill to a large house on the right, where a gate blocks your progress ahead. Bear around to the left and then climb on a loose rocky track that leads up to another gate. Pass through this and follow a rough and eroded track as it zig-zags up onto easier ground. Cross the source of a small stream, and continue to the foot of a steep zig-zag track that climbs steeply up the escarpment.

3 Follow this track, bearing both right and left and then, as the gradient eases, continue ahead along a broad and often boggy track. Take this past a few small cairns to a large one, known as the Blacksmith's Anvil, that sits on top of the ridge. Turn left here and continue to follow the track south over Chwarel y Fan.

4 Walk straight on, along the line of the ridge, to reach the summit of Bal-Mawr. Go down to the left and pass a good track on your left-hand side. Keep ahead to reach a cairn and then descend to the left. Drop down to a fork at which you need to keep right to follow the brook to a crossroads of paths. Maintain your direction (signposted 'Cwm Bwchel').

5 Continue through two fields, down past a house, and over another stile. Ignore another stile on the right and continue down to another at the bottom of the field. Cross this and bear right to cross another and a footbridge. Keep walking straight ahead to another stile and then continue to a gate. Follow the stream down through another gate to another footbridge. Cross this and take the lane to the road. Turn left here, then turn right to visit the priory.

6 Go through a gate on the left, in front of the priory (signposted to Hatterrall Hill), and follow the main track to a stream, where you turn left to a gate. Continue through a succession of fields and through a small copse to reach an interpretation board. Follow the path up onto the ridge and continue to a crossroads; Offa's Dyke is where you turn left.

7 Walk along Offa's Dyke, pass the trig point and continue for another mile (1.6km) to a cairn and a marker stone at a crossroads of paths. Turn left and follow the path down around a sharp left-right zig-zag to a wall. Turn right here, then turn left over a stile. Walk down, over another stile to a hedge at the bottom of the next field, then turn right to continue to another stile on the left. This leads on to a tarmac lane. Turn right and follow this through a yard, where it becomes a rough track. Keep ahead to a sharp left-hand bend and keep straight ahead, up steps and over a stile. Continue straight ahead through more fields to join another lane and follow this down, past two chapels, to the road. Turn left to return to your car.

WHAT TO LOOK OUT FOR

The abbey's west range was converted into a house in the 18th century. Sadly the church fell into ruins: the east window collapsed in 1800 and the west window in 1830, then four piers in the arcade of the south nave fell in 1837. Thereafter there were a number of attempts to strengthen the remains with iron ties. Notably the central tower was reinforced in this way in 1936–37.

Distance 9.5 miles (15.3km)

Minimum time 5hrs 30min

Ascent/gradient 2,460ft (750m) ▲▲▲

Level of difficulty ●●●

Paths Easy-to-follow paths, steep slopes, open moorland, muddy lowland trails, 10 stiles

Landscape Classic U-shaped valleys topped with broad heather-strewn moorland

Suggested map OS Explorer OL13 Brecon Beacons National Park Eastern Area

Start/finish Grid reference: SO 255314

Dog friendliness Some difficult stiles, care required near livestock. No dogs in grounds of priory

Parking Narrow pull-in at southern edge of Capel-y-ffin

Public toilets Next to Llanthony Priory

1100 Henry I succeeds his brother William II as king.

1102 The Council of London outlaws marriage for members of the clergy.

1114 Henry's daughter Matilda marries Holy Roman Emperor Henry V. They have no children. After Henry dies, she marries Count Geoffrey of Anjou in 1128.

1120 Henry's son Prince William is drowned when the 'White Ship' sinks off Barfleur. Matilda is now heir.

1135 Before his death Henry I promises the crown to his daughter Maltida. However, she and her husband, Geoffrey of Anjou, are disliked by the English barons and quarrel with the King, and on his deathbed Henry names Stephen de Blois as heir.

A Medieval Walk from Fountains

A fascinating walk commands views of the magnificent ruins of Fountains Abbey

When 13 monks from St Mary's Abbey in York first settled on the site of what became Fountains Abbey in 1132, this was a wild and desolate place. Many years later, in 1207, a monk from Fountains Abbey recalled his brothers' first sight of the valley of the River Skell in that winter of 1132: 'a place remote from the world, uninhabited thickset with thorns'.

The monks who founded Fountains Abbey were members of the Benedictine order. They had left St Mary's Abbey, York, after becoming dissatisfied with the way it was being run. They enlisted the help of Archbishop Thurstan, who directed them to this place. After settling at Fountains, they joined the Cistercian order early in 1133. Then in 1135 Hugh, Dean of York, retired to Fountains Abbey, bringing his riches with him as an endowment, and its success was assured.

The abbey acquired extensive property – it is said that in the 13th century you could travel for more than 30 miles (48km) westwards without leaving abbey estates – and rose to become the richest monastery in England. Its church was 360ft (110m) long, larger than many cathedrals.

In the early 16th century Abbot Marmaduke Huby erected a huge tower as a symbol of what he believed to be the abbey's enduring power. Yet less than 30 years later, in 1539, all came to an end when King Henry VIII dissolved the larger monasteries. The King confiscated the abbey's riches, dispersed the monks and left the buildings desolate. The estate was eventually sold to Sir Stephen Proctor, who in 1611 built Fountains Hall, whose south front is visible early in the walk. This is a fine Jacobean house, with many mullioned windows. Much of the stone was taken from the monastic remains.

Pleasure Gardens

Beyond Fountains Abbey are pleasure gardens laid out in 1716–81 by John Aislabie and his son William. This is one of the great gardens of Europe, contrasting green lawn with stretches of water, both formal and informal. Carefully placed in the landscape are ornamental buildings, from classical temples to Gothic towers. The Aislabies' mansion stood at the north end of the park; it was destroyed by fire in 1945.

Above right: *Fountains Abbey is Britain's largest monastic ruin*

Right: *Beautiful vaulted arches in the cellarium, where the brothers ate and slept*

Walk 31 Fountains – once England's richest monastery

Gaze on the remains of this grandest of abbeys, built up from modest beginnings by Cistercian brothers – and see a 14th-century manor house

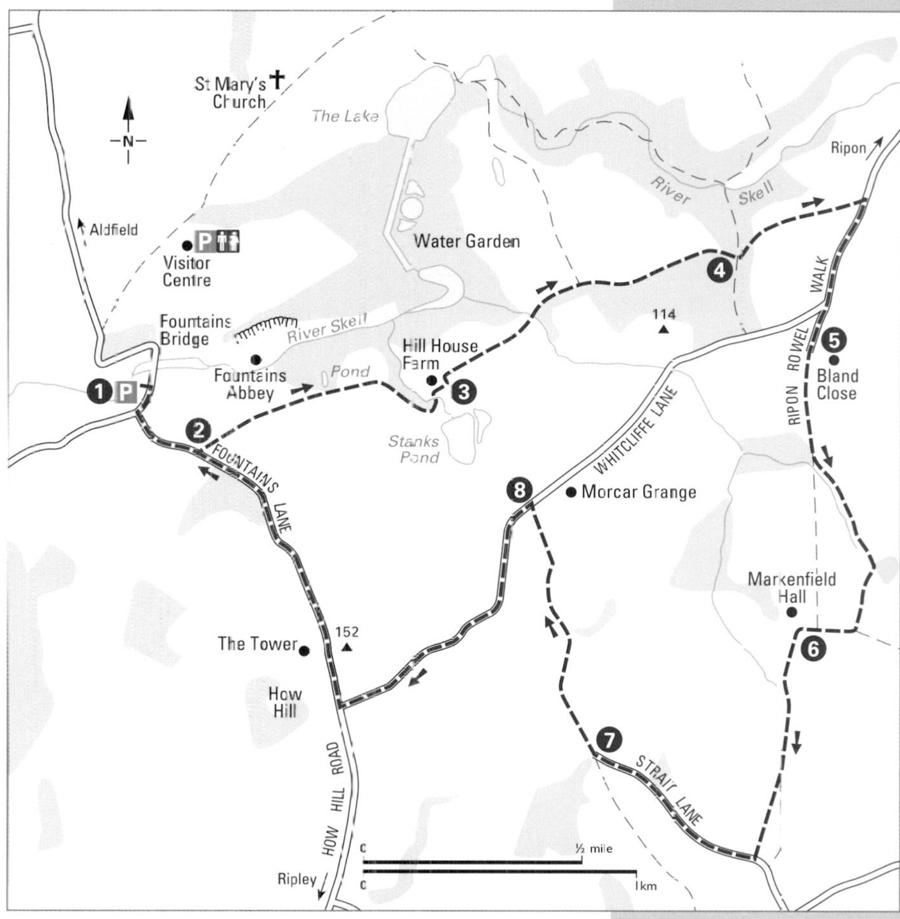

1 From the car park turn right uphill, signed 'Harrogate'. At the fork go left, signed 'Markington, Harrogate'. Just after the road bends right, go left at a footpath sign through a gate.

2 Follow the grassy path just inside the ancient abbey wall, past a small pond. Go through a waymarked gate and then follow the track as it curves round to the right through another gate, before it bends left to a gate leading into Hill House Farm.

3 Turn right, then follow the footpath signs to go left at the end of a large shed and then right. Go through a metal gate onto a track. At the end of the hedge, go ahead down the field to a gate into the wood. Follow the track, passing the ruined archway, to descend to a crossroads of tracks.

4 Go straight on, signed 'Ripon'. The track climbs to a gate with a Ripon Rowel Walk sign. Follow the track beside the line of trees to a gate that gives onto Whitcliffe Lane. Turn right. At the top of the rise go straight ahead on the metalled road.

5 Go over the cattle grid by Bland Close, then leave the lane to go straight ahead with the hedge on your right as far as a gateway. Continue along the waymarked track, eventually with woodland to your right. Follow the park wall, go through a gateway to reach a gate onto a lane. Turn right then to reach some farm buildings situated by Markenfield Hall.

6 Follow the wall to the left, going through a metal gate and straight ahead down the track, over a stile by a gate. Follow the track, then a waymark sign, across a field to a stile by a gate. Turn right up the narrow Strait Lane, to emerge into a field.

7 Follow the waymarked path beside the hedge. Go through a gate in the field corner and continue ahead with the hedge to the right. Go through two more gates. At a third gate, do not go through, but bend left through a hedge gap and proceed down the field side, with the hedge on your right, until you reach a gate. Go through the gate on to Whitcliffe Lane.

8 Turn left and follow the lane, which leads in the direction of How Hill Tower, an 18th-century folly, before carrying on to a T-junction. Turn right here and follow the road back to the car park.

MARKENFIELD HALL

The highlight of the southern end of the walk is Markenfield Hall, a rare early 14th-century fortified manor house. The bulk of the house was built in *c.*1310 for Canon John de Markenfield, but its great hall was originally a freestanding building and dates to *c.*1280. Open for four weeks in the summer, the house shows how a medieval knight and his family lived; it is part home, part farm.

Distance 6.5 miles (10.4km)

Minimum time 3hrs

Ascent/gradient 328ft (100m) ▲▲▲

Level of difficulty ●●●

Paths Field paths and tracks, a little road walking, 3 stiles

Landscape Farmland and woodland

Suggested map OS Explorer 298 Nidderdale

Start/finish Grid reference: SE 270681

Dog friendliness Dogs should be on lead on field paths

Parking Car park located at west end of abbey, and at Visitor Centre

Public toilets Fountains Abbey Visitor Centre

WHILE YOU'RE THERE

As well as visiting the abbey and the gardens, take the time to visit nearby Ripon. Its cathedral has a Saxon crypt, and in the stately market place is Britain's oldest free-standing obelisk, designed in 1702 by Nicholas Hawksmoor, one of England's great baroque architects. You can also discover Ripon's links to author Lewis Carroll and learn how the city inspired his *Alice's Adventures in Wonderland*; or see how the law was administered and the wicked were punished on the 'law and order trail'.

1139 Matilda lands at Wareham to claim her inheritance. There is conflict for nine years as the two sovereigns dispute the succession to the throne.

1148 Unable to rally support, Matilda leaves Britain.

1154 Stephen dies and is buried at the Cluniac monastery in Faversham, Kent.

1154–89 Henry II is king. He appoints his adviser Thomas Becket Chancellor of England, and then Archbishop of Canterbury. Becket unexpectedly wishes to serve only the Church.

1164 Henry limits the Church's power of jurisdiction over the clergy and causes a row between himself and the Archbishop.

Magnificent Manorbier

A delightful excursion passes the sleepy, 12th-century birthplace of Gerald of Wales

Above right: *Manorbier's most famous son was Gerald of Wales*

Below: *High curtain walls and towers survive, and its site on a promontory gave extra defence*

The attractive but sleepy coastal village of Manorbier is dominated by the mighty castle in which medieval churchman Gerald of Wales – known above all for his chronicles of medieval life – was born. The original castle was a motte and bailey design with a wooden keep built by Odo de Barri in the late 11th century, but the stone building that stands tall and proud over the beach and village these days was constructed in the early 12th century by Odo's son and Gerald's father, William. The castle has an angular northeast tower and a round south-east one; its great hall was built in *c*.1140. The splendid vaulted chapel, which still contains some of its original frescoes, was built in *c*.1260.

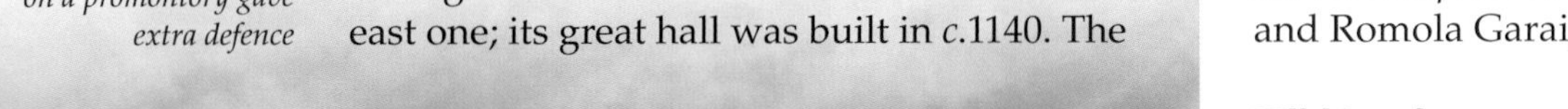

Since the de Barris, Manorbier Castle has passed through many hands, including those of the Crown. It is now privately owned, but open to the public for tours. As well as the splendid views over the bay from the top of the castle walls, you will also see stately rooms, occupied these days by waxwork models of various figures, including Giraldus, hard at work on his accounts. Movie fans may know that the 2003 movie *I Capture the Castle*, starring Bill Nighy and Romola Garai, was shot at Manorbier.

Wild Landscape on Caldey

The name Manorbier derives from 'Maenor of Pyrrus' or 'Manor of Pyr'. Pyrrus was the first Celtic abbot of Caldey, a nearby island first inhabited by monks in the 6th century AD and known in Welsh as Ynys Pyr, or Pyr's Island. Its landscape is wild and unspoilt and its buildings are inspirationally simple. There is a working Benedictine monastery and a number of ornate churches, including 12th-century St Illtud's, with its ancient sandstone cross.

Time for a Beach Picnic?

In addition to delivering historical interest, this delightful short walk runs along the heads of some magnificent cliffs, and visits a wonderful and remote sandy cove. The outward leg passes close to the famous castle, leading to a section across farmland that is open and breezy, with fine views over the coast.

Once reached, the narrow belt of white sand that makes up magical Swanlake Bay provides ample reward for your efforts. Flanked on both sides by impressive sandstone crags, and cut off from easy road access by the farmland that you've just traversed, it sees few visitors and provides a stunning setting for a picnic.

Walk 32 The 'pleasantest spot in Wales'

Explore the quiet corner of Pembrokeshire in which a great churchman was raised

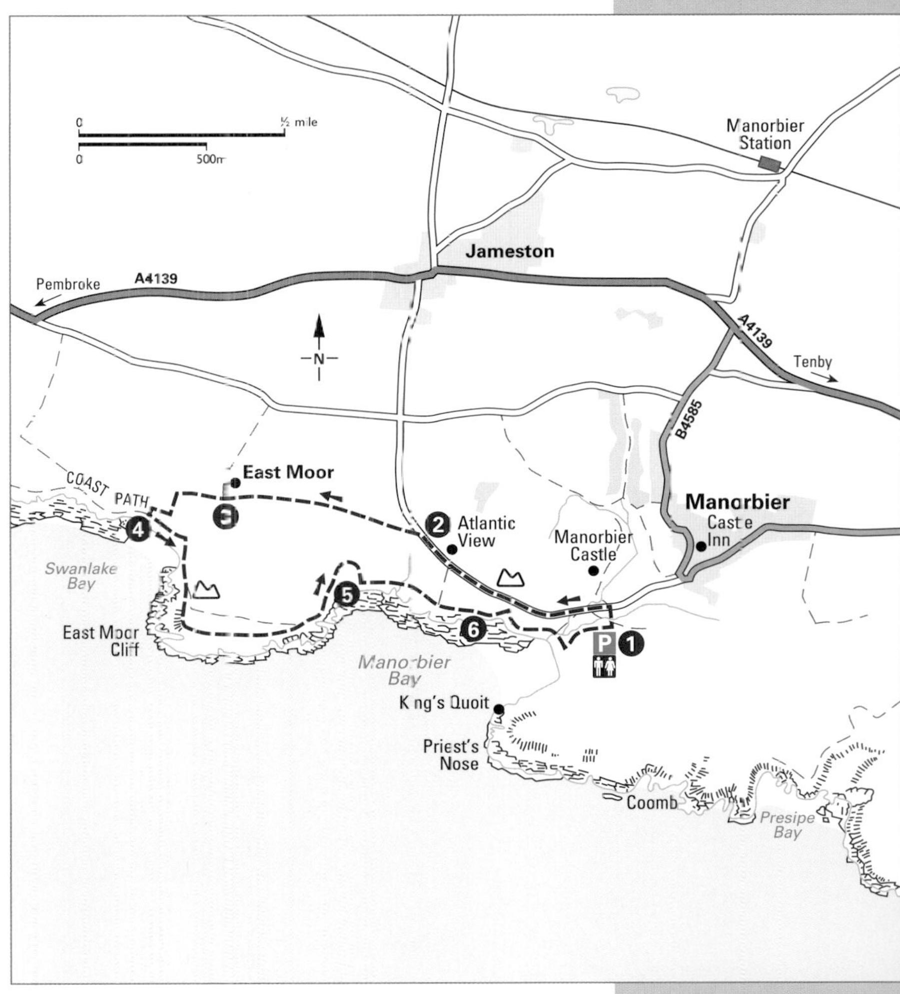

1 Walk out of the car park entrance and turn left towards the sea. Stay on the road as it bears around to the right and climbs steeply above the coast. Pass the impressively situated and well named Atlantic View cottage on your right before reaching a double gate on your left.

2 Cross the stile and walk along the field edge, with a bank and fence on your right, to reach a stone step stile. Cross the stile and continue heading in the same direction to a wooden stile close to the farm, which you also cross. Continue to a gate by the farmhouse, which brings you into a small enclosure, then to a wooden stile that leads you away from the buildings.

3 Continue again along the edge of the field to another gate. Go through the gate and turn left to drop down the field edge to a zig-zag that leads onto the coast path. Access to the beach is via a route available more or less directly beneath you.

4 Turn left onto the coast path and follow it over another stile and then steeply uphill. You'll eventually reach the top on a lovely airy ridge that swings east and then north to drop steeply down into a narrow dip above Manorbier Bay.

5 Cross another stile and climb out of the dip to continue walking easily above the rocky beach. This path leads to a drive, beneath a large house.

6 Continue beneath the Dak and uphill slightly to a gate, where the coast path drops off to the right. Follow the path as it skirts a small car park and then winds down through the gorse and bracken towards the beach. At the bottom, cross the stream and turn left to follow a sandy track back to the car park.

WHILE YOU'RE THERE

Take the coast path up the southeast side of Manorbier Bay to inspect the impressive King's Quoit, a Stone Age burial chamber boasting a 16ft (4.8m) capstone supported by two smaller stones. Carry on to visit the Priest's Nose, a sandstone headland with several interesting caves. The cliffs along this part of the coast show dramatic irregularities in their old red sandstone. At East Moor Cliff, the eastern headland of Swanlake Bay, huge blocks create impressive bastions.

'GERALD OF WALES'

Giraldus Cambrensis, alias 'Gerald of Wales', was born Gerald de Barri, the grandson of Odo, the first Norman lord of Manorbier, in 1146. In addition to his role as a chronicler, he is best known for his attempts to set up an independent Church for Wales, a movement denied by King Henry II of England. In 1184 he entered the service of Henry II, and the following year made a trip to Ireland in the party of the future King John: afterwards he wrote *Topographica Hibernica* and *Expugnatico Hibernica* ('Irish Geography' and 'The Conquering of Ireland', 1188–89). In 1188 Gerald made a preaching tour of Wales, alongside Archbishop Baldwin of Canterbury, as part of an attempt to raise troops for the Third Crusade; afterwards he wrote *Itinerarium Cambriae* ('Welsh Itinerary', 1191) and *Cambriae descriptio* ('Description of Wales', 1194). These books are a key source of information for historians about Norman Wales, its geography and people. Later Gerald tried to become Archbishop of St David's but was frustrated in these efforts. Gerald was very fond of Manorbier, which stands among some of South Pembrokeshire's prettiest countryside. He praised his birthplace as the 'pleasantest spot in Wales'.

Distance 3 miles (4.8km)

Minimum time 1hr 30min

Ascent/gradient 290ft (88m) ▲▲▲

Level of difficulty ●●●

Paths Coast path, clear paths across farmland, 5 stiles

Landscape Sandy coves and dramatic coastline

Suggested map OS Explorer OL36 South Pembrokeshire

Start/finish Grid reference: SS 063976

Dog friendliness Difficult stiles, poop scoop on beaches. Keep on lead and off grass near house on the Dak

Parking Pay-and-display car park by beach below castle

Public toilets At start

1066 – 1300

1167 Henry II invades Ireland, demanding the submission of the Irish kings.

1170 Thomas Becket is murdered by four of Henry's knights while he is at prayer in Canterbury Cathedral.

1189 Richard crowned King. Recognises Scotland as independent state in return for money for Crusades.

1189–99 Richard I spends most of his reign crusading in the Holy Land. His defeat of Kurdish Muslim leader Saladin in the Third Crusade enables Richard to reach an agreement that guarantees safe passage to Christians on pilgrimage to the Holy Land.

1194 Llywelyn the Great declares himself Prince of all Wales.

Holy Orders at Jedburgh

An engaging walk in the Scottish Borders delivers impressive views of a 12th-century abbey

Jedburgh Abbey is one of the most impressive medieval buildings in Scotland. It was built for French Augustinian canons in 1138 by King David I, on the site of an earlier Anglo-Saxon monastery, and was specifically designed to make a visual impact. This was not because the King was exceedingly devout, but was owing to the fact that Jedburgh is close to the border with England: David needed to make a statement of authority to his powerful Norman neighbours.

The abbey is one of four in the Borders – the others being at Dryburgh, Kelso and Melrose – all were built after the Norman Conquest. These magnificent foundations are stretched across the Borders like a string of ecclesiastical jewels.

Top right: *Jedburgh Abbey, looking east*

Background: *Romanesque arches lead the eye upwards*

Right: *Some of the carved details have been restored*

'Black Canons' at Jedburgh

Each of the Border abbeys belonged to a different religious order. The Augustinian canons residing at Jedburgh were also known as 'Black Canons' owing to the colour of their robes. Canons – unlike monks – were all ordained clergymen allowed to administer Holy Communion. Dryburgh Abbey was founded by Premonstratensian canons, who wore white robes and lived a more secluded life than the Augustinians; Kelso Abbey, which became one of the largest monasteries in Scotland, belonged to the Benedictine order, while Melrose was founded by Cistercian monks.

The Cistercians took their name from the forest of Cîteaux in France, where their first community was established. Often known as 'White Benedictines', again because of their cloaks, Cistercians adhered strictly to the Rule of St Benedict. Their regime was designed to purify their lives. They banned the use of practical goods such as bedspreads, combs and even underwear. Most manual labour in a Cistercian abbey was carried out by poor, and generally illiterate, lay brothers; the 'choir' monks devoted their time to reading, writing and private prayer.

Abbeys Under Fire

These medieval abbeys all suffered in the battles that ravaged the Borders for centuries. Jedburgh, for example, was stripped of its roofing lead by King Edward I's troops, who stayed here during the Wars of Independence. It came under attack many times and was burned by the Earl of Surrey in 1530. After the Reformation, all the abbeys fell into decline. Today they remain picturesque reminders of a previous age. The beauty and grandeur of Jedburgh Abbey is still clearly evident. It certainly dominates this border town, and sits serene and seemingly untroubled by the bustle and hassle of modern life.

Walk 33 One of Scotland's finest medieval buildings

Inspect the remains of the grand abbey built by King David I for Augustinian canons

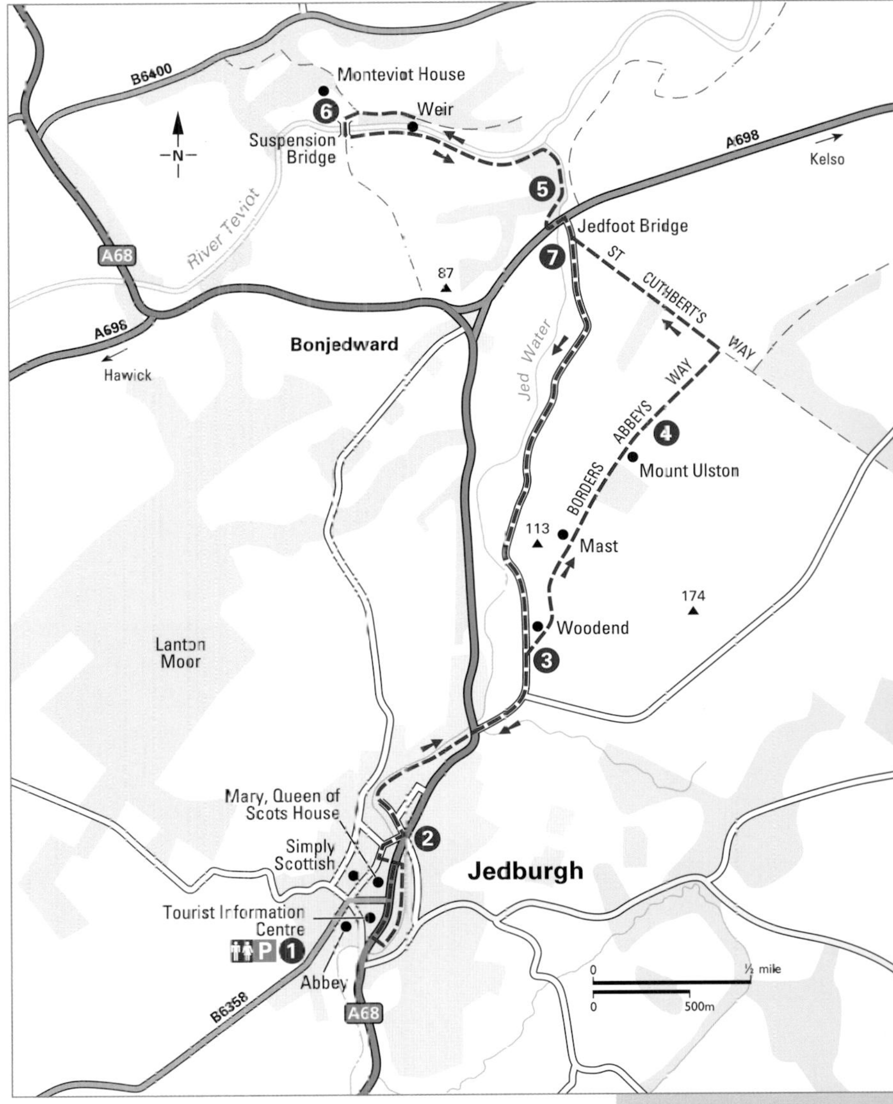

1 From the car park, walk back to the A68. Cross the road into Duck Row. Take the path on the left to walk beside the river, under an old bridge, then onto the road. Turn right across the bridge.

2 Turn left, following the sign for Borders Abbeys Way. Where the road divides, turn left and follow the lane along beside a builders' yard to join 'Waterside Walk'. When you reach the main road, cross and follow the tarmac lane as it heads uphill. Keep straight on, passing a turning on the right, until you reach a fork, situated just before a farmyard on the left.

3 Turn right here to walk in front of a small farmhouse called Woodend. Turn left onto a footpath and pass the front of Mount Ulston house. Head uphill, past a radio mast. Maintain direction to join the narrow grassy track – this can get very muddy, even in the summer.

4 Continue along this track until you reach the fingerpost at the end, where you turn left to join St Cuthbert's Way. The going becomes much easier now as you are walking along a wide, firm track. When you reach the tarmac road, turn right and join the main road. Turn left, go over the bridge, then cross the road. Hop over the crash barrier and go down some steps to continue following St Cuthbert's Way.

5 You're now on a narrow, grassy track, which runs beside the river. You have to nip over a couple of stiles, then walk across a meadow often grazed by sheep. Walk past the weir, then go through the gate to cross the suspension bridge – take care as it can get extremely slippery here.

6 You now pass a sign for Monteviot House and walk through the woods to reach a fingerpost, where you can turn right to enjoy views over the river. If you wish to extend your walk, you can continue along St Cuthbert's Way until it joins the road, then retrace your steps. Whatever you choose, you then retrace your steps back over the suspension bridge, carrying on along the riverside and then heading back to the main road. At this point turn left across a bridge, then immediately go to the right down a tarmac lane.

7 Ignoring the track off to the left, follow the road back to Jedburgh. Cross the A68 and return back along 'Waterside Walk' to the car park.

Distance 4.5 miles (7.2km)

Minimum time 3hrs

Ascent/gradient 295ft (90m) ▲▲▲

Level of difficulty ●●●

Paths Tracks, meadow paths and sections of road, 2 stiles

Landscape Gentle hills and fine old abbey

Suggested map OS Explorer OL16 The Cheviot Hills

Start/finish Grid reference: NT 651204

Dog friendliness Keep on lead near sheep and on road

Parking Main car park by Tourist Information Centre

Public toilets At car park

WHILE YOU'RE THERE

In the town centre you can visit Mary, Queen of Scots, House, a 16th-century fortified house where Mary stayed while visiting Jedburgh in 1566. Mary was resident here for several weeks recovering from an illness caught after she fell into a bog in the course of a lengthy moorland ride to Hermitage Castle, where she went to visit her injured lover (and later husband), the Earl of Bothwell. Many years later Mary was to regret the fact that she had not died in Jedburgh. The house belonged to the Kerr family of Ferniehirst Castle, near Jedburgh. Monteviot House Gardens (Point 6) are open to the public from April to October. There's a river garden with views over the Teviot, a walled rose garden and a fine herb garden.

1066 – 1300

1209 Cambridge University is founded.

1215 King John signs the Magna Carta, a charter of rights and privilege. The first step towards democracy, it is a milestone in English constitutional history.

1216 John dies, leaving England in the hands of Henry III, a nine-year-old boy. Until 1227, when Henry takes over government himself, England is ruled wisely by two regents nominated by John in his will. Henry's rule is less wise.

1236 Henry marries Eleanor of Provence and provokes the fury of English barons by bestowing favours on foreign noblemen. Civil war breaks out, led by Simon de Montfort, Earl of Leicester.

A True Welsh Fortress

A walk through exquisite Welsh countryside near Cadair Idris visits the remains of a once-imposing castle built by Llywelyn the Great

Top right: *Ruins of the well and Round Tower at Castell y Bere*

Above: *The view from the castle walls*

The village of Abergynolwyn, where this walk begins, is built out of Welsh slate and from the proceeds of that slate. It lies in the emerald valley of the Dysynni and beneath the great spruce woods of the Dyfi Forest. However, on this walk we turn our backs on the purple rock to head northwards for the rolling green hills and the delectable oak woods of Coed Cedris that cloak their lower slopes.

At the top of these woods you're transported into a high cwm. The Nant yr Eira trickles out from the rushes, but by the time you're descending into the valley of the Cadair, it is cascading through its own shady ravine.

Guarding the Dysynni Valley

In the middle of the plains, perched on a flat-topped crag, are the ruins of a true Welsh fortress, Castell y Bere. Built in *c.*1221 by Llywelyn the Great, it held out longer than any other Welsh castle when King Edward I and his armies invaded Wales in 1277. By this time Llywelyn ap Grufydd had become Prince of Wales, but had been killed at Builth, leaving his brother Dafydd to defend the castle. Dafydd fought long and hard but was defeated in 1283.

He escaped capture for a while and hid out on the slopes of Cadair Idris. Eventually, however, he was betrayed by his own people and was dragged to Shrewsbury, where he was brutally hung, drawn and quartered. So Wales was defeated and the castle laid waste.

Afterwards Edward I had the castle refortified and set up a garrison there. In 1294–95 the fortress was besieged by Welsh leader Madoc ap Llywelyn. The fortifications were badly damaged but the rebellion was crushed. The castle contained a rectangular, a round and two D-shaped towers. Today the towers and curtain wall can be seen. The D-shaped towers were a distinctive feature of castles built by Welsh lords.

Walk 34 A Welsh prince's formidable stronghold

Tour the still-impressive remains of the castle that briefly defied King Edward I

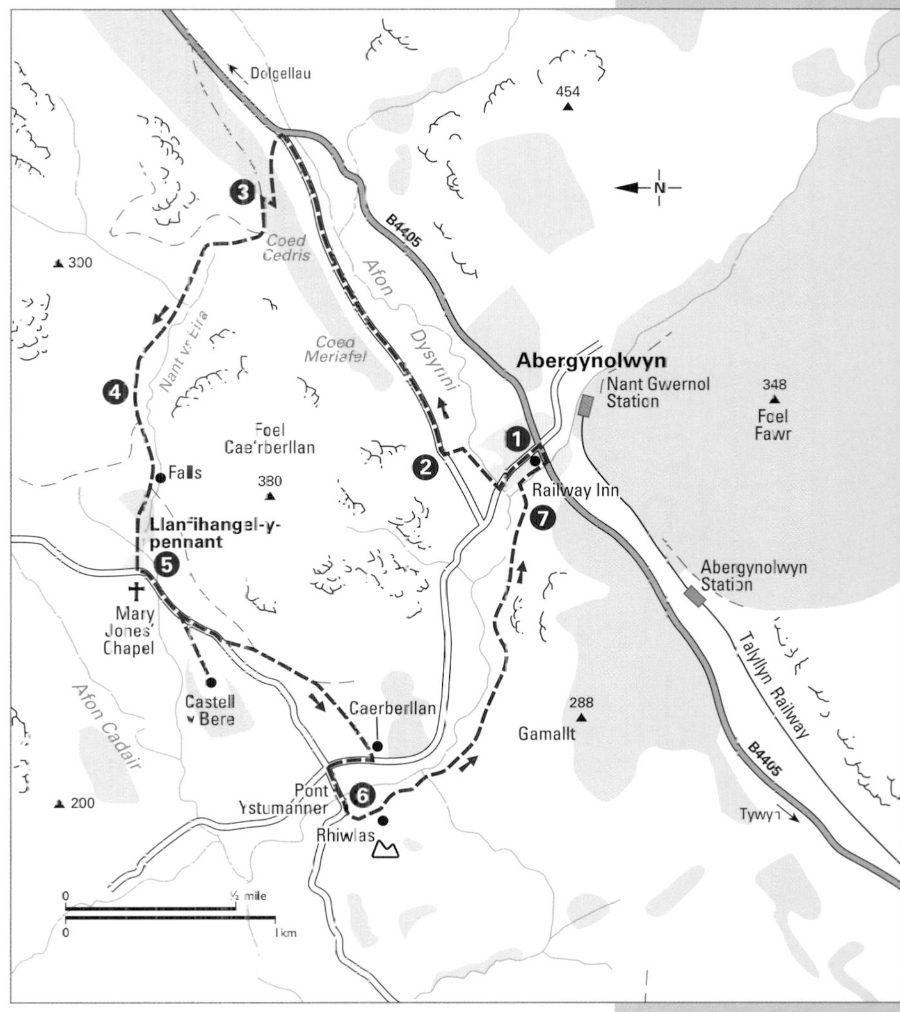

1 Cross the road to the Railway Inn and take the lane signposted to Llanegryn. At the far side of the bridge spanning the Dysynni River, turn right through a kissing gate and trace above the north banks. At a second step stile the path turns left before climbing some steps alongside some tall leylandii to reach a country lane.

2 Turn right along the lane, which heads east through the Dysynni Valley and beneath the woodlands of Coed Meriafel. At the junction with the B4405 turn left, over a stile, and climb northwest across a field. Continue over two more stiles to a woodland path. Follow this to reach a forestry track near the top of the woods.

3 Turn left along the track which climbs out of the woods before veering right to a gate and adjacent stile, giving entry into a large field. Go straight ahead to pick up a ruined, overgrown wall. Where this ends, bear left to descend a high grassy cwm with a stream developing just to your left. Ford another stream which joins from the right near a ruin.

4 The green path develops a flinted surface. Leave it just where it starts to climb, and instead rejoin a streamside path on the left. This descends into the woods and stays close to the stream. After passing several cascades it comes out of the woods to reach a track, which in turn leads onto the road at Llanfihangel-y-pennant just opposite the chapel.

5 Turn left past the chapel and Castell y Bere (detour through gates on the right for a closer look). Just beyond the castle, take a path on the left that climbs to the gate at the top right-hand corner of the field. Turn right along a green track which passes Caerberllan farm to come to the road. Turn right, go left at the crossroads and cross Pont Ystumanner (a bridge).

6 On the other side, a footpath signpost highlights a track on the left, which passes below Rhiwlas farm and then continues as a green path above the river. The path eases across the slopes of Gamallt and swings left with the valley.

WHAT TO LOOK OUT FOR

Caerberllan farm is a splendid building dating from 1590 and renovated in 1755. Caer means 'fort' and the name suggests there was once a Roman fort here. A 12th-century stone-built chapel is associated with Mary Jones, an 18th-century weaver's daughter whose 30-mile (48km) barefoot trek to Bala in search of a Welsh-language Bible inspired local Nonconformist minister, Thomas Charles, to found the British and Foreign Bibles Society.

7 Beyond a river gorge, the path approaches the back of Abergynolwyn village and turns left to pass across an old iron bridge that spans the river. Coming off the bridge, turn right along an unsurfaced street in order to return to the village centre.

Distance 5 miles (8km)

Minimum time 3hrs

Ascent/gradient 656ft (200m) ▲▲▲

Level of difficulty ●●●

Paths Field paths and tracks, 14 stiles

Landscape Pastoral hills and valleys

Suggested map OS Explorer OL23 Cadair Idris & Llyn Tegid

Start/finish Grid reference: SH 677069

Dog friendliness Dogs should be on leads at all times

Parking Car park by Community Centre in Abergynolwyn

Public toilets At Community Centre

1265 Simon de Montfort captures the King and summons the first English Parliament at Lewes. However, de Montfort is killed at the Battle of Evesham, leaving Henry III to resume control.

1267 Under the Treaty of Montgomery, Llywelyn ap Gruffydd receives recognition as Prince of Wales and agrees to pay homage to Henry III.

1272 Edward I becomes king when Henry III dies.

1275 Statute forbids Jews to lend money at interest.

1282 Edward I demands homage from the Welsh prince, Llywelyn ap Gruffydd. When Llywelyn refuses, Edward seizes Gwynedd and mid-Wales, securing his victories with a ring of fortresses.

A King's Lowest Ebb

A fine walk visits the edge of the Fens, close to where the ill-fated King John reputedly lost royal treasure

In October 1216, things were not looking good for King John of England. The previous year he had been forced to sign Magna Carta, which saw him abrogate much of his power to the barons, and 11 months later Prince Louis of France invaded the country, intending to seize the English crown for himself. King Alexander of Scotland had reached Cambridge and had to be ousted, and John was losing supporters by the fistful. To top it all, he was ill, probably with dysentery – unpleasant at any time, but especially so when being forced to travel at speed along a medieval road.

Above right: *Silver coins from the time of John and Henry III*

Below: *King John reluctantly handed power to his noblemen at Runnymede, Surrey, in 1215*

King John's Lost Treasure

On 11 October, John started to move from his Norfolk base into Lincolnshire. Because time was of the essence, with hostile forces all around, he was obliged to take the shortest and quickest route. This happened to be across the Wellstream Estuary in Walpole St Andrew. Impatient to be on his way, John did not wait for the tide to recede – and the result was devastating. The heavy baggage wagons became bogged down in the mud and many of the servants driving them drowned. He also lost some of his chapel goods.

Did John lose the crown jewels in the Wash as the monk chroniclers at St Albans later claimed? Did the tide come racing in, a mass of water that sucked the King's entire baggage train, all his money and most of his army into quicksands and whirlpools? Probably not, although the legend persists and the Walpoles have seen countless treasure hunters searching for the fabled wealth lost to the sea.

Within a few days John was dead. His servants stole his personal goods, the Abbot of Croxton laid claim to his intestines for burial in his abbey, and his nine-year-old son was crowned King Henry III.

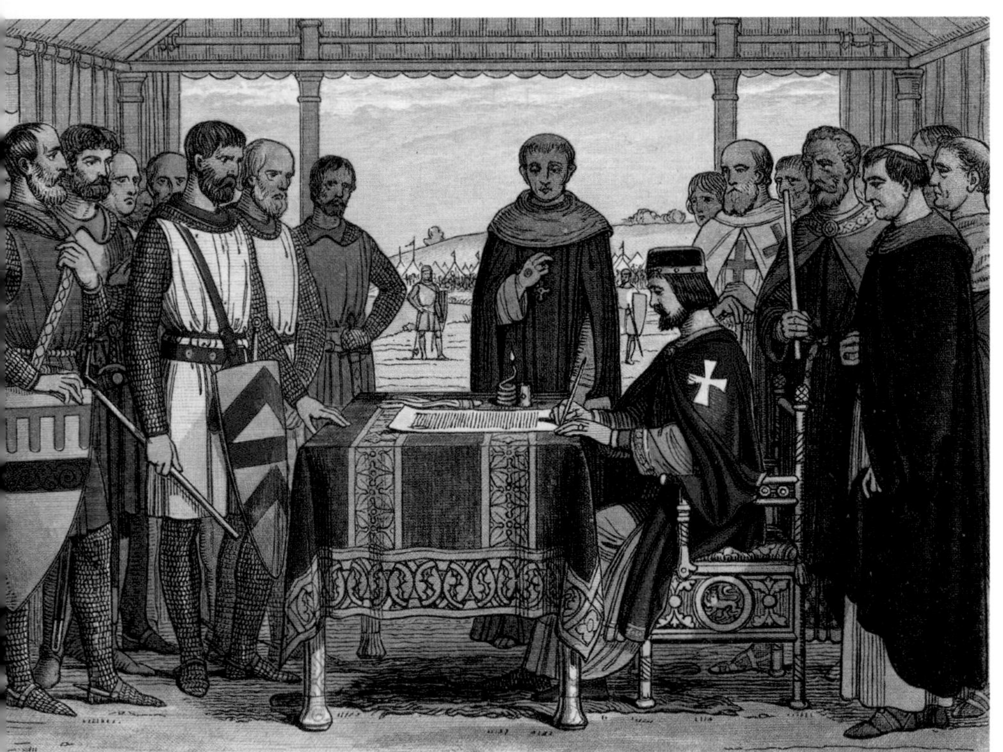

The Walpoles – and the 'Cathedral of the Fens'

The Walpoles offer a good deal more than legends, however. There are four of them – St Andrew, St Peter, Cross Keys and Highway. The church at Walpole St Peter is no less than 160ft (50m) long, and so magnificent that it is known as the 'Cathedral of the Fens'. It was originally built in Saxon times, but the bulk of it was swept away by terrible floods in 1337, so that much of what you see today dates from reconstruction in the mid-14th to 15th centuries.

The money for raising such a fine building came from the fertile surrounding lands. Also fine is Walpole St Andrew's Church, which had bequests in 1443 and 1463. Meanwhile, little Walpole Highway's St Edmund's Church was built in 1844 as a chapel of ease for those people who found Walpole St Andrew's too far to travel.

Walk 35 Crown jewels sunk in the Wash?

Step back in time to see where a washed-up monarch met with the costliest of disasters

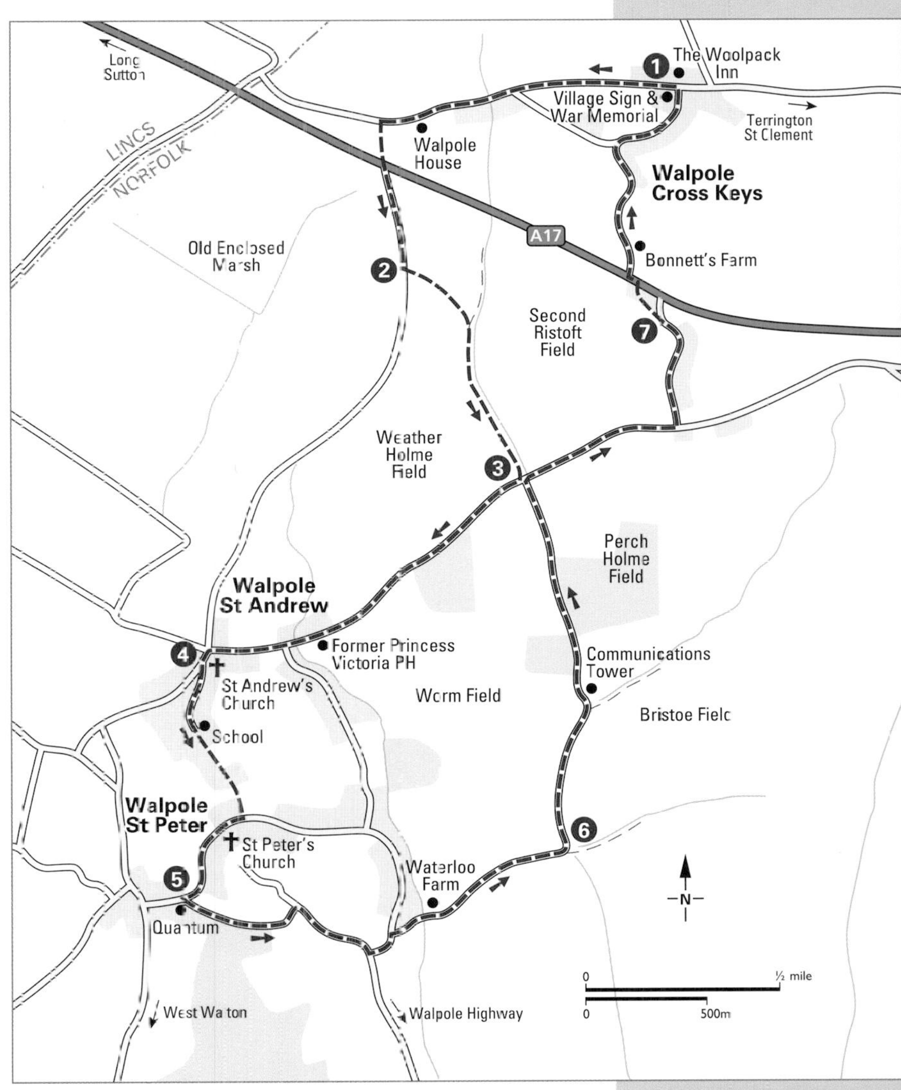

1 With the village sign behind you, turn left along Sutton Road, using the pavement on the right-hand side. After about 0.75 mile (1.2km) you will see a track signed 'No Through Road' on your left. Follow this track, cross the A17 with care, and then head down the lane opposite, signed 'No access to the Walpoles'. This lane follows the line of ancient sea defences; continue along it for about 350yds (320m).

2 Turn left onto the unmarked footpath that cuts diagonally across a field. Cross a second field to a broken line of trees, then go through a gap in the trees and turn right onto a grassy track. Eventually you pass some farm buildings to arrive at a crossroads.

3 Turn right and walk down the lane into the village of Walpole St Andrew. Continue until you reach the old Princess Victoria pub, dating from 1651, now a private house. Keep straight ahead at the junction along Wisbech Road until you see St Andrew's Church to your left.

4 Bear left at the crossroads at St Andrew's Church. Take the first turn on your left and walk down this road towards Anthony Curton Church of England Primary School. Take the footpath that runs down the side of the school and through a housing estate before emerging near St Peter's Church in Walpole St Peter. Turn right, using the pavement on the right as the road winds around to another junction.

5 Turn sharp left at the house called Quantum and stay on this road as it winds through the village. Turn left at Chalk Road. After the road bends, turn right into Bustards Lane and continue until you reach a bend with a farm track straight ahead.

6 Keep to the road as it bends left and walk until you see a communications tower on your right. Keep left again and after 0.5 mile (800m) you will reach the junction you made earlier at Point 3. Go right, with greenhouses to your left, until you reach another junction. Turn left, and follow the lane until you see a tall fence and a hedge of Leylandii trees.

7 Bear left beside a reconstruction of the old Walpole railway station platform, passing the Old Railway Inn, now a house, to reach the A17. Follow the pavement to the left, then cross over at the end of the railings, using the central island. On the other side, walk to the left of the piled pallets and up the lane past scattered houses and a fruit farm. At the T-junction turn right along Station Road and continue back to the start of the walk.

WHILE YOU'RE THERE

Other marshland villages with mighty 'cathedrals' are West Walton, Wiggenhall St Mary, Terrington St Clement, Walsoken and Tilney All Saints. At West Walton, just to the southwest of Walpole St Peter, St Mary's Parish Church was built in 1225–40 and has a nave with six side bays on each side and a 15th-century hammer-beam roof. The church has a tranquil atmosphere; its church tower is unusual in being freestanding and 60ft (18m) away from the main church – the tower is supported by four arches. At Terrington St Clement, 7 miles (11km) west of King's Lynn, the Church of St Clement was built in the 14th century by Edmund Gonville, rector, the founder of Gonville Hall (now Gonville and Caius College, Cambridge). It is vast – 168ft (51m) in length – and cruciform in shape, with an imposing tower next to the west front. At Walsoken, 1.5 miles (2.4km) northeast of Wisbech on the Norfolk–Cambridgeshire border, All Saints Parish Church has a late Norman nave and chancel of c.1146, and an imposing medieval west tower.

Distance 7.25 miles (11.7km)

Minimum time 3hrs

Ascent/gradient Negligible ▲▲▲

Level of difficulty ●●●

Paths Footpaths, lanes

Landscape Pancake-flat fenland and prairie-style fields

Suggested map OS Explorer 236 King's Lynn, Downham Market & Swaffham

Start/finish Grid reference: TF 520199

Dog friendliness Good

Parking Near war memorial and Woolpack Inn, Walpole Cross Keys

Public toilets None on route

1066 – 1300

1284 Llywelyn ap Gruffydd is ambushed and killed. The Statute of Rhuddlan sweeps away Welsh laws and imposes English rule and an English Prince of Wales – the future King Edward II.

1286 Alexander III of Scotland dies and the Kingdom falls into dispute between John Balliol, John Comyn and Robert the Bruce.

1296 Royal edict expels Jews from England.

1296 William Wallace of Scotland makes an alliance with France in the fight for Scottish independence.

1298 Edward I invades Scotland and seizes the throne, triggering a series of vicious wars between the two nations.

Stirling's Braveheart, William Wallace

A town trail uncovers the truth about the ultimate Scottish hero

William Wallace's heroic status is immediately obvious on your arrival in Stirling, which is dominated by the enormous monument erected in his memory. He was born at Ellerslie, near Kilmarnock, early in the 1270s and little is known of his early life. He might have remained unknown were it not for the fact that in 1286 the Scottish king, Alexander III, was found dead on the sands at Kinghorn, Fife. His only direct heir was Margaret of Norway – and many powerful Scots did not want a woman on the throne. When Margaret died on her way to Scotland, the succession was plunged into further confusion. The only likely contestants were John Balliol and Robert Bruce. King Edward I of England was asked to advise, chose Balliol, and then exerted his authority by demanding revenues from Scotland. Balliol later infuriated Edward by signing a treaty with England's enemy, France, and Edward retaliated by sacking Berwick in 1296, killing thousands. The Scots began to resist, Balliol was deposed as king, and the Wars of Independence began.

Wallace Wages War

Wallace joined the struggle. In 1297 he killed the English Sheriff of Lanark and led attacks on English forces. Later that year he won the battle that was to make his reputation, defeating Edward's army at Stirling Bridge. Wallace now had considerable power. In 1298 he was made Guardian of Scotland, but he was defeated by Edward I later that year at Falkirk. He was eventually captured in 1305, executed at Smithfield in London – and at once became a martyr for Scottish independence.

Top: *William Wallace, with Andrew Moray, won a famous victory over the English at Stirling Bridge on 11 September, 1297*

Above: *Looking down from Stirling Castle on the churchyard and Church of the Holy Rude (founded 1129)*

Walk 36 Scottish Guardian who defeated a king

Explore the place in which Scotland's celebrated war leader won a crushing victory

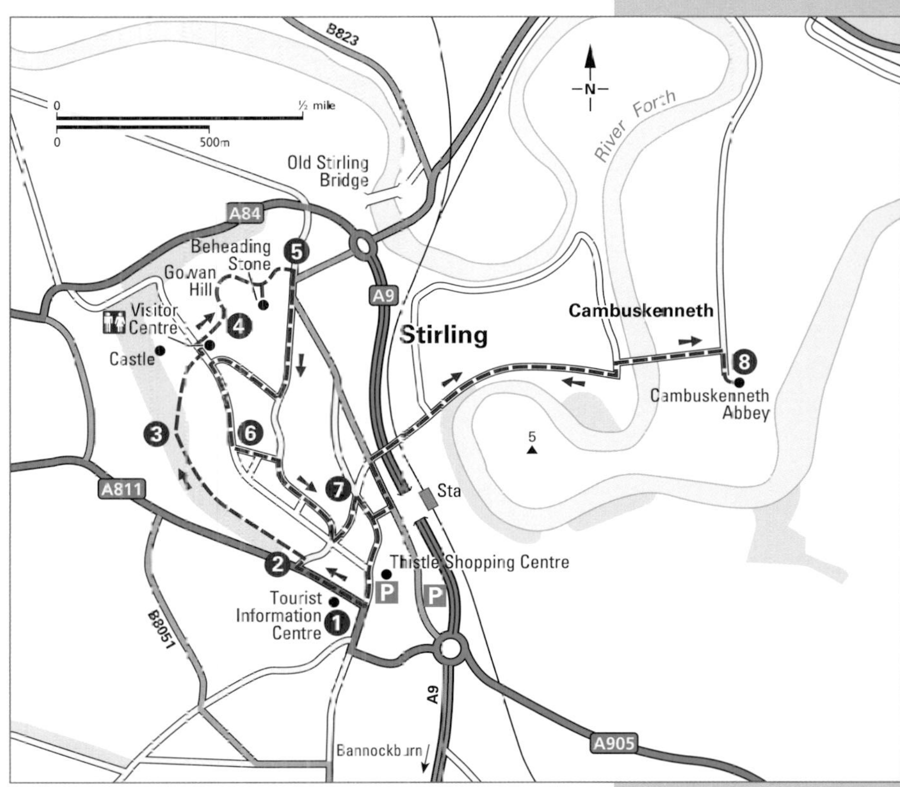

1 From the Tourist Information Centre on Dumbarton Road, cross the road and turn left. Walk past the statue of celebrated poet Robert Burns then, just before the Albert Halls, turn right and walk back on yourself. Just past the statue of Rob Roy, turn left and take the path along the Back Wall.

2 Almost immediately (after around 20yds/18m), turn right up the flight of steps that takes you onto the Upper Back Wall. It's a steady climb now, up past the Church of the Holy Rude, where King James VI was crowned in 1567, and then on past Ladies' Rock – where ladies of the castle once sat to watch tournaments.

3 Continue following the path uphill to reach Stirling Castle. Cross the car park to take the path running downhill just to the side of the visitor centre, so that the castle is on your left. At the cemetery, turn right along the footpath signposted to Moto Hill. Continue up steps and across the cemetery to the gap in the wall.

4 Follow the track downhill onto Gowan Hill. There are several branching tracks but you continue on the main path – heading for the cannons on the hill ahead. At a junction turn right down a track signposted to Lower Bridge Street. Turn onto a grassy slope to the right to see the Beheading Stone. Retrace your steps to the wide track and then follow it to reach the road.

5 Turn right along Lower Bridge Street, then fork right into Upper Bridge Street. Continue straight ahead, then 50yds (46m) beyond Settle Inn, turn right up a cobbled lane that looks a little like the access drive to a house. Follow this uphill, then go left at the top. Eventually you'll pass the Castle Esplanade, followed by Argyll's Lodging, and will reach a junction.

6 Turn left, passing first Hermann's Restaurant and then the Mercat Cross. Turn right at the bottom, heading down Bow Street, then take a turn to the left along Baker Street. When you reach Friars Street (which is a pedestrianised street), turn left and walk down as far as the end.

7 Turn right now, then first left to reach the station. Turn left, then right over the bridge, then bear left in front of new development to reach the riverside. Maintain direction and join Abbey Road. Bear left at the end, go right over the footbridge and continue along South Street, turning right at the end to visit the remains of Cambuskenneth Abbey.

8 Retrace your steps back to the station. Turn right, then left, then right again at the Thistle Shopping Centre. Go along Port Street, then turn right along Dumbarton Road to the start.

Distance 5 miles (8km)

Minimum time 2hrs 30 min

Ascent/gradient 279ft (85m) ▲▲▲

Level of difficulty ●●●

Paths Ancient city streets and some rough tracks

Landscape Bustling little city topped with magnificent castle

Suggested map OS Explorer 366 Stirling & Ochil Hills West

Start/finish Grid reference: NS 795933

Dog friendliness Mostly on lead, not good for those that dislike crowds

Parking On streets near Tourist Information Centre or in multi-storey car parks

Public toilets At visitor centre by the castle

WALLACE MONUMENT AND STIRLING CASTLE

You can add a loop to this walk by crossing Old Stirling Bridge and walking up the road to the Wallace Monument. Designed by architect John Thomas Rochead in the Victorian Gothic style, the 220ft (67m)-tall tower of sandstone was completed in 1869. There are magnificent views from the top, which is accessed by an internal, 246-step spiral staircase. After you've scaled the heights to the statue, come back to the road and turn left, then right, over the railway to Cambuskenneth Abbey, where you can pick up the main route at Point 8.

Stirling Castle was the favourite residence of most of the Stuart monarchs. The Great Hall, with its two tall oriel windows and five vast fireplaces, was built for King James IV in 1503. Visit the Chapel Royal, built by James VI in 1594 for the baptism of his son, Prince Henry, and also the restored 16th-century kitchens. You can also see where Mary, Queen of Scots, lived.

DOMINI MIL

MEDIEVAL BRITAIN
1300–1485

PLAGUE & CONFLICT

For most people, life in medieval Britain was hard work but reasonably predictable, within a fairly rigid social order. However, in the mid-14th century the old world was changed beyond recognition – by the Black Death. The country lost one-third of its people, feudal ties dissolved and a wage economy was born.

Britain in the first half of the 14th century was familiar with upheaval and war. The enmity between England and Scotland rumbled on, exploding into battle at Bannockburn in 1314, when Edward II's troops were routed by Robert the Bruce. In 1337 the more warlike Edward III sent his knights across the Channel to enforce his claim to the French throne, setting in train the Hundred Years' War that would last until 1453. Yet in most communities the daily routine was predictable, if tough – until, in 1348, an epidemic swept in from Europe that seemed to herald Judgement Day itself.

The Black Death was a form of bubonic plague, carried by fleas on the rats that infested ships and towns. The first signs of infection were swellings, or 'buboes', on the armpits or groin; these were followed by coughing, chills and delirium. Victims were usually dead within days. By the time the epidemic had run its course, Europe's population had been halved, Britain's reduced by one-third. Estates and villages were left to rot, with no one to plant or harvest crops, tend or slaughter cattle, produce or sell goods. Those still capable of work found that the feudal rules tying them to their lord's land no longer applied: they could move around, selling their labour to the highest bidder. When the Crown tried to rein in this burgeoning wage economy, imposing a poll tax on everyone over the age of 14, the peasants revolted, only retreating from confrontation with King Richard II when their leader, Wat Tyler, was cut down by his bodyguard.

Faced with the uncertainty of earthly existence, people turned in their thousands to the comforting rituals of religion, trekking to pilgrimage centres in the hope of sharing in the miraculous powers of holy relics. With their stalls and souvenirs, inns and religious sites of interest, pilgrimage routes were as much a holiday as a journey of faith.

POWER STRUGGLES

The ravages of plague and food shortages continued to have their repercussions. A minor Welsh noble, Owain Glyndwr, indignant at the loss of a legal dispute over land rights, attracted a huge following of disaffected countrymen when he took arms against the king, now Henry IV. At its height the rebel movement was calling its own parliaments and signing international alliances, but in 1413 the English gained the upper hand and Glyndwr vanished into hiding.

Two years later, the English celebrated another great and very famous victory – against the French in Agincourt; and in 1420 the Treaty of Troyes pronounced Henry V heir to the throne of France. But the English kingdom's future was far from settled: a tussle over the crown sparked 30 years of intermittent fighting between the houses of Lancaster and York.

In 1485 the Lancastrian claimant, Henry Tudor – son of Margaret Beaufort, the great-granddaughter of John of Gaunt, Duke of Lancaster – returned from exile in Brittany and marched to Bosworth to face the Yorkist king, Richard III. After a fierce battle, Richard was killed. The new king's followers performed an impromptu crowning ceremony in the field. The Tudor era was under way.

KEY SITES

Glentrool, Dumfries & Galloway: Where Robert the Bruce triumphed in 1307.

Bodiam Castle, Sussex: Picturesque fortified manor house of Sir Edward Dalyngrigge

Canterbury Cathedral, Kent: Scene of Becket's martyrdom that attracted medieval pilgrims.

Stafford Castle, Staffordshire: 14th-century stone castle built by Ralph de Stafford.

Otterburn battlefield, Northumberland: Site of the Earl of Douglas's victory in 1388.

Warwick Castle, Warwickshire: Ancestral home of the Earls of Warwick

Left: *Crests in Canterbury Cathedral, a major pilgrimage destination in the 14th century*

1300–1485

1306 Robert the Bruce sets out to oust the English, having killed his main Scottish rival, John Comyn. He is crowned Robert I of Scots at Scone.

1307 Edward I dies and his son becomes Edward II.

1314 Robert the Bruce routs the feckless Edward II's army at Bannockburn.

1315–17 Floods create food shortages and cause an economic crisis.

1318 Scottish raiders reach York.

1327 Owing to a poor choice of advisers, Edward II is deposed by Parliament. He is executed at Berkeley Castle and his son Edward succeeds the throne.

1327–77 Edward III reigns as king.

1328 Scotland's independence is recognised. Bruce, now officially King of Scotland, dies in 1329 and is succeeded by his son, David II.

1337 Edward III claims to be heir to the French throne, and the Hundred Years' War with France begins.

The Battle of Glentrool – Road to Independence

Forest trails lead to the site of Robert the Bruce's turning point during the bitter Wars of Independence

Above: *Robert the Bruce, King of Scots*

Background: *Inscription on the Bruce's Stone at Loch Trool*

Below right: *The tumbling waters of a burn cascade down towards Loch Trool*

The year 1314 is etched deep in the Scottish consciousness: Robert the Bruce's victory over the English at Bannockburn is regarded as the culmination of the Wars of Independence. But it could be argued that an earlier skirmish, when the two nations clashed at Glentrool in 1307, was a more important step on the road to Scottish independence.

Scotland was an independent country long before these wars, but had been left without a monarch following the death of Alexander II in 1286 and that of his only heir, Margaret of Norway, on her journey to Scotland. The Guardians of Scotland (the country's de facto rulers during the interregnum or period between reigns) asked Edward I of England to adjudicate on the various claimants to the succession.

Edward used this as an excuse to re-assert his claim as overlord of Scotland. He chose John Balliol as king but made him swear an oath of fealty, then later removed him, leaving Scotland to be run by English officials. Sir William Wallace was appointed Guardian of Scotland by the nobility and led the resistance against the English. However, he was betrayed by the nobles in 1305, taken to London and executed.

Meanwhile Robert the Bruce advanced his claim to the Scottish throne and launched attacks on the English in the southwest. He was crowned King of Scots on 25 March, 1306, but suffered a series of defeats and fled to Rathlin Island, off the Antrim coast. There he regrouped before returning to Scotland early in 1307.

Glen Trool Ambush

An English army was dispatched to capture him, but he set up an ambush. Using a small part of his force to lure the English onto the southern shores of Loch Trool, he concealed the bulk of his men on the slopes above the loch. The English were forced to dismount and follow in single file and, when they were at their most vulnerable, the Scots blocked the path and hurled a barrage of heavy boulders down on them.

Walk 37 Around Loch Trool

Explore where the Bruce ambushed English troops and enjoy one of Scotland's finest views

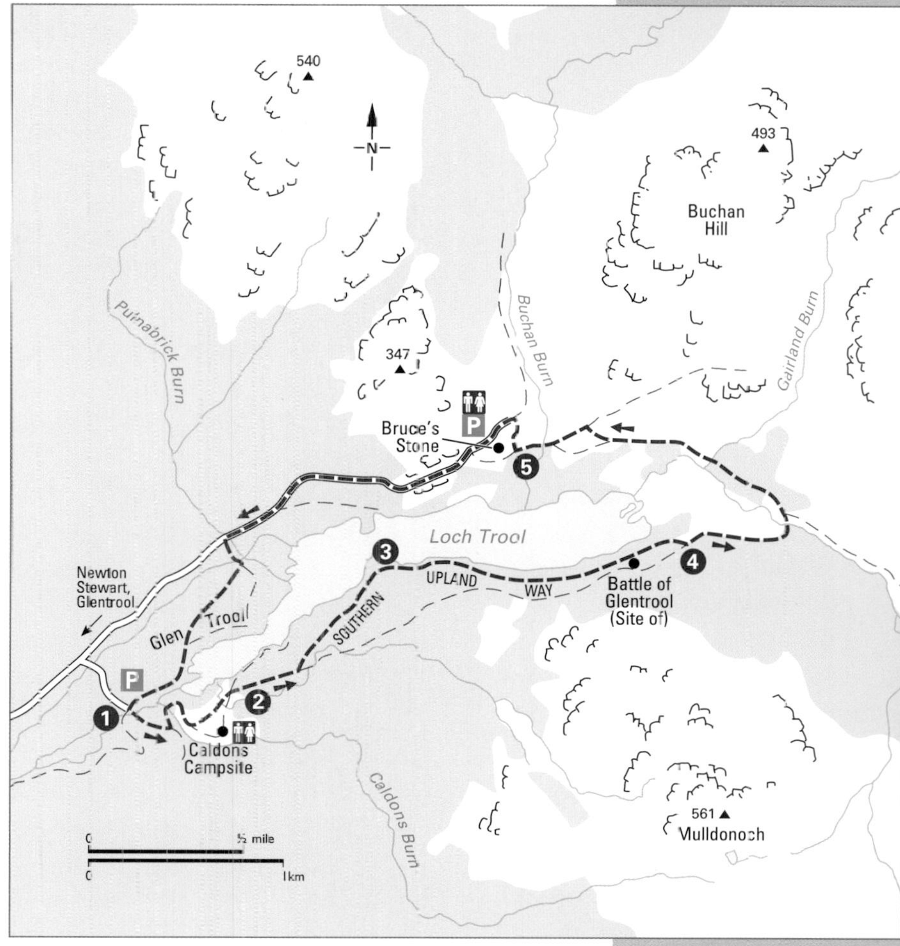

1 Leave the car park and follow the Southern Upland Way markers. Cross the bridge over the Water of Trool. Cross another bridge over the Caldons Burn. Next, take a left turn onto a footpath that runs along the banks of the river. Cross over a bridge.

2 Follow this well waymarked trail and then at a fork by a waymarker turn right, before heading uphill and into the forest.

3 Keep on the path uphill and through a clearing, then go through a kissing gate and re-enter the woodland. Continue along the southern side of Loch Trool until you reach an interpretation board near the loch end. This marks the spot where Robert the Bruce and his army cleverly lured the superior English forces into a well-planned ambush and routed them.

4 Follow the path from here, leaving the woodland and heading downhill and to the left, before leaving the Southern Upland Way. Turn left, go through two gates and over a wooden bridge. Cross the bridge over Gairland Burn and continue. Eventually reaching the bridge over the Buchan Burn, cross over and take the path to the left, branching off uphill.

5 Follow this to the top and Bruce's Stone, which was raised to commemorate the victory at the Battle of Glentrool, the first victory in the Wars of Independence. From here, looking across the clear waters of the loch to the tree-clad hills opposite, is one of the finest views in Scotland. Follow the track past the stone, then turn left onto the narrow road. Head through the car park and keep going until you reach a waymarker on the left which leads to a forest trail, and take this to return to the start of the walk.

WHAT TO LOOK OUT FOR

From the south side of Loch Trool look across the water to see the celebrated Bruce's Stone on its vantage point on the far bank. Behind the Stone is the massive backdrop of Merrick, at 2,765ft (843m) the highest hill in the Southern Uplands, with the lower Benyellary in front and to the left, connected by the narrow ridge of the Neive of the Spit. If you're feeling energetic, a path to the summit of both peaks starts from a spot near Bruce's Stone.

TREATY OF EDINBURGH

After victory at Glentrool the Bruce won further victories against the English, culminating in the Battle of Bannockburn in 1314. Edward I counterattacked in 1317–19, seizing the border town of Berwick. In 1322 Scottish nobles appealed to the Pope to support independence in the Declaration of Arbroath. Support was granted in 1324, and in 1328 England recognised Scotland as an independent nation in the Treaty of Edinburgh.

Distance 5 miles (8km)

Minimum time 2hrs

Ascent/gradient 300ft (91m) ▲▲▲

Level of difficulty ●●●

Paths Forest trails, metalled roads, 1 stile

Landscape Hillside, loch and woodland

Suggested map OS Explorer 318 Galloway Forest Park North

Start/finish Grid reference: NX 396791

Dog friendliness Great walk for dogs

Parking Caldons

Public toilets Caldons Campsite

1338–39 A French fleet raids Southampton, Portsmouth, Dover and Folkestone.

1340 At the naval battle of Sluys, Edward III defeats the French fleet and takes control of the Channel.

1344 Edward III, an embodiment of medieval chivalry, holds a Round Table jousting tournament at Windsor.

1346 David II of Scotland invades England but is defeated and imprisoned. He is released in return for a huge ransom, but after his death in 1371 the debt proves impossible to maintain, and conflict between the two countries continues in the reign of Robert II.

1346 Edward III defeats the French at the celebrated Battle of Crécy despite being outnumbered by three to one. Edward's 15-year-old son Edward, Prince of Wales, wins glory in battle. King John of Bohemia is among those killed on the French side.

1347 The key French port of Calais surrenders to Edward III. Edward demands the lives of six leading citizens. When they emerge to meet their deaths he is persuaded by his queen, Philippa, to spare them.

Discovering Stafford Castle

A short walk from Stafford town leads around one of the county's oldest monuments

In the 11th century, a castle was built on the hill to the west of Stafford by William the Conqueror to keep Saxons in check. It was at this time that the earthworks around the present-day castle were built. They involved avenues, deep ditches, steep slopes and an impressive motte, or steep-sided earth mound, at the centre of the castle complex. The castle proper would have been a three-storey timber keep on the motte, and would have doubled as the lord's residence and his military headquarters.

It was not until 1347 that Ralph de Stafford began building the first stone castle on the site. He raised a rectangular keep with four corner towers. In 1350 Ralph was created the first Earl of Stafford. The castle stayed in the family until 1521, when Henry VIII had Edward Stafford executed on a dubious charge of treason; he actually had a distant claim to the throne. The Staffords recovered their property and titles 25 years later but failed to recover their fortune. By the end of the 16th century, the castle was in ruins and remained so until the Civil War broke out in 1642. Isabel, Lady Stafford, was requested by Charles I to defend the castle against Parliamentarians, and resisted months of siege.

A Gothic Revival

The castle continued to be neglected until Sir George Jerningham had the ruin cleared of debris in the early 19th century and rebuilt the eastern towers in what was an early example of Gothic Revival architecture. Alas, he did not complete the renovation and the castle was more or less neglected thereafter. Today, however, the castle is preserved, with a visitor centre providing a useful insight into the chronicle of the castle, and in particular its Norman founders.

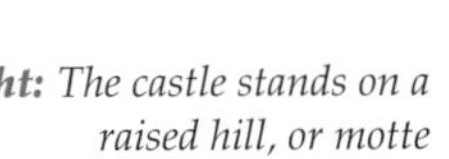

Right: *The castle stands on a raised hill, or motte*

Below: *Parts of the 14th-century stonework survive*

Walk 38 Hilltop stronghold

See the remains of a 14th-century stone castle rebuilt as part of the Gothic Revival

1 From the roundabout by Broad Eye Windmill head away from the town, over the river. After 100yds (91m) go left along Castle Street and over the railway bridge to the roundabout. Cross and walk along the path to the next road.

2 Cross over, turn right, then bear left by a line of trees, going left again at a footpath sign and keeping the houses to your right. Follow the gravel track all the way up through the middle of the golf course and, at the very top, keep going straight across the field ahead of you, following a faint grass trail to a gap in the woods. Turn left for a path along the edge of the trees to the castle's Visitor Centre. The centre makes an ideal starting point for any visit, packed as it is with information on the Norman Conquest and featuring a short film on the history of the castle itself. There's also a shop selling snacks, souvenirs and guides, not just on the castle, but on other castles, churches and historical buildings throughout Staffordshire.

3 After following the castle's self-guided walk (0.75 mile/1.2km) go back the way you came, along the bottom of the wood to the gap, and skirt left around the outside of the wood. At the corner of the wood, go through the hedge and head right. Continue down the field edge path with the hedge on your right. Descending through these fields also serves to illustrate how tough it must have been for Saxon forces to charge in the opposite direction; even assuming they survived the onslaught of arrows from Norman long-bows, by the time they got anywhere near the castle they would have been absolutely spent.

4 When you come to a junction and a hedge ahead, go left, and two fields on turn hard-right on a wide track downhill. Follow this round to the right and back towards Stafford. When the track runs out, bear right onto the road and then left across a roundabout. Just before the next roundabout (Point 2) head left, retracing your steps back into Stafford.

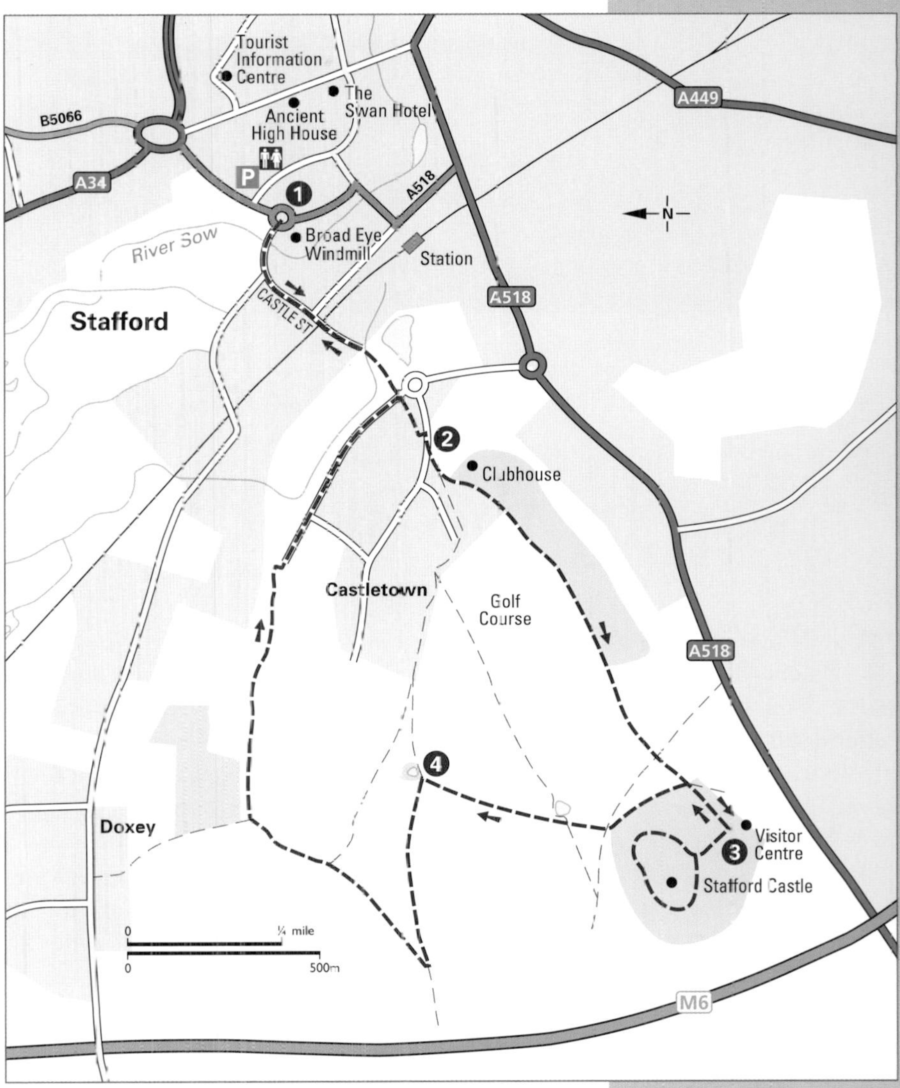

WHAT TO LOOK OUT FOR

Near the start of the walk, in Stafford, look out for the Ancient High House, the largest timber-framed townhouse in England. King Charles I stayed here in 1642 at the beginning of the Civil War and the following year, when the town was captured and the castle besieged by the Parliamentarians, it became a prison for Royalist officers. It's open to visitors Tue–Sat, 10am–4pm, throughout the year.

Distance 4 miles (6.4km)

Minimum time 1hr 30min

Ascent/gradient 240ft (73m) ▲▲▲

Level of difficulty ●●●

Paths Pavement, gravel tracks and grass trails

Landscape Town, golf course, hilltop and farmland

Suggested map OS Explorer 244 Cannock Chase

Start/finish Grid reference: SJ 918233

Dog friendliness Keep on lead near livestock

Parking Pay car parks in town centre

Public toilets Stafford Castle Visitor Centre and in town centre

1348 A virulent disease carried by flea-infested rats sweeps through Europe and reaches London. The Black Death sweeps across England, Scotland and Ireland in several waves, killing one third of the population.

1348 At Windsor Edward III establishes the chivalric brotherhood of the Most Noble Order of the Garter, dedicated to the Virgin Mary and St George.

1351 The King is given power over Church appointments in the Statute of Provisors.

***c.*1360** William Langland writes *Piers Plowman.*

1366 The Statute of Kilkenny forbids the speaking of Gaelic in English-controlled parts of Ireland.

***c.*1375** The alliterative poems *Pearl* and *Sir Gawain and the Green Knight* are written by an unknown poet or poets in central England.

Villages Shaped by the Black Death

A fascinating excursion links two settlements transformed by the plague

The village of Swainby largely owes its existence to tragedy, for with the coming of the Black Death in the 14th century the inhabitants of the original village, just up the hill at Whorlton, deserted their homes and moved here. There were seemingly already a few houses here: Swainby means 'the village of the land workers', and its existence was recorded as early as the 13th century, but the village's future was transformed by the influx of residents.

Medieval Ruins

In the deserted village of Whorlton little survived except the church and the castle, both now partially ruined. On any but a sunny day, Holy Cross Church can be a disturbing place, with its avenue of yew trees leading to the arches of the nave, now open to the skies. The chancel is roofed, and a flap in the doorway allows you to look inside to see a fine early 14th-century oak figure of a knight. It is probably Nicholas, Lord Maynell, who fought with Edward I in Wales and hunted in the woods here.

The gatehouse of Maynell's castle, just along the road, is the only substantial part left. It was built at the end of the 14th century, and was besieged 250 years later during the English Civil War (1642–51). You can still see on the walls the marks of cannon balls from the Parliamentarians' guns. East of the castle, which occupied more than 6 acres (2.4 ha), are further earthworks, which protected the village.

Industrial Frontier Town

Centuries later, Swainby was shocked out of a peaceful rural existence by the opening of ironstone mines in Scugdale. The village took on many aspects of an American frontier town, suddenly full of miners and their equipment, awash with their smoke and clatter. As well as ironstone, jet was mined in the Swainby area in the 19th century, including on Whorl Hill, which you will walk around (Points 7–8). Most of the jet pits were small, employing no more than a dozen men, but they could be very profitable, especially during the boom time for jet, with many encouraged by the example of Queen Victoria's black mourning jewellery.

Like coal, jet is fossilised wood. It comes in two types, hard and soft; hard jet was probably formed in sea water and soft jet in fresh water. It has been prized for more than 3,000 years, and was known to the Celts as Freya's Tears. Because it is easy to work and takes a fine polish, jet workshops could turn out large quantities of jewellery relatively quickly. Although some jet objects are still made, especially in Whitby, the industry had virtually died out by the 1920s.

Above: *Flea-bitten rats bore the plague that killed millions across Europe*

Below: *Headstones in the graveyard at deserted Whorlton*

Walk 39 Tough times in medieval Yorkshire

Investigate abandoned Whorlton and Swainby, in an area that was later a centre of mining

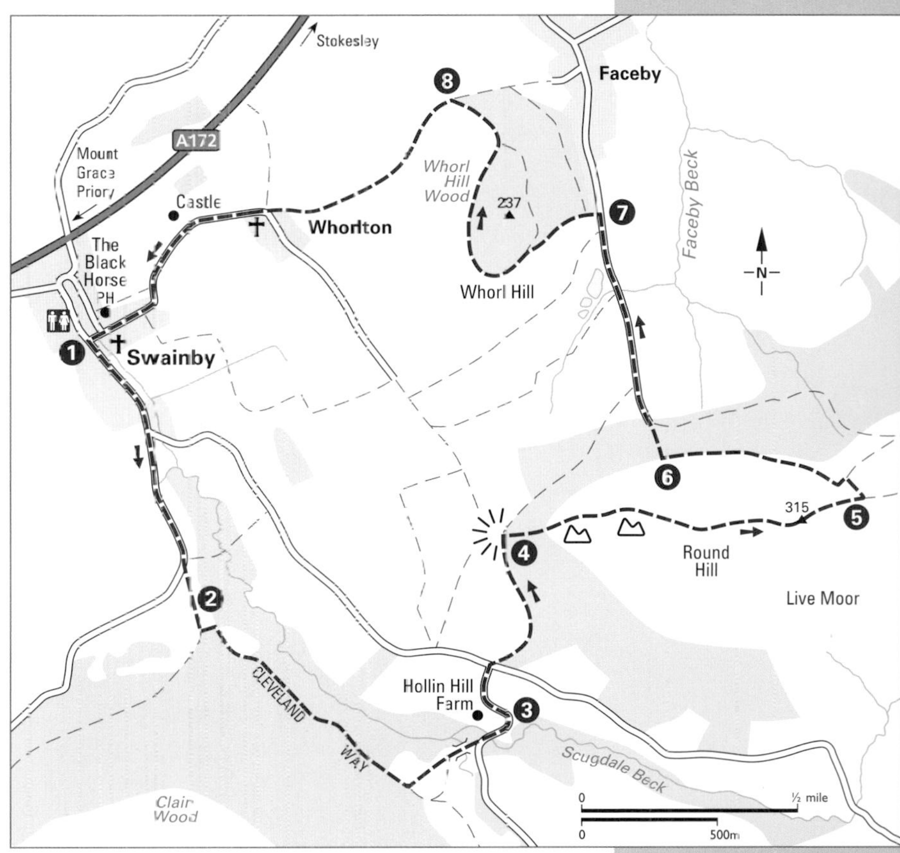

1 With the church on your left, walk down the village street to the right of the stream. Continue walking past a sign 'Unsuitable for Buses and Coaches' and go straight ahead uphill. As the road bends around to the right, follow the bridleway sign to Scugdale, walking up the track that lies ahead.

2 Go through a gate and turn left to join the waymarks for the Cleveland Way National Trail. Walk through the woodland, turning left, just after a seat, down to a gate. The footpath goes half-right, towards blue-topped posts and downhill to another gate. Cross the stream on the footbridge to reach a lane, with another footbridge over Scugdale Beck. Turn left.

3 Follow the lane past Hollin Hill Farm to a T-junction with telephone and post boxes. Cross the lane and go through a Cleveland Way signed gate. Walk up the path beside woodland to a gate – there's a view of the valley from this ridge.

4 The path beyond bends right to a stile and goes on to a paved track in the wood. Go straight ahead at a crossing track to another gate, and continue to follow the paved path up to the heather moorland, passing a cairn. After the first summit, the path descends beyond a large and a small cairn into a dip. Just before the paved path ends, look out for a narrow path off to the left, down through the heather.

5 After about 100yds (91m) you will reach a concrete post. Bear left and follow the narrow path down the gully to a fence beside a wood. Turn left to a signpost. Carry on walking straight ahead, eventually going over a spoil heap to reach a gate on your right.

6 Through the gate, go straight down the hill through woodland. At the bottom, bear right, then left to cross a stile by a gate and go down the lane. Just after the first house on the left, take a footpath over two stiles.

7 Walk up through the woodland onto a grassy track. Turn left, and left again at another track. At a T-junction, turn left again and follow the track downhill to a stile. Turn left to go over another stile. Go straight ahead along the signed track.

WHAT TO LOOK OUT FOR

From the highest part of the walk, which takes you up onto the northern edge of the North York Moors plateau, you are rewarded with extensive northward views over the vast industrial complexes surrounding Middlesbrough. It was the production of iron from the hills that really put Middlesbrough on the map; it had a population of just 40 in 1829, 7,600 in 1851, when the first blast furnace opened, and 20,000 nine years later. Prime Minister Gladstone called the town 'an infant Hercules'. Beyond the River Tees, the area of Seal Sands is home to an oil refinery and chemical works. It is the terminal of the 220-mile (354 km) pipeline bringing oil and gas from the Ekofisk field in the North Sea. If you are on the hills at dawn or dusk, you may see the flare stacks glowing on the skyline.

8 Go over a stile beside a gate and carry on along the hillside. Over a stile with steps beyond, turn left at the bottom and follow the field-edge. Go through a gateway beside a paddock to another gateway onto a metalled lane. Follow the lane back to Swainby village.

Distance 6 miles (9.7km)

Minimum time 3hrs

Ascent/gradient 1,098ft (335m) ▲▲▲

Level of difficulty ●●●

Paths Tracks and moorland paths, lots of bracken, 6 stiles

Landscape Farmland and moorland, dotted with some woodland

Suggested map OS Explorer OL 26 North York Moors – Western

Start/finish Grid reference: NZ 477020

Dog friendliness On short lead on moorland

Parking Roadside parking in Swainby village

Public toilets In Swainby village

1376 In England, the heir to the throne, the Black Prince, dies a year before his father, Edward III.

1377 After a reign of half a century, Edward III dies. His grandson becomes Richard II.

1377 French ships attack and burn Rye and Hastings, in southern England.

1378 Henry Yevele, master mason, begins rebuilding the nave of Westminster Abbey.

1380 Preacher and lay reformer John Wycliffe and his followers begin translating the Bible into English.

1381 The introduction of a poll tax to supplement government funds leads to the Peasants Revolt. The young king agrees to the peasants' demands, but withdraws his promises when the revolt is over.

1382 Geoffrey Chaucer writes *Parliament of Fowls.*

1390 Robert III succeeds to the Scottish throne. He dies in 1406. His son James I, imprisoned by the English, is prevented from returning to Scotland.

Beautiful Bodiam

A Sussex ramble leads to a handsome fortified manor house built to defend the county against French raiders

Right and below: *Shields high on a wall, a narrow arrow slit, a portcullis and the castle seen across the moat from the southeast, showing one of the four-storey 60ft (18m) circular corner towers, and to the left the postern tower in the centre of the two-storey south wall*

No medieval lord was allowed to build a castle or even put a single battlement on his manor house without obtaining a formal licence to crenellate from the king. In 1385 the ill-fated King Richard II granted Bodiam manor's owner, Sir Edward Dalyngrigge, such a licence. French and Spanish raids had recently devastated Rye and Winchelsea; Sir Edward's case was further strengthened by his claim that Bodiam could defend the Rother Valley from the ravages of the French. Indeed the river was then fully navigable up to Bodiam Bridge for quite large vessels.

Heavily Defended

The castle was completed quickly. Rectangular in layout, it possessed four corner towers 60ft (18m) tall and a two-storey defensive wall set with further towers and gatehouses in the centre of each side. When Sir Edward died in 1295 the castle was complete, set within elaborate water defences. The moat – or rather a very large lake some 500ft (152m) by 350ft (107m) fed by water diverted from the Rother – is now a vital element in its modern picturesque appearance.

The original defences comprised three drawbridges leading to the main entrance across the moat and two defending the now vanished postern or rear entrance. There were 'arrow slits' designed for small cannon. In Tudor times the complex and heavily defended drawbridges and islands were replaced with a straight causeway. Within the castle there were 33 fireplaces and 28 lavatories or 'privies', the latter discharging directly into the moat, and generously sized windows to domestic apartments.

The castle interior was gutted after a siege by Parliamentary forces in 1643 during the English Civil War, but the outer walls survived more or less intact. The building was taken in hand in 1919 by Lord Curzon, a former Viceroy of India, who later passed it to the National Trust.

Walk 40 A picturesque lakeside fortress

Enjoy a visit to Sir Edward Dalyngrigge's beautiful castle set within water defences

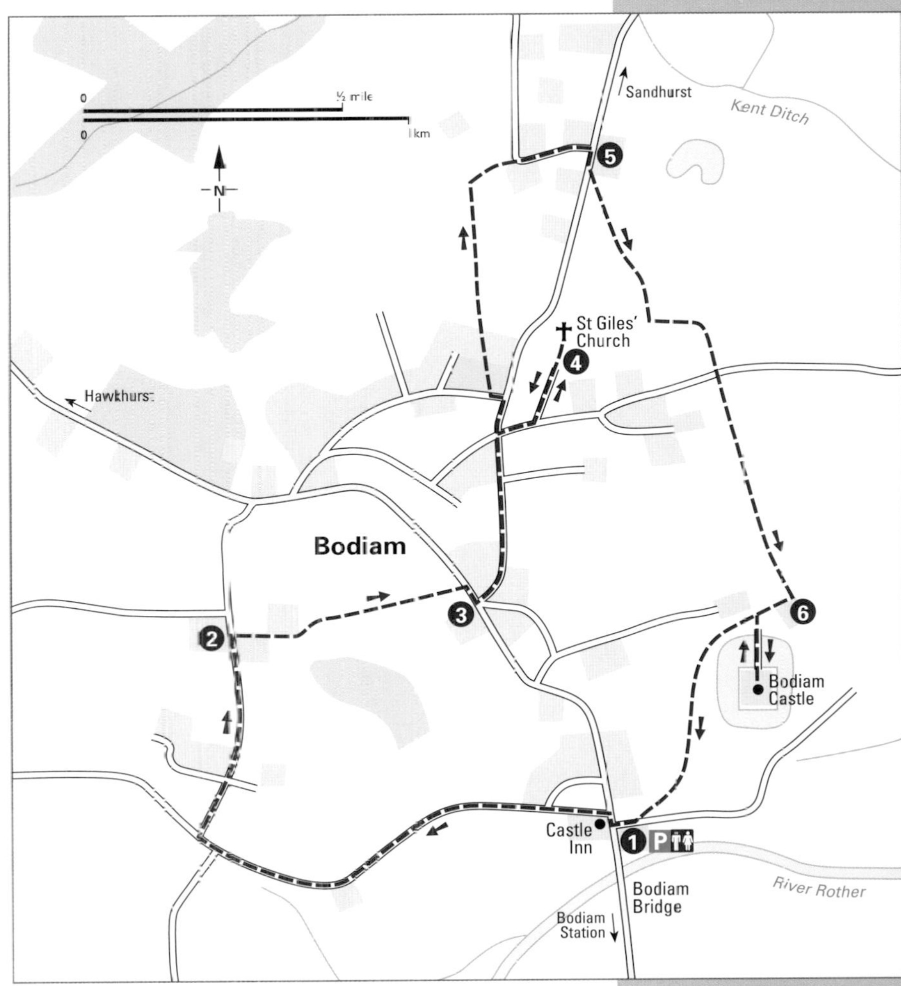

1 Leave the car park and turn right, then left by the Castle Inn to walk left of the small village green along a lane marked 'Private Road', with views south towards Bodiam station on the Kent and East Sussex Railway, if lucky with a steam-hauled train simmering gently. Continue past the Old Cricket Pavilion, now a cottage. At a track T-junction you turn right uphill, the lane climbing to pass well to the right of some converted oasthouses.

2 At the crest and opposite a large modern farm building go right, then to a hand gate between two pairs of five-barred field gates. Descend to the left of cottages to a guidepost. Skirt a red-brick farm building, passing a great number of dachshunds in the kennel runs, and then head left towards a stile. Over the stile go right alongside a hedge and over a stile onto the road.

3 Cross the road to the lane going to the right of the Old School House, formerly a Victorian schoolmaster's house, with the modern school behind it. Walk along the pavement northwards and at the sign for St Giles' Church follow the path and go through the lychgate into the churchyard.

4 Retrace your steps to the road. In Levetts Lane bear right through the woods to the footpath between Nos 35 and 34. Over a stile descend into the valley through pasture. Go through a field gate, then cross to another. Once over this one, head right to another field gate and onto a lane, then continue ahead past Bramble Cottage to a road junction.

5 At the lane turn right and shortly bear half-left into a field to climb towards an oak tree ahead. Climb over a stile, then go left and over another stile, shortly bearing right to climb a third stile. Cross a track to a tree gap and to the left of a double field gate continue ahead alongside a post and wire fence, the battlements of Bodiam Castle ahead in its valley. The path descends between vineyards to a stile.

ST GILES' CHURCH

St Giles' pretty parish church, with its sweeping tiled roofs, is well away from Bodiam's village centre, set in a churchyard surrounded by trees and overlooking a deep-cut sunken lane where the road drops into the valley of the Kent Ditch, a minor tributary of the Rother. The church mostly dates to the 14th century, although the darker, lower parts of the oblong tower may be 12th century.

6 Once you have climbed across the stile you are in the grounds of Bodiam Castle. Follow the path down in order to pay a visit to Sir Edward Dalyngrigge's castle, then afterwards skirt to the right of the beautiful building as you return to the car park.

Distance 2.5 miles (4km)

Minimum time 1hr 30min

Gradient 130ft (40m) ▲▲▲

Level of difficulty ●●●

Paths A stretch of road, lanes and field paths, 6 stiles

Landscape River valley and gentle hills

Suggested map OS Explorer 136 High Weald

Start/finish Grid reference: TQ 784253

Dog friendliness On a lead by Knowle Hill Kennels (horses in the fields), and northwest of Bodiam church where there are sheep

Parking National Trust car park at Bodiam Castle (free for NT members)

Public toilets Bodiam Castle car park

1300–1485

1387 Geoffrey Chaucer begins his poetic masterpiece *The Canterbury Tales.*

1399 While Richard II is in Ireland, his cousin, Henry Bolingbroke, lays claim to the throne. On his return, Richard is deposed by Bolingbroke.

1400 Death of Chaucer.

1401–15 Owain Glyndwr, a descendant of the last independent Prince of Wales, leads the campaign for a return to Welsh autonomy.

1404 The first Welsh parliament meets at Machynlleth and the second parliament meets a year later at Harlech Castle, where Owain is crowned Prince of Wales.

A Canterbury Trail

An atmospheric walk leads through streets that have attracted pilgrims for centuries

As you walk through the streets of Canterbury, you cannot help but be aware that you are following in the footsteps of millions of pilgrims. They have been drawn to Canterbury Cathedral every year since 1170, when Thomas Becket was murdered at the cathedral, and have included some notable historic figures. Yet, out of all these people, the most famous pilgrims of all are fictional – they are the characters created by Geoffrey Chaucer in his epic poem *The Canterbury Tales* (1387): 'And specially from every shires ende, Of Engelond to Caunterbury they wende'.

Soldier, Roving Ambassador

Chaucer is acknowledged as the father of English literature, but writing was not his main occupation. Born in *c.*1340-42, while the Hundred Years War (1337–1453) was raging between England and France, he joined the army in 1359 after spending some years working in the royal household. He was taken prisoner in France, but released after the English paid a ransom for him. Chaucer then became a roving ambassador, travelling throughout Europe on diplomatic missions. He could read French, Latin and Italian and when he travelled he took the opportunity to study foreign literature, which he put to good use in his own works. Back in England, he took on official posts including customs controller of furs, skins and hides, and Knight of the Shire for Kent. He also found time to write several long poems and translate many works of prose.

Lively Characters

Chaucer wrote *The Canterbury Tales* around 1387 and created a cast of lively, believable characters that tell us a great deal about life in the 14th century. There is the earthy Wife of Bath, who has already had five husbands and seems to have set out on pilgrimage to catch her sixth; the too-worldly Prioress, who puts on affected table manners and speaks French; and the corrupt Friar, who is not bothered about the needy but sells absolution to anyone who can afford it. The poem, in Middle English, is known all over the world. Chaucer is buried in Westminster Abbey.

Above: *A pilgrimage is captured in the cathedral glass*

Below: *Canterbury Cathedral is a magnificent example of Perpendicular Gothic architecture*

Walk 41 City of pilgrims and St Thomas Becket

See where Chaucer's pilgrims and countless faithful flocked to honour an English martyr

1 Go right from Castle Street car park, then right again down Gas Street to pass the castle. At the end turn left on Centenary Walk. Where this finishes go right and walk beside the road. Cross a bridge, turn left, go under another bridge and carry on along the river to the other side of the road.

2 Cross some grassland, go over a bridge and through a children's play area. Walk across the car park and turn left up the road to join the Stour Valley Walk.

3 Go under a bridge and continue to a level crossing. Cross the railway, then stroll up past Whitehall Farm. Walk under the bridge, through a gate and over a stream. The path bends round and the main road is on your left. At a junction turn right along the North Downs Way.

4 Go over a bridge and up a lane. To your left is Golden Hill – from which pilgrims traditionally had their first view of the city. When you come to a track, turn left and follow it round. Go right along Mill Lane as far as the main road. Take the underpass to cross Rheims Way, walk down London Road, then turn right into St Dunstans Street.

5 Walk into Canterbury to the Westgate, turn left along Pound Lane and into St Radigund Street.

6 Continue into Northgate, go left then right down Broad Street. You're now walking around the outside of the city walls. Turn right along Burgate, past a tiny 16th-century building called the Pilgrim's Shop. Soon come to a pedestrianised area that brings you out at the Butter Market and war memorial. On your right is the entrance to the cathedral.

7 Turn left, cross the Parade into St Margaret's Street and turn right down Beer Cart Lane. Turn left into Stour Street and on the right is the city museum, and almost opposite, down Jewry Lane, is Canterbury Wholefoods where you can finish your walk. To return to Castle Street, retrace your steps along Stour Street, turn left along Rosemary Lane and then right.

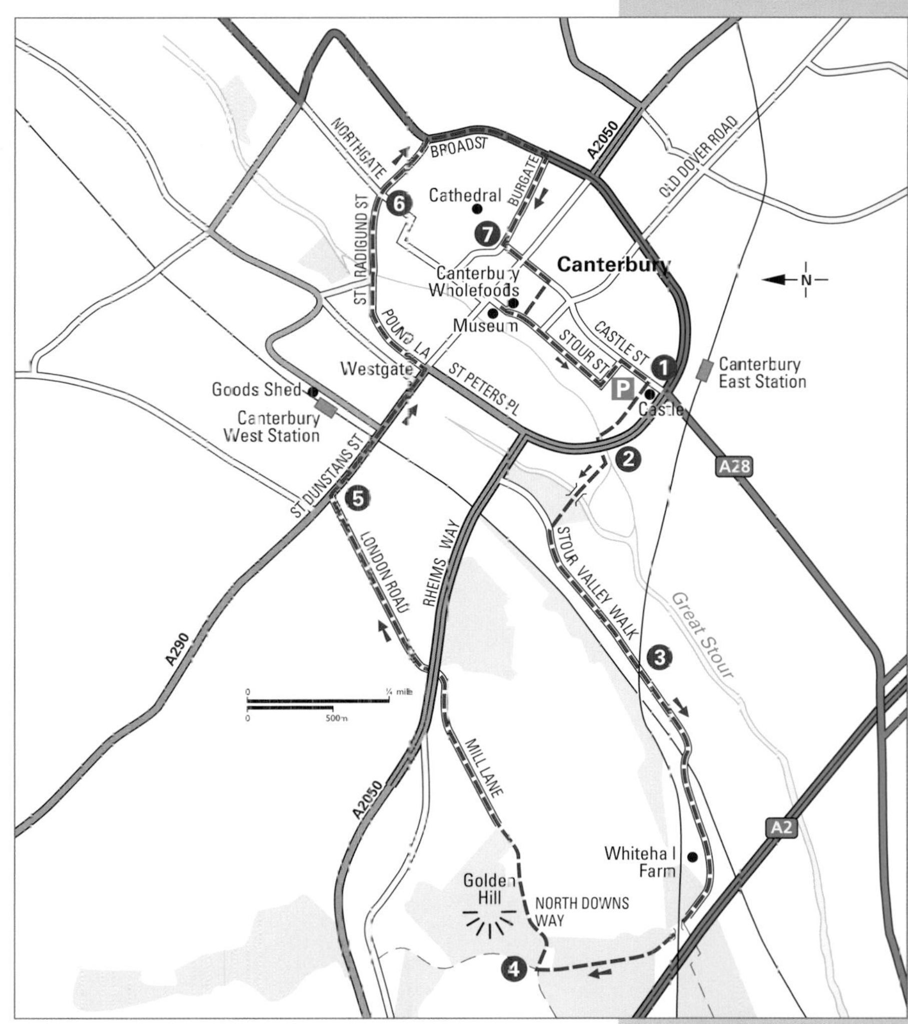

CANTERBURY CATHEDRAL

Canterbury Cathedral was the first cathedral built in England. It was founded in AD 597 by St Augustine. The present structure dates back to 1071. It was a murder that first attracted pilgrims to the cathedral. Thomas Becket, the Archbishop of Canterbury, was killed by men loyal to King Henry II in 1170. The primate had only just returned from exile after a disagreement with Henry over constitutional reform. Following the murder, the King was overcome with guilt and made a pilgrimage to the cathedral, walking barefoot to show his humility. Becket was buried at Canterbury and was credited with so many miracles that he was soon canonised. The city was established as a site of pilgrimage.

Distance 3.75 miles (6km)

Minimum time 1hr 45min

Ascent/gradient 115ft (35m) ▲▲▲

Level of difficulty ●●●

Paths Streets and footpaths

Landscape Cathedral city

Suggested map OS Explorer 150 Canterbury & the Isle of Thanet

Start/finish Grid reference: TR 146574

Dog friendliness Keep on lead in city but can mostly run free on footpaths

Parking Castle Street or one of several car parks in Canterbury

Public toilets Castle Row, off Burgate and off High Street

1405–08 The east window of York Minster is made by John Thornton of Coventry. It is 78 by 31ft (24 by 9m) – England's largest stained glass window.

1413 King Henry IV dies. His son becomes Henry V.

1415 Henry V leads the English army to a famous victory over the French at the Battle of Agincourt.

1420 Henry's marries Catherine of France. Charles VI of France accepts him as heir to the French throne.

1422 Henry V dies. His son, nine months old, inherits the English and French thrones as Henry VI.

1429 Joan of Arc begins to put into action her vision of ridding France of the English.

1431 After being captured in 1430, Joan of Arc is condemned as a witch and burnt at the stake in Rouen.

Otterburn and Percy's Cross

A military-themed walk skirts a famous medieval battlefield

Otterburn's fame rests on the battle fought there in 1388. This period was characterised by unrest along the Scottish border. In 1388 a force of 50,000 Scottish soldiers crossed the border in two divisions: the main group crossed near Carlisle, while a smaller force under the earls of Douglas, Moray and Dunbar, attacked through Northumberland.

Having reached Durham, the eastern division, laden with plunder, returned north. At Newcastle they engaged in skirmishes with a force led by the Earl of Northumberland's son, Sir Henry Percy, nicknamed 'Hotspur' because of his lightning raids against the Scots. Douglas captured Hotspur's pennant and threatened to raise it on his own castle. To avenge this insult, Hotspur pursued Douglas northwards. He caught up with him at Otterburn.

The Battle of Chevy Chase

Heavily outnumbering the Scots, Percy attacked on the moonlit night of 19 August. During the battle Douglas was mortally wounded, but the Scots fought so well that Percy was captured and held to ransom. An estimated 100 Scots were killed compared with more than 1,000 English.

Otterburn became known as 'the battle won by a dead man' because Douglas died before its end; this great encounter inspired the ballad 'Chevy Chase', one of the earliest poems in the English language. Subsequently Harry Hotspur, his father and his brother helped depose Richard II and replace him with Henry IV. Hotspur later turned against the King, and died at the Battle of Shrewsbury in 1403. He is also a notable character in Shakespeare's history plays *Richard II* and *Henry IV Part One.*

Above right: *The Battle of Otterburn was described in Jean Froissart's* Chronicles

Below: *Peaceful moorland stands where a battle once raged*

Walk 42 Scene of 'the battle won by a dead man'

Wander where Sir Henry Percy – 'Hotspur' of Shakespearian fame – was defeated by Scots

1 From the car park, walk through Otterburn. About 100yds (91m) after passing the Church of St John the Evangelist, turn right onto the road to Otterburn Hall. At the top of the incline, go onto the public bridleway on the left, past farm buildings and into a field. Follow the bridleway alongside the wall and through a gate into the next field. Continue, now with the wall, which gives way to a wire fence, on your right.

2 Go through the next gate and, keeping in the same direction, cross the field to a gate through the opposite wall. Go through the gate and across marshy ground past a small plantation, now mostly cut down, to a junction with a metalled road. Follow this to the right, across a cattle grid and around the bend to the left, up a gentle incline.

3 About 100yds (91m) after the bend, follow a grassy track across the hillside to the right, past a sheep pen. This leads to a gate, beyond which is a military warning notice. Go through the gate and continue across moorland, gently downhill. The ground is boggy and the track indefinite in places, but it leads to a better track, which follows a fence on your right to join a metalled road at Hopefoot farm.

4 Follow the road to the right, crossing a bridge over the stream, then go through woods, to join the old main access road to the army camp at Hopefoot Cottages. Turn right and follow the road past Doe Crag cottages and across a bridge to the entrance to Otterburn Hall. Go through the gate opposite this onto a footpath, signposted to Otterburn and leading across a field.

5 Follow the track, passing a sports centre on your right. At a bend in the wire fence, the track forks. Follow the left fork downhill, across two small footbridges, then go through a kissing gate and carry on along the river bank. The track may be muddy and overgrown at times. After crossing a stile, the track brings you into Otterburn, just opposite the Percy Arms. Turn left and return to the car park.

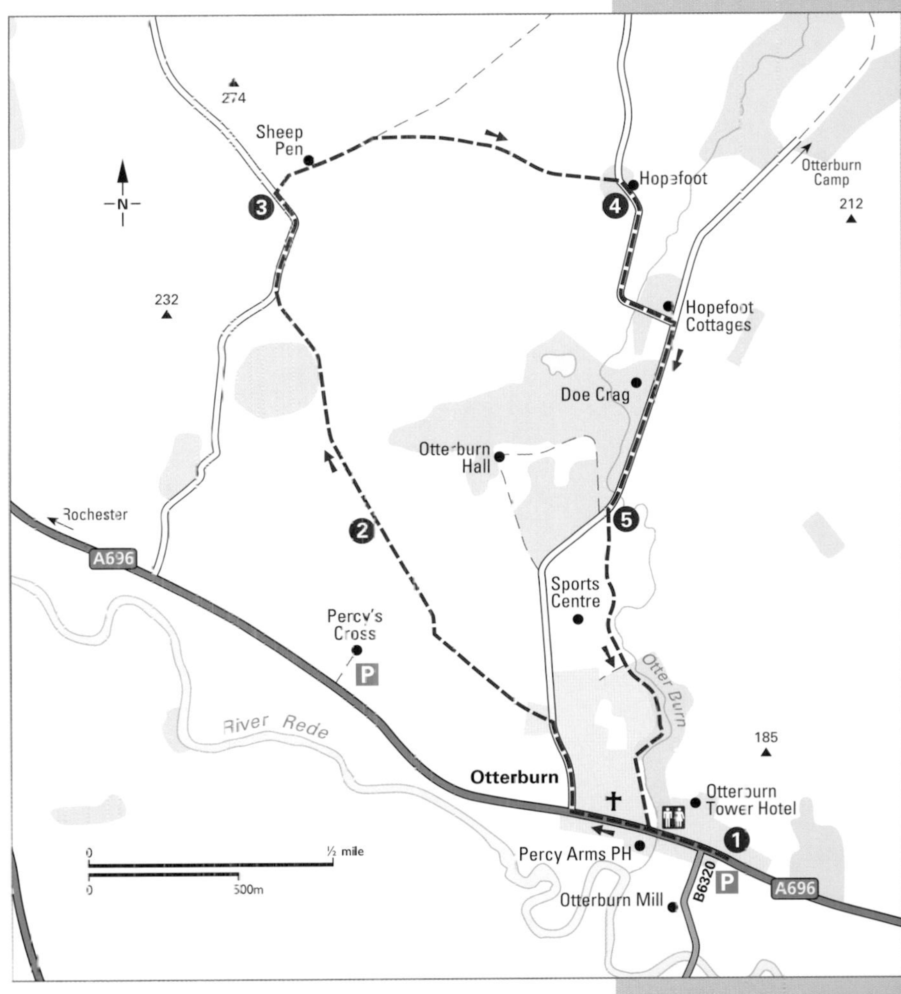

WHAT TO LOOK OUT FOR

The site of the Battle of Otterburn is not known for certain, but it is thought to be somewhere near the second field you cross after leaving the village between Points 1 and 2. The remains of Percy's Cross, which commemorates the battle, can be seen in the small conifer wood at the bottom of this field, to your left, where the field adjoins the A696. There is a car park in the wood, marked on the map.

Five miles (8km) north of Otterburn in the village of Rochester is Brigantium, a reconstruction by archaeologists of many of the Stone Age, Iron Age and Romano-British remains to be found in Northumberland. Just above the site of Brigantium is the Roman fort of Bremenium.

Distance 4.5 miles (7.2km)

Minimum time 2hrs

Ascent/gradient 300ft (91m) ▲▲▲

Level of difficulty ●●●

Paths Bridleway, moorland track and metalled road, 1 stile

Landscape Open moorland with extensive views

Suggested map OS Explorer OL42 Kielder Water & Forest

Start/finish Grid reference: NY 889929

Dog friendliness Keep on lead on roads and near sheep

Parking Roadside car park at eastern end of Otterburn village

Public toilets Beside bridge in Otterburn

1437 The Scottish king, James I, whose zeal for reform makes him many enemies among the Highland lords, is assassinated. His son becomes James II.

1441 Henry VI founds King's College, Cambridge.

1445 At Titchfield Abbey, Hampshire, Henry VI weds Margaret of Anjou.

1449 The French recapture Normandy.

1450 Former soldier Jack Cade leads a revolt against Henry VI among Kentish peasants. Rebels reach Blackheath and the King retreats, but the rebellion disperses. Cade is later killed near Lewes.

1450 Glasgow University is established.

1453 The Hundred Year War ends, leaving the French victorious. England has lost all her French lands except Calais.

On the Hill of the Graves

An upland walk leads past the scene of a great victory for Owain Glyndwr

***Top right:** Red kites have a wingspan up to 76in (195cm)*

***Above:** Nant-y-moch was dammed in 1964 to generate hydroelectric power*

Pumlumon Fawr is one of the three major mountains of Wales, along with Snowdon and Cadair Idris. This noble peak commands views across Wales. From its summit there is a memorable vista: to the west, Nant-y-moch slips away into brown hills and inky forests, leading the eye to the thin blue line of Cardigan Bay; in the south, the angular ridges of the Brecon Beacons, Black Mountains and Mynydd Ddu fill the view, while to the north Cadair Idris reigns.

Bryn y Beddau and the Battle of Nant Hyddgant

Early on in this walk you pass beneath the rocks of Bryn y Beddau, a rather unremarkable piece of quarried moorland. But the name means 'hill of the graves', and therein lies a stirring tale. In 1401 the troops of Owain Glyndwr met those supporting the English king, Henry IV, on the northern slopes of Pumlumon. Glyndwr had only 400 men, the English had 1,500; the Welsh troops were hemmed in on all sides. The scene was set for the famous Battle of Nant Hyddgant. The Welshmen realised they would have to fight like fury or die. Many did both. They lost 200 fighters but in the process a famous victory was theirs. The battle gained Glyndwr a considerable following among his countrymen – one which would sweep him to power and help him to the title of Prince of Wales. The dead from the battle were buried here at Bryn y Beddau.

On the return part of the circuit you'll be looking downstream and towards the Hyddgen Valley. Desolate and uninhabited these days, it is the site of a tragic tale of a shepherd who was caught in a blizzard. His wife, alarmed that his horse returned alone, took a lamp and went in search of him. Eventually she found him unconscious and tried to drag him back home, but sadly both died on that ferocious night. It is said that at the end of each day a light can be seen, wavering, as it travels from the valley to the spot where the shepherd fell.

Walk 43 Where Owain Glyndwr's Welsh warriors triumphed against the odds

View the mountain battlefield on which King Henry IV's troops were humbled

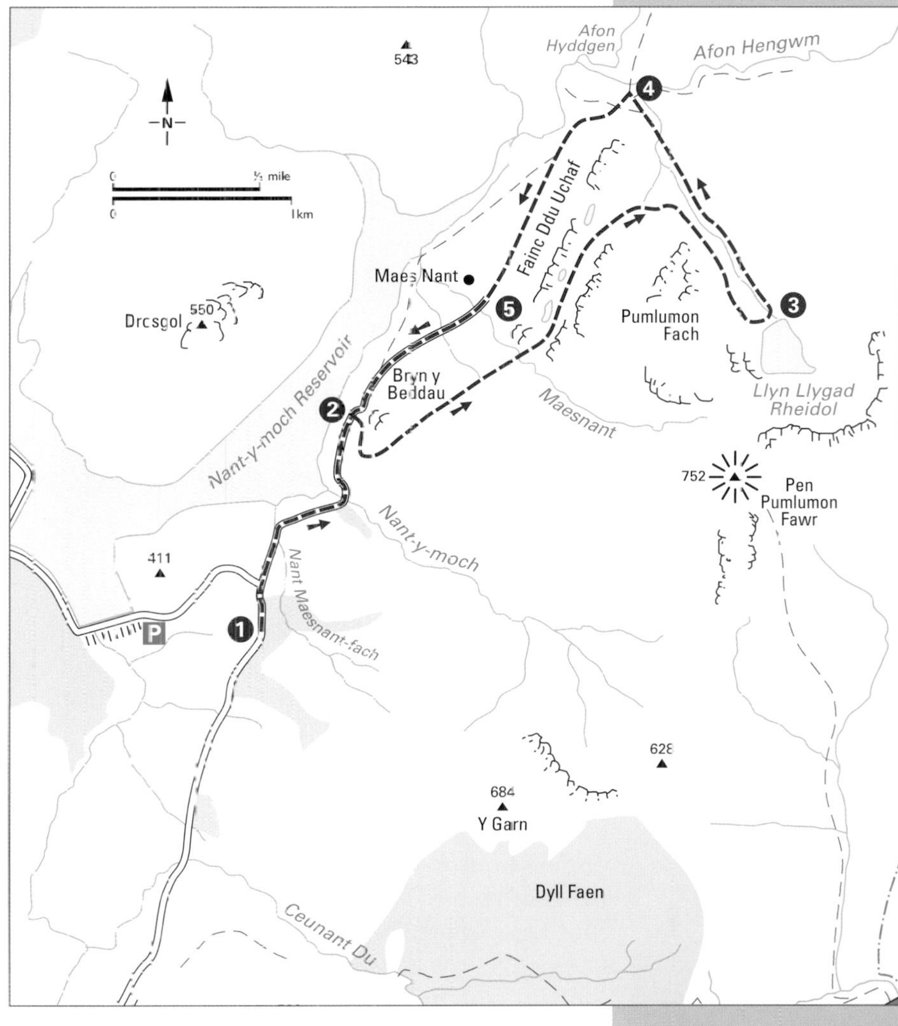

1 From the car parking spaces beneath the woods east of the Nant-y-moch dam (near the spot height 392m on OS Explorer maps) walk north along the road and take the right-hand fork. The road descends to cross the streams of Nant Maesnant-fach and Nant-y-moch before traversing rough moorland along the east shores of Nant-y-moch Reservoir. The reservoir, stocked with native brown trout, is popular with anglers during the season.

2 Beneath the quarried rocks of Bryn y Beddau, a rubble track on the right-hand side of the road doubles back up the hillside then swings round to the left. The steep sides of Pumlumon now soar away to the skyline on your right, with the little stream of Maesnant tumbling down them. Follow the track which climbs further, then levels out to pass some shallow lakes, which lie above the rocks of Fainc Ddu Uchaf. Now high above the bare valleys of the Hyddgen and Hengwm, the track swings south beneath the crags of Pumlumon Fach to arrive at Llyn Llygad Rheidol's dam.

3 To get to the footpath along the other side you'll have to ford the stream a short way downhill – take care if the stream is in spate. The path, which runs parallel to the eastern banks of the stream, is sketchy in places, especially where you ford a side stream. It descends peaty terrain where mosses and moor grasses proliferate.

4 When you reach a small stand of conifers in the Hengwm Valley, turn left to follow an old cart track which fords the Afon Rheidol, close to its confluence with the Afon Hengwm. The track heads west and soon the Hengwm Valley meets that of the Afon Hyddgen. The track swings to the southwest and passes between the squat cliffs of Fainc Ddu Uchaf and the western shores of Nant-y-moch Reservoir.

5 Go through the gate above the outdoor pursuits centre at Maes Nant and continue along the tarmac lane, joining in the outward route. Return to the car park and the start of the walk.

WHAT TO LOOK OUT FOR

The red kite can often be seen flying here, with its wide angled wings, distinctive reddish colouring and forked tail. Red kites had become nearly extinct with only a few breeding pairs here in Central Wales, but these days are more widespread. They have been imported from Spain to make up the numbers, and feeding centres have been set up to encourage the bird to stay in the area. At the Bwlch Nant-yr-Arian Forestry Centre (just off the A44, west of Ponterwyd) you can watch the red kites feeding every day at 3pm (2pm winter). The centre is open 10am–5pm in summer and 10am–dusk in winter.

Distance 5.5 miles (8.8km)

Minimum time 3hrs

Ascent/gradient 623ft (190m) ▲▲▲

Level of difficulty ●●●

Paths Good track up, sketchy return path, streams to ford

Landscape Wild moorland

Suggested map OS Explorer 213 Aberystwyth & Cwm Rheidol

Start/finish Grid reference: SN 752861

Dog friendliness Dogs are okay off lead outside summer months when sheep will be in lowland fields

Parking Off-road parking – room for several cars by woods at start of walk, car park by Nant-y-moch dam

Public toilets Nearest at Ponterwyd

1455 The Wars of the Roses begin as the Protector, Richard, Duke of York, is dismissed and Henry VI takes over rule of the government. Yorkists defeat the royal army at the Battle of St Albans.

1461 Edward, Duke of York, deposes Henry and is crowned king; he is deposed briefly in 1470 but restored in 1471 and reigns until his death in 1483.

1471 Henry VI is murdered.

1474–5 William Caxton prints the first book in English, *The Recuyell of the Historyes of Troy.*

1483 Edward V succeeds to the throne but is declared illegitimate. He and his brother vanish without trace and Richard, Duke of York, becomes Richard III.

1483 Martin Luther is born in Germany. He becomes founder of the Reformation, and dedicates his life to establishing a religious doctrine that is not based on corruption and dogma.

1483–85 Richard III reigns as king. In 1485 he is defeated at the Battle of Bosworth Field by Henry Tudor, who founds the Tudor dynasty.

The Battle of Bloreheath

A gentle walk leads around one of the bloodiest battlegrounds on English soil

Below: *The bloody Wars of the Roses lasted for 30 years*

Bottom: *The peaceful scene at Bloreheath today*

At Bloreheath, just to the west of the village of Loggerheads, history was made. It was there that one of the early battles of the Wars of the Roses was fought, in 1459. The Wars of the Roses were a conflict between the House of Lancaster, led by King Henry VI, and the House of York, led by Richard, Duke of York. (The wars took their name from the badges worn by adherents of the two sides: a white rose for York and a red rose for Lancaster.) They lasted 30 years, 1455–85.

Henry was a weak ruler, who periodically fell into madness and was unable to impose his authority on feuding barons; Richard had a claim to the throne through his uncle Edmund Mortimer, Earl of March, who had been excluded from the succession when Henry IV took the crown in 1399. Richard was twice Protector and Defender of the Kingdom, in 1454-55 and again in 1455-56, but was both times deprived of the position by the royal camp. Richard's allies were scattered all over England, and to consolidate his forces he ordered Neville, Earl of Salisbury, to march from his castle in Yorkshire to his own pile in Ludlow, about 40 miles (64km) south of Bloreheath. Aware of this march, Henry's queen consort, Margaret, directed James Touchet, Lord Audley, to intercept Salisbury.

Audley knew that the road to Ludlow would take Salisbury through a defile near Bloreheath, and assembled 10,000 soldiers on the heath overlooking the road. On Sunday 23 September the two sides opposed each other across the valley, with Salisbury on the slopes where Audley's Cross now stands and Audley on the other side. Salisbury had nothing in the way of firearms, and was heavily outnumbered. The scene was apparently set for a rout.

Reckless Charge

However, Salisbury had other ideas. He sensed that Audley might be tempted into a cavalry charge to impress Queen Margaret, so he withdrew his pikemen from the front – leaving an opening for an advance. Audley ordered his cavalry down the hill, but found he had underestimated the difficulty of ascending the steep, muddy slope of the brook at the bottom. Exposed and vulnerable, the horses were no match for Salisbury's archers who had been waiting in the wings. The result was unequivocal: twice Audley's forces charged and twice they were mown down. A third assault involved more than 4,000 infantry.

Audley himself was slain in the hand-to-hand fighting that ensued, and today Audley's Cross marks the spot at which he died. The battle lasted all day. By nightfall, more than 2,000 Lancastrians lay dead on the blood-soaked battlefield, while Yorkist casualties were just 56. But ultimately it was to no avail; after 30 years of war the Lancastrians kept the throne.

Walk 44 Early victory for the white over the red rose

Have a good look at one of the few medieval battlefields to survive largely unchanged

1 Head along the A53 in the direction of Market Drayton and take the first left along Kestrel Drive. Just after the Robins head left along the gravel track down the back of some houses. When you reach the end of a cul-de-sac, go left on a wide woodland track. After skirting a large, deep hollow turn right. At a clearing bear left past an iron bar across a wide track and, at the fork, go right, past the football pitch, then turn left uphill to reach a major path junction.

2 Take the fourth path on your left and where this finally runs out, follow a narrow path through the undergrowth to reach a wide gravel track. Turn right through the gate and continue for 0.5 mile (800m), until the main track goes right.

3 Head over a stile and along the footpath with a hedge to your right-hand side. At the bottom of the field bear right towards the right-hand corner of the bank of trees. Go through a gate here and head up towards Knowleswood farm (which is now derelict) and another gate.

4 Continue straight ahead and, at the bottom of the field, go right over a stile and drop down through a small dip. At the bottom of the dip go through a gate and head right along a concrete track. At a fork go left to the Nook Farm and, after a mile (1.6km) reach Home Farm. Turn right here along Flash Lane and up the gentle hill to Blore Farm. When you get to a junction keep going straight and, after 200yds (183m), head left through a hedge over a stile. Follow this hedge right to a stile in the right-hand corner of the field. This stile probably provides the best vantage point from which to view the main battlefield, now private farmland, which was centred on the shallow valley to your left.

5 Continue to the bottom right-hand corner of the next field before bearing diagonally right across another field to the right-hand end of a bank of trees. Cross the small stile and follow the faint track straight across the middle of the next field to another stile.

6 Follow the path through a young plantation to a fence ahead and cross a stile. Keep following the faint track alongside a wood to your right and, when you come to a clearing, head diagonally across the field to the left-hand end of the trees. At the corner of this field, cross a stile and then a footbridge to reach a wide track, which you follow right and then up the hill as far as a large, lone oak at the top. Turn left here in order to cross a stile and walk back onto the A53.

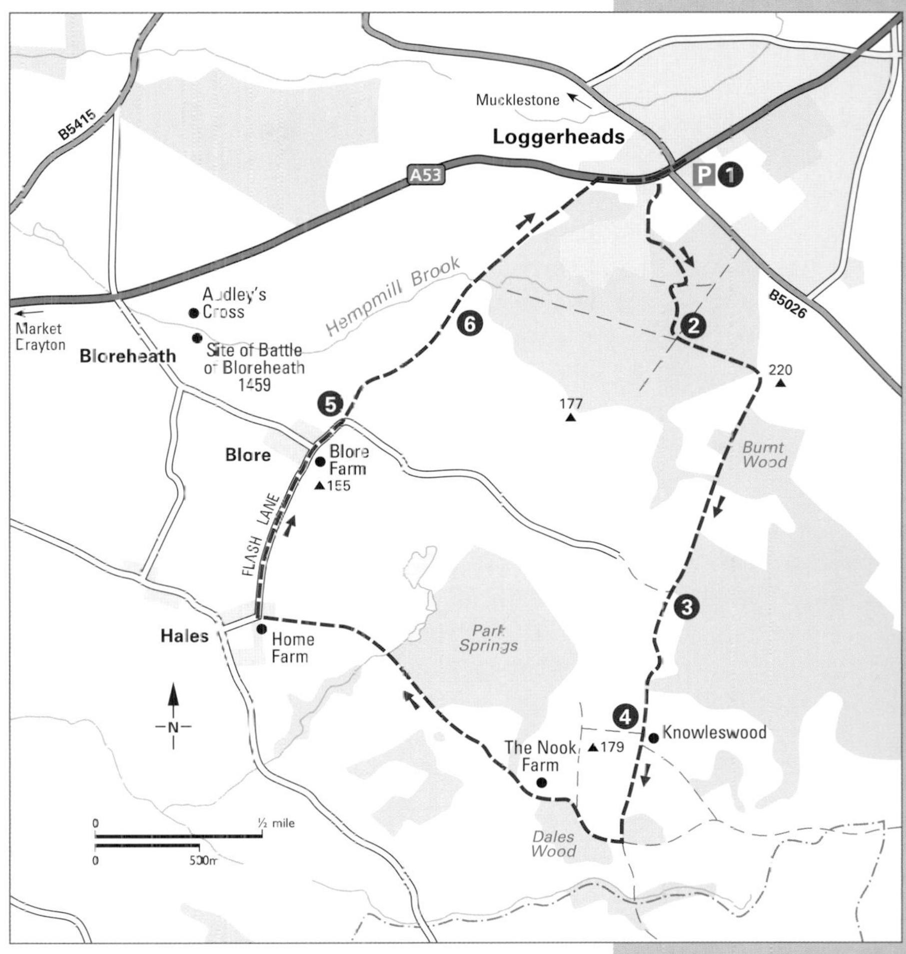

WHAT TO LOOK OUT FOR

It is difficult to walk across the battlefield today, but the surrounding landscape still includes many of the features that were present in 1459. Most obvious is Hempmill Brook, across which Audley's army charged. The site is one of only a handful of medieval battlefields to have escaped modern development. It is said that Queen Margaret watched the defeat of the Lancastrian forces from the church tower at Mucklestone. Fearing for her safety, she made plans for her escape, instructing the local blacksmith, William Skelhorn, to put the shoes on her horse the wrong way round, to disguise her escape. Unfortunately for Skelhorn, the Queen had him executed so that he couldn't reveal the deception. The anvil supposedly used by Skelhorn stands in front of St Mary's, Mucklestone.

In Loggerheads look out for the 'Loggerheads' pub, formerly known as the 'Three Loggerheads', whose sign featured two fools' heads and a third, that of an onlooker. The word loggerhead, meaning 'blockhead' or 'fool', is believed to derive from the word 'logger' which was used colloquially to refer to a block of wood for hobbling horses. The village of Loggerheads itself takes its name from the pub.

Distance 5.5 miles (8.8km)

Minimum time 2hrs

Ascent/gradient 240ft (73m) ▲▲▲

Level of difficulty ●●●

Paths Gravel tracks, roads and grass trails, 11 stiles

Landscape Woodland and farmland

Suggested map OS Explorer 243 Market Drayton

Start/finish Grid reference: SJ 738359

Dog friendliness Keep on lead near livestock

Parking Ample parking in Loggerheads village

Public toilets None on route

Warwick and its 'Kingmaker'

An easy walk visits one of England's most celebrated castles

Warwick Castle sits imperiously above the River Avon near the centre of the town. It is the ancestral home of the Earls of Warwick. Richard Beauchamp, 13th Earl (1382–1439), served three kings (Henry IV, Henry V and Henry VI) and was present at the trial and execution of Joan of Arc in 1431, before dying in Rouen in 1439. Richard Neville, 16th Earl (1428–71), played a key role in the deposition of two kings – Henry VI and Edward IV – and so gained the name 'Warwick the kingmaker'.

The original castle was a timber motte and bailey fortification built in 1068 by William the Conqueror. A stone castle was built on the site in *c.*1260, and then key elements were added in the 14th century: the imposing Caesar's Tower (147ft/45m high) in *c.*1350 and Guy's Tower (128ft/39m high) in *c.*1395. Caesar's tower is notable for its double parapet and a dark basement dungeon: according to local accounts, it is known also as Poitiers Tower, either because prisoners from the 1356 Battle of Poitiers were imprisoned in the dungeon or because profits deriving from ransoms paid by knights captured in the battle paid for the tower's building.

Above: *Richard Beauchamp, 13th Earl, was a Knight of the Order of the Garter*

Below: *An imposing view of Warwick Castle from the River Avon*

A Day in Warwick

No trip to Warwick is complete without a visit to Warwick Castle. You can spend a whole day there: as well as Guy's Tower and Caesar's Tower there are the Gatehouse, the Clock Tower and the Old Bridge over the River Avon – and all are impressive. Inside you can see the tapestry of the gardens of

WHAT TO LOOK OUT FOR

Tear yourself away from the castle to continue the walk through the county town of 'Shakespeare Country'. The town displays a fascinating blend of Georgian and Tudor architecture. In Castle Street you pass the timbered home of Thomas Oken – now housing a doll museum. Oken (*d.*1573) was a merchant trading in silk and luxury goods and a famous Warwick benefactor. St Mary's Church is up the road opposite. You can climb its great 174ft (53m) tower for a breathtaking view of the town and the surrounding countryside. Inside the church is the 15th-century Beauchamp Chapel where the body of Richard Beauchamp lies. Nearby in St Mary's is the tomb of Ambrose Dudley, Earl of Leicester. Before heading back to the racecourse you'll pass Lord Leycester's Hospital, at the West Gate of Warwick. This was originally the Guild House of St George which became the Almshouse in 1571, founded by Robert Dudley. Now it is probably the most famous medieval building in this fine town.

Versailles, Cromwell's helmet and Queen Anne's travelling trunk. Outside are gardens designed by 'Capability' Brown.

Do walk carefully as you enter the eerie Ghost Tower – for you may not be alone. It was here, in 1628, that the castle's then owner, Sir Fulke Greville, was fatally stabbed by a manservant because he did not bequeath sufficient funds to him in his will.

Entry to the castle is not cheap – the castle is run on commercial lines by the Tussauds Group – but it is reasonable out of high season. It's open 10am–6pm April to September, 10am–5pm October to March.

Entertainment Medieval Style

For the nobility, at least, medieval life had many diversions. As well as tournaments, jousting, single combat contests and hunting parties, there were menageries, with collections of hawks and dogs, bears and lions. Little excuse was needed for a feast: beef, mutton, venison and boar were served, together with fish and game birds, often in rich and spicy sauces. Pastries, sweets and puddings were also popular, all washed down with imported wine. Jesters, jugglers and acrobats provided a floor show to music from the minstrels' gallery and, once the tables had been cleared, it was time to dance.

Walk 45 An earl's stronghold

Investigate one of England's most celebrated castles

1 Walk to the end of the racecourse car park and go left towards the golf clubhouse, the Warwick Golf Centre.

2 Beyond, go right and take the wide green track between the golf course and the driving range. In about 300yds (274m), cross over the racetrack and go through a kissing gate onto a footpath alongside modern housing. Continue ahead and, at the corner of common land, go right through a kissing gate onto a lane and descend to the road. Go left along the pavement beneath the railway bridge, then left opposite St Michael's Road through a gate onto grassland by the Saltisford Canal. Follow this grassy area to the tow path, passing a large narrowboat mooring area, and climb the steps up to the canal bridge and onto the pavement beside a road. Go right, along the pavement, and in 50yds (46m) you will come to a canal bridge over the Grand Union Canal and the busy A425.

3 Cross the road with care. Go left over the canal bridge and, immediately across it, descend to take the tow path into Warwick, about 1.5 miles (2.4km) away, passing by a lock gate with the Cape of Good Hope pub opposite and then going along the back of residential properties. Shortly after passing by a Tesco store and just before reaching the aqueduct over the River Avon, go left down steps to join the 'Waterside Walk', turning right at the stream.

4 Proceed right under the aqueduct and follow the river bank footpath. At Castle Bridge climb steps onto the pavement of the A425 (Banbury) road and cross with care.

5 Stroll onto the bridge for the classic view of Warwick Castle, then turn around and follow the pavement towards Warwick town.

6 In 220yds (201m) go left and meander down picturesque Mill Street for the second classic view of the castle. Return to the main road and go left through the main entrance gate to Warwick Castle grounds. Bear right and leave the grounds via a wall gate into Castle Street, signed 'Exit to Town'. Stroll up Castle Street, passing by Oken's House, until you reach the Tourist Information Centre on the corner of the High Street. Turn left here and walk along the High Street, going beneath the archway of the Lord Leycester Hotel. Go right into Bowling Green Street and, in 50yds (46m), turn left down Friars Street to reach Warwick Racecourse and the St Mary's Area 3 car park.

Distance 5 miles (8km)
Minimum time 2hrs
Ascent/gradient 33ft (10m) ▲
Level of difficulty ●
Paths Canal and riverside paths, street pavements
Landscape Canalside and historic town
Suggested map OS Explorer 221 Coventry & Warwick
Start/finish Grid reference: SP 277647
Dog friendliness Off lead along tow path, otherwise under control
Parking Racecourse car park (St Mary's Area 3 car park, at north end of racecourse)
Public toilets None on route

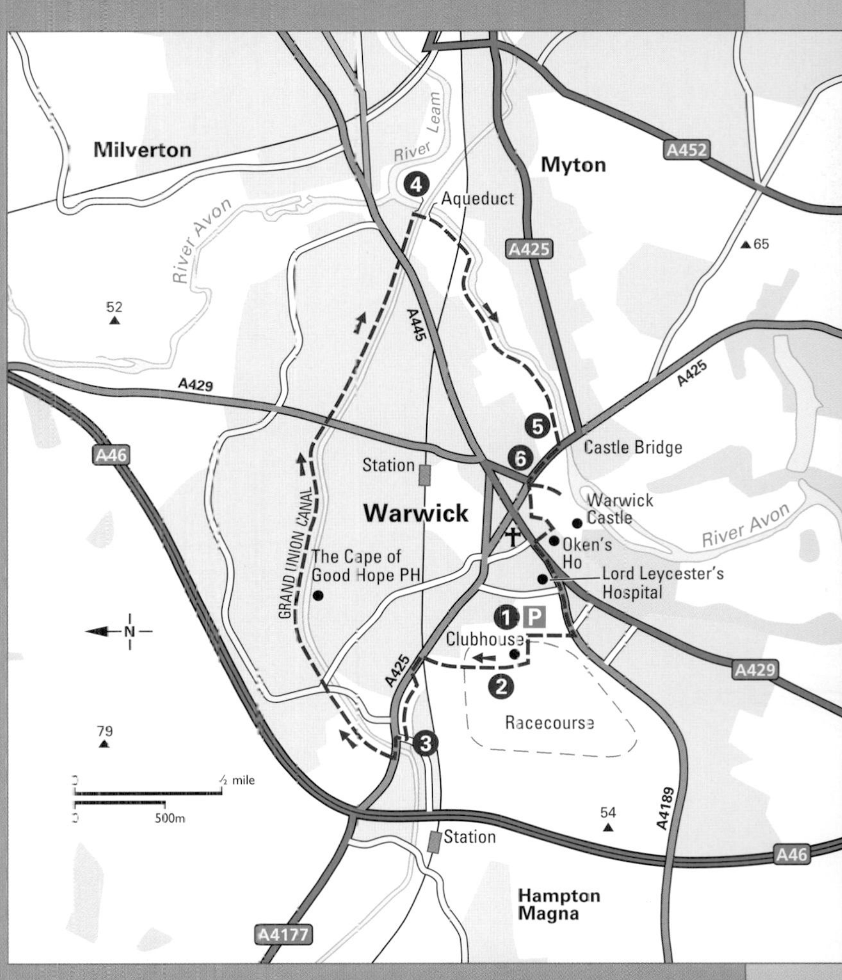

THE TUDORS
1485–1603

BUILDING A DYNASTY

The Tudors reigned for only 118 years, but their dynasty has captured the British imagination more than any other. From the accession of Welshman Henry Tudor as Henry VII in 1485 to the death of the Virgin Queen, Elizabeth I, in 1603, theirs was an era of unforgettable characters and profound social change.

With Henry VII's marriage to Elizabeth of York, the Wars of the Roses were effectively brought to a close. When the King died, his young heir – the sporty, musical, dashing Prince Henry – was welcomed as a bright new star. As King Henry VIII, he made a major impact on the European stage, too: his mentor Cardinal Wolsey arranged a magnificent peace summit with France at the Field of the Cloth of Gold, near Calais; and the King's anti-Lutheran pamphlet earned him the Pope's gratitude and the title 'Defender of the Faith'.

Domestic matters soon cast their shadow over Henry's reign – specifically, the absence of a male heir. Henry had married Catherine of Aragon in 1509, but by 1527, with only a daughter, Mary, surviving, he was seeking a way out. Having failed to gain a papal annulment of the marriage, Henry took direct action, declaring himself Supreme Head of the Church of England and pronouncing his own marriage invalid. In 1533 he married the vivacious Anne Boleyn and within a year she bore him another child: Elizabeth. Three years later Anne was dead, executed on trumped-up treason charges. Henry's third wife, Jane Seymour, died giving birth to his longed-for son, Edward. There followed three more wives, but no more children.

Henry took full advantage of his new role as head of the reformed Church, dissolving and looting hundreds of monasteries. By the end of the 1530s the countryside was littered with the disintegrating shells of religious buildings, and the previously Catholic population found itself abruptly converted to the Protestant cause.

KEY SITES

Bosworth battlefield, Leicestershire: Where Henry Tudor defeated Richard II to found a dynasty.

Compton Wynyates, Warwickshire: Beautiful rose-brick Tudor manor house.

Hailes Abbey, Gloucestershire: Once one of England's grandest Cistercian monasteries.

Sudeley Castle, Gloucestershire: Final resting place of Catherine Parr, Henry VIII's last wife.

Longleat House, Wiltshire: Glorious Elizabethan 'prodigy house' built by Sir John Thynne

Stratford-upon-Avon: Shakespeare's birthplace.

AFTER THE HENRIES

Edward VI was a sickly child of nine when he became king, and reigned for only six years, guided by staunchly Protestant courtiers. The devoutly Catholic Mary married the Spanish king, Philip II and became a ruthless persecutor of Protestants, instigating the infamous 'turn or burn' policy. Mary died in 1558 and her successor, Elizabeth, aimed for a middle course, avoiding religious extremes. She also resisted Parliament's pressure to marry her off to secure the dynasty's future.

The succession was a thorny issue: Mary, Queen of Scots, claimed the English throne as granddaughter of Henry VII, and after her Scottish opponents had forced her to abdicate, fled to England, where, for nearly 20 years, she was moved from place to place, a dangerous figurehead for Elizabeth's enemies. Eventually, a plot was uncovered to snatch the crown for Mary, and she was executed – sparking the wrath of Catholic Spain. When the Spanish Armada, sent to wreak vengeance, was battered by the English and foundered in rough seas, Elizabeth's popularity hit an all-time high.

Elizabeth's long reign was a golden age: music flourished, with composers such as William Byrd and Thomas Tallis making their names; William Shakespeare was a leading light of English drama; Francis Drake and Walter Raleigh typified the spirit of adventure and exploration; and the building and woollen trades boomed. Gloriana, the 'Virgin Queen', would long remain a charismatic symbol of the Tudor age at its best.

***Left:** Magnificent Hampton Court Palace was built by Cardinal Wolsey and given to King Henry VIII*

1485 Henry VII is crowned king and his marriage in 1486 to Elizabeth of York, Edward IV's daughter, unites the houses of Lancaster and York.

1495–98 In Milan, Leonardo da Vinci paints *The Last Supper* in the Sante Maria delle Grazie convent.

1503 Henry VII Chapel, Westminster Abbey, is begun.

1508–12 In the Vatican, Michelangelo paints the Sistine Chapel ceiling.

1509 Henry VIII accedes to the throne. He marries Catherine of Aragon, a daughter of Ferdinand and Isabella of Spain. The future of the Tudor dynasty looks assured.

1513 James IV of Scotland invades England in support of his French allies, but he and many of the Scottish court are killed at the Battle of Flodden Field.

Doing Battle at Bosworth

This country ramble brings history to life on one of England's most famous battlefield sites

The Battle of Bosworth Field, which took place on 22 August 1485, is one of the key events in English history. Not did it only finally bring to an end the long-running Wars of the Roses between the houses of York and Lancaster, but it also signalled the start of a new era, as the Middle Ages gave way to the powerful Tudor dynasty.

The Yorkist Richard III had only been ruler for a couple of years before Henry Tudor landed in Pembrokeshire with a small and rather ragbag force and advanced on the Midlands. The two armies met at Ambion Hill, south of Market Bosworth, with Richard's larger force occupying the higher ground and Henry's scattered below. Nowadays their positions are marked by their standards, which flutter from tall flagpoles. A third standard, located some way to the north, belonged to a faction led by Sir William Stanley, who crucially decided to pitch in on Henry's side at the last moment and, in so doing, tipped the scales by cutting off and surrounding the King. Richard was defeated and Henry Tudor became Henry VII of England.

***Above:** The Tudor rose, painted on a 15th-century ceiling at Haddon Hall, Derbyshire*

***Right:** A memorial on the Bosworth battlefield*

There are interpretative panels all the way along the 1.75-mile (2.8km) Battle Trail, showing the position of the armies and how the fateful day unfurled. The fascinating exhibition at the Heritage Centre (closed January) is supplemented by regular workshops and also re-enactments by local groups throughout the summer months.

The Controversial Monarch

A memorial stone marks the place where Richard was slain, but as the last of the Plantagenets (and the last king of England to die in battle) he has since received something of a bad press from historians and chroniclers, most notably William Shakespeare. The bard's *Richard III* was probably written in 1591: there are few more villainous characters in English literature than Shakespeare's Richard III, who famously declares, 'I can smile, and murder while I smile', but whether the reputation is deserved is doubtful. Although he may have been involved previously in the infamous murder of the Little Princes (Edward IV's sons Edward V and Richard, Duke of York) in the Tower of London, there is scant evidence to suggest that he was any worse as a king than other rulers of the time. Moreover, he seemed to be an able administrator and leader. Today there is a society established to clear Richard's name and they meet every year, around the date of the Battle of Bosworth, at the Church of St James in nearby Sutton Cheney, where the ill-fated king supposedly heard his last Mass before going in to battle.

Walk 46 Fall of an ill-fated king on a Leicestershire field

Follow the Battle Trail and see where English history changed direction on a single day

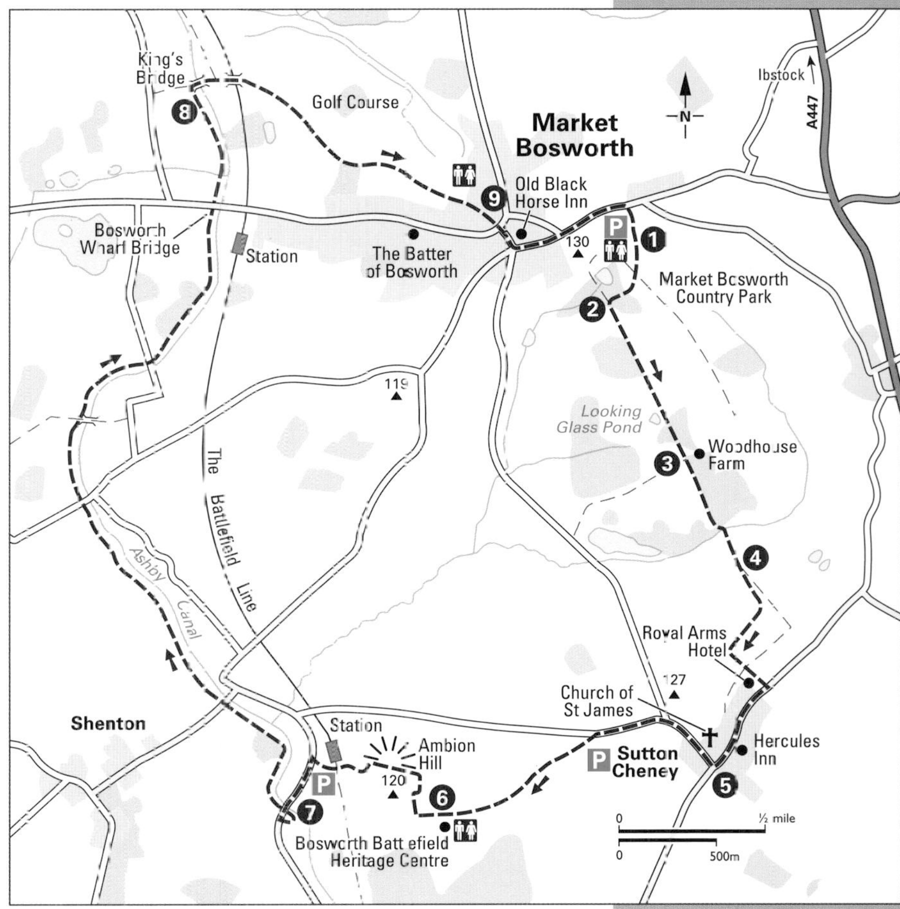

1 Walk down the wide track from the car park to reach the children's playground and adjoining spinney, and continue across the wildflower meadow to the woods beyond. Follow the main gravel path through the trees and then bear left at a fork. Keep a look out for the wide kissing gate on the left.

2 Go through this and follow the path for just under 0.5 mile (800m) along the edge of woodland and past Looking Glass Pond.

3 Go over a stile and on, passing to the right of Woodhouse Farm. The path continues down along the left-hand side of a field, then crosses a stream to climb the right-hand side of the next.

4 As the hedge falls away, the well-walked path heads out across the middle of the field before turning right approaching – but not quite at – the top. The path keeps to the top of the next field, then turns left across another field to reach the car park of the Royal Arms Hotel. Turn right and walk through Sutton Cheney until, just past the church entrance, you take a right turn at the road junction (signposted 'Shenton').

5 Follow the lane as it forks left and in 550yds (503m) turn off left through Cheney Lane car park and follow the clearly marked path across the fields in the direction of the Heritage Centre.

6 Walk past the centre below the car park and continue across a picnic area to a junction of paths. You can turn briefly left here to visit King Dick's Well and the memorial to Richard III. To continue the main walk, turn right and follow the waymarked Battle Trail across Ambion Hill to reach Shenton Station. Cross the railway line by the gate and turn left out of the car park entrance onto the lane. Walk along as far as the canal bridge.

7 Go over the bridge in order to double back and turn left beneath the bridge onto the tow path of the Ashby Canal, signposted 'Market Bosworth'.

8 After 2.5 miles (4km) of easy and peaceful tow path walking, leave the canal at King's Bridge (No 43), the one after Bosworth Wharf Bridge. Cross this, then the railway bridge beyond for a field-edge path across stiles. This path heads half-right across a golf course – aim to the left of the house in front of hilltop woodland. Go over another stile and along the top of a field before joining an unmade lane which takes you into Market Bosworth.

9 At the end join the narrowing road (Back Lane), left and ahead, that comes out in the Market Place. Cross and walk past the Old Black Horse Inn, then turn left into Rectory Lane. At the end of the lane is the country park.

WHAT TO LOOK OUT FOR

Market Bosworth Country Park occupies the site of medieval parkland once grazed by England's only herd of pure black fallow deer. Originally it formed part of the landscaped grounds of the 17th-century country house of Bosworth Hall (now a hotel and spa), but in the 1970s Leicestershire County Council purchased 87 acres (35ha) and established an arboretum featuring oaks, maples and conifers, as well as a lake and a meadow containing wild flowers. There is a picnic area and children's play zones.

Distance 8.25 miles (14.1km)

Minimum time 4hrs

Ascent/gradient 279ft (85m) ▲▲▲

Level of difficulty ●●●

Paths Easy lanes and tow path, may be muddy, 8 stiles

Landscape Gently rolling woods and arable land

Suggested map OS Explorers 232 Nuneaton & Tamworth; 233 Leicester & Hinckley

Start/finish Grid reference: SK 412031 (on Explorer 232)

Dog friendliness Generally very good (care required on street sections)

Parking Market Bosworth Country Park (pay-and-display)

Public toilets At car park, Bosworth Battlefield Heritage Centre, Shenton Station and Market Bosworth

1514 Hampton Court is built for Cardinal Wolsley, but later he gives it to the King.

1516 A daughter, Mary, is born to Henry VIII and Queen Catherine.

1517 German theologian Martin Luther publishes his *95 Theses*, questioning the Roman Catholic Church.

1520 Henry meets Francis I of France at the Field of the Cloth of Gold, a diplomatic summit, near Calais.

1529 Pope Clement VII refuses to grant Henry VIII a divorce. Wolsey falls from power and influence.

1530 In Peru Spanish conquistadors invade the lands of the Inca; the Inca Empire is destroyed by 1535.

1531 A convocation of the English Church recognises Henry VIII as 'sole protector and Supreme Head'.

1533 In January, Henry marries Anne Boleyn in secret; in September a baby, the future Elizabeth I, is born.

1534 Under the Act of Supremacy Henry is confirmed as Supreme Head of the Church of England.

A Perfect Mansion at Compton Wynyates

A scenic walk over high ground delivers spectacular views of one of Warwickshire's finest houses

Regarded as one of the most visually striking mansions in England, Compton Wynyates is all that remains of the village of Compton-in-the-Hole, which was depopulated by Sir William Compton during the reign of Henry VIII. The reason was simple: Sir William wanted to create a spacious park around his new home, built in brick on the site of an earlier structure, and the village was in the way.

Lying in a secluded fold of the hills, about 12 miles (19km) southeast of Stratford-upon-Avon, Compton Wynyates first came into the possession of Philip de Compton in about 1204 and has been in the same family ever since. The original moated house was demolished and a new brick and stone building begun in about 1481 by Edmund de Compton, part of which still survives in the vicinity of the courtyard. Rebuilding of Compton Wynyates took about 40 years to complete.

The house passed to Edmund's son who, at the end of the 15th century, was a young page to Prince Henry. He was knighted by Henry VIII following the Battle of Tournai in 1512 and the King also gifted him the old castle at Fulbroke, near Warwick. However, so keen were the Compton family to improve and enlarge Compton Wynyates that they demolished the castle to provide extra materials. Undoubtedly, the timber roof of the hall and the oriel window facing the courtyard came from Fulbroke. Many other distinguished features from that period include the battlemented towers and the great porch, which bears the arms of Henry VIII and Catherine of Aragon above the door.

The variety of colour in the brickwork is breathtaking, with hardly two bricks being the same shade. As you look down the drive towards the house, you may catch a hint of pale rose, orange, dark red and blue. Henry VIII stayed here on several occasions, as did Elizabeth I, James I and Charles I, but it was during the English Civil War (1642–51) that Compton Wynyates experienced its darkest days: the house was besieged and finally captured by the Parliamentarians, before eventually being returned to the Compton family. The church was demolished at this time.

Secret Passages, Fine Decorations

Privately owned and sadly not open to the public, Compton Wynyates comprises a network of secret passages, hidden rooms and fine stairways. There are almost 100 rooms and about 300 windows. The dining room has a fine Elizabethan or early Jacobean ceiling and there are many portraits of Compton ancestors. Carved panels depicting the Battle of Tournai and a 16th-century tapestry of Cupid picking grapes are among many other historic features.

Above: *The all-powerful king. The entrance to Compton Wynates bears the motto 'My Master King Henry VIII'*

Top: *The mansion is bordered by formal topiary gardens*

Walk 47 Red-brick manor house in a green valley

Take a tour through lovely country and gaze on a house that hosted Henry VIII and Charles I

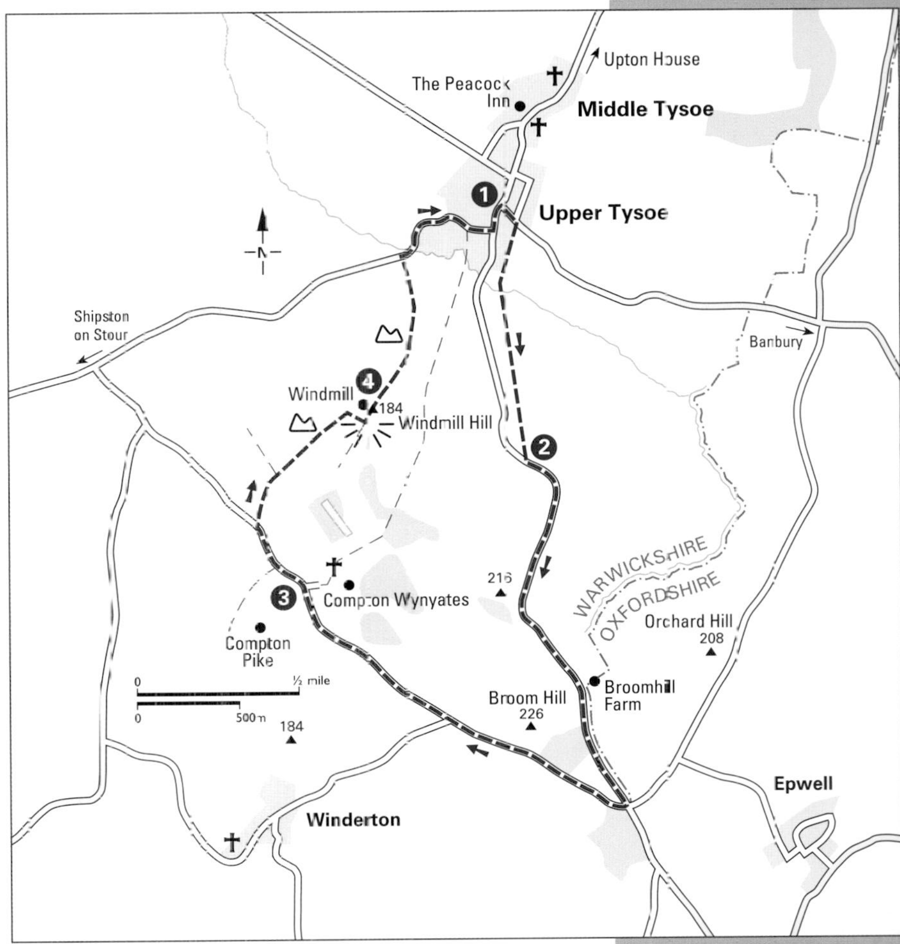

1 Make for the southern end of Upper Tysoe and look for the turning signposted 'Shenington and Banbury'. Follow the road, keeping Middleton Close on the left, and turn right just before the speed derestriction signs at a gate and footpath sign. Keep alongside allotments, then follow the field boundary to a kissing gate in the corner and continue across the field to the next stile. Keep ahead in the next field, passing beneath power lines, and make for a plank bridge and stile in the boundary hedge. Go straight on up the field slope and, on reaching the brow of the hill, look for a stile and plank bridge in the hedge by the road.

2 Turn left and follow the road as it curves right and up the hill. Pass Broomhill Farm and continue ahead to the first crossroads. Turn right here, signposted 'Compton Wynyates', and pass a turning on the left to Winderton. Follow the lane along to the main entrance to Compton Wynyates on the right.

3 Keep walking ahead, passing a house on the left-hand side, and as the road begins to curve left look for a galvanised gate and stile on the right. Join the green lane and follow it to the next gate and stile. Continue ahead and, when the track curves to the left, go straight ahead over a stile and up the edge of the field. Pass a ruined stone-built barn and make for the top corner of the field. Take some steps up the bank before climbing steeply but briefly up to a stile. Keep a stone wall and a restored windmill on your left-hand side and look over to the right for a splendid view of Compton Wynyates house.

4 Make for a stile a few paces ahead and then follow the path over the high ground, keeping to the right of the windmill. Make for a hedge corner ahead, pass through the gap and then descend the field slope, keeping the hedge on your right. Pass into the next field and keep close to the right-hand boundary. Aim a little to the left of the bottom right corner of the field and make for a stile leading out to the road. Turn right and return to the centre of Tysoe.

WHAT TO LOOK OUT FOR

The windmill near Compton Wynyates dates to at least 1725. The 'Wynyates' in the house name may derive from 'wind gate', perhaps a reference to the gap in the hills where the windmill stands. Tysoe Church is a rare Grade I-listed building dating back to the 11th century, with an octagonal Perpendicular font, ancient brasses and window glass.

COMPTON PIKE

Compton Pike can be seen across the fields as you approach the main entrance to Compton Wynyates. The pike – more a spire really – is a beacon thought to have been erected at the time of the Spanish Armada in 1588. It may also have been put up to indicate the position of the old village of Compton-in-the-Hole, depopulated by Sir William Compton.

Distance 6 miles (9.7km)

Minimum time 2hrs 30min

Ascent/gradient 298ft (90m) ▲▲▲

Level of difficulty ●●●

Paths Field paths, tracks and roads, 9 stiles

Landscape Undulating countryside on edge of Cotswolds

Suggested map OS Explorer 206 Edge Hill & Fenny Compton

Start/finish Grid reference: SP 338437

Dog friendliness Keep dogs on lead or under control across farmland

Parking Spaces in Tysoe

Public toilets None on route

1535 Sir Thomas More is executed for his refusal to accept the King as Head of the Church.

1535 Sir Thomas Cromwell is appointed Vicar General with powers to inspect churches and monasteries.

1536 Anne Boleyn is executed on the grounds of high treason, and Henry marries Jane Seymour.

1536 French Protestant reformer John Calvin publishes his *Institutes of the Christian Religion.*

1536 The Act of Union between England and Wales is passed. The Dissolution of the smaller monasteries takes place in England, and in 1539 the remaining monasteries are suppressed. Henry makes gifts or sells the land at enormous profit.

1537 The Queen, Jane Seymour, Henry's most favoured wife, gives birth to a son (the future Edward VI), but dies shortly afterwards.

1540 Henry marries Anne of Cleeves and divorces her within a year. Thomas Cromwell is executed.

1540 St James's Palace in London is completed.

Remembering the 'Reivers' at Newcastleton

Gentle walking passes through borderlands where cattle raiding was a part of 16th-century life

The area around Newcastleton was once what tabloid newspapers would describe as 'war-torn'. Ownership of these borderlands was hotly disputed between England and Scotland for hundreds of years and there were frequent battles and skirmishes. Because places like Newcastleton were so remote from the centres of power in both London and Edinburgh, they were difficult to defend and had a reputation for lawlessness. Feuds often developed between powerful local families, and violent raids and cases of cattle rustling (reiving) were common – cattle were a valuable asset. These were ruthless people who could probably have shown the Vikings a thing or two. A raid would commonly be followed by an illegal revenge attack or sometimes a legal 'Hot Trod'. This was a pursuit mounted immediately after a raid and had strict rules – including one stating that a lighted turf had to be carried if the trod crossed the border. When reivers were caught they were often taken hostage (the ransom money was very handy), taken prisoner, or even killed. Not surprisingly the countryside became studded with sturdy castles and fortified 'pele' towers.

Right: *The Armstrong family motto – 'I remain unbeaten'*

Below: *A romantic rendition of the often ruthless reivers*

The Border Armstrongs

The most powerful family in this area were the Armstrongs. They held large tracts of land: their main seat was Mangerton Tower, the remains of which you can see on this walk. The principal reiving clan in the Borders, the Armstrongs were said to be able to muster 3,000 mounted men whenever they wished to launch a raid into England. They were ruthless and violent, running a rather successful protection racket.

The Border wars ceased and the power of the reiving clans was finally dispersed only when the Union of the Scottish and English crowns took place in 1603 – when King James VI of Scots become James I of England, following the death of Elizabeth I. Keen to gain control and make his mark as an effective ruler of the new united kingdom, James banned weapons and established mounted forces to police the area. Reiving families – often identified with the help of local informers – were scattered and members transported or even executed. After Archibald Armstrong of Mangerton was executed in 1610, the Armstrongs lost their lands to the Scotts, another powerful local family.

Walk 48 Where Armstrongs had the upper hand

Get to grips with a landscape that was once a cattle-rustling family's Border stronghold

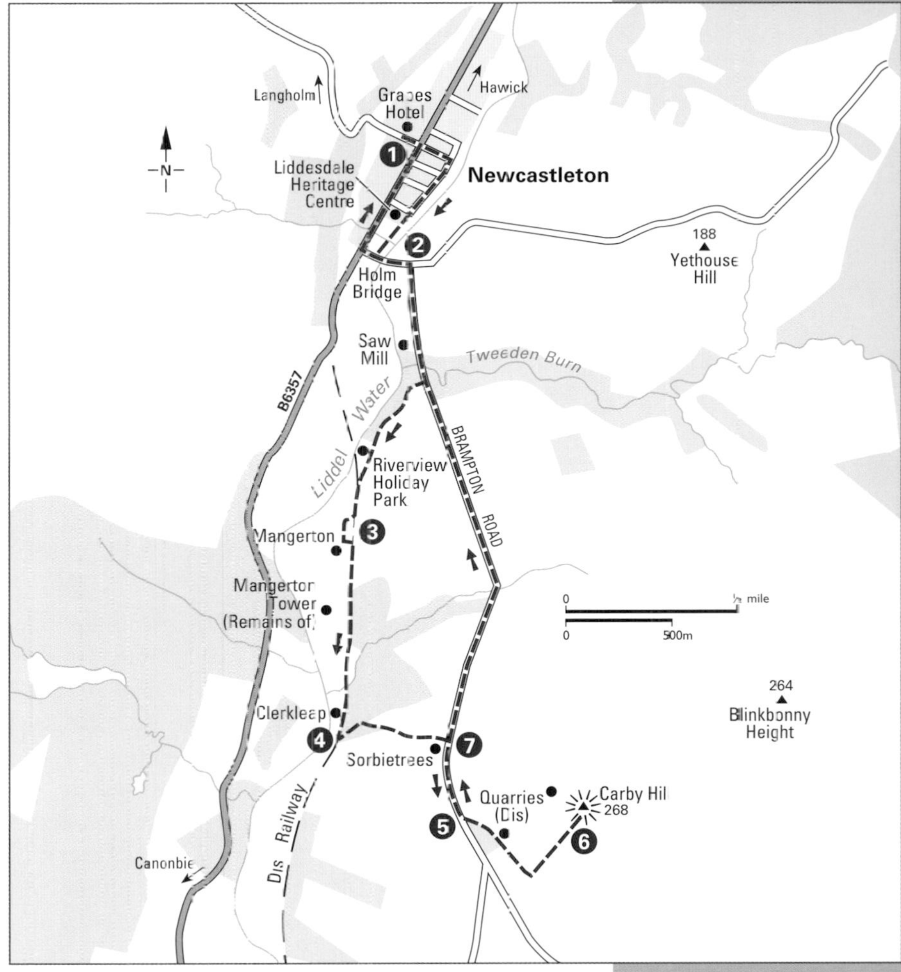

1 From Douglas Square in the centre of Newcastleton, with your back to the Grapes Hotel, walk along Whitchester Street (or any of the other streets opposite) and go down to the river, the Liddel Water. Turn right, then walk along the river bank and join the footpath downstream to reach Holm Bridge. Here, turn left at the top of the steps and then cross over the bridge.

2 After about 100yds (91m), turn right and follow the Brampton Road, passing static caravans on either side. You will eventually pass an old saw mill with a corrugated iron roof and will then reach the Tweeden Burn Bridge. Go across the bridge and walk uphill, then turn right and join the metalled track signed for the Riverview Holiday Park. Continue on this road until you near the farm buildings.

3 At the farm entrance, fork left onto the bed of the old railway line, which has joined you from the right. This line once linked Carlisle to Edinburgh but was closed following the Beeching cuts of 1963. Follow the line as it leads past the remains of Mangerton Tower, which are in a field to your right, and continue ahead until you reach Clerkleap cottage.

4 Walk 50yds (45m) beyond the cottage and turn left over a rotting gate. A rough path leads up left, then turns right to join a rough track. This leads through woodland and on, uphill, to join the road by Sorbietrees farm. Turn right now and walk along the road, past the farm, to a small stand of conifers on the left. Turn left through the gate.

5 Bear right now and head up the left-hand side of the trees. Walk past the top of the wood, following a dry-stone wall up below a former quarry to the field's top corner. Climb over the field gate ahead. Now open grassy slopes lead up left, to the cairn and fallen walls on the summit of Carby Hill. The views are truly great from here. Known locally as Caerba Hill, this was the site of a prehistoric settlement.

6 Retrace your steps to reach the road again, then turn right and walk back past Sorbietrees farm.

7 At the farm, continue on the main road as it bears right and follow it back over the Tweeden Burn Bridge and up to the Holm Bridge. Cross the bridge and walk straight on for 100yds (91m), then turn right onto the B6357 and walk back to the village square via the little Heritage Centre.

WHILE YOU'RE THERE

Liddesdale Heritage Centre and Museum is the place to come to learn more about the history of the area and its people. It occupies the former Townfoot Kirk in Newcastleton. There are displays on local churches, shops and trades including shoemaking, clogging and weaving as well as farming. Trainspotters will love the Waverley Line memorabilia, which includes a seat from the station platform and an old railway clock. And if you're trying to trace your family tree you can make use of the centre's genealogical records.

Distance 5.75 miles (9.3km)

Minimum time 2hrs 45min

Ascent/gradient 689ft (210m) ▲▲▲

Level of difficulty 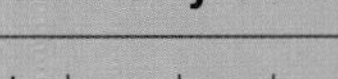

Paths Quiet byroads and farm tracks, one grassy climb

Landscape Rolling borderlands and moors

Suggested map OS Explorer 324 Liddesdale & Kershope Forest

Start/finish Grid reference: NY 483875

Dog friendliness Dogs on lead; sheep, cows and ponies graze on route

Parking Douglas Square

Public toilets Langholm Street, next to fire station

1540 The Dissolution of Monasteries, begun in 1536, continues with the closure of Waltham Abbey.

1540 Henry marries Catherine Howard, but has her executed for treason two years later.

1542 In Scotland, Mary, Queen of Scots, accedes the throne a week after her birth.

1543 Henry marries Catherine Parr and enjoys her quiet companionship until his death.

1543 Polish-born mathematician and astronomer Nicolaus Copernicus publishes his *De Revolutionibus Orbium Coelestium* (*On the Revolutions of Celestial Spheres*) in which he makes the radical argument that the Sun is the centre of the universe.

1544 Thomas Cranmer's *Exhortation and Liturgy* is the Church's first English-language prayer book.

1545 Henry VIII's warship, the *Mary Rose*, sinks off Portsmouth, Hampshire.

1545 The Council of Trent defines Roman Catholic doctrine, marking the start of the Counter Reformation.

Thomas Cromwell and Hailes Abbey

This pleasant ramble leads to the spot from which Henry VIII's commissioner supervised the abbey's winding up

In the 11 years from 1536 to 1547 just about every English religious institution that was not a parish church was either closed or destroyed – this was the Dissolution of the Monasteries, Henry VIII's draconian policy to force the old Church to give up its wealth. The smaller monasteries went first, then the larger ones and finally the colleges and chantries. All their lands and tithes became Crown property. Much of the land was sold off to laypeople, usually local landowners. The Church as a parish institution was considerably strengthened as a result of the Dissolution, but at the expense of the wider religious life. The suppression of the chantries and guilds, for example, meant many people were deprived of a local place of worship.

***Background:** Medieval floor tiles from Hailes Abbey*

***Below:** Empty cloister arches at Hailes Abbey*

Hailes Abbey

Hailes Abbey was one of the most powerful Cistercian monasteries in the country, owning 13,000 acres (5,265ha) and 8,000 sheep. It was a particular target for reformers. In 1270 Edmund, Earl of Cornwall, the son of its founder, had given the monastery a phial supposed to contain the blood of Christ. Thereafter the monastery became a major pilgrimage centre, to which pilgrims came to see 'the Holy Blood of Hailes'.

Thomas Cromwell was the King's Commissioner responsible for seeing to the closure of the monasteries. He is reputed to have surveyed the destruction of the monastery from a vantage point near Beckbury Camp. There is still a fine view of the abbey from here, as you should find as you pass Point 5 on this walk.

The monastery lands were confiscated by the Crown and then sold to a speculator, who sold the land on in lots. In *c*.1600 the abbey site was bought by Sir John Tracy. The monks were dispersed: a few managed to secure positions as parish clergy, while others took up posts with the cathedrals at Bristol and Gloucester.

Charming Remains

Hailes Church, where the walk starts, is all that remains of the village of Hailes. It predates the abbey and survived the Dissolution, perhaps because it had been a parish church and was not directly linked to the neighbouring monastery. It has real charm, but is sadly overlooked by the many visitors to the monastery's ruins. Although small, it has several special features, including a panelled chancel – floored with tiles from the monastery – and a nave with 14th-century wall paintings. Didbrook Church (near Point 2) also survived the upheavals. Built in Perpendicular style, it was rebuilt in 1475 by the Abbot of Hailes, following damage caused by Lancastrian soldiers after the Battle of Tewkesbury.

Walk 49 One of England's most powerful abbeys and a major pilgrimage centre

Wander a corner of Gloucestershire in which a grand Cistercian monastery once stood

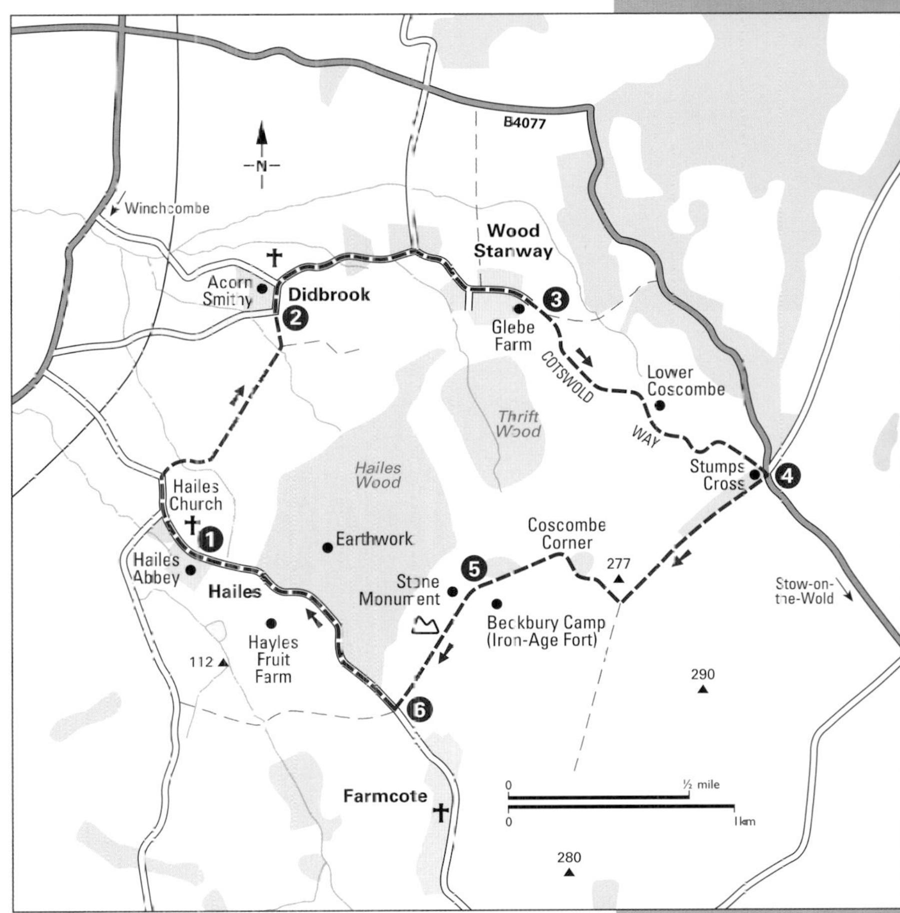

1 From Hailes Church turn right and follow the lane to a T-junction. Turn right here and after 200yds (183m) turn right again onto a footpath through a gate. Walk across an area of concrete, go over a stile next to a gate and follow a track as it goes right and left, turning at an old oak tree, eventually becoming a grassy path beside a field. Go over a stile, followed by a stile and footbridge. After about 75yds (69m) turn left, through a gate, and cross a field alongside the right-hand hedge to reach a gate at a road.

2 Turn right and follow the road as it meanders through the pretty village of Didbrook, then a stretch of countryside. At a junction turn right for Wood Stanway. Walk through this village, bearing left at a cherry tree on a grass island, into the yard of Glebe Farm.

3 Ignore a bridleway sign and gate on the left and at a gate go onto a track on the left of a field and walk ahead, looking for a gate on the left. You are now on the Cotswold Way, well marked by arrows with a white dot or acorn. Cross into a field and go half-right, keeping to the left of some electricity poles, to a gate in a hedge. Bear half-left across the next field, heading towards farm buildings. Through a gate turn sharp right, up the slope (guide posts), to a gate on your right. Through this turn immediately left up the field to a guide post. Go through a gate. Follow the footpath as it winds its way gently up the slope. At the top walk along the crest, with a dry-stone wall to your right, to a reach gate at a road.

WHILE YOU'RE THERE

If you have time to visit Hailes Abbey, rent a recorded commentary that explains the layout of the ruins. Farmcote Church is a gem, hard to find but worth the effort: overlooking Hailes, it is located high up in a silent, tranquil corner of the wolds. It is little more than a chapel but ancient, and a visit makes for an uplifting experience.

4 Turn right and then right again through a gate to a track. Follow this for 0.5 mile (800m), passing through a gate, until at the top (just before reaching some trees) you turn right to follow another track for 50yds (46m). Turn left through a gate into a field and then turn sharp right to follow the perimeter of the field as it goes left and passes through a gate beside the ramparts of an Iron Age fort, Beckbury Camp. Continue ahead to pass through another gate which leads to a stone monument with a niche. According to local lore, it was from here that Thomas Cromwell watched the destruction of Hailes Abbey in 1539.

5 Turn right to follow a steep path down through the trees. At the bottom go straight across down the field to a gate. Pass through the gate, then continue down to another gate and, in the field beyond, head down to a stile beside a signpost.

6 Over this turn right down a lane, all the way to a road. To the left is Hayles Fruit Farm with its café. Continue ahead along the road to return to Hailes Abbey and the start point by the church.

Distance 5 miles (8km)

Minimum time 2hrs

Ascent/gradient 605ft (185m) ▲▲▲

Level of difficulty ●●●

Paths Fields, tracks, farmyard and lanes, 4 stiles

Landscape Wide views, rolling wolds and villages

Suggested map OS Explorer OL45 The Cotswolds

Start/finish Grid reference: SP 051302

Dog friendliness Mostly on lead – a lot of livestock in fields

Parking Beside Hailes Church

Public toilets None on route

1547 Henry VIII dies, riddled with disease.

1547 Edward VI reigns with the help of two Protectors, but only outlives his father by six short years before he dies in 1553 of tuberculosis.

1549 The *Book of Common Prayer*, drawn up by Thomas Cranmer, is introduced under the Act of Uniformity. There are uprisings in Devon and Cornwall against the new prayer book.

1549 Robert Kett leads a rebellion in Norfolk against enclosures of land.

1549 Lord Protector Edward Seymour, Duke of Somerset, loses power to John Dudley, Duke of Northumberland. Somerset builds Somerset House, a magnificent palace on the Strand in central London.

1553–58 During Mary Tudor's short reign, she earns herself a lasting reputation as the zealous persecutor of the Protestant faith. Despite her gentle personality, she is obsessed throughout her reign with returning the English Church to Rome.

Montgomery – Land of the Marcher Lords

This enjoyable outing with breathtaking views visits a once-imposing medieval castle

Montgomery is a fine country town with its origins in medieval times. Tucked beneath a castle-topped crag, many of the houses have Georgian facades, but these were additions to much older dwellings. The centrepieces of the town are the elegant red-brick town hall with a clock tower on top, and the half-timbered Dragon Hotel, a 16th-century coaching house. Plaques on the walls of the old houses tell you of Montgomery's proud history, but you can learn more by calling into the Old Bell Inn, which has been converted into a museum.

Controlling the Welsh Marches

After William I conquered England in 1066 he gave the task of controlling the Welsh Marches to his friend and staunch supporter, Roger de Montgomery. Montgomery set up a motte-and-bailey timber castle at Hendomen, a mile (1.6km) north of the present town. There were continuous skirmishes with the Welsh, especially with the coming to power of Llewelyn the Great, Prince of Wales. Henry III had the current castle built in 1223 on a rock overlooking the plains of the River Severn. A gatehouse and two D-shaped towers protected the inner ward; in 1228-9 the middle and outer wards were begun. The castle repelled attacks by Llyewelyn the Great in 1228 and 1231, and by Dafydd ap Llywelyn in 1245.

In 1541 Henry VIII handed the stronghold to the Herberts, a powerful Welsh dynasty. The castle saw its last action during the Civil War: the Herberts were Royalists and at first held the castle, but were defeated in a great battle in which their 5,000 troops were attacked by 3,000 Parliamentarians. In 1649 the Parliamentarians demolished the castle. Nevertheless, when you view its remains today, you still get a feeling of impregnability as you look down on the plain.

Iron Age Remains

The other castle you see on the walk, though, is much earlier. When emerging from the woods, the sight of the giant earthworks of Ffridd Faldwyn makes it obvious that this hilltop Iron Age fort was of great importance. It was built in four stages, all completed before the Roman conquest. Artefacts, including neolithic tools, are held in the National Museum of Wales in Cardiff.

__Below left:__ Montgomery Castle was built on a high outcrop of rock

__Below:__ A view over the Severn Valley as seen from Montgomery Castle

Walk 50 Ruins of a fortress that defied Welsh princes

Admire the remains of a castle given to the powerful Herberts by the Tudors

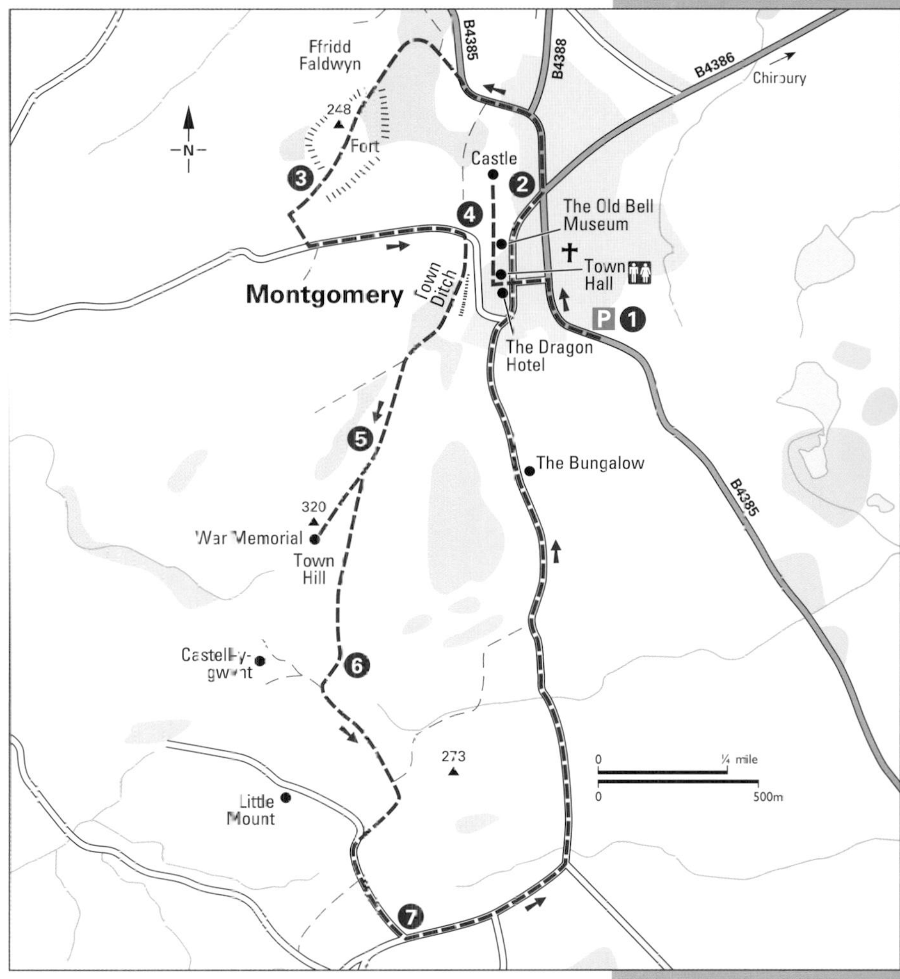

1 From the car park head north, then left along Broad Street, where you'll see the Town Hall and the Dragon Hotel. A signpost to the castle points up the lane behind, the path then leaving right through a kissing gate. It's a must to see and is free. Return to this point. Head north up Arthur Street, past the Old Bell Museum

2 Reaching the main road, go left and keep left with the B4385 in the direction of Newtown. Leave just past the speed derestriction sign, over a stile on the left. Bear right across a field towards trees. This path climbs through woodland, then swings left (southwest) to reach the old hilltop fort above Ffridd Faldwyn.

3 Over the stile at the far side of the fort, bear left down the field to the roadside gate. Turn left along the road, which takes you back towards Montgomery.

4 As the road turns sharp right just above the town, leave it for a footpath on the right that is signposted for the Montgomeryshire War Memorial. The path begins beyond a kissing gate and climbs steadily up the hill to join a farm track, which at first runs parallel to the Town Ditch, part of the 13th-century fortifications.

5 As it enters high pastures, the track begins to level out and traverse the eastern hillside. Here you can make a detour to the war memorial that can be seen clearly ahead at the top of the hill. Return to the track and follow it through a gate and past some pens with gorse and hawthorn lining the way on the left.

6 Keep going in the next field. Walk ahead through a wide gap and head down the field to leave by a gate and stile. Follow a track down to a junction southeast of Little Mount farm and go left to a lane.

7 Keeping left at successive junctions, walk back to Montgomery. Turn right along Kerry Street and make your way into the square.

Distance 5.25 miles (8.4km)

Minimum time 3hrs

Ascent/gradient 951ft (290m) ▲▲▲

Level of difficulty ●●●

Paths Well-defined paths, farm tracks and country lanes, 3 stiles

Landscape Pastoral hills overlooking wide plains of the Severn

Suggested map OS Explorer 216 Welshpool & Montgomery

Start/finish Grid reference: SO 224963

Dog friendliness Farming country – dogs on lead. Not allowed in castle grounds

Parking Car park on Bishops Castle Street on B4385 at south end of town square

Public toilets Behind Town Hall

WHAT TO LOOK OUT FOR

The Old Bell Museum gives a fascinating insight into the history of the town, its castles, workhouses and archaeological excavations. In 1279–80 Montgomery built new town walls of stone to protect itself from attack. Not much remains of the walls themselves, but in places you'll see the Town Ditch that accompanied them. You can see the ditch alongside the track climbing to the war memorial and to the east of town behind the church. In St Nicholas's Church, founded in the 13th century, look for the Elizabethan tomb of Richard Herbert, father of poet George Herbert, and the double rood screen.

1554 Queen Mary marries Philip of Spain, but the union is unpopular. Mary also returns England to papal authority, and thousands of Protestants are given the option to 'turn or burn'. Among those who choose to burn is Thomas Cranmer; he dies in 1556.

1558 Following the death of 'Bloody Mary', the accession of Elizabeth I is welcomed with relief.

1558 Mary, Queen of Scots, daughter of James V of Scotland, marries the French Dauphin.

1560 The Scottish Parliament proclaims the nation Protestant, ending their alliance with France.

1562 Sir Francis Drake voyages to America for the first of many slave-trading expeditions.

Winchcombe and Sudeley Castle

A rewarding walk circles above a thriving Cotswold town and the burial place of Catherine Parr

At the end of a long drive just outside Winchcombe is a largely 16th-century mansion called Sudeley Castle. The first castle was built here in 1140 and fragments dating from its earlier, more martial days are still in evidence. It became a royal castle under Edward IV; in the Wars of the Roses Richard III used it as his base before the Battle of Tewkesbury in 1471. Henry VIII later visited with Anne Boleyn.

In 1547 the castle was given to Thomas Seymour by King Edward VI. As the brother of King Henry VIII's third wife, Jane Seymour (mother of the young Edward), Seymour was the King's uncle. In April 1547, after Henry's death, Seymour then married the dead king's sixth wife, Catharine Parr, and lived at Sudeley with her; he was her fourth husband. He was Lord High Admiral of England but remained in the shadow of his brother Edward, who was Lord Protector in the reign of Edward VI. Thomas Seymour was executed for treason in 1549.

Top: *A wild-eyed gargoyle on St Peter's Church, Winchcombe*

Right: *One king, six wives – Catherine Parr is bottom left*

Below: *The Knot Garden at Sudeley mimics the pattern on a dress worn by Elizabeth I in a portrait hung in the castle*

The Queen Who Outlived Henry VIII

Catherine Parr is buried in Sudeley's chapel. She was born in 1512 and educated in Henry's court. She was first married at nine, but widowed six years later. Back at court, she was at the centre of a group of educated women, using her influence with the King to protect her second husband, Lord Latimer, from the machinations of courtly politics. When Latimer died in 1543, Catherine was one of the wealthiest and best-connected women in England, and an obvious choice of wife for Henry. She looked after him and his affairs during the years until his death in 1547. Then she quickly married Seymour and moved to Sudeley, where she died in childbirth in 1548.

After Thomas Seymour's death, Queen Mary gave the property to Sir John Brydges, the first Lord Chandos in 1554. Sudeley Castle was a Royalist stronghold during the Civil War but was disarmed by the Parliamentarians. It was left to decay until its purchase in 1863 by John and William Dent, brothers from Worcester.

Winchcombe's Older Royal Connections

Winchcombe also has a considerable history. In Anglo-Saxon times it was a seat of the Mercian kings and the capital of Winchcombshire. It became a significant place of pilgrimage due to the presence of an abbey established in 798 and dedicated to St Kenelm, son of its founder, King Kenulf. The abbey was razed in the Dissolution of the Monasteries, but the town's parish church survived. It was rebuilt in 1468.

Walk 51 Royal castle with Tudor connections

View a Gloucestershire manor that Henry VIII visited and where Catherine Parr died

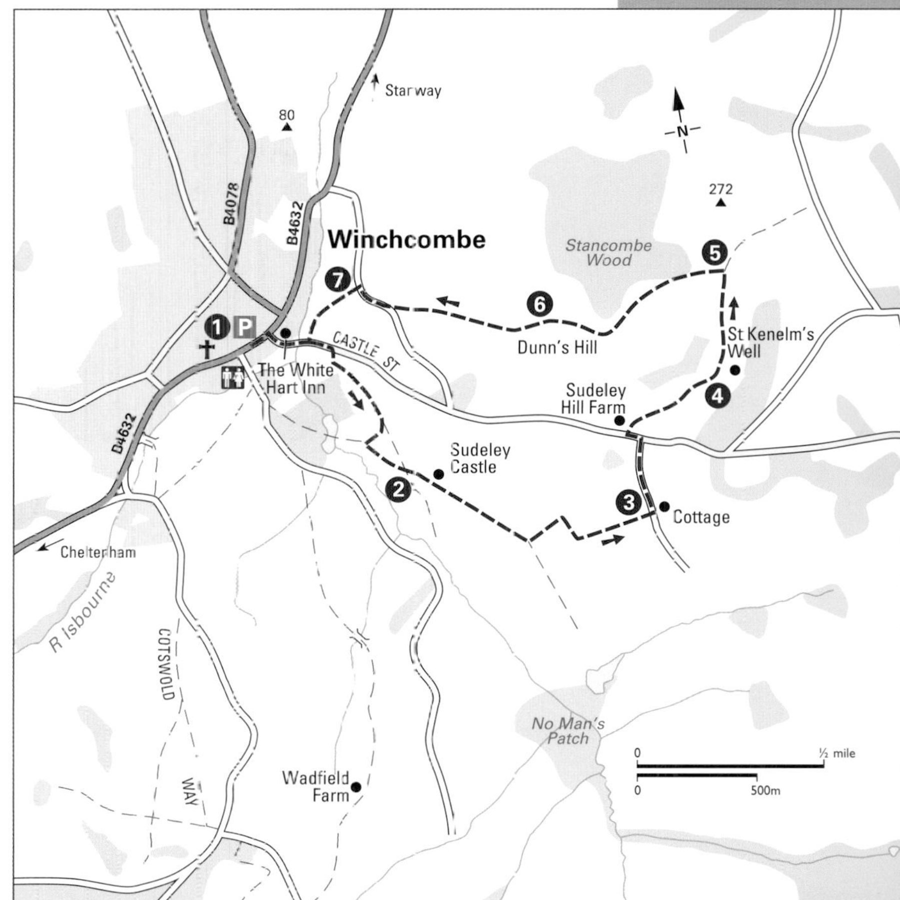

1 From the parking area on Abbey Terrace in Winchcombe, walk towards the town centre past a Lloyds TSB bank and turn right, down Castle Street. Where it levels out, cross a river bridge, and after a few paces bear right to leave the road near the Sudeley Castle Country Cottages and ascend to a kissing gate. Follow the path through the middle of a long field to a kissing gate. At a drive, with the castle visitor centre ahead, turn right for 50 paces, then left through a gate.

2 Walk between fences, with a play fort on the right, to a kissing gate. Follow the left fence past Sudeley Castle, then across its parkland (guide posts). Over a stile in the far corner turn left and after 25 paces climb another stile and walk alongside the left-hand field boundary, then right at the corner alongside a fence. At the willows go left over stile and walk uphill beside hedging towards a cottage.

3 Through a gate turn left onto a lane and follow this to a junction, turning left. After about 50 paces and just before Sudeley Hill Farm turn right and over a stile. Head half-left uphill and over another stile. Over this cross the middle of the field, then bear to the left of a cottage to a stile.

4 Over this you see St Kenelm's Well, a 17th- to 19th-century building in a fenced enclosure. Pass to the left of this along a track. Cross a stream and go through a gate (or over the stile) and climb half-right towards a gate at the right end of woodland.

WHAT TO LOOK OUT FOR

At St Peter's Church, Winchcombe, look out for the 60–70 gargoyles, reputedly portraits of locals; inside, note the embroidery behind a screen, said to be the work of Henry VIII's first wife, Catherine of Aragon. Behind Sudeley Hill Farm, look out for St Kenelm's Well, largely rebuilt in the 19th century, a holy well connected with the martyred prince, patron saint of the vanished Winchcombe Abbey.

5 At a woodland fence corner turn left, short of the gate, and go left alongside the fence, over two stiles alongside a small fenced field. Beyond this the path drops, fairly close to the woods on your right, and curves left to a gate. Through this continue alongside the wood, then a line of trees, to a gate and stile in the far corner.

6 Descend half-right towards Winchcombe, heading to the furthest corner. Over a stile descend, a fence on your right. At the fence corner continue half-right across the field. Through the hedge into the next field continue half-left towards a gate. Over the nearby stile cross the field corner to another stile and a footbridge. Half-left in the next field head for the gap to the right of a cottage. Through the gate turn right onto a lane, passing a heavily buttressed kitchen garden wall on your left.

7 After about 100yds (91m) turn left through a kissing gate and head across the field towards Winchcombe church tower. Then veer left before the river valley bottom to a kissing gate by a stone cottage. Follow this path to Castle Street and turn right over the river bridge and back into the town centre.

Distance 4 miles (6.4km)

Minimum time 2hrs

Ascent/gradient 490ft (150m) ▲▲▲

Level of difficulty ●●●

Paths Fields and lanes, 13 stiles

Landscape Woodland, hills and town

Suggested map OS Explorer OL45 The Cotswolds

Start/finish Grid reference: SP 024282

Dog friendliness On lead (or close control) throughout – much livestock

Parking Free on Abbey Terrace; also car park on Back Lane

Public toilets On corner of Vineyard Street

1563 An outbreak of bubonic plague kills 20,000 people in London.

1563 John Foxe's *Actes and Monuments* (*Book of Martyrs*) is published.

1568 Mary, Queen of Scots, flees from Scotland to England, but is imprisoned by Queen Elizabeth.

1576 James Burbage builds London's first theatre.

1586 Sir Walter Raleigh introduces tobacco and potatoes into England from the Americas.

1587 Elizabeth I signs a death warrant for Mary for alleged plots against the monarch. The execution of Mary triggers a reaction from Philip of Spain.

1588 Determined to depose Elizabeth, Philip sends an armada of 130 ships to attack England, but most of the fleet is destroyed by English gunfire, and the survivors fall prey to bad weather as they retreat.

1589 Author and courtier Sir John Harington invents the first water closet (flushing toilet), but it does not come into general use for another 300 years.

Longleat House and Grounds

Glorious woodland and parkland walking leads to an opulent Elizabethan mansion

Your first view of Longleat is an unforgettable one. As you stroll down the azalea- and rhododendron-lined path to Heaven's Gate, nothing prepares you for the superb panorama that stretches to the distant Mendip Hills. Central to this composition is Longleat House, an exquisite Elizabethan stone manor in a glorious wooded, lakeside setting that looks more like a fairy-tale palace from a distance.

Majestic Mansion

Architect and builder Sir John Thynne completed the Elizabethan mansion in 1580 on a site chosen for its beauty. The house was revolutionary in its design as it showed no thought for defence, its great bayed walls of stone and mullioned glass windows setting a new trend in Elizabethan architecture. The house was his second at Longleat. He had purchased the Augustinian Priory there in *c.*1540 and began building his first house around six years later. This was burned down in 1567, but at once he set to work constructing a new one. He worked to his own designs, but employed several surveyors, as architects were then known. These included Frenchman Allan Maynard and Englishman Robert Smythson, who later built the celebrated Hardwick Hall in Derbyshire.

Thynne's house at Longleat was designed– like other 'prodigy houses' built by Sir William Cecil (Burghley House, Lincolnshire) and Sir Christopher Hatton (Holdenby House, Northamptonshire) – to be grand enough for a royal visit. Sure enough, Queen Elizabeth I visited Longleat in 1575, in the course of her summer progress. At this point the house was incomplete, being just two storeys tall; the third storey was probably added after Thynne's death in May 1580 by his son, another John Thynne. The facade of the house makes use of the three classical 'orders' or column styles of ancient Greece and Rome: Doric, Ionic and Corinthian. It has Doric at ground-floor level, Ionic on the first floor and Corinthian on the second storey.

***Right:** Longleat was England's first house to be built in the classical Renaissance style*

Walk 52 A taste of Tudor majesty in golden stone

Admire Sir John Thynne's many-windowed 'prodigy house' set in a beautiful wooded estate

1 Cross the road and follow the path into the trees. Disregard the straight track left, bear right and then left along a gravelled path through mixed woodland to double gates and reach the viewpoint at Heaven's Gate.

2 Facing Longleat, go through the gate in the left-hand corner. In 180yds (165m) at a crossing of paths, turn right, then keep right at a fork and head downhill through woodland to a metalled drive by a thatched cottage. Turn right onto the waymarked bridleway and pass the cottage gate. Now follow the path left, heading downhill close to the woodland edge to reach a lane by the Garden Cottage.

3 Turn left along White Street to a crossroads and turn right going downhill. Ascend past the church to a T-junction and then turn right. Turn left opposite the school, following the bridlepath up a track and between sheds to a gate. Bear left with the grassy track, pass through two more gates and then bear slightly right to a gate and stile on the edge of woodland.

4 Follow the path through the copse and soon bear off right diagonally downhill to a gate. Turn left along the field edge in order to reach a track. Turn right, go through a gate beside a thatched cottage and follow along the metalled lane (Pottle Street). In around 200yds (183m), climb the stile on your right and cross the field to another stile before rejoining the lane.

5 Turn right and follow this quiet lane to a crossroads. Proceed straight across and follow the road through Horningsham village, passing the thatched chapel, to the crossroads opposite the Bath Arms.

6 Go straight across the crossroads, walk down the estate drive and through the gatehouse arch into Longleat Park. With the magnificent house ahead of you, walk beside the metalled drive with the lakes and weirs to your right. At a T-junction in front of the house, keep ahead to visit the house and follow the path left to reach the other tourist attractions.

7 For the main route, turn right and walk beside the drive, heading uphill through the Deer Park. Bear left with the drive and climb steeply, then turn sharp right through a wooden gate onto a metalled drive. With beautiful views across the parkland, gently ascend Prospect Hill and reach Heaven's Gate viewpoint. Retrace your steps to the car park.

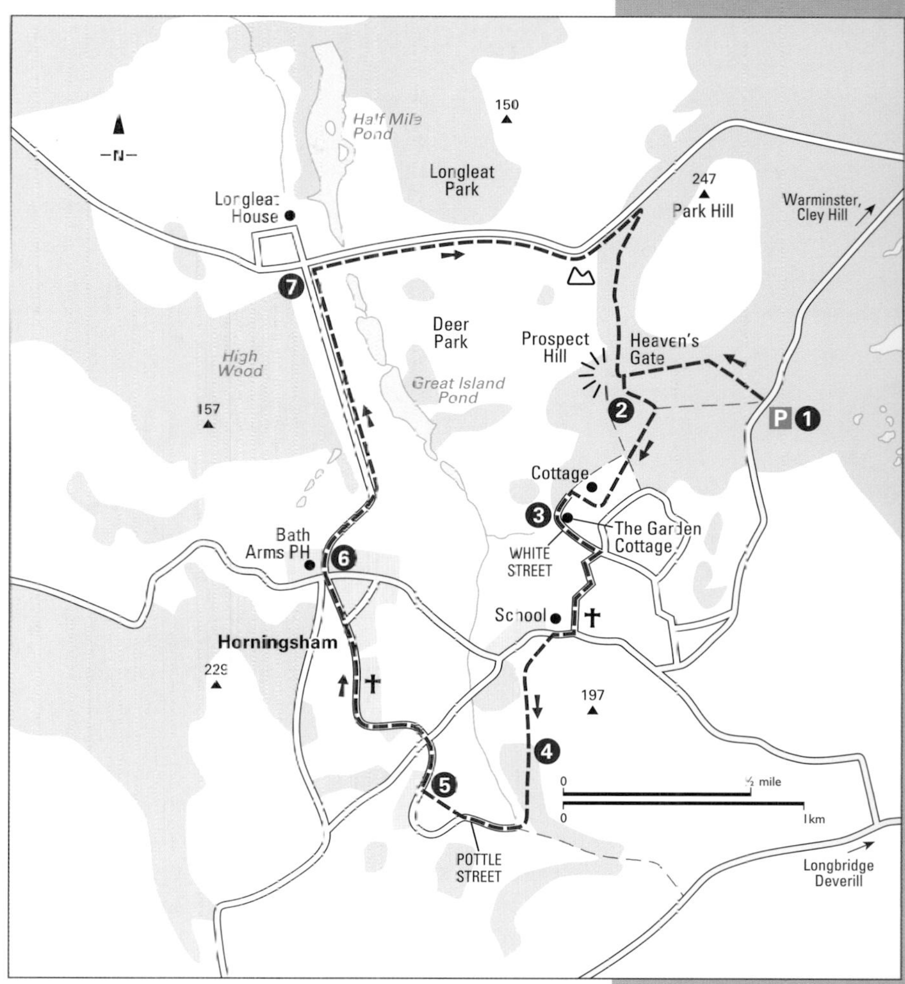

WHILE YOU'RE THERE

A tour of Longleat House is highly recommended. Much the interior was remodelled in the 19th century, but the Great Hall, which is 35ft (11m) tall and boasts a superb hammerbeam roof, remains as it was in Thynne's day. Longleat contains a mixture of furnishings and artefacts. Notable treasures include a 33ft-long (10m) 16th-century oak shuffle-board, a 17th-century gilt steeplechase cup and a library table commissioned from John Makepeace. Rich 17th-century Flemish tapestries, Genoese velvet and ancient Spanish leather clothe the walls, while painted ceilings, inspired by Italian palace interiors, including the Ducal Palace in Venice, and marble fireplaces ornament the state rooms.

Visit England's oldest Free Church as you stroll through nearby Horningsham. This Meeting House was provided by Sir John Thynne in 1566 for the Scottish workmen who built Longleat. Also in Horningsham, note the pollarded lime trees outside the Bath Arms. Planted in 1793, they are known as the Twelve Apostles. Not far away at the Church of St Peter and St Paul in Longbridge Deverill you can see the Thynne tomb.

Distance 5.25 miles (8.4km)

Minimum time 2hrs 30min (longer if visiting Longleat attractions)

Ascent/gradient 508ft (155m) ▲▲▲

Level of difficulty ●●●

Paths Field, woodland and parkland paths, roads, 4 stiles

Landscape Wooded hillside, village streets, parkland

Suggested map OS Explorer 143 Warminster & Trowbridge

Start/finish Grid reference: ST 827422

Dog friendliness On lead through grounds

Parking Heaven's Gate car park, Longleat Estate

Public toilets Longleat attractions complex

1485–1603

1590 William Shakespeare's *Henry VI Part I* and *Titus Andronicus* are his first performed plays.

1595 Shakespeare's *Romeo and Juliet, A Midsummer Night's Dream* and *Richard II* are first performed.

1599 The Globe Theatre is built on the south bank of the Thames in London by the Lord Chamberlain's Men.

1601 The Earl of Essex, stepson of the Queen's 'favourite', the Earl of Leicester, leads a revolt against Elizabeth's government and is executed.

1603 Elizabeth dies, a childless spinster. The English throne passes to King James VI of Scots and thereby unites the two crowns of Scotland and England. He rules in England as King James I.

The Golden Age of Mining in Newlands

A delightful romp above two lovely valleys leads close to the Elizabethan-era Goldscope copper mine

Both Borrowdale and the Newlands Valley, like many parts of Lakeland, have seen extensive periods of industry from an early age. From the top of Maiden Moor, scree can be seen issuing from the workings of an old mine in Newlands. This is Goldscope, a name that first appears in records during the reign of Elizabeth I, who imported German miners to work here. The name is a corruption of 'Gottesgab' or 'God's gift', so called because it was one of the most prosperous mines in Lakeland.

Copper was mined here as early as the 13th century from a vein 9ft (2.7m) thick. The mine also produced large quantities of lead, a small amount of silver and a modicum of gold. But the mine's greatest period of production was in the 16th century, when Elizabeth made a serious attempt to exploit England's own resources to reduce dependency on imports. Ironically, it was German miners who largely worked Goldscope, encouraged by the award of hidden subsidies in the form of waived taxes. Copper ore was taken by packhorse to Derwent Water by way of Little Town, then transported to a smelter on the banks of the River Greta, at Brigham. From here the copper went to the Receiving House in Keswick to receive the Queen's Mark.

Top right: *A delivery van of 1954 at the Pencil Museum, Keswick*

Below: *Looking across Derwent Water to Catbells and Friar's Crag*

Bottom right: *The pencil factory in the early 19th century*

Slate and Graphite

The Rigghead Quarries in Tongue Gill produced slate from levels cut deep into the fellside, and a number of adits are still open, although they are dangerous and should not be explored. But the real secret of these fells is wad, more commonly known as graphite, plumbago or black cawke – or the lead in your pencil. Its discovery dates from the early 16th century, when shepherds used a black mineral found on tree roots for marking sheep. Pencils appeared around 1660 as wooden sticks with a piece of graphite in the tip.

Keswick became the world centre of the graphite and pencil industries, and the first record of a pencil factory appears in 1832. The Cumberland Pencil Company was first set up in nearby Braithwaite in 1868 and moved to its present site in Keswick 30 years later.

Walk 53 When German miners dug Lakeland copper

Explore land highly valued for its mineral deposits – and enjoy views of Derwent Water

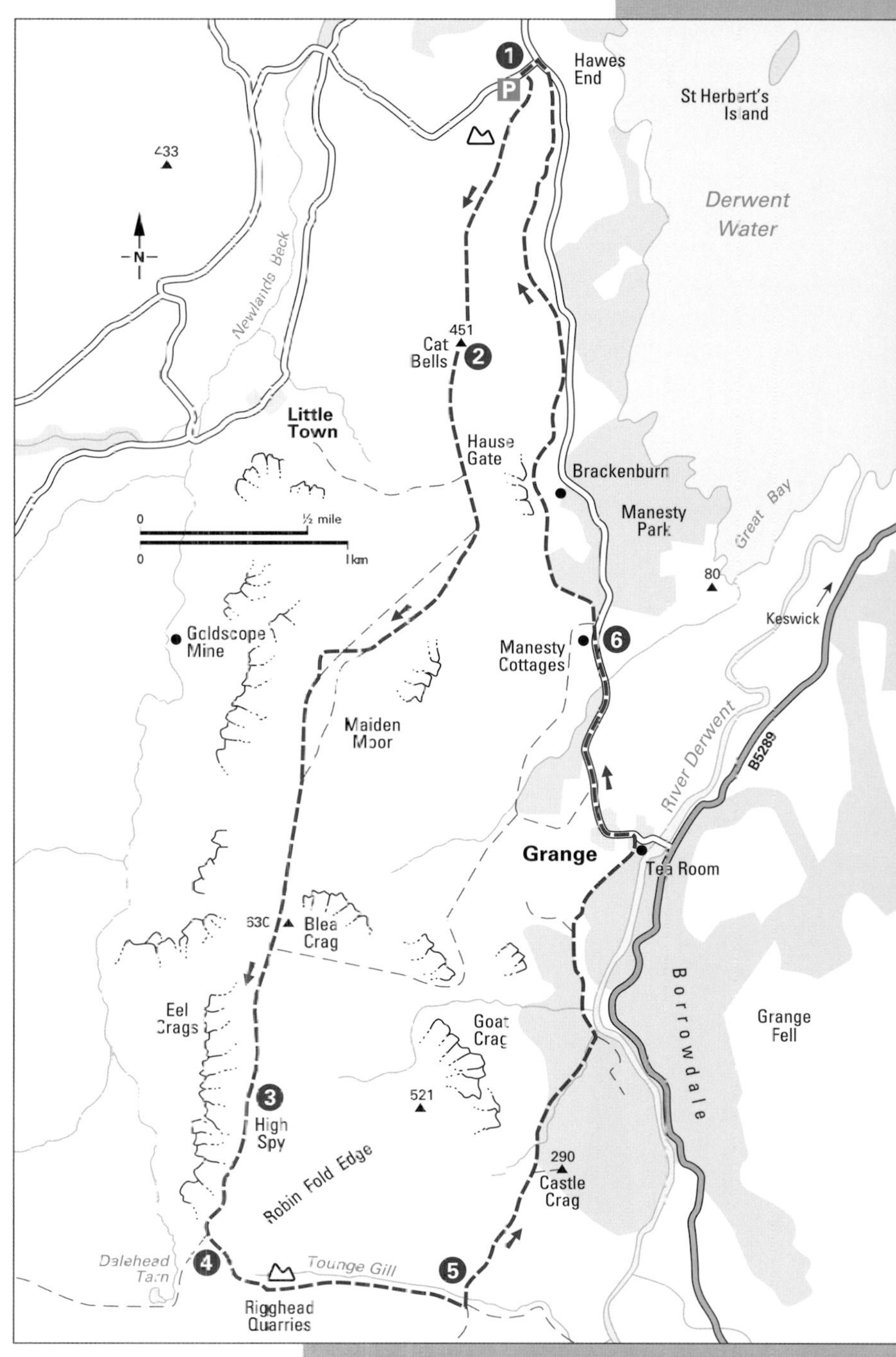

1 At Hawes End, walk up the road and at a bend take a stepped and rocky path rising steeply. Follow this steadily, climbing through small rocky outcrops before reaching Brandlehow. The onward route keeps to the centre of a grassy ridge, before rising through more rock outcrops to Cat Bells.

2 From Cat Bells descend easily to the broad col of Hause Gate. Go forward across Hause Gate on a grassy path and carry on ahead onto the broad expanse of Maiden Moor, across which a good path leads to the summit of High Spy.

3 Head down a path towards the col housing Dalehead Tarn. Gradually, the ravine of Tongue Gill appears over to the left, but finding the right moment to quit the Dalehead Tarn path is a hit and miss affair. Such paths as there are across to Tongue Gill are indistinct and invariably wet underfoot; keep heading for a fence.

4 Stiles across the fence give onto a path leading to a cairn at the start of a path down to Rigghead Quarries. Take care descending the steep slate paths until the gradient eases alongside Tongue Gill itself. Keeping to the right bank, follow the gill to a path T-junction, and turn left to a gate and stile, and footbridge.

5 The path climbs gently and soon crosses a shallow col near Castle Crag. Go past the crag, descending, soon to enter woodland at a gate. Take a narrow footbridge spanning Broadslack Gill and follow a path down to the banks of the River Derwent. Just before the river, cross a footbridge on the left, and a little further on, keep to a path roughly parallel with the river until you reach a wall. Take a broad track following the wall and eventually walk out to a surfaced lane. Go right and walk up to Grange village. Go left and follow the road.

6 Just after Manesty Cottages, branch left onto a path climbing gently above the road to a stile and gate. Through this, go forward onto a gently rising broad track and, when it forks, bear right, heading for a path above an intake wall. Pressing on beyond Brackenburn, the footpath, which affords lovely views of Derwent Water, soon dips to make a brief acquaintance with the road at a small quarry car park. Beyond this gap, immediately return to a gently rising path. This is an old road, traversing the lower slopes of Cat Bells that will ultimately bring you back to the road at Hawes End and the car park.

Distance 9 miles (14.5km)

Minimum time 4hrs

Ascent/gradient 2,460ft (750m) ▲▲▲

Level of difficulty ●●●

Paths Generally good paths, indistinct above Tongue Gill, 4 stiles

Landscape Fell ridge tops, quarry workings, woodland, riverside path

Suggested map OS Explorer OL4 The English Lakes (North-western Area)

Start/finish Grid reference: NY 247212

Dog friendliness No special problems, though fell sheep roam tops

Parking Wooded parking area at Hawes End

Public toilets None on route

Note Walk not advised in poor visibility

Shakespeare's Stratford

A gentle walk along the River Avon leads to buildings once known by England's most celebrated playwright

Visitors flock in their millions to Stratford-upon-Avon to see sites connected with the early life of poet and playwright William Shakespeare. The author of *Hamlet*, *Romeo and Juliet*, *A Midsummer Night's Dream*, *Henry V* and many other plays was born in Henley Street in 1564. He was baptised in Holy Trinity Church, then attended King Edward VI's Grammar School in Church Street.

He married a local woman named Anne Hathaway in 1582 and they had three children: Susannah, Hamnet and Judith. However, a country market town was no place for a playwright and poet, so some time in the mid-1580s he headed for London. By 1592 he was the talk of the town, counting Queen Elizabeth and her court among his plays' many admirers. His poetry was first published around this time and he began to accumulate serious wealth. By 1597 Shakespeare was able to buy New Place, then one of Stratford's grandest properties, next door to Nash's House on the corner of Chapel Street and Chapel Lane. The early 1600s saw his theatre company gain a royal title ('the King's Men'), and in these years the Bard wrote many of his best-known tragedies, such as *Othello*, *King Lear* and *Macbeth*.

Retired to Stratford

Shakespeare began to spend less time in London and more time at home in Stratford. His son Hamnet had died, aged 11, in 1596, but the boy's sister Susannah survived and married Dr John Hall in 1607. The couple lived in Hall's Croft, in the old part of the town. Shakespeare died on 23 April, 1616 and was buried at Holy Trinity. You can see his tomb, and that

Below left: *Holy Trinity Church, where Shakespeare was baptised and is buried*

Below: *The Bard's birthplace in Henley Street. He was born on 23 April, 1564*

Bottom: *The former Grammar School, Church Street, at which Shakespeare studied*

of his wife Anne Hathaway, who died in 1623. It bears the inscription: *'Good friend for Jesus sake forebeare/ To dig the dust encloased heare!/ Bleste be the man that spares the stones/ And curst be he that moves the bones.'*

There are other things to see in Stratford-upon-Avon apart from the Shakespeare heritage. The medieval 14-arched Clopton Bridge forms a splendid gateway to the town. The Town Hall is a fine Palladian building, and Harvard House in the High Street dates from 1596. It takes its name from the owner's daughter, Katherine Rogers, who married Robert Harvard of Southwark in London in 1605. Their son John went on to bequeath Harvard University in the US, and the university now owns Harvard House.

WHAT TO LOOK OUT FOR

As well as Holy Trinity Church, Shakespeare's birthplace and the former Grammar School, look out for the Falcon Hotel in Chapel Street – probably one of the poet's regular haunts. Opposite is the Guildhall and a row of almshouses. In the Canal Basin narrowboats form a colourful foreground for photographs of the Gower Memorial, which depicts Shakespeare and characters from his plays. In the 1970–80s, swans virtually disappeared from the Avon due to poisoning by lead fishing weights. Today, thankfully, they are back.

Walk 54 In the footsteps of the Bard

See Shakespeare's birthplace, burial place – and, perhaps, one of his plays

1 From the car park, walk along the banks of the River Avon opposite the famous Royal Shakespeare Theatre. Pass the weir until you come to a footbridge over the river, just in front of the A4390 road bridge.

2 Go right over the footbridge and bear right past the flats that replaced the old watermill, into Mill Lane. Continue up Mill Lane and go through the churchyard of Holy Trinity Church, walking around the church to see the river view. Leave the churchyard through the main gate into Old Town and follow the pavement. Just before reaching the turn into Southern Lane, go right into New Place Gardens and walk up to the Brass Rubbing Centre. Continue past the ferry and stroll through the attractive Theatre Gardens by the side of the Avon, exiting into Waterside and passing by the frontage of the old theatre building.

3 Go left up Chapel Lane, taking time to wander through the Knot Gardens on your way up to Chapel Street. At the top of the lane is the Guild Chapel to Shakespeare's Grammar School, with New Place Gardens to the right.

4 Go right along Chapel Street, passing The Shakespeare and the Town Hall into High Street. Harvard House is on the left, near the black-and-white Garrick Inn. At the end of High Street, bear left around the traffic island into Henley Street and walk along the pedestrianised area that takes you past Shakespeare's Birthplace and the museum. At the top of Henley Street, bear right and then left into Birmingham Road. Cross the road at the pedestrian crossing and afterwards go left up to the traffic-lights.

5 Head right up Clopton Road for 100yds (91m), then descend to the tow path of the Stratford-upon-Avon Canal at bridge No 66. Follow this, going southeast. Cross the canal at bridge No 68 and continue along the tow path into Bancroft Gardens by the canal basin where you will see an array of colourful narrowboats and the Royal Shakespeare Theatre. Cross the old Tram Bridge to the car park on the right.

Distance 2.5 miles (4km)
Minimum time 1hr 30min
Ascent/gradient Negligible
Level of difficulty ●
Paths Riverside paths and street pavements
Landscape Historic streets
Suggested map OS Explorer 205 Stratford-upon-Avon & Evesham
Start/finish Grid reference: SP 205547
Dog friendliness On lead along streets
Parking Recreation Ground pay-and-display car park
Public toilets At car park and top of Henley Street

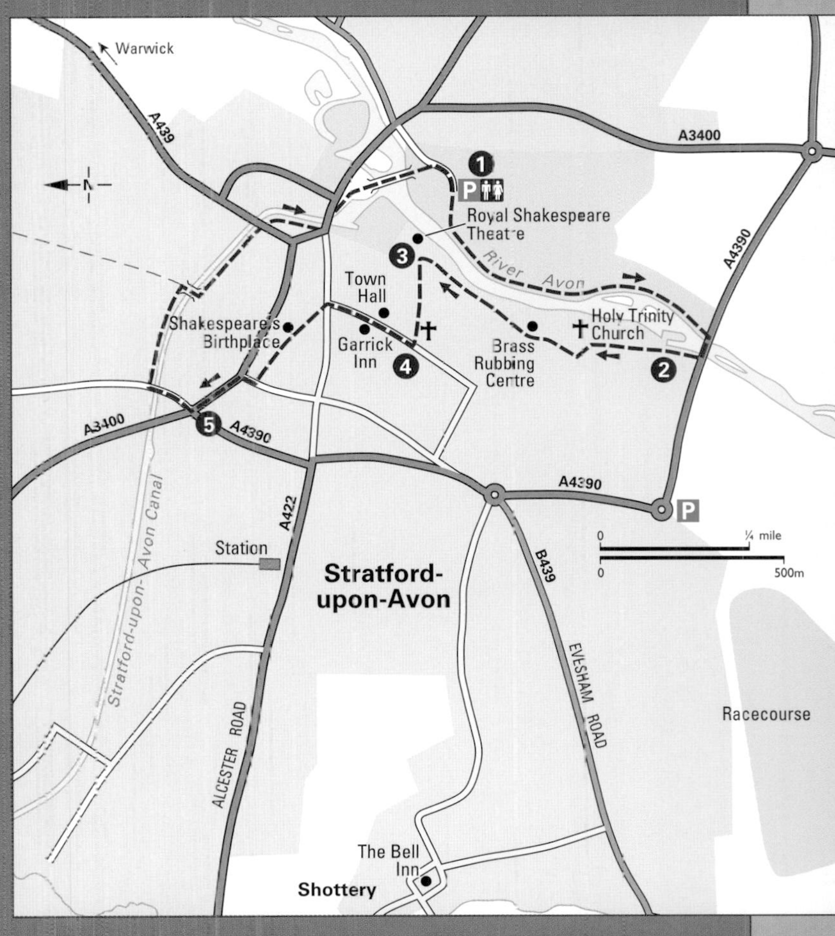

GUNPOWDER TO WIG POWDER

During the 17th century Britain endured a roller-coaster ride through religious and political controversy, and was nearly torn apart by years of bitter fighting in the English Civil War, followed by the Restoration of the Monarchy. Yet by the dawn of the 18th century, the foundations of a modern nation state had been laid.

King James VI of Scots, son of Mary, Queen of Scots, became James I of England when Queen Elizabeth I died on 24 March 1603 without an heir. He left Calvinist Edinburgh to take up his throne in London, where Puritans were pushing to get rid of all remnants of Catholic ritual in the Church. Their bid to abolish bishops went too far for the new king, but when, in 1605, Guy Fawkes and his Catholic conspirators tried to blow up the Houses of Parliament, James hardened his stance and reimposed anti-Catholic penalties.

James was a notable patron of the arts. William Shakespeare's play *Measure for Measure* was written in his honour; during his and his son Charles I's reigns drama and poetry flourished in the hands of playwrights John Webster and Ben Jonson and poets John Donne and John Milton; royal funds were splashed out on the Banqueting House in Whitehall Palace, designed by Inigo Jones. Asked to vote the king money to cover these costs and to pay for war with Spain, Parliament presented its 'grievances'.

Acceding to the throne on James's death in 1625, Charles I found himself in similar difficulties, seeking funds for wars with Spain and France, and alienating Parliament with his 'High Church' views. In 1629 the Commons passed resolutions condemning the King, while the Speaker was held down in his chair. For the next 11 years Charles ruled without calling a parliament. The interlude ended with the king's defeat by Scottish Presbyterians resisting the English-style religious practices. Parliament returned and the wrangle continued. In 1642 Charles entered the House of Commons with troops to arrest the ringleaders, only to find that 'his birds had flown'. Neither side was prepared to yield, so both prepared for civil war. Seven years of bitter fighting beginning in 1642 devastated the country, dividing families and destroying crops, buildings and lives. After Charles's execution in 1649 the nation was left in a state of exhaustion and shock. Lord Protector Oliver Cromwell's vicious campaigns in Ireland and puritanical domestic policies made him a hate-figure to many, and after his death Charles II was restored to the throne in 1660 to widespread acclamation.

AFTER THE RESTORATION

Theatres reopened for the first time since 1642, but religious conflicts continued, and a split between the King's supporters and opponents – Tories and Whigs – marked the beginnings of a political party system. In the mid-1660s two disasters hit – the Plague and the Great Fire of London. But despite all this, poor harvests and wars against the Dutch, parts of Britain prospered. American and West Indian colonies supplied tobacco, cotton, rice and sugar. Fortunes were made; money opened doors to power and influence. In 1688 the 'Glorious Revolution' took place: the Catholic king – Charles's brother, James II – was deposed in favour of William of Orange, and Parliament established a constitutional Protestant succession. Everywhere, the old certainties of religion, power and knowledge were being challenged. Two years earlier, Isaac Newton had put forward his laws of physics, changing man's view of the universe for ever.

KEY SITES

Edge Hill, Warwickshire: Battleground for one of the first major clashes of the Civil War in 1642.

Wardour Castle, Wiltshire: Where Royalist Lady Arundel defied a besieging army in 1643.

Sedburgh, Cumbria: Where George Fox, founder of the Quakers, preached a key sermon in 1652.

Eyam, Derbyshire: Village struck by the plague in 1665 and put into voluntary quarantine.

London: Some 53 new churches were built in the wake of the Great Fire of 1666.

Castle Howard, Yorkshire: One of England's great houses, begun in 1699 by John Vanbrugh.

***Left:** With the Restoration came a taste for opulence in reaction to the Puritanism of previous years*

1603 – 1714

1603 When James I accedes to the English throne, having ruled for 36 years as James VI of Scots in Scotland, religion is a burning issue. The King is caught between the Puritans who are pressing for reform and the Catholic influences of his court.

1605 James gives way to his Puritan advisers and introduces penal laws against Catholics.

1605 Alarmed by his religious policies, a group of Catholic conspirators plan to blow up the King, his family and the Houses of Parliament. Guy Fawkes is discovered and caught before he is able to light the fuse of several barrels of gunpowder.

1611 Shakespeare's late plays, *The Winter's Tale* and *The Tempest*, are performed for the first time.

Edge Hill and a Theatre of War

This climb on a wooded escarpment offers fine views over a 17th-century field of battle

***Above right:** Looking down on the battlefield from Edge Hill*

***Below:** Brutal fighting claimed more than 4,000 lives at the Battle of Edge Hill*

The scene may look peaceful now, but around 370 years ago the fields below the tree-lined escarpment known as Edge Hill were anything but quiet. This tranquil corner of south Warwickshire was the setting for the first major battle of the English Civil War in 1642. On the morning of Sunday 23 October Charles I's army departed from Cropredy Bridge, a few miles away in neighbouring Oxfordshire, arriving at Edge Hill, which was already occupied by Prince Rupert's army, at noon. A staggering 14,000 Royalist troops spread out across the entire hillside, from the Knowle to Sunrising Hill, and as many as 10,000 Parliamentarians, under the command of the Earl of Essex, were massed in the fields below. Led by Prince Rupert, the cavalry of the King's right flank charged and routed the enemy, pursuing the men beyond the village of Kineton, several miles to the northwest. They began to celebrate.

An Inconclusive Battle

Elsewhere, the Royalists were not doing so well. Commanding the left flank, the Commissary-General attacked the enemy's right. At first his efforts proved successful, but on reaching a line of hedgerows and ditches near Little Kineton, he was driven back. At the same time the King advanced his centre, also with success, until he, too, was forced to halt – his way blocked by trees and hedges. Open to attack on both sides, the army's centre gave way and the royal standard-bearer, Sir Edmund Verney, was killed.

Prince Rupert re-emerged from Kineton and relieved the King's centre, thus averting defeat; the battle still raged as darkness descended over the escarpment, and the Earl of Essex and his forces withdrew to Kineton for the night. The King slept in a nearby barn and then breakfasted in Radway the following morning. Neither side seemed keen to continue the battle and Charles resumed his march to London unopposed while Essex withdrew to Warwick. Inconclusive though it was, the battle claimed the lives of more than 4,000 men on a single day.

There were occasions during the Civil War when it looked as if Charles might win. But two factors ruined his chances. One was the military genius of Oliver Cromwell, whose successes at Marston Moor (1644) and Naseby (1645) confirmed him as the foremost cavalry leader, and the other was the intervention of the Scots. The first Civil War finally ended in 1651.

Walk 55 Green fields of a Civil War battleground

Look down on a peaceful landscape in which Royalists once clashed with Parliamentarians

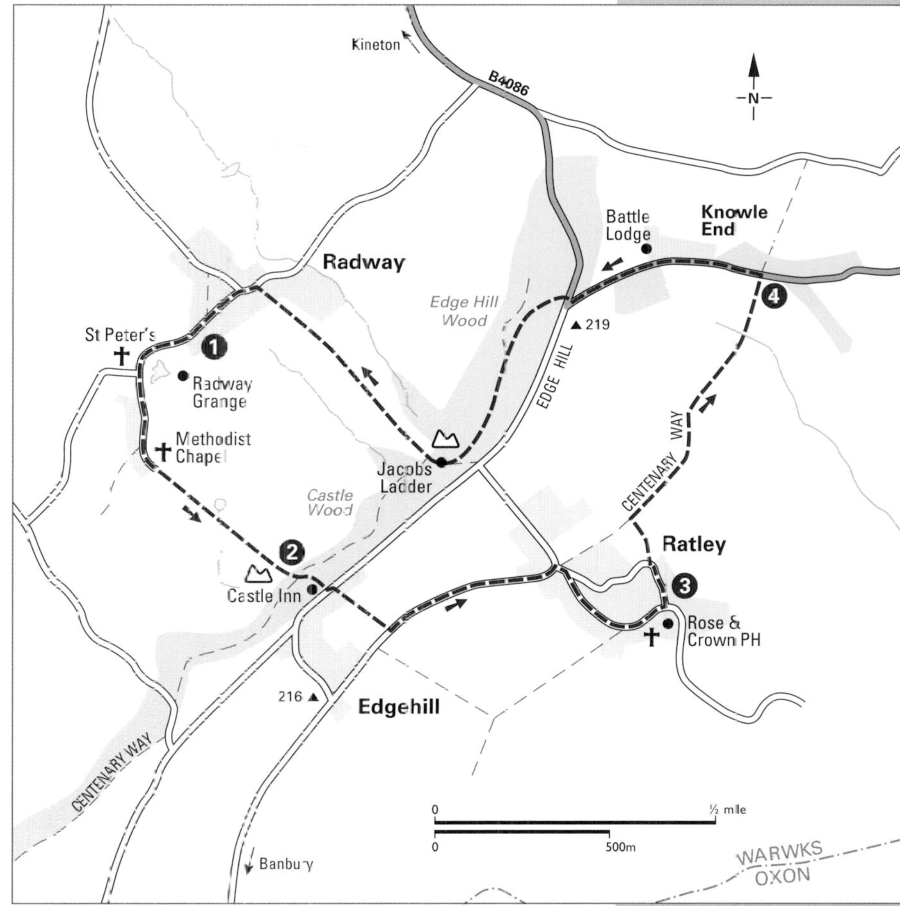

1 Walk through the village of Radway to the church. Veer left here into West End and pass beside the grounds of Radway Grange on your left. Curve left by a pond and some thatched cottages. The 19th-century Methodist chapel can be seen here. Follow the lane as it becomes a stony track and go through two kissing gates into a field. Walk ahead to a third gate and continue ahead across the sloping field towards Radway Tower, now the Castle Inn. Look for an inspection cover near the left-hand field boundary and maintain the same direction, climbing steeply towards the wooded escarpment.

2 Make for a gate and enter the wood. Continue straight over the junction and follow the markers for the Macmillan Way up the slope to the road. With the Castle Inn on your right, turn left for several paces to take a right-hand path running between Cavalier Cottage and Rupert House. Turn left at the road and walk along to Ratley. At the T-junction turn right and follow the High Street down and round to the left. Pass the church and keep left at the triangular junction.

3 With the Rose & Crown over to your right, follow Chapel Lane and, when it bends left, go straight ahead up some steps to a stile. Keep the fence on the left initially before striking out across the field to a stone stile in the boundary wall. Turn right and follow the Centenary Way across the field to a line of trees. Swing left and now skirt the field down to a galvanised kissing gate, cut across the field to a footbridge and then head up the slope to reach a gap in the field boundary.

4 Turn left and follow the road past some bungalows. Pass Battle Lodge and make for the junction. Cross over and join a woodland path running along the top of the escarpment. On reaching some steps on the left, turn right and descend steeply via a staircase known as Jacobs Ladder. Drop down to a gate and then follow the path straight down the field to a kissing gate at the bottom. Go through a second kissing gate beyond, then pass alongside a private garden to reach a drive. Follow it to the road and turn left for the centre of Radway.

WHAT TO LOOK OUT FOR

Radway Grange was once owned by Walter Light, whose daughter married Robert Washington in 1564. The couple were the great-great-great grandparents of George Washington, the first President of the United States. The house was later owned by the architect Sanderson Miller, who carried out improvements in the 18th-century Gothic Revival style. One of Miller's friends was the writer Henry Fielding, who read his manuscript of *The History of Tom Jones* (1749) in the dining room. Earl Haig, Commander-in-Chief of British Forces during the First World War, also rented Radway Grange.

Distance 3.5 miles (5.7km)

Minimum time 1hr 30min

Ascent/gradient 280ft (85m) ▲▲▲

Level of difficulty ●●●

Paths Field and woodland paths, country road, 2 stiles

Landscape Edge Hill escarpment

Suggested map OS Explorer 206 Edge Hill & Fenny Compton

Start/finish Grid reference: SP 370481

Dog friendliness On lead in Radway and Ratley, under close control on Centenary Way

Parking Radway village

Public toilets None on route

1611 The King James or Authorised Version of the Bible in English is published.

1618 Inigo Jones begins design of the Banqueting House in Whitehall.

1620 *The Mayflower* sets sails from Plymouth to North America, carrying the Pilgrim Fathers. During the following two decades, 20,000 emigrants travel from England to join the colony.

1625 Charles I accedes the throne, but within a year causes controversy by dissolving Parliament.

1642 The English Civil War breaks out when Charles I attempts to arrest five MPs for treason. The royal court moves to Nottingham as outrage mounts and opposition grows in the capital.

1642 A Parliamentary ordinance bans stage plays and orders the closure of all theatres.

1644 Parliament orders that Sundays be strictly observed and bans the celebration of Christmas.

Old and New Wardour Castles

A gentle ramble through the Nadder Valley and rolling parkland passes the scene of two dramatic Civil War sieges

Below and bottom: *The two faces of shattered Wardour Castle*

Inset: *A staircase inside the castle ruins*

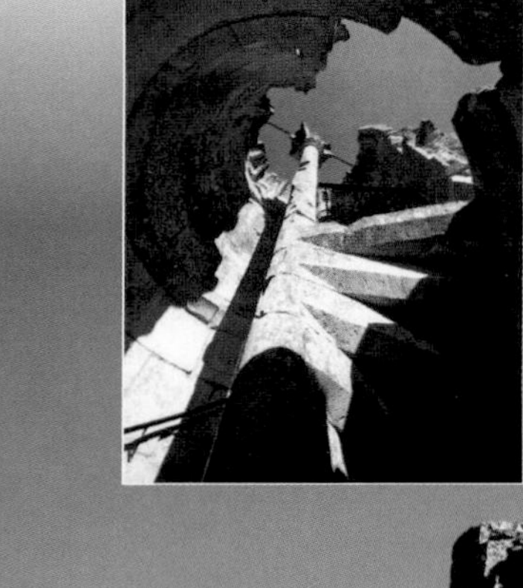

The austere ruins of Old Wardour Castle stand in a peaceful lakeside setting deep in south Wiltshire countryside. On a spur of high ground, protected by acres of secluded woodland, they overlook the Palladian mansion of New Wardour Castle and the tranquil Nadder Valley.

Civil War Sieges

During the Civil War in 1643, the castle had to be defended against a Commonwealth army. A garrison of only 50 soldiers and servants, along with Lady Arundell, conducted an heroic defence of Old Wardour, holding out for six days against 1,300 of Cromwell's regulars led by Sir Edward Hungerford. The Parliamentarian leader was notorious for depriving the most prominent Royalist families of their houses and property. Lady Arundell surrendered only when offered honourable terms, which the Roundheads immediately broke, sacking the castle and imprisoning her. Rather than destroy the castle, the Parliamentarians decided to install a garrison there and use it to protect themselves from a strengthening Royalist army in Wiltshire.

However, Henry, Lord Arundell's son, resolved to recover his confiscated property and his home. After several unsuccessful demands for the Parliamentarians to surrender, the young Arundell lay siege to the castle in January 1644. During the siege, a gunpowder mine was laid in a drainage tunnel underneath the castle. When it exploded a large portion of the structure collapsed, leaving it uninhabitable.

New Wardour Castle

Old Wardour was never restored after the Civil War. In the early 18th century the ruins were surrounded by landscaped gardens, creating the flavour of a romantic ruin. New Wardour Castle was designed in a Palladian style by James Paine for the 8th Lord Arundell and built, in 1769–76, on the other side of the park. It remained the seat of the Arundell family until 1944. This fine building has since been a school, and was converted into apartments during the 1990s.

Walk 56 Royalist castle that held an army at bay

Inspect the ruins of Old Wardour, where Lady Arundell defied her Parliamentarian besiegers

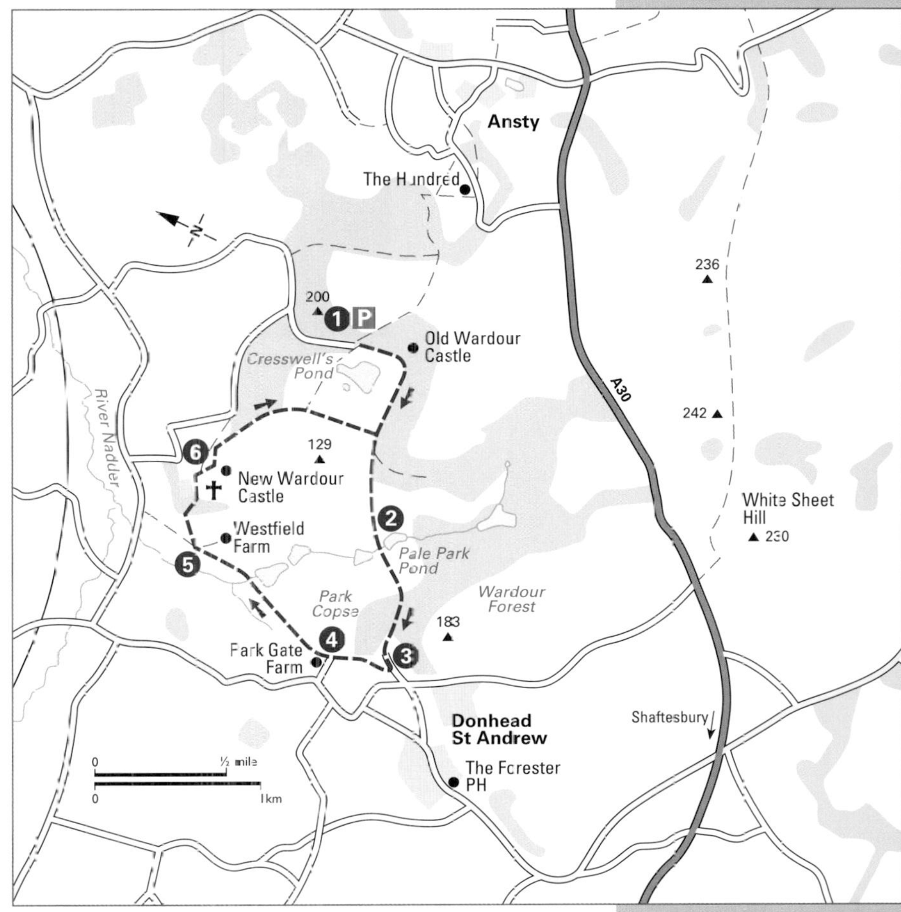

1 From the parking area, turn left along the drive and pass between the castle and Cresswell's Pond. Pass the Gothic Pavilion, then at Wardour House (private) bear right with the trackway. Gently climb the wide track, skirting woodland, then at a fork keep right. At the end of the woodland, cross a stile by a field entrance and walk ahead along the right-hand side of the field, heading downhill to a stile.

2 Follow the path beside Pale Park Pond to a squeeze gate, then ascend across the field to a further squeeze gate into woodland. Shortly, bear right to continue along the main forest track, before leaving Wardour Wood beside a gate onto a gravel drive.

3 At the end of the drive, cross the stile on your right. Head downhill across the field to a metal gate and then follow the waymarked path through Park Copse, soon to bear left down a grassy clearing to a squeeze gate beside a field entrance. Follow the right-hand edge towards Park Gate Farm.

4 Cross a stile on to the farm drive and turn right (yellow arrow) to cross the concrete farmyard to a gate. Follow the path beside the hedge to a further gate, with the River Nadder on the left, then proceed ahead along the right-hand field-edge to a double stile in the far corner. Bear diagonally left across the field, aiming for the left-hand side of a cottage. Go through a gate and maintain direction to reach a stile.

5 Cross the farm drive and the stile opposite and head straight uphill, keeping to the left of the tree and directing yourself towards a stile and woodland. Follow the path right on through the trees and soon bear left in order to pass a building on your left. New Wardour Castle is now visible on your right. Keep close to the bushes as you make your way across the grounds towards the main drive and then turn right along a gravel path.

6 Join the drive and walk past New Wardour Castle. Where the track forks, keep right to a stile beside a gate. Follow the grassy track ahead across parkland towards Old Wardour Castle. Climb a stile beside a gate and proceed ahead, following the track uphill towards a T-junction of tracks. Turn left and follow your outward route back to the car park.

WHAT TO LOOK OUT FOR

In the grounds of Old Wardour Castle (entrance charge), seek out the elaborate rockwork grotto and the remains of a stone circle, both part of 18th-century landscaping improvements carried out Lancelot 'Capability' Brown. Film buffs may recognise the castle as a location in the 1991 movie *Robin Hood: Prince of Thieves.*

Distance 3.75 miles (6km)

Minimum time 1hr 45min

Ascent/gradient 278ft (85m) ▲▲▲

Level of difficulty ●●●

Paths Field and woodland paths, parkland tracks, 11 stiles

Landscape River valley, undulating parkland

Suggested map OS Explorer 118 Shaftesbury & Cranborne Chase

Start/finish Grid reference: ST 938264

Dog friendliness Dogs can be off lead on downland track

Parking Free parking at Old Wardour Castle

Public toilets Old Wardour Castle (if visiting ruin)

1603 – 1714

1645 Royalist hopes of victory are dashed when Oliver Cromwell brings his New Model Army to Naseby.

1647 Charles is captured and imprisoned at Carisbrooke Castle, Isle of Wight, despite rallying support from the Scots.

1648 Cromwell routs the Scots at Preston.

1649 Charles I is beheaded in London. England is proclaimed a Commonwealth.

1651 Charles II is crowned in Scotland and invades England, but Cromwell defeats him at Worcester.

1653 Under the Instrument of Government, Cromwell is proclaimed Lord Protector of the Commonwealth.

Sedbergh and the Quakers

A delightful walk leads from Sedbergh to the Quaker hamlet of Brigflatts

Top: *The Friends Meeting House at Brigflatts dates to 1675*

Right: *George Fox urged Friends to 'walk cheerfully over the world'*

Below: *The Quaker burial ground at Brigflatts, in use since 1656*

The solid, stone-built town of Sedbergh, one of the largest settlements in the Yorkshire Dales National Park, is noted for its Quaker associations. In 1652 the founder of the Religious Society of Friends, George Fox, came to the town and preached from a bench beneath a yew tree in the churchyard to a great crowd of people attending the Hiring Fair. On Firbank Fell, northwest of Sedbergh, Fox again preached to a large crowd, this time from a large stone, still known as Fox's Pulpit. This meeting is said to mark the inception of the Society of Friends. (They are also known as Quakers – according to one account because early Friends trembled or quaked when inspired by the Holy Spirit.)

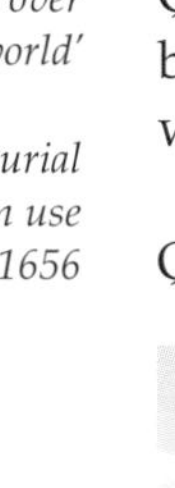

The best reminder of the early days of the Quakers in the area is to be found in the tiny hamlet of Brigflatts. Fox stayed here with Richard Robinson in a farmhouse in 1652, and in 1674 the Friends of the district decided to build a Meeting House. Completed the following year, it still survives, and is the oldest in the North and the third oldest in England. From the outside, it looks like a typical whitewashed cottage of the period, though, unlike most cottages, it had a stone roof from the start. Each winter the cracks in the slate were stuffed with moss to stop the rain getting in. George Fox was there in 1677, noting 'a great concourse…there were about 500–600 persons present. A very good meeting it was.' Around the beginning of the 18th century the gallery was put up to accommodate the large gatherings. Just up the lane from the Meeting House is the small and peaceful burial ground, first used in 1656.

Walk 57 First days of the Society of Friends

Walk in the footsteps of George Fox to the oldest Quaker Meeting House in the North

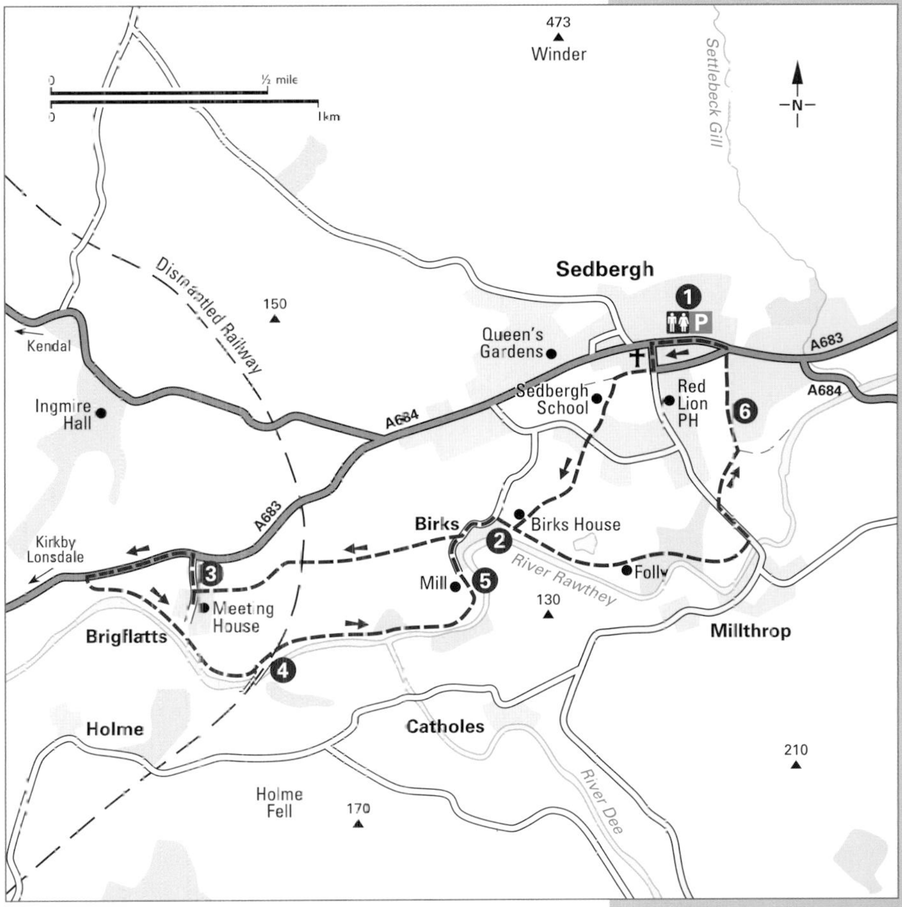

1 From the car park, turn right along the main street. At the junction with the main road turn left. At the churchyard, turn right, signed 'Cattle Market or Busk Lane'. At the next signpost, go left behind the pavilion, then straight ahead through two kissing gates to a road. Cross and go down a track beside playing fields. Go through a kissing gate near a barn and follow a green path to pass Birks House.

2 Go through a kissing gate to a lane and turn left. Pass several houses then go right, through a metal kissing gate, and bear half-left to a waymarker, roughly following the Brigflatts sign. Follow the wall and then cross a field to a small bridge under the old railway. Drop down and bear slightly left, proceeding along a path across fields as far as a gate that gives onto a quiet lane opposite the Quaker Burial Ground.

3 Turn left to visit the Meeting House, then return to the gate, continuing on up the lane to the main road. Turn left. Just beyond the bend sign, go through a signed metal kissing gate in the hedge on the left. Follow the narrow path to meet the River Rawthey and walk upstream to a large railway bridge.

4 Go through the gate and slant up the embankment. Cross and descend back to the river. Continue along the riverside, passing the confluence of the Rawthey and the Dee, and reach a tarmac lane by an old mill.

5 Follow the lane back into Birks. Go right, though the kissing gate signed 'Rawthey Way' (you went through this the other way earlier in the walk). By the hedge around Birks House, bear right and down towards the river. Walk alongside another playing field to a stile. Climb slightly left to go past a folly. Follow the left side of a wood, then enter at a kissing gate. At a footpath sign, bear right down a sunken path. Leave the wood and follow a clear path across a field to emerge onto a road by a bridge. Turn left. By the 'Sedbergh' sign, go right, though a stile. Cross the field to another stile, then bear left alongside a wall to another kissing gate.

6 Cross a drive, go downhill and then carry on straight on along a lane to the main road. Cross the road then turn left at the 'No Entry' sign, proceeding along Sedbergh's main street to the car park.

Distance 4.5 miles (7.2km)

Minimum time 1hr 30min

Ascent/gradient 131ft (40m) ▲▲▲

Level of difficulty ●●●

Paths Mostly field and riverside paths, 7 stiles

Landscape Playing fields give way to rich farmland, dominated by fells

Suggested map OS Explorer OL19 Howgill Fells & Upper Eden Valley

Start/finish Grid reference: SD 659921

Dog friendliness Keep dogs on lead when animals in fields

Parking Pay-and-display car park just off Sedbergh main street (which is one-way, from west)

Public toilets By car park

HOWGILL FELLS AND CAUTLEY SPOUT

The Howgill Fells, very different from the rest of the Yorkshire Dales, are huge, rounded humps of hills that seem to crowd in on each other like elephants at a watering hole. They are formed from pinkish sandstone and slate, 100 million years older than the limestone that underlies much of the rest of the National Park. The hills have few of the stone walls you will see elsewhere in the Dales – they are mostly common grazing land for the local farms and escaped the passion for enclosure in earlier centuries. One of the spectacular sights of the Dales, the great ribbon of waterfalls known as Cautley Spout, is worth the drive from Sedbergh in the direction of Kirkby Stephen – park by the Cross Keys, a temperance inn. You can view the falls from there or walk part of the way towards them on a good path.

1658 Oliver Cromwell dies. He is succeeded as Lord Protector by his son, Richard.

1658 Richard Cromwell resigns.

1660 Charles II is restored to the throne by a new Parliament. The Restoration brings with it a shrewd king, and religious tolerance presides over a new era, which sees a fresh blossoming of English literature, drama, scientific discovery and architecture.

1665 The outbreak of the Great Plague in London kills 14,000 people a week, resisting preventive measures such as scented posies and 'purifying bonfires'. The plague claims 80,000 lives before slowing its course.

1666 The Great Fire breaks out in a baker's shop in Pudding Lane, London, and burns for three days, destroying 13,000 houses and 80 churches. Only a few die in the blaze and the fire destroys the last vestiges of the plague, but medieval London is all but lost.

1667 John Milton's great poem *Paradise Lost* is published for the first time. It was written in 1658–64.

An Enemy of the King

This bracing mountain walk leads past the home of a leading Civil War politician and military leader

There are few people living in Nantcol these days – just a handful of farmers. When you set out along the narrow tarmac lane to the mountains you're struck by the sheer isolation of the place. Yet Maes-y-garnedd, the first farm along the route, had an important role in the events if the English Civil War (1642–51) – for it was then the home of Colonel John Jones, Member of Parliament for Merionnydd.

The Barmouth and Harlech areas were strong supporters of the Crown, Harlech being one of the last strongholds to surrender to the Parliamentarians. But Jones was not a Royalist: he married Cromwell's sister and took an active part in the war, and was one of the signatories of Charles I's death warrant in 1649. Colonel Jones gained much power from his associations, but the death of Cromwell and the Restoration was untimely, for Charles II remembered him and condemned him to death. Diarist Samuel Pepys noted that the steaming remains of Jones's hung, drawn and quartered body were dragged through the streets of London.

A Fearsome Place, a Glorious Lake

The tarmac lane ends just beyond the farm and a good stony path climbs into Bwlch Drws-Ardudwy, a dark pass between the cold grey ramparts of Rhinogs Fawr and Fach. This was a drovers' route along which the Welsh Black cattle would have been driven to the markets of the Marches and the Midlands. The drovers would have been armed and mob-handed, but for the solo traveller in times gone by this would have been a fearsome place: an area frequented by robbers and highwaymen.

Beyond the pass you reach first the shallow lake of Llyn Cwmhosan, with its pale yellow marsh grass contrasting with dusky heather, and then the magnificent Llyn Hywel, one of the great sites of Wales. Rhinog Fach appears as a pyramid of boulders and scree, capped by crag. On the other side of the hollow lies Y Llethr, highest of the Rhinogs, displaying a little more greenery, but still cutting quite a dash. In between the peaks are slabs of rock plunging at 45 degrees into the deep waters of the lake.

Below: *Looking beyond the valley of Cwm Nantcol, Rhinog Fawr (left) and Rhinog Fach (right)*

Walk 58 Welsh republican executed for regicide

Head past Colonel John Jones's farm on your way to the magnificent Llyn Hywel

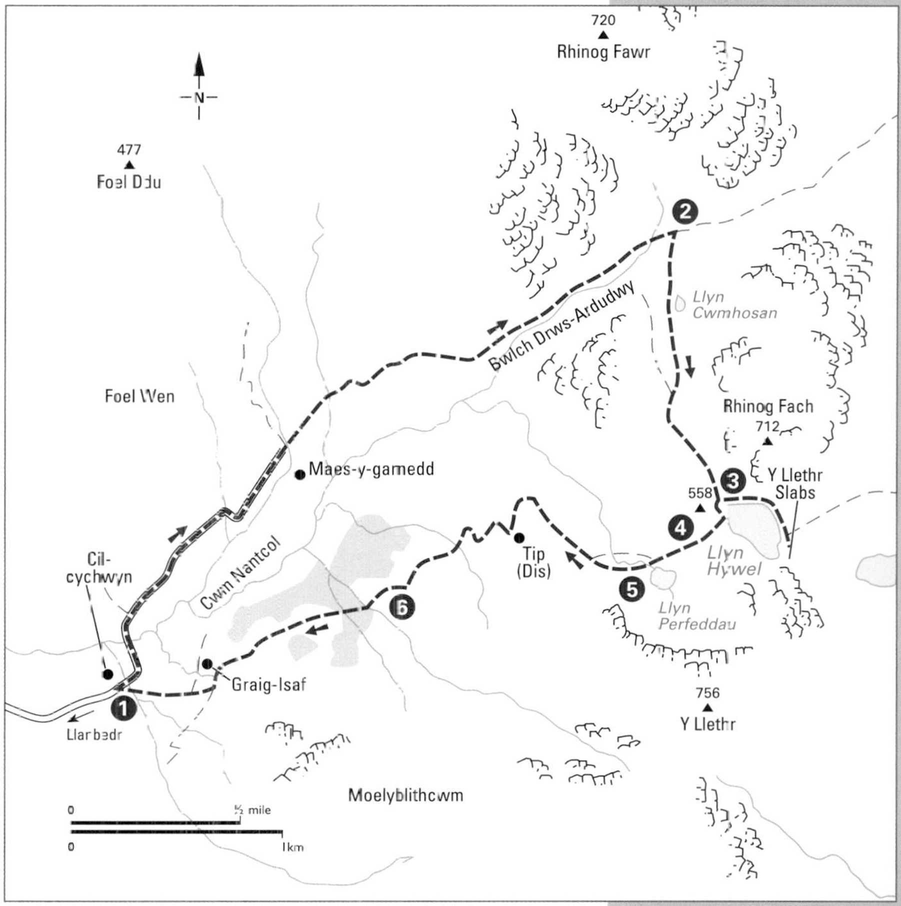

1 From the farm at Cil-cychwyn, follow the narrow lane up the valley until you reach its end. Here continue on a narrow wall-side path, initially hidden, through upper Nantcol. The path traverses the lower south flanks of the splendid Rhinog Fawr before entering the dark pass of Bwlch Drws-Ardudwy.

2 On reaching a marshy basin beneath Rhinog Fawr and Rhinog Fach look for ladder stiles over the wall on the right. The first of these leads to a very steep short-cut that bypasses Llyn Cwmhosan. It is preferable to take the second stile and follow a narrow path climbing through heather and passing the west shores of Llyn Cwmhosan, and beneath the boulder and screes of Rhinog Fach's west face. Beyond this, the route comes to the shores of Llyn Hywel.

3 For the best views take the path left of the farm, crossing bouldery screes, and up to the top of the huge Y Llethr Slabs, that plummet into the lake. Retrace your steps to the lake's outlet point, then continue along the west shore.

4 Turn right to follow a sketchy, narrow path down to Llyn Perfeddau which soon becomes visible. Nearing the lake, keep straight ahead on a faint path where the clearer path goes off to the right.

5 Follow the wall running behind the lake then, after about 0.5 mile (800m), go though a gap in the wall to follow a grassy path that rounds a rocky knoll high above Nantcol before passing an old mine. Descend leftwards to a prominent track that winds past some mine workings before adopting a straighter course, passing a ruined farm.

6 Through woodland and high pasture, the track passes Graig-Isaf farm before reaching the valley road at Cil-cychwyn.

THE RHINOGS

The Rhinogs, or the Harlech Dome as they are known to geologists, have an overlying strata of rock formed in the Cambrian era more than 500 million years ago, long before the surrounding mountain ranges. Mainly consisting of greywackes (grits), these were formed beneath the sea but were uplifted during a collision of continental plates. Look at the layers of angular slabs of rock that form Rhinog Fawr's southern face to see the immense folding in this anticlinal system.

The mountains – known as Rhinogydd in Welsh – are widely covered in heather. The best known peaks are Rhinog Fawr (2,363ft/720m) and Rhinog Fach (2,337ft/712m), but the highest in the range is in fact Y Llethr (2,481ft/756m). A 30 sq km area of the range is designated a Special Area of Conservation and National Nature Reserve. You're likely to encounter a few wild goats, for the mountains are home to a lively and noisy population of these animals.

On the walk's return leg, the heather is particularly thick around the lake of Llyn Perfeddau. Here you can pause to see Rhinog Fach perfectly reflected in the water before returning to Cwm Nantcol.

Distance 5.5 miles (8.8km)

Minimum time 3hrs 30min

Ascent/gradient 1,378ft (420m) ▲▲▲

Level of difficulty ●●●

Paths Peaty paths through heather and farm tracks, 1 stile

Landscape Gnarled gritstone peaks with heather slopes

Suggested map OS Explorer OL18 Harlech, Porthmadog & Bala

Start/finish Grid reference: SH 633259

Dog friendliness Can be off lead in upper heather-clad regions of walk

Parking Small fee for parking at Cil-cychwyn farm or Maes-y-garnedd

Public toilets None on route

1603 – 1714

1675 The Royal Observatory is founded at Greenwich by Charles II for the discovery of 'the longitude of places for perfecting navigation and astronomy'.

1675–1710 Architect Sir Christopher Wren builds St Paul's Cathedral, on Ludgate Hill, London. The cathedral is remarkable for its fine 278ft (85m) dome and the impact it makes on London's skyline.

1678 John Dryden's *All for Love* is first performed.

1684 Isaac Newton, mathematician and scientist, publishes his revolutionary Theory of Gravity.

1685 James II accedes the throne, but because he is a Catholic he is regarded with suspicion, and is described as being 'as very papist as the pope himself'.

Eyam – the Plague Village

This thought-provoking walk tours the village that cut itself off

Above right: *The Riley Graves outside Eyam*

Below: *A Saxon preaching cross in the churchyard*

Bottom: *St Lawrence's, Eyam*

Eyam (pronounced 'eem') is best known as the community that placed itself in quarantine when the plague arrived, desperately trying to prevent it from spreading throughout Derbyshire. The plague came to Eyam via a batch of infected cloth from London in summer 1665 and soon the local tailor's family had been struck down. The deadly disease quickly spread to the entire community – and when it was over, 14 months later, had claimed the lives of 260 villagers out of a population of around 800.

Under the leadership of Rector William Mompesson, villagers agreed a self-imposed exile to stop the plague spreading beyond Eyam. Supplies were left on the edge of the village and families agreed to swiftly bury their own dead at or close to their homes. Today you can see many of the sites associated with this time, including cottages and houses with plaques recording who died where. You can also extend the walk east of the Square by half a mile (800m) to visit the Riley Graves, a tragic and touching spot where a mother buried her whole family.

Saxon Settlers

Yet it would be wrong to think that Eyam's history is just about the plague. In Eyam churchyard, for instance, a Saxon preaching cross from the 8th century recalls a time when settlers were attracted by the plentiful supply of water.

Since then, here as in many other Peak District communities, farming and mining have been the two main occupations. Lead, barytes and fluorspar have all been all extracted at various times, but when a major works on the edge of the village closed some years ago it signalled a large-scale regeneration project that has resulted in new housing and recreation facilities – all of which you can see at the end of the walk.

Jacobean Manor House

Eyam also has its fair share of interesting and beautiful old buildings. Eyam Hall, which you pass on Church Street, is an imposing Jacobean manor house whose associated farm buildings have been converted into a craft centre. In contrast, only a few paces along the street is a simple terraced row of cottages, including the 'Plague Cottage' where the 'visitation' (as it was called) first struck in Eyam.

Although there are plenty of interesting interpretation boards dotted around the village, your walk should begin or end with a visit to Eyam Museum, which chronicles the entire history of the village. The museum is open Tuesday–Sunday, March–November. For a more detailed guide to the village buy a copy of 'The Eyam Map', produced by villagers as a special millennium project and full of illustrated detail.

Walk 59 Eyam's infectious historical charm

Pay your respects to 17th-century victims of the plague in a fine Peak District village

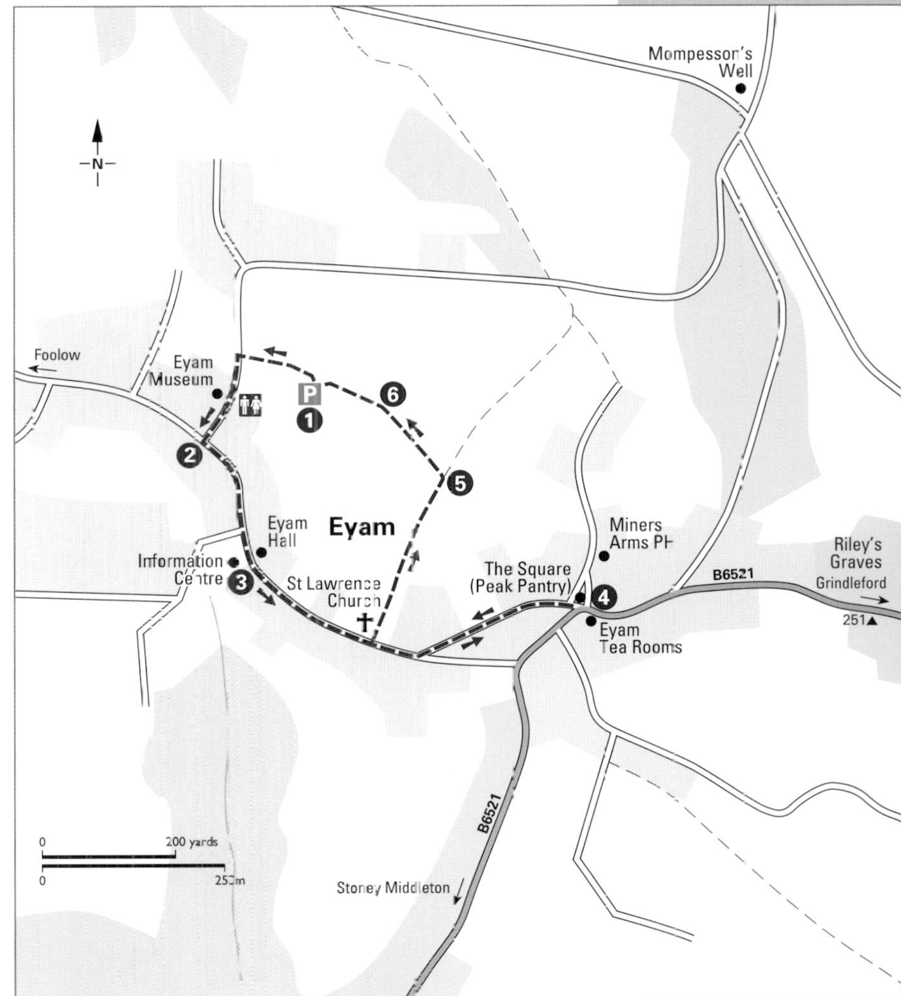

1 After parking in the Parish Council's free car park (not the District Council one just below, which charges) go out of the car park and turn left, down Hawkshill Road. Eyam Museum is on the right, which you can either visit now or at the end of the walk.

2 At the junction at the bottom of the road turn left Walk along Church Street through the middle of the village. On the right, opposite Eyam Hall, is a seasonal information centre in the old market hall.

3 Continue along Church Street past the sheep roast stand, the Plague Cottage and the church. Just after the school fork left at the junction and follow the road down to the Square in the heart of the village.

4 After visiting the cafés or a pub and inspecting the various interpretation boards, retrace your steps to St Lawrence's Church. Go right at the gate into the churchyard, signed 'public footpath', and either visit the church or follow the path around the building. Head for the exit at the northeastern corner.

5 Go through the black kissing gate and turn left for a dirt track uphill, with the graveyard on your left. Above on the right is a football pitch. At the top of this track you come to a gate.

6 Go through the gate, then a second, with the children's play area and the village cricket green on the left. Go straight on to reach the car park.

WHAT TO LOOK OUT FOR

If you go up Hawkshill Road and follow it to the top of the steep hillside you come to Mompesson's Well (by the turning to Bretton). The well was where food and other supplies were left for collection by the villagers, who in return paid with money they placed in the running water to be sanitised. Some food was supplied free by the Earl of Devonshire from the gardens at nearby Chatsworth House. Opposite Eyam Hall, on a small green, are Eyam stocks. At one time every town had to have this form of punishment, which was meted out to miscreants who failed to obey the law. Individuals would be locked in the stocks by their hands and feet for a specified time and then subjected to the ridicule of passers by.

Distance 1 mile (1.6km)

Minimum time 1hr

Ascent/gradient 98ft (30m) ▲▲▲

Level of difficulty ●●●

Paths Pavements and one unsurfaced but hard track

Landscape Village street scene

Suggested map OS Explorer OL24 White Peak

Start/finish Grid reference: SK 216767

Dog friendliness On lead on streets

Parking Parish Council car park

Public toilets Near car park

The Flaming City

This fascinating linear walk traces the route of the Great Fire of London of 1666

Londoners of the 17th century must have wondered what they had done to deserve such calamities when, only months after they had fought off the Great Plague, they had to face a fire of monumental proportions. The fire began at a bakery in Pudding Lane. It was 2am on Sunday 2 September, 1666 when the baker discovered the fire. He escaped to safety along a roof, but his young assistant was not so lucky. Neither were the 13,000 houses, 87 churches and 40 livery halls that perished in the inferno over the following days.

The flames were fanned by east winds. The fire raged throughout Sunday, Monday and Tuesday but finally grew less powerful on Wednesday and was extinguished on Thursday 6 September. Londoners attempted to flee the flames, some to Moorfields, and others up to the high ground of Highgate and Hampstead. Remarkably, only eight people lost their lives in the fire itself – although how many later died after being left homeless is unknown. It took five days to contain the fire, partly because of the high number of houses with timber roofs and the rudimentary fire-fighting equipment available at the time.

A City Rebuilt

The event at least offered an opportunity to give the city a facelift but, due to the sheer cost and to property rights, most of the rebuilding followed the original street lines. The remaking of London did, however, create a safer, more sanitary English capital than before. Within six years the city had been rebuilt and its boundaries extended – and London was in the midst of an economic boom. By 1700 the population had increased five-fold to 500,000 inhabitants.

With the new population and new houses came a demand for new furniture – excellent news for cabinetmakers. In terms

Far left: *St Stephen's Walbrook was one of 53 London churches built by Sir Christopher Wren in the wake of the Great Fire. A 15th-century church on the site had been destroyed by the flames. The church's 63ft (19m) dome was based on Wren's initial design for St Paul's*

Left: *The Monument was built in 1671–77 to mark the rebuilding of the city. Designed by Wren and physicist Robert Hooke, it is 202ft (61m) tall – the exact distance from its location just north of London Bridge to the place in Pudding Lane where the fire began*

Below: *Wren's most famous London church was the majestic St Paul's Cathedral, finished in 1710. Its entrance is through the Great West Door*

of technical development, the city's manufacture of chests and cabinets led the way. Perhaps one of the most common items produced by a cabinetmaker was the table, with candlestands and mirror ensemble, which had been introduced from France and soon became a standard item of furniture in many English homes. To meet heavy demands furniture was, for the first time, offered across a range of quality and price.

Brisk trade with North America, the East Indies, East India and the Far East introduced new styles such as lacquer-ware. Although France led the way in furniture design, Oriental items such as screens were very popular. Most Londoners made do with 'japanned' furniture that was varnished in a cheaper imitation of lacquer, much of which survives today. Cane chairs too, were introduced from the Far East and most middle-class homes had one or more 'English chairs'.

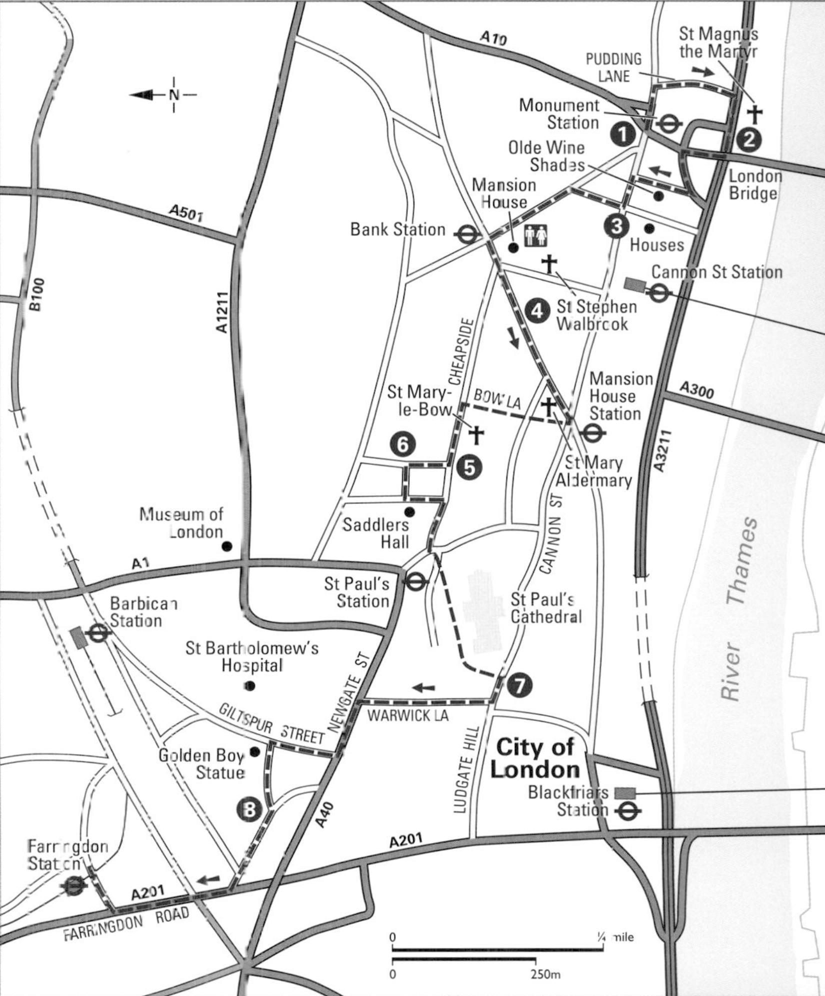

Walk 60 The City that rose from the ashes

See where the Great Fire began and some of the beautiful churches built in the wake of its destruction

1 Take the Fish Street Hill exit from the Monument tube station and bear right towards the Monument. Follow the cobbled street for 20yds (18m) to see the plaque that marks the spot on the corner of Pudding Lane where the ill-fated bakery once stood. Bear right, then cross Lower Thames Street at the pedestrian crossing to reach St Magnus the Martyr Church.

2 A few paces further to the right of the church, climb a set of steps and, ignoring the first exit, continue to arrive on the west side of London Bridge. Continue ahead, away from the river, along King William Street and shortly turn left along Arthur Street and then sharp right into Martin Lane, past the Olde Wine Shades. At the end turn left into Cannon Street. (For a detour to see the red brick houses that survived the fire, turn next left into Laurence Poultney Hill.)

3 Cross the road and turn right into Abchurch Lane. At the end bear left along King William Street towards Bank tube station. Keep to the left, past the front of Mansion House, and notice the street on the left, Walbrook: this is the site of one of Wren's finest churches, St Stephen Walbrook Church. Turn left into Queen Victoria Street.

4 Continue ahead, then turn right into Bow Lane, past St Mary Aldermary and a row of shops, to St Mary-le-Bow at the end. Turn left into Cheapside which, despite being the widest road in the City, also went up in flames.

'GOLDEN BOY'

The statue on the building at the corner of Cock Lane of the 'Golden Boy' marks the spot where the fire is thought to have ended. On this site, until 1910, stood a pub called The Fortune of War, where body-snatchers would leave bodies and wait to hear from the surgeons of the nearby St Bartholomew's Hospital.

5 Cross this road, and turn right into Wood Street. On your right was the site of one of London's debtors' prisons.

6 Turn left into Goldsmith Street and, at the Saddlers Hall opposite, turn left and rejoin Cheapside. Turn right and cross the pedestrian crossing to St Paul's Cathedral. Walk through the churchyard, bear left to reach Ludgate Hill.

7 Turn right and right again into Ava Maria Lane, which becomes Warwick Lane. At the end turn left along Newgate Street. At the traffic lights turn right along Giltspur Street, then left into Cock Lane.

8 Where another road meets it, turn right along Snow Hill, past an angular building, and right at Farringdon Street (which becomes Farringdon Road). At the second set of traffic lights turn right, to reach Farringdon tube, where the walk ends.

Distance 2.25 miles (3.6km)
Minimum time 2hrs
Ascent/gradient Negligible ▲▲▲
Level of difficulty ●●●
Paths Paved streets
Landscape Alleys and roads in busy City of London
Suggested map AA Street by Street London
Start/finish Monument tube station; Farringdon tube station
Dog friendliness Not recommended for dogs
Public toilets Monument, Mansion House

1603–1714

1688 James II attempts to gain toleration for the Catholic Church but sparks rebellion and provokes hostility in the House of Commons. MPs invite the King's Protestant Dutch son-in-law, William of Orange, to invade. James flees to Ireland, a deposed king.

1689 William III and Mary II begin their rule as joint monarchs in a constitutional monarchy.

1690 William confronts James in Ireland. James is defeated at the Battle of the Boyne and is forced into exile in France, without his crown.

1692 In 'the Massacre of Glencoe', troops commanded by Campbell of Glenlyon under the orders of William III slaughter men, women and children of the Clan MacDonald at Glencoe in Scotland.

The Braes o' Killiecrankie

This fine walk leads from Killiekrankie to Loch Faskally

Ye wouldna been sae swanky o/ If ye'd hae seen where I hae seen/ On the braes o Killiecrankie o'…' This song, commemorating victory in the Battle of Killiecrankie in July 1689, is still sung wherever anyone with an accordion sits down in a pub full of patriotic tourists. In fact, both sides in the battle were Scots.

When James II was ousted from England in a bloodless coup in 1688, the Scots Parliament (the Estates) voted to replace him with William of Orange. The Stuarts had neglected and mismanaged Scotland, persecuting the fundamentalist Protestants (Covenanters) of the Southern Uplands. John Claverhouse, 'Bonnie Dundee', had earned the rather different nickname 'Bluidy Clavers' in those persecutions. He now raised a small army of Highlanders in support of King James. The Estates sent a larger army north under another Highlander, General Hugh Mackay, to sort things out.

Dundee, outnumbered two to one, was urged to ambush Mackay in the Pass of Killiecrankie. He refused, on the grounds of chivalry. The path above the river was steep and wide enough for only two soldiers; a surprise attack on such difficult ground would give his broadsword-wielding Highlanders too great an advantage against Mackay's inexperienced troops. Just one of the Lowlanders was picked off by an Atholl sharpshooter at the Trouper's Den, and the battle actually took place to the north of the pass.

Claymore Victorious

Killiecrankie was the last time the claymore conquered the musket in open battle – and this was due to a deficiency in the musket. Some 900 of the 2,500 Highlanders were shot down as they charged, but then the troopers had to stop to fix their bayonets, which plugged into the muzzle of the musket. By this time the Highlanders were upon them, and they broke and fled.

The battle lasted just three minutes. Half of Mackay's army was killed, wounded, captured or drowned in the Garry. One escaped by leaping 18ft (5.5m) across the river – the 'Soldier's Leap'. Dundee died in battle. A month later his army was defeated at Dunkeld, and 25 years later in 1713, when the Highlanders next brought their claymores south for the Stuarts, the troopers had learnt to fix a bayonet to the side of a musket where it did not block the barrel.

***Above:** 'Bonnie Dundee' died in a cavalry charge during the Battle of Killiecrankie*

***Below:** The Pass of Killiecrankie is a deep river gorge*

Walk 61 Where Highland claymores conquered Mackay's muskets in 1689

Marvel at the length of a soldier's river leap as a prelude to a pleasant country ramble

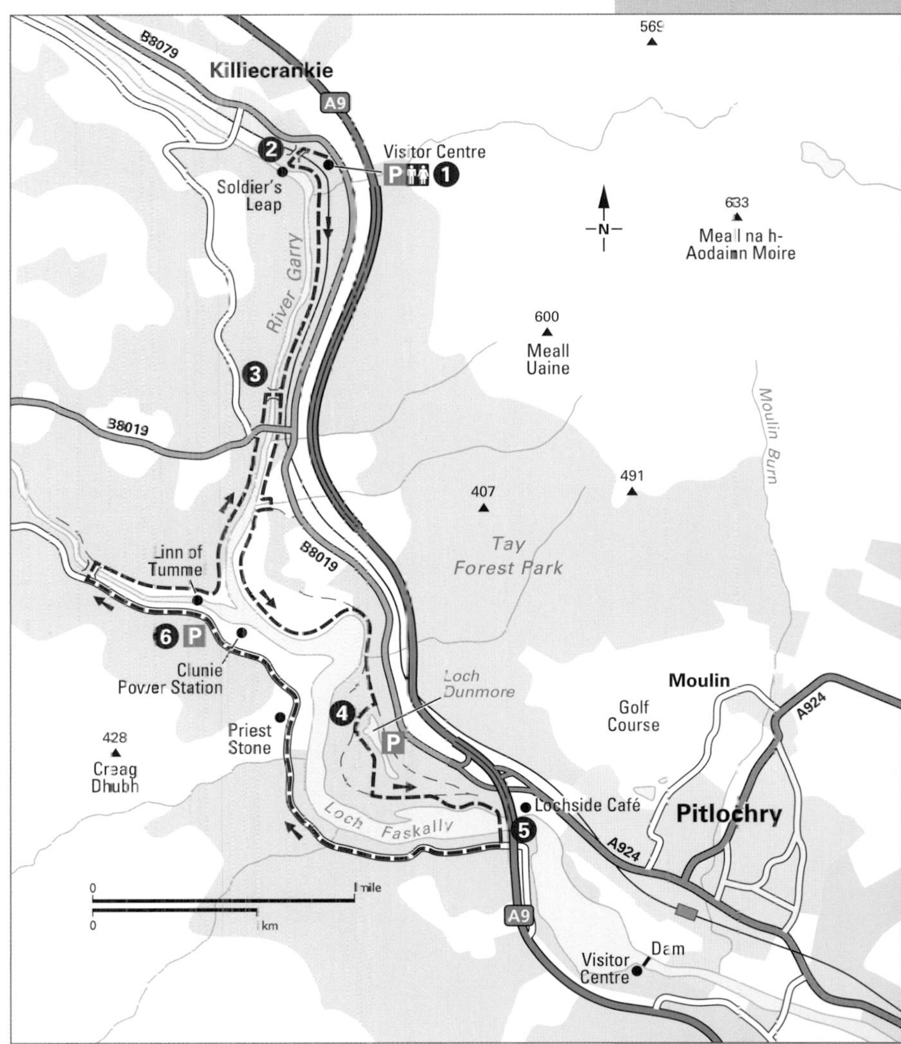

1 From the back corner of the Visitor Centre steps, signed 'Soldier's Leap', lead down into the wooded gorge. A footbridge crosses the waterfall of Trouper's Den. At the next junction, turn left ('Soldier's Leap'). Ten steps down, a spur path on the right leads to the viewpoint above the Soldier's Leap.

2 Return to the main path, signed 'Linn of Tummel', which runs down to the River Garry below the railway viaduct. After following this path for 1 mile (1.6km) you reach a footbridge.

3 Don't cross this footbridge, but continue ahead, signed 'Pitlochry', along the riverside under the tall South Garry road bridge. The path bears left to a footbridge. Cross and turn right, signed 'Pitlochry', back to the main river. The path runs around a huge river pool to a tarmac lane; turn right here. The lane leaves the lochside, then passes a track on the right, blocked by a vehicle barrier. Ignore this track; shortly afterwards turn right at a signpost, 'Pitlochry'.

4 Immediately bear left to pass along the right-hand side of Loch Dunmore, following red-top posts. A footbridge crosses the loch, but turn away from it, half-right, onto a small path that becomes a dirt track. After 270yds (250m) it reaches a wider track. Turn left, with a white/yellow waymarker. After 220yds (201m) the track starts to climb; here the white/yellow markers indicate a smaller path on the right, which follows the lochside to a point below the A9 road bridge.

5 Cross Loch Faskally on the Clunie footbridge below the road's bridge and turn right, taking the quiet road that leads around the loch. In 1 mile (1.6km), at the top of the grass bank on the left, is the Priest Stone. After you pass the Clunie Power Station, you reach a car park on the left. Here a sign indicates a steep little path leading down to the Linn of Tummel.

6 Return to the road above for 0.5 mile (800m), to cross a grey suspension bridge on the right. Turn right, downstream, to pass above the Linn. A spur path back right returns to the falls at a lower level, but the main path continues along the riverside (signed 'Killiecrankie'). It bends left and goes down wooden steps to the Garry, then continues upstream and under the high road bridge. Take the side-path up onto the bridge for the view of the river, then return to follow the descending path signed 'Pitlochry via Faskally'. This runs down to the bridge, Point 3. Return upstream to the start.

Distance 8.75 miles (14.1km)

Minimum time 4hrs

Ascent/gradient 492ft (150m) ▲▲▲

Level of difficulty ●●●

Paths Wide riverside paths, minor road

Landscape Oakwoods on banks of two rivers

Suggested map OS Explorer 386 Pitlochry & Loch Tummel

Start/finish Grid reference: NN 917626

Dog friendliness Off lead on riverside paths

Parking Killiecrankie Visitor Centre

Public toilets At start

CLUNIE POWER STATION AND PITLOCHRY DAM

Loch Faskally is artificial, and you will pass the Clunie Power Station on the walk. Its stone arch commemorates the five people who tragically died during the construction of the Clunie Tunnel, which brings water from Loch Tummel down to Killiecrankie. At the Pitlochry dam that forms Loch Faskally, Scottish and Southern Energy has a visitor centre celebrating its hydro-electric schemes. Look for the window into the salmon ladder beside the dam: from March to October, you can watch the fish battle their way up towards Killiecrankie. The loch itself attracts visitors angling for its brown trout and pike.

1694 The Bank of England is established by the government, on the advice of a group of businessmen who raise £1.5 million to lend to the government in return for a regular interest payment into the bank. The enterprise is to be a roaring success.

1695 A new coinage is introduced, funded by a tax on windows. Many windows are bricked in.

1700–1789 The 'Age of Reason' begins, under the influence of thinkers such as John Locke, Jean-Jacques Rousseau, Immanuel Kant and Thomas Paine.

1702 Jethro Tull invents the horse-drawn seed drill.

1702 After the death of King William (following that of Mary in 1694), Queen Anne accedes to the throne.

Glorious Castle Howard

A truly delightful walk leads around the well ordered estates of one of the country's most famous stately homes

One of the greatest of England's stately homes, Castle Howard was designed in 1699 by John Vanbrugh for Charles Howard, 3rd Earl of Carlisle. Vanbrugh was not an architect; he had made his reputation first as a soldier, then as a playwright – author of *The Relapse: Or Virtue in Danger* (1696) and *The Provok'd Wife* (1697), so he was an odd choice. Nevertheless, he rose to the task in superb style. The north front, which we see from the first part of the walk, is hugely dramatic, with its giant columns, curving wings and crowning dome. One early visitor, Horace Walpole, wrote, 'I have seen gigantic palaces before, but never a sublime one.'

Everyone who visits Castle Howard will soon realise that this great house is set in a landscape that has been carefully manipulated as a setting for the house. The impressive 3.75-mile (6km) long, ruler-straight avenue that passes through the fortified Carrmire Gate and the Pyramid Gate, is only the start. Virtually everything of the estate you will see on the walk has been altered – hills rounded or levelled, rivers re-routed and dammed, lakes dug. All this was to create what the 18th-century writers called 'a perfect landskip', based on Italian paintings and dotted with classical buildings.

Top right: The Temple of the Four Winds

Above: The South Front, with the Atlas Fountain

Below: The Mausoleum

Pyramid and Mausoleum

There are three pyramids at Castle Howard. One is over the Pyramid Gate, one is in Pretty Wood and the third, the 'Great' Pyramid, is a landmark on the second part of this walk.

To the right as you approach the ornamental bridge over the New River, created in the 1740s, is the Mausoleum, the final resting place for many generations of the Howard family. Beyond the bridge is the Temple of the Four Winds. This building is at the end of a terraced walk from the house; it is said that this was originally the main street of the village of Henderskelfe, swept away by the 3rd Earl and his architect in their grandiose scheme. Beyond, notice the garden wall; the ground is higher on the house side, and is retained by a solid, rustic wall with a ditch in front of it – an early 'ha-ha', which allowed uninterrupted views of the countryside without the inconvenience of sheep in the drawing room.

Walk 62 A 'sublime palace' set in a perfect landscape

Take in fine views of the loveliest of landscapes, created to offset the house it contains

1 From the roadside car park, turn left to reach the crossroads and then turn right towards Coneysthorpe. Walk right through the attractive village, and, just beyond the 'Slow' road marking, go right through a tall white gate in a wall.

2 Go half-left, following the Bog Hall sign. Cross the track and head towards the further telegraph pole, passing the cemetery on your left. Go through a gate, then bend right along the edge of a field and, when you reach the double gate, turn right again along the edge of the wood. Continue along the track to reach a bridge.

3 Do not cross the bridge, but turn left along the track, continuing as it bends right through the farm buildings, following the Welburn and Centenary Way (CW) signs. The track passes a wood and winds over a bridge. At the next farm buildings follow the Centenary Way sign to the right.

4 At the T-junction, turn right along the metalled lane. The Pyramid comes into view. As you near the Pyramid, you will reach a staggered crossroads. Turn right here, signed 'Coneysthorpe', and descend to the bridge over the dammed stream, with the Mausoleum on the right and Castle Howard on the left.

5 Cross the bridge, go through the gate then bear left, keeping the Temple of the Four Winds on your left. The path goes on over the ridge, then turns left towards the park wall. Follow the wall as it bends around to the left, go though a kissing gate beside a white gate.

6 After about 50yds (46m), just beyond a gate on your left, go left off the track down a grassy path. Follow this, keeping parallel to the estate wall to another track. Cross the track, then bear half-left to reach another track. Turn right here and follow this track back to the tall white gate in Coneysthorpe. Turn left through the gate, and retrace your route back to the car park.

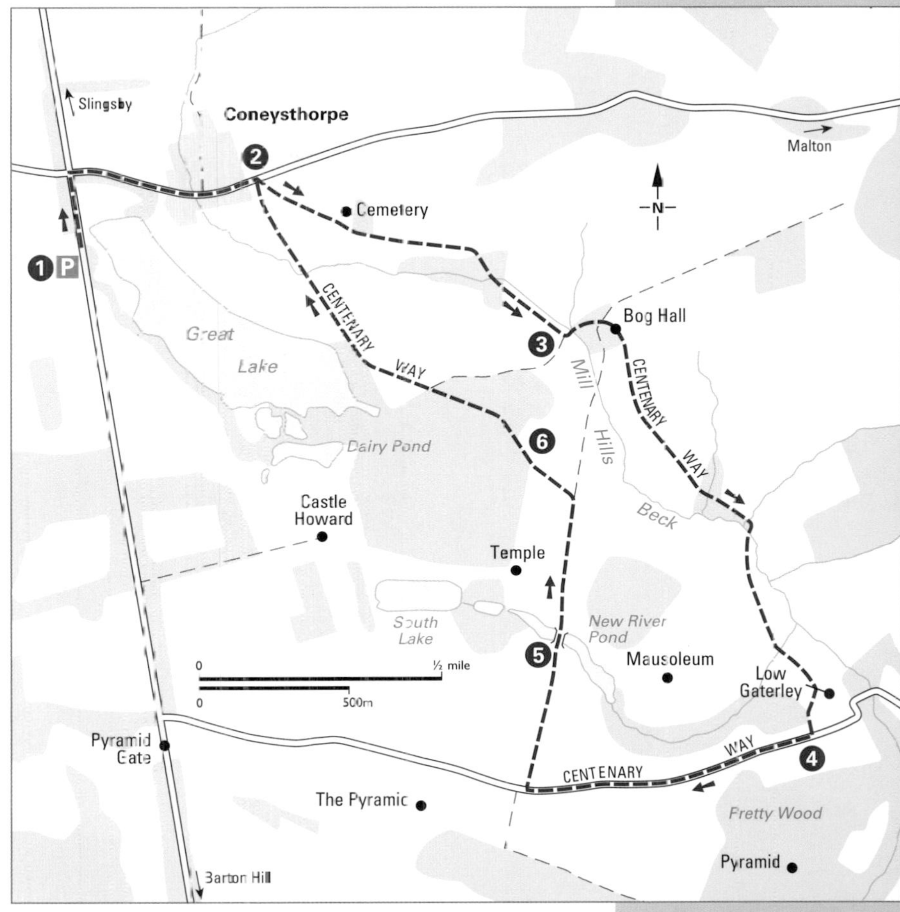

THE ATLAS FOUNTAIN

Not everything at Castle Howard is 18th century. The largest piece of sculpture in the gardens is the grandiose Atlas Fountain, with the Titan holding up the globe and surrounded by Tritons spouting water from their shells. This was put in place when the Victorian garden designer W. E. Nesfield laid out a new parterre at Castle Howard's south front. It was sculpted by Prince Albert's favourite artist, John Thomas. Thomas's 'labours in this important and arduous undertaking have been unwearied, and his success has kept pace with his exertions', commented the *Art Journal* in 1851. The Atlas Fountain came to Castle Howard after being on display at the Great Exhibition in that year.

Distance 5.25 miles (8.4km)

Minimum time 2hrs

Ascent/gradient 256ft (78m) ▲▲▲

Level of difficulty ●●●

Paths Field paths and estate roads, no stiles

Landscape Estate landscape and farmland

Suggested map OS Explorer 300 Howardian Hills & Malton

Start/finish Grid reference: SE 708710

Dog friendliness Dogs should be on lead for much of walk

Parking Roadside car park near lake northwest of Castle Howard, near crossroads

Public toilets None on route (toilets at Castle Howard)

1603 – 1714

1704 The royal estate of Woodstock is given to the Duke of Marlborough in gratitude for his victory over the French at the Battle of Blenheim. The building of Blenheim Palace starts in 1705.

1707 The Act of Union between England and Scotland combines the two parliaments into a single governing body.

1709 At Coalbrookdale, Shropshire, Abraham Darby develops a method of using coke to smelt iron.

1711 Horse racing is founded at Ascot by Queen Anne. Her Majesty's Plate is run for 100 guineas.

1711 German-born composer George Friederic Handel's first London opera, *Rinaldo*, is performed.

1711 *The Spectator* periodical is first published.

1713 The war with France ends.

1714 The death of Queen Anne also marks the end of the Stuart monarchy, making way for a new royal house, that of the Hanoverians. The first king of the house of Hanover is George I.

The Romance of Rob Roy in Callander

Steep wooded paths lead you through the crags in a land once familiar to an outlaw clan

***Top:** The graves of Rob Roy, his wife and two sons in Balquhidder*

***Above:** The hardy Highland cattle were the rustlers' prize*

As you climb through the trees above Callander, it is easy to imagine yourself back in the late 17th century, when Rob Roy and his clansmen lived as outlaws in the heart of the Trossachs. For some, Rob Roy is a Highland hero, for others a notorious cattle thief – whatever the truth behind the myth, he is certainly one of the most colourful characters in Scottish history.

Rob Roy (Gaelic for 'Red Robert') was more properly known as Robert MacGregor. Born in 1671, he was the son of Donald MacGregor of Glengyle. This clan had been outlawed in 1603, and was known as 'the nameless clan' because they were even forbidden to use their name. The MacGregors had a reputation for violence. They defended their lands and cattle vigorously against assaults from neighbouring clans, which included the Campbells, who acted as government agents. Rob Roy, living as a cattle herder in Balquhidder, kept an armed band of men to protect him and his cattle – and offered their services to neighbours who paid him protection money. He began to extend his influence and eventually made a claim to be the chief of the clan.

In 1712 he borrowed money from the Duke of Montrose for a speculative cattle deal, and suffered heavy losses. His lands were seized, his properties plundered and his wife and children turned out of their home in midwinter. These were already troubled times, for the Jacobite rebellion had begun in 1689. This was an uprising in support of the Catholic James II, who had been replaced on the throne in 1688 by the Protestant rulers William III and Mary II – and there were frequent battles between government forces and the 'Jacobite' supporters of King James. Rob Roy, who had fought on the Jacobite side at Sheriffmuir, now gathered his clansmen and took revenge on the Duke of Montrose, supporter of the government.

Loved by the Good

As a result, Rob Roy was outlawed and stories began to appear about his dramatic escapes. He even began to be seen as a sort of Robin Hood figure, generously helping the poor by stealing from the rich: local people would help him and warn him if troops were in the area. However, Rob Roy's luck didn't last – he was captured in 1727 and sentenced to transportation. However, he was later pardoned and went back to Balquhidder, where he seems to have settled down and lived quietly for the rest of his life. He died in 1734 and is buried in Balquhidder.

Walk 63 Through Red Robert's lawless lands

Fall in love with the isolated hills in which Rob Roy's followers rustled cattle

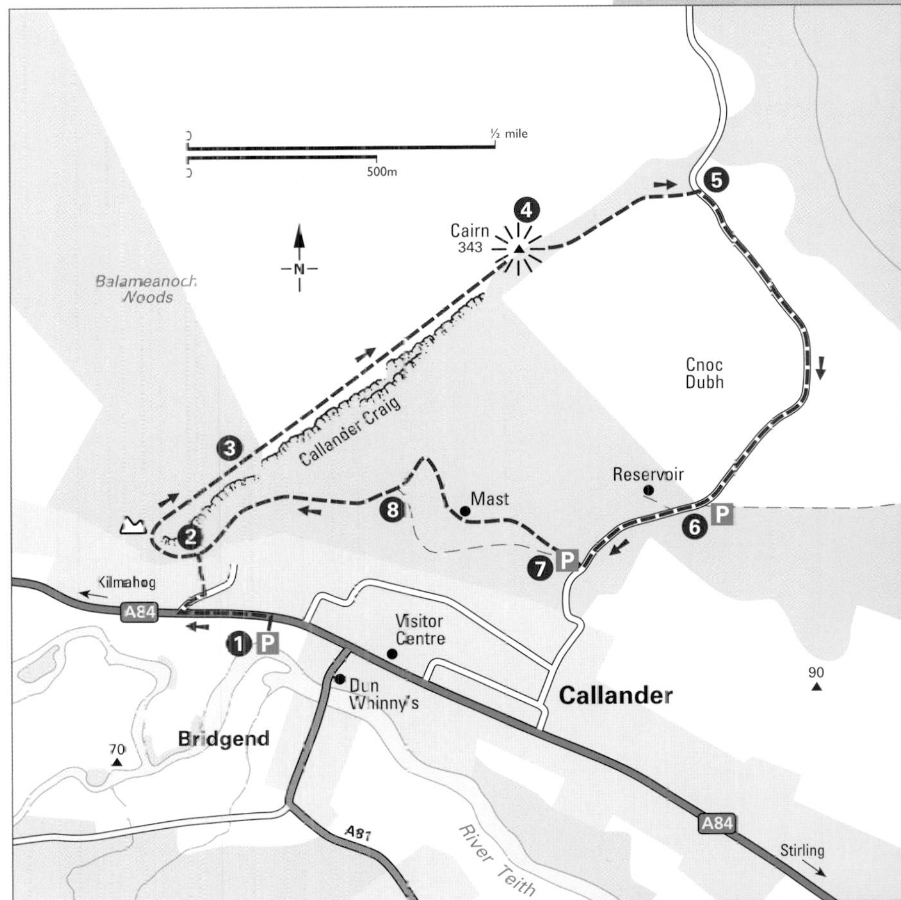

1 From the Riverside car park, walk back to the main road, then turn left. Follow this, then turn right along Tulipan Crescent. Just in front of some modern flats, turn left and follow the wide track. Where the track splits, take the path on the left that is signposted 'The Crags'.

2 The path now winds steeply uphill through the trees and can get slippery if there's been a lot of rain. Keep following the path and cross a footbridge. Climb to reach a wall on the left-hand side, after which the path narrows. Follow it to pass a large boulder.

3 Continue following the path, which eventually bears left, up some steps to a fence. Cross another footbridge, scramble over some rocks and go through a metal kissing gate. You eventually come to a memorial cairn, created in 1897 for Queen Victoria's Diamond Jubilee. On a clear day there are stunning panoramic views of the surrounding countryside from here.

4 Leaving the cairn, the path now begins to wind downhill. This part of the walk is rocky in places and you will need to take some care as you descend. Follow the path right down to the road.

WHILE YOU'RE THERE

In Callander you will find many of the tourist attractions linked to the ancestry of the Highland clans. The word 'clan' comes from the Gaelic word 'clann'. This originally meant 'children' but gradually came to refer to 'kindred'. The earliest clan was Clann Duib, or Clan Duff. They were the ruling family of Fife. The head of the clan was referred to as MacDuib, or MacDuff. In the centre of Callander look out for the Rob Roy and Trossachs Visitor Centre's audio-visual presentation. Rob Roy and his clansmen, you will discover, were known as the 'Children of the Mist' – because they would appear out of the mist to steal cattle or collect their protection money. The romance of Rob Roy inspired authors and filmmakers – including Sir Walter Scott whose novel *Rob Roy* was published in1817.

5 Turn right along the road – you can see the Wallace Monument near Stirling in the far distance. You will soon pass a sign on the right-hand side for the Red Well, where the water runs a distinctly reddish colour owing to the presence of iron traces in the local rock. Continue until you reach a car park on your left. You can make a detour here to see the Bracklyn Falls.

6 After the car park, stay on the road for about 0.25 mile (400m), passing a track up to a reservoir on your right, then turn right into the Forestry Commission car park (signposted 'The Crags').

7 Continue to walk through a car park onto a broad Forestry Commission track. Continue walking past a telecommunications mast next to the end of the track. At the end of the track, turn left and then walk downhill until you reach a wooden seat and a footbridge.

8 Take the path that runs to the right of the seat (but don't cross the footbridge). Follow the path as it runs downhill and takes you back to the place at which you entered the woods. Turn right, then go left along the main road and walk back into Callander to the car park at the start of the walk.

Distance 4 miles (6.4km)

Minimum time 2hrs 30min

Ascent/gradient 896ft (273m) ▲▲▲

Level of difficulty ●●●

Paths Forest tracks and some rocky paths

Landscape Mixed woodlands, great views of hills and lochs

Suggested map OS Explorer 365 The Trossachs

Start/finish Grid reference: NN 625079

Dog friendliness Can run free, steep climb and crags might not suit some

Parking Riverside car park

Public toilets Callander

THE BRIDGE WAS CAST AT COALBROOK-DALE
AND ERECTED IN

THE GEORGIAN AGE

1714 – 1837

BIRTH OF INDUSTRY

After no fewer than 18 pregnancies, Queen Anne – sister-in-law and successor of William III and the final monarch of the House of Stuart – died in 1714 with no surviving children. A new king arrived at the invitation of the government: the Elector of Hanover, George I. The Georgian era had begun.

George was not universally welcomed. The 'Old Pretender' James Francis Edward Stuart – son of James II, the king deposed in 1688 – pressed his claim to the throne, but fled to France after the ill-fated Jacobite uprising of 1715. A few years later came a different crisis, the South Sea Bubble, an 18th-century version of the Wall Street Crash. The South Sea Company went under in 1720, and hordes of its investors, from government ministers to household servants, faced ruin.

Britain spent much of the 18th century at war, and along the way gathered lands and gained the naval prowess celebrated in the 1740 ditty 'Rule Britannia'. At home, agriculture and industry were progressing rapidly and new inventions came thick and fast. Successful experiments in stock-breeding prompted landowners to turf out their tenants to make way for more sheep and cattle. In 1730 Charles 'Turnip' Townshend revolutionised farming methods with crop rotation. The textile industry was mechanised – and many spinners were put out of work – by James Hargreaves' Spinning Jenny; Richard Arkwright devised a hydraulic spinning frame in 1769, and in the same year James Watt patented his steam engine. Improved smelting techniques increased iron production, and a network of canals carried materials from source to market.

REFORM AND REVOLUTION

London was now the financial and social hub of a growing empire. People gathered in the city's coffee houses to read newspapers and discuss the day's issues, and satire found an eager audience. William Hogarth's prints provided graphic social comments on greed, decadence and ambition. Political corruption became a target for radicals such as John Wilkes, whose popular support foreshadowed the campaign for parliamentary reform and the 1832 Reform Act, which extended the vote to all 40-shilling freeholders – those owning freehold property worth at least £2 (40 shillings) a year. The Jacobite threat resurfaced in 1745, now led by Charles Edward Stuart – son of the 'Old Pretender' and known as the 'Young Pretender'. After the massacre of his followers on Culloden Moor the following year, Charles escaped to Skye, disguised in women's clothes.

In 1763 Britain emerged from the Seven Years' War with France and the government set about replenishing its funds with heavy taxes. When a stamp duty was imposed on the American colonies, an angry response escalated into war. By 1783 the former colonies had won their independence. Revolutionary ideas carried home by America's French allies contributed to the French Revolution, at first welcomed by British radicals such as William Wordsworth and political philosophers such as Thomas Paine. But soon revolution turned to terror, and before the end of the century Napoleon Bonaparte was leading his armies through Europe. British patriots found heroes in Admiral Lord Nelson, who died fending off the French at the Battle of Trafalgar in 1805, and the Duke of Wellington, victor at Waterloo in 1815. Meanwhile, the future George IV, acting as Prince Regent during one of his father's bouts of madness, commissioned John Nash to create Brighton Pavilion in the fashionable resort, and the Georgian era ended with a foretaste of the 19th century's imperial swagger.

KEY SITES

Blenheim Palace, Oxfordshire: Masterpiece of the English Baroque style, completed in 1722.

Temple Newsam, Yorkshire: Park beautifully landscaped by 'Capability' Brown in the 1760s.

Gwennap Pit, Cornwall: Where John Wesley delivered open-air sermons to Cornish miners.

Ironbridge Gorge, Shropshire: Preserved site of early advances in the iron industry.

Dove Cottage, Cumbria: Home to Romantic poet William Wordsworth, 1799–1807.

Left: *The iron bridge near Coalbrookdale, Shropshire, symbolises the way industry transformed Britain*

1714–1837

1714–27 George, Elector of Hanover in Germany, reigns as George I.

1715 The first Jacobite rebellion, in support of James Francis Edward Stuart (son of the James II and known as the 'Old Pretender') in Scotland, is easily crushed.

1717 Handel's *Water Music* is first performed.

1718 The Transportation Act authorises the deportation of convicts to new territories.

1719 Daniel Defoe's *Robinson Crusoe* is published.

1720 Investors lose their savings in the 'South Sea Bubble', the share collapse of the South Seas Trading Company that takes the government down with it.

1720 Nicholas Hawksmoor is working on three London churches: Christ Church Spitalfields, St Anne's Limehouse and St George's in the East.

1720 Prince Charles (the 'Young Pretender') is born.

1721 J. S. Bach presents the Brandenburg concertos to the Margrave of Brandenburg-Schwedt.

Blenheim Palace Parkland

A gentle constitutional through peaceful countryside leads to England's largest stately home

When King George III first set eyes on Blenheim Palace, he remarked, 'We have nothing to equal this.' Few would disagree with him. The views of the palace, the lake and the Grand Bridge from the waterside path on this delightful walk are stunning. Set in a magnificent 2,000-acre (810ha) park landscaped by 'Capability' Brown, the great Baroque house covers a staggering 7 acres (2.8ha) and is England's largest stately home.

Blenheim Palace took nearly 20 years to build and was finally completed in 1722. The architect John Vanbrugh was commissioned to design the house for John Churchill, 1st Duke of Marlborough (1650–1722), following Churchill's victory over the French at Blenheim in 1704. Inside, there are various state rooms and tapestries, the Long Library – considered by many to be the finest room in the house – and the room where Winston Churchill was born in 1874.

Churchill's Just Reward

As a soldier and as a statesman, John Churchill was responsible for suppressing the French king Louis XIV's imperialist ambitions in Europe. Churchill's spirit and determination enabled him to defeat the French at Blenheim on 13 August 1704. In gratitude, Queen Anne conferred the Royal Manor of Woodstock on the Duke of Marlborough and his heirs in perpetuity, and a sum of £500,000 was voted by Parliament for the building of Blenheim Palace.

The Duke's wife Sarah – who was Princess Anne's favourite companion before Anne became queen in 1702 – supervised the building work. She rejected Sir Christopher Wren's designs in favour of those produced by John Vanbrugh, but was a thorn in his side throughout the project and finally forbade Vanbrugh from seeing the finished building in 1725, even refusing him entry to the grounds.

Characterised by ornament and exuberance, Blenheim Palace is not to everyone's taste, although the immense scale of the house has to be seen as a tribute to the skill and ingenuity of its creators. The vast parkland and gardens, too, are renowned for their beauty and range with Vanbrugh's Grand Bridge as the focal point.

Left: *The park was landscaped by 'Capability' Brown*

Below: *Blenheim is the finest embodiment of the English Baroque style*

Walk 64 A tribute to the Duke of Marlborough

Admire a magnificent palace built to express a nation's gratitude to a great general

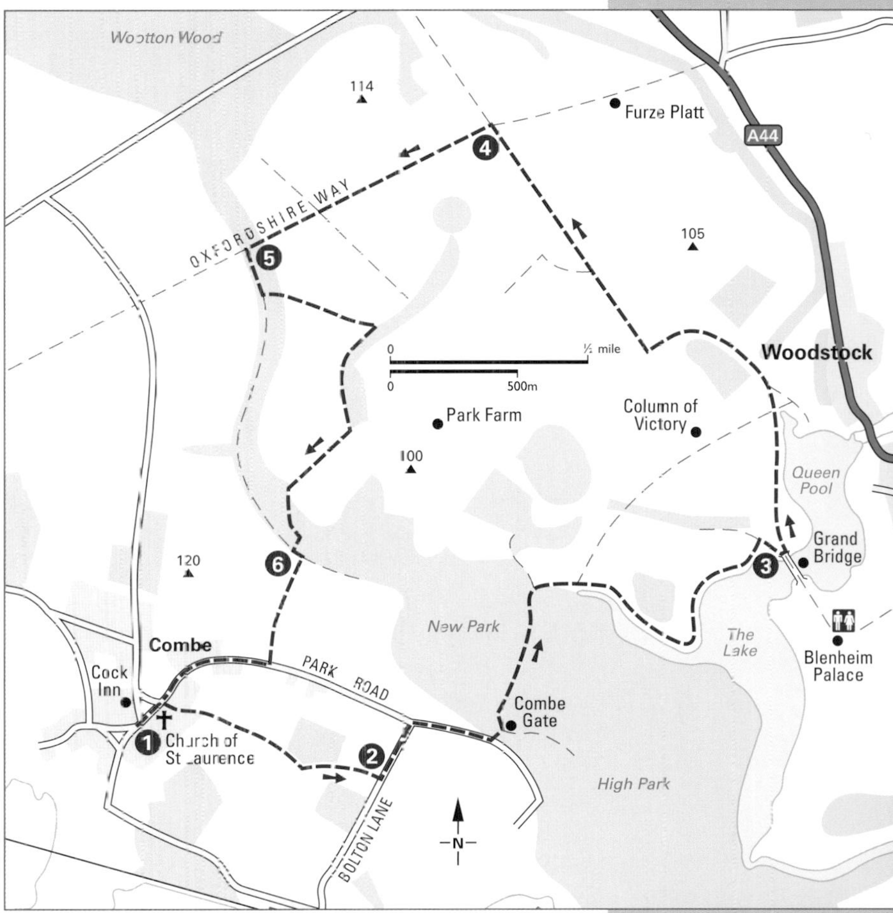

1 From the green, take the road signposted 'East End'. Swing right by the village pump into the churchyard and keep left of the church. Exit through the gap in the boundary wall, flanked by two gravestones, and begin skirting the right-hand edge of the sports field. After about 50yds (46m), branch off into the trees, then head diagonally across the field. Cross into the next field and keep to the right edge of the wood. In the next field, turn left (trees on the left) and go up to the woodland corner. Pass through a gap in the hedge and cross the field.

2 Exit to the road, turn left and keep right at the next junction. Walk to Combe Gate. Go through the large kissing gate into the grounds of Blenheim Palace, keep left at the junction and follow the drive through the parkland. As it sweeps left to a cattle grid, veer to the right by a Public Footpath sign. Follow the grassy path to a stile. Keep right when the path divides and walk beside the western arm of the Lake.

3 Eventually you reach a tarmac drive. Turn right and walk down towards the Grand Bridge. As you approach it, turn sharp left, passing between mature trees and keeping the Queen Pool on your right. Cross a cattle grid and keep ahead through the park. With the Column of Victory on your left, follow the drive as it sweeps around to the right.

4 Turn left at the second cattle grid, in line with Furze Platt (right). Join the Oxfordshire Way, go through a gate and follow the grassy track beside trees, then along a gravel track between fields. At length cross a track and continue towards woodland. Enter, and turn left after a few paces to join a clear track.

5 After about 150yds (137m) take the first left, crossing a footbridge to reach a field edge. Keep right here, following the obvious path across a large field beside fencing. When you reach a track, turn right. Keep alongside trees to a junction. Turn right and follow the grassy track down to and through a wood, then diagonally left across a strip of pasture to an opening. Go up to a track and cross it to a ladder stile.

6 Turn left to a hedge, then turn right, keeping it and a ditch on your right. Skirt a field to the road, turn right and walk back into Combe.

COMBE CHURCH

The original building, which was located in the valley about 1 mile (1.6km) from its present site, was built during the Norman period. The present church, dedicated to St Laurence, was built in about 1395. The design of the church is an example of the Early Perpendicular style, with a stone pulpit and medieval stained glass.

Distance 7 miles (11.3km)

Minimum time 3hrs

Ascent/gradient 150ft (46m) ▲▲▲

Level of difficulty ●●●

Paths Field paths and tracks, parkland paths and estate drives. Some quiet road walking, 2 stiles

Landscape Farmland and parkland

Suggested map OS Explorer 180 Oxford

Start/finish Grid reference: SP 412159

Dog friendliness On lead in grounds of Blenheim Palace

Parking Spaces in centre of Combe

Public toilets Blenheim Palace, for visitors; otherwise none on route

1721 Sir Robert Walpole is elected First Lord of the Treasury, making him effectively Prime Minister and the most powerful man in Britain.

1726 Jonathan Swift publishes *Gulliver's Travels.*

1727 George I dies; his son George Augustus becomes George II.

1731 The 'Architect Earl', Richard Boyle, 3rd Earl of Burlington, designs the Assembly Rooms, York.

1732–35 William Hogarth paints his series of eight pictures, *A Rake's Progress.*

1736 Witchcraft is abolished as a punishable crime in Scotland following repeal of a 1604 statute.

1739 John Wesley delivers an open-air sermon in Bristol and founds the first Methodist Chapel.

1742 *The Messiah*, George Frideric Handel's most popular choral work, is first performed, in Dublin.

1742 Swedish astronomer Anders Celsius proposes his celsius temperature scale.

A Wander Around Wedgwood Country

An intriguing outing explores the life and times of the Staffordshire Potteries' most famous son

During the 18th and 19th centuries, white stoneware was all the rage in polite society, thanks in part to an influx of expensive white china from the Orient. In the quest for a cheaper alternative, potters experimented with powdered flint from the local mills. Flint, when mixed with clay, helps to whiten it, but there were so many problems with the process and such a high level of wastage that for a time English china was more expensive than silver. In the 1760s, however, Josiah Wedgwood perfected cream ware and a few years later, when Queen Charlotte purchased an entire tea set, marketing genius Josiah cannily changed the name to Queen's Ware. The rest, as they say, is pottery.

The Wedgwood family came from Burslem, a district of what is now Stoke-on-Trent. Craftsman Gilbert Wedgwood was recorded as the first Master Potter in the family in 1640 – and his most famous descendant, Josiah, was born in 1730. Josiah worked in his father's pottery from the age of nine, and in 1744 he was apprenticed to his older brother Thomas. An attack of smallpox seriously reduced Josiah's output (his right leg later had to be amputated as a result of the illness), but the time it gave him to research and experiment in his chosen craft stood him in good stead in later years.

First Pottery Factory

After a number of partnerships Josiah set up his own pottery in Burslem in 1759. Until then pottery had been something of a cottage industry, but Wedgwood built the first pottery factory. A decade later, with business booming, Josiah built a bigger factory in Burslem called Etruria – at the time, Greek vases were thought to be Etruscan in origin. This became a model for other pottery manufacturers. He applied rigorous techniques to producing innovative pottery. The results of his efforts can still be purchased today and include 'Jasperware' (characterised by unglazed pale-blue stoneware with white relief portraits or classical scenes) and black basalt ware, also known as 'Egyptian ware', a hard stone-like material used for vases and busts of historical figures.

Above right: *An exquisite Wedgwood Portland vase*

Right: *The walks passes Barlaston Hall, once the centre of Wedgwood operations*

Walk 65 A land transformed by a master potter

Take the air in a corner of Staffordshire where the Wedgwood family broke the mould

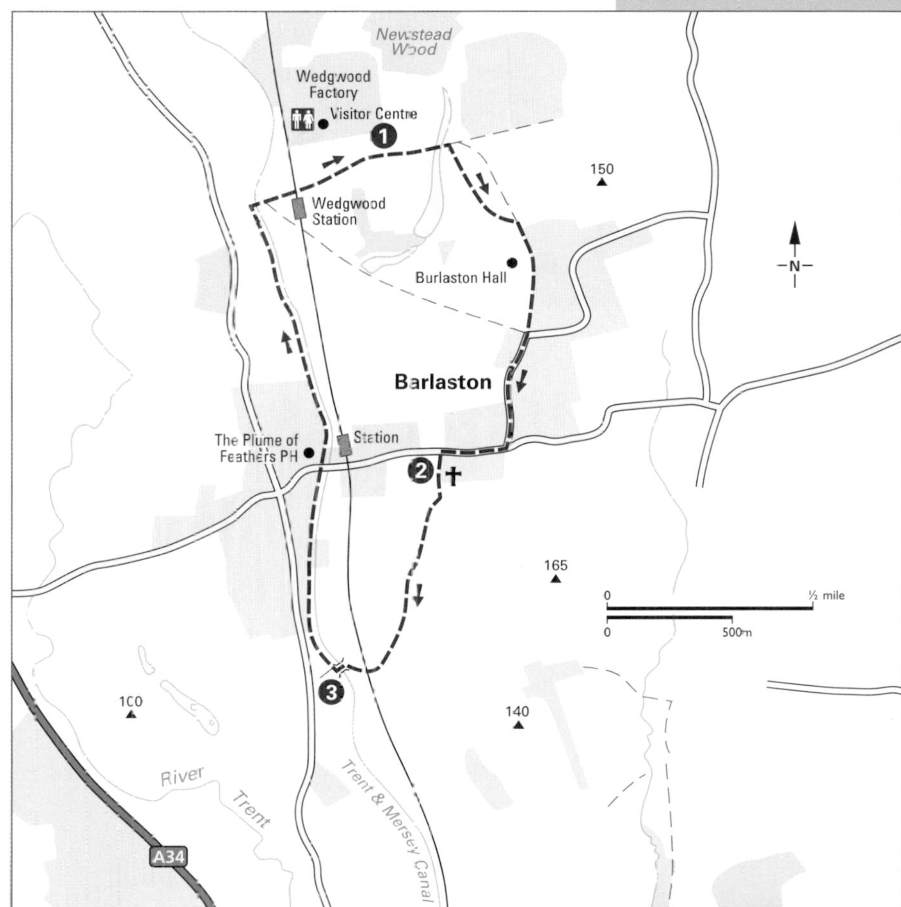

1 From the Visitor Centre drive, head left across the lake and then right up the drive towards Barlaston Hall. Go past this hall and continue along the metalled road as far as the crossroads in Barlaston. At the crossroads turn right and after 250yds (229m), just past the Church of St John the Baptist on your left, head left along a wide gravel track.

2 The track passes through a broad expanse of open farmland, with sweeping (if not altogether dramatic) views of the Trent and Mersey canal to the right and, beyond, the flood plain of the Trent Valley. After about 800yds (732m), at the third gate, go right on a less obvious path around the edge of the field to reach a stile. After crossing the stile head right along a wide track, then cross the railway via an underpass, before bearing right to a bridge over the canal. Go over the bridge and take the steps down to the left.

3 At the bottom of the steps head left and then follow the canal all the way to the first bridge (at Barlaston) and then the second (at Wedgwood Station). Head left here, up to the metalled road, and then right, back towards the visitor centre.

THE WEDGWOOD STORY

The Wedgwood Story Visitor Centre is a multi-million pound attraction featuring a museum, shop, two restaurants and of course the Wedgwood factory itself. As well as a fine display of rare and valuable exhibits, the museum also traces the rich history of the Wedgwood company and visitors can walk the factory floor to see the production process, from throwing to firing. You can take your turn at the potter's wheel, try your painting skills or talk to Wedgwood's craftsmen in the demonstration area. If you still have any energy for shopping, take time to browse for souvenirs, ornaments and tableware, including some exclusive lines. The centre is open year-round (except Christmas week and New Year's Day), Monday to Friday 9am–5pm, weekends 10am–5pm.

WHAT TO LOOK OUT FOR

The Trent and Mersey Canal, completed in 1777, linked the River Trent at Derwent Mouth near Derby with the Bridgewater Canal at Preston Brook, near the mouth of the Mersey River. This effectively meant the country could be navigated all the way from the west coast to the east, and that fine clay from the West Country could be shipped to the doorstep of Wedgwood's factories. James Brindley designed and built both the Bridgewater and the Trent and Mersey, the latter comprising some 93 miles (150km) of waterway and 76 locks, not to mention a tunnel almost 1.75 miles (2.8km) long beneath the heart of Stoke-on-Trent.

The Palladian country house of Barlaston Hall was built by architect Sir Robert Taylor in 1756–58. In 1931–45 it was the Wedgwood headquarters, then after 1945 it was home to the Wedgwood Memorial College, but in the 1980s – badly damaged by subsidence – was bought and restored by a heritage trust. Today it is once again a private home.

Distance 3.25 miles (5.3km)

Minimum time 1hr 15min

Ascent/gradient 180ft (55m) ▲▲▲

Level of difficulty ●●●

Paths Roads, gravel tracks and tow paths, 3 stiles

Landscape Village, farmland and canal

Suggested map OS Explorer 258 Stoke-on-Trent

Start/finish Grid reference: SJ 889395

Dog friendliness Must be kept on lead near livestock

Parking Roadside parking near Wedgwood Visitor Centre entrance

Public toilets Wedgwood Visitor Centre (customers only)

1745 In the second Jacobite rebellion the 'Young Pretender' Bonnie Prince Charlie captures Edinburgh and defeats the English at Falkirk.

1746 The Jacobites' luck runs out at Culloden Moor, ending their bid to regain the throne. Bonnie Prince Charlie flees to the Hebrides, pursued by government agents, and at last is forced to return to France.

1748–49 Samuel Richardson's novel *Clarissa* is published in two parts.

1749 Henry Fielding publishes the novel *Tom Jones.* The book scandalises polite society, and is blamed for the two earthquakes that hit London that year.

1752 Benjamin Franklin discovers electricity.

1756–63 The Seven Years' War with France is fought.

1760 George II dies, and is succeeded by his grandson George William Frederick as George III.

1760 The clearances begin in the Scottish Highlands and Islands; by the end of the century three-quarters of the land is in the hands of a few wealthy landowners.

Temple Newsam's Stately Countryside

Explore a tranquil 'Capability' Brown landscape just a short distance from Leeds city centre

Below: *'Capability' Brown's grounds at Temple Newsam in spring*

Bottom: *Temple Newsam House dates mainly from the 17th century*

Temple Newsam is one of England's finest historic houses, dating right back to the 11th-12th centuries, but substantially rebuilt after 1622. The impressive surrounding parklands were laid out by the landscape architect Lancelot 'Capability' Brown in the late 1760s for Charles Ingram, the 9th Viscount of Irvine.

The earliest record of the property is a mention in the Domesday Book as 'Neuhusam', meaning 'new house'. The preface 'Temple' comes from the fact that it was owned by the Knights Templar between 1155 and 1307, when the order was quashed following papal decree and the property seized by the State. Subsequent owners faired little better: Sir Philip Darcy was executed in 1537 for his part in the Yorkshire uprising known as the Pilgrimage of Grace, and the property was seized again in 1565 when Temple Newsam owner Lord Henry Darnley married Mary, Queen of Scots, and was later suspected of attempting to murder her to win her throne. Sir Arthur Ingram, who bought the Temple Newsham Estate in 1622, built the basis of the mansion we see today, incorporating part of the existing brick-built house in the new west wing. Regarded by some as a wise financier and by others a rogue, the native of Rothwell made his fortune during the struggle to make James I and Charles I financially independent of Parliament. He was knighted in 1613 and became one of the most powerful men in Yorkshire.

Royal Gift

On display within the house is a pair of 18th-century Brussels tapestries depicting the biblical stories of the discovery of Moses, and the battle of the Israelites and the Amalekites. These were given by the Prince of Wales (the future George IV) to his mistress Lady Hertford, Ingram's daughter. Look out also for furniture masterpieces by Thomas Chippendale, silver and Leeds pottery on display.

Walk 66 Beautiful house in carefully designed setting

Admire 'Capability' Brown's sublime landscaping skills on a peaceful ramble

1 Leave the car park and pass by the left side of the main house. Bear left and follow the main track that sweeps downhill below the Stable Courtyard. Fork right to make your way beyond the estate buildings, down to a junction by a pond.

2 Leave the hard-surfaced track here and take the narrow path ahead, signed for the Little Temple, across a patch of grass and over the pond's outflow into woodland. The edged path rises to follow the right edge of a clearing, to a junction.

3 Turn left here, past the Little Temple on the path signed 'Easy going path to lakes'. This gently descends through rhododendrons, zig-zagging at the bottom to a junction with the lakeside path. Bear right, then left down the brick-surfaced track met at a crossroads, to the water's edge.

4 Turn right past two wooden footbridges to a fork. Here, your walking route continues ahead left – but making a short diversion to the right, to explore the Rose Garden and Georgian Walled Garden, will more than repay the minimal effort involved.

5 Returning to the junction, resume your earlier direction. Bear hard left at the next opportunity to double back down the opposite side of the lakes and go past the two footbridges. The trail sweeps up to a junction and bears right to wind its way back to the house, stables and car park beyond.

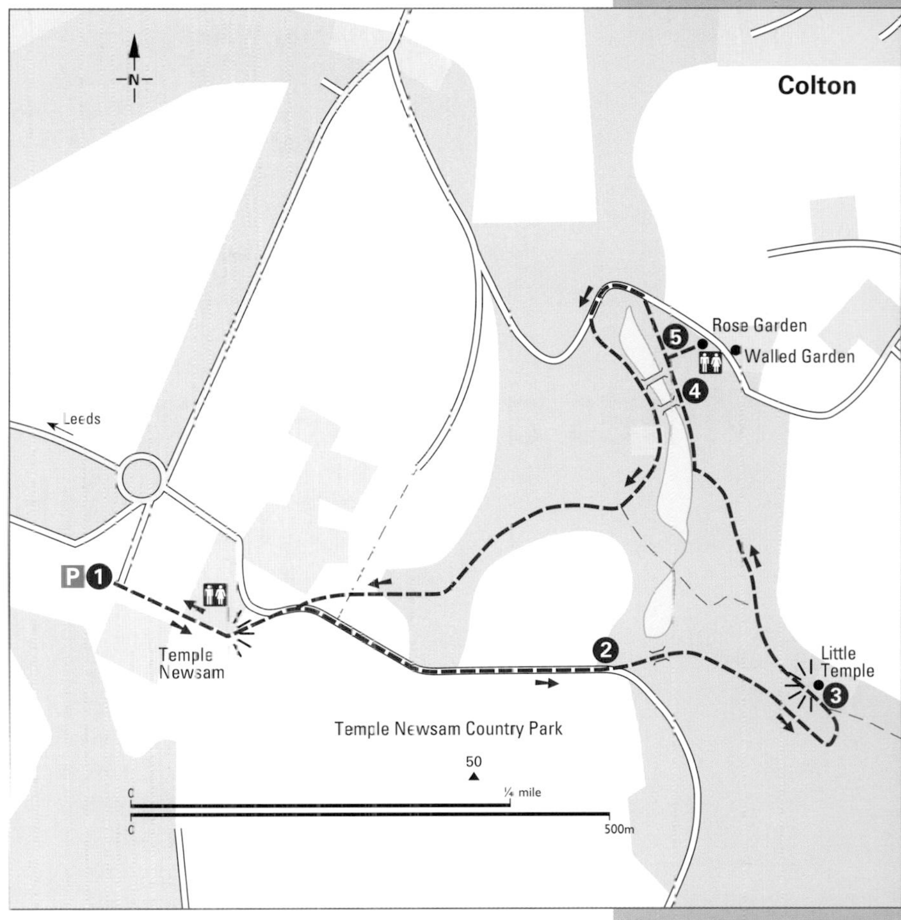

WHILE YOU'RE THERE

Temple Newsam's Home Farm was the maintenance base for the grand estate in years gone by. Today, visitors explore its cobbled yards, admire the 17th-century Great Barn and delight in Europe's largest rare breeds farm, which has more than 400 animals including sheep, poultry, cattle, goats and pigs.

WHAT TO LOOK OUT FOR

On a hillside gazing across to Temple Newsam House, you will find the Little Temple, created in the 18th century to enhance the already splendid view from the house. In landscaping the grounds, 'Capability' Brown opted for a natural design, breaking up the symmetry imposed by the house and opening up fresh vistas to west and south. Stables and other functional buildings were screened by fresh tree planting and a new approach along a long driveway, which passed between gateways guarded by sphinxes, was created.

Distance 1.5 miles (2.4km)

Minimum time 30min

Gradient 151ft (46m)
▲▲▲

Level of difficulty ●●●

Paths Good tracks and paths throughout

Landscape Parkland, gardens, lakes and woodland

Suggested map OS Explorer 289 Leeds

Start/finish Stable Courtyard, Temple Newsam
Grid reference: SE 357321

Dog friendliness Dogs should be under control

Parking Pay-and-display in the House Car Park, off Temple Newsam Road, Leeds

Public toilets In Stable Courtyard at start and at the Rose Garden

1761 The Bridgewater Canal opens, running from Manchester to Runcorn to transport coal.

1764 James Hargreaves invents the Spinning Jenny.

1764 The Royal Academy is founded in London.

1769 James Watt patents his steam engine.

1769 Josiah Wedgwood's pottery factory Etruria opens in Burslem, Staffordshire.

1773 In North America, Bostonians show their fury at trade controls and taxes imposed by Britain by dumping a shipload of tea into the harbour.

1775 The American War of Independence begins.

Mines and Methodism at Redruth

A tramp through Cornwall's mining heartland visits a celebrated Methodist preaching venue

The old Cornish town of Redruth gained its name from mineral mining. In medieval times, the process of separating tin and copper from waste materials turned a local river blood-red with washed-out iron oxide. The Cornish name for a nearby ford was Rhyd Druth, the 'ford of the red', and the village that grew around it became Redruth. The innovative engineering that developed in tandem with mining turned Redruth and the adjoining town of Camborne into centres of Cornish industry, bringing wealth and prosperity.

Into the often bleak world of 18th-century mineral mining came the brothers John and Charles Wesley, their religious zeal as hot as a Redruth furnace. It is highly appropriate that one of the most revered locations in Methodism is Gwennap Pit, near Redruth. Here the grassy hollow of a caved-in mine shaft was first used for secular gatherings and events, which included cockfighting. But before long the pit was commandeered as a sheltered venue for preaching. John Wesley preached here on no fewer than 18 occasions in 1762–89.

Above right: *Gwennap Pit became the 'Cathedral of the Moor'*

Below: *Looking across the moors from Carn Brea*

Wide Views from the High Ground

The first part of this walk leads from the heart of Redruth past such mining relics as the chimney stack of the Pednandrea Mine to the high ground of Gwennap and Carn Marth. From Gwennap Pit you head for the summit of Carn Marth and to one of the finest viewpoints in Cornwall. From above the flooded quarry on the summit you look north to the sea and to the hill of St Agnes Beacon. Northeast lies the St Austell clay country, southwest is the rocky summit of Carn Brea with its distinctive granite cross; southeast you can even see the cranes on Falmouth dockside. From the top of Carn Marth, the return route is all downhill back to the heart of Redruth.

Walk 67 The mine shaft that became a 'cathedral'

Wander – and sit – where Wesley preached Methodism to Cornish miners in the open air

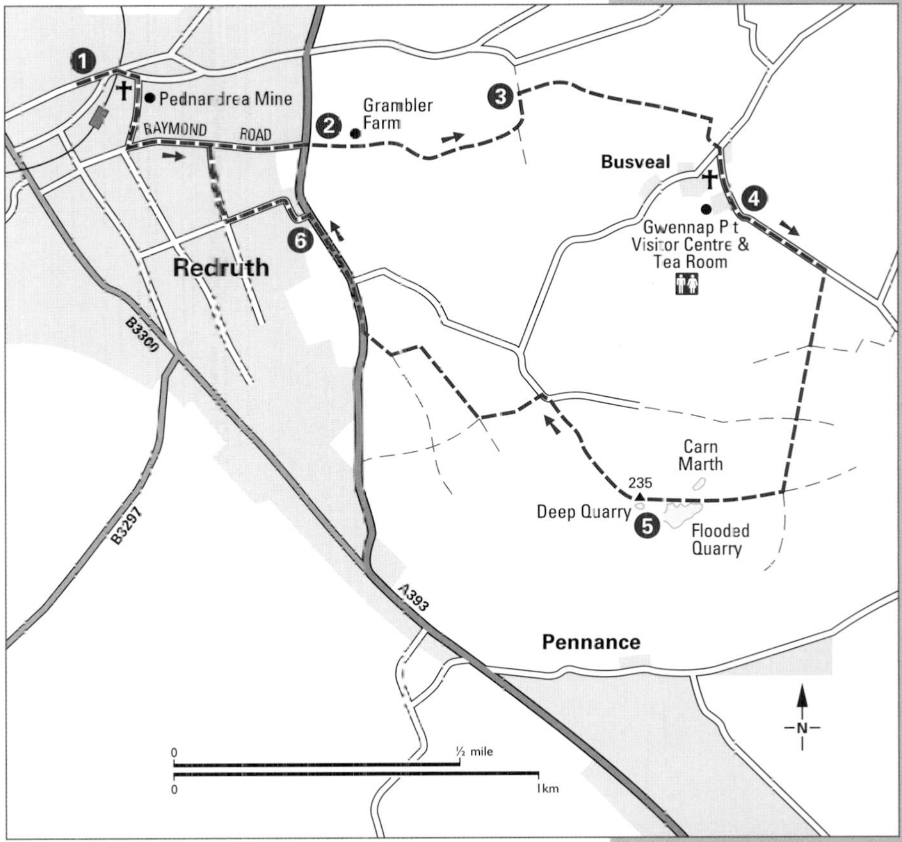

1 From any of the car parks, make your way to Fore Street, the main street of Redruth. Walk up to a junction (the railway station is down to the right) and take the middle branch, to the left of the Wesley Centenary Memorial Building (now the YMCA) and signposted 'To Victoria Park'. This is Wesley Street. In just a few paces turn right on Sea View Terrace; the chimney stack of the Pednandrea Mine is up to the left a few paces along the road. Pass Basset Street on the right and, where streets cross, go left, all the way up Raymond Road to a T-junction with Sandy Lane.

2 Cross the road with care, then follow the track opposite, signposted 'Public Bridleway' and 'Grambler Farm'. Go through a gate by the farm and continue to an open area. Bear left here and follow a track between hedges. When you reach a junction with another track turn left, signposted 'Gwennap Pit'.

3 Go right and over a stile next to a field gateway with breeze block gateposts. Cross a stile at the next gate and then keep straight ahead across the next field. Cross another stile and continue between wire fences by a house to a final stile. Walk down a lane to a junction of surfaced roads and follow the road opposite for 100yds (91m) to Gwennap Pit.

4 Follow the road away from Gwennap Pit. Ignore the first few turn offs and in about 300yds (274m) turn off to the right along a broad track, signposted 'Public Bridleway'. Keep straight ahead at two crossings, then, at a final crossing beside a ruined building, turn right and make your way along a stony track that leads up the hill to the prominent summit of Carn Marth.

5 Pass a flooded quarry on your left, then follow a rocky path round to the right past a trig point and on along the fenced-in rim of a deep quarry. Keep ahead at a junction and go down a track to reach a surfaced road. Turn left and in 30yds (27m) turn left along a track, signed 'Public Bridleway'. Follow the track to a T-junction with the main road at a house called Tara. Cross with great care, turn right and continue for 300yds (180m).

6 Go left at a junction, taking the way signposted as a cycle route, and follow a lane round right, then left into a broad avenue of houses. Go on to the crossroads, then turn right along Trefusis Road. At the next junction turn left into Raymond Road and then turn right at the next crossroads into Sea View Terrace. Turn left down Wesley Street and on into Fore Street.

THE BROTHERS WESLEY

John and Charles Wesley are seen as founders of Methodism. After study at Oxford University, both travelled to Georgia in North America but returned to England in the late 1730s. John began open-air preaching in 1739 under the influence of his friend George Whitefield. The first Methodist groups were founded in London and Bristol that year.

WHAT TO LOOK OUT FOR

A visit to Gwennap Pit and its visitor centre is a must, but Redruth itself rewards exploration. The fine Victorian Gothic buildings in Fore Street and the Italianate Clock Tower of 1828 reflect the boom period of Redruth's growth. The Pednandrea Mine Chimney Stack swas part of a mine that operated in 1710–1891 producing copper, tin, lead and arsenic. The original height of the stack was 126–140ft (38–43m). The field hedgerows are bright with wild flowers and butterflies in season. Look for the brownish-red peacock butterfly (*Nymphalidae*), easily identified by its 'peacock-eye' markings.

Distance 4 miles (6.4km)

Minimum time 2hrs 30min

Ascent/gradient 442ft (135m) ▲▲▲

Level of difficulty ●●●

Paths Field paths, rough tracks and surfaced lanes. Can be muddy after rain, 6 stiles

Landscape Small fields and open heathland with quarry and mine remains

Suggested map OS Explorer 104 Redruth & St Agnes

Start/finish Grid reference: SW 699421

Dog friendliness Dogs on lead through grazed areas

Parking Several car parks in Redruth

Public toilets Redruth car parks; Gwennap Pit Visitor Centre, when open

Revolution at Coalbrookdale

An absorbing walk leads through the wooded hills and valleys where the Industrial Revolution began

People have been smelting iron for many centuries, but production was originally small-scale because smelting was dependent on timber that first had to be made into charcoal – a slow and laborious process. All that changed at Coalbrookdale in 1709 when Abraham Darby I perfected a method of smelting iron with coke instead of charcoal. It may sound a small thing, but it sparked a revolution that changed the world. At long last iron could be made cheaply in large quantities and it came to be increasingly used in many areas of engineering. By 1785 the Coalbrookdale district had become the foremost industrial area in the world.

Coalbrookdale was celebrated for its innovations: the first iron bridge, the first iron boat, the first iron rails and the first steam locomotive. Tourists came from far and wide to see the sights, and artists came to paint it all – furnaces lighting up the night sky was a favourite subject. Decline eventually set in due to competition from the Black Country and South Wales and the area fell into decay. Since the 1960s, the surviving industrial relics have been transformed into a collection of museums and the gorge has been designated a UNESCO World Heritage Site. Perhaps even more remarkable than the industrial heritage is the way nature has reclaimed sites of industrial despoilation and made them beautiful again.

Taking Care of the Workers

The ironmasters built decent houses for their workers and took an interest in their moral well-being. When you walk through Dale Coppice and Lincoln Hill Woods you will be using the Sabbath Walks, designed by Richard Reynolds to provide healthy Sunday recreation for his workers.

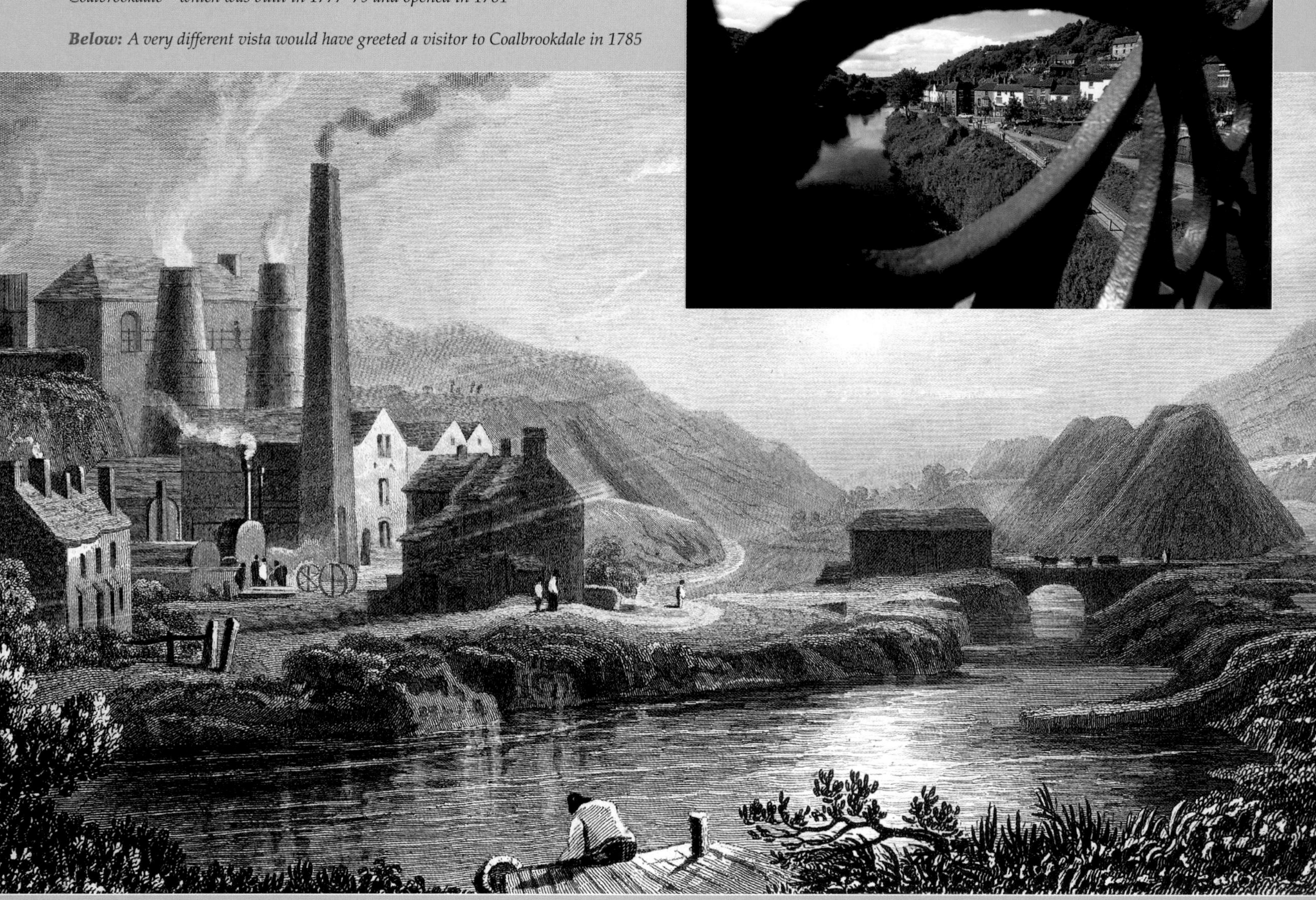

Right: *You can still walk across the world's first iron bridge – over the Severn near Coalbrookdale – which was built in 1777–79 and opened in 1781*

Below: *A very different vista would have greeted a visitor to Coalbrookdale in 1785*

Walk 68 The land that iron built

Explore where ironworkers laboured – and took their rest on a sabbath

1 Follow the River Severn upstream, using the Severn Way. Take care as the path is narrow and there's a big drop to the river in places. Pass under two bridges. After the second one, bear away from the river towards Buildwas Road. At the road, turn left for a few paces then cross to a footpath that ascends through woodland. Keep close to the edge until a waymarker directs you obliquely to the right.

2 Cross a stile and continue in the same direction over pastureland. Pass under a pylon, then join a farm track climbing to a gate. Turn right and follow the hawthorn hedge to a junction. Turn left and follow three field-edges, then go up through the middle of a meadow to a lane. Turn left and continue on the lane.

3 Leave the lane just before it bridges a road, turning right on a farm access track (Shropshire Way). Just before Leasows Farm, go through a gate on the right, then down the field to enter Lydebrook Dingle at a stile. A path descends through the wood, with numerous steps. Continue along a path called Rope Walk.

4 Descend some steps on the left into Loamhole Dingle. Cross Loamhole Brook at a footbridge and climb 41 steps on the other side. Turn right and follow the undulating boardwalk to Upper Furnace Pool. Cross its far end on the first of two footbridges to meet the road.

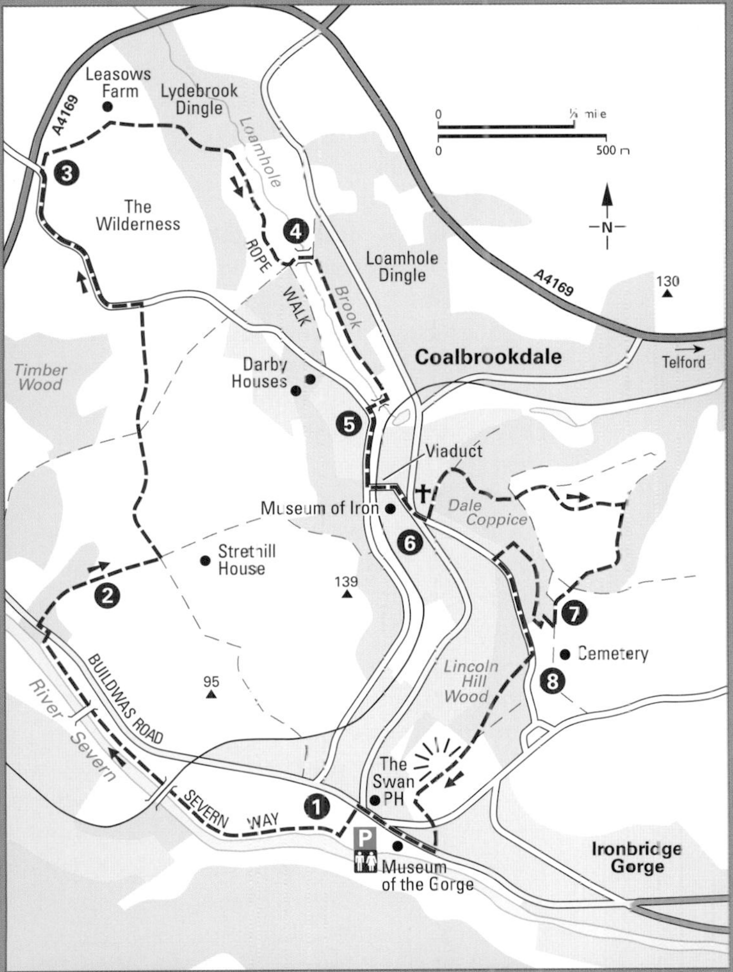

5 Your onward route is to the left, but a short detour right leads to the Darby Houses, Tea Kettle Row and the Quaker Burial Ground. Resuming the walk, go down to Darby Road and turn right beside the viaduct and the Museum of Iron. Turn left under the viaduct at a junction with Coach Road. Follow the road past the museum and Coalbrookdale Works to a junction.

6 Cross into Church Road. Immediately after the Wesleyan chapel turn left, then go up steps to enter Dale Coppice. Follow signs for Church Road at two junctions, then keep following the steps, bearing left up through the woods. Leave the wood to enter grassland and go forward a few paces to meet a track. Turn left, then shortly fork right, staying on the track. Bear left at another junction, then bear right at the next two. Dale Coppice is on your right, a cemetery on your left.

7 Part way along the cemetery, a small wooden gate accesses Dale Coppice. Turn right, then soon left, going downhill to a junction marked by a bench. Turn right, then left when a sign indicates Church Road, then left again down the road.

8 Turn right into Lincoln Hill Wood and follow signs to the Rotunda, presently arriving at a viewpoint where the Rotunda formerly stood. Descend a very steep flight of steps to a junction. Turn right, then left down more steps and left again, signposted to Lincoln Hill Road. Cross the road to a footpath opposite, that descends to the Wharfage. Turn right past Lincoln Hill lime kilns and The Swan to Dale End Riverside Park.

Distance 5 miles (8km)
Minimum time 2hrs
Ascent/gradient 770ft (235m) ▲▲▲
Level of difficulty ●●●
Paths Woodland paths, lots of steps (mostly descending), may be fallen trees at Strethill, 2 stiles, some paths very overgrown
Landscape Wooded hills of Severn Gorge
Suggested map OS Explorer 242 Telford, Ironbridge & The Wrekin
Start/finish Grid reference: SJ 664037
Dog friendliness Excellent, but keep under strict control at Strethill (sheep)
Parking Dale End Riverside Park, just west of Museum of the Gorge
Public toilets In Museum of the Gorge car park

WHAT TO LOOK OUT FOR

Upper Furnace Pool in Loamhole Dingle is the pool that powered the bellows that blew the furnace where Abraham Darby first smelted iron with coke. The area of open water has been reduced by a profuse growth of marsh horsetail.

The Museum of Iron brings the Darbys' achievements to fascinating life and includes the Darby Furnace where it all began. Equally interesting are the ironmasters' homes and the workers' houses at Tea Kettle Row.

1778 The Australian Penal Colony is established. Thousands of convicts are offloaded at Port Jackson, later to become Sydney Harbour.

1779 Abraham Darby III casts the world's first iron bridge to span the river Severn, near Coalbrookdale.

1783 The British recognise American independence.

1789 Edmund Cartwright invents the power loom.

1789 The French Revolution starts.

1789 George Washington becomes the first President of the United States of America.

1793–1802 War rages between Britain and France.

1794 The Cardiff coal dock opens; within 50 years Cardiff is the world's biggest coal-shipping port.

1796 Napoleon Bonaparte is made Commander of the French armies and takes power in 1799.

1796 English surgeon Edward Jenner develops a vaccine against smallpox.

Revolutionary Utopia at New Lanark

A rustic promenade visits a model industrial community

If you take this walk you will get a glimpse of Utopia, for the planned industrial village of New Lanark was the embodiment of one man's vision of an ideal world. New Lanark was built as a cotton spinning centre in 1785 by David Dale and Richard Arkwright, and is so well preserved that it is now a UNESCO World Heritage Site. It owes its fame to Dale's son-in-law, Robert Owen, who took over its management in 1798 and made it the focus of a revolutionary social experiment.

Right: *The mill wheel, powered by the River Clyde*

Below: *Looking over the back of Caithness Row to Robert Owen's school*

Forward-thinking Pioneer

Owen was a very efficient businessman and ran a strict regime, monitoring wages, insisting on good timekeeping and dismissing employees for persistent drunkenness and theft. His methods made New Lanark extremely profitable. He was also an extremely fair employer. He believed in humane capitalism and felt that businesses were more successful if the workers were well treated.

Owen disapproved of cruel treatment of workers and refused to allow corporal punishment to be used as a form of discipline. His staff were provided with good housing, free medical care and a co-operative store.

Unlike most industrialists of his day, he did not allow children under ten to work in his mills, and established the world's first nursery school. He ensured that all children received a rounded education: by the age of seven they were attending lessons on everything from history and geography to nature study and dancing. Education did not end when children began working in the mills, moreover, for all employees were encouraged to attend evening classes, lectures and dancing classes in the wonderfully named Institute for the Formation of Character.

He tried hard, without success, to persuade other industrialists to adopt his caring regime. Disillusioned, he sold New Lanark in 1825 and travelled to America where he bought a settlement in Indiana, which he named New Harmony. He intended to turn it into a utopian community, freed from the strictures of 19th-century Britain. This experiment did not work as well as he hoped, either, and he returned to Britain in 1828, where he continued to campaign for workers' welfare. Owen died in 1858. He never managed to create Utopia, but inspired several other model villages such as Saltaire, Port Sunlight and Bournville, and influenced attitudes for years to come.

Walk 69 Heritage site that honours a pioneer

See where Robert Owen attempted to implement his vision of humane capitalism

1 From the car park, walk downhill into New Lanark. Bear left and walk to the Scottish Wildlife Trust Visitor Centre. Turn up the stone steps on the left, following the signs leading to the Falls of Clyde. The path soon goes down some steps to reach the weir, where there is a lookout point.

2 Continue along the path. You will pass Bonnington Power Station on your right, where the path divides. Take the right-hand path, which takes you into woodland and up some steps. You soon come to Corra Linn waterfall, with another lookout point.

3 Your path continues to the right, signposted 'Bonnington Linn, 0.75 miles'. Go up some more steps and follow the track to go under a double line of pylons. Follow the path to reach the weir, cross it, then turn right into the Wildlife Reserve.

4 After 100yds (91m), turn right off the track down a narrow path, which crosses a footbridge and then follows the river, rejoining the main path downstream. Bear right here in order to reach Corra Castle. Continue walking along by the river, cross a small footbridge, then follow the wide path that leads through the woods. When you meet another path, turn right.

5 Follow the path to pass houses on your left. At the road turn right, then right again to cross the old bridge, which brings you into a cul de sac. Go through the gate on the right – it looks like someone's drive but is part of the Clyde Walkway.

6 Walk past the stables, then turn left through a gate to follow the riverside path. Beyond another gate, continue up some steps to pass beside a water treatment plant and then bear right along a tarmac lane. Follow the lane past some houses and carry on until you see a sign to Jooker's Johnnie on your left. Just 20yds (18m) further on, turn right down a driveway, then right again at a sign for the Clyde Walkway.

7 Your path zig-zags down to the river. At the water's edge turn left, and follow the forest track back to New Lanark. When the path meets the road turn right, then left at the church for the car park.

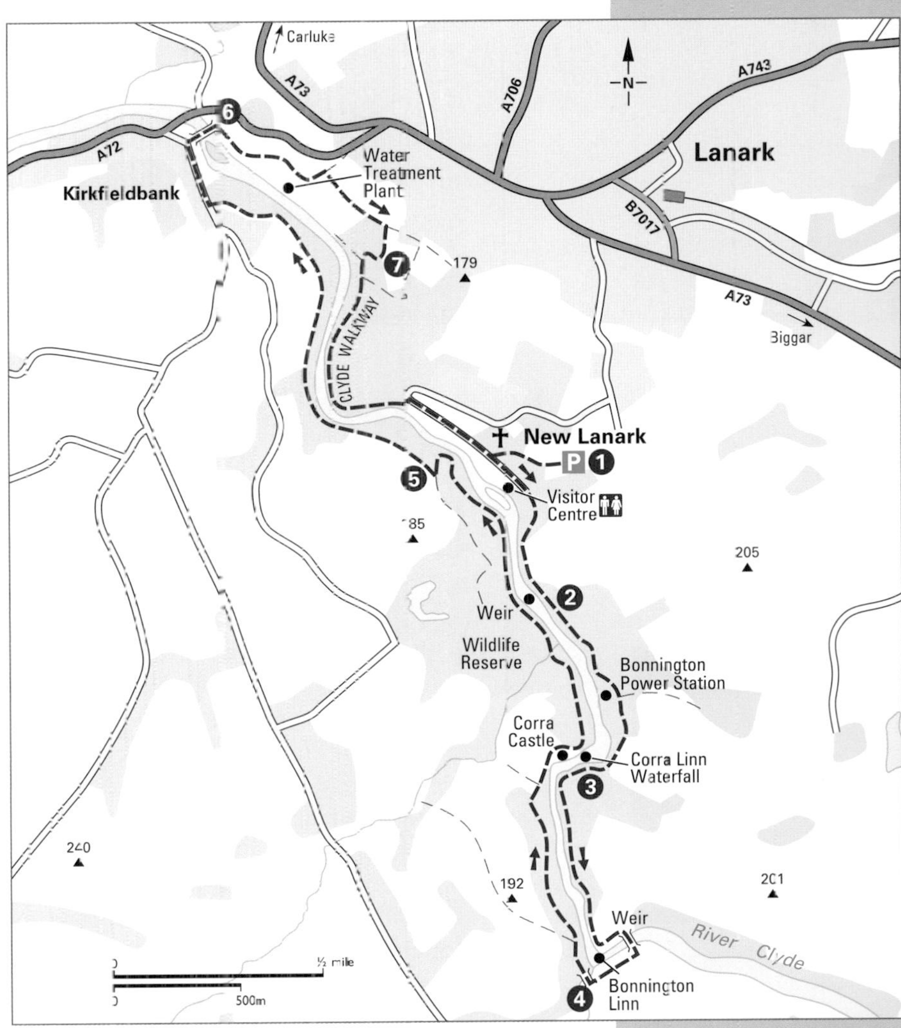

RED-ARMED BATS

The ruins of Corra Castle are home to a colony of natterer's bats. These medium-sized bats are found throughout Britain. In winter they tend to hibernate in caves and mines, while during the summer they prefer to roost in old stone buildings and barns. Their limbs have a slight pink tinge, giving rise to their nickname – the 'red-armed bat'.

WHAT TO LOOK OUT FOR

Peregrines nest near the Corra Linn falls from April to June each year, and high-powered telescopes have been set up to allow you to view the peregrine nests without disturbing the birds. Peregrines are a protected species, with only around 800 pairs in Scotland, and they are sadly threatened by egg collectors, shooting and poisoning.

Distance 6.5 miles (10.4km)

Minimum time 3hrs

Ascent/gradient 476ft (145m) ▲▲▲

Level of difficulty ●●●

Paths Clear riverside tracks and forest paths, a few steep steps

Landscape Planned industrial town and some stunning waterfalls

Suggested map OS Explorer 335 Lanark & Tinto Hills

Start/finish Grid reference: NS 883426

Dog friendliness Mostly off lead

Parking Main car park above New Lanark

Public toilets Visitor Centre, when open

1798 Poets William Wordsworth and Samuel Taylor Coleridge publish their collection *Lyrical Ballads*.

1801 The Act of Union with Ireland achieves its first aim, to unite the Irish and Westminster parliaments; but George III refuses to give Catholics their freedom, and Prime Minister William Pitt the Younger resigns as a result.

1803–15 The Napoleonic Wars rage.

1807 The Slave Trade Reform Bill is passed and by 1833 the trade is abolished in the British colonies.

1808 Poet and artist William Blake publishes *Milton (Book I)*, which contains the lyric 'And did those feet in ancient time...', now better known as 'Jerusalem'.

1809 The 2000 Guineas horse race is first run at Newmarket.

1811 John Nash draws up plans for the design of Regent Street, London.

1811–16 Factory machinery is destroyed in riots led by Ned Ludd and his 'Luddites'.

Wordsworth Country Around Dove Cottage

Vigorous climbing in the footsteps of an energetic poet leads to a moorland tarn and breathtaking views

Above: *The house formerly known as Town End*

Below: *A view of the fells from Alcock Tarn*

The name 'Dove Cottage' would have been meant nothing to William Wordsworth and his family. The little house beneath the woods and towering ridge of Heron Pike was known to the poet and his family as Town End, and it had previously been an ale house called the Dove and Olive Bough. The Wordsworths arrived there on foot, just before Christmas in the winter of 1799. They paid £8 a year in rent and left nine years later for a variety of homes, before ending up a few miles away at Rydal in 1813.

Artistic Complex

Dove Cottage today is a whole complex of academic and artistic endeavours as well as a museum, art gallery and tea room. It is fair to say that the Wordsworths would probably not realise this was the same place that William settled in to write 'Daffodils'. Some things may be familiar, however. The mercilessly steep section of this walk that leads from the back of Forest Side and takes you up into Greenhead Gill, is still perhaps as stiff a climb as Wordsworth described it in his poem 'Michael', written around 1800:

If from the public way you turn your steps,
Up the tumultuous brook of Greenhead Ghyll,
You will suppose that with an upright path,
Your feet must struggle in such bold ascent,
The pastoral mountains front you, face to face
But courage! for around that boisterous brook
The mountains have all opened out themselves
And made a hidden valley of their own.

Missing from the gill in Wordsworth's day would be the parapet of the Thirlmere aqueduct and associated pieces of water supply equipment, but the slope is still a 'bold ascent'. Another addition since 'Michael' is the tarn in the hollow beneath Butter Crag. Alcock Tarn was once a boggy depression and took its name from the rocks that rise above on the slopes of Heron Pike. Mr Alcock of the Hollins in the valley below enlarged it with a dam and stocked it with trout at the end of the 19th century. Alcock Tarn was bought by the National Trust in the 1940s.

Walk 70 'Bold ascent' celebrated by Romantic poet

Take courage from Wordsworth's example as you climb to Alcock Tarn

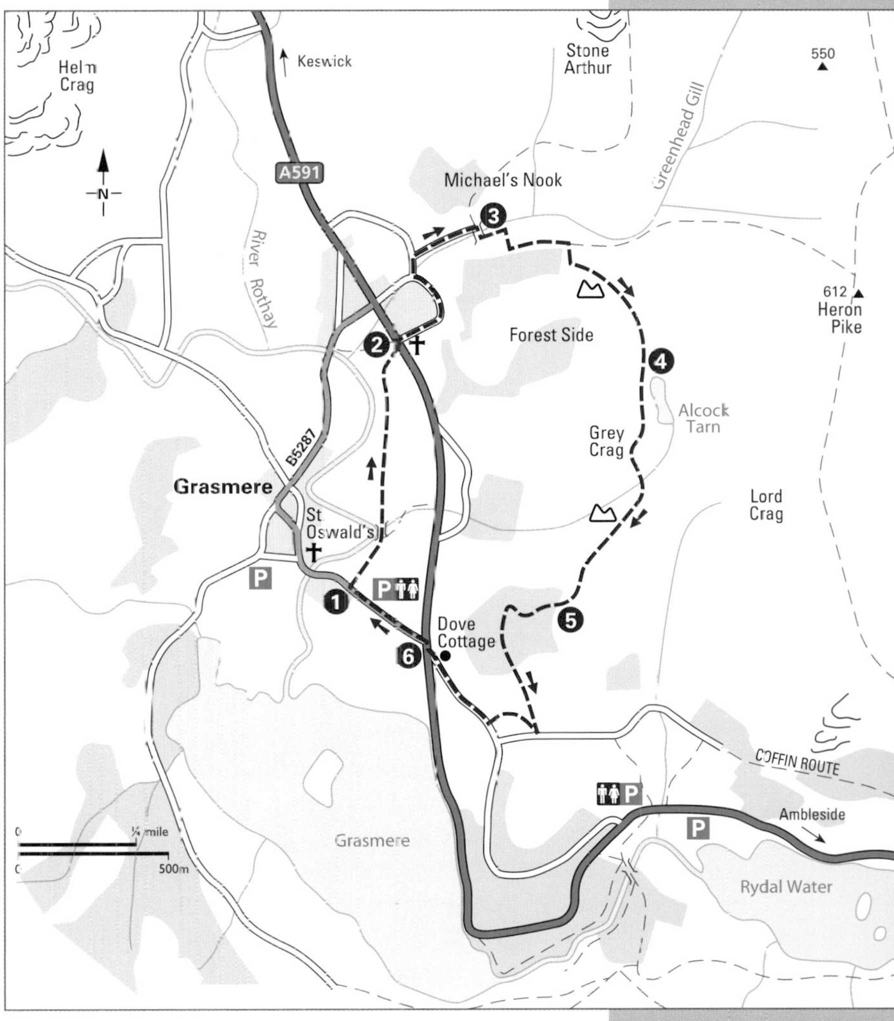

1 From the far end of the car park, close to the toilets, locate a snicket round the back of the school and follow it, turning right at a junction and passing the old Workman's Reading Room. Keep ahead at a crossing of paths by a small bridge and go through a kissing gate to join a meadow path. It bears to the left of a stand of pines and meanders its way through several gates to reach the main road.

2 Turn left along the pavement for a few paces, before crossing over to the lane adjacent to the Catholic church. Walk up this quiet residential lane, staying with it as it swings round to the left. At a junction, turn right and continue until a footpath sign on the right points you up towards Alcock Tarn. At the top of this lane, go through a gate onto the open fell.

3 Turn immediately right over a little bridge to walk up the right-hand side of the beck as you look up. The path ascends steeply and is paved in places, at the side of a plantation. Beyond a bench, keep going upwards. The slope lessens momentarily to round the head of a wall before cutting back to continue zig-zagging up the hill. A line of crags fills your immediate horizon until you work your way beyond them, swinging round to the right and levelling off, though the tarn remains hidden. A wall joins you on one side and a gate takes you through a crossing wall. Passing several little boggy tarnlets you go through another gate to reach Alcock Tarn.

4 Half-way along, a little bluff on the right affords great views of the valley below. Pass the tarn and its dam and take the right fork, aiming for a gap in the wall. A way now descends beside the rocky promontory of Grey Crag, a zig-zag path beginning just beneath the crag itself. The descent is steep and rocky in places but navigation is fairly straightforward, keeping to an engineered route down to a gate. Through this the descent continues past a bench and a little reservoir by a stand of trees. At a junction of tracks keep left, above a plantation. Go through a metal gate into the woods and you soon reach a second gate.

5 Keep ahead around the grounds of Wood Close, descending to a lane. Don't go out onto the lane, but turn right, descending on a track that emerges at Woodland Crag Cottage. Turn left along the access road and left again with a tarmac lane. After a few paces a right-hand dodge cuts off the corner down to a road. Turn right, and eventually right again at the road by a coffin resting stone. Emerge at Dove Cottage, walking past the museum and gallery to the main road.

6 Turn right in order to cross beyond the mini-roundabout, then follow the road back along towards Grasmere and the car park.

GRASMERE SPORTS

The little flourish of crag that marks your descent route is known as Grey Crag. It is the principal destination of the Guides Race at the annual Grasmere Sports, held late August, with the runners taking the direct route from the sports field up the steep field below the fell and back again. The record for the seniors' race is just over 12 minutes!

Distance 3 miles (4.8km)

Minimum time 2hrs

Gradient 984ft (300m) ▲▲▲

Level of difficulty ●●●

Paths Road, paths and tracks

Landscape Woods, field, fell, tarn and lake

Suggested map OS Explorer OL7 The English Lakes (South Eastern Area)

Start/finish Grid reference: NY 339072

Dog friendliness Some places grazed by sheep

Parking Grasmere National Park Authority pay-and-display car park by the sports ground on the southern side of the village

Public toilets At car park

1714–1837

1813 Jane Austen's novel *Pride and Prejudice* is first published. It was written in 1796–97.

1814 Walter Scott's first novel, *Waverley*, is published.

1815 The Duke of Wellington defeats Napoleon Bonaparte at the Battle of Waterloo, marking the end of the Napoleonic Wars.

1815 The Corn Laws are passed to regulate prices and imports, causing public outrage as a few landowners profit while the poor starve.

1820 On the death of George III, Prince Regent George Augustus Frederick becomes George IV.

1824 The National Gallery in London opens.

1825 The first railway line, the Stockton and Darlington, opens.

1828 Arthur Wellesley, Duke of Wellington, is made prime minster.

1830 On the death of George IV, his brother William Henry becomes William IV at the age of 64.

Brunel's Great Tunnel Through Box Hill

A fascinating ramble leads around Box Hill, famous for its stone and Brunel's greatest engineering achievement

Box is a large straggling village that sits astride the busy A4 in hilly country halfway between Bath and Chippenham. Although stone has been quarried here since the 9th century, Box really found fame during the 18th century when the local stone was used in the construction of Bath's magnificent buildings. The digging of Box Tunnel uncovered immense deposits of good stone and by 1900 Box stone quarries were among the most productive in the world. Little trace can be seen above ground today, except for some fine stone-built houses in the village and a few reminders on Box Hill.

Appointed Engineer

In 1833, the newly created Great Western Railway appointed Isambard Kingdom Brunel as engineer. His task was to build a railway covering the 118 miles (190km) from London to Bristol. The problems he encountered on the way would help to make him the most famous engineer of the Victorian age. After a relatively straightforward and level start through the Home Counties, he came to the hilly Cotswolds.

The solution at Box was a tunnel, and at nearly 2 miles (3.2km) long and with a gradient of 1:100, this was the longest and steepest in the world at the time. It was also very wide: already controversial, Brunel ignored the gauge of other companies, preferring the 7ft (2.1m) one used by tramways and roads (and, it was believed, Roman chariots). He made the tunnel dead straight – and, never one to 'hide his light' – calculated the alignment so the dawn sun would shine through on his birthday, 9th April. Unfortunately he did not allow for atmospheric refraction and was two days out!

All was on a grand scale: a ton of gunpowder and candles were used every week, 3 million bricks were fired to line the soft Cotswold limestone and 100 navvies lost their lives working on the tunnel. After two and a half years the way was open, and although Brunel would ultimately lose the battle of the gauges, his magnificent line meant that Bristol was then a mere two hours from the capital.

Noises in the Dark – and Disappearing Trains?

Like many large, dark holes, the tunnel has collected its fair share of mystery associations – with tales of noises, people under the hill and trains entering the tunnel, never to re-emerge. However, as is often the case, the explanations are rather more mundane. To test excavation conditions, Brunel dug a small trial section alongside what is now the eastern entrance, and the military commandeered this section during World War II as a safe, secret store for ammunition, records and top brass.

Above right: *Isambard Kingdom Brunel*

Below: *The magnificent West Portal of the tunnel at Box*

Walk 71 A rail wonder of the Victorian age

See where the Great Western Railway overcame the immovable object of Box Hill

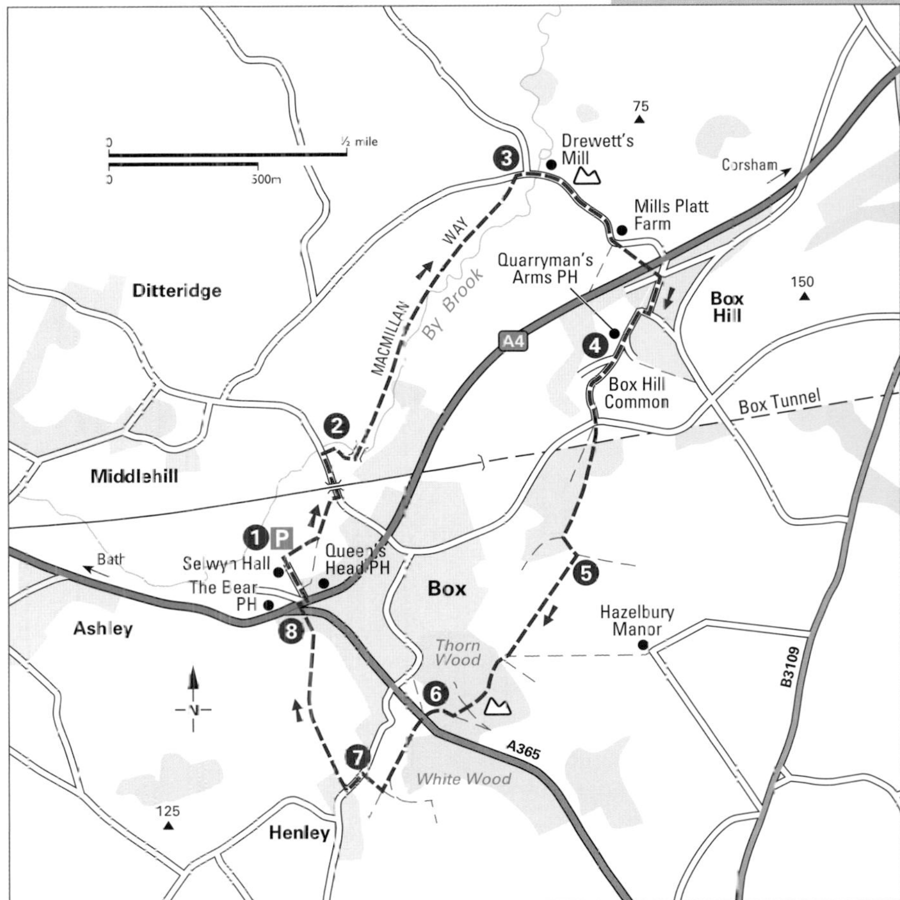

1 Facing the recreation ground, walk to the left-hand side of the football pitch to join a track in the corner close to the railway line. When you reach the lane, turn left, pass beneath the railway, cross a bridge and take the arrowed footpath, to the right, before the second bridge.

2 Walk beside the river, cross a footbridge and turn right. Cross a further footbridge and continue to a stile. Walk through water-meadows close to the river, then go through a gate and maintain direction. Shortly, bear left to reach a squeeze stile in the field corner. Follow the right-hand field-edge to reach a stile leading onto a lane.

3 Turn right, then right again at the junction. Cross the river, pass Drewett's Mill and steeply ascend the lane. Just past Mills Platt Farm, take the arrowed footpath ahead across a stile. Continue steeply uphill to a stile and cross the A4. Ascend steps to a lane and proceed straight on up Barnetts Hill. Keep right at the fork, then right again and pass the Quarryman's Arms.

4 Keep left at the fork and continue beside Box Hill Common to a junction. Take the bridleway straight ahead into woodland. Almost immediately, fork left and follow the path close to the woodland edge. As it curves right into the beech wood, bear left and follow the path through the gap in the wall and then immediately right at the junction of paths.

5 Follow the bridle path to a fork. Keep left, then turn right at the T-junction and take the path left to a stile. Cross a further stile and descend into Thorn Wood, following the stepped path to a stile at the bottom.

6 Continue through scrub to a stile and turn right beside the fence to a wall stile. Bear right to a further stile, then bear left uphill to a stile and the A365. Cross over and follow the drive ahead. Where it curves left by stables, keep ahead along the arrowed path to a house. Climb a few steps, bear right to pass Washwell cottage and follow the drive uphill to a T-junction.

7 Turn left, then on entering Henley, take the path right, across a stile. Follow the field-edge to a stile and descend through a paddock to a stile. Continue to a stile and gate.

8 Follow the drive ahead, bear left at the garage and take the metalled path right, into Box. Cross the main road and continue to the A4. Turn right, then left down the access road back to Selwyn Hall.

WHAT TO LOOK OUT FOR

In Box look for the Blind House, one of a dozen in Wiltshire for disturbers of the peace, and Coleridge House, named after the Romantic poet Samuel Taylor Coleridge, who often broke his journey here on his way to Nether Stowey in Somerset. The former Candle Factory on the Rudloe road produced the candles used during the building of Box Tunnel.

Distance 3.25 miles (5.3km)

Minimum time 1hr 45min

Ascent/gradient 508ft (155m) ▲▲▲

Level of difficulty ●●●

Paths Field and woodland paths, bridleways, lanes, 16 stiles

Landscape River valley and wooded hillsides

Suggested map OS Explorer 156 Chippenham & Bradford-on-Avon

Start/finish Grid reference: ST 824686

Dog friendliness Can be off lead on Box Hill Common and in woodland

Parking Village car park near Selwyn Hall

Public toilets Opposite Queen's Head in Box

1832 The Great Reform Bill raises the electorate from 478,000 to 814,000 men. The reforms are moderate, but it is the first of a series of political reforms that culminate in a one-man (and eventually also one-woman) one-vote democracy.

1834 In Tolpuddle, Dorset, six agricultural labourers form a 'friendly society' but are promptly arrested and sentenced to transportation. The action provokes an outcry and the 'martyrs' are pardoned two years later.

1834 Charles Babbage designs the Analytical Machine, a forerunner of the first computers.

1834 The Houses of Parliament are destroyed by fire – the biggest conflagration since the Great Fire of London in 1666. The rebuilt Parliament designed by Sir Charles Barry and A.W.N. Pugin opens in 1844.

1835 The Municipal Corporations Act introduces local government in England and Wales.

1837 Charles Dickens begins publication of *Oliver Twist* as a serial in *Bentley's Miscellany*.

Weaving Along the Stroud Valley

A walk in Chalford leads past former weavers' cottages and one-time woollen mills

Wool has been associated with the Cotswolds for centuries. During the Middle Ages the fleece of the 'Cotswold Lion' breed of sheep was the most prized in all of Europe. Merchants from many countries despatched their agents to purchase it from the fairs and markets of the wold towns in the northern part of the region – most famously Northleach, Cirencester and Chipping Campden. Woven cloth eventually became a more important export and so the industry moved to the southern Cotswolds, whose valleys and faster-flowing streams were suited to powering woollen mills.

Mechanisation

The concentration of mills in the Stroud area was evident by the early 15th century. Indeed, the area's importance was such that when a 1557 Act of Parliament restricted cloth manufacture to towns, the villages of the Stroud district were specifically exempted. By 1700 the lower Stroud Valley was producing about around 49 million square feet (4.6 million square metres) of cloth every year. At this time the spinning and weaving was done in domestic dwellings or workhouses, the woven cloth then being returned to the mill for finishing.

The Industrial Revolution was to bring rapid change. There was great opposition to the introduction of mechanical spinning and shearing machines. This was heightened in 1795 by the development of the improved broadloom with its flying shuttle. The expectation was that, as well as compelling weavers to work in the mills, it would bring mass unemployment.

Progress marched on, however, and by the mid-19th century there were more than 1,000 looms at work in the Stroud Valley. They came with their share of political unrest too, and in 1825 and 1828 strikes broke out. The industry went into decline as steam replaced water power and it migrated northwards to the Pennines. By 1901 only 3,000 people were employed in the cloth industry, compared with 24,000 in the mid-17th century. Today, only one mill remains.

Graceful Elevations

This walk begins in Chalford, an attractive village built on the steep sides of the Stroud Valley. Its streets are lined with 18th- and 19th-century clothiers' terraces and weavers' cottages. On the canalside the shells of woollen mills are still in plentiful supply.

The 18th-century church contains fine examples of craftsmanship from the Arts and Crafts period of the late 19th and early 20th century. Nether Lypiatt Manor is a handsome manor house now owned by Prince and Princess Michael of Kent. Known locally as 'the haunted house', it was built in 1702 for Judge Charles Cox. Its classical features and estate railings, all unusual in the Cotswolds, inspired wealthy clothiers to spend their money on the addition of graceful elevations to their own houses.

Background: *Naturally dyed wools from the Cotswolds*

Below: *Belvedere Mill, Chafford*

Walk 72 Cloth country

Discover the impact of the Industrial Revolution in the Cotswold valleys

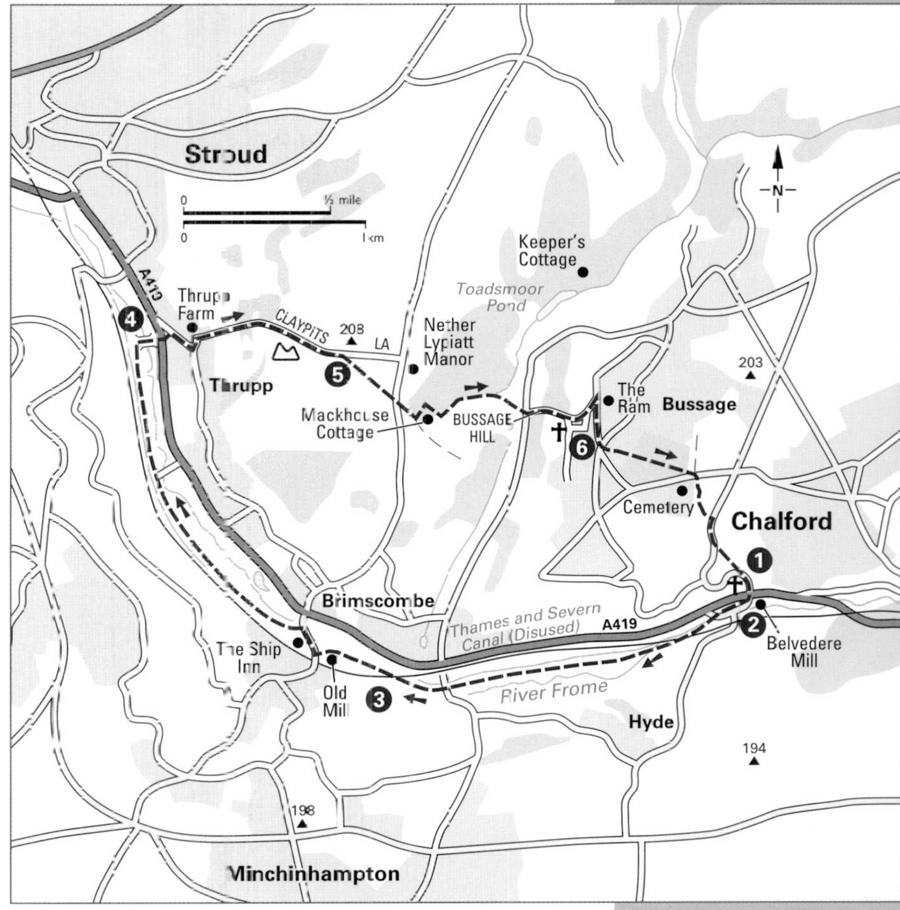

1 Walk towards Chalford Church. Immediately before it, cross the road and locate a path going right, towards a canal roundhouse. Note the Belvedere Mill across to your left, and follow the tow path beside the Thames and Severn Canal on your right.

2 Cross a road and continue along the tow path as it descends steps. Now follow this path for about 2 miles (3.2km). It will soon disappear under the railway line via a gloomy culvert, so that the railway will now be on your right, beyond the old canal. Old mills and small factories line the route.

3 Shortly before arriving in Brimscombe the tow path passes beneath the railway. Soon after, it becomes a road leading into an industrial estate. At a road opposite a large old mill, turn left to come to a junction. Cross at the junction and turn right. Immediately after the Ship Inn turn left along a road among offices and workshops. Continue straight on along a path, keeping factory walls to your right. The canal reappears on your left. As you walk on into the country you will pass beneath three brick bridges and a metal footbridge.

4 At the next bridge, with a hamlet on your left, turn right to follow a path to the A419. Cross this and then turn left. Beside the bus stop turn right up a short path to meet Thrupp Lane. Turn right, and at the top, turn left once more into Claypits Lane. Turn right just before Thrupp Farm and climb up steeply.

WHILE YOU'RE THERE

On the far side of the Stroud Valley, there are a number of places to go. Woodchester has a celebrated and well-preserved Roman mosaic, which unfortunately is kept covered – it was last displayed in 1973 and there are no plans to uncover it again. There is also an unfinished 19th-century Gothic mansion at Woodchester. Rodborough Common is the site of an 18th- and 19th-century fort. At Selsley is a church filled with stained glass by members of the Arts and Crafts Movement.

5 After a long climb, as the road levels out, you will see Nether Lypiatt Manor in front of you. Turn right, beside a tree, over a stile into a field. Go half-left to the far corner. Cross a stone stile and follow a narrow path beside trees to a road. Descend a lane opposite. Where it appears to fork, follow the 'Mackhouse Cottage' sign, descending. Enter woodland, descending steadily, and fork right near the bottom. Keep a pond on your left and cross a road to climb steeply again, up Bussage Hill. After 100yds (91m) pass a lane on the left. At a pair of signs indicating speed de-restriction, fork left. Soon notice a woodland path on the left, but continue on the road to The Ram. Turn right.

6 Walk for nearly 0.25 mile (400m) to a telephone box then, at a bus shelter, turn left to follow a path among houses into woodland. Go ahead until you meet a road. Turn left and immediately right down a path beside a cemetery. Descend to another road. Turn right for 100yds (91m) – care is needed on this short road stretch – then turn left down a steep lane among trees, leading back to Chalford. At the bottom turn left to the lay-by.

Distance 6 miles (9.7km)

Minimum time 3hrs

Ascent/gradient 495ft (150m) ▲▲▲

Level of difficulty ●●●

Paths Fields, lanes, canal path and tracks, 3 stiles

Landscape Canal, road and railway, valley and steep slopes, villages

Suggested map OS Explorer 168 Stroud, Tetbury & Malmesbury

Start/finish Grid reference: SO 892025

Dog friendliness Good, with not too many stiles and little livestock

Parking Lay-by east of Chalford Church

Public toilets None on route

THE VICTORIAN AGE
1837–1901

AGE OF OPTIMISM

Queen Victoria's reign saw the British Empire achieve the peak of its influence and confidence, extending so far around the globe that 'the sun never set' over its territories – it was so vast there was always part of its territory in daylight. In this era, also, Britain emerged as the world's leading industrial power.

The age of the machine gathered speed in the 19th century; factories and mills became the focus for new communities; cheap housing was thrown up and families at the bottom of the industrial heap lived in terrible squalor. In his novel *Sybil or The Two Nations*, future prime minister Benjamin Disraeli described a society split into 'haves' and 'have-nots'; the misery and poverty of the expanding industrial cities was also vividly documented by Charles Dickens and Elizabeth Gaskell. Throughout the century, urban centres were worlds of extremes. Grand civic buildings and monuments, neo-Gothic libraries, schools, churches and railway stations typified the self-assurance of the age, while back-to-back houses and belching chimney stacks characterised a grimmer reality in working-class areas. In the face of glaring inequalities the Chartist movement called for a 'people's charter' guaranteeing democratic rights: universal male suffrage, a secret ballot and salaries for MPs, to make parliament accessible to those without private incomes. The road to reform, however, was long; progress was slow and piecemeal.

GREAT EXPECTATIONS

Victorian Britain was proud of its achievements and of the progress made in industry and science. In 1851 the Great Exhibition opened at the Crystal Palace, in Hyde Park, London. The brainchild of Victoria's prince consort, Albert, this was a showcase of international crafts, inventions and cultures, dominated by 7,000 British exhibits. More than 1 million visitors a month were attracted, and with the funds generated Albert established the Victoria and Albert Museum. In 1861, however, Prince Albert died of typhoid fever and Victoria entered a period of protracted grief, closeting herself away from all public appearance and ceremony. Her absence from the public stage provoked mockery and complaint from the press and public. Some anti-monarchical sentiments took a more extreme form and there was more than one suspected anarchist plot; other threats to the establishment were perceived in the Fenian Movement, calling for Irish independence. Meanwhile the Liberal government of William Ewart Gladstone ushered in reforms to cope with the changing face of Britain. A secret ballot was introduced; schooling was extended; and efforts were made to address the 'Irish Question', though attempts to introduce Home Rule in Ireland fell flat.

As the 20th century approached, new discoveries encouraged the development of a consumer society. The electric telegraph made communications faster. Photography, cinema and gramophones heralded a new kind of mass entertainment. Motor cars and bicycles began to appear on the roads, and at the turn of the century powered flight became a possibility. Victoria celebrated her Golden Jubilee in 1887 and her Diamond Jubilee in 1897; these, the 50th and 60th anniversaries of her accession, were greeted with wide acclaim. By the time she died, in 1901, her reign had seen Britain transformed beyond recognition.

KEY SITES

Consett, County Durham: Where Consett Steel Works thrived, from 1849 onwards.

Former tin mines at Pendeen, Cornwall: Where copper and tin were dug.

Dale Dike Reservoir, South Yorkshire: Scene of terrible disaster when a dam burst in 1864.

Castell Coch, near Cardiff, Wales: Victorian fairy-tale castle built by the 3rd Marquess of Bute.

Wanlockhead, Dumfries & Galloway: Victorian gold and lead mines were highly profitable.

Whitechapel, London: Scene of Jack the Ripper's gruesome murders of prostitutes in 1888.

Mount Snowdon, Gwynedd: The mountain railway, using a rack-and-pinion system developed in the Swiss Alps, opened in 1896.

Left: *The Victorian era is celebrated for architecture, among many other things. This is Brighton station*

1837 Victoria is crowned Queen of England at the age of 18. Her reign will last for almost 64 years.

1838 The first camera, called a daguerreotype, is developed by Frenchman Louis Daguerre.

1840 The 'penny post' is introduced; along with the telegraph, it revolutionises communication.

1843 Charles Dickens publishes *A Christmas Carol.*

1843 William Wordsworth becomes Poet Laureate.

1845–48 The Irish potato crop is wiped out by blight, and hundreds of thousands die of starvation. Landlords evict families unable to pay their rent, and masses emigrate to America and England in search of work.

Consett Steel and the River Derwent

A fascinating ramble leads along the banks of the river that first brought steel-making to Consett

Even into the late 1970s views of Consett would still be described as 'terrible and magnificent'. As Henry Thorold's *Shell Guide to County Durham*, published in 1980, recorded, 'Vulcan's great forges stand there on the hillside enveloped in steam; cooling towers, cylinders, chimneys, incredible and intimidating.' It was true then – just. But the steel mills of Consett closed in that very year, bringing to an end a story of growth and enterprise that began in 1837 when iron ore was discovered here. The first works opened four years later: by the 1880s the Consett Iron Company, founded in 1864 as a successor to the Derwent Iron Company, employed more than 6,000 people in the town.

The closure a century later could have devastated Consett. Instead, it has reinvented itself as a place of service and manufacturing, which also looks back with pride to its history of steel making. Dividing Northumberland and Durham, this stretch of the River Derwent was the cradle of the northern steel industry. The name of Forge Cottage, just over the footbridge at the start of the walk, indicates that iron-working had been long established in the valley. German steel makers, producing fine swords, lived in Shotley Bridge as early as the 1690s – the village later became the fashionable place for the upper middle classes of Consett to live.

Steelworks Site

The section of the walk along Pemberton Road seems quiet today. But until 1980 the whole of the area to your right, now landscaped, was one of the most industrialised in the country. Here stood one of the British Steel Corporation's mills, its huge buildings alive with noise, smoke and heat. Today it provides an area for recreation and enjoyment, crossed by paths that follow the old railway lines that served the works.

Above right: *Hownsgill Viaduct, near Castleside*

Below: *Snowy fields at Consett*

Walk 73 Hotbed of Victorian industry

Investigate a quiet river and woodland where steel once reigned

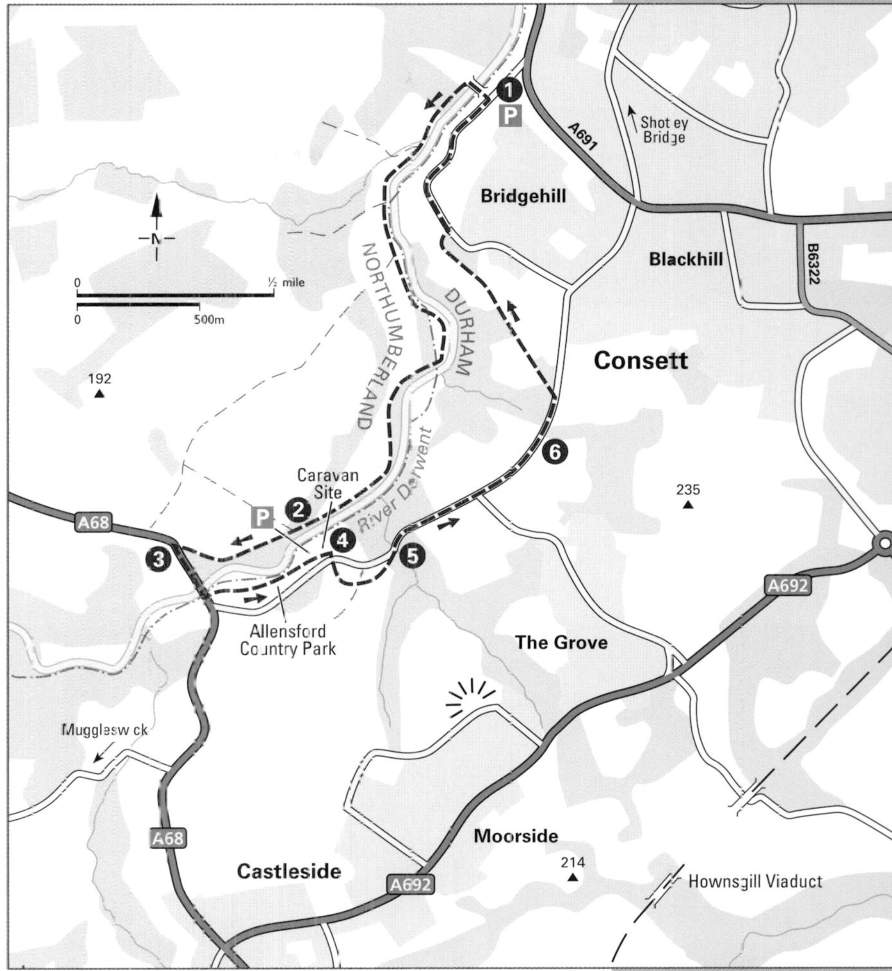

1 From the roadside parking area, locate steps down to the footbridge and cross over the River Derwent. Walk upstream along the tree-lined path, ignoring turnings to the right as it meanders between riverside meadows and the Derwent. Pass another bridge and, where the path divides, carry on alongside the river. Eventually reach an area of beech woodland where the path rises onto a wider track.

2 Follow the track, keeping left when it forks – there are waymarks on this section. The path follows a wire fence, and eventually bears right over a tiny stone bridge skirting a house to reach the A68.

3 Turn left down the hill. Go over the road bridge, passing from Northumberland into Durham. Where a road joins from the left, go left through the entrance into Allensford Country Park. Bear round to the right, and walk through the grassed riverside area to a car park. Go through the car park to reach a road by the entrance to the caravan site.

4 Cross the road to a stile marked 'Derwentside Local Nature Reserve Allensford Wood'. Follow the path, which goes up two sets of steps. At the top follow the grassy path. Where it divides, bear to the left and follow the winding path into woodland and continue downhill. When you reach a crossing path, turn left to the road.

5 Turn right and follow the road (taking care because this stretch can be busy). It rises through woodland, then passes through a more open area. After 0.5 mile (800m), pass a road off to the right. In 0.25 mile (400m) beyond, look for a footpath that descends on your right to meet the road, by trees.

6 Continue to follow the road for 400yds (366m). As the roads rises, take a signed footpath left, downhill into woodland. The path opens out into a track, then becomes a path again. Follow the path for 0.5 mile (800m) to reach a lane. Turn left here, and walk downhill. Continue down the lane, passing Grove House on the left and carry on to reach the parking area.

WHAT TO LOOK OUT FOR

Developed by Durham County Council – and right on its northern boundary – Allensford Country Park consists of 14 acres (5.7ha) of riverside grassland. As well as pleasant walks, there are play facilities for children and access for people using wheelchairs. Within the park is Allensford Wood – the walk takes you through part of it. It is semi-natural ancient woodland that is mainly of oak and birch. There has been some recent replanting with native species. A series of trails criss-crosses the wood; the routes are marked with a symbol of a walking man.

Otters have been spotted in the River Derwent, though you will be lucky to see one. Evidence of their proximity may be found, however, if you are alert to the marks they leave. Be on the lookout for the animals' characteristic footmarks, with their lopsided five-pointed toe marks that turn inwards. Look, too, for the mark of the tail dragging behind the animal. You may also spot places where otters have made mudslides, or where they have scraped up sand into a mound. Adult male otters can be up to 2ft 6in (76cm) long and have a tail – which is thick and tapered and acts as a rudder when the animal is swimming – of up to 20in (50cm). Their short brown fur provides excellent insulation, and otters have the ability to close their nostrils and ears to keep out the water.

Distance 4 miles (6.4km)

Minimum time 1hr 45min

Ascent/gradient 311ft (95m) ▲▲▲

Level of difficulty ●●●

Paths River and streamside paths with some roadside walking, 1 stile

Landscape Pastoral landscapes with reminders of industrial past

Suggested map OS Explorer 307 Consett & Derwent Reservoir

Start/finish Grid reference: NZ 088522

Dog friendliness Can be off lead for most of walk – look for notices

Parking Roadside parking on Shotley Grove Road off A691

Public toilets Allensford Country Park (may be closed in winter)

1846 The Corn Laws are repealed, allowing imported food to compete with British crops.

1847 Charlotte Brontë publishes *Jane Eyre*; her sister Emily publishes *Wuthering Heights*; the third sister, Anne, publishes *Agnes Grey*.

1848 The Chartists demand votes for all men.

1851 T. and W. Bowler of Southwark sell the first bowler hat, designed for gamekeepers.

1851 The Great Exhibition, housed in a huge cast-iron and glass crystal palace in Hyde Park, is a resounding success, attracting 6 million visitors. The profits are used to establish the Science, Natural History and Geology and the Victoria and Albert museums.

1853 Mrs Gaskell's novel *Cranford* is published.

1854–6 Britain and France join forces against Russia in the Crimean War over the Russian Tsar's bid to control Turkey and the Black Sea.

1854 Florence Nightingale and 38 nurses travel to Crimea to care for the wounded.

Victim of a Victorian Scandal

An excursion by the river Irvine leads close to the impressive Loudoun Castle, where a disgraced Victorian lady lies buried

***Above:** The romantic shell of Loudoun Castle, designed by Archibald Elliot around 1807.*

On Wednesday 10 July, 1839, a strange funeral procession made its way through the streets of London. Strange because it was 4:30am and because this early morning procession had an eerie line of empty carriages following the hearse. The carriages represented the highest families in the land and were preceded by the equally empty state coach of the young Queen Victoria. The hearse was bound for the docks, carrying the coffin of Lady Flora Hastings for the sea voyage back to Scotland and burial in the family vault at Loudoun Castle. Despite the hour the streets were lined with people who stoned the state coach as it passed. This was the culmination of a period of deep unpopularity that saw Victoria, queen for just two years, booed at state events and during theatre visits as a direct result of what the public perceived as her unfair treatment of Lady Flora.

The youngest daughter of the Marquis of Hastings, Flora had grown up at Loudoun Castle before moving to London to be lady-in-waiting to Victoria's mother, the Duchess of Kent. Following complaints of severe pain and displaying a swollen abdomen she consulted the royal physician, Sir James Clark. He was unable to determine the cause of her symptoms, but following his examination a rumour started circulating that Flora was pregnant. Despite an intimate examination by two other doctors the rumours persisted. Lady Flora was ostracised at court and shunned by Victoria. Several newspapers got hold of the story and published a tale of jealousy, scandal and intrigue in court circles, naming the guilty parties.

Defending the Family Honour

Flora's brother, Lord Hastings, was incensed and threatened court action and pistols at dawn. Her uncle published a detailed account in another paper and as a result public opinion sided with Lady Flora, who was cheered whenever she appeared. Faced with such hostility, Victoria conducted a PR exercise by having Lady Flora attend her in public while continuing to ignore her in private. When Lady Flora died, an independent post mortem revealed that she had suffered from a swollen liver.

It may have been Victoria who started the rumour rather than her physician, and Victoria continued to consult him. However, in December 1861 the same physician wrongly diagnosed Prince Albert as suffering from a 'feverish sort of influenza'. By the time William Jenner was called in and discovered that Albert was in the advanced stages of typhoid fever, it was too late to save him – and he died on 14 December.

Walk 74 A lady wronged

As you make a pleasant tour of Loudoun, spare a thought for the tragic final days and unhappy end of a queen's lady in waiting

1 From Lady Flora's Institute, go west along Main Street and turn left into Craigview Road. Cross a bridge, then turn right and follow the road you are on as far as a T-junction. Turn left here, then, where the road forks, keep to the right, going along the side of the factory. Turn left into Stonygate Road and follow this to join the Irvine Footpath.

2 Keep on this path, passing Strath and on to the kennels. Turn right at the gate and follow the path round the perimeter. The walkway continues along the river bank on a well-defined, if somewhat muddy, path. Keep on this, going through some woodlands until a white cottage comes into view.

3 Keep right along the riverside path and cross playing fields to go through another gate, then along a street to a T-junction.

4 Turn right, cross the road and continue, heading out of town, crossing the 'Muckle Brig' and the Galston bypass to continue on a pavement heading along the A719 towards Loudoun Academy. Pass the academy on the right, then the entrance gates to Loudoun Castle.

5 Turn left opposite the gates and head along a narrow country lane for 0.5 mile (800m) to Loudoun Kirk Bridge. Turn left and go into Loudoun kirkyard. Return from there, cross a small bridge and turn right onto the signposted footpath heading to Galston. After around 100yds (91m) the path bends right and a narrow grassy footpath forks left. Go left.

6 Keep on this well-trodden path to the T-junction at Galston bypass, then turn right and head along a pavement, across a bridge, then turn right and head downhill. Turn left at a waymarker and go through the underpass to the other side of the bypass. Turn left and walk along a footpath, which runs beside the river.

7 At the end of the path turn right, head along a narrow lane, then turn left into Titchfield Street. Turn right at the next junction, cross the road and take the next left, passing two school buildings and a cemetery to reach a staggered junction. Cross the B7037 and continue along Clockstone Road.

8 Turn left at the T-junction. Take the next right beside a house and follow this road downhill, then back up to pass Piersland farm. Head downhill from here and cross a gate where the road turns left to go under a railway bridge. Turn right after the bridge and retrace your steps to the start.

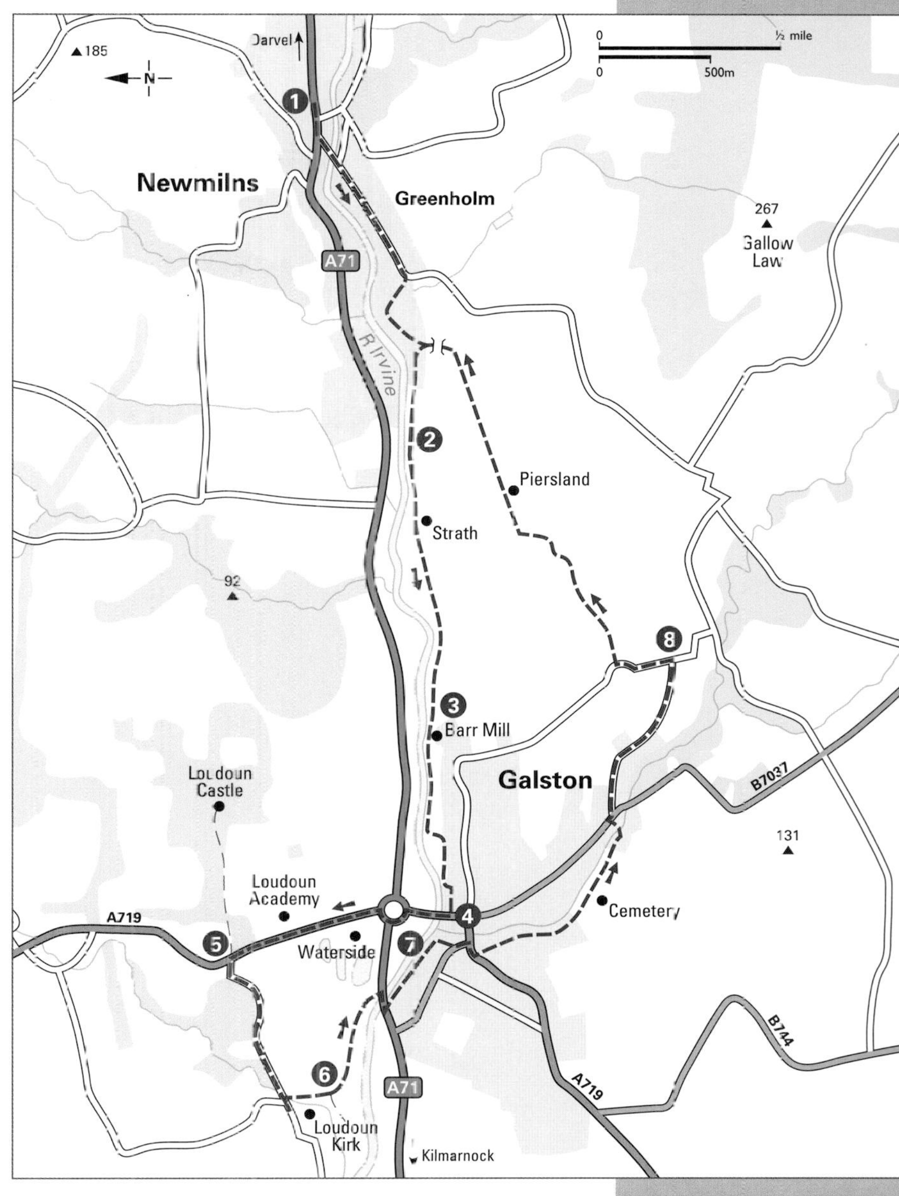

WHAT TO LOOK OUT FOR

On the section running along the river bank look across the river to Loudoun Castle, one of the most impressive ruins in Scotland. The castle was built in the early 19th century on the site of a previous keep. Known as the 'Windsor of Scotland', it was destroyed by fire on 1 December 1941, and lay derelict for years before being renovated. A theme park was opened on the site, but has now closed.

WHILE YOU'RE THERE

Nearby Kilmarnock was once the centre of the rail industry. Andrew Barclay's Victorian locomotive works built steam engines that went all over the world. The first steam passenger railway was the Kilmarnock to Troon line, which crossed the Laigh Milton Viaduct, the oldest in Scotland.

Distance 7.5 miles (12.1km)

Minimum time 4hrs

Ascent/gradient 187ft (57m) ▲▲▲

Level of difficulty ●●●

Paths Footpaths and roads

Landscape River valley

Suggested map OS Explorer 334 East Kilbride Galston & Darvel

Start/finish Grid reference: NS 539373

Dog friendliness On lead at lambing and near livestock

Parking Lady Flora's Institute

Public toilets None on route

1837 – 1901

1855 Photographs showing the graphic reality of the Crimean War are taken by Roger Fenton, founder of the Royal Photographic Society.

1857–58 The Indian Mutiny breaks out against British rule in India after widespread famine in the country. The mutiny is suppressed by British troops, who massacre thousands of Indian men and women.

1859 Charles Darwin's thought-provoking publication *On The Origin of Species by Means of Natural Selection* causes outrage. Science and religion seem finally to have reached a parting of the ways.

1861 The death of Victoria's consort, Prince Albert, leaves the Queen inconsolably grief-stricken. She withdraws from public life.

There's Copper in Them There Hills

An energetic walk leads up to the old copper mines of Mynydd Sygyn and through the truly spectacular Pass of Aberglaslyn

This route heads for the rugged hills that form one side of the great Aberglaslyn gorge. At the back of the car park you pass under a railway bridge that belonged to the Welsh Highland Railway and pass the site of an old crushing plant. Here, copper ore from the mountain would have been prepared for shipment, using the railway. Beyond the plant, the path follows a playful stream and climbs steadily through the lonely Cwm Bychan. Here, beneath splintered, craggy mountains patched with heather and bracken, you come across a line of rusting gantries. These are part of an old aerial ropeway, built to carry ore down to the crushing mill.

Above: *The River Afon at Beddgelert*

Below: *Looking up the Aberglaslyn Gorge*

Mining had taken place hereabouts since Roman times, but after the First World War the extraction became uneconomical. In 1922 the mines closed. Continuing to the col above, the route comes to a huge area of mining spoil and a meeting of routes. Ours turns south, and soon we are following a rugged rocky path zig-zagging down to a grassy basin below, before continuing along a craggy ridge. Here the ground drops away steeply into the valley of the Afon Glaslyn. If it is early summer the scene will be emblazoned by the vivid pink blooms of rhododendrons, which smother the hillside.

Hundreds of feet below lie the roof tops of Beddgelert, a pretty village with a fine two-arched bridge spanning the Glaslyn; if you get a feeling of *déjà vu*, the hillsides around here were used to stand in for China in *The Inn of the Sixth Happiness* (1958), starring Ingrid Bergman.

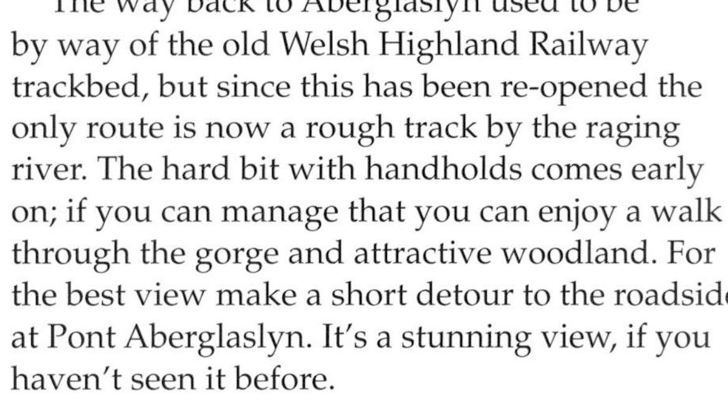

The way back to Aberglaslyn used to be by way of the old Welsh Highland Railway trackbed, but since this has been re-opened the only route is now a rough track by the raging river. The hard bit with handholds comes early on; if you can manage that you can enjoy a walk through the gorge and attractive woodland. For the best view make a short detour to the roadside at Pont Aberglaslyn. It's a stunning view, if you haven't seen it before.

Llyn Dinas and the Sygun Mines

An extension to the walk, beginning at Point 3, leads to the beautiful lake of Llyn Dinas and also offers views of the Sygun copper mining complex. You'll see it displayed in all its magnificence, surrounded by oak woods, rhododendrons, and the crags of Snowdon's foothills. Small-scale mining had gone on for centuries but the Sygun mines were opened up on a larger scale in 1836. However, they only achieved spasmodic success and production stopped in 1903. They're now open as an award-winning tourist attraction.

Walk 75 Beautiful waters, valuable element

Enjoy wonderful lake views as you explore remote hills near Beddgelert, where copper was dug by hardy miners for centuries

1 The path starts to the left of the toilet block and goes under the old railway bridge, before climbing through Cwm Bychan. After a steady climb the path reaches the iron pylons of the aerial cableway.

2 Beyond the pylons, keep straight on, ignoring paths forking left. A grassy corridor leads to a col, where there's a stile in a fence that is not shown on current maps. Bear left beyond the stile and head for a three-way footpath signpost by the rocks of Grib Ddu.

3 Follow the path on the left signed 'To Beddgelert and Sygun' and go over another ladder stile. Turn left, then follow the path down round a rocky knoll and then down the hillside to a signpost. Just beyond the sign is the cairn at Bwlch-y-Sygyn and over to the left is a shallow, peaty pool in a green hollow.

4 The path now heads southwest along the mountain's northwestern ridge, overlooking Beddgelert. Ignore any lesser paths along the way.

5 Watch out for a large cairn, highlighting the turn-off right for Beddgelert. The clear stony path weaves through rhododendron and rock, goes through a kissing gate in a wall halfway down, then descends further to the edge of Beddgelert, where a little lane passing the cottage of Penlan leads to the Afon Glaslyn.

6 Turn left to follow the river for a short way. Don't cross the footbridge over the river but turn left to follow the Glaslyn's east bank. Cross the restored railway line and then continue between it and the river.

7 Below the first tunnel, the path is pushed right to the water's edge. Handholds screwed into the rocks assist passage on a difficult but short section. The path continues through riverside woodland and over boulders until it comes to Pont Aberglaslyn.

8 Here, turn left up some steps and follow a dirt path through the woods. Just before the railway, follow a signed path down and right to the car park.

Extension

From the signpost described in Point 3, follow the stony path, signed 'To Dinas', which descends gradually north-east down the hillside. Your eyes will be captured by the craggy hills to the right. The serrated top is that of Moel Meirch and those vertical cliffs to the right of it belong to Craig Llyn-llagi. Snowdon's summit comes in and out of view on the left, but its satellite, Y Lliwedd, is ever present. As the path veers left to round a rocky knoll, Llyn Dinas comes into view. On reaching the shoreline, Point A, turn left, go through a kissing gate and then follow a level path alongside the Afon Glaslyn. Ignore the bridges which entice you to the far banks. Adjacent to the second bridge you'll see the remains of an old crushing plant, including water-wheels. This is part of the Sygun copper mining complex, Point B, the main part of which stands on the hillside just above. The path joins a tarmac track that curves left towards the mines before veering right to resume its course down the valley.

The track becomes a lane and passes a campsite. Leave it where it crosses the river and go over a stile to a path leading into Beddgelert. Don't cross the first bridge in the village but continue downriver to a metal footbridge to rejoin the main walk at Point 6.

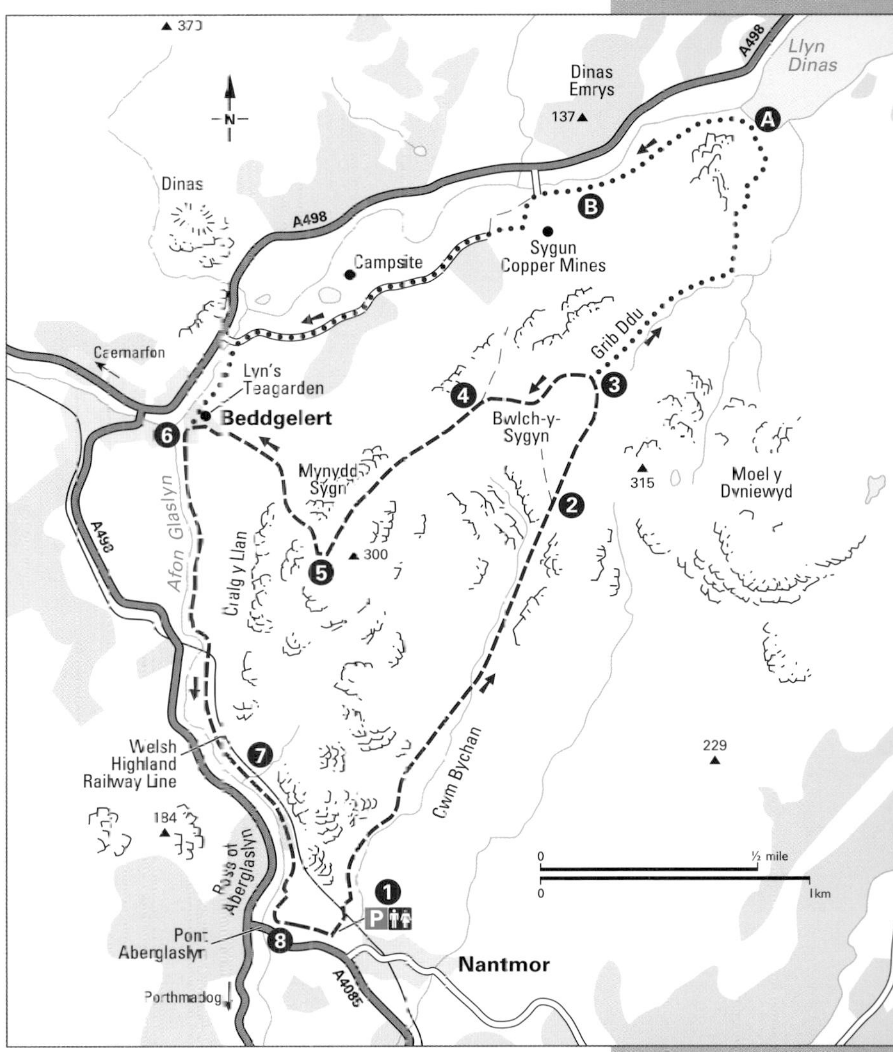

WHILE YOU'RE THERE

Try one of the self-guided tours of the Sygun Copper Mines. See veins of copper ore in chambers coloured by an array of stalactites and stalagmites. If you take the extension walk, look out for Dinas Emrys, a rocky hill on the far banks of the Glaslyn; it once had great ramparts built into the rock.

Distance 4 miles (6.4km) [Extension 6 miles (9.7km)]

Minimum time 2hrs 30min [Extension 3hrs 30min]

Ascent/gradient 1,181ft (360m) ▲▲▲ [Extension 820ft (250m) ▲▲▲]

Level of difficulty ●●● [Extension ●●●]

Paths Well maintained paths and tracks, 2 stiles; section of path in Aberglaslyn gorge requires use of handholds

Landscape Hills and gorge

Suggested map OS Explorer OL17 Snowdon

Start/finish Grid reference: SH 597462

Dog friendliness Dogs should be on lead at all times

Parking National Trust pay car park, Aberglaslyn

Public toilets At car park

1861–65 The American Civil War is fought between Southern slave masters and people in the Northern states, seeking abolition of the slave trade.

1863 The mass production of cars by Henry Ford begins in the United States.

1863 The Football Association is set up in London.

1865 C. L. Dodgson publishes *Alice's Adventures in Wonderland* under the name Lewis Carroll.

1867 Doctor Barnardo opens his first children's home in Stepney, London.

1868 The Liberal William Ewart Gladstone becomes prime minister. He will serve four times before 1894.

1869 John Sainsbury opens his first dairy shop.

1870 Primary education is made compulsory.

1871 Cricketer W.G. Grace scores 2,739 runs in a single season.

1874 Benjamin Disraeli becomes prime minister.

The Tinners' Trail at Pendeen

This absorbing outing leads through the historic tin- and copper-mining country of the Land's End Peninsula

The Cornish tin- and copper-mining industry saw its heyday in the Victorian era. Since then it has suffered a long decline, as it lost out to cheap ore from surface strip mines in Asia and to the vagaries of the international market. Today all the mines in Cornwall are redundant.

At Pendeen on the north coast of the Land's End peninsula the area's last working mine, the Geevor Tin Mine, closed in 1990 after years of uncertainty and false promise, and despite vigorous efforts by the local community to save it. Tin- and copper-mining began in the area towards the end of the 18th century; the East Levant Mine was operational here until 1840. Then the North Levant Mine worked in 1851–91 and at its height in the 1880s employed more than 175 miners. In the early 19th century Cornish mines were the world's largest suppliers of copper, but after around 1860 overseas copper suppliers became more important and the Cornish mines concentrated on tin.

Today, the modern buildings of Geevor have been transformed into a fascinating mining museum, but it is the ruined granite chimney stacks and engine houses of the 19th-century industry that have given this mining coast its dramatic visual heritage.

Sea Spray and the Crown's Mine

Early in the walk you reach the Geevor Tin Mine and then the National Trust's Levant Engine House. From Levant the coast path runs on to Botallack, where the famous Crown's Mine Engine Houses stand on a spectacular shelf of rock above the Atlantic. The workings of the Crown's Mine ran out for almost 1 mile (1.6km) beneath the sea, and the mine was entered down an angled runway using wagons.

You can visit the Crown's Mine Houses by following tracks down towards the sea from the route of the main walk. Flooding was a constant problem for these mines and some of the earliest steam engines were developed to pump water from the workings. On the clifftop above the Crown's Mine the National Trust has restored the 19th-century facade of the Botallack Count House. This was the assaying and administrative centre for all the surrounding mines.

Below: *Chimneys at the Levant Mine*

Bottom: *Old workings at the Geevor Tin Mine*

Below right: *The dramatically situated Crown's Mine Engine Houses at Botallack*

Walk 76 Once-bustling centre of Victorian copper- and tin-mining

Explore a landscape rich in history and character above the Cornish waves

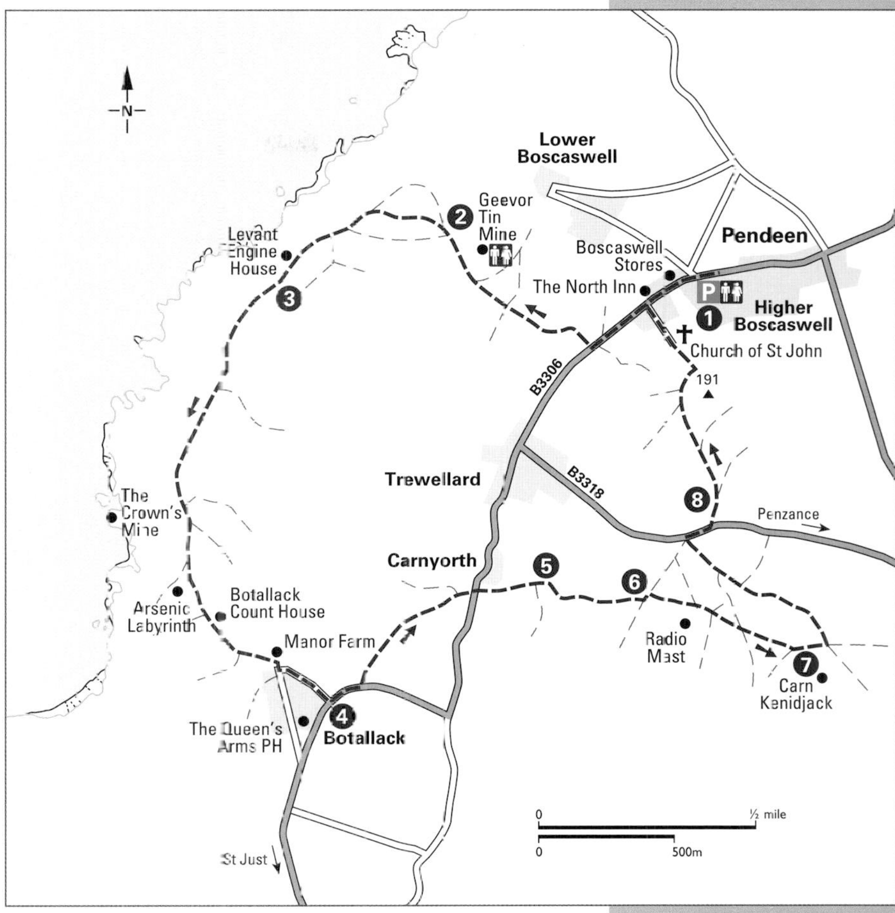

1 Turn left out of the car park and follow the road to the entrance of the Geevor Tin Mine. Go down the drive to the reception building and keep to its left. Go over a stile and follow a road between buildings.

2 Just beyond the buildings, turn left to walk along a track, signposted 'Levant'. Pass a huge boulder and follow the track towards a very tall chimney stack ahead. Continue ahead across open ground to reach the Levant Engine House.

3 Go through Levant car park and then follow a rough track to reach the Botallack Count House. Keep on past Manor Farm and reach the public road at Botallack. The Queen's Arms pub is straight down the road ahead.

4 Turn left, then left again at the main road (watch for fast traffic), then turn left along Cresswell Terrace to a stile. Follow field paths to Carnyorth. Cross the main road, then follow the lane opposite, past a row of cottages, to reach a solitary house.

5 Keep left of the house and then go over a stile and cross over the field to the opposite hedge to reach a hidden stile just beyond a water trough. Follow a path through small fields towards a radio mast. Cross a final stile on to a rough track.

6 Go left, then immediately right at a junction. Keep on past the radio mast, then follow a path through gorse and heather to the rocky outcrop of Carn Kenidjack (not always visible when misty).

7 At a junction abreast of Carn Kenidjack, go left, then sharp left again along a path past a small granite parish boundary stone, eventually emerging on a road. Turn right and in about 140yds (128m), go left along an obvious broad track opposite a house.

8 Keep left at a junction and then straight ahead at the next junction. When abreast of two large rocks on the left, go right between two smaller stone pillars. Keep straight ahead across rough ground and then go alongside an overgrown wall. Go left over a big stone stile directly above the church and descend to the main road. Turn right to the car park.

BEAM ENGINE AT WORK

The National Trust's restored engine house at Levant Engine House contains a remarkable reconstruction of a Cornish beam engine, the great driving force of every Victorian mine. The engine is regularly 'steamed up' to go through the stately rocking motion that powered deep water pumps and facilitated the movement of ore from below ground.

WHAT TO LOOK OUT FOR

Just below the track that runs past the Botallack Count House lie the ruins of an arsenic labyrinth. Mineral ore was often contaminated with arsenic. In the 19th century, during times of low tin prices, this arsenic was collected by roasting ore in a calciner and passing the smoke through enclosed tunnels, known as the labyrinth. The cooling vapour deposited the arsenic on the labyrinth walls as a powder. This powder was then exported, mainly to North America where it was used as a pesticide against the boll weevil in the cotton fields.

The Geevor Tin Mine is well worth a visit. Part of the experience is an underground tour and a look the old treatment sheds.

Distance 5 miles (8km)

Minimum time 4hrs

Ascent/gradient 328ft (100m) ▲▲▲

Level of difficulty ●●●

Paths Coastal footpath, field paths and moorland tracks, 6 stiles

Landscape Spectacular coastal cliffs, old mining country and open moorland

Suggested map OS Explorer 102 Land's End

Start/finish Grid reference: SW 383344

Dog friendliness Keep dogs under control in field sections

Parking Free car park in centre of Pendeen village, opposite Boscaswell Stores, on the B3306

Public toilets Pendeen car park and Geevor Tin Mine

1876 Queen Victoria is proclaimed Empress of India.

1876 Alexander Graham Bell patents his invention of the telephone.

1879 The Tay Bridge between Dundee and Wormit collapses in a terrible storm on 28 December while a train is crossing; 78 die.

1883 Robert Louis Stevenson's adventure novel *Treasure Island* is published.

1884 The Greenwich Meridian is approved; Greenwich Mean Time becomes the global standard.

1884 The Fabian Society, forerunner to the Labour Party, is founded.

1884 The Statue of Liberty is presented to the United States as a gift from France in recognition of a hundred years of Independence.

1886 The first Crufts Dog Show is held by Charles Cruft at the Royal Aquarium, Westminster.

1886 The Severn railway tunnel opens.

Bradfield and the Dale Dike Dam Disaster

A quiet waterside walk visits the site of a 19th-century industrial tragedy

Just before midnight on Friday 11 March, 1864, when the Dale Dike Dam tragically collapsed, 650 million gallons (2,955 million litres) of water surged along the Loxley Valley towards Sheffield. They swept aside 415 houses, 106 factories and shops, 20 bridges and countless cottage and market gardens for 8 miles (12.9km), and killed 244 people.

During the Industrial Revolution Sheffield expanded rapidly, as country people sought employment in the city's steel and cutlery works. This put considerable pressure on the water supply. The 'Bradfield Scheme' was the Sheffield Waterworks Company's ambitious proposal to build massive reservoirs in the hills around the village of Bradfield, about 8 miles (12.9km) from the city. Work commenced on the first of these, the Dale Dike Dam, on 1 January 1859. It was a giant by the standards of the time with a capacity of over 700 million gallons (3,182 million litres) of water, but some 200 million gallons (910 million litres) less than the present reservoir.

The Disaster of 1864

Construction of the dam continued until late February 1864, by which time the reservoir was almost full. Friday 11 March was a stormy day and as one of the dam workers crossed the embankment on his way home, he noticed a crack, about a finger's width, running along it. John Gunson, the chief engineer, turned out with one of the contractors to inspect the dam.

At 10pm, Gunson concluded that it was nothing to worry about, but as a precaution lowered the water level. He re-inspected the crack at 11.30pm, noting that it had not visibly deteriorated. However, then the engineer saw to his horror that water was running over the top of the embankment into the crack. He was making his way to the bottom of the embankment when he felt the ground beneath him begin to shake and saw the top of the dam breached by the straining waters. He just had time to scramble up the side before a large section of the dam collapsed, unleashing a solid wall of water.

Below: *The Dale Dike Dam was rebuilt in 1875*

Walk 77 Deadly waters

Pay your respects at the memorial to those killed in the devastation of 1864

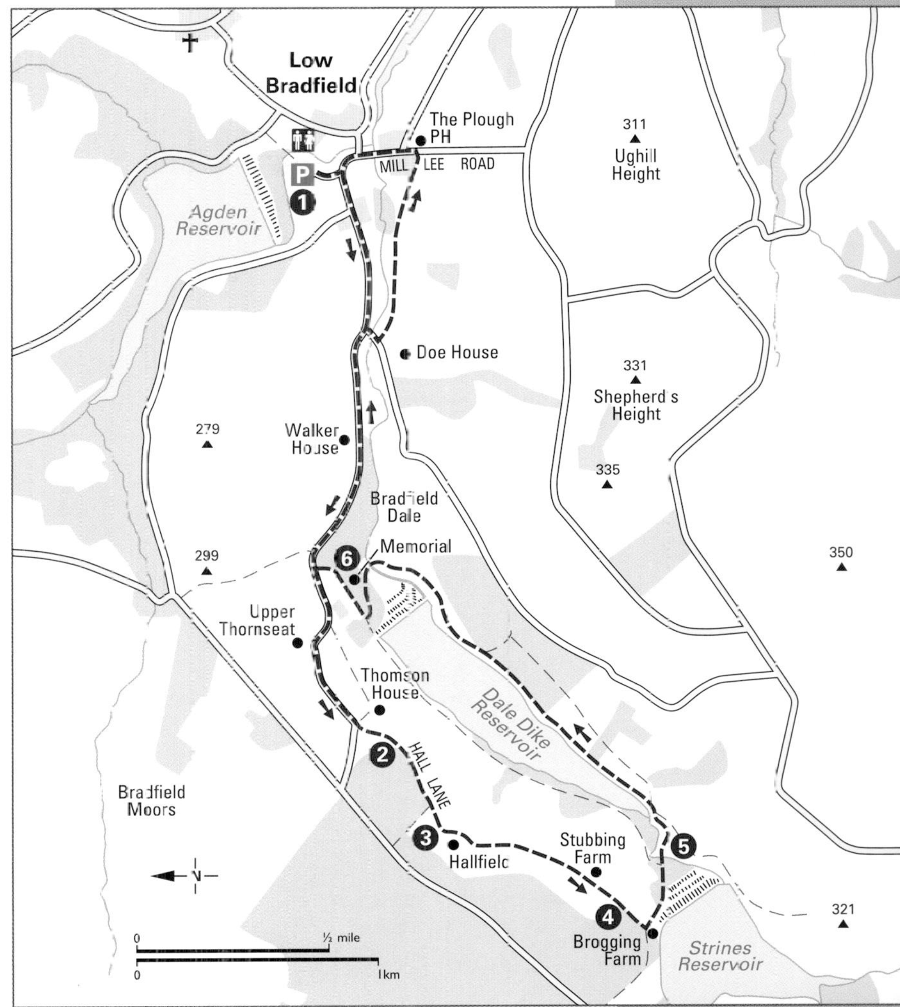

1 Exit the car park and turn right onto the road. At the second junction go right towards Midhopestones. Follow this road uphill passing, on the right, a former inn, Walker House farm and Upper Thornseat. When the road turns right, with Thomson House below, turn left onto an overgrown track.

2 From here go through a gate in front of you and onto Hall Lane, a public bridleway. Follow this along the edge of a wood then through another gate and continue ahead on the farm road. Another gate at the end of this road leads to the entrance to Hallfield.

3 The right of way goes through the grounds of Hallfield but an alternative permissive path leads left through a gate, round the perimeter of the house and through another gate to rejoin the bridleway at the back of the house. Follow the bridleway through a gate and then past Stubbing Farm.

4 The next gate leads to Brogging Farm and the dam at the head of Strines Reservoir. Look out for a sign near the end of the farmhouse and turn left. Go slightly downhill, over a stile, follow the path, then cross a stile and go through a wood.

5 Cross the stream by a footbridge, go right at a junction and then carry straight on at the next junction with the stream on your left. Afterwards follow the path along the bank of Dale Dike Reservoir as far as the dam head. From here continue through the woods, going down several sets of steps, and continue on the path, looking out for the memorial stone erected to honour those who were killed in 1864.

6 Follow the path until it reaches the road. Cross the stile, turn right onto the road and proceed to the road junction. Turn right, cross the bridge then look for a public footpath sign just before the entrance to Doe House. Cross the stile on the left and follow the path all the way to its end on Mill Lee Road opposite the Plough. Turn left and follow this road downhill, through the village and back to the car park.

WHAT TO LOOK OUT FOR

A memorial was erected at the dam in 1991 to commemorate those who lost their lives in the flood. It is a simple memorial stone surrounded by a small garden. Next to it there is a white stone bearing the letters CLOB. This is one of four stones that mark the Centre Line of the Old Bank and are the only trace today of where the earthen embankment of the previous dam stood.

WHILE YOU'RE THERE

Don't miss the Parish Church of St Nicholas, which dates from 1487. It contains a Norman font gifted by the Cistercian monks at Roche Abbey and a Saxon cross found at Low Bradfield in the late 19th century. But it is the Watch House at the gates of the church that sets it apart. Built in 1745 to prevent body snatching from the graveyard, it is the last one to survive in Yorkshire.

Distance 5.5 miles (8.8km)

Minimum time 3hrs 30min

Ascent/gradient 394ft (120m) ▲▲▲

Level of difficulty ●●●

Paths Minor roads, bridleways, forest paths, 4 stiles

Landscape Woodland, reservoir and meadows

Suggested map OS Explorer OL1 Dark Peak

Start/finish Grid reference: SK 262920

Dog friendliness Keep on lead near livestock

Parking Car park by Low Bradfield cricket ground

Public toilets Low Bradfield, rear post office

Castell Coch and the New South Wales

An idyllic walk leads from the beautiful 'Red Castle' to a wild, windswept hillside – the new-look Valleys at their scenic best

At the bottom of the Taff Vale, just a few miles north of Cardiff, is a castle easily capable of rivaling the most romantic of fortified dwellings in Bavaria. With its red sandstone walls and conical towers, Castell Coch was built in the late 1870s on the site of a 13th-century fortress. It was a country retreat for the 3rd Marquess of Bute, who in the 1860s was thought to be the richest man in the world and based his empire in Cardiff.

Fantasy Style

Architect William Burgess, who also designed St Finbar's Cathedral in Cork, created at Castell Coch a design of pure, unadulterated fantasy, with a working drawbridge and portcullis, three circular towers and a dream boudoir that features a lavishly decorated domed ceiling. The grandest of all the castle's rooms has to be the drawing room, three storeys high with a ribbed and vaulted ceiling, further decorated with birds and butterflies. The two-storey chimney piece boasts statues of the Three Fates, which show the thread of life being spun, measured and finally cut. Characters from Aesop's Fables are also depicted.

Every bit as captivating up close as it is from a distance, the castle is well worth a visit, but perched on a clifftop amid stunning deciduous woodland, it is also a great place to start a walk. Conveniently, two waymarked trails run close to the castle and these, together with a labyrinth of forest tracks, provide an invigorating circular route that shows some of the many different faces of the regenerated Valleys.

The route away from the woods follows a section of the Taff Trail, a 55-mile (89km) waymarked route that leads from Cardiff Bay to Brecon via the Taff Valley, Llandaff, Pontypridd and Merthyr Tydfil. Most of the trail, including the lower section of this walk, is along disused railway lines, along with forest tracks and canal paths. From the Taff Trail, this walk follows an airy section of the 21-mile (34km) Ridgeway Walk (Ffordd-y-Bryniau), which traces a fascinating hilltop line across what was once the Borough of Taff Ely until the local government reorganisations of the mid-1990s. The section following climbs steeply onto the narrow ridge of Craig yr Allt, a spectacular viewpoint which on the one hand feels as wild as the mountains further north, but at the same time gives a view of the industrial side of the Valleys.

Bottom: *Castell Coch is built in reddish sandstone, and known as the Red Castle*

Below left: *The main entrance is across a bridge*

Below right: *Victorian Gothic is seen at its most extravagant in the Drawing Room*

Walk 78 Fairy-tale castle and stunning woodland

Take your pleasure in the regenerated Valleys and see the Middle Ages recreated on a Welsh hillside

1 From the car park, walk up to the castle entrance and turn to the right to walk to a stone information plaque. Take the path next to this and climb steeply on a good path past a waymark post and through a gap in a fence to a junction of tracks.

2 Turn sharp left, signposted 'The Taff Trail', by a picture of a viaduct, and follow this broad forest track around the hillside and then down, where it meets the disused railway line close to some houses. Pass through the barrier on the right and follow the clear track for over a mile (1.6km) until you pass a picnic area and come to another barrier.

3 Go through the barrier then, as you come to a disused bridge, turn right over a stile, signposted 'Ridgeway Walk'. Take this and follow it up for a few paces and then around to the right. Ignore one turn left and then turn sharp left to zig-zag back across the hillside, where you turn right again. Follow this around to the left again, aiming at the mast and then, as you reach the field edge, bear right once more. This leads up to a post on a narrow ridge where you turn left.

4 Climb steeply up the ridge and continue ahead, keeping the high ground to your left, until you reach a clear path that leads left, up to the ridge top. Follow this and bear right at the top to walk easily along, drinking in the great views. Keep ahead to drop slightly and then bear left onto a broad track.

5 Follow it down through the bracken to a stile. Cross this and take the track down to a gate that leads onto a tarmac drive. Turn left and continue past some houses on the right-hand side to a junction. Turn right and climb up to another junction, where you bear right.

6 Carry on past the golf club, then fork right onto a narrow lane that drops and bears around to the left. Turn right here to walk past the Forestry Commission sign and then turn immediately left, onto a clear footpath marked by a post.

7 Follow this path, ignoring tracks on both the right and left, until the posts become blue and you come to a T-junction by a sign forbidding horse-riding. Cross the small brook and afterwards turn left to continue steeply downhill, going past a turning on the left to the Countryside Visitor Centre.

8 The track eventually swings around to the right and descends to meet the drive. At this point turn right to climb up the drive and go back to the castle.

Distance 5.5 miles (8.8km)
Minimum time 2hrs 30min
Ascent/gradient 920ft (280m) ▲▲
Level of difficulty ●●
Paths Forest tracks, disused railway line and clear paths, short section of tarmac, 2 stiles
Landscape Mixed woodland and open hillside with views over residential and industrial developments
Suggested map OS Explorer 151 Cardiff & Bridgend
Start/finish Grid reference: ST 131826
Dog friendliness Care needed when walking near livestock; dogs are not allowed in castle
Parking Castell Coch
Public toilets In castle and nearby Countryside Visitor Centre

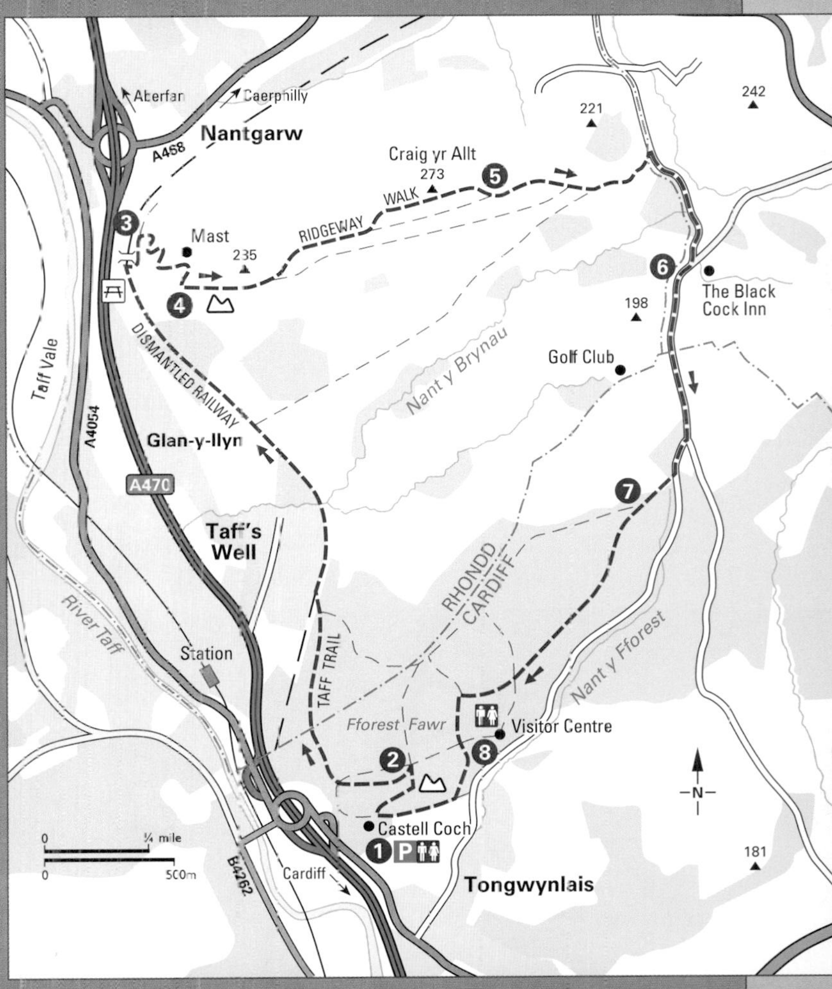

WHAT TO LOOK OUT FOR

Fforest Fawr is a great place to spot woodland birds and mammals. Grey squirrels are common and have become unpopular in some quarters due to their inquisitive nature, insatiable appetite and ability to destroy bird feeders. They are often blamed for the demise of the smaller red squirrel in this country, but research has shown that this is more likely due to habitat loss, courtesy of development. The area is part of the Fforest Fawr Geopark, created in 2005 to protect the natural environment and promote sustainable tourism.

1837 – 1901

1886 Workers at the Royal Arsenal in Woolwich found Arsenal football club, later to be known as the 'Gunners' by their supporters.

1887 St John Ambulance service is founded.

1888 The first pneumatic tyre is developed by John Boyd Dunlop. It is fitted to a bicycle.

1888 Jack the Ripper commits a series of horrific murders in Whitechapel. The police fail to trace the Ripper, and after eight weeks the murders simply stop.

1889 The Eiffel Tower is completed in Paris, designed by Gustave Eiffel as the entrance to the World's Fair.

1890 Queen Victoria opens the Forth Bridge.

Wanlockhead: Scotland's Highest Village

An instructive ramble reveals secrets of Victorian gold- and lead-mining

Above right: *Remains of the old mine workings*

Below: *A beam engine display at the lead mining museum in Wanlockhead. The village is at an altitude of 1,531ft (461m)*

Rich deposits of lead in this part of the Southern Uplands resulted in the establishment of Scotland's highest village at Wanlockhead. Lead mining here was at its peak in the late 19th century, when some 850 people lived in the village. Because of the richness of its deposits, the settlement and its mines became known as 'God's treasure house'.

The first village had been established locally in the 17th century. It was permanent but primitive: accommodation consisted of one-room cottages with often as many as eight people living in them. The hardy early residents cooked over the open fire in the middle of the room and smoke was vented through a hole in the roof. In the 19th century, cottages were bigger, with an attic room and a proper cooking range. In 1871 the miners founded a co-operative society, bought all their supplies there and received a share of the profits. Amazingly this continued until 1971.

A Thriving Community

The miners valued the little leisure time they had and were very active in forming local clubs and societies. There were curling, bowling and quoiting clubs, a drama group and even a silver band. The Library, the second oldest subscription library in Europe, was founded in 1756 by the minister and a small group of villagers. Wanlockhead fared better than most libraries with a donation of books from the local landowner, the Duke of Buccleuch. He also funded the building of a new school and the salary of the teacher.

The miners' children learned to read, write and count and could also take lessons in Latin and Greek. A government inspector visiting in 1842 was so impressed by the standard of learning he concluded that 'the children of the poor labourers of Wanlockhead are under as good, or perhaps better system of intellectual culture than even the middle class children of South Britain generally.'

As the price of lead slumped, and mines became exhausted, the miners gradually drifted away. The last of the mines, Glencrieff, closed in 1934 and the village went into decline until only 30 people remained. In the 1960s the local authority offered to re-house them elsewhere but they resolutely refused to leave. Thanks to their determination, an influx of new blood, renovation of houses and the opening of the Museum of Lead Mining, Wanlockhead has survived as a community into the 21st century.

Walk 79 'God's Treasure House' on a remote hill

See where Victorian lead miners worked hard but lived well and enjoyed varied leisure hours

1 With the museum to your back, turn left and join the Southern Upland Way. Head uphill on steps then, at the top, cross to a stone building with a large white door. Turn right onto a rough road, cross the main road and take the public footpath to Enterkine Pass. Follow this to the front of a white house.

2 Turn left onto the course of an old railway line. Follow this, cross a road, then go through a long cutting to reach a fence. Go over a stile to get to Glengonnar Station, then follow the narrow path that runs along the left side of the railway tracks from here. Eventually the path runs onto a rough road and in the distance you will see two terraced houses.

3 At the point where telephone wires intersect the road, turn left at the pole on the left-hand side and follow the line of the fence down to some sheep pens. Turn right at the end of the pens and walk out to the main road.

4 Turn right then almost immediately left onto a hill road. Walk uphill on this until the road bears sharp right and a dirt track forks off to the left. Turn left onto the track and keep on it until you reach a gate. Cross over, then veer left onto a faint track. Follow the track downhill to the point where it comes close to the corner of a fence on your left.

5 Cross the fence and go straight ahead on a very faint track, picking your way through the heather. Eventually, as the track begins to look more like a path, you will reach a fork. Go to the right here and cross the flank of the hill, passing through some disused tips.

6 The path at this point is little more than a series of sheep tracks and may disappear altogether but that is not a problem. Ahead of you is a large conical spoil heap and, provided you keep heading towards it, you know you will be going in the right direction.

7 Towards the end of the hill the track heads left, starts to make its way downhill, then passes behind a row of cottages. Veer right, downhill, after the cottages to join the road. Turn left and continue past Glencrieff cottages, then turn right, leaving the road and heading downhill again. Cross a bridge and climb up on to the Southern Upland Way. Turn left along it and follow this back to the car park.

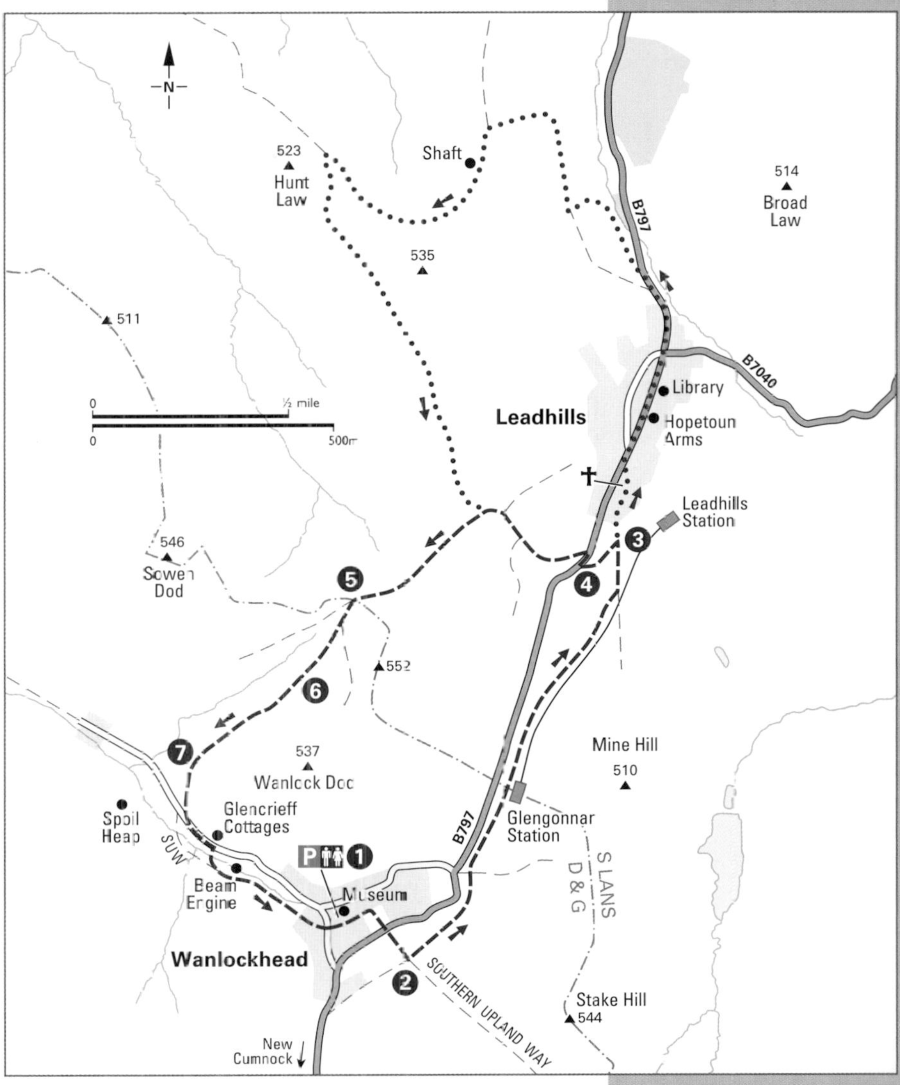

Extending the Walk

From Point 3 you can carry on into the mining village of Leadhills, where you will find the first public subscription library in Europe. A pleasant loop can be made by heading across the mining ground on the far side of the village to intersect some hill tracks, which will eventually lead you back into Wanlockhead.

MUSEUM OF LEAD MINING

A visit to the Museum of Lead Mining will enhance your understanding of the area and your enjoyment of the walk. The entire history of gold- and lead-mining in this area is covered and the admission fee includes a visit to a former miners' cottage and a trip into one of the mines – be sure to wear warm clothing! You can also explore the miners' library – founded in 1756, this is the second oldest subscription library in Europe, after one established in 1741 in the nearby village of Leadhills. During the summer there are gold-panning demonstrations and courses, and the opportunity to hire a pan and head off to try your hand in the local rivers. The museum is open from April to October, daily.

Distance 3.75 miles (6km)

Minimum time 3hrs

Ascent/gradient 525ft (160m) ▲▲▲

Level of difficulty ●●●

Paths Footpaths, hill tracks, hillside and old railway lines, 1 stile

Landscape Hills, mining relics and village

Suggested map OS Explorer 329 Lowther Hills, Sanquhar & Leadhills

Start/finish Grid reference: NX 873129

Dog friendliness Keep on lead near livestock

Parking Museum of Lead Mining car park

Public toilets At car park

1837 – 1901

1894 The Manchester Ship Canal opens and Manchester becomes the first inland port.

1894 Arthur Conan Doyle's detective novel, *The Memoirs of Sherlock Holmes*, is published.

1895 The radio is invented by Italian inventor Guglielmo Marconi.

1895 Oscar Wilde's play *The Importance of Being Earnest* opens to huge acclaim.

1895 The National Trust is founded.

1897 Queen Victoria's Diamond Jubilee is celebrated in style on 22 June. Her reign is recognised as being one of unprecedented achievement.

Guts and Garters in the Ripper's East End

A fascinating city walk follows the bloody path of Jack the Ripper through Whitechapel streets

***Topright:** A cobbled lane in Whitechapel*

***Above:** The Victorian era is vividly recalled in the alleys of Whitechapel*

In the space of 10 weeks during the autumn of 1888 five women, all prostitutes, were brutally murdered by an unidentified serial killer later dubbed 'Jack the Ripper'. This name was first used in a letter claiming responsibility for the attacks; the letter is thought by many to have been a hoax, but the name stuck. More than 100 years later the murderer's true identity remains a mystery. Jack the Ripper has become one of the most notorious serial killers of all time and the subject of many films and documentaries.

At the time of the murders Whitechapel was home to the poor and destitute, and pollution from sewers was commonplace. If you escaped death by starvation you had a high chance of succumbing to disease. Infant mortality was soaring. More than 80 per cent of the population were considered criminals.

Given these facts, prostitution may not have seemed such a bad option for many women. As illiteracy was high among the poor, no doubt news of the killings was spread by word of mouth, although in the literate world at the time, the murder of a prostitute would hardly have raised too many eyebrows.

Modus Operandi

The first victim, 42-year-old Mary Ann Nichols, was found with her throat cut from left to right, suggesting that the killer was left-handed; her stomach had also been slashed several times. Annie Chapman, aged 47, was the second victim and, as well as having her throat cut, certain organs had been removed from her abdomen. The third victim, 45-year-old Elizabeth Stride, also had her throat cut, but apparently a passing pony and trap, driven by the man who discovered her corpse, interrupted the killer. Victim number four was Catherine Eddowes, aged 46, who was found less than an hour after Stride. Her uterus and left kidney had been removed – the kidney was later sent to the chairman of the Whitechapel Vigilance Committee in a package along with a note.

Crowds began to gather at the murder sites and vigilante groups became active, frustrated by the failings of the police investigation. Yet records show that the Ripper was able to spend more time with his last victim, Mary Jane Kelly. She was the only one in her twenties, and was murdered at her home. However, she was so badly mutilated she could be identified only by her eyes and hair. A few years after the Jack the Ripper murders some of the street names were changed to avoid notoriety; other sites are now buried beneath new buildings, but this walk will take you very close to all five sites.

Walk 80 One of the world's most notorious serial killers

Take a deep breath and step back in time to re-examine a gruesome Victorian crime

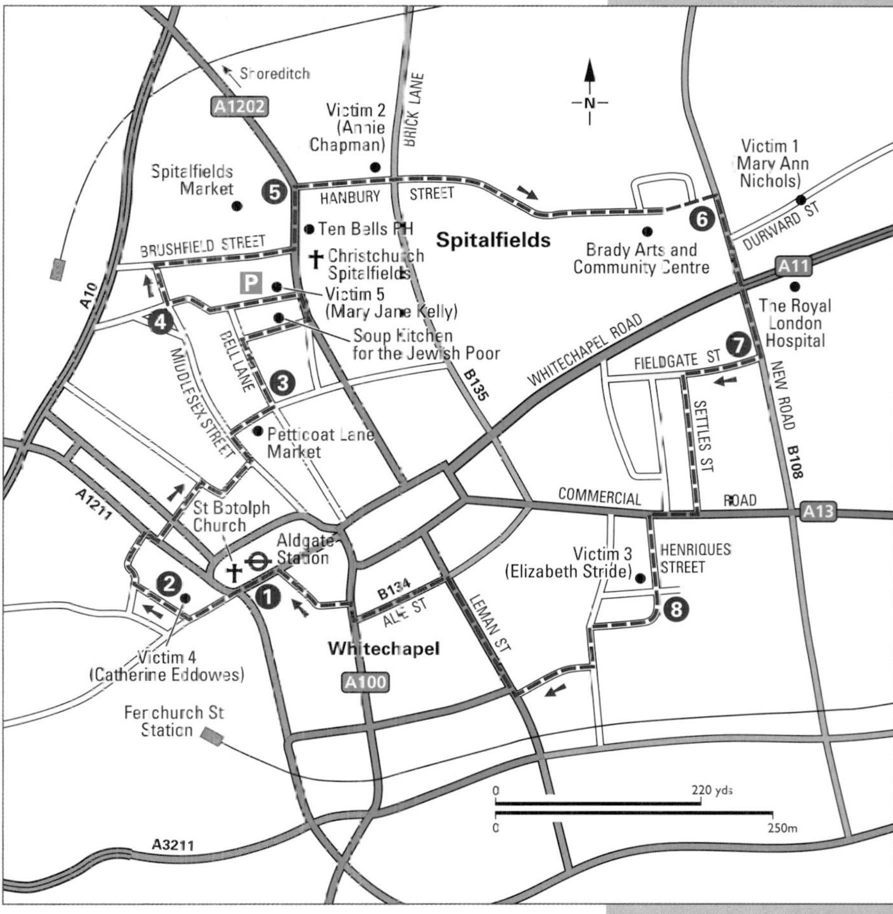

1 With Aldgate tube station behind you, walk towards St Botolph without Aldgate Church on the right. Cross the road at the pedestrian lights and continue ahead, past the school. Turn right on Mitre Street. A few paces further is Mitre Square, where the fourth victim, Catherine Eddowes, was discovered by the benches.

2 Continue ahead, turning right into Creechurch Lane and past some posts marking the boundaries of the City of London. Go across two main roads to reach Stoney Lane. At the end bear right into Gravel Lane, and once past the parade of shops, turn left along Middlesex Street. Take the first right into Wentworth Street, more commonly called Petticoat Lane and host to the famous, thriving market.

3 Turn left into Bell Lane and right into Brune Street, where you'll see the remains of a Victorian soup kitchen. At the end turn left and left again into White's Row, where the fifth body, that of Mary Jane Kelly, was found (the site is now a car park). Cross Bell Lane and follow Artillery Lane as it narrows to form an alleyway (Artillery Passage).

4 Turn right into Sandy's Row, past a synagogue, then right and left to reach Brushfield Street. Turn right again past Spitalfields Market and you'll end up at Hawksmoor's majestic Christ Church Spitalfields, the white building ahead. Bear left to cross at the pedestrian lights and turn left along Commercial Street.

5 As the road bends, turn right into Hanbury Street, where the Truman's Brewery denotes the murder scene of Annie Chapman, the second victim. Cross Brick Lane and continue along this road for another 500yds (457m), past the Brady Arts and Community Centre and along an alleyway.

6 Turn right at the main road and look out for Durward Street on the left, which leads to the site of the first murder (Mary Ann Nichols), although little now remains of the original streets. Continue ahead and cross the busy traffic on Whitechapel Road into New Road.

7 At Fieldgate Street turn right and then take the third left into Settles Street. When you reach the end bear right and cross over at the pedestrian lights, to turn left into Henriques Street. The school here stands on the site of the Ripper's third murder, Elizabeth Stride. Notice the signs 'Cookery/Laundry' above the school's entrance door.

8 Continue ahead along the road at it swings to the right. At the end, turn left and then immediately right into Hooper Street. Continue ahead, then turn right into Leman Street. Turn right and at the crossroads turn left along Alie Street. At the end cross the road and bear right and then left along Little Somerset Street, which comes out opposite where you began the walk at Aldgate tube.

WHAT TO LOOK OUT FOR

Between 1880 and 1914 Whitechapel became home to hundreds of eastern European Jewish refugees. At the soup kitchen in Brune Street the 'Jewish Poor' came for some basic hot soup. The soup kitchen was built – with an ornate facade – by wealthy Jews to help their poorer cousins. Note the Dickensian 'Way In' and 'Way Out' signs above the doors.

Distance 2.75 miles (4.4km)

Minimum time 1hr 30min

Ascent/gradient Negligible ▲▲▲

Level of difficulty ●●●

Paths Paved streets

Landscape Plenty of narrow streets and some main roads

Suggested map AA Street by Street London

Start/finish Aldgate tube station

Dog friendliness On lead

Public toilets None on route

1898 After the Opium Wars (1830–64), the Chinese government signs a 99-year lease giving Britain power over new territories north of Kowloon.

1898 H.G. Wells's science fiction novel, *The War of the Worlds*, is published.

1898 Marie and Pierre Curie discover radium.

1898 Ebenezer Howard, proponent of garden cities, writes *Tomorrow: the Peaceful Path to Real Reform* (later known as *Garden Cities of Tomorrow*).

1899–1902 The Second Boer War is fought in southern Africa between the British Empire and two Boer republics, the Orange Free State and the South African Republic.

1899 Edward Elgar's *The Enigma Variations* is first performed, in London. Each variation is a musical portrait of one of his friends.

1901 Queen Victoria's death on 22 January is mourned by the nation. Victoria's 64-year reign had been one of imperial expansion, massive industrial growth and profound social change.

Snowdon's Marvellous Mountain Railway

An energetic mountain walk climbs in view of one of the Victorian age's more unusual engineering marvels

In Victorian times the interest in mountains was in its infancy. Being Wales's highest peak, Snowdon – and the village of Llanberis at its foot – became the centre of attention.

A branch line of the London and North Western Railway had opened from Caernarfon to Llanberis in 1869; from Llanberis people either walked or took a donkey up the mountain. Pressure mounted to build an extension that would carry visitors to the top of Snowdon, but for twenty years local landowner George William Duff Assherton Smith resisted attempts to build the railway, fearing it would spoil the scenery; only when plans were put in place to build a railway from Rhyd Ddu on the other side of Snowdon did he relent and allow his land to be used for constructing a railway from Llanberis.

Built in a Year

The Snowdon Mountain Tramroad and Hotels Company was formed. Work was begun in December 1894 and completed in just over a year. The first carriage reached the summit in January 1896 and the railway was opened to the public at Easter 1896. The trains used a rack-and-pinion system developed by German engineer Dr Roman Abt and used in the Swiss Alps: the engine pushes the train up the mountain, powered by a rotating pinion beneath the engine; both engine and carriage have independently operating brakes.

REBUILT 1988 Nº2 GILFACH DDU WORKS

Early Setback

Unfortunately, on the very first day of operations, a descending train ran out of control and was derailed round a bend, before tumbling down steep slopes. One passenger who jumped from a falling carriage was killed. Since then the steam engines on the rack-and-pinion railway have chugged up the mountain pushing their red and cream carriages for 4.5 miles (7.2km) to the summit without incident. Though a few resent the trains' presence, most walkers are comforted by the whistles that pierce the mountain mists or the plumes of smoke billowing into a blue sky.

Above right: *A brass plaque on the restored engine*

Below: *The steep gradient offers magnificent views*

Walk 81 Engines on Wales's highest peak

Doff your cap to the memory of the railway engineers who conquered Snowdon

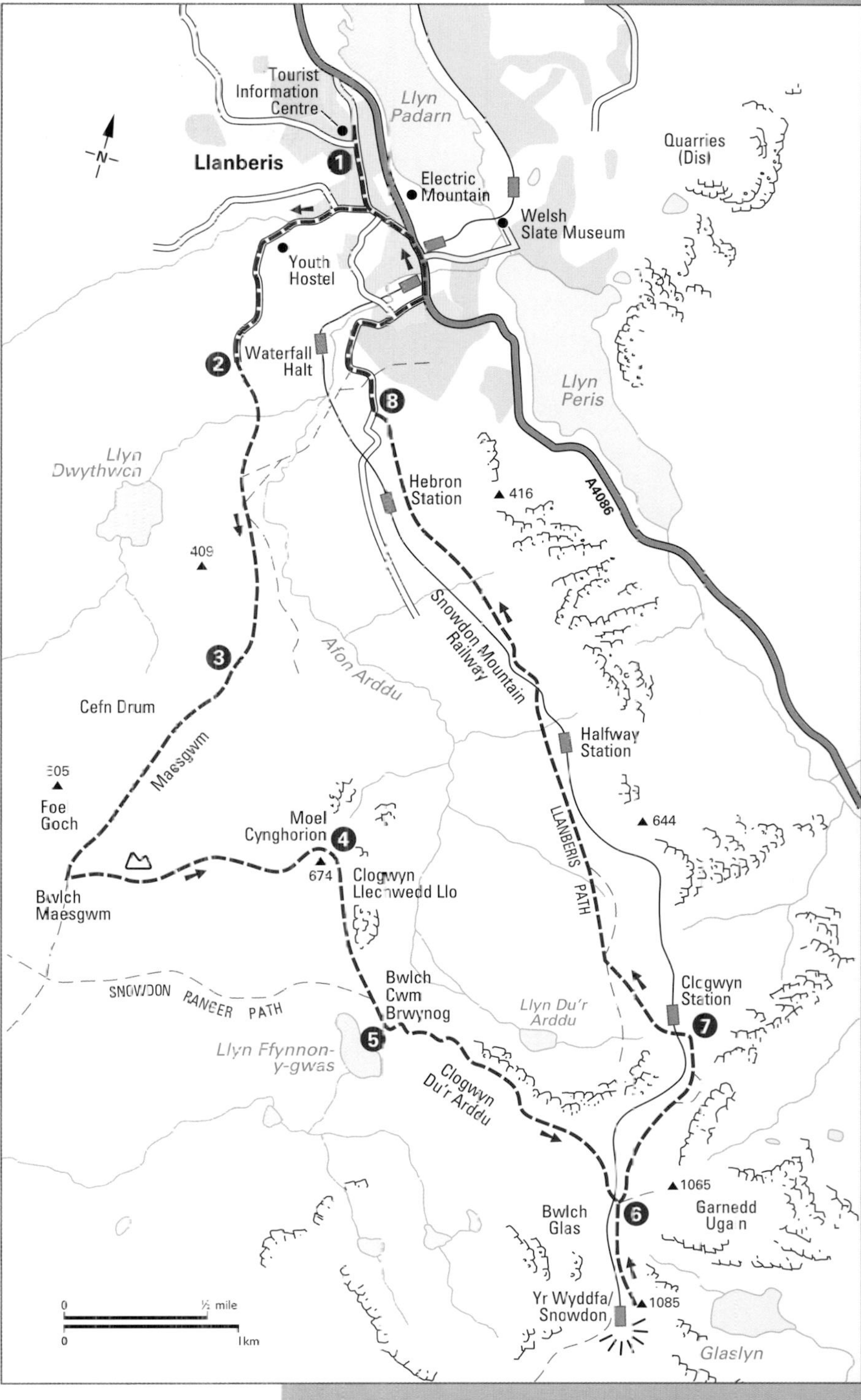

1 From the Tourist Information Centre in the heart of Llanberis, head south along the High Street (Stryd Fawr) before turning right up Capel Coch Road. Go straight ahead at a junction, where the road changes its name to Stryd Ceunant, and follow the road past the youth hostel. The road winds and climbs towards Braich y Foel, the northeast spur of Moel Eilio.

2 Where the tarmac ends at the foot of Moel Eilio, continue along the track, which swings left (southeast) into the wild cwm of the Afon Arddu. On the other side of the cwm you will have the chance to see the trains of the Snowdon Mountain Railway, puffing up and down the line.

3 On reaching the base of Foel Goch's northern spur, Cefn Drum, the track swings right into Maesgwm and climbs to a pass, Bwlch Maesgwm, between Foel Goch and Moel Cynghorion. Go through the gate here, then turn left and follow the route for the steep climb by the fence and up the latter-mentioned peak.

4 From Cynghorion's summit the route descends along the top of the cliffs of Clogwyn Llechwedd Llo to another pass, Bwlch Cwm Brwynog, which overlooks the small reservoir of Llyn Ffynnon-y-gwas. Here you join the Snowdon Ranger Path.

5 Follow the zig-zag route up Clogwyn Du'r Arddu, whose cliffs, on the left, plummet to a little tarn, Llyn Du'r Arddu, which sits uneasily in a dark stony cwm. Near the top the wide path veers right, away from the edge, meets the Snowdon Mountain Railway, and follows the line to the monolith at Bwlch Glas. Here you are met by both the Llanberis Path and the Pyg Track, and look down on the huge cwms of Glaslyn and Llyn Llydaw.

6 The path now follows the line of the railway to the summit. Retrace your steps to Bwlch Glas, but this time follow the wide Llanberis Path traversing the western slopes of Garnedd Ugain and above the railway. (Make sure you don't mistake this for the higher ridge path to Garnedd Ugain's summit.)

7 Near Clogwyn Station you come to Cwm Hetiau. The path goes under the railway and below Clogwyn Station before recrossing the line near Halfway Station.

8 The path meets a lane beyond Hebron, and this descends back into Llanberis near the Royal Victoria Hotel. Turn left along the main road, then take the left fork, High Street, to get back to the car.

Distance 10 miles (16.1km)

Minimum time 6hrs 30min

Ascent/gradient 3,839ft (1,170m) ▲▲▲

Level of difficulty ●●●

Paths Well defined paths and tracks, 1 stile

Landscape High mountain cwms and tarns

Suggested map OS Explorer OL17 Snowdon

Start/finish Grid reference: SH 577604

Dog friendliness Sheep, trains and crags: best on lead throughout

Parking Several car parks throughout Llanberis

Public toilets Just off High Street, south of Tourist Information Centre

WOLFERTON
WOLFERTON

THE EDWARDIAN AGE
1901–1918

A NEW CENTURY

As the 20th century opened, the world was shrinking. Aeroplanes, cars, the telephone and the cinema were extending global communications and seemed to promise increased understanding and even peace. But within two decades such hopes had been buried in the trenches of the First World War.

Edwardian Britain was the hub of a rich empire, and still a society divided into sharply defined classes. Women were starting to make inroads into education and the professions, but only in exceptional cases. On the whole, women played a backstage role in public life, and in the early years of the century there was a growing call for change. Many men and women pressed for further electoral reform – demanding the vote not only for all men, but for some women as well. Frustrated at their lack of progress, a section of the suffrage movement (those pressing to extend voting rights) employed headline-grabbing tactics. Known as 'the Suffragettes', women such as Emmeline Pankhurst chained themselves to railings and led public demonstrations to bring attention to their cause. The need for reform was, in fact, acknowledged in a series of policies that sought to tackle industrial Britain's problems of poverty and inequality. While the new Labour Party brought the working-class voice into the political forum, Chancellor of the Exchequer Lloyd George laid the foundations of a welfare state, taxing luxury items such as motor cars to pay for old age pensions. Nevertheless women had to wait until 1918 for even a limited right to vote, because the normal business of government (which also included Home Rule for Ireland) was suspended during four years of devastating warfare.

Meanwhile technology was progressing quickly, with advances in medicine, communications and entertainment. In 1903 the Wright Brothers made the first successful man-powered flight, in North Carolina; the next goal was to travel long distances by air. Frenchman Louis Blériot won a Daily Mail prize of £1000 when, on 25 July 1909, he made the first flight across the English Channel. Within five years the world was at war; the air force brought a new dimension to international conflict.

THE GREAT WAR

Hundreds of thousands of men suffered in rat-infested, waterlogged trenches as battles raged to gain a few feet of muddy field on the European front. The effects of shelling and mustard gas were recorded by young poets such as Siegfried Sassoon and Wilfred Owen. Nevertheless, it took a long time for the full magnitude of events to filter back to those at home, who had, on the whole, greeted the outbreak of hostilities with patriotic fervour.

By the time the war ground to a close, a generation of young men had virtually been wiped out. The survivors were promised homes fit for heroes, but too many came back to unemployment and despair. Meanwhile, women had proved their ability to do 'men's work', stepping into the breach in factories and on public transport; and at the same time the common experiences of officers and the lower ranks had at least begun to break down some class barriers. In just four years, lives and attitudes had been shattered. The only generally held certainty was that this had been the war to end all wars.

KEY SITES

Chipping Camden, Gloucestershire: Where the Guild of Handicrafts was established in 1902.

Sandringham Estate, Norfolk: royal residence, a favourite of King Edward VII.

Hidcote Manor Gardens, Gloucestershire: One of England's finest gardens, begun in 1907.

Strumble Head Lighthouse, Pembrokeshire: Lighthouse on St Michael's Island, built in 1908.

Cannock, Staffordshire: Site of First World War training camp, with Allied and German cemeteries.

Broughton, Scottish Borders: Hill country that inspired Scottish writer John Buchan, author in 1915 of *The Thirty-Nine Steps*.

Llanystumdwy, Gwynedd: Birthplace of David Lloyd George, prime minister 1916–22.

***Left:** The former railway station at Wolferton, near the Sandringham Estate, as used by Edward VI*

Arts and Crafts in the Campdens

A lovely Cotswolds walk between Chipping and Broad Campden follows the rise and fall of the Guild of Handicraft

In the idyllic rural setting of Chipping Camden Charles Ashbee established the Guild of Handicraft, in 1902. Born in Isleworth in 1863, Ashbee studied history at King's College, Cambridge, then took a job at Bodley and Garner, a company specialising in Gothic Revival architecture. He became involved with, and subsequently a leader of, the burgeoning Arts and Crafts Movement, the leading light of which was the poet and artist William Morris. In 1887–88 Ashbee founded the Guild and School of Handicraft in Mile End Road, London. Its educational programme laid great emphasis on training in the Arts and Crafts tradition with the emphasis on furniture design. He moved it to Chipping Camden in 1902.

Ashbee's work shows in its sparseness and restraint all the key elements of the Arts and Crafts Movement. He also drew attention to the activities of other artists: notably he promoted the work of Frank Lloyd Wright. In his essay 'Should We Stop Teaching Art?' (1911), he discussed the changing nature of industrial patronage and organisation, reflecting his move towards reconciling the use of industrial methods.

The move to Chipping Campden (and later to Broad Campden, where Ashbee converted a derelict Norman chapel into a place to live in 1905) was not an altogether successful one and by 1908 the Guild of Handicraft was no more – having fallen prey to competition from other, cheaper producers like Liberty's. Ashbee died in 1942. However, the craft tradition he pioneered has not altogether died out. In Sheep Street in Chipping Campden, where the original Guild shops stood just off the High Street, the silversmiths at David Hart's continue to produce beautiful, handcrafted work.

Broad Camden

Chipping Campden is perhaps the finest of all Cotswold towns. Its near neighbour, Broad Campden, does not possess a spectacular high street, but it does have some pretty houses (several, unusually for the Cotswolds, thatched), an attractive pub and a 17th-century Quaker Meeting House.

Above: *An exquisite silver butter bowl and knife made by Ashbee in 1901*

Below: *The Market Hall, Chipping Camden, built in 1627 by Sir Baptist Hicks*

Walk 82 Country retreat for city Handicraft Guild

Explore the genteel town in which Charles Ashbee and students produced handmade crafts

1 From Chipping Campden High Street, walk through the arch next to the Noel Arms Hotel and continue ahead to join a path. Pass some playing fields through a gate, and at a junction with a road go left into a field and then quickly right to follow the edge of the field parallel with the road.

2 After 600yds (549m), fork right and come to a kissing gate. Follow a drive, walk past a house and then cross the drive to a gate. Pass through into an alley and follow it to pass the Quaker Meeting House.

3 Emerge at the green with the church to your left. At a junction, continue ahead to walk through the village, passing the Malt House. The road bears left and becomes straight. After the turning for Blockley, go left down a road marked 'Unsuitable for Motors', then after around 70yds (64m) turn right along the drive of 'Hollybush'; a stone wall is running along on your left. After two stiles continue along the left, lower margin of an orchard.

4 Go through a kissing gate, then cross a bridge and turn sharp right to walk along the right edge of a field, with the stream on the right. Go right to the end of the field to cross the stream and in the next field go straight across, bearing a little right, to a gap. Go up the centre of the next field to a kissing gate and cross into a field.

5 Turn left and then go half-right to pass to the right of a house. Through a kissing gate go half-right to another. Go through and head quarter-right down to another kissing gate in the corner. In the next field go half-right, with a tree-lined stream on your right and Campden Church away to the right, to a stream near a stone arch known as Lady Juliana's Gateway.

6 Do not cross the stream but, roughly 70yds (64m) after the arch, turn right through a gate past a former watermill and then follow the path as it turns left to a drive. Turn right and follow the drive to a road (Calf Lane). At the road turn right and at the top make a turn to the left into Church Street (turn right to visit the church, if you wish) to return to a junction with the main street.

Distance 2.5 miles (4km)
Minimum time 1hr 15min
Ascent/gradient 83ft (25m) ▲▲▲
Level of difficulty ●●●
Paths Fields, road and track, 2 stiles
Landscape Farmland, hills, village
Suggested map OS Explorer OL45 The Cotswolds
Start/finish Grid reference: SP 151391
Dog friendliness Suitable in parts but livestock in some fields
Parking Campden High Street or parking area on main square
Public toilets Short way down Sheep Street

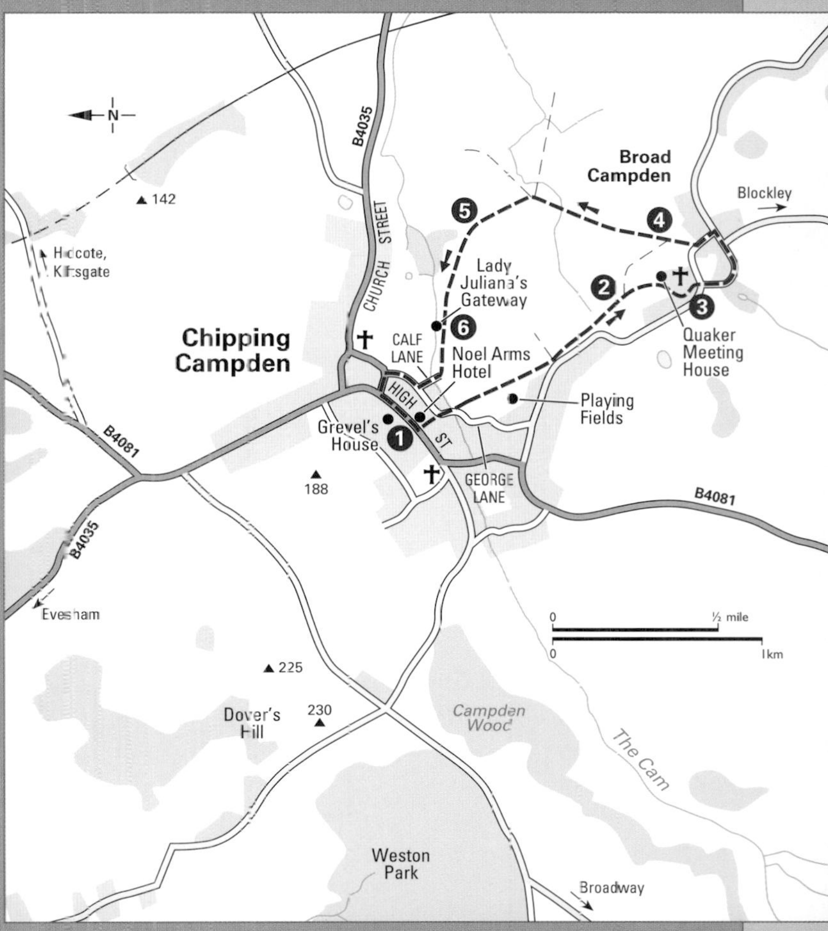

WHAT TO LOOK OUT FOR

Among the many fine houses in Chipping Campden is the 14th-century Grevel's House, opposite Church Lane. This belonged to William Grevel, a wealthy wool merchant, who was largely responsible for the church in its current form and is believed to have been the model for the character of the Merchant in Geoffrey Chaucer's poetic masterpiece *The Canterbury Tales*.

WHILE YOU'RE THERE

The gardens at Hidcote Manor and Kiftsgate Court are only a short drive away. If you would like to visit Shakespeare's birthplace, there is a bus service from Chipping Campden to Stratford-upon-Avon, a 45-minute journey. About 4 miles (6.4km) southwest is Broadway Tower, set in a country park overlooking the Vale of Evesham and a favourite haunt of William Morris, key figure in the Arts and Crafts Movement.

1901 The former Prince of Wales is crowned King Edward VII on 9 August in Westminster Abbey.

1902 Polish-born novelist Joseph Conrad's novella *Heart of Darkness* is published.

1902 The Boer War ends with the signing of the terms of surrender in the Treaty of Vereeniging.

1903 The Women's Social and Political Union is formed by Emmeline Pankhurst.

1903 In the US, the Wright Brothers Wilbur and Orville make the first controlled powered flight in a heavier-than-air aircraft, at Kitty Hawk, North Carolina, on 17 December. On the longest of four flights the *Wright Flyer* covers 852ft (260m).

1903 Architect Charles Rennie Mackintosh designs the Willow Tea Rooms in Glasgow.

1904 J.M. Barrie's play *Peter Pan* is first performed. It is later granted copyright in perpetuity, with proceeds to Great Ormond Street Children's Hospital.

1904 Licensing of motor cars is introduced.

Sandringham and Wolferton

A forest stroll takes in a historic railway station and a country park – while offering views of a stately home and royal residence

In 1862 revenues from the Duchy of Cornwall had raised such a large sum of money for its owner, the Prince of Wales, that he was able to buy himself a fine house. The Prince – the future King Edward VII – chose Sandringham, set in 7,000 acres (2,835ha) of beautiful rolling countryside. The house, however, was not at all to his liking, so he set about rebuilding it in a style he felt reflected his status. The result was the rambling Jacobean-style palace in red brick and stone that you can visit today – providing that no member of the Royal Family wants to stay in it, of course.

Sandringham is the private property of the Queen, along with much of the surrounding countryside. In 1968, she expressed the wish that the general public should also enjoy the estate and some 600 acres (243ha) of woodland and open heath were set aside as the Sandringham Country Park. Access to the park is free (there is a charge to enter Sandringham Gardens) and visitors can enjoy the peaceful waymarked nature trails, as well as the observation hide to watch the wildlife around Jocelyn's Wood nature reserve. Visitors to the house and its gardens can also see some of the most spectacular parkland in the country, with an intriguing mixture of formal arrangements and ancient, rambling woodland.

Above: *Edward commissioned architect A.J. Humbert, who built in the Jacobean Revival style, with many turrets, gables and mullion windows*

At Wolferton

When Sandringham was owned by the fun-loving Prince of Wales, monarchs and statesmen on their way to visit him would pass through the unassuming railway station at nearby Wolferton. In 1898 the track from King's Lynn was upgraded and two staterooms were added to the station, so that visiting dignitaries could arrive in style. When the railways came under the axe in the 1960s, Wolferton looked set to follow the fate of many other small stations, but a British Rail inspector bought the property. The station was restored and the waiting rooms converted into a museum. Unfortunately, the Sandringham Estate refused permission for the museum to put up any advertising signs, so in 2001 the owner decided to sell it. Although since purchased as a private house, the pretty, rust-red ironstone station, which can easily be seen from the road, still looks much as it might have done in the 19th century. There are no tracks, and flowers occupy the place where grunting, hissing steam engines would once have stood, but it is easy to imagine the commotion of its former life.

Walk 83 Edward VII's grand and spacious country home

Step out through beautiful countryside once admired by the Edwardian great and good

1 Cross the road from the car park and bear right on the lane towards Wolferton. The walled gardens of the Old Rectory mark the end of the mixed woodland. Continue straight ahead at the junction, past St Peter's Church. The road bends to the right, passing the old railway gatehouse and cottages (1881) bearing the fleur-de-lis emblem. Stay on this road as it makes a complete circuit of the village, eventually leading to the pretty buildings of the former Wolferton Station.

2 After the station, follow the road to the left and go up a hill until you reach the car park for the Dersingham nature reserve and a gate beyond it.

3 Go through the gate and take the track to your left, signed 'Wolferton Cliff and Woodland Walk'. The path climbs to a cliff top looking out over a forest, which 6,000 years ago was the seabed (now 1.5miles/2.4km distant). Follow the track until you see the 330yd (302m) circular boardwalk around the bog to go down some steps to your left. Walk down the steps to explore the bog walk. Emerging from the boardwalk, take the sandy track to your left, skirting the woods to return to Scissors Cross. Take the left fork out of the car park and walk along this road to the A149.

4 Cross the A149 and take the lane opposite, passing a house named The Folly. After a few paces you will see a lane to your left marked 'scenic drive'. Turn left to walk through the gates.

5 Walk along the drive or take the footpath on the right through Sandringham Country Park. When you see a processional avenue leading to Sandringham House on your right, leave the drive and look for a gap in the trees to your left. Follow the trail past a bench and down some steps, then stay on the yellow trail (waymarked in the opposite direction) as it winds through Jocelyn's Wood before returning to the main drive. Turn left and walk along the drive to the car park and Visitor Centre.

6 From the Visitor Centre, head for the lower car park and pick up the yellow trail again, which follows the main road, but is tucked away behind the trees of Scotch Belt. Cross a lane, then take the road ahead to your left for 200yds (183m) before picking up the path on your right as it passes through Brickkiln Covert.

7 At the crossroads, where the footpath comes to an end, turn right down a quiet lane with wide verges. You are still in woodland, although the trees here tend to be silver birch rather than the oaks and pines seen earlier. Cross the A149 to reach Scissors Cross.

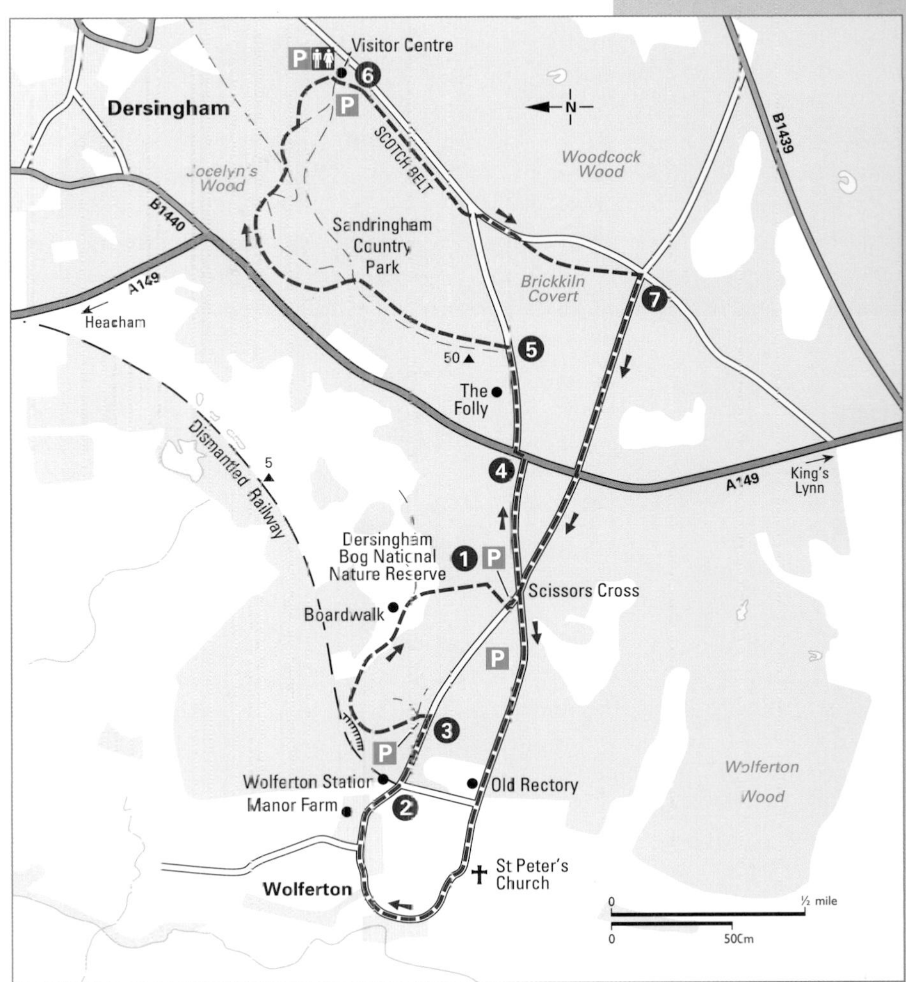

WHILE YOU'RE THERE

This walk takes you through the country park, but not into the Sandringham Estate. On paying an entrance fee to the estate you have access to gardens, woodland walks, the house itself and a museum containing vintage royal coaches and cars, historic photographs and a tribute to Sandringham Company soldiers who died in the First World War.

Distance 6.5 miles (10.4km)

Minimum time 3hrs

Ascent/gradient 131ft (40m) ▲▲▲

Level of difficulty ●●●

Paths Marked forest trails and country lanes, some steps

Landscape Country park and woodland nature reserve

Suggested map OS Explorer 250 Norfolk Coast West

Start/finish Grid reference: TF 668280

Dog friendliness Dogs should be kept on lead in nature reserves

Parking Scissors Cross car park on road to Wolferton

Public toilets At Sandringham Visitor Centre

1904 Lhasa is captured by the British, forcing the Dalai Lama to flee from Tibet to India.

1905 The 'Bloody Sunday' massacre in St Petersburg sows the seeds of the Russian Revolution.

1905 The Automobile Association is formed by a small group of automobile owners.

1906 San Francisco is hit by a massive earthquake, devastating the city and killing 2,500 people.

1907 The building of Hampstead Garden Suburb is begun under the guidance of Henrietta Barnett.

1907 Major General Sir Robert Baden Powell organises a camp for 20 boys on Brownsea Island in Dorset. This marks the foundation of the Boy Scouts, and leads later to the formation of the Girl Guides.

1907 Edward VII opens the Central Criminal Court, Old Bailey, London.

1907 Rudyard Kipling wins the Nobel Prize for Literature, the first English writer to do so.

Quenching the Thirst at Dovestones

This fine circular outing leads beside moorland reservoirs dating to the Edwardian years

In 1875, as the demands of Manchester's industrial population grew, the need to supply the city with safe and sufficient drinking water became paramount. The planners turned their attention towards the Pennines, that formidable upland barrier that soaks up so much of north England's rain. Before long, a series of reservoirs sprang up across the hills that separated urban Lancashire and Yorkshire and, just as the counties' rivers and streams had previously been harnessed for the mills, the moorlands were now drained and the tiny Pennine valleys dammed to create artificial lakes. The first of four reservoirs known collectively as Dovestones was Yeoman Hey, created in 1880, and the second, Greenfield, followed in 1902. When Chew Reservoir was built, in 1914, it was the highest in Britain, at around 1,600ft (488m). Dovestone Reservoir, the largest of the group, came later, in 1967.

Keeping Oldham Watered

Today the four reservoirs supply drinking water to Oldham and communities in the Tame Valley. Here at Dovestones, water collects in Chew Reservoir, high on the top of the bleak moorland, before travelling via an underground pipe almost 1 mile (1.6km) long to emerge at Ashway Gap, below Dean Rocks. Water is then held in the two main reservoirs at the valley bottom, Dovestone and Yeoman Hey, before being piped further down the valley for treatment at a large plant at Buckton Castle in Mossley.

Left: *Canadian geese are among the visiting birds at Dovestone Reservoir*

Below: *Looking down over moorland to Dovestone Reservoir from ruined Bramley's Cot*

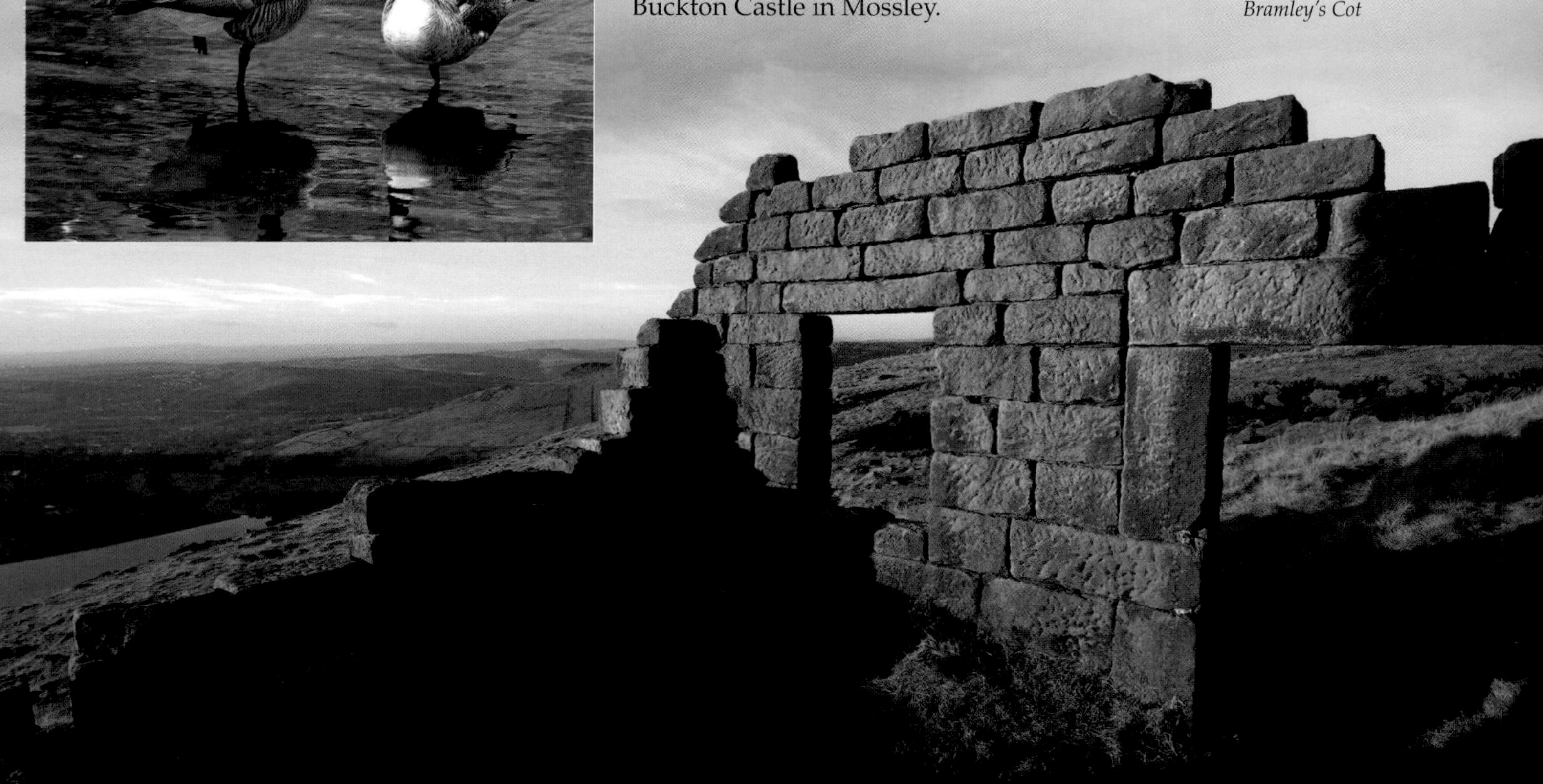

Walk 84 Water for the industrial northwest

Enjoy reservoir views in a grand tour along the edge of the moors

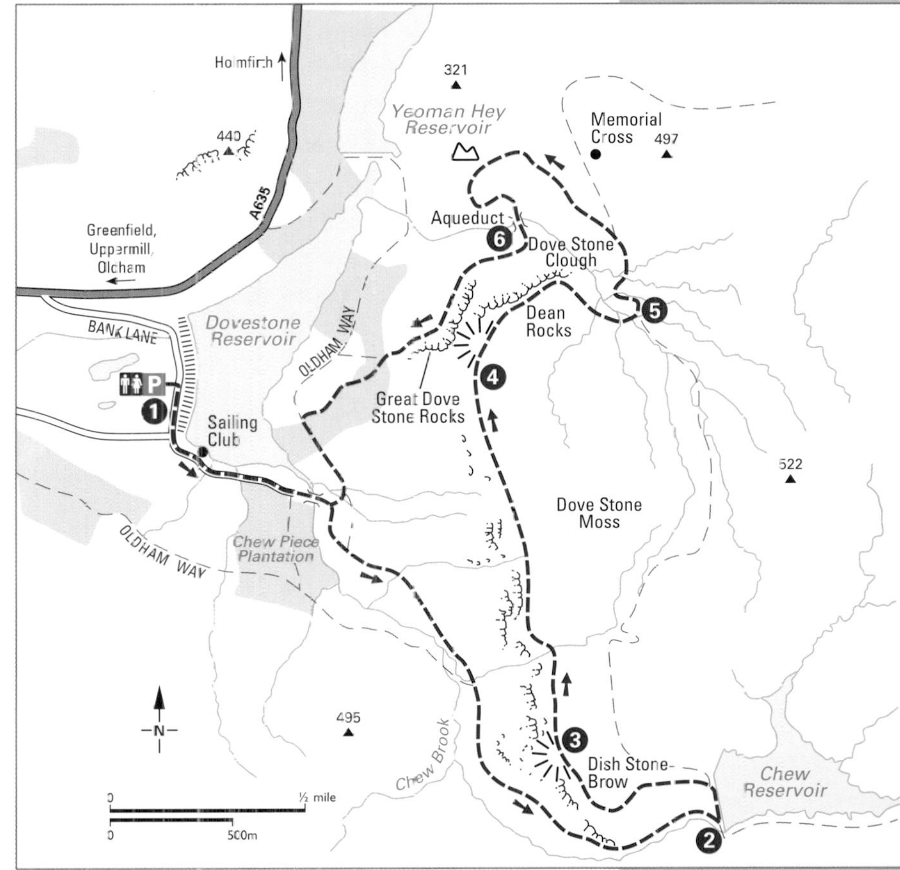

1 From the car park walk up to the top of the Dovestone Reservoir dam and turn right, along the road past the sailing club. Where the plantation ends go over a bridge and straight on to follow a private, vehicular track as it makes its way steadily up to the very top of the Chew Valley.

2 When you reach Chew Reservoir turn left and walk along by the dam wall until just before it kinks right. With your back to the reservoir (and near a sign warning of the dangers of deep water) drop down to the moorland and follow the very wide, straight track opposite that heads back towards the edge of the hillside. It first bears left, then swings back to the right, and soon becomes a thin path that weaves its way between the loose rocks around Dish Stone Brow.

3 With Dovestone Reservoir coming into view far below, continue along the high rim of the hillside past a series of rocky outcrops. If you occasionally lose sight of the path don't worry, just keep to the wide strip between the steep drop on your left and the banks of peaty bog on your right.

4 Nearing Great Dove Stone Rocks continue to follow the rocky edge as it swings back to the right. Beyond Dean Rocks is a clear path that winds its way around the head of a narrow valley known as Dove Stone Clough.

5 Cross over the stream as it flows over a rocky shelf and, as you continue across the slope on the far side, the narrow path slowly begins to drop down the grassy hillside. Fork left and ignore a higher path towards a prominent stone memorial cross ahead. Soon the path curves steeply down to the left and there are numerous criss-crossing tracks through the long grass and bracken. If you are in any doubt then just aim for the unmistakable aqueduct below you, at the foot of Dove Stone Clough, and cross it by using the high footbridge.

6 Walk along the path below the rock face and the fence on your left, and across an area of slumped hillside littered with rock debris. Eventually the path joins a wide, grassy strip that gently leads down between fenced-off plantations of young conifers. Go through the gate and drop down through the open field to reach the popular reservoir-side track. Turn left and then follow this track all the way back to the car park.

POTS AND PANS AND WINES

Looking westwards from the moors above Dovestone Reservoir, a small but distinctively pointed hill a mile (1.6km) beyond the reservoir catches the eye. This is known as Pots and Pans and its odd-shaped rocks contain weathered holes that are rumoured to have been specially deepened to hold the wine of well-to-do grouse shooters!

WHILE YOU'RE THERE

A visit to the Saddleworth Museum and Art Gallery, which is located just 2 miles (3.2km) from Dovestones on the High Street in Uppermill, is highly recommended. The former canalside woollen mill is stuffed full of curiosities and intriguing snippets of local history – from farming to brass bands, Roman soldiers to weaving mills, local prehistory to modern Morris dancers; there is also information on the building of the canal. The museum is open daily and has displays and hands-on exhibits for children.

Distance 8 miles (12.9km)

Minimum time 3hrs

Ascent/gradient 1,296ft (395m) ▲▲▲

Level of difficulty ●●●

Paths Mostly on good tracks but with some rocky sections, occasionally very steep, 2 stiles

Landscape Open and exposed moors, with sheltered valleys

Suggested map OS Explorer OL1 Dark Peak

Start/finish Grid reference: SE 013034

Dog friendliness Condition of access to moors is that dogs must be on lead

Parking Dovestone Reservoir, pay at weekends

Public toilets At car park

1908 Under the Old Age Pensions Act the first state pensions are created.

1908 The *Daily Mail* sponsors the first Ideal Home Exhibition, at Olympia in west London.

1908 Kenneth Grahame's classic children's novel, *The Wind in the Willows*, is published.

1909 Frenchman Louis Blériot makes the first successful flight across the English Channel, taking off near Calais and landing near Dover Castle on 25 July. The 43-minute flight in the *Blériot XI* monoplane wins him a £1000 prize offered by the *Daily Mail*.

1909 Belgian chemist Leo Baekeland invents Bakelite, an early form of plastic.

1910 *In Old California*, directed by D.W. Griffith, is the first movie shot in Hollywood, California.

1910 Bertrand Russell and A.N. Whitehead publish the first volume of their *Principia Mathematica*.

1910 Edward VII dies and is succeeded by his son George Frederick Ernest Albert as George V.

Ebenezer's Welwyn Vision

A wander through Welwyn sheds light on the Garden City Movement that was born in the Edwardian age

Hertfordshire is a key place in the Garden City Movement. Within the county are Letchworth, started in 1903, and Welwyn Garden City, started in 1920. The movement was the inspiration of utopian socialist Ebenezer Howard, who published the cumbersomely titled *Tomorrow: A Peaceful Path to Real Reform* in 1898. This book inspired the foundation of the Garden City Association in 1899 and then was rewritten in 1902 with the somewhat snappier title *Garden Cities of Tomorrow*. Howard started work on Letchworth in nearly 4,000 acres (1,620ha) of land to the west of Baldock. Then after the First World War he embarked upon his next venture, using lessons learnt at Letchworth to refine his ideas. He bought 1,688 acres (684ha) southeast of Welwyn at auction in May 1919, adding a further 694 acres (281ha) in October of the same year. In April 1920 he formed Welwyn Garden City Limited and the first houses were occupied by Christmas.

Right: *The Saturday Market*

Below: *Spring sunshine on the Parkway*

Parkway and Campus

The aim of Letchworth and Welwyn Garden City was to create a complete town, with industry and commerce providing a viable economic base. The railway that cuts through the middle of Welwyn, running north to south, had a profound influence on its layout, which was masterminded by a young architect named Louis de Soissons.

The principal boulevard is Parkway, which has parallel avenues of trees. Parkway and the semi-circular Campus at its north end have the same axis as the railway, which also served to separate the city into two: on the east side working-class housing and factories, on the west middle-class housing, much of it occupied by commuters to London. Our route crosses the Campus, goes down Parkway and then west to wind through the middle-class housing. The style of buildings here is 'Cottage Georgian', which works well at this scale. However, to the east of Parkway the larger-scale 1930s buildings, also by de Soissons, are in an over-blown Neo-Georgian style, complete with pedimented porticos or temple fronts. Welwyn's cereal factory, designed by de Soissons in 1925, is now a listed building. After the Second World War a third generation of planned towns arrived; Hertfordshire received Stevenage, Hemel Hempstead and Hatfield.

Walk 85 Cottage Georgian in a Garden City

Investigate the forerunner of new towns such as Stevenage and Hatfield

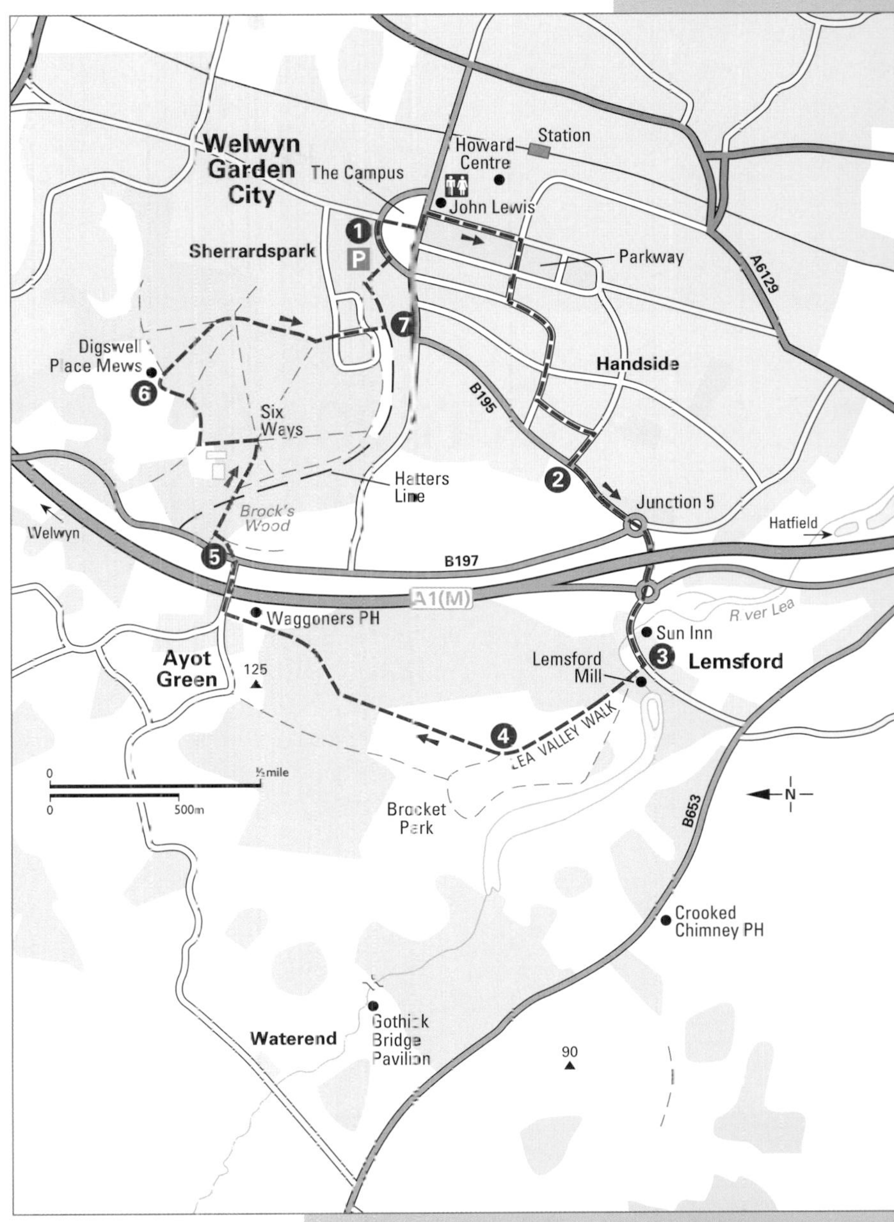

1 Cross the Campus, a semi-circular, leafy open space, and pass to the right of a large department store, along Parkway. At the second traffic lights cross right, into Church Road. At its end turn left into Guessens Road, which curves right. Cross Handside Lane into Youngs Rise and then turn left into Elm Gardens. At the end turn right into Applecroft Road.

2 Turn left into the Links. Leaving Welwyn Garden City, go under the A1(M) bridge and straight on into Lemsford village, with the River Lea to your left.

3 At Lemsford Mill turn right to cross the river on a modern bridge. Follow the footpath and bear right at a junction, now on the Lea Valley Walk. You are soon in Brocket Park, this part a golf course. Carry straight on where the right-hand fence ends. Cross a tarmac path to a footpath post – a thatched tennis pavilion is behind the fence here.

4 Turn right but follow the drive for only about 20 paces, then carry straight on across the golf course, guided by waymarker posts. The footpath climbs right, out of a dry valley and, passing a cottage, you head out of Brocket Park. Go through a kissing gate and turn left into Brickwall Close, with the Waggoners pub on the right. At Ayot Green turn right and cross over the A1(M).

5 At the T-junction turn left and almost immediately right, down to a stile leading into some woods. Go diagonally left, not sharp right. When you reach a bridleway junction bear right, the path descending to cross the course of an old railway line. At Six Ways (which has carved totem poles) turn sharp left onto a bridleway. Pass through a car park to a lane. Turn right, with the parkland to Digswell Place on your left.

6 At Digswell Place Mews turn right by a waymarker post, to return to the woods. At a bridleway post bear right uphill – the path carries on straight through the woods. Ignore all turns to the left and right until you come to a waymarked bridleway running off right. If you miss it, you soon come to houses and a school. Follow the bridleway as it bends left to houses and gardens. Pass alongside their fences, eventually bearing left to merge with a track and leave the woods. Go straight over Reddings into Roundwood Drive and onto a tarmac path between gardens.

7 Turn left onto the old railway trackbed (the Hatters Line). Turn right up a fenced ramp, out of the cutting and back into the Campus West car park.

Distance 4 miles (6.4km)

Minimum time 2hrs

Ascent/gradient 120ft (37m) Negligible ▲▲▲

Level of difficulty ●●●

Paths Town roads, parkland paths and woodland tracks, 2 stiles

Landscape Garden City, 18th-century parkland (and golf course) and mixed woodland

Suggested map OS Explorer 182 St Albans & Hatfield

Start/finish Grid reference: TL 235133

Dog friendliness On lead on town roads and golf course

Parking Campus West Long Term car park (free on Sundays) off B195 in Welwyn Garden City

Public toilets John Lewis store, Welwyn Garden City

1911 King George V is crowned.

1911 A Norwegian, Roald Amundsen, beats the British expedition to the South Pole, led by Captain Robert Scott, in December. Scott's party reaches the South Pole on 2 January 1912, but none of the team survives the return journey; tragically, the party die just a few miles from their main depot.

1912 The invasion of Greece, Bulgaria, Serbia and Montenegro by the Turkish Army sparks the start of the Balkan Wars (1912–13).

1912 On 14 April R.M.S. *Titanic*, the 'unsinkable' flagship of the White Star Cruise Line, hits an iceberg off Newfoundland and within hours disappears into the Atlantic. Some 1,517 crew and passengers are lost.

Gardens Around Mickleton

A lovely excursion takes you within striking distance of two of the finest planned gardens in England

Above right: *A decorated bench amid white and gold planting at Hidcote Manor*

Below: *The classical temple and pool at Kiftsgate Court*

Hidcote Manor Garden, part of the little hamlet of Hidcote Bartrim, is considered by many people to be one of the greatest of English gardens, and certainly one of the most influential. It is the fruit of more than 40 years of work by Major Lawrence Johnson, an East Coast American who purchased the 17th-century manor house in 1907 and gave it to the National Trust in 1948. Hidcote grew from almost nothing – when Major Johnson first arrived there was a just a cedar tree and a handful of beeches on 11 acres (4.5ha) of open wold. To some extent it reconciles the formal and informal schools of garden design. Hidcote is not one garden but several. It is laid out in a series of 'outdoor rooms', with walls of stone and of hornbeam, yew and box hedge. These rooms are themed, having names such as the White Garden and the Fuchsia Garden. There is also a wild garden growing around a stream, as well as lawns and carefully placed garden ornaments that help to create a bridge between the order within and the disorder without.

Kiftsgate Court

The other garden seen on this walk is Kiftsgate Court, the lesser known of the pair but one that nonetheless demands a visit. The house itself is primarily Victorian, while the garden was created immediately after the First World War by Heather Muir, a close friend of Major Johnson, the creator of the nearby Hidcote Manor Garden.

Kiftsgate's gardens are designed around a steep hillside overlooking Mickleton and the Vale of Evesham, with terraces, paths, flowerbeds and shrubs. Like Hidcote, its layout is in the form of rooms and the emphasis is more on the plants themselves, rather than on the overall design. The steeper part of the garden is almost a cliff: it is clad in pine trees and boasts wonderful views across the vale below.

Have a Butcher's!

This walk begins in Mickleton, at the foot of the Cotswold escarpment, below these two fine gardens. The parish church lurks behind a striking house in the Cotswold Queen Anne style. It has a 14th-century tower and a monument to an 18th-century quarry owner from Chipping Campden, Thomas Woodward. In the village centre is a Victorian memorial fountain designed by William Burges, the architect of Cardiff Castle. There is also a fine butcher's shop here, a sight to behold in autumn, when it is festooned with locally shot pheasants.

Walk 86 Restful ramble from a Cotswold village

At the edge of Gloucestershire, explore the rural setting of two widely renowned gardens

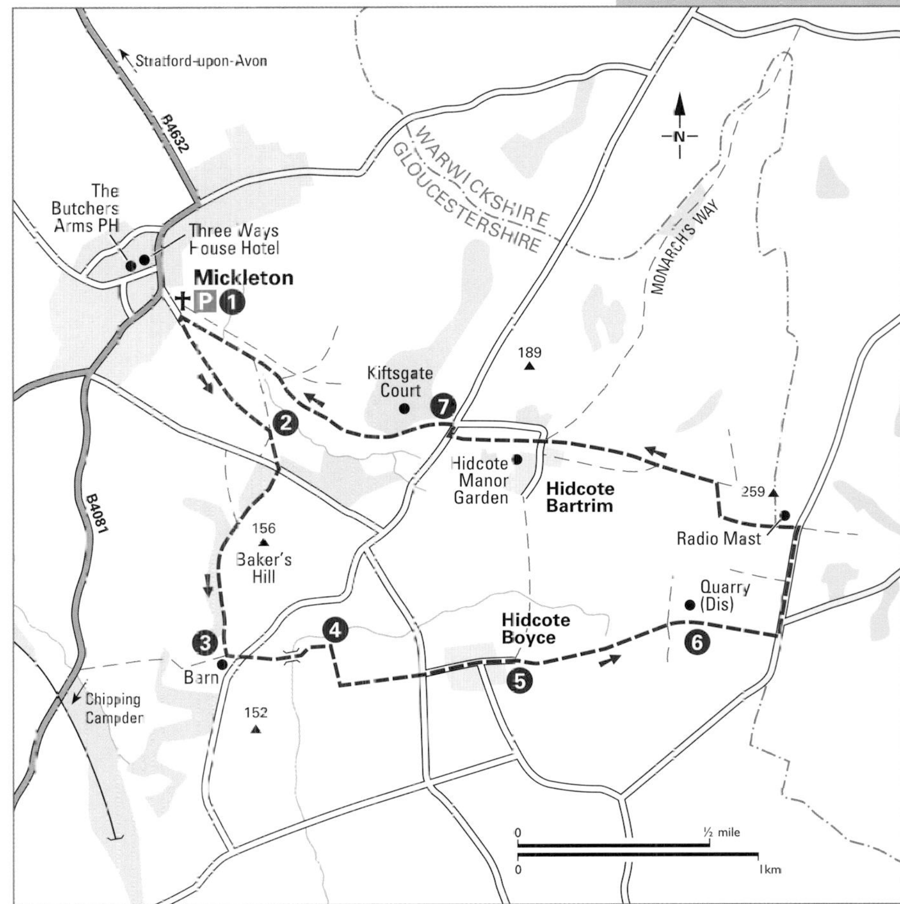

1 With your back to the church, turn right up a bank to reach a kissing gate to the left of Field House. Continue across a field on a right diagonal to a kissing gate at a thicket. Follow a path through trees and go through another kissing gate to emerge into a field, and follow its left margin to reach a kissing gate at the end.

2 In the next field go half-right to a gate in the corner. Cross a road and go up some steps to a stile or a gate. Turn right to walk around the edge of the field as it bears left. After 250yds (229m), take a path among trees, a steep bank eventually appearing down to the right. The path brings you to a field and then a Dutch barn.

3 At the barn turn left briefly onto a track. Just about opposite the barn, keep left of a hedge, following along the edge of a field to the bottom corner. Go through a gap to a bridge, with a stile on each side, across a stream and turn left.

4 Follow the margin of the field as it goes right and then right again. Continue until you come to a field gate on the left. Go through this and walk until you reach another field gate at a road. Walk ahead through Hidcote Boyce. Where the road goes right, stay ahead to pass through a farmyard.

5 Beyond a kissing gate take a rising track for just over 0.25 mile (400m). Where this track appears to fork, stay to the left to enter a field via a field gate. Bear left and then right around a hedge and head for a field gate. In an area of grassy mounds stay to the left of a barn and head for a gate visible in the top left corner.

6 Follow the next field-edge to a road. Turn sharp left to follow the lesser road. Immediately before a radio transmission mast turn left onto a track and follow this all the way down to pass through Hidcote Manor Garden's car park entrance. Go straight on for 30 paces to turn left through a gate, and then immediately right to walk a path parallel to the road with Hidcote's trees on your left. Through a beech copse enter a field through a kissing gate and cross it to a gate on the far side.

7 At the road turn right and then, before Kiftsgate Court, turn left through a gate and descend through a field. Pass through some trees and follow the left-hand side of the next field until you come to a gate on the left. Go through this and cross to another gate, ignoring a footbridge to your left. Follow the edge of the next field to a gate. Go through and head to Mickleton Church and a path between graveyards back to the start via a gate.

WHILE YOU'RE THERE

It would be a shame to miss the two fine gardens. Kiftsgate Court is open Saturday to Wednesday 2–6pm, in May–July, and on Sunday, Monday and Wednesday 2–6pm in April, and August–September. Home-made teas are available but dogs are not welcome. Hidcote Manor Garden is open daily, 10.30am–6.30pm, but closed Thursday and Friday, March–November, and Friday only in June/July. There is a good restaurant and plant sales centre.

Distance 5 miles (8km)

Minimum time 2hrs 15min

Ascent/gradient 625ft (190m) ▲▲▲

Level of difficulty ●●●

Paths Fields, firm tracks, some possibly muddy woodland, 5 stiles

Landscape Woodland, open hills and villages

Suggested map OS Explorer 205 Stratford-upon-Avon & Evesham

Start/finish Grid reference: SP 162434

Dog friendliness On lead in livestock fields, good open stretches elsewhere

Parking Free car park at church

Public toilets None on route

1913 Suffragettes gain their first martyr when Emily Dickinson throws herself in front of the King's horse at the Derby and is trampled to death. Captured on film, the incident becomes a symbol for the desperate struggle and frustration of the women's movement.

1913 The Royal Horticultural Society organises the first Chelsea Flower Show.

1913 The Panama Canal is opened, creating a shorter shipping route between the Atlantic and Pacific oceans.

1914 George Bernard Shaw's *Pygmalion* opens.

1914 The heir to the Austro-Hungarian throne is assassinated by a Serbian. Austria declares war on Serbia and Russia mobilises its troops to defend Serbia.

Strumble Head and its Shapely Lighthouse

A rewarding walk on the wild side of the Pembrokeshire coast leads past an impressive 1908 lighthouse

Built in 1908 to help protect the ferries that run between Fishguard and Ireland, the Strumble Head Lighthouse guards a hazardous stretch of coast that wrecked at least 60 ships in the 19th century alone. The tower stands 55ft (17m) tall and its light is 148ft (45m) above the water.

Its revolving lights, which flash four times every 15 seconds, were originally controlled by a massive clockwork system that needed rewinding every 12 hours. The original lens system weighed more than 4 tonnes and was set in a mercury bath to limit friction. This heavyweight set-up was replaced in 1965 by an electrically powered system, and the lighthouse was later converted to unstaffed operation in 1980.

It is possible to cross the daunting narrow chasm that separates Ynys Meicel (St Michael's Island), where the lighthouse stands, from the mainland by an aluminium bridge. An original iron bridge, now redundant, incorporated in the handrail and steps a system to supply oil to the lighthouse from a tank on the mainland.

Take the High Road

As you walk to and from Strumble Head, the cliffs tower high above pounding Atlantic surf and the sky is alive with the sound of seabirds. Atlantic grey seals, porpoises and even dolphins are regularly to be spotted in the turbulent waters far below. Garn Fawr, a rocky tor that lords high above the whole peninsula, brings a touch of hill walking to the experience.

At Carregwastad Point is a stone obelisk that marks the spot of the last hostile invasion of Britain. On 22 February 1797, a small French force known as the Légion Noire came ashore and set up camp at Tre-Howel, a local farm. The invaders were quick to take advantage of a huge haul of liquor that had been salvaged from a recent wreck and, subsequently unfit to fight, were forced to surrender within two days.

Top: *Atlantic grey seals live all along this coast*

Right: *The lighthouse on St Michael's Island*

Walk 87 Lighting up a dangerous coast

Look down from the coastal path on seals and dolphins in treacherous South Wales waters – and see the lighthouse that guards them

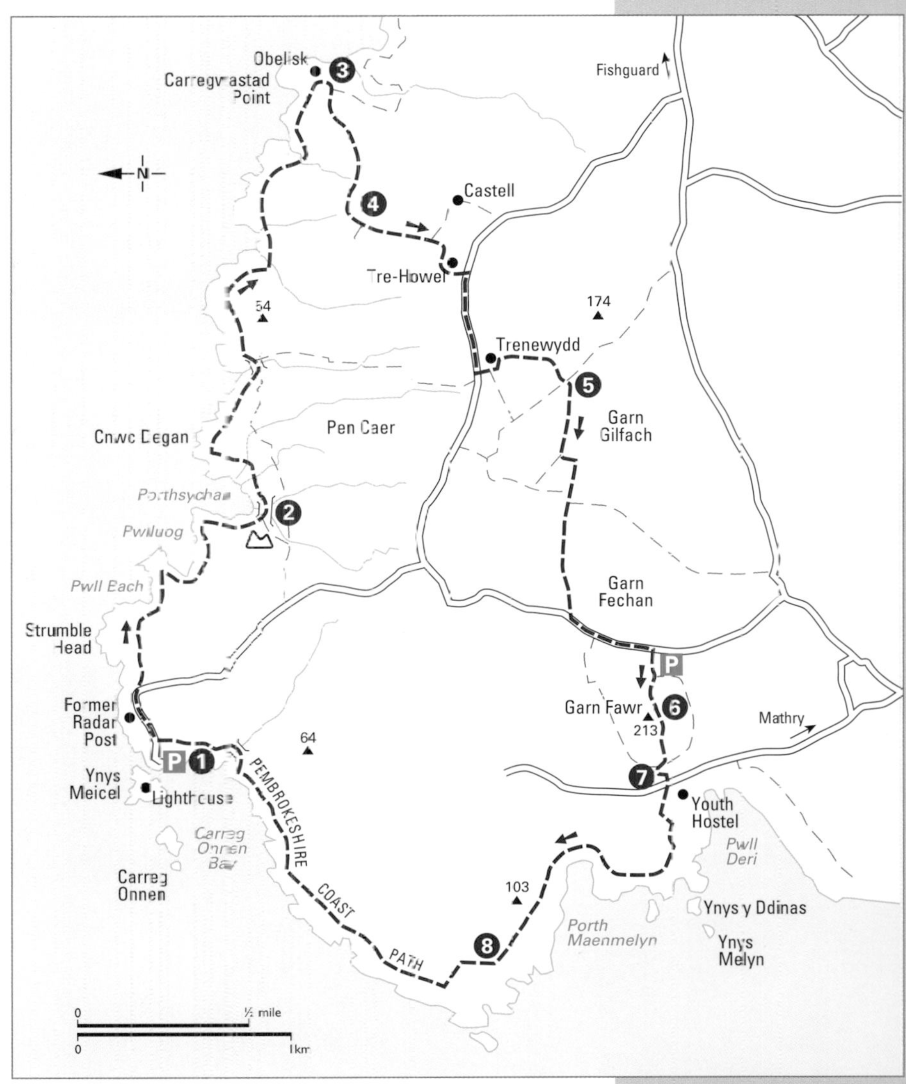

1 Walk back up the road and cross a gate on the left onto the coast path. Pass above the bays of Pwll Bach and Pwlluog, then drop steeply to a footbridge behind the pebble beach of Porthsychan.

2 Follow the coast path waymarkers around Cnwc Degan and down to another bridge, where a couple of footpaths lead away from the coast. Continue along the coast, passing a cottage on the right and climbing and dropping a couple of times, before you reach the obelisk at Carregwastad Point.

3 Follow the main path inland and cross a stile on to a farm track, where you turn right, away from the coast path. Continue with this path, which is vague in places, up through the gorse to a wall, then turn right onto a good track. Take this through a succession of gates and around a left-hand bend.

4 Ignore a track to the right and continue up the cattle track, eventually bearing right into the farmyard where you follow a walkway past livestock pens before swinging left, after the buildings, to the road. Turn right and follow the road past a large house to a waymarked bridleway on the left. Pass Trenewydd and go through a gate onto a green lane. Follow this up to another gate and onto open ground.

5 Turn right and follow the wall to another gate. This leads to a walled track that you follow to the road. Turn left and climb to the car park beneath Garn Fawr. Turn right, on a hedged track, and follow this up, through a gap in the wall, and over rocks to the trig point.

6 Climb down and cross the saddle between this tor and the other, slightly lower, one to the south. From here head west towards an even lower outcrop and pass it on the left. This becomes a clear path that leads down to a stile. Cross this and turn left, then right onto a drive that leads to the road.

7 Walk straight across and onto the coast path. Bear right and cross a stile to drop down towards Ynys y Ddinas, the small island ahead. Navigation is easy as you follow the coast path north, over Porth Maenmelyn and up to a cairn.

8 Continue along the coast, towards the lighthouse, until you drop to a footbridge above Carreg Onnen Bay. Cross a stile into a field, then another back onto the coast path and return to the car park.

WHAT TO LOOK OUT FOR

The small hut beneath the car park at the start was a Second World War radar post that has been converted into a bird observatory – a great place for spotting migratory birds leaving in autumn and arriving in the spring. As well as obvious seabirds, look out for early swallows and swifts, also large numbers of warblers and other small migrants. In addition, this is one of the best walks in Pembrokeshire to spot Atlantic grey seals: these lumbering marine giants reach over 8ft (2.4m) in length and can weigh as much as 770lbs (350kg). They are usually seen bobbing up and down (bottling) in the water just off the coast, but in autumn when the females give birth to a single pup they often haul up onto inaccessible beaches where the young are suckled. The pups shed their white coat after around three weeks, when they are weaned and taught to swim before being abandoned. The males are bigger than the females, with a darker coat. The best places to see seals on this walk are the bays of Pwll Bach and Pwlluog.

Distance 8 miles (12.9km)

Minimum time 3hrs 30min

Ascent/gradient 920ft (280m) ▲▲▲

Level of difficulty ●●●

Paths Coast path, tracks, rocky paths, 13 stiles

Landscape Headland, secluded coves and rocky tor

Suggested map OS Explorer OL35 North Pembrokeshire

Start/finish Grid reference: SM 894411

Dog friendliness Take care near cliff tops and livestock

Parking Car park by Strumble Head Lighthouse

Public toilets None on route

1901 – 1918

1914 Germany declares war on Russia and France on 1 August, and invades Belgium two days later.

1914 On 4 August Britain declares war on Germany, and by early September the Battle of Marne stops the German advance at the Marne River. German and British troops dig themselves into the ground, and four years of bloody trench warfare ensues.

1914 The Irish Home Rule Bill is passed by the Liberal government, despite the opposition of the Conservatives and the Ulster Unionists. Because of the war, however, little attention is paid to the growing political unrest in Ireland.

1914 Irish writer James Joyce publishes his short story collection *Dubliners*.

Cannock's Memorials

This ramble serves as a poignant reminder of less peaceful times

Top right: *The German War Cemetery is the only one of its kind in the UK*

Above: *Autumn walking on the landmark hill of Cannock Chase*

With the outbreak of the First World War, Cannock Chase was chosen as the setting for an army training camp. Between 1914 and 1918, 250,000 British and Commonwealth troops passed through here on their way to the trenches. Many would not return. The camp occupied much of the area covered by this walk. There were training areas and firing ranges and also a railway, sewage works, a prisoner of war camp, a powerhouse and pumping station, and quarters for troops and officers. Equally important were the veterinary hospital at Chase Road Corner (horses were still a large part of military life) and the Great War Hospital at Brindley Heath, for wounded soldiers brought back from the front.

Commonwealth and German Cemeteries

Many German, British and Commonwealth soldiers who died in the War Hospital were buried in the Commonwealth Cemetery, which today is a quiet, immaculately preserved place. Equally moving is the German War Cemetery, just to the northeast. It was established by the German War Graves Commission, an organisation charged with caring for the graves of victims of war and tyranny. The commission was asked by the German government to take care of over 1.4 million graves, in 343 cemeteries throughout 24 different countries.

After the German-British War Graves Treaty of 1959, most of the German soldiers in cemeteries around Britain were exhumed and transferred to the cemetery at Cannock Chase, and today it is the only German war cemetery in the UK. It is the final resting place for 2,143 servicemen who died in the First World War and 2,797 who died in the Second World War. In all, 1,307 Germans remain in other British cemeteries (including the Commonwealth Cemetery here) and are looked after by the Commonwealth War Graves Commission. Read the poem on the wall of the visitor centre; it says it all.

Walk 88 Staging post on the road to the trenches

Tour a former army training camp and pay your respects to the war dead

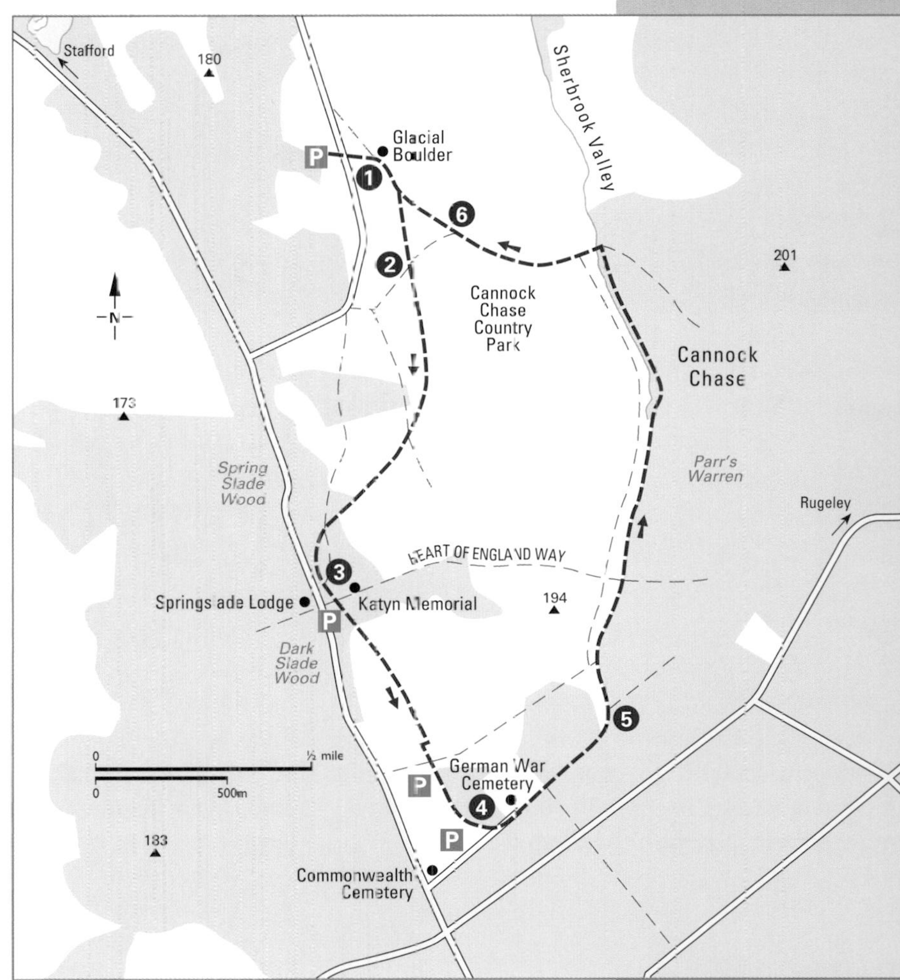

1 From the Glacial Boulder, walk away from the road following a narrow path past the trig point and then turn right along the wide gravel track. When you get to a fork, go right, following the Heart of England Way footpath sign.

2 At a crossroads of paths, continue in the same direction (ignoring a footpath off to the right). At the next path junction, again carry straight on as the path curves gradually around to the right. Continue along this track across several more path crossroads until your route curves around to the left, passing alongside the road. At the point where another wide track comes in from the left, go straight on rather than taking the shortcut down to the road.

3 After crossing the narrow surfaced road opposite Springslade Lodge, continue up a dirt track and across a path crossroads. After about 500yds (457m), you come to a T-junction in the path which requires a dog-leg right then left to keep going in the same direction through a car park. Continue in this direction to a second car park and, as the track curves around to the left, another metalled road.

4 Turn left past the German War Cemetery until the road becomes a wide gravel track. Continue along this track, down into the woods, and when you get to the fork go left down the hill.

5 Continue along the bottom of the valley for a mile (1.6km), staying to the right of the stream and ignoring all paths heading off, until you get to the obvious ford where the conifers end. Cross the stream here using the stepping stones. At the junction on the other side, head away from the stream following a track that leads to the left around the bottom of a hill ahead, rather than going to the right, straight over the top of it. Follow this track as it curves round to the right, all the way to the top of the hill.

6 Continue across the plateau until the path starts to descend the other side, at which point you rejoin the path, following it as it heads to the right and leads back towards the start and the car park.

KATYN MEMORIAL

The Katyn Memorial, near Springslade Lodge, is a tribute to the 14,000 members of the Polish armed forces and professional classes executed in 1940 in Katyn Forest, near Smolensk, Russia, by the Soviet secret police on the orders of Stalin. The Poles had been prisoners of war following the Soviet Union's invasion of Poland while Germany was invading from the west.

WHAT TO LOOK OUT FOR

To the right of the visitor centre are the massive grave stones marking the deaths of four Zeppelin crews shot down over England in the First World War. They were originally buried in Potters Bar, Burstead and Theberton. Much harder to find are the graves of the 90 unknown soldiers buried here; one near to the centre is marked simply: 'Zwei unbekannte Deutsche Soldaten'.

Distance 4 miles (6.4km)

Minimum time 1hr 30min

Ascent/gradient 361ft (110m) ▲▲▲

Level of difficulty ●●●

Paths Gravel tracks, dirt paths and roads

Landscape Heather and woodland

Suggested map OS Explorer 244 Cannock Chase

Start/finish Grid reference: SJ 980181

Dog friendliness Beware of cyclists at all times

Parking Ample parking at start point

Public toilets None on route

1915 The R.M.S. *Lusitania*, a ship carrying munitions and civilian passengers, is torpedoed and sunk by a German U-boat. The attack provokes moral outrage and soldiers are dispatched to quell anti-German riots. In the US feelings also run high.

1916 Tsar Nicholas II of Russia is executed along with his family as the Russian Revolution gets under way.

1915 John Buchan's *The Thirty-Nine Steps* is published.

1915 P.G. Wodehouse creates the character of Jeeves, wise and ingenious valet to Bertie Wooster.

1916 A German zeppelin crashes on British soil at Potters Bar, Hertfordshire.

1916 Frustrated over the Irish Home Rule Bill's lack of progress, members of the Sinn Fein Party seize buildings in Dublin and proclaim a provisional government. (These events are known as 'the Easter Uprising'.) The leaders are captured and shot.

1916 Copies of D.H. Lawrence's novel *The Rainbow*, prosecuted for obscenity, are seized by police.

'Thirty-Nine Steps' in Broughton

An exhilarating walk leads through John Buchan country

The rugged hills around Broughton were once familiar to John Buchan, Scottish author of the spy thriller *The Thirty-Nine Steps* (1915). Although he was born in Perth (in 1875), Buchan has close links with this area as his grandparents lived here and he spent many summer holidays in the village. A keen hillwalker, it is almost certain that he followed the same tracks that you take on this exhilarating circuit.

'Shockers'

Buchan's most famous fictional creation is the upper-class hero Richard Hannay, who featured in *The Thirty-Nine Steps*. But this was not his only novel. He wrote many other adventure stories (or 'shockers' as he liked to call them) – four of them featuring Hannay, as well as a book of poetry and several historical works including biographies of Sir Walter Scott and Oliver Cromwell. After Oxford University, he became a barrister. During the First World War he was Director of Information, and then wrote a 24-volume history of the war. In 1927 he became a Member of Parliament and was made a Companion of Honour in 1932 – publishing more works all the time. In 1935 he was appointed Governor-General of Canada and was given a peerage – taking the title Baron Tweedsmuir of Elsfield. Tweedsmuir is a hamlet close to the village of Broughton, and the area featured in a number of Buchan's works. Broughton was the village of 'Woodilee' in his lesser-known novel *Witch Wood* (1927), while much of the action in his adventure novels is played out on the moody moors and lonely hills of the Borders. John Buchan died in Canada in 1940.

Below: *Buchan tramped the Borders hills in all weathers, and loved the landscape*

Walk 89 Border hills that inspired a celebrated son of Perth to tales of derring-do

Wander where Buchan may have dreamt up escapades for his spy-hero Richard Hannay

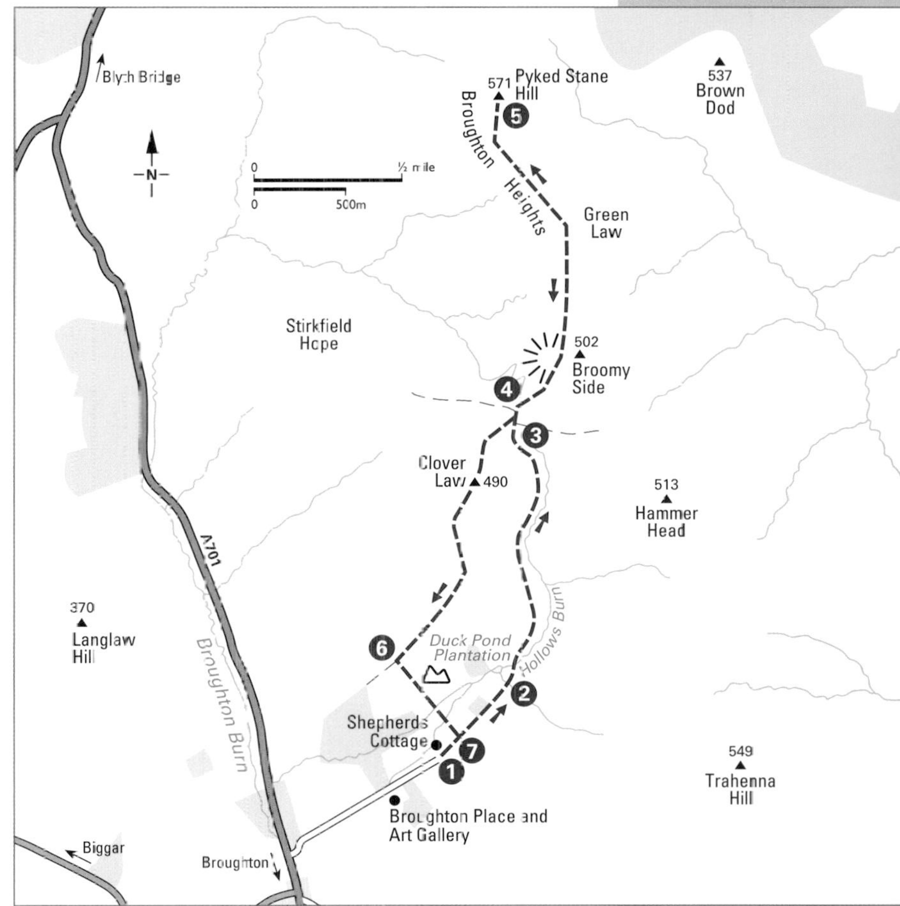

1 From the parking place, go through the gate and follow the obvious, grassy track that runs in front of the cottage. You will soon pass a copse on the left-hand side, then pass the attractively named Duck Pond Plantation, also on the left-hand side. Carry on along the track, which becomes slightly rougher now, then cross a small footbridge over a burn.

2 Your track continues ahead past feathery carpets of heather and bracken – listen out for the skylarks in the summer. Continue walking steadily and the path will soon level out and lead you past a gully on the right-hand side. Follow the track until it bends, after which you come to a meeting of tracks.

3 Take the track that bears left and head for the dip that lies between the two hills – Clover Law on the left and Broomy Side in front. You should just be able to spot the fence 100yds (91m) on the skyline. Make for that fence and, as you near it, you'll eventually spot a gate, next to which is a wooden stile.

4 Cross the stile, then turn right and follow the fence line. You soon get superb views to the left – well, you do on a clear day. Continue following the fence and walk up the track until you reach the trig point on Broughton Heights – the final ascent is a bit of a puff – but thankfully it is not too long.

5 Now retrace your steps to reach the stile again, nip over it, but this time turn right and follow the narrow track that climbs Clover Law. Continue walking in the same direction, following the fence line as it runs along the top of the ridge. When you near the end of the ridge, keep your eyes peeled for a path to the left, down an old earth boundary bank.

6 Follow the track as it runs down roughly in the direction of the cottage – it's quite a steep descent. At the bottom you'll come to an old wall and a burn, which you cross, then continue ahead to cross over another burn and across a field to reach the main track.

7 Turn right here and walk past the little cottage again, through the gate and back to your car. If you want to visit Broughton Place and its art gallery, just continue walking down the track to reach the house on your left.

WHAT TO LOOK OUT FOR

If you're a real John Buchan fan you can make a pilgrimage to the John Buchan Centre, which is at the far end of Broughton village. It is housed in an old church in which Buchan and his relatives once attended services. This small museum is full of photographs, books and general memorabilia that illustrate the life and achievements of the author. There is a display of Buchan's military uniforms, and a feature dedicated to the many movie and TV adaptations that have made *The Thirty-Nine Steps* so well known, starting with the 1935 Alfred Hitchcock film. The centre is open at weekends and each day from May to October, 2–5pm. There is a small admission charge.

Distance 5 miles (8km)

Minimum time 2hrs 30min

Ascent/gradient 1,575ft (480m) ▲▲▲

Level of difficulty ●●●

Paths Hill tracks and grassy paths, 1 stile

Landscape Rolling hills and exposed ridge

Suggested map OS Explorer 336 Biggar & Broughton

Start/finish Grid reference: NT 119374

Dog friendliness Good, but keep on lead because of sheep

Parking Parking in front of cottage past Broughton Place and art gallery

Public toilets None on route

1916 Tanks are used for the first time against German troops at the Battle of the Somme.

1917 Mata Hari, an exotic dancer turned German spy, is executed in France.

1917 On 6 April the US declares war on Germany, restoring hope to the Allied forces.

1918 Germany signs the armistice agreement on 11 November, marking the end of the war.

1918 Political reforms give women over 30 the right to vote in a general election for the first time, in recognition and appreciation of their tremendous efforts during the war. The emancipation of women had at last taken an enormous step forward.

In the Country of Lloyd George

A coastal tour crosses a land that nurtured 'the greatest Welshman since the age of the Tudors'

David Lloyd George came from modest beginnings in Llanystumdwy. This village on the banks of the Dwyfor is separated from the coast by 0.5 mile (800m) of fields and coastal marshes. When you are barely out of the car park at the start of the walk, you pass Highgate, his boyhood home, and the Lloyd George Museum. In the woods you will come across the grave and a memorial to this last Liberal prime minister of Great Britain. It is a spot where he loved to sit. That Lloyd George was a great man is not in dispute, but his life was not without controversy. Although he was one of the early pioneers of the Welfare State and led Britain to eventual victory in the First World War, he was also linked with several dubious private moneymaking deals and gained a reputation for allowing peerages to be awarded to wealthy political benefactors.

__Above right:__ A bust of David Lloyd George at his birthplace, Llanystumdwy

__Below:__ Lloyd George's boyhood home in Criccieth

A flamboyant man, Lloyd George just did not fit in with his rather stuffy Edwardian contemporaries. He is reputed to have been a womaniser, and at one time he had a wife in Criccieth and a mistress, his parliamentary secretary, whom he later married, in London.

Winston Churchill made the following tribute in Parliament, following Lloyd George's death in 1945. 'As a man of action, resource and creative energy he stood, when at his zenith, without rival… He was the greatest Welshman which that unconquerable race has produced since the age of the Tudors… and those who come after us will find the pillars of his life's toil upstanding, massive and indestructible.'

Woodland Walking, Coastal History

The walk leads through woodland by the Dwyfor riverside – and this is as good as woodland walking gets. The Dwyfor's crystal clear waters chatter to the rocks below and in spring the forest floor is carpeted with primroses, bluebells, garlic and wood anemones. The early part of the walk heads away from Criccieth and the coast, but soon the route takes us back across fields into this town with a history in two episodes. Criccieth Castle had major strategic importance in the 13th–15th centuries, but despite this Criccieth remained a small fishing port until the Victorian penchant for sun and sand saw it expand. You will pass rows of Victorian terraces on the way to the coastal path that takes you by the sand and pebble beach back to the Dwyfor and David Lloyd George's village.

Walk 90 Welsh village in which David Lloyd George began and ended his days

Explore the countryside and coastal haunts of the last Liberal prime minister

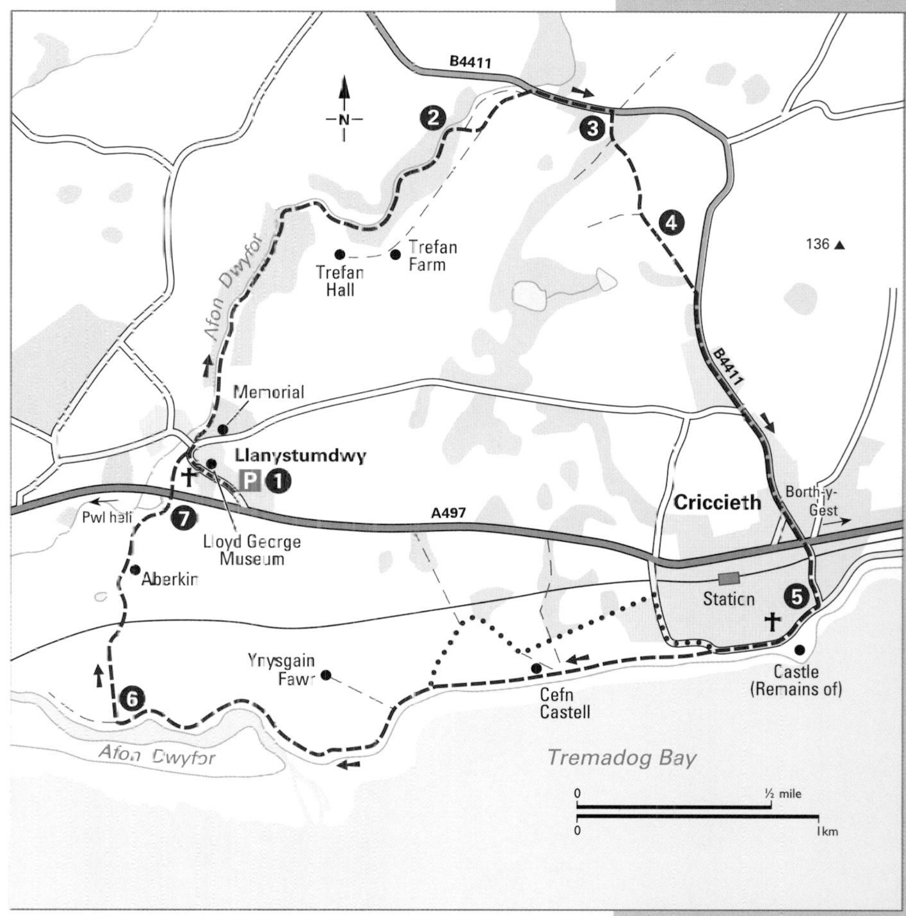

1 Turn right out of the car park and go through Llanystumdwy village, past the museum to the bridge over the Afon Dwyfor. Turn right along the lane, then follow the footpath on the left past the memorial and down to the wooded river banks.

2 After 1.5 miles (2.4km) the path turns right, then goes under a stone archway to meet a tarmac drive. Turn left along this, carry on to the B4411 and turn right.

3 After about 500yds (457m), turn right down an enclosed drive. As another drive merges from the left, turn half-left along a path shaded by rhododendrons. After a few paces, go though the kissing gate, then cross the field guided by a fence on the left. Through another kissing gate the path veers half-right, following a fence which is now on the right.

4 Beyond another gate the now sketchy route cuts diagonally (southeast) across two fields to rejoin the B4411, a mile (1.6km) or so north of Criccieth. Follow the B4411 into town. Keep straight on at the crossroads, and bear left after the level crossing to reach the promenade.

5 Follow the coast road past the castle and continue until it turns firmly inland. From here, tide permitting, simply follow the coast path or walk along the sands. Otherwise, follow the road to a bridleway on the left. Go past Muriau and then to the right of Ty Cerrig. Cross a track and a field then turn right on a green track, nearly to the railway. Head left, back to the coast east of Ynysgain Fawr. Follow the coast path west through coastal grasslands and gorse scrub to the estuary of the Dwyfor and some crumbled concrete sea defences.

6 At a metal kissing gate, waymarks point inland. Follow these, with the fence on your right. The route becomes a farm track that cuts under the railway and passes through the yard of Aberkin farm before reaching the main road.

7 Cross the main road and go through the gate on the opposite side. A short path leads to a lane, which in turn leads to the village centre. Turn right for the car park.

THE GREAT CASTLE

Criccieth Castle stands on a huge volcanic crag that juts out into Tremadog Bay. The twin-towered gatehouse is believed to have been built by Llewelyn the Great, around 1240. It was captured and modified by King Edward I in 1283. Edward's architect, Master James of St George, added a two-storey rectangular tower, built a second storey on the gatehouse and strengthened several towers in the wall. Yet it was a Welshman who was responsible for the castle's downfall. In 1404 Owain Glyndwr captured it, then burnt it to the ground.

WHILE YOU'RE THERE

Visit the Lloyd George Museum, where you can follow the life of this statesman from boy to man. There are excellent audio-visual commentaries and a rather freaky but lifelike talking head. Open Easter to October or by arrangement.

Distance 6 miles (9.7km)

Minimum time 4hrs

Ascent/gradient 300ft (91m) ▲▲▲

Level of difficulty ●●●

Paths Generally well defined paths and tracks, 4 stiles

Landscape Woodland, fields, town streets, coastline

Suggested map OS Explorer 254 Lleyn Peninsula E

Start/finish Grid reference: SH 476383

Dog friendliness Dogs can run free in woods as well as on the coast

Parking Large car park at east end of village

Public toilets Near museum at Llanystumdwy and at Criccieth

Note Small section of coast path engulfed by highest tides. Make sure you know times of tides before setting off

DEPRESSION AND WAR
1918–1945

JAZZ AGE TO ATOMIC AGE

The First World War was ended by the Armistice of November 1918, but peace did not bring prosperity to everyone – far from it. The age of the Charleston dance and 'the Bright Young Things' was also a period of mass unemployment and the hunger march, of the General Strike and the Wall Street Crash.

Conventions were thrown aside and taboos broken in the 1920s. Skirts grew shorter and parties wilder; literature became more explicit, as writers such as D.H. Lawrence dealt with sex and working-class culture. But the Jazz Age was the experience of a privileged minority. For many more people, life in post-war Britain was a struggle to make ends meet. A dispute between coal miners and mine-owners threatening to cut already meagre wages drew in workers from other industries, and in 1926 a General Strike seemed about to bring the country to a standstill. Three years later the New York stock market crashed, and the repercussions were felt across the Western world. Personal fortunes were lost and whole sectors of industry floundered: the Jarrow 'hunger march' to London of 1936 highlighted the plight of ship-builders unable to make a living.

There could be no greater contrast than the world presented in the increasingly popular movies, all-singing and all-dancing since the introduction of sound in 1929. They provided a regular dose of escapism and a taste of Hollywood glamour in ordinary lives. In the 1920s, also, the radio began to appear in households across the country. Under the sole guardianship of the BBC, established in 1922, radio promised to 'inform, educate and entertain'. In 1936 television made its début, but only to a limited audience.

With the increased use of the car came the spread of suburbs, as families flocked from cities to live in new housing estates that were springing up on their rural edges. Streamlined architecture, using the stylised curves and corners of Art Deco, took its place alongside the ornate finery and terraced brick of the Victorian age. Some of the most notable buildings met the needs of modern electrical industries – consumer-goods factories such as the Hoover Building in Perivale.

BACK TO THE FRAY

The opposing forces of Fascism and Communism were drawing up battle lines. About 2,000 volunteers joined the Republican forces of Spain against General Franco in 1936, while at home British Fascists looked to Oswald Moseley, figurehead of the 'blackshirts'. But the main concern of the British press was the abdication of King Edward VIII, who gave up the throne in 1936 to marry divorcée Wallis Simpson. As Hitler's Germany set about annexing and occupying territories and persecuting its Jewish population, Britain pursued a policy of appeasement, until the German army invaded Poland in 1939 and made war inevitable.

Winston Churchill took the helm as prime minister in 1940, as France fell and British cities suffered devastating 'blitz' bombing. In the following year the United States entered the war and those who were billeted 'over here' made a deep impression with their easy-going informality. On 6 June 1944 British, Commonwealth and American forces landed on the Normandy beaches to begin the final thrust that would end in Germany's surrender. The war with Japan dragged on until August 1945, when the first atomic bombs were dropped on Hiroshima and Nagasaki, and the world faced up to the realities of the nuclear age.

HISTORIC SITES

Dartington Hall, Devon: An experiment in rural regeneration and education.

Chopwell, Tyne & Wear: Coalmining village dubbed 'Little Moscow' in the 1920s.

Penzance, Cornwall: 1930s Art Deco lido and other architectural treasures in a beautiful setting.

Kinder Scout, Derbyshire: where ramblers led a celebrated 'mass trespass' in 1932.

St Ives, Cornwall: centre for leading British artists, including sculptor Barbara Hepworth, from the 1930s onwards.

Bletchley Park, Bedfordshire: the secret wartime code-breakers' HQ.

Left: The widely admired Art Deco Hoover Building in Perivale, West London.

1919 The Treaty of Versailles is signed, and the terms burden Germany with huge reparations. The formidable German navy is handed over to Britain, and Germany is forbidden from rebuilding her armed forces.

1919 In the wake of the Versailles peace conference British economist John Maynard Keynes publishes *The Economic Consequences of the Peace*. This very influential book predicts the damaging consequences of imposing a punitive peace on Germany.

1919 Nancy Astor is elected Britain's first female MP.

1919 John Alcock and Arthur Brown make the first non-stop transatlantic flight, piloting a Vickers Vimy from Newfoundland to Ireland in 16 hours 27 minutes.

1919 The ballet *The Three-Cornered Hat*, commissioned by Sergei Diaghilev of the Ballets Russes, with choreography by Léonide Massine and sets by Pablo Picasso, opens in London.

1919 Brothers Ross and Keith Smith make the first flight from London to Australia, flying a Vickers Vimy bomber, in 27 days and 20 hours.

The Vision That is Dartington

A gentle rural ramble leads around the delightful Dartington Hall Estate

The story of Leonard and Dorothy Elmhirst, who bought the historic but rundown Dartington estate in 1925, is a fascinating one. Born in Yorkshire in 1893, Leonard had studied agriculture at Cornell University, New York, and worked as secretary to Indian poet and artist Rabindranath Tagore before he bought the derelict hall and 1,000 acres (405ha) of the estate at Dartington in 1925. Elmhirst was a member of the Bloomsbury set of artists and writers and was interested in farming and forestry, and in increasing rural employment opportunities. His American wife Dorothy Whitney Straight, whom he met while studying in the United States, believed passionately in the arts as a way of promoting personal and social improvement. Their joint aim was to create a foundation in which both dreams could be realised, and Dartington Hall provided the perfect setting. They commissioned architect William Weir to oversee the renovation of the buildings.

The Dartington Hall Trust, a registered charity, was set up in 1935. Under its auspices the Dartington International Summer School and Schumacher Environmental College are run. Dartington College of Arts, a specialist arts education centre, was founded in 1961 and operated until 2008, when it merged with University College, Falmouth.

Below: Looking across the Tiltyard at the Great Hall

Devon's 'Most Spectacular Medieval Mansion'

Dartington Hall was described by architectural authority Nikolaus Pevsner in his classic book on the buildings of Devon as 'the most spectacular medieval mansion' in Devon. The great hall and main courtyard at Dartington were built for John Holland, Duke of Exeter, at the end of the 14th century, and although all the buildings have since been carefully restored, to walk through the gateway into the courtyard today, with the superb Great Hall with its hammerbeam roof opposite, is to step back in time.

Sir Arthur Champernowne, Vice Admiral of the Devon Coasts, came to own the manor in 1554, and made various alterations, and the estate stayed in the hands of the Champernowne family until 1925. Further restoration work was carried out in Georgian times, but by the time the Elmhirsts came on the scene the hall was derelict.

Former Estate Church

St Mary's Church can be found on the northern edge of the estate just off the Totnes road. You pass the site of the original estate church just to the north of the Hall: it was demolished in 1873, leaving only the tower, which can be seen today. The new church, which is wonderfully light and spacious, was built in 1880, following the exact dimensions of the original building, and re-using various items from it, such as the south porch with its lovely star vault, the chancel screen, font, pulpit and roof. A tablet in the outer east wall records the rebuilding and consecration of the church by Frederick, Bishop of Exeter.

Walk 91 Medieval mansion amid a glorious estate

Appreciate the beautiful Devon setting for an experiment in rural life and education

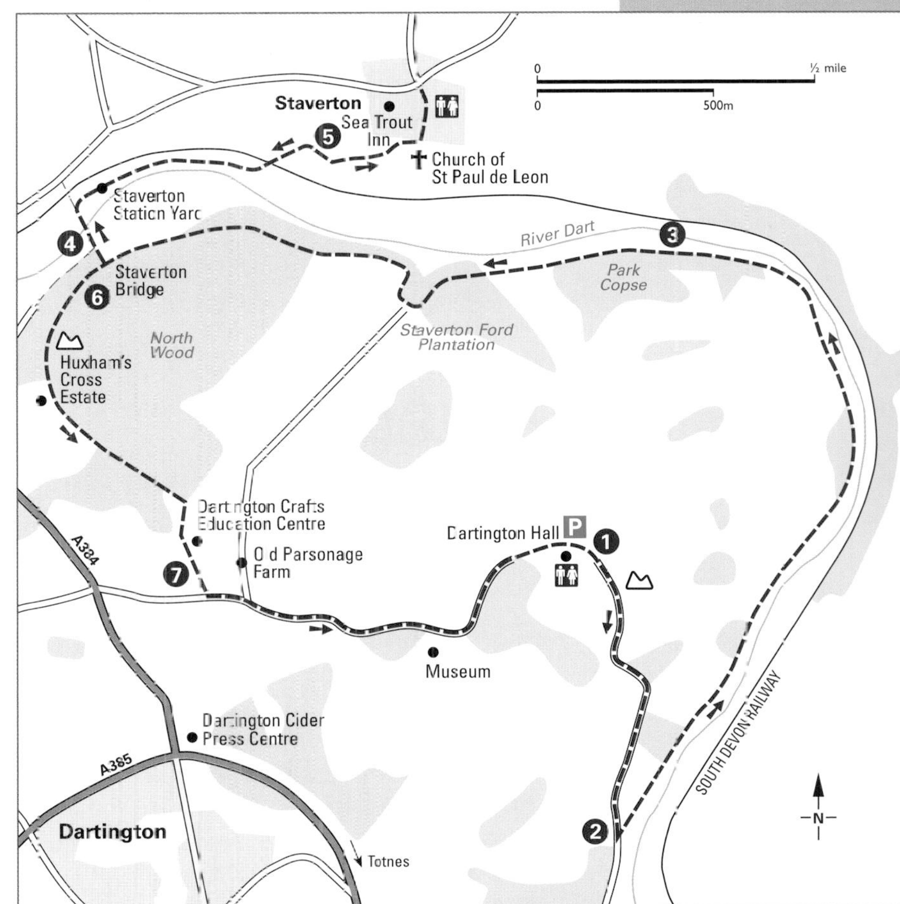

1 From the car park turn left downhill. Follow the pavement until you reach the River Dart.

2 Turn left through a gate (no footpath sign) and follow the river northwards. This part of the walk is likely to be very muddy after rainfall. The Dart here is broad, tree-lined and slow-moving. Pass through one gate, then another, through woodland and a gate. Continue through riverside meadows, and eventually pass through an open gateway onto a wooded track.

3 Walk along the river edge of the next field (Park Copse left). At the end of that field a gate leads into Staverton Ford Plantation. Where the track bears left go through the gate in the wall ahead, then right to follow a narrow path back towards the river, bearing left over a footbridge. This path runs parallel with the Dart, becoming a broad woodland track through North Wood. When you see buildings nearby through the trees on the right, leave the track and walk downhill to a metal gate and a lane.

4 Turn right to cross Staverton Bridge. At the level crossing turn right to pass through Staverton Station yard into a park-like area between the railway and river. Follow the path across the single-track railway and walk on to meet a lane by Sweet William Cottage.

5 Turn right and follow the lane to its end. Go straight ahead on a small gritty path to pass the Church of St Paul de Leon, who was a 9th-century travelling preacher. Turn left at the lane to pass the public toilets, and left at the junction to the Sea Trout Inn. After your break retrace your steps to the metal gate past Staverton Bridge.

6 Turn immediately right to rejoin the track. Follow this until it runs downhill and bends left. Walk towards the gate on the right, then turn left on the narrow concrete path. The houses of Huxham's Cross can be seen, right. Keep on the concrete path, which leaves the woodland to run between wire fences to meet a concrete drive at the Dartington Crafts Education Centre. Follow the drive to meet the road.

7 Turn left to pass Old Parsonage Farm. Keep on the road back to Dartington Hall, passing the gardens and ruins of the original church (right), until you see the car park on the left.

SOUTH DEVON RAILWAY

The South Devon Railway runs from Buckfastleigh to Totnes. Staverton Station has featured in many television programmes and films, such as *The Railway Children* directed by Lionel Jeffries in 1970. The station at Buckfastleigh has old locomotives and rolling stock on display, a museum and café, riverside walks and a picnic area. Nearby is Dartmoor Otters & Buckfast Butterflies. While you're there, consider spending some time at the Dartington Cider Press Centre. There is local food, a bookshop, crafts gallery, cook shop, toy shop, delicatessen, plant shop and more. The centre is open seven days a week, with free parking.

Distance 6.5 miles (10.4km)

Minimum time 2hrs 30min

Ascent/gradient 164ft (50m) ▲▲▲

Level of difficulty ●●●

Paths Fields, woodland tracks and lanes, 4 stiles

Landscape River meadows, parkland and mixed woodland

Suggested map OS Explorer 110 Torquay & Dawlish

Start/finish Grid reference: SX 799628

Dog friendliness Keep on lead; only guide dogs allowed in Dartington Hall grounds

Parking Opposite entrance to Dartington Hall

Public toilets Outside entrance to Dartington Hall

Note Larger organised groups require permission from the Property Administrator (tel: 01803 847000) in advance

1918–1945

1920–1933 Prohibition on alcohol is declared in the United States.

1920 Following a spate of killings carried out by members of the Irish Republican Army, Britain declares martial law in Ireland.

1920 Gustav Holst's *The Planets* is first performed.

1920 Agatha Christie introduces the character of Hercule Poirot in *The Mysterious Affair at Styles*.

1922 After three years of vicious warfare between Irish nationalist and British forces, Prime Minister Lloyd George introduces the Government of Ireland Act, which establishes two parliaments in Ireland. The Irish Free State comes into being and civil war ensues.

1922 Italy has a new leader, fascist dictator Benito Mussolini. His 'trademark' is his black shirt, and his fascist followers are known as 'Blackshirts'.

1922 The BBC is established.

1922 English Egyptologist Howard Carter discovers the tomb of Tutankhamun at Luxor, Egypt.

Derwent Valley's Past

An outing in historic country visits a one-time centre of steelmaking and political activism

Coal mining created the village of Chopwell that we see today, with its red-brick buildings and no-nonsense atmosphere – and miners' activism earned it the name 'Little Moscow' in the 1920s. The coal won from local mines was predominantly used for making coke to stoke the furnaces of the Consett Iron Company. When coal production declined after the First World War, many miners were made redundant or put on short-time working. These conditions allowed Communist sympathisers to assume the running of the village.

A miners' strike from July 1925 to December 1926 led to accusations of a Communist takeover of the local Labour Party. A national newspaper declared that 'the village is known far and wide as the reddest in England'. Streets were renamed after Marx, Engels and Lenin, and it is said that there were Communist Sunday schools in the village, as well as *Das Kapital* on the lectern of the local church. For a time the hammer and sickle flag flew over the town hall.

The Cradle of Steel

The area between Blackhall Mill and Derwentcote Ironworks was once the centre of the steel industry in Britain. Steel was made here initially to supply the sword manufacturers of Shotley Bridge, eastwards along the river.

Derwentcote, the earliest steel-making furnace to have survived, was built around 1720 and worked until the 1870s. Another furnace at Blackhall Mill lasted until 1834, when a flood washed away its mill dam; the mill was demolished in the early the 20th century. Derwentcote, now cared for by English Heritage, is open to visitors on summer weekends.

Along the Line

Beyond Derwentcote the walk enters Byerside Wood and joins the old railway line that now forms the 12.5-mile (20.1km) footpath and cycle route of the Derwent Valley Country Park. This runs from Consett to Gateshead and connects conveniently with other former railway routes, including the Waskerley Way and the Consett and Sunderland Railway Path.

Below left: *The Derwentcote steel furnace has been restored*

Below: *Autumnal colours in beautiful Chopwell Wood*

Walk 92 Communists in 'England's reddest village'

Tour the mining settlement dubbed 'Little Moscow' that flew the hammer and sickle flag

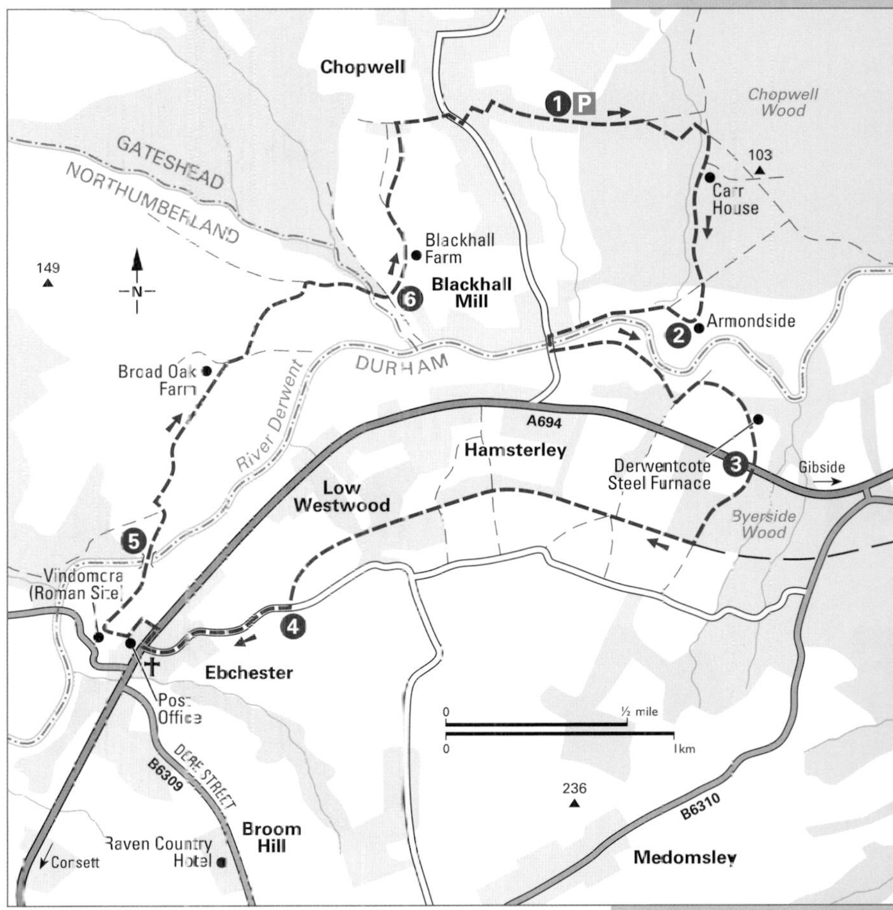

1 Walk up the entrance road to Chopwell Park. Turn right past a metal barrier and bear right, into the wood. Follow the woodland track to a junction in about 200yds (183m). Pick out a narrow path on the right, marked by a wooden post amongst broom and gorse. Follow this winding path, eventually over a little bridge and up to join a forest road. Turn right, onto the road marked Forestry Commission road and follow the track downhill, passing Carr House on the left. The path drops down to the right and continues downhill. As the forest track swings right, turn left through a gate and continue down between the fields to Armondside farm.

2 Bear right and follow the track to the road in Blackhall Mill. Turn left, over the bridge. Just beyond it, turn left by a footpath sign and follow the field-edge path to the right of the hedge. Follow the fenced riverside path. You may find there are some diversions along here where the floods of September 2008 caused landslides. At a crossing path, turn left, uphill. At the top go sharp left, following waymark signs. Go left of the buildings, over a stile and across the field. Go over two wooden stiles then right. Follow the track uphill, passing Derwentcote Steel Furnace, to the main road.

3 Cross and take a signed footpath almost opposite. Go over a stile and, at a crossing path, turn right to another stile. Follow the path through woodland to the former railway track. Turn right and follow the track, which crosses another track (barriers at each side) and eventually rises to another barrier onto a metalled lane.

4 Turn right and descend into Ebchester. Bend right by the Community Centre to meet the main road. Cross over and turn right in front of the post office. Turn left at the footpath sign beyond. Follow the fence on your left, bend left at the end beside the wall, then follow the footpath downhill to reach a metalled lane. Turn right along the lane to a footbridge.

5 Cross the bridge. The footpath bends right before going straight ahead across the field to a stile. Follow the green lane uphill, pass a farmhouse and follow the track through several gates. Where the main track bears left, go straight ahead. Go through a gate and along the field edge. Go though two gates to a T-junction of tracks.

6 Turn left, up the track towards a farm. About 300yds (274m) after the farm go right, through a gate and walk across the field to a stile, hidden in a hedge. Continue up the field to another stile, right of the houses, and along a narrow lane. At the end, turn right along the tarmac lane. At the main road turn right and then left, following the signs to 'Chopwell Park Car Park'.

Distance 7 miles (11.3km)

Minimum time 2hrs 30min

Ascent/gradient 541ft (165m) ▲▲▲

Level of difficulty ●●●

Paths Tracks, field paths and old railway line

Landscape Woodland and riverside, farmland and industrial remains

Suggested map OS Explorer 307 Consett & Derwent Reservoir

Start/finish Grid reference: NZ122579

Dog friendliness On lead, except on former railway line

Parking Roadside parking in Chopwell; follow signs for 'Chopwell Park Car Park'. Car park, itself, opens irregularly

Public toilets None on route

WHAT TO LOOK OUT FOR

The 949-acre (384ha) Chopwell Wood was once a wild area of oaks and hazel. This was much affected by coal mining in the 19th and early 20th centuries, when a railway ran through it. It was taken over by the Forestry Commission in 1919, and its trees were largely felled during the two World Wars. Restocking, beginning in 1952, has left it a mainly coniferous forest, with larch, pine and spruce, although there are still patches of earlier broadleaved woodland remaining. The wood provides habitats for a wide variety of animals. In the area, the National Trust's Gibside Estate is 4 miles (6.4km) east of Chopwell. Once home to the Bowes-Lyon family, the estate has riverside and forest walks, and several ornate buildings, including an 18th-century chapel and 140ft (42.7m) Column of British Liberty.

1918 – 1945

1922 The publication of the poem 'The Waste Land' causes a public sensation. Poet T.S. Eliot uses the work to describe the darkness of post-war Britain and the frailty of the human condition.

1923 Adolf Hitler addresses the first Nazi Party Rally in Munich on 27 January. He is later sentenced to five years in prison, where he writes *Mein Kampf.*

1923 German inflation spirals and bartering replaces paper currency.

1923 In her novel *Whose Body?* Dorothy L. Sayers introduces the character or Lord Peter Wimsey.

1924 On 2 November the *Sunday Express* publishes the first crossword in a British newspaper.

1924 Wembley Stadium opens.

1925 The Exposition des Arts Décoratifs et Industriels Modernes is launched in Paris. The Art Deco style (from Arts Décoratifs) is born.

1925 Irish playwright George Bernard Shaw is awarded the Nobel Prize for Literature.

Sezincote House and John Betjeman

A Cotswold stroll reveals Indian influences on Sezincote, a regular haunt of the poet as a young man

Top: *The onion dome and corner minarets at Sezincote House*

Above: *Indian influence extends to interior decorations*

For anyone with a fixed idea of the English country house, Sezincote will come as a surprise. It is, as the poet John Betjeman said, 'a good joke, but a good house, too'. Built in the early 19th century on the plan of a typical large country house of its era, in every other respect it is thoroughly unconventional. A large copper onion dome crowns the house, while at each corner of the roof are finials in the form of miniature minarets. The walls are of Cotswold stone, but the Regency windows and decoration owe a great deal to Eastern influence.

Betjeman was a regular guest at Sezincote during his undergraduate days, when he was a student at Magdalen College, Oxford. 'Stately and strange it stood,' he wrote, 'the nabob's house, Indian without and coolest Greek within, looking from Gloucestershire to Oxfordshire.' In his blank verse autobiography *Summoned By Bells*, published in 1960, he recalls approaching the house down the drive 'under the early yellow leaves of oaks', and notes how the 'onion domes' and other features burst upon the visitor to the '"Home of the Oaks", exotic Sezincote'.

Hindu Architecture

Sezincote House is a reflection of the fashions of the early 19th century. Just as engravings brought back from Athens had been the inspiration for 18th-century Classicism, so the colourful aquatints brought to England from India by returning artists such as William and Thomas Daniell were a profound influence on architects and designers. Sezincote was one of the first results of this fashion.

The owner of Sezincote, Sir Charles Cockerell, was a 'nabob', a Hindi-derived word for a European who had made their wealth in the East. On his retirement from the East India Company he had the house built by his brother, Samuel Pepys Cockerell, an architect. The eminent landscape gardener Humphry Repton helped Cockerell to choose the most picturesque and evocative elements of Hindu architecture from the Daniells' drawings. Samuel Pepys Cockerell had made his first experiments with Indian-influenced architecture in designing a house for Warren Hastings, first Governor-General of British India, at Daylesford, Gloucestershire.

At Sezincote some modern materials, such as cast iron, were used to complement the intricacies of traditional Mogul design. The garden buildings took on elements from Hindu temples, with a lotus-shaped temple pool, Hindu columns supporting a bridge and the widespread presence of snakes, sacred bulls and lotus buds. The Prince of Wales was an early visitor. The experience obviously made some impression as the intensely Mogul-influenced Brighton Pavilion arose not long after.

Walk 93 Eastern inspiration for the Brighton Pavilion and for a very British poet

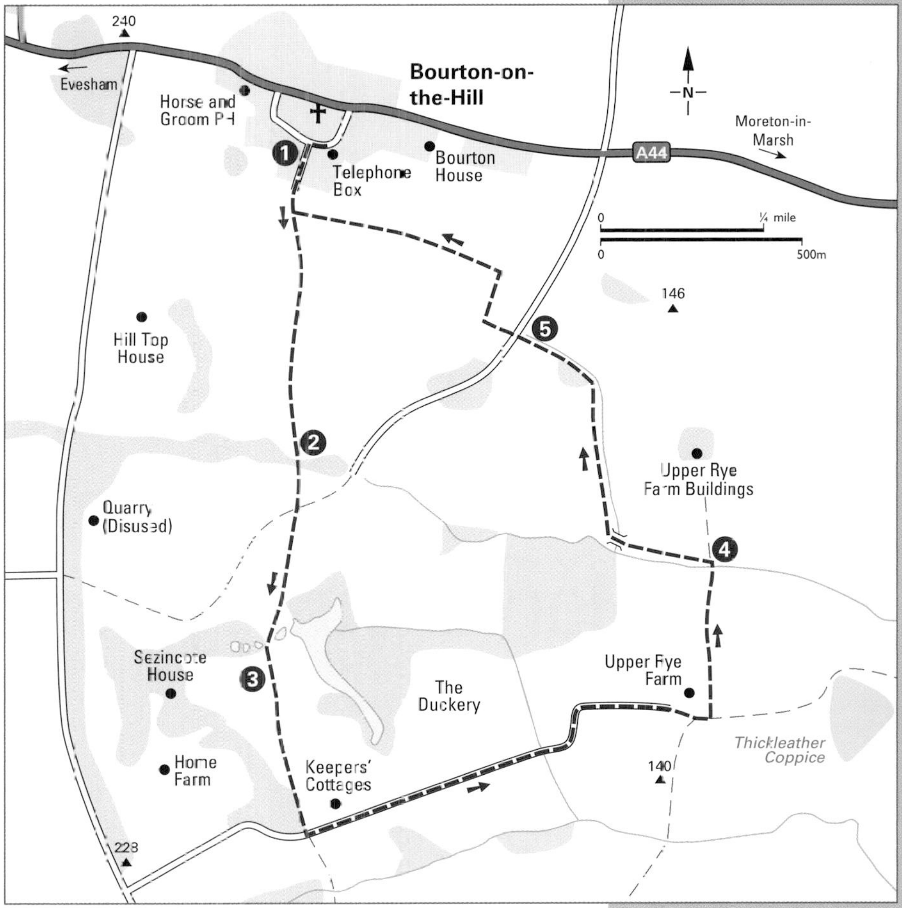

View the house John Betjeman celebrated as 'exotic Sezincote' – as well as the lovely Cotswold village of Bourton-on-the-Hill

1 Walk up the road from the telephone box with the church to your right. Turn left down a signposted track running between walls. Go through a gate into a field and then continue forward in order to pass through two more field gates.

2 Continue to a stile, then carry on to two kissing gates amid a tree belt. This is the Sezincote Estate – go straight ahead, following markers and crossing a drive. Dip down, keeping to the right of woodland, to two field gates among trees, with ponds on either side. Go ahead and into a field, from where Sezincote House is visible away to the right.

3 Walk into the next field via a gate and go right to the end, aiming for the top, right-hand corner. Pass through a field gate and kissing gate to a narrow road and turn left. Walk down this road, passing the keepers' cottages to your left, and through a series of three gates. The road will bottom out, curve left and right and bring you to Upper Rye Farm. Pass well to right of the farmhouse, go through a gate and, immediately before a barn, turn left along a track and a road.

4 After a second cattle grid, go left over a stile. Follow the left edge of the field to a footbridge between step-through stiles. Go over it and turn right. Now follow the right-hand margin of the field to a stile in the far corner. Cross this in order to follow a path through woodland until you come to step-through stiles on each side of a footbridge and a field and continue on the same line to another stile.

5 Cross a track to another stile into Sezincote's Millennium Oak Plantation and walk onwards. After a few paces, with Bourton-on-the-Hill plainly visible before you, turn right and follow the path to the next corner. Turn left and pass through three gates. After the third one, walk on for about 60 paces and finally turn right through a gate to return to the start.

Distance 3 miles (4.8km)

Minimum time 1hr 30min

Ascent/gradient 85ft (25m) ▲▲▲

Level of difficulty ●●●

Paths Tracks, fields and lanes, 7 stiles

Landscape Hedges, field and spinney on lower part of escarpment

Suggested map OS Explorer OL45 The Cotswolds

Start/finish Grid reference: SP 175324

Dog friendliness Keep under close control – likely to be a lot of livestock

Parking Street below Bourton-on-the-Hill church, parallel with main road

Public toilets None on route

BOURTON-ON-THE-HILL

This walks begins and ends in Bourton-on-the-Hill, a pretty village that was once on the main road between London and Worcester and which today would be exceptional were it not for traffic streaming through it on the A44. St Lawrence's Church owes its impressive features to the fact that the village was formerly owned by Westminster Abbey, whose income was handsomely supplemented by sales of wool from the vast flocks on the surrounding hills. The church was founded in 1157, but only a few pillars on the south side of the nave survive from this period. There is a 14th-century tower, a 15th-century clerestory and a 15th-century octagonal font. The stone screen in the south nave dates to the 15th century but was not originally part of the church – discovered in a builder's yard, it was fitted only in 1927.

Further down the village, the 18th-century Bourton House has a 16th-century barn in its grounds. Among the village's many pretty cottages, the finest is no doubt the 17th-century Slatter's Cottage.

1918 – 1945

1926 Britain experiences its first General Strike. It lasts ten days, 3–13 May.

1926 A.A. Milne's children's book, *Winnie-the-Pooh*, is published.

1927 Al Jonson stars in the first feature-length 'talkie', *The Jazz Singer.*

1927 Charles Lindbergh makes the first solo flight across the Atlantic, from Long Island to Paris. He pilots the monoplane *Spirit of St Louis*.

1927 Virginia Woolf publishes *To the Lighthouse*.

1928 All women over the age of 21 are given the vote – on equal terms with men.

1928 The discovery of penicillin by Alexander Fleming is announced.

With Fleming on Darvel's Marvellous Byways

A walk around the town of Darvel leads along the boyhood paths of this town's most famous son – the discoverer of penicillin

Lochfield Farm, the birthplace of Alexander Fleming, was the ideal childhood home for a boy with an insatiable curiosity about nature. Together with his brothers, the young Alexander spent much of his time on the moors – identifying birds, animals and plants and catching trout by hand in the nearby burns.

At the age of 13 he moved to London to live with his brother Tom. After finishing his education at London Polytechnic, Alexander spent four years working in a shipping office until an uncle left him a legacy that enabled him to take a course of private tuition. He gained first place in the examination that would allow him to enter medical school and subsequently took first place in every exam he sat. By 1906 he had joined the Inoculation Department at St Mary's Hospital in Paddington, and by 1909 was a Fellow of the Royal College of Surgeons. The war interrupted his career at St Mary's, but he became Professor of Bacteriology there in 1928.

In 1928, while clearing up some old virus cultures in his laboratory, Fleming noticed that although all were covered in moulds, one was significantly different. This particular mould was dissolving the virus colonies round about it and was spreading across the dish, destroying the rest. The mould was one of a class called *penicillium*. Discovering what we now know as penicillin was just the beginning. Isolating, extracting and finding a means of using it to treat infection took ten years and it was the 1940s before this 'magic bullet' was commercially available. Since then it has saved countless thousands of lives, and a huge industry has grown round the research and development of other antibiotics.

Honours Near and Far

Honours were heaped upon Fleming. In 1945, he received the Nobel Prize for Medicine and on 26 October, 1946, returned to his native Darvel to receive 'the proudest title I could have… the Freedom of Darvel'. Fleming died from a heart attack on 11 March, 1955; he is buried in St Paul's Cathedral, London.

Above: *Darvel celebrates its most famous son*

Below: *A snowy scene in Ayrshire, with Loudoun Hill in the distance*

Walk 94 In tribute to a great Scottish scientist

Start from the Sir Alexander Fleming memorial and see the farm where he was born

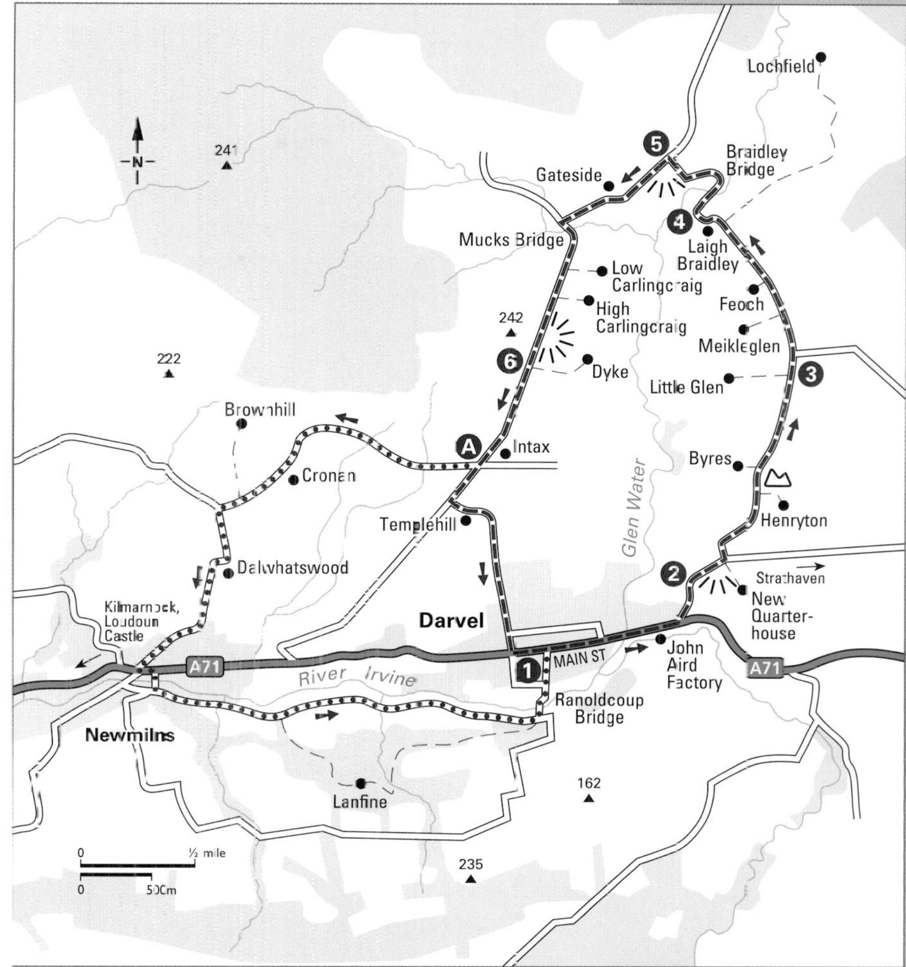

1 From the Alexander Fleming Memorial, cross the square to the pedestrian crossing, cross over the road, turn right and go along Main Street. Near the outskirts of the town go across Darvel Bridge and take the second turning on the left just past the John Aird factory. Go uphill on this road and pass the cemetery.

2 Keep going uphill to reach a crossroads near New Quarterhouse farm. Follow the waymark arrow pointing left. The road continues uphill, passing Henryton on the right and then Byres on the left. Near Byres there is a conveniently situated bench by the roadside if you want some respite on this steep climb.

3 Little Glen is the next farm on the left-hand side, and shortly afterwards the road forks. Take the left turn. The next two farms passed on this road are Meikleglen and Feoch which come in quick succession. Just before the next farm on the left, Laigh Braidley, a farm road leads off to the right. This is the entrance to Lochfield, Alexander Fleming's birthplace, which is not open to the public. Continue past Laigh Braidley.

4 After Laigh Braidley the road turns sharply left, then right and goes downhill to cross the Glen Water at Braidley Bridge. As you descend the hill look slightly to the right and uphill and you will see the steading of Lochfield, which is still farmed. Follow the road uphill from the bridge. There's another bench by the roadside at the T-junction near the top of the hill. Enjoy a well-earned rest here and appreciate the splendid view back across the Irvine Valley.

5 Ignore the waymark and turn left, heading along a lane and past Gateside. When the road forks take the left fork, cross Mucks Bridge and continue uphill. The lane now passes the roads to Low then High Carlingcraig, then levels out. As you continue along the top of this hill look to the left for the distinctive outline of Loudoun Hill.

6 When you reach Dyke the road heads downhill again. Go over a crossroads at Intax and continue a short distance to some bungalows on the right. Just past here take a left turn. After Hilltop the road turns sharply right and downhill. As you approach the town the lane continues into Burn Street. At the T-junction turn left and follow this back to Hastings Square.

Extending the Walk

You can extend this walk into the town of Newmilns, once the centre of the Irvine Valley weaving industry. At Intax (Point A) turn right and follow the lanes down past Cronan and Dalwhatswood into town. You can return to Darvel along a pleasant riverside track before crossing the River Irvine at Ranoldcoup Bridge to get back to Hastings Square.

Distance 7 miles (11.3km)

Minimum time 3hrs

Ascent/gradient 459ft (140m) ▲▲▲

Level of difficulty ●●●

Paths Country lanes and pavements

Landscape Hillside, moorland, pasture and townscape

Suggested map OS Explorer 334 East Kilbride, Galston & Darvel

Start/finish Grid reference: NX 563374

Dog friendliness Keep dogs on lead in lanes

Parking On-street parking at Hastings Square at start of walk

Public toilets None on route

1928 The Scottish National Party is founded.

1928 D.H. Lawrence has his novel *Lady Chatterley's Lover* privately printed in Florence, Italy.

1929 On 24 October the Wall Street Crash in America costs thousands of investors their livelihoods. The world economy is in crisis.

1930 The first football World Cup is won by host nation Uruguay. They defeat Argentina in the final 4–2.

1930 Arthur Ransome publishes *Swallows and Amazons*, first in a series of much-loved books.

1932 The Ramblers' Association leads a mass trespass on Kinder Scout.

1932 Aldous Huxley's novel, *Brave New World*, is published.

1933 Adolf Hitler is appointed Chancellor of Germany, and by 1934 is made President of Germany.

1933 Charles Laughton stars in Alexander Korda's film *The Private Life of Henry VIII*.

Art-Deco-on-Sea at Penzance

A pleasant stroll starts by taking in two 1930s masterpieces

Top: *The elegant Jubilee Pool, with the water of Mount's Bay beyond*

Above: *Clean Art Deco lines at the stylish Yacht Inn*

There is a Mediterranean ring to the name Penzance that goes well with the town's sunny south-facing aspect on the shores of Mount's Bay, one of the largest bays in Britain. This is a town whose mellow climate even encourages the growth of palm trees and where you really do have a sense of taking your pleasure 'abroad'. During the first part of the walk you pass the 1930s Art Deco swimming lido, known as the Jubilee Pool, and the nearby Yacht Inn, a classic of 20th-century marine architecture. The triangular Jubilee Pool is so called because it was built in 1935, King George V's Silver Jubilee. Designed by Borough Engineer Captain F. Latham, this stylish lido extends into the waters of Mount's Bay. In 1993 it was Grade II listed. In 2010 it celebrated its 75th anniversary.

Wealth of Tin and Copper

Penzance was made a borough as early as 1614 and received an even greater economic boost in the later 17th century when it became a 'stannary' or 'coinage' town, with the right to assay and tax tin and copper from the many mines on the Land's End peninsula. The town continued to grow and reached its commercial apogee in the 19th century.

In addition to the Art Deco attractions, there are other fine buildings in Penzance, many from the Regency period and its immediate aftermath. Regent Square, through which your route passes, is a splendid example. The town also has a legacy of fine open spaces, such as the Morrab Gardens, which evolved during the same period. There are many more architectural gems. The walk then leads to Chapel Street, Penzance's finest thoroughfare, which has a mix of styles and boasts the one-time home of Maria Branwell, the mother of the famous Brontë sisters. Ultra-modern style is represented at the Exchange art gallery, while Penzance's Market Jew Street brings you back to the busy commercial town.

Walk 95 Mellow setting for stylish architecture

Take a tour of Penzance's varied attractions, from Art Deco back to Regency squares

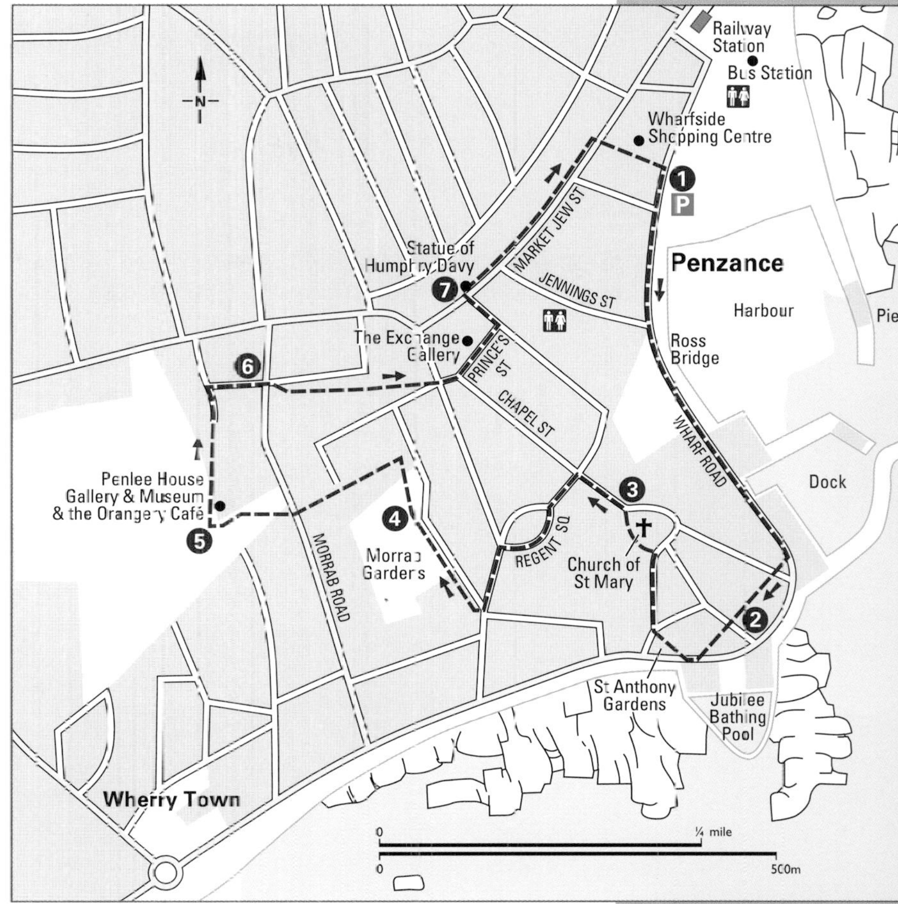

1 Exit the Harbour Car Park onto Wharf Road and cross the road using the pedestrian crossing in front of the Wharfside Shopping Centre. Turn left and pass the old Lifeboat Station, cross the junction and continue across Ross Bridge. Bear right in front of the Dolphin Tavern and go up the cobbled lane to the right of the pub.

2 Cross a junction, slightly leftwards, to the seafront road. In a few paces turn right into the peaceful St Anthony Gardens. Walk through the gardens and exit in the far left-hand corner opposite the Yacht Inn. Cross left to South Place. Turn right and climb steps beneath a granite archway into St Mary's churchyard. Climb more steps and continue into Chapel Street.

3 Turn left then left again opposite the Admiral Benbow pub and into Voundervour Lane. Keep left at the next junction and go through Regent Square. On leaving the square, cross the road, turn left and, in a few paces, turn right. Go through a gap in railings just beyond a line of lock-up garages. Turn right and enter Morrab Gardens.

4 Leave by the gate in the top right-hand corner of the gardens. After about 30yds (27m) go left down an alleyway in front of a terrace of handsome houses. Keep straight ahead across a junction of lanes and across a pedestrian crossing in Morrab Road. Turn right and in a few paces go left through the gates of Penlee Park.

NEWLYN SCHOOL

Penzance shares in the artistic heritage of West Cornwall. Nearby Newlyn saw the late 19th-century emergence of the Newlyn School of Painting. This was the label given to a style, based on the French *plein air* or 'open air' tradition, by which artists painted out of doors in a more dynamic fashion. During the walk through Penzance you pass the Penlee House Gallery and Museum, which has a collection of Newlyn School paintings.

5 Just past the Penlee House Gallery and Museum turn right along a leafy walkway. Mid-way along visit the Memorial Garden on the right. On the main route keep straight ahead and follow the walkway round to the right. Go through a gateway and keep uphill to reach Morrab Road.

6 Cross the road (with care) and go along an alleyway between houses. At a junction of lanes keep straight across. At the next junction, by the Globe public house, cross the street, turn right and in a few paces turn left along Prince's Street past the Exchange Art Gallery. Turn left at the next junction to reach Market Jew Street.

7 Cross the street and go up steps behind the statue of Humphry Davy, inventor of the miner's safety lamp. Turn right down the Terrace, a raised, granite walkway. When opposite the Wharfside Shopping Centre, cross the street, go through the centre and down the escalator to the Harbour car park.

Distance 1.25 miles (2km)

Minimum time 1hr

Gradient 115ft (35m) ▲▲▲

Level of difficulty ●●●

Paths Surfaced pavements and lanes throughout

Landscape Townscape and seafront

Suggested map *The Penzance Town Guide*, from the Tourist Information Centre, has a fold-out map

Start/finish Grid reference: SW 476304

Dog friendliness Dogs should be kept under control. Dog fouling regulations are strictly enforced

Parking Penzance Harbour Car Park

Public toilets Penzance Bus Station; entrance to Inner Harbour; Jennings Street (leading down from post office in Market Jew Street)

1918 – 1945

1934 The driving test is introduced.

1935 The FT Ordinary Share index is introduced.

1936 German troops occupy the Rhineland.

1936 George V dies; his son Edward Albert Christian George Andrew Patrick David is King Edward VIII.

1936 The Crystal Palace, which housed the Great Exhibition, goes up in flames.

1936–1939 Civil war is fought between Republican and Nationalist factions in Spain.

1936 Mass unemployment sparks the Jarrow March from Northumberland to London.

In the Footsteps of the Trespass

A dramatic route to Kinder Downfall follows the famous trespassers of 1932

***Top right:** The starting point of the trespass is marked by a plaque*

***Above:** Walking along the edge*

***Below:** High on Kinder Scout*

From the beginning of the 20th century there was conflict between ramblers and the owners of Kinder's moorland plateau. By 1932 ramblers from the industrial conurbations of Sheffield and Manchester, disgusted by lack of government action to open up the moors to walkers, decided to hold a Mass Trespass on Kinder Scout. Benny Rothman, a Manchester rambler and a staunch Communist, was to lead the trespass on Sunday 24 April. The police expected to intercept Benny at Hayfield railway station, but he outwitted them by arriving on his bicycle, not in the village itself, but at Bowden Bridge Quarry to the east. Here he was greeted by hundreds of cheering fellow ramblers. With the police in hot pursuit the group made their way towards Kinder Scout.

Although they were threatened and barracked by a large gathering of armed gamekeepers, the ramblers still managed to get far enough to join fellow trespassers from Sheffield, who had come up from the Snake Inn. Predictably, fighting broke out and Benny Rothman was one of five arrested. He was given a four-month jail sentence for unlawful assembly and breach of the peace.

The ramblers' cause inspired folk singer, Ewan McColl (famous for 'Dirty Old Town' and 'The First Time Ever I Saw Your Face'), to write 'The Manchester Rambler', which became something of an anthem for the proliferating walkers' clubs and societies. However it took until 1951, when the recently formed National Park negotiated access agreements with the landowners, for the situation to improve.

National Park Signs

Just like the mass trespass this walk starts at Bowden Bridge, where you will see a commemorative plaque on the rock face above the car park. After climbing through the Kinder Valley and above Kinder Reservoir you are confronted by those same moors of purple heather and the enticing craggy sides of the Scout. But now it is the National Park signs that greet you, not a gun-toting gamekeeper.

A dark shadow-filled cleft in the rocks is the Kinder Downfall, where the infant Kinder tumbles off the plateau. Now you climb to the edge for the most spectacular part of the walk – the trespass – and continue along a promenade of dusky gritstone rock. Round the next corner you come to that dark cleft seen earlier. In the dry summer months the fall is a mere trickle, but after the winter rains it can turn into a 100ft (30m) torrent. The prevailing west wind often catches the torrent, funnelling it back up like plumes of white smoke. In contrast, the way down is gentle, leaving the edge at Red Brook and descending the pastures of Tunstead Clough Farm. A lane returns you to the Kinder Valley.

Walk 96 Where trespassing walkers defied the police and armed gamekeepers

Pay your tributes to the fearless folk celebrated in Ewen McColl's 'The Manchester Rambler'

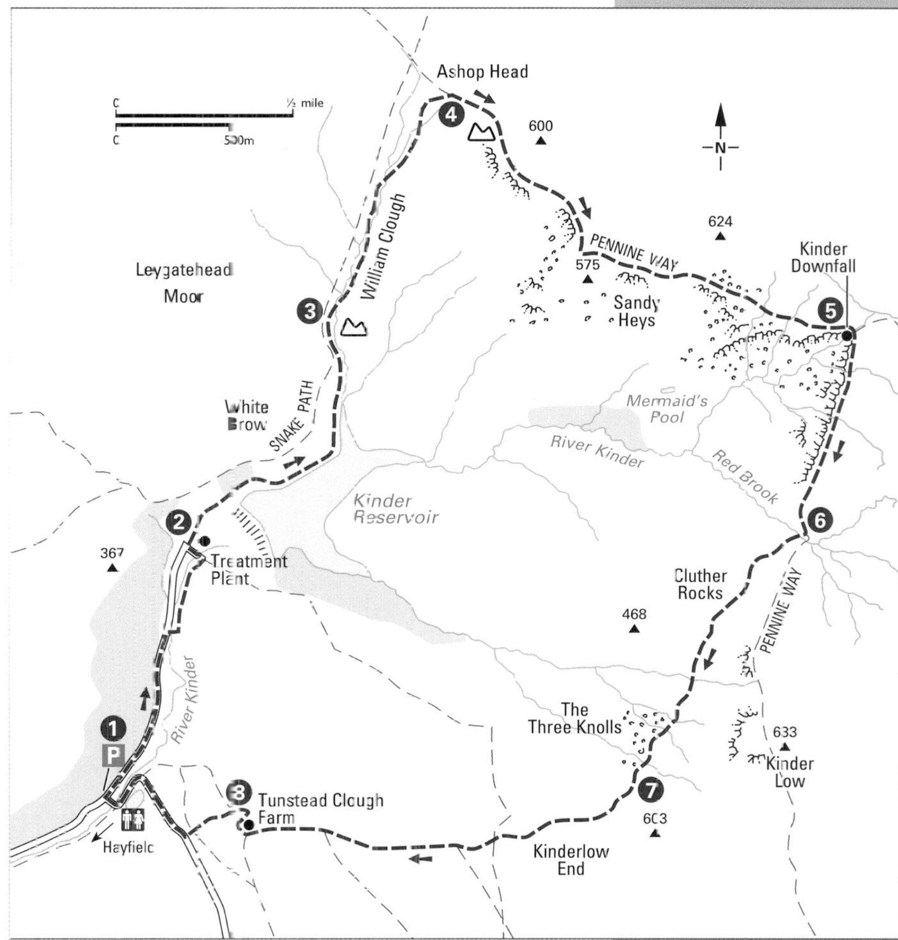

1 Turn left out of the car park and walk up the lane, which winds beneath the trees and by the banks of the River Kinder. After 550yds (503m), leave the lane at a signposted footpath after crossing a bridge. Follow the path as it traces the east bank of the river before turning left to rejoin the road at a point just short of the treatment plant buildings.

2 Here you fork left through a gate onto a cobbled bridleway, following this as it climbs above the buildings. The bridleway continues alongside the reservoir's north shore, turning sharp left on White Brow. Go beyond a gate but don't cross over the footbridge: instead follow the path as it climbs alongside William Clough, where it is joined by the Snake Path from the left.

3 The path crosses and recrosses the stream as it works its way up the grass and heather clough. In the upper stages the narrowing clough loses its vegetation and the stream becomes a trickle in the peat. Climb to Ashop Head, where you meet the Pennine Way at a crossroads of paths.

4 Turn right to walk along the slabbed Pennine Way path across the moor towards Kinder Scout's north-west edge, then climb those last gritstone slopes on a pitched path to gain the summit plateau. Now it's easy walking along the edge.

5 After turning left into the rocky combe of the River Kinder, the Mermaid's Pool and the Kinder Downfall (waterfalls) come into view. Descend to cross the Kinder's shallow rocky channel about 100yds (91m) back from the edge, before turning right and continuing along the edge.

6 Beyond Red Brook, leave the plateau by taking the right fork, which descends southwestwards, contouring round grassy slopes beneath the rocky edge.

7 After passing the Three Knolls rocks and swinging right beneath the slopes of Kinderlow End, go through a gate in a fence (grid reference 066867) before taking a right fork to reach another gate in the wall dividing the moor and farmland. Go over a stile next to it and then turn left through a gateway. Descend the trackless pastured spur, passing through several gates and stiles at the field boundaries to pass to the left of Tunstead Clough Farm.

8 Turn right beyond the farmhouse to follow a winding track that descends into the upper Sett Valley. At the crossroads of lanes at the bottom, go straight ahead, and along the road to emerge at Bowden Bridge.

WHILE YOU'RE THERE

In 2007, the 75th anniversary of the Mass Trespass was marked by the opening of the Trespass Trail, a 14-mile (22.6km) walk following the route of the original hardy trespassers up onto Kinder Scout. A booklet guide to walking the trail is available from Hayfield Information Centre.

WHAT TO LOOK OUT FOR

When you are deep in your thoughts, absorbed in the pleasures of wilderness walking, some comic bird with a flash of red on his head will probably wreck the moment by cackling loudly before scuttling from under your feet. This red grouse will have been absorbed in the pleasures of the tasty heather shoots you are passing. The gamekeeper makes sure that the ungainly red grouse have all they need to breed successfully – a mixture of young heather and more mature plants for cover.

Distance 8 miles (12.9km)

Minimum time 5hrs

Ascent/gradient 1,450ft (440m) ▲▲▲

Level of difficulty ●●●

Paths Well defined tracks and paths, quite a few stiles

Landscape Heather and peat moorland and farm pastures

Suggested map OS Explorer OL1 Dark Peak

Start/finish Grid reference: SK 048869

Dog friendliness Walk is on farmland and access agreement land, dogs should be kept on lead

Parking Bowden Bridge pay car park

Public toilets Across bridge from car park

1918–1945

1936 Cheshire-born Fred Perry wins Wimbledon for the third consecutive year. To date, he is the last British player to have won the trophy in the Men's Singles.

1936 In December, Edward VIII is presented with an ultimatum – the throne or American divorcee Mrs Simpson. He chooses Mrs Simpson, and signs the Instrument of Abdication passing the throne to his brother, George VI. Edward and Mrs Simpson are married on 3 June 1937 in France.

1937 King George VI is crowned.

1937 Pablo Picasso paints *Guernica* in response to the bombing of that town (in the Basque country) by German and Italian bombers in the Spanish Civil War.

The Artists of St Ives

A vigorous outing provides a taste of cliffs, fields and sea views that moved Ben Nicholson and others

The picturesque old fishing town of St Ives is renowned for its narrow, cobbled streets, lovely cottage-lined courtyards and superb sandy beaches and coastline. These – and its equable climate – attract thousands of visitors each year to this part of beautiful west Cornwall. But another group of enthusiasts was drawn here by the natural scenery and qualities of light and space – and not to relax, but to work. The celebrated St Ives colony of artists was founded in the great *plein air* movement of the 19th century and ever since has attracted hundreds of artists from all over the world.

Top right: Looking across to the Island

Right: Tate St Ives

Below: Low tide in the harbour

Nicholson and Hepworth

Painter Ben Nicholson once remarked that he found drawing a pencil line as exhilarating as taking a coastal walk from St Ives to Zennor. Born in Buckinghamshire in 1894, Nicholson first came to St Ives with fellow-artist Christopher Wood in 1928 and met fisherman-artist Alfred Wallis. Wood died tragically young two years later, but Nicholson went on to become one of Britain's major abstract artists. In 1939 he returned to live in Cornwall with his wife, the sculptor Barbara Hepworth. They lived first at Carbis Bay and then in St Ives. Over the next two decades they turned St Ives into one of the leading centres of British art, attracting gifted younger artists such as Peter Lanyon, Patrick Heron and many others.

In the 1950s, following their divorce, Nicholson moved to Switzerland, but Hepworth – an immensely innovative non-figurative sculptor and a powerful artist – remained in St Ives until her death in 1975. The Barbara Hepworth Museum and Sculpture Garden (a permanent exhibition of her work at her former home) is a significant attraction in the town and well worth a visit. Bernard Leech, one of the foremost potters of the 20th century, also made his mark here when he established a pottery in St Ives in 1920 on his return from studying in Japan.

Tate St Ives

On his departure to Switzerland, Nicholson left his studio to Patrick Heron – whose magnificent stained-glass window can be seen in the Tate St Ives. This impressive building, designed by Eldred Evans and David Shalev and opened in June 1993, houses work produced by St Ives's artists from the late 1880s to the present day.

Walk 97 Coastal tramp near an artists' colony

Revel in the light, sea air and wonderful wide skies that inspired generations of artists

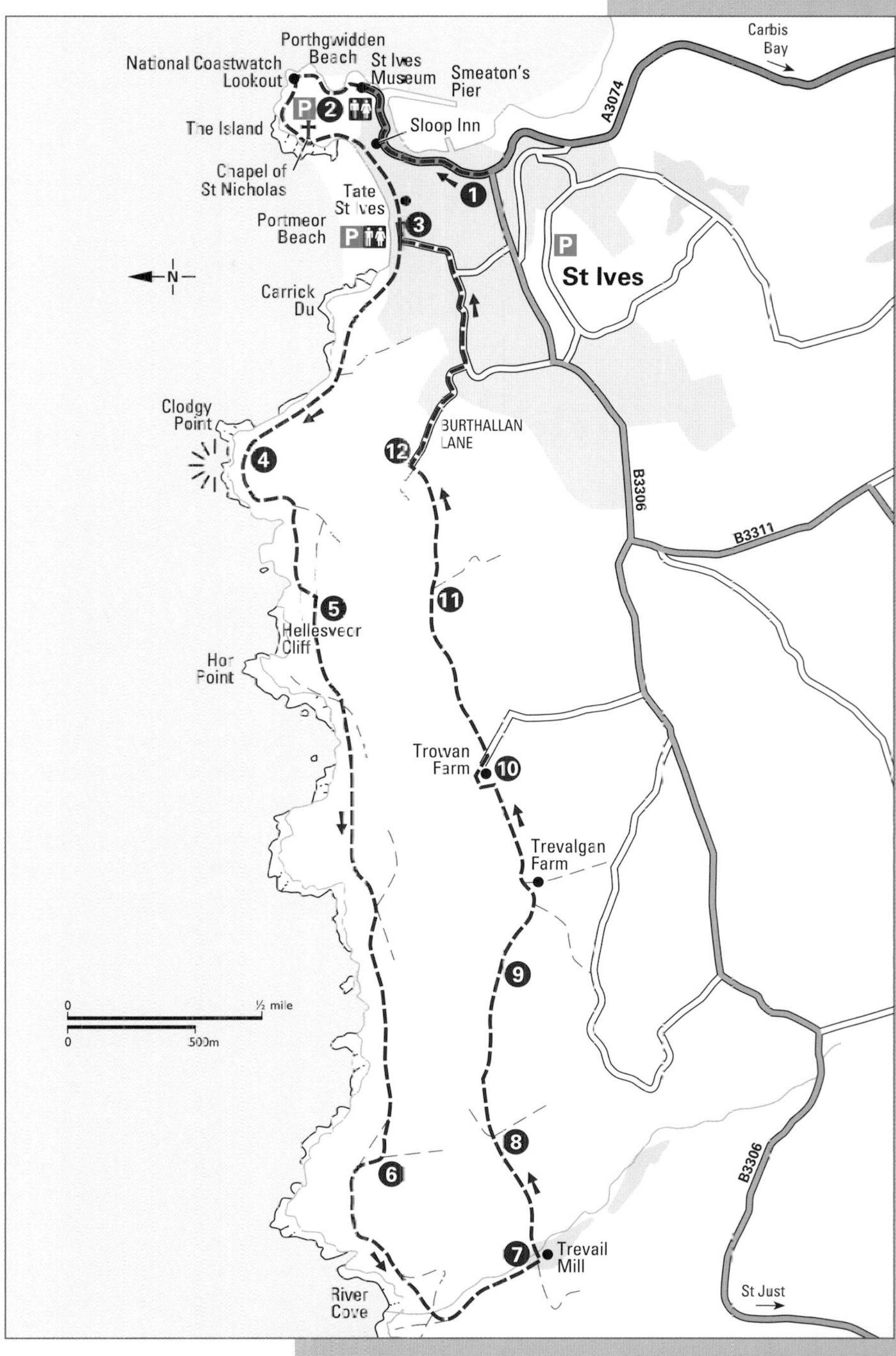

1 Walk along the harbourfront towards Smeaton's Pier. Just before the pier entrance, turn left, signed to 'St Ives Museum'. Where the road bends, keep straight on into Wheal Dream. Turn right past St Ives Museum, then follow a walkway to Porthgwidden Beach.

2 Cross the car park above the beach and climb to the National Coastwatch lookout. Go down steps behind the building at the back of the lookout, then follow a footway to Porthmeor Beach. Go along the beach. At the beach end, go up to the car park.

3 Go up steps beside the public toilets, then turn right along a surfaced track past bowling and putting greens. Continue to the rocky headlands of Carrick Du and Clodgy Point.

4 From Clodgy Point walk uphill and follow the path to the right. Continue along a boggy and very rocky path. In about 0.5 mile (800m) go left at a junction by a small acorn signpost and big yellow-lichened boulder.

5 At a T-junction with a track just past a National Trust sign, 'Hellesveor Cliff', turn right on the coast path.

6 Keep right at a junction just past an old mine stack and shed that lie a few fields inland. Continue to River Cove. On the other side of the cove, climb to where the path levels off at a junction. Follow the inland path.

7 At a junction with a track, go left through a kissing gate, then follow signs past Trevail Mill. Go through another kissing gate and climb steadily.

8 Cross a track and follow the hedged-in path, signposted 'Bridleway'. In about 40yds (36m) go left over a stile by a black and white pole. Follow field-edges ahead over intervening stiles.

9 Keep in the field with a granite upright. Cross a stile. Where the field hedge bends sharply right, head across the field towards two gates. Cross a stile and continue to another stile at Trevalgan Farm. Go between buildings and in 50yds (46m), turn left at a gate, bear round right and cross a stile. Continue to Trowan Farm.

10 At Trowan Farm, pass a granite post; continue between houses, then go through a wooden field gate. Follow field paths over several stiles.

11 Cross a lane, then a stile and follow the left-hand edges of small fields. Pass a field gap on the left and turn left just before another and a rusty gate. Cross two stiles and pass between high hedges to a surfaced lane.

12 Turn right (Burthallan Lane) to a T-junction with the main road. Turn left and follow the road downhill to Porthmeor Beach.

Distance 8 miles (12.9km)

Minimum time 4hrs

Ascent/gradient 394ft (120m) ▲▲▲

Level of difficulty ●●●

Paths Coastal and field paths, many stiles

Landscape Very scenic coast and small inland fields

Suggested map OS Explorer 102 Land's End

Start/finish Grid reference: SW 522408

Dog friendliness Dogs on lead through grazed areas

Parking The Island car park, St Ives

Public toilets Smeaton's Pier, Porthgwidden Beach and Porthmeor car park

1918–1945

1939 On 15 March German forces take Prague as they march into Czechoslovakia.

1939 On 1 September Germany invades Poland. Britain declares war on 3 September.

1940 Winston Churchill is elected prime minister; he holds the post for the duration of World War II.

1940 In July–October RAF Fighter Command leads the defence of British skies in the 'Battle of Britain'.

1940–41 London, Coventry, Plymouth and other British cities suffer under a 'Blitz' of German bombing.

1941 Operation Barbarossa, Germany's failed invasion of the Soviet Union, turns the tide of the war.

1944 On 6 June Allied forces land in Normandy, launching the final assault on Germany.

1945 On 2 May V.E. Day celebrations mark the end of the war in Europe.

1945 The Allies drop atomic bombs on Hiroshima and Nagasaki, Japan.

Skyline Walking – and a Memorial – Above the Caerfanell Valley

An outing on spectacular escarpments passes a monument commemorating victims of a 1942 air crash

***Below:** The crash site*

***Bottom:** The memorial, with poppy wreaths for remembrance*

On 6 July 1942 a Wellington bomber came down on the Brecon Beacons in bad weather, in the course of a routine training flight. On this walk you will pass the forlorn wreckage of this warplane and a memorial to those who perished in her– a reminder that the suffering of the Second World War touched even the most remote parts of Britain.

The walk sums up everything good about walking in the Brecon Beacons, encapsulating almost every sort of landscape found in the national park. There are magnificent views of moorland, mountains and valleys before you have the sobering encounter with the aircraft's remains. The route starts by climbing steeply onto an impressive peak from where you track easily along a steep sandstone escarpment, so typical of the area's high mountain scenery. The airy path crosses the head of a precipitous waterfall, rubs shoulders with an expansive moorland plateau and provides views that will remain in your memory for a long time.

Final Flight

As you approach the clearly visible cairn beneath Waun Rydd, on the walk's return leg, a sharp eye will spot flashes of red against the impeccable stonework. Drawing closer, you can see that the red belongs to poppy wreaths hung over a memorial. A plaque lists the names of the Canadians who lost their lives when the Wellington bomber R1645 crashed in poor visibility. The twisted wreckage, a deathly shade of dull grey, lies strewn around the bracken-covered hillside below the cairn.

Walk 98 Glorious country touched by conflict

Pause to reflect on war's inevitable suffering amid the serene beauty of the Brecon Beacons

1 Walk back out of the car park, either crossing the cattle grid or a stile to the left of it, then turn immediately right onto a stone track that heads uphill, with the stream on your left. Follow this track steeply up to the top of the escarpment and keep straight ahead to cross the narrow spur, where you bear around, slightly to the left, to follow the escarpment.

2 Stay on the clear path, with the escarpment to your right, for about 1.5 miles (2.4km), till you meet a number of paths at the head of the valley.

3 Take the sharp right turn to follow a narrow track slightly downwards and around the head of the valley, towards the cliffs that can be seen clearly on the opposite hillside. Keep left at a fork and then continue to the crash memorial.

4 Almost directly above the memorial, you'll see a rocky gully leading up onto the ridge. On the left-hand side of this, as you look at it, is a faint track that climbs steeply up. Take this to the top and turn right onto a narrow but clear track. Follow this track easily above the crag, to a distinctive cairn at the southern end of the ridge. Just north of the cairn you'll see a small stream.

5 Follow this down for 10ft (3m) to join a clear grassy track that trends leftwards at first, then follows a clear groove down the spur. This becomes an easy footpath that crosses a broad plateau and then leads to a junction at a wall. Turn right here and drop down to the Afon Caerfanell.

6 Cross the stile on your left at the bottom and follow the narrow footpath downstream, past a number of waterfalls. Eventually you'll pass the largest of them and come to a footbridge.

7 Cross the footbridge and then a stile to follow the track into the forest. Pass some ruined buildings on your right, and before you cross the small bridge, turn right onto a clear path that leads uphill into the forest with waterfalls on your left.

8 Continue uphill on the main track, taking optional detours to the left and right to see other waterfalls. Eventually you'll meet a broader forest track where you turn left and then right to return to the car park.

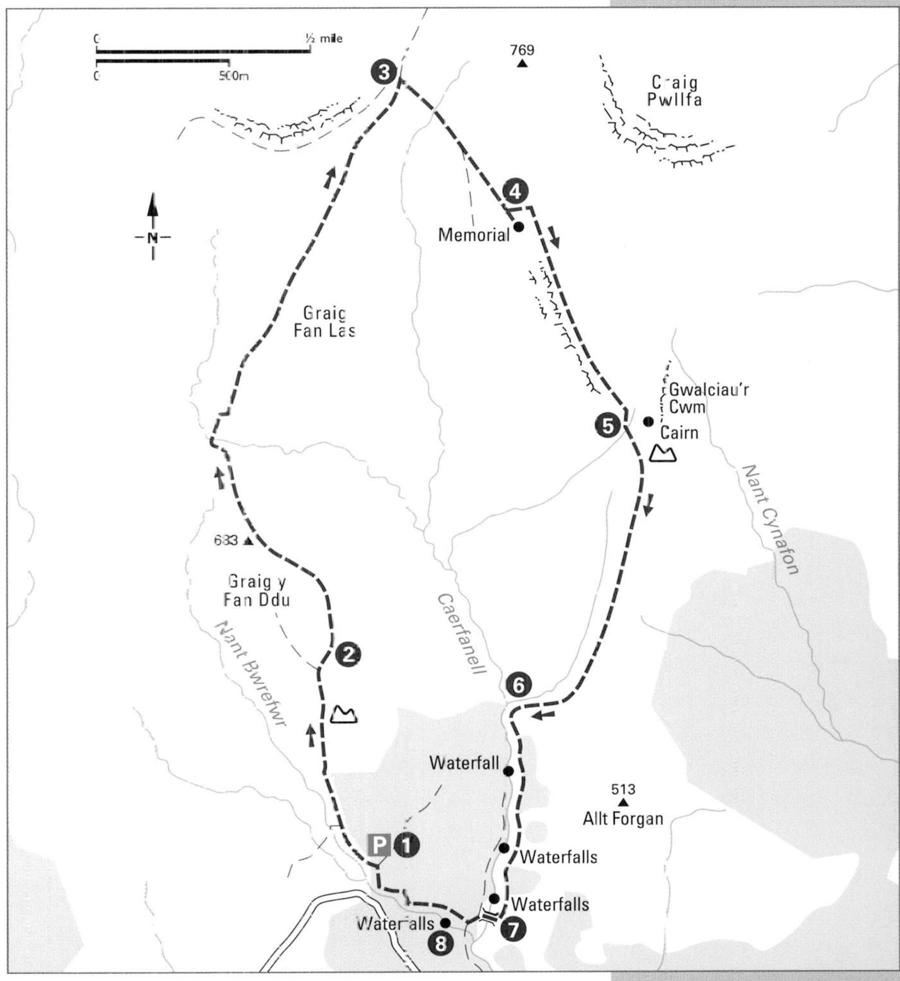

WHAT TO LOOK OUT FOR

The diminutive crag that shades the memorial is named Cwar y Gigfran after the raven: *gigfran* is Welsh for raven, and these powerful birds can often be seen performing aerobatics above the outcrop. Ravens are the largest members of the corvid family, easily distinguished by their size from carrion crows, rooks, jackdaws and the rarer chough. They are synonymous with remote upland areas and rugged coastal regions, where they tend to nest on crags and perform tumbling flight displays. The majority of their nourishment in the mountain environment comes from sheep carrion, but they are endlessly resourceful and incredibly skillful hunters too.

Elsewhere on the walk, you will see small, mottled brown birds – either skylarks or meadow pipits. The skylark is slightly larger, lighter in colour, has a stouter beak and a small crest on its head. The pipit makes a dipping flight, while the skylark is well known for its continuous song, usually performed as it hovers high above you.

Distance 5.5 miles (8.8km)

Minimum time 3hrs 30min

Ascent/gradient 1,542ft (470m) ▲▲▲

Level of difficulty ●●●

Paths Clear tracks, some mud and wet peat, 3 stiles

Landscape Moorland, escarpments, valley, coniferous plantation

Suggested map OS Explorer OL12 Brecon Beacons National Park Western & Central areas

Start/finish Grid reference: SO 056175

Dog friendliness Care needed near livestock, 1 dog-proof stile

Parking Large car park at start, 3 miles (4.8km) west of Talybont Reservoir

Public toilets None on route

Secrets of Bletchley Park

A fascinating walk leads around a key site of Britain's Second World War effort

Bletchley Park. The name may sound ordinary enough but what took place here during the Second World War is quite remarkable. This was the home of Station X – where more than 10,000 people worked in total secrecy in a small, nondescript town in the heart of the English shires.

Brain Teasers

It was here that mathematicians, linguists, crossword enthusiasts and Oxbridge scholars battled for hours on end, in wooden huts and brick-built blocks, to break the seemingly unbreakable. Their role was to study the German military cipher machine, 'Enigma', and devise a programme to enable the Allies to decode the Nazis' secret radio messages. The odds against success were phenomenal, but they did succeed, shortening the war against Germany by as much as two years.

One of the key figures in the story of Bletchley Park was Alan Turing, a mathematical genius considered to be one of the pioneering fathers of the modern computer. It was he who invented the 'Bombe', an electro-mechanical machine of clattering code wheels intended to significantly reduce the time needed to break the daily-changing Enigma keys.

But why Bletchley Park? Midway between the universities of Oxford and Cambridge and a few minutes' walk from a mainline railway station, it seemed a perfect venue for the Government Code and Cypher School. As the threat of war loomed, Bletchley Park became a key communications centre. In August 1939, code breakers arrived at Bletchley Park. They posed as members of 'Captain Ridley's shooting party' so as not to arouse suspicion. Ridley was the man in charge of the school's move to Bletchley. For the next 40 years, no one outside Bletchley Park knew exactly what went on here, and the Germans never realised Enigma had been broken.

Below left: *An enigma machine – British intelligence intercepted and decoded German messages*

Below and background: *The 'Bombe' at Bletchley Park*

Walk 99 Where 'Captain Ridley's shooting party' shot down a German code

Puzzle over the enigma of Station X on this urban walk around Bletchley

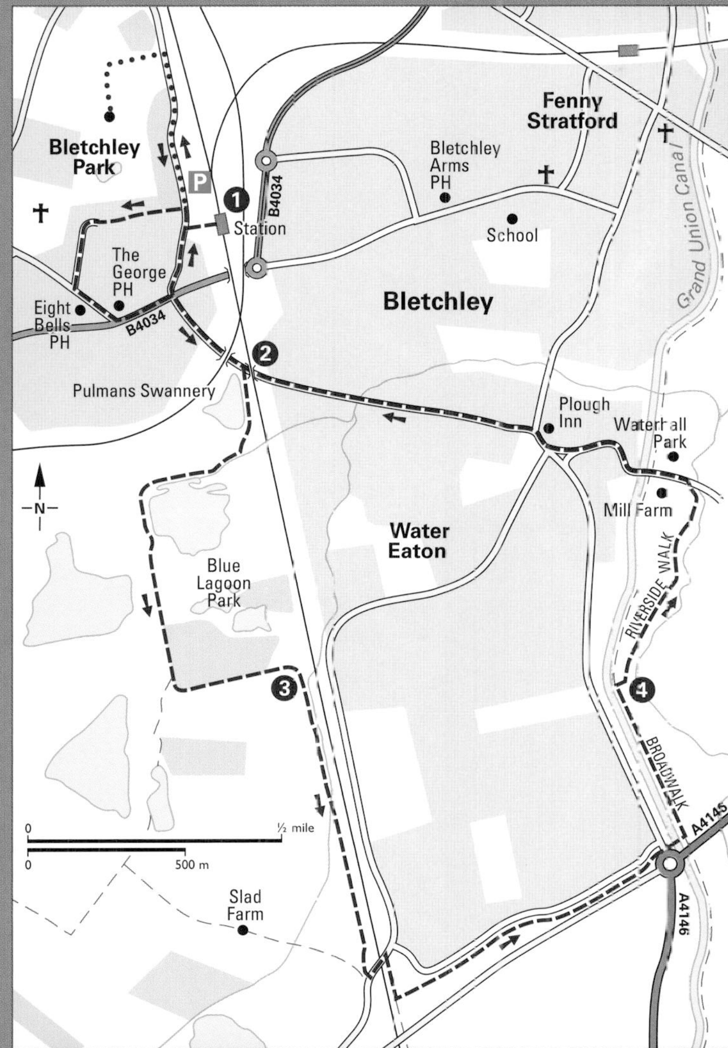

1 From the station car park cross the road and to visit Bletchley Park turn right, its entrance now about 300yds (274m) further along Sherwood Drive. After the visit retrace your steps towards the station and turn right onto the footpath opposite. This brings you into Wilton Road, the former entrance into Bletchley Park. Turn left along Wilton Avenue and left into Church Green Road. Bear left at the junction with Buckingham Road and head towards Central Bletchley. Turn right into Water Eaton Road, pass beneath the Bletchley–Oxford rail line, and bear right at the footpath sign, just before the next railway bridge.

2 Pass a pond, Pulmans Swannery, on the right and follow the fenced path to a stile. Continue to a fork, keep right and follow a track in an anti-clockwise direction round the edge of the lake. Avoid a ford and a footbridge and continue on the lakeside path. At the northwest corner of the lake, look for some steps and a footbridge on the right. Turn left immediately beyond them and follow a path parallel to power lines. Eventually bear left at a grassy track and follow it towards the railway line. Turn right immediately before a stile and keep to the right of the site of a house. Swing left at a fence to reach a stile, and then walk ahead with the railway line on your left.

3 Pass through a tunnel of trees and alongside farmland, eventually crossing a footbridge but always keeping the railway on your left-hand side. Then, when you reach the former drive to Slad Farm, make your exit onto the road. At this point bear left, cross the railway bridge and turn immediately right at yellow posts. Follow the path for a short distance to a field corner and then swing around to the left in order to join a bridleway. Keep the houses of Bletchley on your left, beyond the trees and the hedgerow. On reaching the road, between two roundabouts, cross the canal bridge ahead and afterwards swing left to follow the Broad Walk. When you reach a sign for the Riverside Walk, turn right and then swing left after about 75yds (69m).

4 Keep the river a short distance away to the right. Draw level with a farm over to the right, cross a footbridge over a pond and turn left. Head for the Watermill and Mill Farm, avoiding the car park for Waterhall Park. Cross the bridge over the Grand Union Canal and keep right. Ahead now are several thatched and timber-framed cottages. Turn left in front of them and keep right at the main road junction, heading towards the Plough Inn. Cross the road at the roundabout, following the sign for the station. Continue ahead through a residential area, pass beneath the two railway bridges seen near the start of the walk, go straight over at the junction and back to the station car park.

Distance 6 miles (9.7km)
Minimum time 1hr 45min
Ascent/gradient Negligible
Level of difficulty ●
Paths Roads, park and field paths, canal tow path and riverside walk, 2 stiles
Landscape Mixture of suburban streets and farmland
Suggested map OS Explorer 192 Buckingham & Milton Keynes
Start/finish Grid reference: SP 868337
Dog friendliness Under control in Blue Lagoon Park, along Broad Walk and by canal. Dogs are permitted in grounds of Bletchley Park
Parking Bletchley Station and approach road
Public toilets Bletchley Station and Bletchley Park

WHILE YOU'RE THERE

After the war the intelligence services continued to use part of the park as a training centre, and the site was also used as a training college for teachers, post office workers and air traffic controllers. It was decommissioned in 1987 and in 1992 the Bletchley Park Trust was established to preserve the historic site. There are many and varied attractions here, so allow plenty of time for your visit. Props from the film *Enigma* (2001) are on display and you can follow the Cryptology Trail, learning how messages were intercepted and delivered to Bletchley Park. Also available for inspection is a replica of Colossus, the world's first programmable electronic computer. If you need a breath of fresh air there is a children's playground, and you can take a gentle stroll to admire the wildlife beside the lake.

INTO THE NEW MILLENNIUM

In the 60-odd years since 1950, Britain has passed from postwar austerity through sweeping social changes and profoundly challenging times for its once-proud industries. In these decades, the country has grappled with its identity – as a declining empire, a European power and a multiracial, multinational society.

In the post-war years the last vestiges of empire fell away. Mahatma Gandhi's long campaign of peaceful resistance to British rule in India culminated in Indian independence in 1947, and in the ensuing decades a series of former colonies followed suit. Britain entered the 1950s a war-weary and austere place, although the Festival of Britain in 1951 made a concerted, and successful, effort to lift public spirits. The economy did pick up and by the late 1950s jobs were plentiful, and immigrants were encouraged, especially from the Commonwealth countries, to swell Britain's workforce.

A new generation, with disposable income and a liberal outlook, exploded into the 1960s and created the permissive age. London and Liverpool were the unofficial capitals of pop, and Mary Quant revolutionised street fashion with mini skirts, high boots and a look that celebrated the Space Age. Motorways crisscrossed the country and cars became accessible to more families – as did television, complete with a new commercial channel to promote new products. Throughout the 1960s Britain had been negotiating to enter the European Common Market, and in 1973 the Conservative prime minister, Edward Heath, oversaw the country's accession to the Common Market. Britons had already come to terms with a new currency, replacing pounds, shillings and pence with a decimal system.

However, crisis hit Britain and the rest of the Western world in the mid-1970s, when an Arab-Israeli war provoked a dramatic rise in oil prices. Fuel tanks ran empty; petrol was rationed and prices rapidly increased. Demands for higher wages to meet the rising cost of living stoked industrial conflict, and strikes and picket lines became an enduring image of the 1970s. The emergence of punk music and fashion seemed to epitomise an angry and disillusioned decade.

In the 1980s service industries and computing flourished but older industries suffered, with the closure of coal mines and steel plants and the decline of ship-building. While entire communities faced the prospect of long-term unemployment, 'yuppies' – young, upwardly mobile professionals – indulged in conspicuous consumption. The 1980s also brought the revival of a decades-old proposal for a tunnel between Britain and France. In 1986 a Channel Tunnel agreement was signed between the British and French governments; in 1994 two passenger tunnels and one service tunnel were opened.

BRITAIN LOOKING FORWARD

In the 1990s and the early years of the 21st century, Britain was taking stock of itself and its place in the world. Devolution of power from Westminster to Scotland and Wales; the continued search for a solution in Northern Ireland; issues of immigration, multi-ethnicity and an increasingly pluralistic society; international terrorism and British support for the United States-led 'War on Terror'; the love-hate association with Europe; economic difficulties and cutbacks in the wake of a major global financial crisis in the late 2000s – all shaped the nation. Yet in difficult times Britain retains a sense of hope and endeavour and enters the second decade of the 21st century as fascinated with its future as it is with the past.

KEY SITES

Glenkiln, Dumfries & Galloway: Work of great 20th-century sculptors set in a stunning landscape.

Milton Keynes: Purpose-built 1960s city, tailored to accommodate the car.

Aberdeen: Former fishing port whose future was guaranteed by the 'Black Gold' of North Sea Oil.

Falkirk Wheel, Falkirk: Ultramodern iconic rotating boat lift constructed to connect the Forth and Clyde Canal to the Union Canal.

London Eye: Enduringly popular millennial wheel offering unrivalled views of the capital.

Left: The London Eye was built to celebrate the millennium but endured to become an icon of the city

1947 The marriage of HRH Princess Elizabeth and Lieutenant Philip Mountbatten takes place.

1947 British rule in India comes to an end.

1947 The first Edinburgh Festival of the Arts is held.

1948 The affordable Morris Minor car goes on sale.

1948 The annual Aldeburgh Festival in Suffolk is founded by the composer Benjamin Britten and his life partner, the tenor Peter Pears.

1948 On 30 January Mahatma Gandhi is assassinated in New Delhi.

1948 The Olympic Games is held in London.

1948 The Welfare State is created in response to the 1942 Beveridge report of Aneurin Bevan, who recommends state care from 'the cradle to the grave'.

1949 The North Atlantic Treaty Organisation (NATO), a military alliance, is formed and signed by 12 nations.

1949 The Republic of Eire (Ireland) is created.

Manchester Climbers and the Green Knight

A country tramp visits the scene of a 1950s rock-climbing revolution and, perhaps, of a literary chapel

The jagged ridge of the Roaches is one of the most popular outdoor locations in the Peak District National Park. The name is a corruption of the French for 'rocks' – *roches*. It was here on the gritstone crags that the 'working-class revolution' in climbing took place in the 1950s.

Two Manchester lads – builder Joe Brown and plumber Don Whillans – went on to become legends within the climbing fraternity by developing new rock-climbing techniques wearing gym shoes and using Joe's mother's discarded clothes line as a rope.

Below: *Mosses and other plants thrive in the damp cool of the rocky cleft*

Other, less tangible legends surround this long outcrop, several of them attached to Doxey Pool. Locals speak of a mermaid who lived in the pool, but was captured by a group of men: her ghost can still be heard singing through the mist. Lurking in the darkest depths of the pool is Jenny Greenteeth, a hideous monster with green skin, long hair and sharp teeth, who grabs the ankles of anyone unfortunate enough to get too close, dragging them to a deep and watery grave.

Sir Gawain and the Green Knight

The greatest legend associated with the Roaches is the Arthurian tale of Sir Gawain and the Green Knight. According to the 14th-century poem of this name, a knight on horseback, cloaked entirely in green, gatecrashed a feast at Camelot and challenged the Knights of the Round Table. Sir Gawain beheaded the Green Knight but the latter retrieved his head and asked Sir Gawain to meet with him again, in a year's time, at the Green Chapel; when Gawain did so, he beheaded the Green Knight a second time.

A possible site for this chapel has been identified as Lud's Church, a rocky cleft near the Roaches. In the 1950s Professor Ralph Elliot identified the Roaches as the general location of the chapel. His theory was supported by a group of linguists, working on the poem at the same time, who placed the work in the same 15-mile (25km) radius. Then the professor and a group of students from the University College of North Staffordshire (the forerunner of Keele University) tramped all over the countryside looking for a suitable cave to match the poetic description: *A hole in each end and on either side//, And overgrown with grass and great patches//All hollow it was within, only an old cavern// Or the crevice of an ancient crag.* Lud's Church fitted the bill. This rocky cleft was created by a mass of sandstone slipping away from the hill.

Walk 100 Climbing legends and literary sleuths

Explore a corner of Staffordshire that saw two breakthroughs in the 1950s in very different fields – mountaineering and English literature

1 From the lane go through the main gate by the interpretation panel and follow the path half-right to the end of the rocks. At a gate in the wall on your right, turn left and straight uphill on a rocky track. Go left through a pair of stone gateposts and continue right on a well-defined track.

2 The path is flanked by rocks on the right and woodland to the left and below. Follow it to the right and uphill through a gap in the rocks. Turn left and then continue uphill. Continue following this ridge path. Pass to the left of Doxey Pool and on towards the trig point

3 From here descend on a paved path, past the Bearstone Rock to join the road at Roach End. Go through a gap in the wall, over a stile and follow the path uphill keeping the wall on the left. At the signpost, fork right onto the concessionary path to Danebridge.

4 Follow this path, keeping straight ahead at a crossroads, and go through a wall gate and up towards an outcrop. Carry on along the ridge then head down to a signpost by a gate. Turn right and follow the bridleway signed 'Gradbach'. At the next signpost fork right towards Lud's Church.

5 After exploring Lud's Church continue along the path, through woodland, following the signs for Roach End, eventually taking a paved path uphill. Keep the wall on your left-hand side and at the top, cross a stile onto the gated road and follow this back to the lay-by near Windygates Farm.

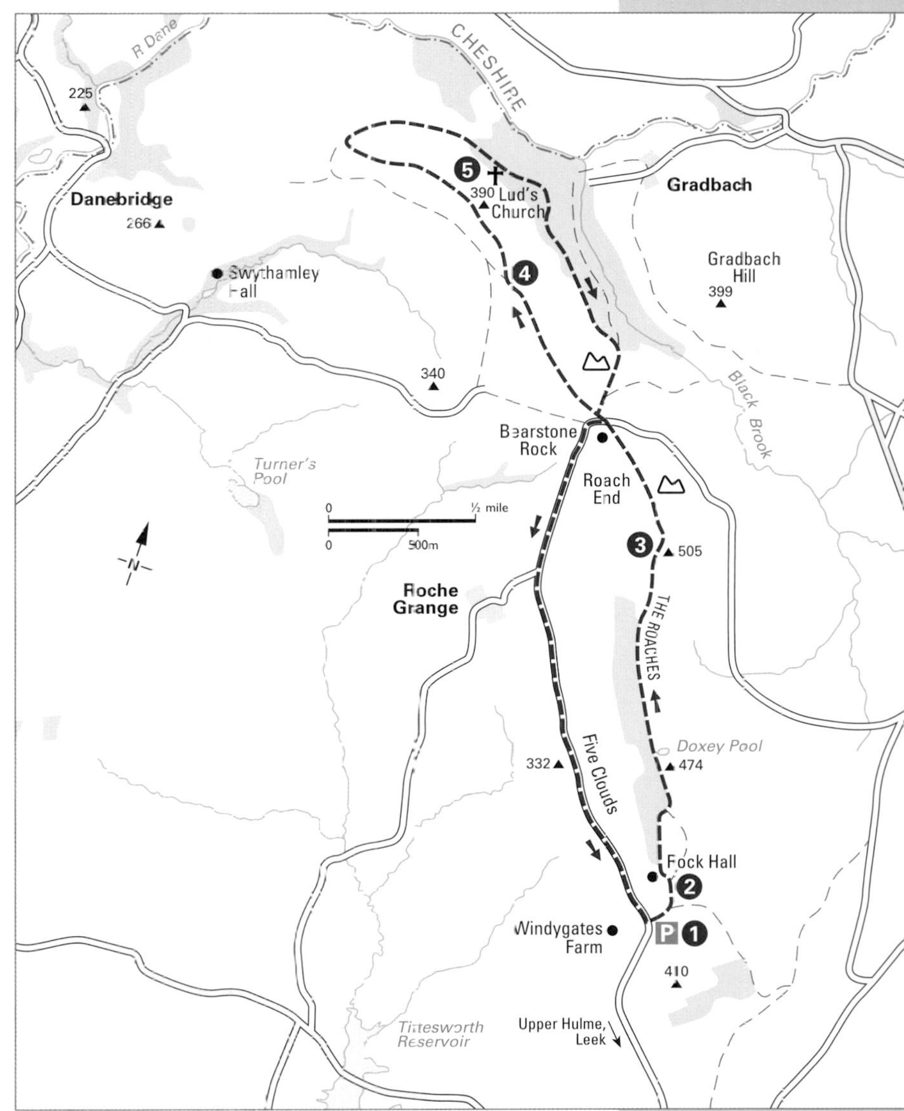

DON WHILLANS HUT

Look out for Rock Hall cottage, built into the rock and containing at least one room that is a natural cave. This listed building is a former gamekeeper's residence, currently owned by the Peak District National Park. Restored in 1989, and now known as the Don Whillans Memorial Hut, the bothy can be booked through the British Mountaineering Council by small groups of climbers.

WHILE YOU'RE THERE

Leek is a magnet for antique hunters. As well as having a large number of antique dealers, the town hosts an open-air craft and antiques market each Saturday in the historic Market Square. Other markets include the Butter Market, selling mainly fresh traditional produce, on Wednesday, Friday and Saturday.

Also worth visiting is the Brindley Water Mill and Museum. Leek was the home of James Brindley, the 18th-century canal engineer who built the Trent and Mersey Canal and the Staffordshire and Worcestershire Canal. He constructed a water-powered corn mill in Leek in 1752. You can view the restored and now working water mill and tour the museum devoted to Brindley and his achievements.

Distance 6.75 miles (10.9km)

Minimum time 4hrs

Ascent/gradient 1,020ft (311m) ▲▲▲

Level of difficulty ●●●

Paths Rocky moorland paths, forest tracks and road

Landscape Moor and woodland

Suggested map OS Explorer OL24 White Peak

Start/finish Grid reference: SK 005621

Dog friendliness Keep on lead near livestock

Parking In lay-by on lane near Windygates Farm

Public toilets None on route

1950 In June BBC radio farming drama 'The Archers' is broadcast for the first time.

1950 North Korea invades South Korea and civil war breaks out.

1950 The Old Vic, repaired after being bombed in 1941, reopens with Shakespeare's *Twelfth Night*.

1951 The Festival of Britain, designed to boost morale, transforms London's bombed-out South Bank into an exhibition complex.

1951 Britain's first National Park is opened in the craggy Peak District of central England.

1952 Agatha Christie's play *The Mousetrap* opens.

1952 George VI dies. His daughter Elizabeth Alexandra Mary succeeds as Queen Elizabeth II.

1953 Edmund Hillary and Sherpa Tenzing conquer Mount Everest.

1953 On 2 June, thousands watch the first televised coronation – of Queen Elizabeth II.

Welsh Base Camp for an Assault on Everest

An energetic ramble in Snowdonia reveals where John Hunt and his team prepared for their historic 1953 expedition to the Himalayas

Below: *Lord Hunt and Tenzing Norgay reunite at Capel Curig*

Bottom: *Reflected glory – the view across Llynnau Mymbyr*

In the 1950s the Pen y Gwryd Inn in Capel Curig became a centre for planning Alpine and Himalayan expeditions. In this inn, run by enthusiast Chris Biggs, John Hunt and his team, who in 1953 were the first to climb Mount Everest, met to make the final preparations before departing for Nepal. The wood ceiling in the Climbers' Bar has been autographed by many climbers, including the summit pair, Sir Edmund Hillary and Tenzing Norgay.

The cottages and inns of Capel Curig stretch 6 miles (9.7km) between Pont-Cyfyng, beneath Moel Siabod, to the Pen y Gwryd, beneath Glyder Fawr. The inns were there at first to serve the quarrymen from the barracks of Siabod and the miners from the copper mines of Snowdon – and then, when the mines and quarries shut down, that new breed of visitor, the walker and the climber. This corner of Wales became the British Alps, Capel Curig taking the role of Zermatt and Snowdon that of the Matterhorn.

Glass-like Waters

This walk leads around the valley, with views of the mountains around Capel Curig and the Llugwy Valley. There is an optional scramble to Capel's very own pinnacle, Y Pincin, where you can see the peaks of Snowdon reflected in the twin lakes of Mymbyr. Later you come out by a footbridge on the shores of Llynnau Mymbyr, and again see Snowdon reflected in glass-like waters. On the other side of the bridge at the Plas y Brenin National Mountain Centre, they are training the next generation of mountaineers.

Walk 101 Treading in the footsteps of Hillary and Norgay in the 'British Alps'

Savour a taste of mountaineering history in a circular walk around Capel Curig

1 The path begins at a ladder stile by the war memorial on the A5 and climbs towards Y Pincin, a large, craggy outcrop cloaked in wood and bracken. Climb over another stile and keep to the left of the outcrop. Those who want to make their way to the top should do so from the northeast, where the gradients are easier. It's fun, and the views from the top are a major incentive, but take care as you go. You will need to retrace your steps to the main route.

2 Continue east through the woods and across some marshy ground, keeping well to the right of the great crags of Clogwyn-mawr. On reaching a couple of ladder stiles, ignore the footpath, which heads off to the right and back down to the road, but instead maintain your direction across the hillside.

3 Just beyond a footbridge over Nant y Geuallt, leave the main footpath and follow a less well-defined one, with marker posts, across marshy ground. This path veers southeast to cross another stream before coming to a prominent track.

4 Turn right along the track, go over a ladder stile, then at a four-way meeting of paths head towards the left. Follow the path as it descends into some woods. Take the right-hand fork going down to the road near the Ty'n y Coed Inn.

5 Turn left down the road, then right, along the lane over Pont-Cyfyng. Go right again beyond the bridge to follow a footpath that traces the Llugwy to another bridge opposite Cobdens Hotel. Don't cross this time, but scramble left over some rocks before continuing through the woods of Coed Bryn-engan, where the path soon becomes a wide track.

6 After passing the cottage of Bryn-engan, the track comes to the bridge at the head of the Mymbyr lakes. Turn right across the bridge, then go left along the road for a short way.

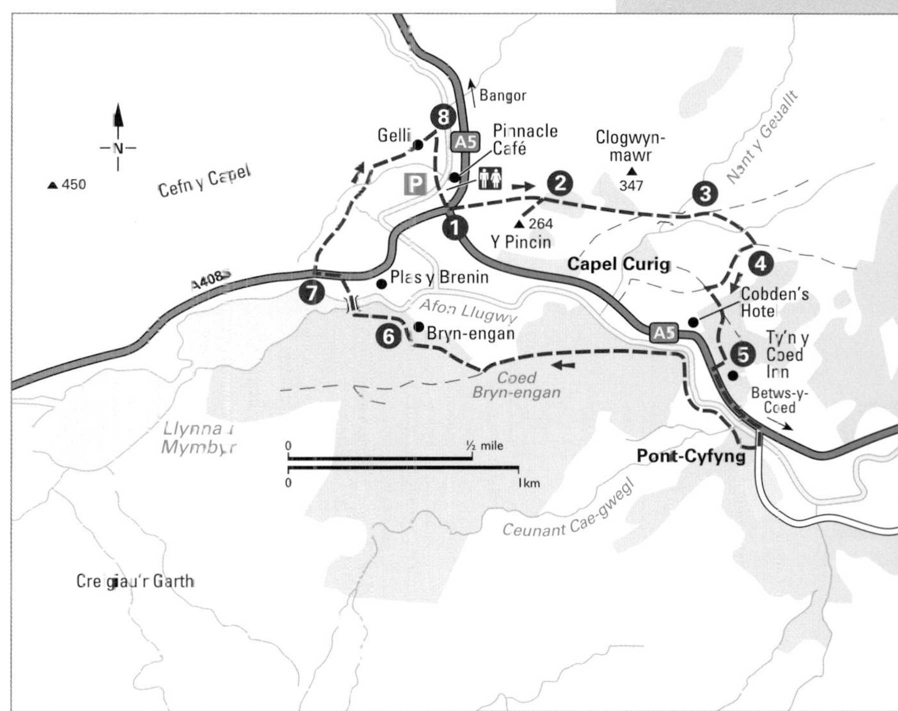

WHILE YOU'RE THERE

Visit the Motor Museum by the railway station at nearby Betws-y-Coed. Based on the Houghton family's collection of vintage vehicles, exhibits include a Bugatti, Aston Martin, Bentley, Bullnose Morris, Model T Ford and MGs. There's also a land speed record jet engine and plenty of motoring memorabilia.

WELSH FOXGLOVE

The foxglove is one of Wales' most common plants. It's big, it's bold, and between June and August this biennial will be boasting columns of vivid pink bell-like flowers. It is also poisonous, but its leaves were the original source for the heart drug, digitalis.

7 Cross the road to the next ladder stile and take a track straight ahead, soon swinging right to hug the foot of the southern Glyder slopes.

8 When you get beyond Gelli farm turn right to follow the cart track back to the car park.

Distance 4 miles (6.4km)

Minimum time 2hrs

Ascent/gradient 295ft (90m) ▲▲▲

Level of difficulty ●●● (doesn't include pinnacle scramble)

Paths Generally clear and surfaced but can be wet in places, 9 stiles

Landscape Woodland, wetland and high pasture

Suggested map OS Explorer OL17 Snowdon

Start/finish Grid reference: SJ 720582

Dog friendliness Dogs should be on lead

Parking Behind Joe Brown's shop at Capel Curig

Public toilets By Joe Brown's shop

1954 Wartime food rationing ends.

1954 Roger Bannister runs the first 4-minute mile.

1955 Ruth Ellis, convicted of the murder of her lover, is the last woman to be sentenced to death in Britain.

1955 ITV begins broadcasting.

1955 Mary Quant opens her first shop on the King's Road in Chelsea.

1957 The first space satellite, Sputnik I, is launched by the Soviet Union.

1958 An 8-mile (13km) stretch of motorway is opened on the Preston Bypass.

1959 The first hovercraft crosses the English Channel.

1960 The first episode of the television soap opera *Coronation Street* is broadcast.

1963 On 22 November US President John F. Kennedy is assassinated in Dallas, Texas. His death sends shockwaves around the world.

Dunaskin Iron Works and a Lost Village

A hill walk leads from a 19th-century industrial monument to a village abandoned in 1954

For just over one hundred years, from the mid-19th century until 1954, people lived in twin villages together known as 'the Hill' on the Knockkippen plateau. Built to house workers at iron ore mines associated with the Dunaskin Iron Works, the villages of Lethanhill and Burnfoothill survived the closure of the mines, the end of smelting at Dunaskin and two world wars. However, sanitation and overcrowding were a problem, and when the local authority decided to concentrate new building in nearby Patna and Dalmellington the quality of the new housing and the clean living space it offered was irresistible. Gradually the population dwindled on the Hill until the last man, James Stevenson, departed on 31 August 1954. All that remains today are the bare outlines of houses among the trees, the war memorial and a simple stone painted white with the poignant inscription 'Long live the Hill 1851–1954'.

Birth and Growth of the Ironworks

During the Industrial Revolution, iron was one of the great growth industries. In 1836 Henry Houldsworth, owner of a mill in Glasgow, created the Coltness Iron Works. Ten years later he and his son John brought the iron industry to the remote Doon Valley. Henry built his iron foundry on the site of Dunaskin farm. The area, although rich in iron, coal and water, was lacking in transport links. Everything for the foundry had to be brought in by train to Ayr and then by horse.

The principal local industries were agriculture and weaving: the population of the Upper Doon Valley was 250 at Patna and 800 in the parish of Dalmellington. Skilled workers were brought in to provide the core of the workforce for the ironworks. They were joined by local men, leaving agricultural work in hope of higher wages, as well as tin miners from Cornwall, itinerant English workers and Highlanders displaced by the Clearances. The company built Waterside village opposite the ironworks and the two villages on the Knockkippen plateau that became known as the Hill. Iron was produced here from 1848 until 1921, when the buildings became a brickworks and then a processing plant for the coal mines until the late 1970s.

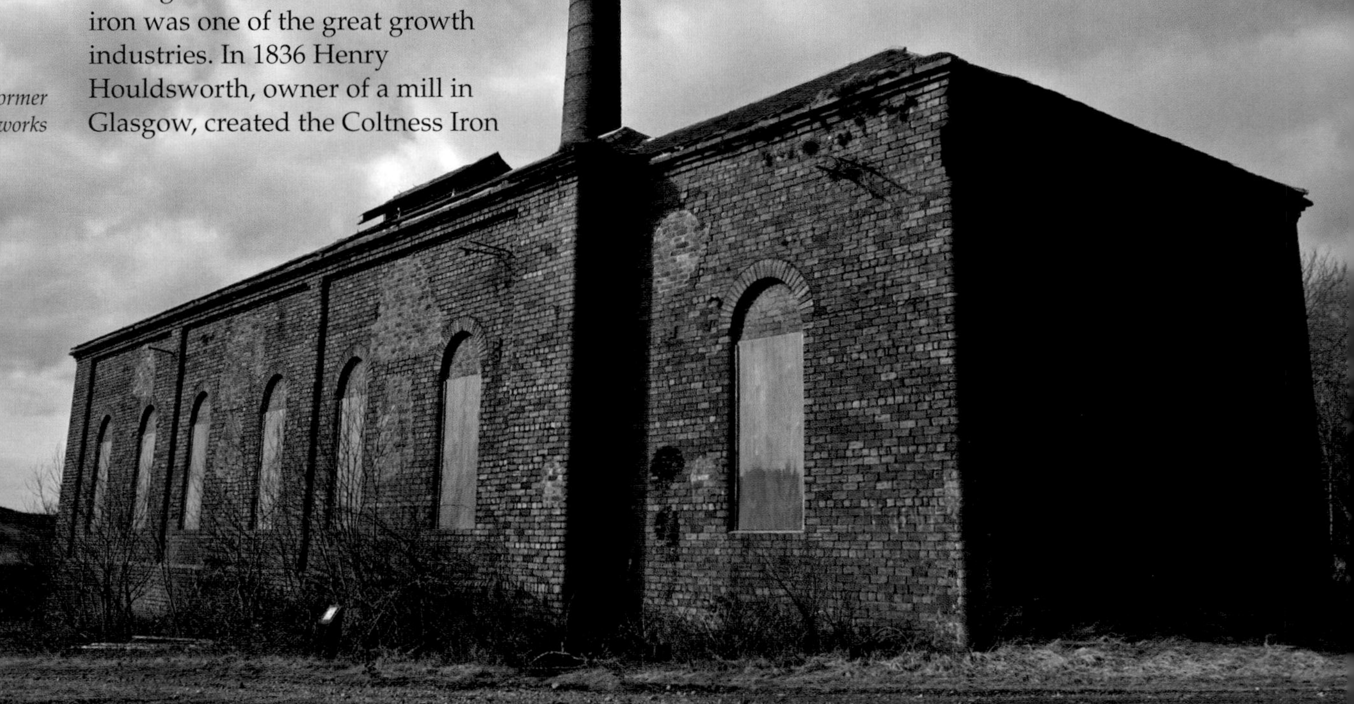

***Below:** The former Dunaskin ironworks*

Walk 102 Industrial heritage in Ayrshire

Explore a remote and largely deserted setting once thronged by iron workers

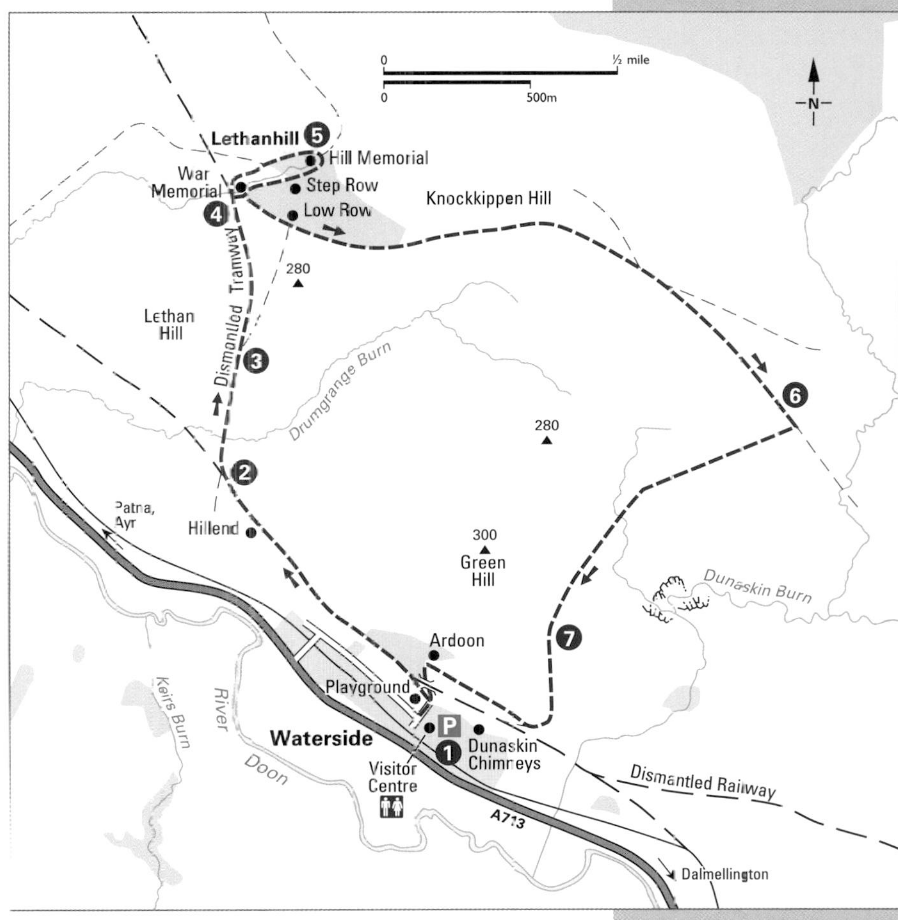

1 Turn right in front of the visitor centre and then follow the road towards the adventure playground. Once there, go uphill on a track to the right of the playground and pass through a kissing gate into woodland. Emerge at a T-junction opposite a railway bridge and turn left onto a grassy trail.

2 When you reach a metal gate across the trail, go through a small wooden one at its side. Climb over the next gate, turn right and head uphill following the line of a disused tramway, between the ends of an old bridge. This is the trackbed of the former horse-drawn tramway, which was used in order to bring the iron ore down from the plateau.

3 At the top of the hill, when the path divides, keep left and follow the path as it goes through two short sections of wall. The ground to your right, in front of the conifer plantation, was once the village football field. Where the path is blocked by a fence, turn right and then go left to walk through a gate and afterwards right on to a metalled lane.

4 Head along here, past the remains of the miners' houses of Step Row, which are clearly visible amongst the trees. A stone memorial to the Hill stands near the site of the former village store. To the right of this, and now within the wood, is the former village square and the remains of more houses.

5 From the stone memorial turn back towards the war memorial, then return to the gate at the corner of the wood and continue along the track beside the wood. In the trees are the remains of Low Row. Go through another gate and continue along the former railway. When it forks, keep right.

6 Continue until the route ahead is blocked by sheets of corrugated iron. Cross the wall and turn right, heading downhill to pick up a faint path. Continue on this to reach a cluster of trees beside a ruined building.

7 Head down from here towards the right of a row of cottages. Go through a gate, turn right then right again at a fork to reach Ardoon. Go past the house, turn left onto a footpath and follow it downhill and under a small, disused railway bridge. Cross the track and carry on, heading back downhill on the footpath which leads back to the Visitor Centre.

Distance 4 miles (6.4km)

Minimum time 3hrs

Ascent/gradient 492ft (150m) ▲▲▲

Level of difficulty ●●●

Paths Old rail and tram beds and rough hillside

Landscape Hill, moorland and industrial buildings

Suggested map OS Explorer 327 Cumnock & Dalmellington

Start/finish Grid reference: NX 440084

Dog friendliness Keep on lead near sheep and at lambing time

Parking Dunaskin Open Air Museum

Public toilets At Visitor Centre

WHILE YOU'RE THERE

Don't miss a visit to one of Scotland's most fascinating railway museums. Just along the road, on the north edge of Dalmellington, is the Scottish Industrial Railway Centre, operated by enthusiasts from the Ayrshire Rail Preservation Group. This is as much part of the local story as the Dunaskin ironworks, and every Sunday in July and August the centre offers trips on a working steam train.

WHAT TO LOOK OUT FOR

The foundations of the former church and schoolhouse can be seen on the ground behind the war memorial. The church was sold to a local silver band and was rebuilt in Dalmellington. Look out also in the remains of the houses of Low Row for floral tributes hung on the trees by former residents who still walk here on a regular basis and are touched by a nostalgia for the old days.

1964 Nelson Mandela, leader of the anti-apartheid struggle in South Africa, is sentenced to life imprisonment for treason.

1964 An audience of 73 million Americans tune in to watch The Beatles on the Ed Sullivan Show.

1964 Winston Churchill retires from politics.

1966 England beat West Germany 4-2 after extra time to win the football World Cup.

1968 American civil liberties leader Martin Luther King Jr is assassinated in Memphis, Tennessee.

1969 On 20 July American astronaut Neil Armstrong is the first man to step on the Moon.

1969 The Concorde supersonic airliner, developed by British and French engineers, makes its first flight.

1971 British currency is decimalised.

1972 A Catholic march ends in bloodshed in Londonderry, Northern Ireland, when paratroopers kill 13 civilians.

Glenkiln's Outdoor Sculptures

An exhilarating tour shows the works of Henry Moore, Epstein and Rodin in a unique countryside setting

During the mid-1950s a Dumfriesshire landowner with a penchant for sculpture acquired a copy of Auguste Rodin's 'John the Baptist' from the Musée Rodin in Paris. The landowner, Tony Keswick, did not hide it away in a vault or even in a gallery. He placed it in open countryside, on his hill farm of Glenkiln.

Keswick had been given the farm by his father in 1924 as a 21st birthday present, but he had rarely visited it until the 1950s. That first Rodin was the start of an amazing art collection. On a visit to the studio of Henry Moore, he recognised that Moore's 'Standing Figure' would be ideal placed on a large flat boulder that stood by the roadside near the farm. This was followed by Moore's 'King and Queen': Keswick tried a number of sites around his land before placing it on a hillside overlooking the reservoir.

Right: *Henry Moore's 'King and Queen' sculpture of 1952–3*

Below: *Auguste Rodin's 'John the Baptist' was the start of a unique display*

Hard Times

Jacob Epstein's 'Visitation' is in the collection of the Tate Gallery in London. Keswick obtained Epstein's own copy purely by chance. He was with the artist when a group of workmen arrived to cart the work off to melt it down. Epstein, although famous, was so hard up that he was selling some of his work for scrap to pay the foundry bill for a bust of Winston Churchill he was working on. Keswick was appalled and promptly bought the statue. It depicts the Virgin Mary with folded hands, head slightly bowed and an expression of utmost serenity on her face. At Glenkiln, she is located amid Scots pine within the tumbledown walls of a long-abandoned sheep fold. To come upon this figure is one of the magical moments of Glenkiln – particularly on a misty winter's day.

Glenkiln has been a popular attraction since Tony Keswick placed his first sculpture out of doors. He encouraged people to come and see the collection, and today it remains as a tribute not just to the artists but to a remarkable man who saw sculpture as a complement to nature.

Walk 103 Remarkable gift of an art-loving landowner

Gaze on great works of art specially chosen and set against the breathtaking backdrop of beautiful Dumfries & Galloway

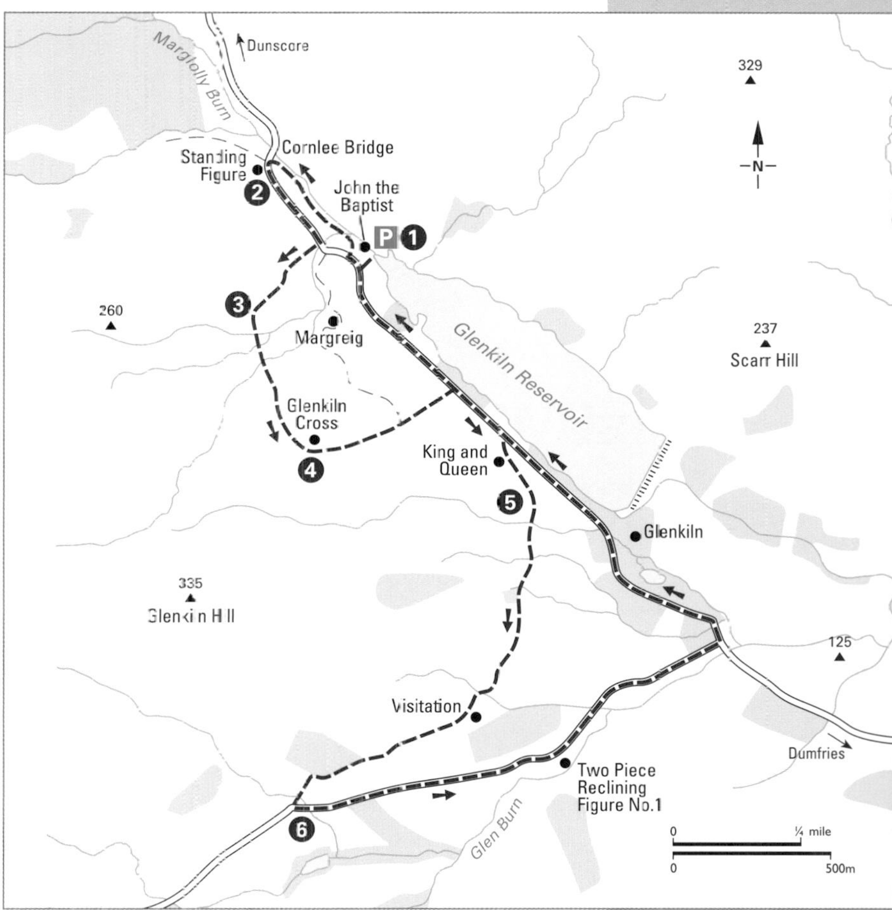

1 From the car park in front of the statue 'John the Baptist', return to the main road and turn right. Cross a cattle grid, then turn right and go past the statue to the Marglolly Burn. Turn left and walk along the bank towards Cornlee Bridge. Just before the bridge turn left and head back to the road. Henry Moore's 'Standing Figure' is before you at the junction with a farm road.

2 Turn left and head back along the main road. Just before the entrance to Margreig Farm on the right is a muddy track running across the field to a gate in the dry-stone wall. Head up and through the gate then keep straight ahead, uphill and towards a telephone pole. At the pole veer left and follow the track uphill. 'The Glenkiln Cross' should now be visible in front of you.

3 There are several footpaths and tracks available here. Take the one that is closest to a large tree in front of you. Cross over a burn at the tree and then take the path that skirts to the left of it. Veer right and then head for the high ground. Once the cross comes into view again, head directly towards it.

4 From the cross turn to face Glenkiln Reservoir and then head downhill towards a telephone pole. Go through a gate in the fence at the bottom of the hill and then turn right onto the road. After a short distance along here a farm track leads uphill to the right. Go through a gate and onto it. To your right on the hillside is Henry Moore's 'King and Queen'.

5 Continue on this track. Go through a gate, pass a small wooded area on your right and then bare hillside until you spot a small stand of Scots pine on the left. Leave the road at this point and continue to the trees and Epstein's 'Visitation'. Return to the road and then continue to the end where you go through a gate, cross over a bridge then turn left on to the road.

6 Go downhill on this road for 0.5 mile (800m), crossing a cattle grid. When you reach the point just before the end of the conifer plantation on the left, look out for Moore's 'Two Piece Reclining Figure No. 1' on your right. Follow the road all the way downhill from here, then turn left at the junction and afterwards continue on this road until you reach the car park.

WHAT TO LOOK OUT FOR

It's easy to miss, but just after going through the gate on the farm track past 'King and Queen', look out for a small block of Dumfriesshire sandstone on the right. It's weathered and a little faded but you can still make out the inscription. On one side is 'Glenkiln' and on the other 'Henry Moore 1898–1986'. This was Tony Keswick's personal memorial to his favourite sculptor.

ROBERT BURNS COUNTRY

Enjoy a visit to Ellisland, the Dumfriesshire farm where Robert Burns wrote 'Tam O' Shanter', and explore the nearby countryside that inspired many of his well loved nature poems. Situated on the A76, a few miles north of Dumfries, this is where Burns came with his bride, Jean Armour, to start a new life as a farmer. Unfortunately the land was poor, the venture failed and the poet moved to Dumfries and life as an exciseman. You can take a guided tour of the farmhouse and visit the associated museum.

Distance 4 miles (6.4km)

Minimum time 2hrs 30min

Ascent/gradient 312ft (95m) ▲▲▲

Level of difficulty ●●●

Paths Country roads, farm tracks, open hillside

Landscape Sculptures, hills, woodland and reservoir

Suggested map OS Explorer 321 Nithsdale & Dumfries

Start/finish Grid reference: NX 839784

Dog friendliness Keep on lead on farmland, particularly at lambing time

Parking Car park in front of statue of John the Baptist

Public toilets None on route or near by

1972 John Betjeman becomes the Poet Laureate.

1973 Britain enters the Common Market under Conservative prime minister Edward Heath.

1973 A ceasefire is declared in the Vietnam war between South Vietnam and its American allies and North Vietnam, backed by Communist states.

1974 In the US, President Nixon resigns amid the Watergate political scandal.

1975 North Sea oil is discovered, and the first supplies piped ashore.

1979 Margaret Thatcher, leader of the Conservative Party, is elected to serve as the first female prime minister. Her policies and imposing personality inspire both fervent devotion and fierce hostility.

1980 The murder of former Beatle John Lennon in New York provokes huge public mourning.

1981 The Humber Bridge, stretching 1440m (4624ft), is first opened to traffic.

How Grey was My Valley

An intriguing walk leads through 1,500 years of history in the footsteps of monks and merchants – and visits the site of Britain's steepest railway

On an industrial site in the Greenfield Valley the steepest conventional passenger railway in Britain ran a service for 42 years, from 1912 until it was closed down in 1954. The railway, which had a gradient of 1 in 27, had been established in 1869, and the passenger service – from Greenfield to Holywell – was introduced in 1912. Today the Greenfield site is home to a fascinating heritage park, but in the 17th and 18th centuries industrial buildings occupied the whole valley. Tall brick chimneys, mill pools, reservoirs and waterwheels were all around, and steam from those chimneys billowed up through the trees as the valley was put to work.

Thomas Williams of the Parys Mine Company established a rolling mill and the Abbey Wire Mill here, while in the Battery Works up the hill the workforce hammered out brass pots and pans that were used for the slave trade. Ships would leave Liverpool laden with brassware for West Africa, where they would load up with slaves for the Caribbean, returning to Liverpool with sugar, tobacco and cotton.

However, in the 20th century the mills shut down one by one. Some were demolished, others were left to crumble just like the valley's first settlement, Basingwerk Abbey. Now in the early 21th century, relics of the old industries sit among pleasant gardens.

Shrine and Abbey

A good head of water served the Greenfield Valley well over the centuries, and that water gushes out from a spring high on the limestone hillsides beneath Holywell. According to tradition St Winefride's Well dates back to the 7th century after St Beuno set up a church here. His daughter Winefride taught in the convent and caught the eye of Caradog, the local chieftain. After being spurned by the young nun, Caradog drew his sword and cut off her head. Immediately, a spring emerged where her head hit the ground. Pilgrims flocked to this 'Lourdes of Wales' to take the healing waters. In 1499 Margaret, the Countess of Derby and mother of Henry VII, financed the building of an ornate chapel around the well. In the 12th century, the Savignac Order, which was later to be combined with the Cistercians, set up Basingwerk Abbey at the bottom of the hill. The abbey has been in ruins since the Dissolution of the Monasteries, but a couple of fine sandstone arches remain.

Left: *Sandstone ruins of Basingwerk Abbey*

Below: *Farm machinery in the Greenfield Valley Heritage Park site*

Walk 104 Welsh valley that was home to a thriving industry powered by water

Explore a now quiet corner of North Wales that was buzzing with industry in the 1700s

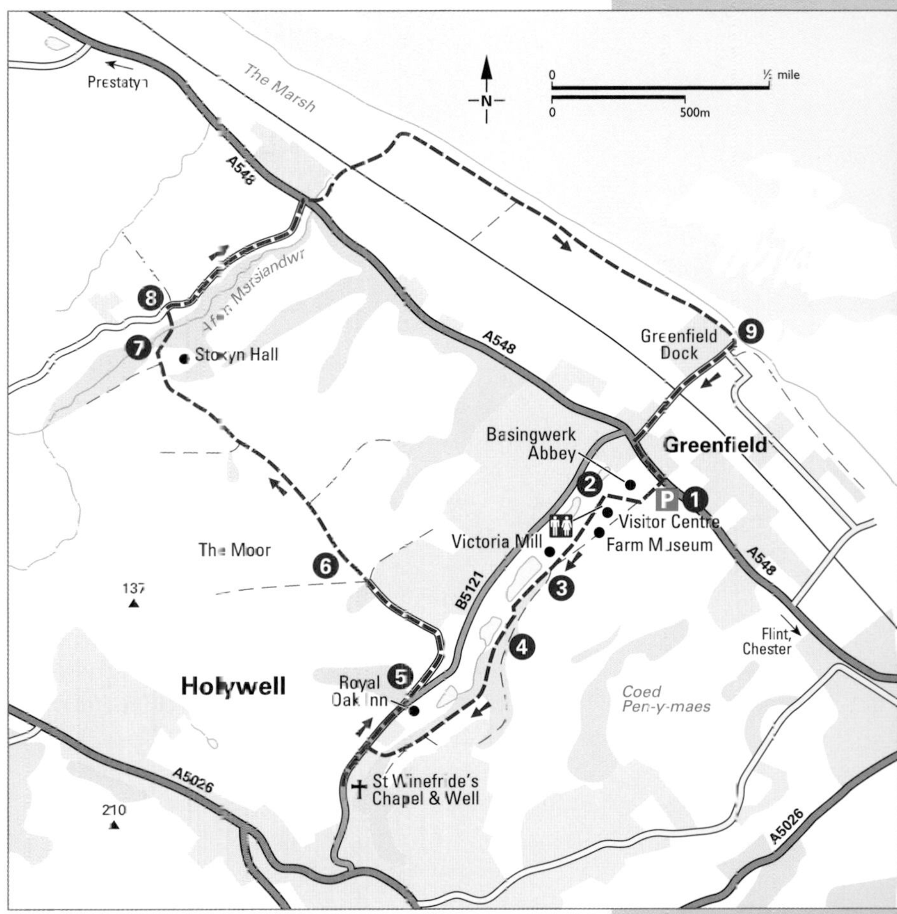

1 Take the footpath that emerges from the back of the car park on the left-hand side and begin the walk by following it around the abbey.

2 Turn left between the Visitor Centre and the old schoolhouse on a track that passes Abbey Farm. Take the left fork by the brick walls of Abbey Wire Mill, following the sign to the Fishing Pool, a lily covered pond.

3 Beyond Victoria Mill take the lower right-hand fork, then bear right past some fixed iron gates to pass the crumbling remains of Meadow Mill. Beyond the mill turn left up some steps, climbing up by a weir and back onto the main track.

4 Turn right along the lower track, eventually passing above Hall's soft drinks factory. Beyond a brick chimney, fork off right down to a kissing gate and wind out to the road. Turn left along the road as far as St Winefride's Chapel and Well. When you've viewed these, go back down the road to the Royal Oak Inn.

5 Climb the lane, called Green Bank, that begins from the opposite side of the road. Beyond the houses bear off right along a waymarked track. Keep ahead past the entrance to a small housing estate on a sunken, hedged path. Enter a field over a stile at the top.

6 Head out to the distant right corner and continue at the edge of the next field. Maintain your north-westerly direction to a stile and keep going to another, part-way down the boundary. Walk on with a hedge on your right, exiting over a stile onto a track.

7 Leave the cart track where it swings round to the right for a second time, and follow a signed footpath that heads across a meadow and then through trees to the banks of Afon Marsiandwr. After crossing the stream follow the path as it climbs out of the woods and crosses a field to reach a country lane.

8 Turn right along the lane, following it down to reach the coast road (A548). Cross the busy road with care. The continuing footpath to the seashore lies immediately opposite you, over a step stile. Cross a field and then a railway track, again with care as trains are not infrequent, and continue walking until you get to the inner flood embankments where you turn right.

9 The footpath comes out by Greenfield Dock. Turn right here along the lane back into Greenfield. Turn left to return to the car park.

DOCK AND FARM MUSEUM

The Greenfield Dock is quiet these days, but at one time there were sailings from here to Liverpool and ferries that operated to the Wirral. When you're walking along the coast you'll see a shallow basin that was formerly a flushing lagoon: here water was flushed out into the docks to remove mud and silt.

The Greenfield Valley Museum and Farm has an exhibition of farming through the ages, with a collection of machinery from the local area displayed in buildings that are about 300 years old. The museum is dedicated to locally born explorer Thomas Pennant, who was a descendant of one of the abbots of Basingwerk.

Distance 5 miles (8km)

Minimum time 3hrs

Ascent/gradient 558ft (170m) ▲▲▲

Level of difficulty ●●●

Paths Woodland paths and tracks, lanes, field paths and coastal embankment, 9 stiles

Landscape Wooded former industrial valley, pastoral hillside and coast

Suggested map OS Explorer 265 Clwydian Range

Start/finish Grid reference: SJ 197775

Dog friendliness Dogs should be on lead

Parking Just off A548 at Greenfield

Public toilets By the Visitor Centre

1981 The first London Marathon takes place.

1981 Prince Charles marries Lady Diana Spencer at St Paul's Cathedral on 29 July.

1982 The Falklands War breaks out between Britain and Argentina. Argentine troops surrender on 14 June, but 255 British and 652 Argentinean lives are lost.

1984–85 A fund-raising drive is launched by singer Bob Geldof to provide aid to starving Ethiopians. The Band Aid record is followed by a Live Aid concert.

1984–85 Pit closures brings about the miners' strike.

1987 In October gale-force winds hit southern Britain, causing chaos.

1988 A Pan Am aircraft explodes over Lockerbie, Scotland, killing more than 300 people.

1989 The Berlin Wall between East and West Germany comes down, 40 years after its construction.

1990 Nelson Mandela, leader of the African National Congress, is released from prison.

Milton Keynes, City of the Future?

An intriguing walk with a strong architectural theme reveals how a brand-new city, begun in 1967, has been shaped and styled

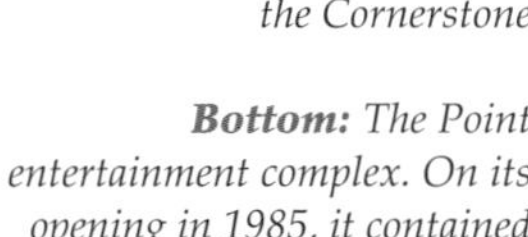

Below: *The Church of Christ the Cornerstone*

Bottom: *The Point entertainment complex. On its opening in 1985, it contained the UK's first multiplex cinema*

Much has happened to Milton Keynes since 1967 when an area of almost 22,000 acres (8,910ha) was designated for the construction of a new city. But why Milton Keynes? The planners and architects of the day considered its location at the heart of England to be just about perfect. Only an hour from London by car on the new M1 motorway and easily accessible by train, the city's communication links were seen as ideal.

Initially it was envisaged that Milton Keynes would consist of high-density settlements connected by monorail to a commercial centre – an innovative move and a far cry from the old concept of garden suburbs as developed by the London planners. However, the monorail system was eventually shelved in favour of a dispersed network of housing within a grid pattern of roads. With its tree-lined boulevards, green squares and stylish office buildings, it is hard not to be impressed by Milton Keynes. It may get a bad press in some quarters, and there are those who feel it has too strong an American influence, but the city has been designed with convenience, mobility and modern living in mind. The task of housing a growing British population remains a priority and, in the late 20th and early 21st century, attention is focused on Milton Keynes as a place to live and work.

A Long History

People first settled in this region in *c*.2000 BC. The earliest known house in the area dates back to the late Bronze Age or early Iron Age. Later the Romans occupied this part of the country, their farms and rural settlements served by two towns – Lactodorum (modern Towcester, Northamptonshire) and Magiovinium (at Fenny Stratford, now part of Milton Keynes). Nearby ran Watling Street, now the A5, linking London, the West Midlands and North Wales.

During the 19th century the Milton Keynes area of Buckinghamshire began to expand, largely due to the dawning of the railway era that brought industrial prosperity to places like Newport Pagnell and Wolverton. The opening of the M1 in 1959 sealed the area's future.

Walk 105 From 'the Point' to the Cornerstone

Judge for yourself the quality of planning and new buildings in Milton Keynes

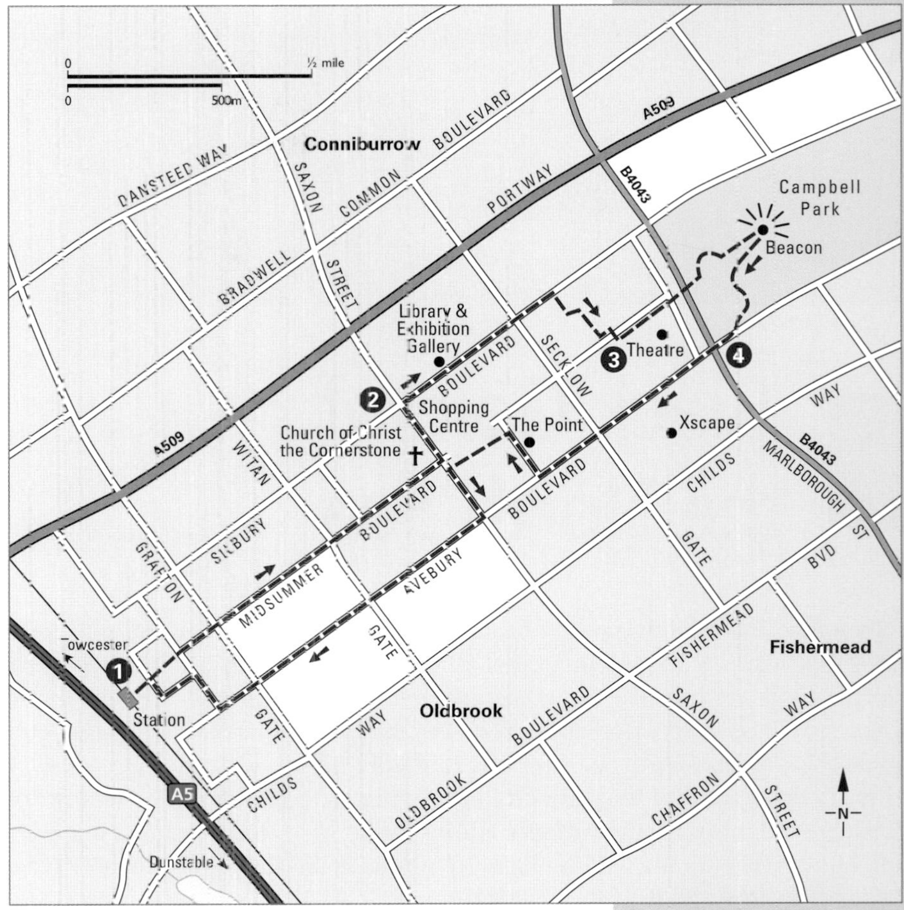

1 With your back to the station, aim slightly left, line up with a row of flag-poles and make for two underpasses. Keep ahead along Midsummer Boulevard, passing the sculpture on the left. Make for the next subway and cross Witan Gate and Upper 5th Street. Swing left just before the next subway to visit the domed Church of Christ the Cornerstone. Keep the church on your left and continue to Silbury Boulevard, passing under the subway ahead.

2 Turn right through a subway and pass Milton Keynes Library and Exhibition Gallery. Pass North 9th Street and a statue of the Lloyds black horse at Lloyds Court. Swing right and pass under the road to approach the shopping centre at Deer Walk. Don't enter the complex here, but instead turn left and walk along to the next entrance, numbered 11, at Eagle Walk. Go straight through, pass a map of the shopping centre and emerge at Entrance 12, Midsummer Boulevard.

3 Turn left to Field Walk and turn right here to cross the boulevard. Bear left to reach the Tourist Information Centre, Milton Keynes Theatre and the city's gallery. Continue ahead under the subway and cross the footbridge into Campbell Park. Skirt the round pond and make for the beacon that represents the highest point in the park. As you approach it, turn sharp right and follow the path as it snakes down through the park. Roughly 30yds (27m) before a circular seat bear sharp right to join a grassy path alongside a fence. Make for a second kissing gate and turn right. Walk along to the next path junction, with a kissing gate on the right. Turn left here, back towards the centre of Milton Keynes. Keep to the left to join a wide concrete ride and follow the waymarked city centre route.

4 Turn right to cross the road bridge to Bankfield roundabout and go along Avebury Boulevard. Cross Secklow Gate and Lower 10th Street, and turn right into Lower 9th Street. Pass the Point and bear left into Midsummer Place shopping centre. Cross the concourse and pass the police station. The Church of Christ the Cornerstone can be seen from here. Turn left towards Debenham's and Avebury Boulevard, turning right to the underpass. Walk down to Grafton Gate, veer right before it and head for Midsummer Boulevard. Go through the underpasses and return to the railway station at the start.

WHAT TO LOOK OUT FOR

Milton Keynes likes to compete at the cutting edge of modern architecture. Equip yourself with information leaflets about the city and head off in search of a host of unusual buildings and eye-catching sculptures. One building to look out for is the Point, which opened in 1985, and takes the form of a striking 70ft (21m) high, mirror-sided ziggurat (a rectangular stepped tower) upon which a red tubular pyramid structure has been superimposed. The Church of Christ the Cornerstone was the first purpose-built ecumenical city-centre church in Britain. The church is 101ft (31m) high, to the top of the lantern, while the cross rises a further 18ft (5m), making it the highest point in the city. Surrounding the church is a cloister and adjacent is the Guildhall, a meeting place for business and commerce in Milton Keynes. The Milton Keynes Theatre opened in 1999 after a 25-year campaign to establish a venue for plays in the town; it has many state-of-the-art features including a ceiling that can be raised or lowered to create a larger or smaller auditorium. The adjacent MK Gallery is the city's art gallery.

Distance 3.5 miles (5.7km)

Minimum time 2hrs

Ascent/gradient Negligible ▲▲▲

Level of difficulty ●●●

Paths Paved walkways, boulevards and park paths

Landscape City centre and park

Suggested map OS Explorer 192 Milton Keynes & Buckingham, or street map from Tourist Information

Start/finish Grid reference: SP 842380

Dog friendliness Probably not most dogs' idea of fun

Parking Car park at Milton Keynes Station

Public toilets Milton Keynes Station and shopping centres

1991 On 16 January Allied forces launch Operation Desert Storm against Iraq. A ceasefire is called by President Bush on 27 February.

1991 The USSR is replaced by the Commonwealth of Independent States.

1991 The Channel Tunnel opens

1997 Tony Blair is elected prime minister, leader of the first Labour government in a generation.

1997 J.K. Rowling's first novel, *Harry Potter and the Philosopher's Stone*, is published.

1997 Diana, Princess of Wales dies in a car accident in Paris, and Britain enters a period of mourning.

1998–2001 The Eden Project eco visitor attraction is built in a disused China clay pit in Cornwall.

1999 Devolution of the Scottish and Welsh parliaments takes place.

2000 The Millennium Dome and the London Eye open, part of huge celebrations for the millennium.

Black Gold of the North Sea

A walk in the old fishing port reveals the riches – and tragedy – brought to Aberdeen by North Sea Oil

The first major oil find in the British sector of the North Sea was in November 1970 in the Forties field, 110 miles (177km) east of Aberdeen. Geologists had speculated about the existence of oil and gas in the North Sea from the mid-20th century onwards, but the difficulty of tapping its deep and inhospitable waters had put them off. However, with the Middle Eastern oil sheiks becoming more aware of the political power of their oil reserves and government threats of rationing, the industry began to consider the North Sea as a viable source of oil: exploration commenced in the 1960s.

By late 1975, after years of intense construction, the hundreds of miles of pipes, massive oilshore rigs, supply ships, helicopters and an army of oil workers were all finally in place. In Aberdeen, at British Petroleum's headquarters, Queen Elizabeth II pressed the button that would set the whole operation moving. Oil flowed from the rig directly to the refinery at far-away Grangemouth. While many ports have suffered decline, Aberdeen remains busy due to the oil trade. The influx of people connected with the industry and a subsequent rise in property prices have brought prosperity.

Piper Alpha Tragedy

Yet this oil prosperity came at a cost – a fact that was brutally brought home on 6 July 1988. On that terrible night a huge fire lit the sky as the Piper Alpha oil platform, 120 miles (193km) offshore, exploded. Helicopters flew all night bringing the dead and injured to Aberdeen. In all 167 people died; many of the survivors live with the scars of that night and the horrific memories of escaping the burning rig.

A memorial to the dead stands in Hazlehead Park, Aberdeen. The subsequent inquiry revealed that safety regulations had been ignored. The industry learned a bitter lesson, and the rigs are now safer places to work. The industry still supports about 47,000 jobs locally, and known reserves are such that oil will continue to flow for many decades yet.

History of a Fishing Port

Aberdeen was a major maritime centre throughout the 19th century, starting when a group of entrepreneurs purchased a paddle tug and launched it as the first steam-powered trawler. The steam trawling industry expanded and by 1933 Aberdeen was Scotland's top fishing port, employing nearly 3,000 men with 300 vessels sailing from its harbour.

By the time oil was coming on stream, much of the massive trawling fleet had relocated to Peterhead. An early morning visit to the fish market will verify that Aberdeen still brings in substantial catches, but the tugs, safety vessels and supply ships for the offshore rigs packed into the harbour far outnumber the trawlers.

Below: *Oil makes the wheels turn in Aberdeen*

Bottom: *A supply vessel at a North Sea rig, at the source of the 'Black Gold'*

Walk 106 Fishing port where oil became the most valuable catch

Admire fine buildings from Aberdeen's past alongside evidence of the city's continuing prosperity, driven by the oil industry

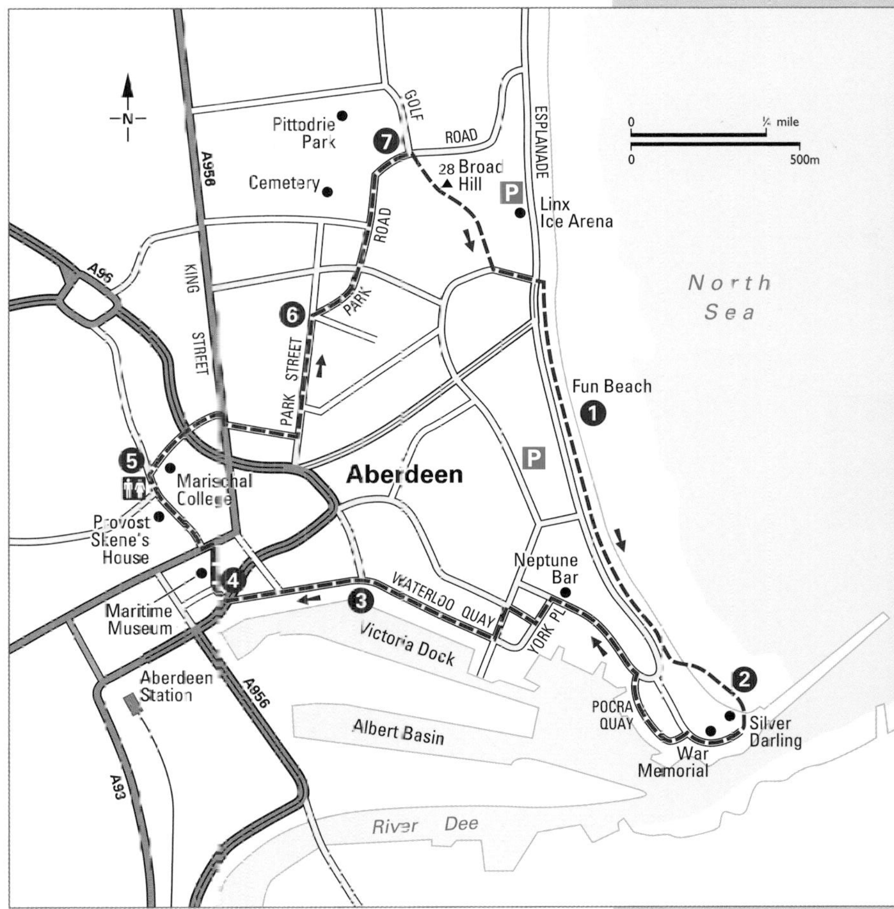

1 From your parking place, head southwards on the promenade, walking beside the shore with the sea on your left. Go down the slipway onto the beach for a short distance to wooden steps on the right and leave the beach to enter a children's play area. (But if the tide is high at the slipway: clamber over the sea wall on your right, and pass along a row of fishermen's cottages.)

2 Walk past the Silver Darling restaurant and into the harbour area. Continue past the war memorial, keeping the blue storage tanks to your left, and along Pocra Quay as it bends right. Turn left into York Street and then, at the Neptune bar, turn left into York Place. Take the first right, the first left and second right to emerge on Waterloo Quay.

3 Where Waterloo Quay becomes Commerce Street turn left into Regent Quay and then at the T-junction cross the dual carriageway at pedestrian lights. Turn left and then first right to reach Aberdeen Maritime Museum and John Ross's House. John Ross was Provost of Aberdeen between 1710 and 1711. If you have time, visit the Maritime Museum.

4 From here head along Exchequer Row and look to turn left into Union Street. Once in Union Street, turn right almost straight away into Broad Street, where you will find Provost Skene's House on the left, reached by passing underneath an office block.

5 Continue ahead past Marischal College, turn right into Littlejohn Street and then cross North Street. At the end of Meal Market Street, turn right into King Street and then go left into Frederick Street. At the junction with Park Street turn left and keep walking ahead until the road crosses a railway.

6 Shortly after the crossing is a roundabout. Head slightly right along Park Road. Follow the road through the Trinity Cemetery and towards Pittodrie Park, which is the home of Aberdeen Football Club, to the junction with Golf Road.

7 At the junction with Golf Road, turn up right, on the well-made path over Broad Hill. There are wide views of the sea and Aberdeen. At the path end, turn left to a roundabout with subtropical plants on the Esplanade. The shoreline promenade leads back to your car.

WHAT TO LOOK OUT FOR

Provost Skene's House, on Broad Street, is the oldest private dwelling in Aberdeen, dating from *c.*1545. It was the home of Provost George Skene from 1676 to 1685, and is preserved almost unchanged as a 17th-century burgher's residence.

You will see plenty of lichens on this walk, particularly on the last section where they hang from the branches of mature birch trees. Lichens are sensitive to pollution and don't grow in places where the air is contaminated. This makes them a useful 'indicator species', meaning that their presence or absence tells you something about the environment. The healthy lichens here are a good sign that the air is particularly clear and clean.

Distance 3.75 miles (6km)

Minimum time 2hrs

Ascent/gradient Negligible ▲▲▲

Level of difficulty ●●●

Paths Mainly pavements; along beach (under water at high tide)

Landscape Old fishing port

Suggested map OS Explorer 406 Aberdeen & Banchory

Start/finish Grid reference: NJ 954067

Dog friendliness Keep on lead

Parking Esplanade at Fun Beach or Linx Ice Arena

Public toilets Upperkirkgate, opposite Marischal College

2001 On 11 September a major terrorist attack hits New York City. Islamic terrorist organisation Al Qaeda claims responsibility. In response the US launches the 'War on Terror' and invades Afghanistan, believed to be one of Al Qaeda's bases.

2003–10 Troops from the US and Britain lead a multinational force in the Iraq War.

2005 On 7 July terrorist suicide bombers attack London: 56 people are killed and hundreds injured.

2007 A banking crisis begins, and appears to threaten global economic meltdown.

2008 Democrat Barack Obama is elected the first African American president of the US.

2010 With no party holding a majority after the general election, the Conservatives and Liberal Democrats form a coalition government and David Cameron becomes prime minister.

2011 On 29 April Prince William of Wales, eldest son of Prince Charles and Princess Diana, marries Kate Middleton in Westminster Abbey.

Reinventing the Wheel at Falkirk

A stroll along Scotland's old canal system leads to a strikingly modern 21st-century wheel

Above: *Opened in 2002, the Falkirk Wheel has become an icon of modern Scotland, and since 2007 has featured on Bank of Scotland £50 notes*

The Falkirk Wheel is the world's first rotating boat lift. It was designed in order to reconnect the Forth and Clyde and Union canals, which stretch across the central belt of Scotland, and so restore a centuries-old link between Glasgow and Edinburgh. Made of sharply glinting steel, the Wheel is 115ft (35m) high and lifts boats from one canal to the other. It can carry eight boats at a time and lift loads of 600 tonnes.

Cruising the Canals

The Forth and Clyde Canal, which ran from Grangemouth to Glasgow, was completed in 1790 and made a great difference to the Scottish economy. It opened up a lucrative trading route to America – raw materials could now easily be transported east, while finished products could be shipped west. The canal was so successful that merchants in Edinburgh built another waterway, running from Edinburgh to Falkirk. Work on the Union Canal began in 1818 and a flight of locks was built to link it to the Forth and Clyde Canal.

The canals were used to transport people as well as goods. Many preferred to travel by barge rather than by stage coach, as the journey was less bumpy and decidedly warmer. Night boats even had dining rooms and gaming tables. By 1835 more than 127,000 people were travelling on the canal each year. Then the canals lost out to the railways from the mid-19th century onwards.

Canals clung to life until the 1960s, when they were finally broken up by the expanding network of roads. However, they are a key part of Scotland's industrial heritage and are being restored. The Falkirk Wheel replaces the original flight of locks linking the two canals, which had been removed in the 1930s. It is as much a work of art as an engineering masterpiece.

Walk 107 Futuristic structure that connects two historic canals

Pass a monument to a 13th-century battle and walk a stretch of Roman wall on the way to a superbly efficient modern machine

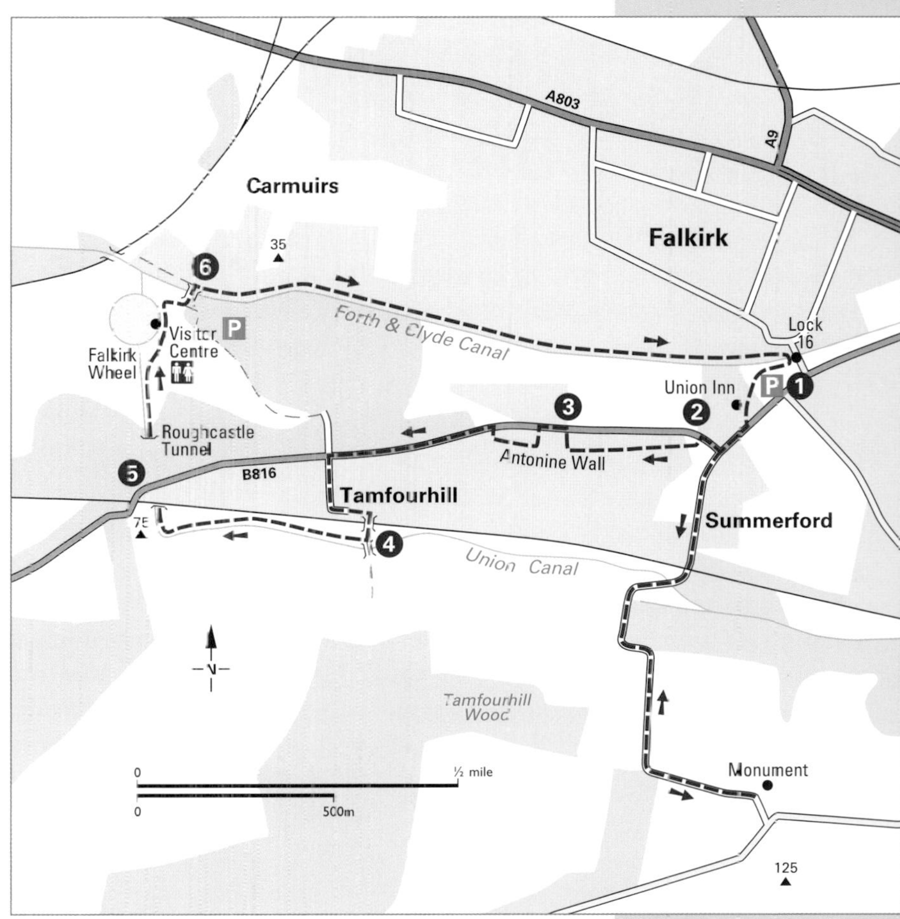

1 Start at the Union Inn by Lock 16. This was once one of the best known pubs in Scotland and catered for passengers on the canal. Turn right now, away from the canal, then go right heading along the road. Turn right along Tamfourhill Road and go through the kissing gate on the left-hand side of the road. Alternatively, don't turn up Tamfourhill Road yet, but continue walking uphill to go under the viaduct. Keep walking all the way up until you come to a monument on the left. This commemorates the Battle of Falkirk of 1298, in which William Wallace was beaten by King Edward I of England's troops. Retrace your steps, going under the viaduct, turning left into Tamfourhill Road, and then heading left through the kissing gate on the left-hand side of the road.

2 This takes you to a section of the Roman Antonine Wall – there's a deep ditch and a rampart behind it. Walk along here, going parallel with Tamfourhill Road. When you reach the point where you can go no further, climb up the bank on the right-hand side and go down the steps to join the road by a kissing gate.

3 Go left to continue along the road – you will soon see another kissing gate on the left leading you to another, much shorter, section of the wall. Leave the wall, rejoin the road and maintain direction to reach a mini-roundabout. Turn left here, along Maryfield Place. When you reach the end, join the public footpath signed to the canal tow path and woodland walks. Follow this track as it winds up and over the railway bridge, then on to reach the Union Canal.

4 Don't cross the canal but turn right and walk along the tow path. This is now a long straight stretch, which is popular with local joggers. Eventually you will reach Roughcastle Tunnel – but remember that the tunnel currently closes at 6pm each evening to protect the Wheel from the risk of vandalism.

5 Walk through the tunnel – it is bright and clean and dry. This will bring you out to the new Falkirk Wheel (and yet another section of the Antonine Wall). You can walk on as far as the Wheel, then walk down to the Visitor Centre at the bottom. Bear right from here to cross the little bridge over the Forth and Clyde Canal.

6 Turn right now and walk along the tow path. Several dog walkers and cyclists tend to come along here – so take care if you are walking with a dog. Keep walking until you come back to Lock 16, then turn right and cross the canal again in order to return to the start of the walk at the Union Inn.

ANTONINE WALL

You pass sections of the Antonine Wall on this walk. It was built in AD 142–143 by Emperor Antonius Pius and stretched for 37 miles (60km), from the Firth of Forth to the Firth of Clyde, marking the most northerly boundary of the Roman Empire.

WHAT TO LOOK OUT FOR

Water voles live along the waterways and are often confused with rats. Immortalised as Ratty in *The Wind in the Willows*, the vole is a threatened species. Voles are vegetarians, have a round snout, and are more likely to be spotted during the day than rats (which like to search for food at night).

Distance 2 miles (3.2km); 4 miles (6.4km) with monument

Minimum time 1hr

Ascent/gradient 197ft (60m) ▲▲▲

Level of difficulty ●●●

Paths Canal tow paths and town streets

Landscape Roman wall, 19th-century waterways, 21st-century wheel

Suggested map OS Explorer 349 Falkirk, Cumbernauld & Livingston

Start/finish Grid reference: NS 868800

Dog friendliness Good along canals

Parking Car park at Lock 16, by Union Inn

Public toilets At Falkirk Wheel Visitor Centre

Keeping an Eye on London

An energising urban river walk passes a towering symbol of 21st-century Britain

This is a well trodden route, and a favourite for many people as it delivers a sense of space in a highly populated city. Early on the route you pass the now iconic structure of the London Eye. Europe's tallest ferris wheel, this is 443ft (135m) high: it bears 32 passenger capsules, each weighing 10 tonnes; the wheel rotates at 0.6 mph (0.9kmh) and a ride all the way around in a capsule takes around half an hour. On a clear day there are superb views across central London and far out to the suburbs; views of glittering lights are good at night.

The London Eye was intended to be a temporary structure to celebrate the new millennium in 2000. It was opened by Prime Minister Tony Blair on 31 December 1999 and then opened to the public on 9 March 2000. It proved such a popular attraction that it has become a permanent fixture, and each 31 December is a focal point for firework displays celebrating the new year. It stands on the riverbank beside County Hall, the former headquarters of the London County Council and subsequently the Greater London Council.

Opposite: *The Oxo Tower is a landmark and advertising column*

Below: *The London Eye is lit up at night*

After passing the Royal Festival Hall, the National Film Theatre and the Royal National Theatre, the walk leads to Gabriel's Wharf. This was once the site of the Eldorado Ice Cream Company. Some 13 acres (5.3ha) in the area were saved from development into office buildings by the Coin Street Community Builders, an association formed in 1984 to create a better community environment. Here you can see some of the 160 box-style houses built in Upper Ground.

Oxo Tower

Close by is the Oxo Tower, originally built in the 19th century as a power station for the Post Office, then acquired in the 1920s by the Meat Extract Company that made the Oxo cubes still available from supermarkets today. Rebuilt in the Art Deco style, the Oxo Tower has 10ft (3m) windows, which, at night, are illuminated in such a way as to spell out the distinctive 'noughts and crosses' of the OXO name in red neon lights to all four corners of London. Extensively refurbished in the 1990s, and winner of several awards for architecture and regeneration, it houses shops on the lower floors and a celebrated restaurant on the eighth floor.

Walk 108 Wheeling in the new millennium

A temporary monument that became a symbol of London

1 Leave Westminster tube station by Exit 1 to follow signs to Westminster Pier. Walk up the steps to your right and cross Westminster Bridge. Turn left along the riverfront. Ahead are the 32 transparent pods of the 2,100-tonne London Eye, a huge modern ferris wheel. Just past Jubilee Gardens, on the right, is the next bridge, Hungerford, sandwiched between two newer pedestrian bridges called the Golden Jubilee Bridges.

2 Continue ahead past the Royal Festival Hall and look to the opposite bank of the Thames for Cleopatra's Needle. After the National Film Theatre and its outdoor café is Waterloo Bridge.

3 The path bends to the right, past the Royal National Theatre and the Hayward Gallery, before reaching the craft shops and restaurants of Gabriel's Wharf. Turn right at the Riviera restaurant and walk through the central path lined on either side with a series of wooden sculptures. Turn left at the end into Stamford Street and 100yds (91m) further on take another left turn into Barge House Street.

4 Ahead, the brown brickwork of the Oxo Wharf somewhat shrouds the entrance to the Oxo Tower. Enter the glass doors to your left and catch the escalator to the eighth floor for a view of the skyline, or continue along the ground floor to the riverside exit.

5 Cross Blackfriars Bridge and turn left to follow the Thames Path along the wide pavement adjacent to the river. The first boat you will pass on your left is the HMS *President*. The next set of buildings to your right after Temple tube station belong to the University of London. Immediately after these comes majestic Somerset House.

6 A further 200yds (183m) ahead the path passes Cleopatra's Needle before reaching Embankment tube. Northumberland Avenue is the next road to appear on your right. About 200yds (183m) further on is Horse Guards Avenue, which is sandwiched between the formidable buildings of the Old War Office and the Ministry of Defence. You are now almost parallel with the London Eye, on the opposite bank of the River Thames. When you reach Westminster Bridge turn right into Bridge Street, to return to Westminster tube and the start.

Distance 2.75 miles (4.4km)
Minimum time 1hr 15min
Ascent/gradient Negligible ▲▲▲
Level of difficulty ●●●
Paths Paved streets
Landscape Riverside walk
Suggested map AA Street by Street London
Start/finish Westminster tube station
Dog friendliness On lead
Public toilets North side of Blackfriars Bridge; south side by London Eye

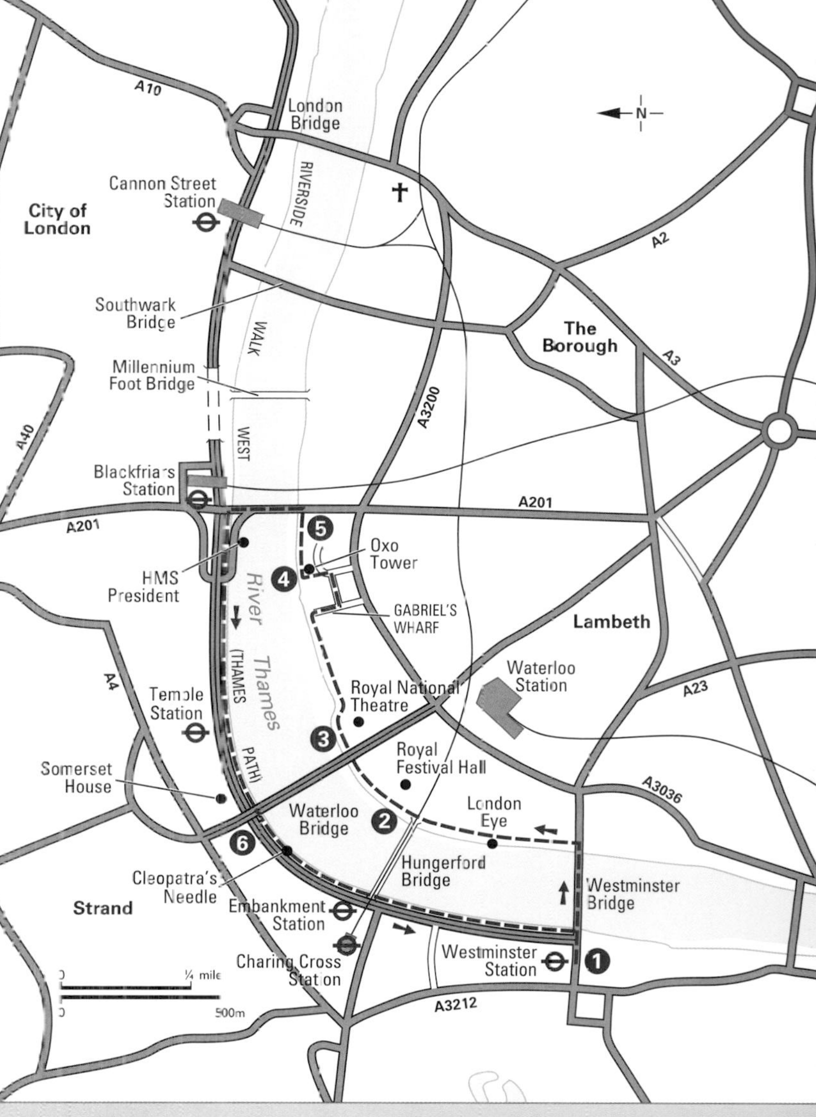

Index

Page numbers in *italic* refer to illustrations

Acknowledgements

The Automobile Association would like to thank the following photographers, companies and picture libraries for their assistance in the preparation of this book.

Abbreviations for the pictures credits are as follows – (t) top; (b) bottom; (c) centre; (l) left; (r) right; (AA) AA World Travel Library.

3 AA/T Souter; 6/7 AA/J Beazley; 8t AA/J A Tims; 8b The Art Archive/Reading Museum/Eileen Tweedy; 9t © Amoret Tanner/Alamy; 9c AA/S Gibson; 10cl © AISA/ The Bridgeman Art Library; 10cr Mary Evans Picture Library; 11t Mary Evans Picture Library; 11b AA/P & G Bowater; 12t The Art Archive/British Museum; 12b © Roberto S. Herrett/Alamy; 13t AA/P Kenward; 13b AA/I Burgum; 14/5 AA/M Moody; 16bl © David Robertson/Alamy; 16bl © Les Gibbon/Alamy; 18b © Joan Gravell/Alamy; 18cr Mary Evans Picture Library; 20tl Mary Evans Picture Library; 20bl AA; 22t The Art Archive/Dorchester County Museum/Eileen Tweedy; 22c AA/T Mackie; 24cl The Art Archive/Devizes Museum/Eileen Tweedy; 24tr The Art Archive/Devizes Museum/Eileen Tweedy; 24b Stephen Spraggon www.Photolibrary.com; 26t © Christina Bollen/Alamy; 26b AA/T Mackie; 28t The Art Archive/British Museum/Eileen Tweedy; 28bl AA/J A Tims; 28br AA/J A Tims; 30t © Mike Hayward/photoshropshire.com/Alamy; 30c © Mike Hayward/Alamy; 32cl AA/S Day; 32b AA/D Hall; 34/5 AA/R Coulam; 36tr Mary Evans Picture Library; 36bl AA/A Baker; 38t Bibliotheque Nationale, Paris, France/ The Bridgeman Art Library; 38b Roger Kidd; 40t AA/S & O Matthews; 40b Photolibrary Wales; 42b AA/R Coulam; 42tr The Art Archive/British Museum/Eileen Tweedy; 44t Keith Wood www.Photolibrary.com; 44b AA/S Day; 46c AA/J A Tims; 46b AA/J A Tims; 48bl AA/J Hunt; 48br AA/R Coulam; 50b/g AA/J Miller; 50b © Adrian Davies/Alamy; 52t AA; 52c AA/C Jones; 54/5 AA/C & A Molyneux; 56t © National Museums of Scotland/The Bridgeman Art Library; 56bl Michael Campbell; 56br Michael Campbell; 58cl © Chris Howes/Wild Places Photography/Alamy; 58bl AA/C Warren; 60t AA/D Forss; 60c AA/R Elliott; 62t © Ange/Alamy; 62b AA/R Newton; 64t © Holmes Garden Photos/Alamy; 64cl © Matthew Richardson/Alamy; 64b Britain on View Lewis Phillips www.Photolibrary.com; 66t The Art Archive/British Museum/Eileen Tweedy; 66c AA/J A Tims; 66b © The National Trust Photolibrary/Alamy; 68t Mary Evans Picture Library; 68b AA/S&O Matthews; 70/1 AA/C Jones; 72t © Angelo Hornak/Alamy; 72bl AA/S Day; 72bc AA/D Hall; 72b/g AA/D Hall; 74/5 AA; 76t © Mary Evans Picture Library/Alamy; 76b AA/J Miller; 78t AA/C Lees; 78b AA/C Lees; 80t Mary Evans/Interfoto; 80c AA/N Jenkins; 82t AA/L Whitwam; 82b AA/D Tarn; 84t © Classic Image/Alamy; 84b © Jeremy Hoare/Alamy; 86t AA/K Blackwell; 86b AA/K Blackwell; 86b/g AA/K Blackwell; 88t © Realimage/Alamy; 88b © Steve Lewis ARPS/Alamy; 90t English School/Fitzwilliam Museum, University of Cambridge, UK/ The Bridgeman Art Library; 90b Mary Evans Picture Library; 92t AA; 92c AA/S Day; 94/5 AA/M Busselle; 96cl AA; 96b/g AA/S Anderson; 96br AA/S Anderson; 98l AA/J Welsh; 98r © Midland Aerial Pictures/Alamy; 100t AA; 100b © M-dash/Alamy; 102t AA/L Noble; 102cl AA/L Noble; 102cr AA/L Noble; 102b AA/J Millar; 104t AA/L Noble; 104br AA/L Noble; 106t © Mary Evans Picture Library/Alamy; 106b © dmark/Alamy; 108t © Wayne Hutchinson/Alamy; 108c © Robert Harding Picture Library Ltd/Alamy; 110c Mary Evans Picture Library; 110b English Heritage www.Photolibrary.com; 112t © British Library Board. All Rights Reserved/ The Bridgeman Art Library; 112b AA/V Greaves; 114/5 AA/R Turpin; 116t © David Lyons/Alamy; 116b AA/M Birkitt; 118c © Robet Estall Photo Agency/Alamy; 118b AA; 120b Cragside, Northumberland, UK/ National Trust Photographic Library/Derrick E. Witty/The Bridgeman Art Library; 122b/g AA; 122b AA/S Day; 124bl © Realimage/Alamy; 124br AA/N Jenkins; 126t AA/K Doran; 126c AA; 126b AA/K Doran; 128 AA/S Day; 130t © Ian Pilbeam/Alamy; 130bl AA/T Mackie; 130br The Cumberland Pencil Company; 132cr AA/C Jones; 132br AA/M Moody; 132l AA/C Jones; 134/5 Mary Evans Picture Library; 136t © Colin Underhill/Alamy; 136b © 19th era/Alamy; 138cl AA/M Moody; 138bl AA/M Moody; 138b AA/M Moody; 140t AA/J Sparks; 140c Mary Evans Picture Library; 140b © John Morrison/Alamy; 142 © Jon Sparks/Alamy; 144t AA/A Midgley; 144cl AA/A J Hopkins; 144b AA/T Mackie; 146l AA/S Montgomery; 146c AA/J A Tims; 146br AA/S Montgomery; 148t © 19th era/Alamy; 148b AA/J Smith; 150t AA/P Bennett; 150c AA/P Bennett; 150b AA/P Bennett; 152c AA/D W Robertson; 152b AA/D W Robertson; 154/5 AA/M Haywood; 156c AA/H Palmer; 156b AA/C Jones; 158t AA/S&O Matthews; 158b © John Keats/Alamy; 160l AA/P Wilson; 160b © Steven Gillis hd9 imaging/Alamy; 162t © Christopher Griffin/Alamy; 162b © Kevin Britland/Alamy; 164c AA/M Haywood; 164b © Mary Evans Picture Library/Alamy; 166c AA/S Anderson; 166b AA; 168t AA/A Mockford & N Bonneti; 168b © Nadia Isakova/Alamy; 170c Illustrated London News; 170b © The Art Gallery Collection/Alamy; 172b/g © Nick Turner/Alamy; 172b © Cotswolds Photo Library/Alamy; 174/5 AA/D Forss; 176t © Clearview/Alamy; 176b © Spike Thompson/Alamy; 178 Photo courtesy of East Ayrshire Council © 2011; 180t AA/D Croucher; 180b AA/N Jenkins; 182cl AA/A Burton; 182bl AA/A Burton; 182br AA/A Burton; 184 © Steven Gillis hd9 imaging/Alamy; 186cl AA/Rebecca Duke; 186cr AA/I Burgum; 186b AA/H Williams; 188t AA/J Beazley; 188b AA/J Beazley; 190t © Toby de Silver/Alamy; 190c © Toby de Silver/Alamy; 192c AA/P Aithie; 192b AA/S Lewis; 194/5 © Peter Moulton/Alamy; 196t © Interfoto/Alamy; 196b AA/H Palmer; 198 AA/T Mackie; 200c Photodisc; 200b © Vincent Lowe/Alamy; 202c © Greg Balfour Evans/Alamy; 202b © Greg Balfour Evans/Alamy; 204t AA/S Day; 204b AA/D Hall; 206t AA/M Moody; 206b AA/N Jenkins; 208t © Colin Underhill/Alamy; 208b AA/C Jones; 210 Simon Butterworth www.Photolibrary.com; 212t © Warren Kovach/Alamy; 213t AA/R Newton; 214/5 © Jon Arnold Images Ltd/Alamy; 216b © Globuss Images/Alamy; 218bl © Leslie Garland Picture Library/Alamy; 218br © Jason Friend/Alamy; 220c AA; 220b © foto-zone:buildings/Alamy; 222t © Hugh Maxwell/Alamy; 222b © dianajarvisphotography.co.uk/Alamy; 224c © Kevin Britland/Alamy; 224b © Andy Hallam/Alamy; 226t AA/M Birkitt; 226c AA/T Mackie; 226b AA/T Mackie; 228t AA/J Wood; 228c AA/J Wood; 228b AA/A Burton; 230cl © Matt Botwood (CStock)/Alamy; 230b © Photolibrary Wales/Alamy; 232b/g © Peter Vallance/Alamy; 232l © By Ian Miles-Flashpoint Pictures/Alamy; 232r © Peter Vallance/Alamy; 234/5 AA/J A Tims; 236 © John Bentley/Alamy; 238c © Trinity Mirror/Mirrorpix/Alamy; 238b AA/M Bauer; 240 Photograph by Michael Scott, Photoaddiction.co.uk; 242c © Gary Cook/Alamy; 242b © Filmshots/Alamy; 244c © The Photolibrary Wales/Alamy; 244b © The Photolibrary Wales/Alamy; 246c AA/M Moody; 246b AA/M Moody; 248c AA/S Whitehorne; 248b © Simon Price/Alamy; 250 AA/J Smith; 252 AA/J A Tims; 253 AA/N Setchfield.

Every effort has been made to trace the copyright holders, and we apologise in advance for any accidental errors. We would be happy to apply any corrections in a following edition of this publication.